Concurrences Books

Tributes

Eleanor Fox – Liber Amicorum
Nicolas Charbit et al. (eds.), 2021

Herbert Hovenkamp – Liber Amicorum
Nicolas Charbit et al. (eds.), 2021

Albert Foer – A Consumer Voice in the Antitrust Arena
Nicolas Charbit et al. (eds.), 2020

Richard Whish – Taking Competition Law Outside the Box
Nicolas Charbit et al. (eds.), 2020

Frédéric Jenny – Standing Up for Convergence and Relevance in Antitrust, Vol. I & II
Nicolas Charbit et al. (eds.), 2019 & 2021

Wang Xiaoye – The Pioneer of Competition Law in China
Adrian Emch, Wendy Ng (ed.), 2019

Douglas H. Ginsburg – An Antitrust Professor on the Bench, Vol. I & II
Nicolas Charbit et al. (eds.), 2018 & 2020

Ian S. Forrester – A Scot Without Borders, Vol. I & II
Assimakis Komninos et al. (ed.), 2015

William E. Kovacic – An Antitrust Tribute, Vol. I & II
Nicolas Charbit et al. (eds.), 2013 & 2014

Practical Books

Global Dictionary of Competition Law
Deborah Healey, William Kovacic, Pablo Trevisan, Richard Whish (eds.), 2022

Perspectives on Antitrust Compliance
Anne Riley, Andreas Stephan, Anny Tubbs (eds.), 2021

Information Exchange and Related Risks – A Practical Guide
Marcio Dias Soares (ed.), 2021

State Aid & National Enforcement
Jacques Derenne, Denis Jouve, Christophe Lemaire, Francesco Martucci (eds.), 2021

Merger Control in Latin America – A Jurisdictional Guide
Paulo Burnier da Silveira & Pamela Sittenfeld (eds.), 2020

Competition Inspections under EU Law
Nathalie Jalabert-Doury, 2020

Competition Digest – A Synthesis of EU, US and National Leading Cases, 4th ed.
Frédéric Jenny (ed.), 2020

Gun Jumping in Merger Control – A Jurisdictional Guide
Catriona Hatton, Yves Comtois, Andrea Hamilton (eds.), 2019

Choice – A New Standard for Competition Analysis?
Paul Nihoul et al., 2016

PhD Theses

Essays in Industrial Organization: Competition and Regulation in Network Industries
Jean-Marc Zogheib, 2021

The Role of Media Pluralism in the Enforcement of EU Competition Law
Konstantina Bania, 2019

Buyer Power in EU Competition Law
Ignacio Herrera Anchustegui, 2017

General Interest

Women & Antitrust – Voices from the Field, Vol. I & II
Evelina Kurgonaite & Kristina Nordlander (eds.), 2020

Conference Proceedings

Antitrust in Emerging and Developing Countries, Vol I & II
Eleanor Fox, Harry First (eds.), 2015 & 2016

Global Antitrust Law – Current Issues in Antitrust Law and Economics
Douglas Ginsburg, Joshua Wright (eds.), 2015

Competition Law on the Global Stage: David Gerber's Global Competition Law in Perspective
David Gerber, 2014

e-Book versions available for
Concurrences+ subscribers

Testimonials

The world faces many significant issues today, such as climate change, plastic waste, food waste, social injustice, and food security, to name but a few. Solving them needs the power of collective action. This book provides strong food for thought for policymakers as they embark on unleashing the power of collective action, but at the same time, ensuring healthy competition.

Wai-Chan Chan, Managing Director, The Consumer Goods Forum

La concurrence, sur les marchés comme sur les circuits, est au cœur des valeurs de Michelin depuis sa création il y a plus de 130 ans. Mais le terrain de jeu est plus large que jamais: la performance concerne aussi les gens et la planète. En tant que société, nous avons fixé collectivement des objectifs ambitieux. Il s'agit maintenant de livrer. De multiples coopérations, à la fois au sein des secteurs et au-delà, seront essentielles au succès. Nous nous félicitons de cet ouvrage qui partage cet esprit et qui devrait aider les parties prenantes à co-construire des normes de droit de la concurrence en tant qu'outil efficace de durabilité.

Yves Chapot, directeur général, Groupe Michelin

Climate change is such a central challenge for humanity that practitioners in all fields of policy must ask what part they should play. This timely collection of essays from many leaders in their fields constitutes a rich addition to the ongoing discussion of the proper role for competition policy in meeting this challenge.

Andrea Coscelli, Chief Executive, UK Competition and Markets Authority

We are running out of time in the fight against climate change. If we are to give our children hope for the future, all aspects of our economy, laws, and regulations need to adapt. This welcome book shows how competition policy can play its part.

Benedict Cumberbatch, Actor

Not so long ago competition rules were invoked to prevent the Dutch Chicken of Tomorrow initiative. This book shows that today, competition rules no longer have to stand in the way of collaboration between competitors to promote environmental sustainability. It provides a comprehensive overview of the complex issues that have so far arisen and gives innovative suggestions on how competition policy can be further shaped to support future sustainability initiatives. It is a must-have for competition practitioners who do not want to miss out on these important developments."

Jolling De Pree, Partner, De Brauw Blackstone Westbroek

In recent years, policymakers and regulators worldwide have acknowledged that climate change and environmental sustainability is a vital challenge cutting across many policy fields. This book provides a rich and unique perspective from competition law and policy practice.

Frank Elderson, Executive Board Member, European Central Bank

This excellent book brings together leading contributors to discuss the challenges and opportunities associated with competition law enforcement and sustainability. An impactful collection that should be read by anyone who is interested in competition enforcement and the future of our planet.

Ariel Ezrachi, Slaughter and May Professor of Competition Law, Oxford University

Just as sustainability has become one of the most defining issues of our time, "Competition Law, Climate Change & Environmental Sustainability" comes on the market. This is an excellent collection of essays by experts and deep-thinkers, including agency heads, industry, lawyers, and academics, into whether and how to receive sustainability into competition law and policy.

Eleanor Fox, Walter J. Derenberg Professor of Trade Regulation, New York University School of Law

As Secretary-General of the European Round Table for Industry (ERT) I very much welcome this book with excellent reflections on the relationship between competition policy and the Green Deal. The Green Deal can be a force that strengthens Europe's place in the world. Europe's climate leadership can potentially create one of the biggest opportunities for its future security and prosperity. It is in all our interests to try to make the most of it. I strongly believe that competition law should be adapted to facilitate the achievement of the objectives under the Green Deal. ERT encourages the Commission to play a lead role so as to ensure a consistent approach across the EU and globally. EU competition policy is central to the functioning of the internal market and is one of our most powerful tools to ensure a level playing field for all European companies. Smarter competition policies that will help European business to also compete successfully at scale on the international stage."

Frank Heemskerk, Secretary-General, European Round Table for Industry

This book is a pioneer on the relationship between antitrust law and environmental sustainability which is an inspiring topic. The wide variety of the perspectives and the diversity of the contributing authors add to its value and make it a useful reference for practitioners.

Jenny Huang, Director Competition Policy, Tencent

Purpose-led business models are rooted in the idea of healthy competition between players. However, system change to protect our planet and to build a more equitable society will also require partnerships and cooperation across sectors and within industries. This innovative book provides rich inspiration for policymakers when defining the important role of competition law in achieving a more sustainable economy.

Alan Jope, Chief Executive Officer, Unilever

Similar to other areas of law, competition law must acknowledge its role in addressing the climate crisis. This groundbreaking book offers rare insights from industry leaders, policymakers, and academics and demonstrates how to modernize competition law to advance environmental and economic sustainability.

Amelia Miazad, Director & Senior Research Fellow, Business in Society Institute Berkeley Law

Competition law and policy can support other public policies and contribute to the achievement of their goals. Now more than ever, competition law and policy should have an active role in the

green and inclusive economic recovery, encouraging sustainability in a transparent manner and providing clear guidance for businesses. This book may be groundbreaking in that sense.

Teresa Moreira, Head of the Competition and Consumer Policies Branch, UNCTAD

"Competition Law, Climate Change & Environmental Sustainability" addresses very topical questions which demand urgent answers. The issues at stake affect us all and together we need to find proper solutions. The book makes a remarkable contribution in this regard.

Andreas Mundt, President, German Federal Cartel Office (Bundeskartellamt)

Climate change has long been at the centre of international debate, both in politics and economics. However, it is only recently that environmental sustainability has entered the discourse on competition policies. The editors of this volume are pioneers in the field. A number of outstanding authors address the issues related to sustainable competition from various perspectives. As a public — and former private — enforcer, let me focus on the part of the book that analyses how sustainability can enter the decision-making process. Martijn Snoep and all the contributors underline how decision-makers may find themselves in a situation in which they are called to rethink the traditional consumer welfare standard.

Gabriella Muscolo, Commissioner, Italian Competition Authority (AGCM)

A highly interesting and timely book edited by an illustrious group of leading practitioners in the field. A book that cannot be missed by anyone who is interested in the debate about what EU competition law can and should do in the face of the climate crisis.

Julian Nowag, Associate Professor, Lund University

Companies across industries are determined to live up to their environmental and social responsibilities Co-operation between peers will be decisive to make it happen. This volume couldn't be more timely in illustrating the important role competition law should play in the process of critical industry transition.

Prof. Dr. Michael Otto, Chairman of the Supervisory Board, Otto Group Holding

Just a few years ago, contemplating the idea that the application of competition law could help tackle environmental concerns would have been criticized. Today, things have changed, as the competition

community recognizes that climate change is the most pressing long-term worldwide issue. This publication represents an interesting compilation of different views on how sustainability considerations can be incorporated into an agency's practice. As an enforcer, I found it very interesting. Moving forward, a question we will face as an international competition community is: What does the future hold for countries where legal frameworks do not incorporate public policy objectives, such as sustainability, in competition law?

Alejandria Palacios Prieto, Chairwoman, Mexican Federal Economic Competition Commission (COFECE)

A valuable and timely collection of essays, addressing from a variety of angles one of the most important issues confronting competition law. This book deserves wide attention from policy-makers, practitioners, and academics.

Sir Peter Roth, President, UK Competition Appeal Tribunal

So how can competition policy encourage (or at least not chill) solutions to climate change, the defining challenge of our time? This timely and important work looks beyond the consumer welfare orthodoxies from various legal, industry, and agency perspectives to assess how environmental considerations can be incorporated in antitrust analysis to promote a sustainable economy. A must-read for policymakers, lawyers, and scholars.

Maurice Stucke, Distinguished Professor of Law, University of Tennessee College of Law

This book makes a significant and innovative contribution to the vigorous ongoing debate on the proper role of environmental sustainability in contemporary competition law and policy. Whatever opinion one adopts on these issues, the series of works included in this book, shed light on a better understanding of all the aspects involved in this debate. Kudos to the editors of this timely contribution.

Pablo Trevisán, Founder, Instituto de Derecho de la Competencia, Former Commissioner Argentine, Competition Authority

Our collective sustainability challenge urges industry players, policy makers and regulators to work toward a common goal. This book addresses many of the policy issues we must address – and explores what is possible and what isn't when collaborating on sustainability topics.

Thierry Vanlancker, Chief Executive Officer, AkzoNobel

This book provides innovative and fresh perspectives to one of the most pressing debates in contemporary competition law. Competition authorities, legislators, and courts alike need to seriously consider how environmental requirements interact with the market mechanism of supply and demand that competition law seeks to protect. Is the environment a mere externality or is sustainability a responsibility that all market players share? Holmes, Middelschulte and Snoep's work will undoubtedly contribute to this timely discussion and hopefully, spark further change.

Marc Van der Woude, President, General Court of the EU

Many congratulations to all concerned - and to the editors in particular - for putting this wonderful series of essays together on one of the most pressing issues of contemporary competition policy: the contribution that competition law can make to sustainable development. The book is superbly structured and will be indispensable for anyone wishing to engage with this most important of subjects

Richard Whish, Emeritus Professor of Law, King's College London

The European Union has set high standards with the EU Green Deal as well as the Recovery plan based on digital and green transition. Competition policy will have a key role to play in achieving these objectives and deliver concrete results for our future generations. It is time for economists, industrialists, lawyers, and decision-makers to find common ground and take their part in this transition. The EU has to pave the way for a new competition policy approach fit to tackle climate change and the sustainability challenge. This book is a great contribution to the on-going debate with different perspectives providing a comprehensive overview of the challenge lying ahead of us.

Stéphanie Yon-Courtin, Member of Parliament, European Parliament

How to consider climate change and environmental sustainability issues when implementing competition laws is an important and unique topic. This book is surprising. It makes us think about what green antitrust laws are and whether environmentally friendly competition policies should be implemented.

Meng Yanbei, Professor and Doctoral Tutor, Renmin University of China Law School

COMPETITION LAW, CLIMATE CHANGE & ENVIRONMENTAL SUSTAINABILITY

Copyright ©2021 by Institute of Competition Law
106 West 32nd Street, Suite 144 New York, NY, 10001, USA
www.concurrences.com
book@concurrences.com

First Printing, March 2021
978-1-939007-72-8 (Hardcover)
Library of Congress Control Number: 2021903458

Cover Design: Yves Buliard, www.yvesbuliard.fr
Book Design and Layout implementation: Nord Compo

COMPETITION LAW, CLIMATE CHANGE & ENVIRONMENTAL SUSTAINABILITY

Foreword by Frans Timmermans

Introduction by Suzanne Kingston SC

Edited by

Simon Holmes
Dirk Middelschulte
Martijn Snoep

Managing Editor
Sonia Ahmad

Foreword

FRANS TIMMERMANS

European Commission Executive Vice-President
for the European Green Deal

Humanity is going through one of the most transformational periods in history. We are battling a pandemic while also faced with the consequences of a digital industrial revolution as well as the existential threats posed by the climate and biodiversity crises.

In late 2019, the European Commission presented the Green Deal to enable Europe to become the first climate-neutral continent. We did so knowing that we needed to switch to a new, sustainable economic model. With the pandemic, the Green Deal has also become our roadmap to recovery.

Coming out of the Covid-crisis, the European recovery package and new multiyear budget enable governments across the European Union to invest massively in their recovery. 30% of these funds should go to climate policy, 20% to supporting the digital transition. And none of it can do significant harm to our planet.

In spending all this money we would be relegating our duty if we spent it on restoring parts of the economy that have no future. We are already placing a heavy debt on the shoulders of our children and grandchildren, and we have to avoid creating locked-in assets. The moment we are in requires us to save jobs not for years but for decades to come.

We are still in the early days of this historical change. Making this transformation a success means managing the transition. Predictability and long-term stability are key. Several elements in the Green Deal, including our Climate Law, help us anchor our commitment and provide the required clarity. We also need rules on competition and state aid that are adapted to the new realities. Public funds should act as a catalyst for private investment. Interest in sustainable investments is growing already, and our competition policy can help facilitate it further.

Time is ticking, but the work is happening as well. The changes needed to put Europe firmly on track to climate neutrality will take shape in the years to come. So while there still is plenty of doom on our horizon, we also have reason for hope. And – to paraphrase Thomas Jefferson – we can continue to find inspiration in the dream of the future rather than the history of the past.

Introduction

PROFESSOR SUZANNE KINGSTON SC[*]
University College Dublin

Should competition law prohibit competitors from agreeing to produce more energy-efficient goods, where this means higher prices for consumers? Is a dominant undertaking that switches to using only pricier recyclable packaging abusing its dominant position? Can the fact that a merger may lead to lower carbon emissions from production in the long-term be taken into account by competition authorities? Should state aid to coal-fired power plants be permitted?

Such questions typify the vigorous ongoing debate on the proper role of environmental considerations in contemporary competition law and policy within Europe. It is a pleasure to introduce this important book which makes a significant contribution to this debate. Its publication could hardly be more timely. There is now an overwhelming scientific consensus that the environmental crisis threatens the very fabric of our societies and our economies. In 2019, a report authored by the world's leading climate science organisations, including the Intergovernmental Panel on Climate Change and the UN Environmental Programme, *United in Science*, found that, without a sharp and urgent decline in greenhouse gas emissions, global warming will surpass 1.5°C, meaning irreversible ecosystem loss and human catastrophe.[1] At present, global greenhouse gas emissions are still growing.[2]

In the words of UN Secretary-General Guterres, climate change is "the defining challenge of our time".[3] Sector-specific responses to this will fail. Action must involve "all sectors of the society and the economy, including industry".[4]

The European Green Deal, the European Commission's flagship initiative declared by President Von der Leyen as a "European man on the moon moment",

---

[*]   Senior counsel at the Irish Bar and professor, University College Dublin.
[1]   Report to the UN Secretary-General's Climate Action Summit: WMO, *United in Science* (WMO 2019) <www.ipcc.ch/2019/09/22/united-in-science-report-climate-summit/>.
[2]   ibid.
[3]   ibid, 3.
[4]   European Parliament, Resolution declaring a climate and environmental emergency 2019/2930 (RSP) (28 November 2019).

has an all-economy approach at its heart. The role of private businesses and consumers in making investment, innovation and purchasing decisions is stated to be fundamental, as an essential complement to (although not a substitute for) legislation that will, if passed, be the most radical EU climate and environmental legislation ever seen.[5] Reliance on state action alone will be insufficient. The European Climate Pact, launched by Vice-President Timmermans in December 2020 as a fundamental element of the European Green Deal, expressly seeks to promote the involvement of citizens, businesses and civil society in taking voluntary action in furtherance of the EU's climate goals.[6] As the Commission states therein, the Green Deal can only succeed if "citizens, communities, companies and organisations play their part, alongside government policies and regulation".[7] As announced by President Von der Leyen, the aim is to "bring about a change of behaviour, from the individual to the largest multinational".[8]

This acknowledgement of the crucial role of private business initiatives in achieving climate and environmental goals reflects the broader paradigm shift that has occurred in global environmental regulation in the past 20 years. Whereas traditional environmental regulation relied almost exclusively upon the state to fashion and enforce environmental rules, there is now consensus that private environmental initiatives form a crucial part of the policy mix.[9] This is based on a profound realisation that it is no longer good enough to sit back and wait for the legislature to act to address environmental degradation. There are many environmental problems that the state cannot possibly address rapidly or effectively enough alone. Environmental problems do not respect jurisdictional borders, and are in many cases caused, and may most effectively be solved, by transnational economic actors.[10] To take just one example, if Amazon fulfils its stated climate pledge to become net-zero carbon by 2040, based on current figures this would avoid emissions of at least[11] 51.17 million metric tonnes of carbon dioxide equivalent per annum, which equates approximately to the entire greenhouse gas emissions of Sweden in 2018.

---

5   Including the proposed European Climate Law which in its current form, as discussed below, contain a binding target for the EU to achieve carbon neutrality by 2050. The proposal is currently being considered by the European Parliament and the Council.

6   Commission, "European Climate Pact" (Communication) COM(2020) 788 final.

7   ibid, 1.

8   Ursula von der Leyen, "A Union that strives for more: Political Guidelines for the next European Commission 2019–2024" (2019) <https://ec.europa.eu/info/sites/info/files/political-guidelines-next-commission_en_0.pdf>.

9   This is reflected, for instance, in the UN Sustainable Development Goals, including UN SDG 12, addressing sustainable consumption and production patterns. See generally, Michael P Vandenbergh "Private Environmental Governance" (2013) 99(1) Cornell L Rev 129.

10 Based on Amazon's published 2019 figures. Sweden's greenhouse gas emissions in 2018 totalled 51.79 million metric tonnes of carbon dioxide equivalent: Amazon and OECD, "Statistical Dataset on National Greenhouse Gas Emissions: <www.aboutamazon.com/planet/climate-pledge> accessed 4 February 2021.

11 It is unclear whether this figure includes, for instance, greenhouse gas emissions from energy required to operate data centres, or emissions from Amazon's supply chain. See further Nives Dolsak and Aseem Prakash, "Amazon Pledges $2 Billion Climate Fund, As Its Carbon Emissions Grow" (*Forbes*, 24 June 2020).

What role does competition law and policy have to play in this? The debate on the role of so-called "non-economic" policy factors in competition law is well known.[12] The Commission orthodoxy has, for almost 20 years, been that such factors must be excluded from competition analysis: the consumer welfare standard requires a narrow economic efficiency assessment entailing proof of quantified economic benefits for consumers within the relevant market.[13]

This is perhaps most evident in the Article 101 TFEU context, addressed in detail in Part I(1) of this volume.[14] The 2004 guidelines on the application of Article 101(3) TFEU emphasise, for instance, that "objective economic efficiencies" are necessary for restrictive agreements to fall outside the Article 101(1) TFEU prohibition.[15] The 2010 horizontal cooperation guidelines place similar emphasis on the need for the parties to an agreement to demonstrate objective economic efficiency gains in order to fall within Article 101(3) TFEU.[16] They also make clear that benefits for consumers who fall outside the relevant market will not be relevant to the Article 101(3) TFEU assessment.[17] Neither the Article 101(3) Guidelines nor the Horizontal Cooperation Guidelines expressly state that environmental benefits may in themselves satisfy constitute "technical or economic progress" within the meaning of the first condition of Article 101(3) TFEU. (By contrast, the previous (2001) horizontal cooperation guidelines expressly indicated that, where there were "net benefits in terms of reduced environmental pressure resulting from" a horizontal agreement, this would constitute technical/economic progress, whether the benefits were achieved "either at individual or at aggregate consumer level".)[18]

Today, the suggestion that environmental benefits should be disregarded by competition authorities and courts appears, I would respectfully suggest, severely outdated.

First, it runs directly contrary to the European Green Deal and its all-economy approach to environmental protection, which demands "deeply transformative policies" underpinned by an economic model that properly values environmental

---

12 See for instance the discussion of Simon Holmes in this volume and see further, Suzanne Kingston, *Greening EU Competition Law and Policy* (CUP 2011), chapter 1; Christopher Townley, *Article 81 and Public Policy* (Hart 2009); and more recently Giorgio Monti. "Four options for a greener competition law" (2020) 11 (3–4) JECL & Pract 124–132.

13 For a defence of this approach, see, e.g., Luc Peeperkorn's contribution to this volume.

14 See the contributions of Theo van Dijk, Maurits Dolmans, Ella van den Brink & Jordan Ellison, and Maarten Pieter Schinkel & Leonard Treuren.

15 Commission, "Guidelines on the application of Article 81(3) [now 101(3)] of the Treaty [2004] OJ C101/97 (Article 101(3) Guidelines), [59].

16 Commission, "Guidelines on the applicability of Article 101 of the Treaty on the Functioning of the European Union to horizontal co-operation agreements" [2011] OJ C11/1 (Horizontal Cooperation Guidelines), [49].

17 ibid ("'consumers' encompasses the customers, potential and/or actual, of the parties to the agreement"). See similarly, Article 101(3) Guidelines (n 15), [84].

18 Commission, "Guidelines on the applicability of Article 81 of the EC Treaty to horizontal cooperation agreements" [2001] OJ C3/2, [193].

and natural resources.[19] As already noted, voluntary initiatives of business are expressly encouraged and acknowledged as playing a vital role in the EU's transformed, sustainable economic model. It would be a perverse outcome if the same businesses being encouraged by the European Green Deal effort to take pro-environmental initiatives were at the same time being *discouraged* from doing so by the chilling effect of potential competition enforcement.[20] As many of the contributions in this book note,[21] competition policy must play its part – and at the very least must not contradict other Green Deal policy initiatives.

Second, such an isolationist approach to EU competition policy has no constitutional legitimacy within EU law. Excluding environmental considerations from competition assessments contravenes the Article 11 TFEU imperative to integrate environmental protection into all other EU policy areas.[22] This is not just an abstract jurisprudential objection. It is fundamental to the rule of law that the Commission must act in accordance with the Treaties. DG COMP, or any other DG, has no administrative discretion to disapply part of the Treaties, whether for reasons of simplifying enforcement and the administrability of the competition rules, or otherwise.

Third, an isolationist approach assumes that environmental benefits cannot constitute economic efficiencies or be measured, which ignores the very significant developments in quantifying environmental goods in the discipline of environmental economics over the past 20 years.[23] Sustainability is, as van Dijk observes in this volume, "increasingly a dimension over which consumers compete with each other". As Mark Carney argues forcefully in his 2020 Reith Lecture series, changes in society's environmental values in turn broaden the market's conceptions of value, thereby transforming moral into market sentiments.[24] This is borne out by the most recent public survey evidence in the EU, showing that 9 out of 10 Europeans see climate change as a serious problem and feel that protecting the environment is personally important to them.[25]

---

19 Commission, "The European Green Deal" (Communcation) COM(2019) 640 final, section 2.1.
20 It is settled case law that, pursuant to the *Ladbroke Racing* line of cases, undertakings remain subject to Article 101 TFEU if Member States (or the EU) merely encourage or make it easier for them to engage in autonomous anti-ompetitive conduct without mandating them by law to do so. See, e.g., Case C–280/08 P *Deutsche Telekom* EU:C:2010:603, [82]; Joined Cases C–359/95 P and C–379/95 P *Ladbroke Racing* EU:C:1997:531, [33]. See further, Kingston (n 12), chapter 11.
21 See for instance the contributions of Holmes, Dolmans and van Dijk.
22 See further Kingston (n 12), chapter 3 and Julian Nowag, *Environmental Integration in Competition and Free-Movement Laws* (OUP 2016).
23 For an excellent overview, see Charles D Kolstad, *Environmental Economics* (2nd edn, OUP 2011); also Frank Ackerman and Lisa Heinzerling, *Priceless: On Knowing the Price of Everything and the Value of Nothing* (The New Press 2004).
24 Mark Carney, "How We Get What We Value: Reith Lectures 2020" (BBC Radio 4, December 2020) <www.bbc.co.uk/programmes/articles/43GjCh72bxWVSqSB84ZDJw0/reith-lectures-2020-how-we-get-what-we-value> accessed 4 February 2020.
25 Commission, "European Climate Pact" (Communication) COM(2020) 788 final, 1.

Integrating environmental considerations does not therefore require a fundamental rethink of the approach to policy factors in competition analysis. The consumer welfare standard is perfectly capable of accommodating environmental benefits. As van Dijk, Dolmans and van den Brink/Ellison discuss in this volume, methods of quantifying environmental benefits, such as assessment of consumers' willingness-to-pay for improved environmental quality, are now well established in the discipline of environmental economics. As Delarue and Walker comment, from an economic perspective there is "nothing conceptually difficult about also believing that things such as sustainable production, decarbonisation, reducing environmental degradation and so on should also be included in a consumer welfare standard." While arguments may be had about how they should best apply in a specific case, this is true for many fields of competition economics.

It can hardly be denied that applying such valuation techniques goes beyond competition economists' traditional comfort zone. Yet the climate emergency requires innovation from competition authorities no less than the rest of society. Such innovation may extend, as noted in van Dijk's contribution for instance, to valuing out-of-market benefits. As highlighted by Kar, Cochrane and Spring, and Iacovides and Vrettos, there are also forceful arguments for applying such valuation techniques to, for instance, valuation of efficiencies in merger analysis,[26] and assessing objective justification under Article 102 TFEU.[27]

Of course, this does not mean that environmental protection aims should be used as a pretext for collusion or "greenwashing", a risk rightly emphasised in Schinkel and Treuren's chapter.[28] A case-by-case approach will be required. But in cases of genuine green private initiatives with objective environmental benefits, where there is no less restrictive means of achieving those benefits, coordinated approaches should not be prohibited. The argument should no longer be about whether such benefits can be considered, but *how* they should be considered. This volume makes an important contribution to that discussion.

Of immense value here are the insights from specific business sectors addressed in Part II, which go beyond the legal and economic framework to explain precisely how sustainable competition policy might impact key economic sectors. As Jérôme Cloarec, head of antitrust at Michelin, puts it, "without legal certainty for the industry, sustainability might remain half-baked". The need for clearer guidance to remove the chilling effect of potential competition enforcement is a vivid and consistent message across the contributions from the automotive, consumer goods, food supply and banking sectors.[29]

---

26 See the contribution of Kar, Cochrane and Spring in this volume.
27 See the contribution of Iacovides and Vrettos in this volume.
28 The avid concern to avoid greenwashing is, of course, not specific to competition policy, and indeed is one of the three core values of the European Climate Pact announced in December 2020 (n 25), 8.
29 See the contributions of de Brousse, Chu, Cloarec, Rose, Linke & Woll, Gayk, Graham, Ferrando & Lombardi, Meagher & Roberts, Bredt and Mullan, Braithwaite & Cheetham-West.

With the exceptions of state aid, where the Commission has had clear guidelines on environmental aid since 1994,[30] it is Member States that are leading the way on this issue. Among the first-movers was the Dutch Autoriteit Consument & Markt (*Chicken of Tomorrow*; *Coal Plant Closure*); as discussed by Snoep in this volume, the Dutch authority published innovative draft guidelines on sustainability in July 2020, and a revised version in January 2021.[31] In Germany, the Bundeskartellamt has indicated that it is prepared to constructively support pioneering environmentally motivated projects: its approach to the *Initiative Tierwohl* is a case in point.[32] The French Autorité de la concurrence has also been active in the field, considering environmental issues in imposing commitments (*Nespresso, Engie*); as discussed by de Silva, in May 2020 it published a working paper on the climate emergency. And beyond the EU, the UK Competition and Market Authority's "Annual Plan 2020 to 2021" commits to developing its understanding of how it can support the transition to a low-carbon economy.[33]

Just as other areas of law are being forced to recognise the scale of the climate emergency – such as human rights law in the wake of the Dutch Supreme Court's *Urgenda* decision[34] – it is now the time for competition law to do so. Competition authorities should send a clear signal to industry that competition policy will not stand in the way of genuine and proportionate pro-environmental initiatives. Policy leadership is required. The current guidance vacuum at EU level should be filled as a matter of urgency. Indeed, if the proposed European Climate Law comes into force, it is arguable that the European Commission will have a legal *duty* to produce such guidance. See Article 5(3) of the Proposal, which obliges the Commission to take the "necessary measures" to ensure that the legally binding objective of climate neutrality in the Union is attained by 2050, and to eliminate inconsistent Union measures.[35]

A good place to start would be the forthcoming horizontal cooperation guidelines, which are presently under review. Beyond this, clear and consistent guidance is also needed on Article 102 TFEU and mergers. Encouragingly, the Commission is actively considering how the competition rules and sustainability policies work

---

30 See the contributions of Webber and Robins in this volume, and Kingston (n 12), chapter 12.
31 ACM, "Draft Guidelines: Sustainability Agreements, Opportunities within competition law (9 July 2020, last updated on 26 January 2021) <www.acm.nl/en/publications/draft-guidelines-sustainability-agreements>.
32 For a summary in English, see Bundeskartellamt, "Bundeskartellamt calls for more consumer transparency in animal welfare initiative" Press release (28 September 2017).
33 CMA, "Annual Plan 2020 to 2021" (19 March 2020) <www.gov.uk/government/publications/competition-and-markets-authority-annual-plan-2020-to-2021/annual-plan-2020-to-2021>.
34 *Netherlands v Stichting Urgenda* Judgment of the *Hoge Raad* (Supreme Court) 20 December 2019 NL:HR:2019:2006. See also, the Decision of the Administrative Tribunal of Paris of 3 February 2021 in *Association Oxfam France, Association Notre Affaire à Tous, Fondation pour la Nature et l'Homme & Association Greenpeace France v République Française* (n°1904967, 1904968, 1904972, 1904976/4-1).
35 Proposal for a Regulation establishing the framework for achieving climate neutrality and amending Regulation (EU) 2018/1999 (European Climate Law) COM(2020) 80 final.

together, as witnessed by its consultation on the matter which, at the time of writing, is ongoing. Within agriculture, for instance, the Commission's May 2020 "Farm to Fork Strategy", part of the Green Deal package, indicates that the competition rules are to be clarified for "collective initiatives that promote sustainability in supply chains".[36] Within state aid, the guidelines on environmental protection and energy[37] are also currently under review. The elephant in the room is that state aid for the fossil fuel industry remains, on the current guidelines, compatible with EU law.[38] Politically, as hot potatoes go, this is undoubtedly a scorcher.[39] On any objective scientific basis, however, this state of affairs appears impossible to justify.

Whatever view one espouses on these issues, it is clear that the role of environmental considerations within economic policies, including competition policy, is perhaps the most critical challenge facing Europe today. The editors are to be commended for their innovative contribution to this vital debate.

---

36 Commission, "A Farm to Fork Strategy for a fair, healthy and environmentally-friendly food system" (Communication) COM(2020) 381 final, section 2.1.
37 Commission, "Guidelines on State aid for environmental protection and energy 2014–2020" [2014] OJ C200/1.
38 The 2014 guidelines expressly do not address the issue of aid to the fossil fuel industry. See the discussion of Nicole Robins in this volume.
39 The issue of aid to the fossil fuel industry has been addressed on multiple occasions by the European Council, which has for some years now committed to the gradual phasing out of such subsidies (see, for instance, European Council Conclusions from 23 May 2013). Regulation 2018/1999/EU on the Governance of the Energy Union and Climate Action [2018] OJ L328/1 requires the Commission to report each year on Member States' progress towards phasing out fossil fuel subsidies. The Commission's most recent report of October 2020 (COM(2020) 950 final) shows that in fact Member State fossil fuel subsidies are still, astonishingly, gradually *increasing* overall (at 1). Overall, fossil fuel subsidies within the EU amounted to €50 billion in 2018.

Contributors

Fiona M Beattie
Macfarlanes

Tembinkosi Bonakele
*South African
Competition Commission*

Marc Braithwaite
*UK Financial Conduct
Authority*

Stephan Bredt
*Ministry of Economics,
Energy, Transport
and Housing of Hessen*

Anton Burger
Oxera

Alec Burnside
Dechert

Rosy Cheetham-West
*UK Financial Conduct
Authority*

Martyn Chu
Danone

Jérôme Cloarec
Michelin

Emma Cochrane
Linklaters

Marjolein De Backer
Dechert

Angélique de Brousse
Johnson & Johnson

Isabelle de Silva
*French Competition
Authority*

Gianni de Stefano
AkzoNobel

Sandrine Delarue
*UK Competition
& Markets Authority*

Eleni Diamantopoulou
ClientEarth

Maurits Dolmans
*Cleary Gottlieb
Steen & Hamilton*

Jordan Ellison
Slaughter and May

Tomaso Ferrando
University of Antwerp

Georgina Foster
Baker McKenzie

Morgan Frontczak
Shell

Andreas Gayk
*Markenverband – German
Brands Association*

Ben Graham
AB InBev

Martijn Han
True Price Foundation

Marios C Iacovides
University of Oxford

Nicole Kar
Linklaters

Boris Kasten
Schindler Management

Ioannis Lianos
*Hellenic Competition
Commission*

Benjamin Linke
Deutsche Bahn

Claudio Lombardi
KIMEP University

Michelle Meagher
*University College
London*

Hugh Mullan
*UK Payment Systems
Regulator*

Grant Murray
Baker McKenzie

Luc Peeperkorn
*Brussels School
of Competition /
College of Europe*

Maarten Pieter Schinkel
University of Amsterdam

Laura Puglisi
Oxera

Hendrik Reffken
Schindler Management

Simon Roberts
*University
of Johannesburg*

Nicole Robins
Oxera

Ian Rose
Volvo Trucks

Bella Spring
Linklaters

Delphine Strohl
Dechert

Wendy Thian
Baker McKenzie

Patrick Thieffry

Christopher Thomas
Hogan Lovells

Leonard Treuren
University of Amsterdam

Ella van den Brink
Google

Theon van Dijk
*Netherlands Authority
for Consumers
and Markets*

Chris Vrettos
Stockholm University

Willem Vriesendorp
*#SustainablePublic-
Affairs*

Mike Walker
*UK Competition
& Markets Authority*

James Webber
Shearman & Sterling

Udo Woll
Deutsche Bahn

Table of Contents

Part I: Legal Themes

Chapter 1: Cooperation

Chapter 2: Abuse of Dominance

Chapter 3: EU Merger Control

Chapter 4: State Aid

Chapter 5: Public Procurement

Part II: Industry Perspectives

Chapter 1: Automotive and Transportation

Chapter 2: Banking and Finance

Chapter 3: Consumer Goods

Chapter 4: Energy

Chapter 5: Food Supply Chain

Chapter 6: Industrial Products

Part III: Agency Outlook

Part IV: Alternative Perspectives

PART I
Legal Themes

Preface:
How Sustainability Can Be Taken Into Account in Every Area of Competition Law

SIMON HOLMES*

Oxford University | UK Competition Appeal Tribunal

I. Introduction

Having written and spoken widely in the last two years on climate change, sustainability and competition law, both personally,[1] and in collaboration with colleagues at the International Chamber of Commerce,[2] I am delighted to introduce the "Legal Themes" part of this book.

It is particularly appropriate that we start with the law, as perhaps the most serious source of confusion, disagreement and, indeed, error in the discussion of sustainability and competition law is a failure to start with the actual law. However useful concepts such as "consumer welfare" or "public interest" may

---

*   Simon Holmes is a visiting professor at the University of Oxford and member of the UK Competition Appeal Tribunal. He is also a legal adviser to the NGO, ClientEarth; a strategic adviser to #SustainablePublicAffairs in Brussels; a member of the Competition Commission of the International Chamber of Commerce (ICC); a member of the International Advisory Board of the IDC (Instituto de derecho de la competencia); an associate member of the UCL Centre for Law, Economics and Society (CLES); and a founding member of the Inclusive Competition Forum. He can be reached at eusebius.holmes@icloud.com.

1   For example: "Climate Change and Competition Law – Note for the OECD" DAF/COMP/WD(2020)94 (OECD 1 December 2020); "Climate Change, Sustainability and Competition Law" (2020) 8(2) JAE 354; and "Climate Change, Sustainability and Competition Law in the UK" (2020) 41(8) ECLR 384.

2   "Competition and Environmental Sustainability" (ICC 26 November 2020), published by the ICC working group on sustainability that I chaired <https://iccwbo.org/publication/competition-policy-and-environmental-sustainability/>.

(or may not) be, they cannot be the correct starting point for an analysis of this issue if they are not part of the law in question.[3]

This book focuses on climate change and environmental sustainability for two key reasons. First, we face a climate emergency and this has to be our number one priority. Secondly, while other concerns (e.g. workers' rights) are important, bringing wider concerns into the "sustainability" net risks diluting or delaying urgent action to help competition law accommodate the fight against climate change.

There is now near-universal acceptance that climate change is an existential threat that requires maximum effort by government, the private sector, and individuals to combat it. The papers in this part of the book explain the scale of the problem and how competition law is relevant to this issue, and set out various solutions as to how competition law (and those in the competition law community) can play a part.

Our authors have different views on many things but there is also consensus on many things, and it is worth highlighting a few of these:

    i.   The seriousness of the climate change crisis. None of our authors are climate-change deniers: they disagree only on the extent to which competition law can play a part in, or is an obstacle to, effective action to combat climate change.

    ii.   Competition law and policy will never play more than a supporting role. In many (perhaps most) cases environmental regulation is the appropriate tool (e.g. regulating air quality or prohibiting the use of unsustainable inputs): the difference of opinion is as to the balance between regulation and private sector initiatives.

    iii.   Sustainability is an aspect of competition (as an aspect of quality and/or innovation) and individual businesses can, and should, compete on the basis of the sustainability of their products: the difference of opinion is over the extent to which it is either lawful or beneficial for business to cooperate to fight climate change and promote sustainability.

On a personal note, I believe there is much more that business must do collaboratively, and which can be done within the current legal framework (at least within the UK and the EU), if we are to fight climate change and move towards a more sustainable future at the necessary pace. However, my views are set out elsewhere.[4] This part sets out the views of a range of authors drawn from leading law firms, economic consultancies and academia. All their papers are excellent

---

3   The concept of "consumer welfare" appears nowhere in the Treaty on the Functioning of the European Union (TFEU) (or any other law with which I am familiar) and has never been endorsed by the Court of Justice of the EU.

4   See, for example, the papers cited in n 1.

in their own different ways. They look at environmental sustainability in the context of the rules governing:

    i.   Cooperation between businesses under Article 101 TFEU[5] (and its national equivalents);

   ii.   Abuse of dominance under Article 102 TFEU[6] (and national equivalents);

  iii.   Mergers under the European Merger Regulation (EUMR);

  iv.   State aid (under Article 107 TFEU); and

   v.   Public procurement (under the EU's various public procurement directives).[7]

To whet your appetite, I will say a few words about each chapter in this part, starting with those looking at cooperation and then going on to look at dominance, mergers, state aid and last, but not least, public procurement.

II. Cooperation

First up is our keynote paper by Maurits Dolmans of Cleary Gottlieb, which sets the scene on the extent of the climate crisis and, using both law and economics, analyses what can and needs to be done. He tackles head-on a number of points made by those who oppose a more sympathetic approach by the competition authorities to the climate crisis. He concludes that we need a "consistent programme of regulation, innovation, taxation, education, reforestation and private cooperation. Competition law should enable this cooperation, including by enabling agreements reflecting the 'polluter pays' principle".

Next up are Ellen van den Brink (Google) and Jordan Ellison (Slaughter & May) with a "Roadmap for Sustainable Cooperation". This paper focuses on one aspect of the debate, Article 101(3) TFEU. It provides a creative and practical solution, namely the "carbon defence", with easily understandable examples. In particular it points out that "a 'fair share' in the citizen/consumer context could be quite different from a 'fair share' in the firm/consumer context.

---

5   Article 101(1) TFEU prohibits anticompetitive agreements. They may be exempted if each of four conditions set out in Article 101(3) are met.

6   Article 102 TFEU makes illegal an abuse of a dominant position by a company (or more technically, an "undertaking").

7   I recognise that these papers are very much focused on EU law. This reflects the experience of the authors and the fact that Europe seems to have been the main region where this has been debated in the recent past (although see the papers in the "Agency Outlook" part of this book discussed later in this preface, looking at some excellent work in Australia and South Africa). Furthermore when speaking at conferences recently I have noted an increasing interest in the topic around the world. For example, all 24 counties of the OECD were present at its round table on Sustainability and Competition Policy on 1 December 2020, and the Concurrences conference on 6 November 2020 attracted over 700 delegates from over 60 countries.

This provides a basis to distinguish agreements to reduce GHG[8] emissions from other agreements."

In this sense it is consistent with the innovative approach taken by the excellent Dutch draft guidelines on sustainability and competition discussed in our next article by Theon van Dijk, chief economist of the Netherlands Authority for Consumers and Markets (ACM). This welcome paper is particularly interesting in providing an example of an economist supporting the more progressive agenda in relation to competition and sustainability, and provides an insight into how the ACM believes it is setting out a practical way forward.[9] It goes a long way towards answering some of the criticisms set out in the paper by Luc Peeperkorn (in the "Agency Outlook" part of this book) of the difficulties of taking into account so-called "out-of-market benefits" – but that is for you to judge.

Luc, as a former European Commission official, takes a different approach. He argues that for competition law to be effective it needs to keep its current focus and that a broader approach to welfare will undermine the rigour and uniform application of EU competition rules. For him, the current approach to competition policy is the best way in which it can help to tackle the climate crisis. Those of us who believe that competition law needs to be more accommodating of cooperation by business to fight climate change will probably find that he takes a rather optimistic view of regulation's ability to do enough and that his approach does not reflect the urgency of the climate crisis or the political mood of the 2020s.

That said, there is much with which we would agree and it is important to understand his point of view – which I am sure still reflects the views of many in the competition enforcement community. In this sense, even if many would like to go further than the ACM draft guidelines, they may well prove to be the necessary compromise if we are to move forward constructively in the fight against climate change. Let us not let the perfect be the enemy of the good.

Our next contribution is from an economist, Maarten Pieter Schinkel (together with Leonard Treuren), one of the leaders of those hostile to competition law being more accommodating of cooperation by businesses to fight climate change.

Maarten Pieter makes a number of very valid points. For example, he warns us of the danger that greater possibilities for businesses to cooperate in fighting climate change could be used as an excuse by governments not to take up their responsibilities and introduce the necessary level of regulation. He also reminds us that businesses have a natural incentive to maximise their profits, and we need to be careful that they do not deliver what he calls "minimal sustainability benefits

---

8   Greenhouse Gas.
9   ACM, "Draft Guidelines: Sustainability agreements, Opportunities within competition law" (9 July 2020, last updated on 26 January 2021).

for maximum price increases". In my view these are very timely reminders but not a reason to do nothing in this area: we need action by both government *and* business if we are to have any chance of fighting climate change on the scale that is required and with the urgency that is needed.

Paradoxically, in my view, Maarten Pieter is both too cynical and too optimistic. Over-cynical about the motives of business leaders genuinely trying to "make a difference". Over-optimistic in relation to the ability of governments and regulation to achieve everything that is necessary, and in relation to the ability of individual companies to introduce sustainable products both profitably and on a sufficient scale.

Like many economists, in my view he places too much emphasis on the need for information to verify sustainability claims. This contrasts with the Dutch draft guidelines on competition and sustainability which recognise that (as in life generally) it is not necessary to reduce everything to a quantification exercise.[10] Those who seek to quantify everything remind me of Oscar Wilde's cynic: someone who knows the price of everything and the value of nothing.

I do not doubt that Maarten Pieter is genuine when he recognises that climate change requires immediate action. However for me much of his analysis is not consistent with the urgency of the need for action. For example, he is concerned that cooperation by businesses to phase out unsustainable products is effectively a redistribution from the poor to the rich. I understand and sympathise with this concern. However, none of us (poor or rich) have the right to cheap products that do not reflect the true costs of the production (once some of the cost of producing them has been offloaded on society as a whole). It is vital that we phase out production methods and products that contribute excessively to climate change. If the resulting products are more expensive (which will not always be the case), then so be it. Where government action is needed is in ensuring that poorer people can pay for the goods that they need without excessive harm to the planet. This may mean providing specific support for, for example, energy bills or, more generally, through broader measures such as minimum wage legislation.[11] Having sustainable products is part of the true cost of living in the 21st century.

Although, it is included in the "Agency Outlook" part of this book, I would also refer anyone interested in cooperation between businesses to fight climate change or help the environment to the article by Georgina Foster, Grant Murray and Wendy Thian of Baker McKenzie giving an Australian perspective on this.

---

10 See ACM Guidelines (n 9), [45] – [54].

11 In the same way, the fact that miners will lose jobs as we phase out coal from the energy system, is not a reason to go on supporting coal to the tune of several billion dollars a year. It *is* a reason to provide adequate funds to support retraining programmes and to help local economies affected by pit closures – in other words, to ensure a "just transition".

Although the Australian statutory framework contains a "public interest" test, the analysis by the Australian competition authority (ACCC) considers factors and evidence which the European competition authorities (and no doubt others) are accustomed to assessing. Cases cited also show how the ACCC is able to strike a balance between looking at short-run price effects and broader longer-term benefits. Finally – and music to my ears – while the ACCC carefully assesses claimed benefits, this is not necessarily a nerdy arithmetical or accounting exercise – it may involve "an instinctive synthesis of otherwise incommensurable factors". Welcome to the real world!

After several articles looking at competition law and cooperation between businesses to fight climate change and other environmental harms, our next two articles look at sustainability and Article 102 TFEU, which deals with abuse of dominance.

III. Abuse of Dominance

The first of these articles is by two progressive academics, Marios Iacovides and Chris Vrettos, who argue that addressing unsustainable business practices through Article 102 TFEU is not only a theoretical possibility and mandated by EU constitutional law, but a real opportunity to address environmental and social injustices. While writers such as Suzanne Kingston and myself have addressed this,[12] this is a relatively unexplored area[13] and this paper is a welcome addition to the literature. It is very well researched (with good footnotes), drawing on work in a range of disciplines including law, economics and ecology.

One particular innovation is the original research looking at the relationship between those firms that have been found to be dominant by the European Commission in the past, and those firms that have been found to have been responsible for "socio-ecological conflict and its negative impacts for society and the environment".[14] Marios and Christos argue that there is a nexus between market power and unsustainable business practices.[15] Agree or disagree with this conclusion,[16] this is certainly something that merits serious consideration

---

12 See Suzanne Kingston, *Greening of EU Competition Law and Policy* (CUP 2011), chapter 9; and "Climate Change, Sustainability and Competition Law" (n 1), 30–36.
13 For example the Commission's public consultation "Competition Policy supporting the Green Deal" (13 October 2020) only asked for contributions on Article 101, merger control and state aid – but not Article 102. Why?
14 Using the Environmental Justice Atlas (EJAtlas). Leah Temper, Daniela Del Bene, Joan Martinez Alier, "Mapping the frontiers and front lines of global environmental justice: the EJAtlas (2015) 22 J Pol Ecology 255.
15 On this see further Michelle Meagher, *Competition is Killing Us: How Big Business is Harming Our Society and Planet – and What To Do About It*" (Penguin 2020).
16 While I found the research interesting, the finding that "dominant" companies are also responsible for negative environmental impacts etc is hardly surprising as many (not all) firms found to have a dominant position are large multinational companies which have the most impact on so many things (good and bad).

(and seems consistent with the current concerns about the relationship between power in digital markets and both anticompetitive practices and harms to society).

The paper makes a powerful plea for our approach to Article 102 not to lose sight of what it was supposed to (and can) achieve. How can we decide whether something is an "abuse" if we have lost sight of the purpose of the prohibition? We have got so trapped in a narrow (so-called) "more economic approach" or narrow consumer welfare standard that "competition lawyers are unable to think outside its narrow market logic confines". Policy can, and must, change – particularly in the light of climate change and the European Green Deal.

The authors argue that by "accepting that unsustainable business practices can be abuses of a dominant position... we focus on what we as a society and Article 102 TFEU care about". As they say, "a market logic may work, but do we really want everything to be filtered through that logic, if that is only possible because we contort concepts (e.g. consumer welfare) and tests that were devised in a different time and on the basis of discredited assumptions and failed ideologies?"

As I argued in my own paper,[17] none of this is as radical as it might seem at first (superficial) sight. As the authors conclude: "our approach is about more competition, just not the toxic kind. It is a call for refocusing competition policy and reconnecting concepts such as 'abuse' with the goals of the system of EU competition law. Our proposals are activist, but they are certainly not radical."[18]

Our next article is by Christopher Thomas, a partner at Hogan Lovells. I have looked at sustainability as a potential "shield", if a company is accused of abusing its dominant position when acting in the interests of the environment or the climate. Like Iacovides and Vrettos, I have also looked at Article 102 as a potential "sword" with which to attack unsustainable practices.[19]

Christopher Thomas does something different. He looks at Article 102 as a potential sword which might be used to attack, not unsustainable practices, but schemes with "laudable sustainability objectives". Citing as an example the famous "Green Dot" case,[20] his paper is a timely reminder that, when analysing

---

Do "dominant" companies have any more negative effects on the environment than firms of equivalent size? See also the comments by Dirk Middelschulte in his preface to the Industry Perspectives part of this book at note [14].

17 "Climate Change, Sustainability and Competition Law" (n 1).

18 For more on "toxic" competition see Maurice E Stucke and Ariel Ezrachi, *Competition Overdose: How Free Market Mythology Transformed Us from Citizen Kings to Market Servants* (Harper Business 2020).

19 See "Climate Change, Sustainability and Competition Law" (n 1).

20 DSD (Case COMP D3/34493) Commission decision C(2001) 1106 [2001] OJ L166/1; Michael Gremminger, Gerald Miersch, "The EU Commission finds that the company which created 'Green Dot' trademark, is restricting competition by abusing its dominant position in the market for

industry-wide schemes to achieve sustainability objectives, one needs to look carefully at their real-world implications for customers and their likely effect on the ability of rivals to compete. "Promoters of sustainability schemes need to exercise the same diligence, and not just assume that 'we're the good guys.'" In this he is, of course, correct.

Similar considerations apply when looking at the actions of individual firms pursuing sustainability objectives as the "'special responsibility' of a dominant firm not to allow its behaviour to impair genuine, undistorted competition... does not disappear simply because it is pursuing worthy environmental objectives". While I agree with such general statements, I do feel he is over-pessimistic when it comes to using sustainability as a "shield". *Hilti* and *TetraPak* which they cite were cases where the dominant companies tied two products together to their own commercial advantage and (at risk of over-simplification) tagged on some safety and health arguments to attempt to justify them. A dominant company that (for example) applies objectively justifiable sustainability criteria to determine who it will supply, or who it will buy from, should in my view have a much better chance of defending itself against allegations of abuse.[21]

Christopher's piece concludes by looking at whether Article 102 could be used as a sword to attack *un*sustainable practices. Although, he discusses this only very briefly, he seems to see limited possibilities for this, particularly as it is arguable whether those suffering harm as a result of damage to the climate or the environment do so "as consumers". However, while prejudice to consumers is a pre-condition for the application of Article 102(b), there is nothing in the other examples (and they are only examples) of abuse in Article 102 limiting the concept in this way.[22] I see scope for a lot more discussion of this in the years to come.

IV. EU Merger Control

Next we move on from "antitrust" to look at another relatively unexplored area: the relationship between environmental sustainability and EU merger control.

Our first article by Nicole Kar, Emma Cochrane and Bella Spring of Linklaters suggests that this might be "EU competition policy's dark horse to support green investment". They recognise that at present considerations of environmental

---

organizing the collection and recycling of sales packaging in Germany (System Deutschland)", 20 April 2001, e-Competitions April 2001, Art. N° 39082 ; upheld in Case C–385/07 P Der Grüne Punkt – Duales System Deutschland v Commission EU:C:2009:456; Anne-Lise Sibony, "Exploitative abuse: The ECJ confirms CFI judgement in relation to excessive licencing fees by the operator of the major recycling scheme in Germany (Der Grüne Punkt)" (2009) Concurrences N° 4–2009 Art N° 29258, 105–106.

21 See further "Climate Change, Sustainability and Competition Law" (n 1), 35–36.

22 This may be contrasted with the second condition for an exemption from the prohibition in Article 101(1) set out in Article 101(3) – which is discussed in several of the articles in this book on cooperation and in my "Climate Change, Sustainability and Competition Law" (n 1), 21–28.

factors in merger control tend to be asymmetric. It is more likely that these factors will be taken into account as (additional) reasons for the EU Commission to *block* a deal, or to require remedies, than as a reason to *clear* an otherwise problematic deal.

However this need not be the case, and the article explains how environmental factors can be part of the substantive merger assessment – both as a positive and negative factor. Intriguingly, they discuss a potential "virtuous circle" by which more merger cases with sustainability objectives or benefits push the Commission to conclude on key issues, such as its approach to the efficiency assessment. This much-needed certainty over the assessment framework could, in turn, encourage merging parties to pursue their own green investment agendas. They are, however, realistic and do not expect the outcome of a merger review to turn on environmental considerations alone. However they do expect environmental factors to play an increasingly important role in the analysis.

Our second article on EU merger control is by a team from the Brussels office of Dechert consisting of Alec Burnside, Marjolein De Backer and Delphine Strohl. While they recognise that the environmentally friendly and sustainable nature of products can form part of an EUMR assessment, they too don't think it likely that either "sustainability efficiencies" or a "decrease in such quality parameters" will be sufficient to change the outcome of a merger review. Indeed, they are less optimistic than the Linklaters team, suggesting that "the more social goals are added into the equation, the more complex the balancing act required. This would seem to go beyond the legitimate scope of EUMR review".

The Dechert team is, however, more optimistic about the possibility ("albeit limited") for Member States to intervene in merger cases on the basis of the legitimate interest provisions (set out in Article 21(4) EUMR). Their innovation is to link this with the evolving foreign direct investment (FDI) regime in Europe which provides the possibility for Member States (in limited circumstances) to take measures to protect interests other than competition – and either block a deal cleared at EU level or impose additional conditions (but not clear a deal that the Commission has blocked). They suggest that the FDI regime could inspire a broader interpretation of the concept of legitimate interest in the future.

They suggest that both the legitimate interest and FDI reviews "may by their nature be more suited to take sustainability and environmental protection into account than merger control".

See what you think.

Having covered the traditional areas of competition law, namely antitrust and merger control, we go on to look at two areas which are (or should be) an equally important part of a healthy competition policy – state aid and public procurement.

V. State Aid

The first article on state aid is by James Webber of Shearman & Sterling. This provides an excellent background to EU state aid and looks at how state aid is being used to promote environmental protection and energy-saving measures, and how it can support the European Green Deal. However, it also identifies the difficulties inherent in the European state aid system, especially the lack of speed and legal certainty and changing political priorities.

James is a lawyer and his perspective is complemented by our second article by Nicole Robins from the economic consultancy Oxera. She focuses on the positive need for state aid to support renewable energy, taking the example of the deployment of renewable hydrogen, and the (negative) need to phase out electricity generated from coal and lignite plants (rightly recognising that state aid rules have a vital role to play in ensuring that the transformation is implemented in an economically and socially viable way). She emphasises the need for "sound economic and financial analysis". This is not surprising coming from an economic consultant, but the point is no less valid for that.

VI. Public Procurement

Our final two chapters in the "Legal Themes" part of this book look at public procurement. This is very much the "poor relation" of competition law and policy. This is a pity as, without effective public procurement rules, there can be no level playing field and competition between countries and companies is inevitably distorted. Furthermore, intelligent use of public procurement rules (both as they currently stand and as how they might be developed) has considerable potential to promote a more sustainable future. The public sector has vast spending power[23] and this should be used, not only to obtain value for money for European citizens, but also to assist in the fight against climate change in general, and to promote the Green Deal, in particular. I am no expert in the area but I believe much greater use could, and should, be made of the "public purse".

The first article is by a Paris-based lawyer, Patrick Thieffry, and contains an interesting discussion of attempts to integrate sustainability into public procurement. In particular it contains a good discussion of attempts to include environmental externalities in the life-cycle costs of products (and respect the "polluter pays" principle). It shows that more thought has been given to these issues in public procurement directives (and related cases) than most competition lawyers or economists (myself included) realise. Those looking at the true costs

---

23 Public procurement constitutes the world's largest marketplace, having a value of some $13 trillion per year. Thiago Uehara, *Public Procurement for Sustainable Development* (Chatham House 19 November 2020).

of producing goods which cause environmental and other social harms (so that products can be properly priced to reflect those costs) could probably learn a lot from our public procurement colleagues.[24]

Last, but certainly not least, the chapter by Fiona Beattie of Macfarlanes, discusses the role of the EU public procurement regimes in furthering environmental policy objectives, and summarises how environmental considerations can be taken into account within the current legal regime. It then identifies some of the practical issues that may hinder the promotion of environmental considerations within public procurement regimes and considers how these challenges could be addressed.

VII. Concluding Remarks

Climate change is the biggest challenge facing humanity now and in the coming years. We must use all the tools and policies at our disposal to combat it. Competition policy, and the powerful tools we have to implement it, are no exception. Exactly how it can play its part is an important and legitimate debate. I hope you enjoy these varied contributions to this debate and are inspired to join some of the many seminars discussing it.

---

24 For an excellent discussion of "true costs" and "true pricing" see True Price Foundation, "A Roadmap for True Pricing. Vision Paper – Consultation draft" (2019) <https://trueprice.org/a-roadmap-for-true-pricing/> accessed 19 January 2020. This includes some helpful ideas on how to determine a "true price" in terms of:
   – Which external costs should be taken into account;
   – How negative externalities should be quantified; and
   – How to "monetise" them.
   (See, in particular, section IV of the paper and its appendix.)

Chapter 1
Cooperation

Sustainable Competition Policy and the "Polluter Pays" Principle

MAURITS DOLMANS*
Cleary Gottlieb Steen & Hamilton

I. The Writing On the Wall

We have known for decades that man destroys the environment. One hundred and fifty years ago, George Perkins Marsh wrote his monumental book *Man and Nature: Or, Physical Geography as Modified by Human Action*, predicting that due to human depredation of the environment, "The Earth is fast becoming an unfit home for its noblest inhabitant." Svante Arrhenius calculated in in 1896 that doubling the concentration of CO_2 in the atmosphere would lead to global warming by four degrees. Revelle and Suess warned about the climate effect of CO_2 emissions in 1957.[1]

In spite of the writing on the wall, we are only starting to acknowledge the threat from extreme weather conditions, wildfires, exhaustion of resources, extinction

* Maurits Dolmans is a partner in the competition law practice of Clearly Gottlieb in London and Brussels. He has extensive experience in information technology, internet, telecom, media and entertainment, as well as in energy and financial services. He has appeared in proceedings before the European Commission and the EU courts, national courts and national competition authorities of several Member States, and ICC and NAI arbitrations.
I am grateful for the thoughts of Simon Holmes, Nadine Watson, Julian Nowag, Areti Maria Kitsou, Quinten De Keersmaecker, David Pérez de Lamo, and Luc Peeperkorn (who kindly commented without agreeing). Errors are mine. For more detail, see Maurits Dolmans, "Sustainable Competition Policy" (2020) 5(4) and 6(1) Competition L & Pol Debate, draft at <https://papers.ssrn.com/sol3/papers.cfm?abstract_id=3608023>. For those who prefer video, see "Sustainable Competition Policy" (Concorrenze webinar, 28 May 2020), <www.youtube.com/watch?v=0lG8_oSI0PY>.

1 Roger Revelle and Hans E. Suess, "Carbon Dioxide Exchange Between Atmosphere and Ocean and the Question of an Increase of Atmospheric Increase of CO_2, During the Past Decades" (1957) 9(1) Tellus 18 <www.rescuethatfrog.com/wp-content/uploads/2017/01/Revelle-and-Suess-1957.pdf>

of wildlife, pollution of air, land and water, the rise of sea levels, and desertification of land and seas. Climate science points unambiguously at the causes: emission of pollutants and greenhouse gases (GHG), including methane and CO_2. We may have created a feedback loop, where temperature increases have triggered uncontrollable methane emissions from melting permafrost, and CO_2 emissions from wildfires and desiccating rainforests.

We must cut global net CO_2 emissions at least in half by 2030 (only nine years from now) and eliminate them altogether by 2050 to have a chance of limiting the average temperature increase to 1.5°C. Worse, just reducing net GHG emissions from human activity to zero is not enough. We need to *lower* GHG in the atmosphere to the levels prevailing before the sudden leap of carbon emissions in the 1950s. That means recapturing and permanently storing not just GHG from 70 years of human activities, but also the methane emitted by melting arctic tundra, and the CO_2 emissions from wildfires and drying and dying rainforests that are turning from carbon sinks into carbon sources.[2] Humanity needs to pull together.

1. Market forces alone cannot save us, because of market failures

Market forces are generally thought to lead to efficient outcomes, a proper allocation of resources, and innovation – leading to cheaper and cleaner production.[3]

Unfortunately, markets are characterised by *negative externalities*. The cost of pollution of air, water and land, and the damage wrought by GHG emissions today and in the future, are generally not included in the price of goods and services. Those costs are real, but are paid by people elsewhere, or in the future, who incur medical costs resulting from pollution, lose their home to wildfires or flooding, or lose a sustainable environment. These costs are, in other words, borne by society as a whole (social cost). Because the market price of a polluting product excludes the social cost, production is higher than the social optimum.

---

2   Myles Allen, "Achieving Net Zero – Challenges for Business and Investors" (AEBA webinar, 3 December 2020). V Masson-Delmotte and others, "IPCC Special Report on the impacts of global warming of 1.5°C above pre-industrial levels and related global greenhouse gas emission pathways, in the context of strengthening the global response to the threat of climate change, sustainable development, and efforts to eradicate poverty" (IPCC 2018) <www.ipcc.ch/site/assets/uploads/sites/2/2019/06/SR15_Full_Report_High_Res.pdf>, 17: "All pathways that limit global warming to 1.5°C with limited or no overshoot project the use of carbon dioxide removal (CDR) on the order of 100–1000 GtCO2 over the 21st century". See also T Gasser and others, "Negative emissions physically needed to keep global warming below 2°C" (2015) Nature Communications 6 7958 <www.nature.com/articles/ncomms8958>, and materials listed in Merritt Turesky and others, "Permafrost collapse is accelerating carbon release" (*Nature*, 30 April 2019) <www.nature.com/articles/d41586-019-01313-4>; Energy & Climate Intelligence Unit briefing, "Negative emissions: why, what, how?" (17 September 2018) <https://eciu.net/analysis/briefings/net-zero/negative-emissions-whywhat-how>.

3   See Luc Peeperkorn, "Competition and sustainability: What can competition policy do?" in Guy Canivet and others, *Sustainability and competition law* (2020) Concurrences N° 4–2020 Art N° 97390.

These externalities can be quantified. Leading economist Sir Nicholas Stern wrote in his 2006 report: "estimates of damage could rise to 20% of GDP or more."[4] Since then, Stern has warned we are "underestimating the risks of inaction and overestimating the cost of action."[5]

Negative externalities arise because of *"collective action problems"* (or "coordination problems"). When pricing goods (or making decisions that affect prices), firms tend to make independent choices designed to maximise their profits individually, based on perceived conflicting interests between them. For example, a firm may want to invest in clean production, but worry that this would raise variable costs, exposing it to the risk of being undercut by rivals drawing on cheaper dirty technology or raw materials. The firm may want to engage in R&D in sustainable production, but worry that it will be unable to recover a return on the associated investment. Unless the innovation leads to lower costs, fear of a first mover disadvantage may lead firms to stay away from investing in the better alternative, even if this leaves everyone worse off. This is an example of a "tragedy of the commons" – the degrading of our environment, due to overuse, in the absence of individual incentives to integrate the true cost of production in the price.[6] Sir Nicholas Stern concluded in 2007 that "climate change is a result of the greatest market failure the world has seen".[7]

Market failures do not exclude *all* competition on the basis of sustainability. As consumers become aware of climate change, environmental degradation and loss of biodiversity, they may come to regard sustainability as a quality improvement. This opens up the possibility for firms to compete on the basis of being cleaner and greener than their rivals.[8] This can adequately address sustainability concerns only, however, if the greener production is also cheaper or if:

 a) Customers' willingness to pay more for a green product (WTP) must be enough to finance investments to avoid the environmental costs to society, e.g., to cover the product's "True Price", including not just the market price but also the unpaid external cost of carbon (the social costs of carbon, or SCC);[9]

---

4   Nicholas Stern, *Stern Review: The Economics of Climate Change* (CUP 2006) <http://mudancasclimaticas. cptec.inpe.br/~rmclima/pdfs/destaques/sternreview_report_complete.pdf>.
5   Naomi Oreskes and Nicholas Stern, "What's the Price of Ignoring Climate Change?" *New York Times* (New York, 5 November 2019) <www.nytimes.com/2019/11/05/opinion/climate-change-economics.html>.
6   James M Buchanan and Yong J Yoon, "Symmetric Tragedies: Commons and Anticommons" (2000) 43(1) JL Econ 1, <www.jstor.org/stable/725744>. Peter Howard and Derek Sylvan, *Expert Consensus on the Economics of Climate Change* (Institute for Policy Integrity 2015) <www.edf.org/sites/default/ files/expertconsensusreport.pdf>.
7   Nicholas Stern, "Climate Change, Ethics and the Economics of the Global Deal" (*Economist's View*, 29 November 2007) <https://economistsview.typepad.com/economistsview/2007/11/nicholas-stern.html>.
8   This section reflects portions written by the author for an ICC paper on "Competition Policy and Sustainability Goals".
9   See True Price Foundation, "A Roadmap for True Pricing" (June 2019) <https://trueprice.org/a-roadmap-for-true-pricing/>. The ACM uses the abatement cost (the cost to prevent and remove pollution and GHG emissions) as a shadow price. See ACM, "Draft Guidelines: Sustainability agreements" (9 July 2020) (ACM Draft Guidelines), 15–16.

b) Sufficiently reliable labelling and monitoring mechanisms must exist to allow consumers easily to determine which products are actually GHG-neutral, and to avoid misleading claims and greenwashing; or

c) Individual firms must be able to achieve the minimum economies of scale and scope to justify an investment to eliminate the pollution or GHG emission.

In markets where WTP > True Price, or where individual firms can achieve sufficient scale to eliminate carbon emissions and pollution individually, it may be enough to agree on objective, relevant and effectively monitored criteria for a green label, and otherwise leave firms to compete.[10] In such markets, agreements on specific sustainability solutions may be counterproductive.[11]

Unfortunately, when assessing WTP, we see market failures on the demand side, too, which mean that the WTP may not be enough to support greener production.[12] Consumers may resist paying more for green products when neighbours don't pay, and thus free ride at their expense. Their expectations are "anchored" by past experience of not paying a True Price, and paying for externalities may be perceived as "unfair", even if it is rational. Other market failures include irrational conduct like "hyperbolic discounting" (underestimating the importance of future environmental damage), and lack of accessible and reliable information about future costs of continuing emissions.

Competition policy should take these points into account when assessing sustainability agreements. Where WTP < True Price, or economies of scale or scope are needed, antitrust authorities should permit agreements that effectively pursue

---

10 If the average WTP > True Price but there are a significant number of consumers unwilling to pay as much as the average consumer, cooperation may still be needed.

11 Schinkel and Spiegel find that if consumers are willing to pay fully for sustainability, an agreement to coordinate on sustainability may create less sustainability than a traditional price/quantity cartel. See Maarten Pieter Schinkel and Yossi Spiegel, "Can Collusion Promote Sustainable Consumption and Production?" (2017) 53(C) IJ Industrial Organization, 371; Maarten Pieter Schinkel and Lukáš Tóth, "Compensatory Public Good Provision by a Private Cartel" Amsterdam Law School Research Paper No 2016-5 (16 December 2019) <https://papers.ssrn.com/sol3/papers.cfm?abstract_id=2723780>. This does not mean that sustainability agreements should not be allowed. The model is based on several assumptions that limit the conclusion: for instance, it assumes every consumer wishes to maximize consumption of market goods, and must be fully compensated for any price increase, in the same market. This excludes compensation of the same consumers in different goods or non-market goods, and excludes consideration of benefits to other consumers or to society. In-market full compensation is in the guidelines for convenience, but it is not a requirement of EU law, as discussed below. Second, every producer is presumed to be a short-term profit maximiser. That ignores that more firms are realising the risks that climate change entails for them in the short, mid and long term. It ignores the trend towards stakeholder capitalism, shareholder activism and ESG investment. In a tinder-dry world, I derive benefit if the fire in my neighbour's house is quenched.

12 Other factors affect WTP, including the concern that the margin over the cost of production will be pocketed by the producer rather than used to avoid pollution and GHG emissions, or for effective carbon offset. Many consumers may be unable to pay. A climate change policy leading to a True Price must therefore encompass a social justice element that includes a living wage adjusted to account for internalisation of SCC in the price of goods.

sustainability goals even if they lead to higher market prices, so long as they lower the True Price at least in equal measure, and meet the conditions of proportionality or individual exemption (as discussed below). Before discussing this, the following sections discuss why reasons often invoked against integration of sustainability goals in competition policy are deficient.

2. Regulation alone cannot save us, because of government failures

Those who oppose sustainability goals in competition policy argue that the most effective and efficient form of coordination is regulation and taxation. Examples are bans on polluting production, emission limits, carbon taxation or emission rights trading systems (ETS). The idea of taxation and ETS is to integrate the social costs of production in the True Price, avoiding price externalities, and so to encourage cleaner production.

Regulation and taxation are needed, but it is unfortunately too late to rely *solely* on True Price to address climate change.[13] GHG emissions since the industrial revolution have unleashed runaway climate feedback processes that lead to GHG emissions from nature, such as the methane from melting permafrost and the CO_2 from wildfires and drying rainforests. This requires a combination of GHG reduction and innovation to extract and permanently sequester carbon – a *negative* carbon policy – at potentially huge expense.

Second, taxation or ETSs to achieve a True Price are necessary, but not sufficient, since price increases only lead to a reduction of demand and substitution at the margin.

Moreover, funds raised by taxes are not necessarily used to mitigate and adapt to climate change, or to avoid pollution.

Third, only few countries have adopted carbon taxes and ETSs, and those that exist cover only a portion of the economy (in the EU, ETSs cover about 45% of GHG emissions).[14] The EU Green Deal proposes lowering caps, reducing free ETS allowances allocated to airlines, and extending emissions trading to the maritime sector and perhaps construction, but will leave many sectors of the economy unaffected. Moreover, existing regulation appears to be inadequate – the right to emit a tonne of CO_2 until recently traded at around €25, well below an effective carbon emission price, which should equal at least the social cost of carbon of \$47–130 (depending on the discount rate applied).[15]

---

13 See, e.g., Anthony Patt and Johan Lilliestam, "The case against carbon prices" (19 December 2018) Joule 2, 2487–2510 ("carbon prices are outdated. They made sense as our primary tool against climate change when our climate policy ambitions were limited and the greatest barrier was cost. Today our ambition is to eliminate CO_2 emissions entirely, and the greatest barriers are associated with infrastructure and institutions.").

14 EU Emissions Trading System, <https://ec.europa.eu/clima/policies/ets_en>.

15 Howard and Sylvan (n 6). The social cost of methane and nitrous oxide is up to \$3,200 and \$39,000 per tonne, respectively. US Environmental Protection Agency, "The Social Cost of Carbon"

Environmental regulation is, moreover, time consuming – EU directives and regulations require years from conception to effective implementation, if adopted at all.

The reality is that taxation and regulation remain inadequate because they are politically controversial until it is too late. There are several causes for this "government failure", including:

> "governments may lack incentives for climate mitigation action, since the benefits of these mostly accrue to citizens of other jurisdictions or countries... Economic agents gaining from the status quo may have the incentive, the means and the ability to coordinate targeted lobbying of government and influencing media... Democratically elected governments are subject to election cycles and can have limited ability to make long-term commitments..."[16]

Some opponents of integrating sustainability and competition policy invoke Nobel Prize winner Jan Tinbergen. According to Tinbergen, a regulator should have one policy goal, and if a government pursues various policy goals, it should have separate instruments for each goal.[17] But sustainability is not *separate* from competition policy.[18] The two goals should be *integrated*, recognising that a fully effective competition policy cannot ignore market failures and external effects, and should take account of the costs of climate change and pollution, certainly where these costs can be quantified, just like it takes account of effects on price, quality, innovation and consumer choice. We cannot afford the spectre of different government agencies pursuing goals that are perceived as inconsistent, with antitrust authorities rejecting arrangements that environmental authorities would encourage. Antitrust authorities should perhaps worry more about another concern of Tinbergen, namely that "personal or institutional inertia and the tendency to maintain the existent are other frequent factors which often impede the execution of a rational policy".[19]

In addition, some argue that competition authorities should ignore sustainability goals because if they do, they should consider *all* 17 UN Sustainable Development

---

<https://19january2017snapshot.epa.gov/climatechange/social-cost-carbon_.html> accessed 2 January 2021. See also Noah Kaufman, "A new way to calculate the price of carbon pollution" (*State of the Planet: Earth Institute, Columbia University*, 17 August 2020) <https://blogs.ei.columbia.edu/2020/08/17/new-way-calculate-price-carbon-pollution/>.

16 Signe Krogstrup and William Oman, "Macroeconomic and Financial Policies for Climate Change Mitigation: A Review of the Literature" (2019) IMF Working Paper No.19/185.

17 Jan Tinbergen, *On the Theory of Economic Policy* (North-Holland Publishing Company 1952). Peeperkorn (n 3).

18 According to the Commission, Article 101(3) TFEU provides "... a legal framework for the economic assessment of restrictive practices and not to allow the application of the competition rules to be set aside because of political considerations..." (Commission, *White Paper on the Modernisation of the Rules Implementing Articles 85 and 86 of the EC Treaty* [2000] OJ C132/1, [57]). But see Joined Cases T–528/93 and others, *Métropole Télévision v Commission* [1996] ECR II-649, [118] ("the Commission is entitled to base itself on considerations connected with the pursuit of the public interest in order to grant exemption").

19 Tinbergen (n 17), 76.

Goals,[20] all of the 20-odd goals listed by the EU treaties or national constitutions, or industrial policy concerns, and doing this is not realistic.[21] That is not a reason not to integrate climate change mitigation in competition policy, however. The climate crisis and looming environmental disasters like the decline of pollinators pose a unique, existential threat to humanity, and (contrary to many other objectives) the damage can be quantified.[22] The European Parliament has declared a climate emergency,[23] and the Commission has recognised it as a top priority.[24] Article 191(2) TFEU mandates that EU policy on environmental sustainability should be based on the "precautionary principle", i.e., requires the EU to take appropriate measures "by giving precedence to the requirements related to the protection of those interests over economic interests."[25]

Moreover, climate change mitigation is an obligation under international law: the 2015 Paris Agreement requires signatories to restrict the increase in the global average temperature to "well below 2°C above preindustrial levels and pursuing efforts to limit the temperature increase to 1.5°C" (article 2(1)(a)). The EU Charter of Fundamental Rights requires the EU to protect the fundamental right to life (article 2(1)) and provides that "a high level of environmental protection and the improvement of the quality of the environment must be integrated into the policies of the Union and ensured in accordance with the principle of sustainable development" (article 37).[26] The Dutch Supreme Court held in *Urgenda* that Articles 2 and 8 ECHR mandate a "positive obligation" for governments "to take appropriate steps to safeguard the lives of those within its jurisdiction" in view of a "real and immediate risk" from climate change. Antitrust authorities would violate these obligations if they did not integrate climate change and environmental protection in competition policy.[27]

In sum, we cannot wait for regulation, taxation, and carbon trading to provide a perfect solution. We need all hands on deck now. That includes competition authorities enabling private initiative. Taking environmental goals into account in competitive analysis is necessary, proportionate, legal and required by law. Other, less urgent objectives should be assessed on their own merits. We cannot let the perfect be the enemy of the good.

---

20   UN, "Make the SDGS a reality" <https://sdgs.un.org/> accessed 2 January 2021.
21   See, e.g., Peeperkorn (n 3), [37] ff.
22   See, for instance, Sander de Bruyn and others, *Environmental Prices Handbook 2017* (CE Delft 2018) <www.cedelft.eu/en/publications/2113/envionmental-prices-handbook-2017>.
23   European Parliament resolution of 28 November 2019 on the climate and environment emergency (2019/2930(RSP)) <www.europarl.europa.eu/doceo/document/TA-9-2019-0078_EN.html>.
24   Ursula von der Leyen, "A Union that strives for more: Political Guidelines for the Next Commission 2019–2024" (2019).
25   Joined Cases T–74/00 and others *Artegodan v Commission* EU:T:2002:283 [184].
26   Case C–723/17 *Craeynest v Brussels Hoofdstedelijk Gewest* [2020] Env LR 4, EU:C:2019:168, Opinion of AG Kokott.
27   Peeperkorn (n 3), correctly points out that "under the ECHR, it is states – and not firms – that are obliged to protect their citizens". This means that there is no *obligation* on firms to take action, but if they do, the *antitrust authorities* are *bound* to allow them if the conditions of proportionality or Art 101(3) are met.

3. Innovation may save us, but we cannot just bet on that

The EU Green Deal includes support for Important Projects of European Interest,[28] and rules for state aid to foster innovation and transition away from hydrocarbons. Jonathan Foley's "Project Drawdown" provides a great inventory of innovation.[29] Some advocate "Los Alamos"-style research labs, staffed by researchers from various countries, all working on carbon capture.[30] Others speculate about "solar radiation management" and geo-engineering.[31]

An effective competition policy encourages innovation to abate and undo climate change and pollution. Some of the market failures mentioned above play a role also in innovation policy, including coordination problems, first mover disadvantages, and the need to achieve scale and spread risks. The EU and other jurisdictions recognise this and have adopted precedents, guidelines and block exemptions to encourage cooperation in R&D. But mere techno-optimism will not save us. Given the risks involved, the exponential increase of problems and possible tipping at unpredictable moments, we cannot sit back and wait for engineers to produce a *deus ex machina*. Until viable technological solutions are proven fully effective and scalable, we must do all we can to abate and undo GHG emissions. That includes effective and efficient cooperation between market players.

4. Sustainability agreements can benefit consumers

While some sustainability agreements may lower costs or increase production as a result of innovation, the expectation is that they will often raise price and lower output. That does not necessarily mean they harm consumers, for the following reason.

The traditional approach is that consumer surplus increases as quality increases (and WTP increases), or prices decrease, in which case output increases:

$$\text{Overall Consumer Surplus} = (\text{WTP} - \text{Market Price}) \times \text{Quantity Consumed}$$

The problem is that where negative externalities arise, the market price is not the True Price. In accordance with the "polluter pays" requirement under Article 191(2) TFEU, producers should pay for consumption of public resources.

---

28 Commission, "Criteria for the analysis of the compatibility with the internal market of State aid to promote the execution of important projects of common European interest" [2014] OJ C188/4 <https://eur-lex.europa.eu/legal-content/EN/TXT/?uri=CELEX:52014XC0620(01)>.

29 Project Drawdown: The world's leading resource for climate solutions <www.drawdown.org/> accessed 2 January 2021.

30 Shi-Ling Hsu, "Capital Transitioning: An International Human Capital Strategy for Climate Innovation" *Transnational Environmental Law* (CUP 2016) <http://myweb.fsu.edu/shsu/publications/XXTransEnvtlLXX.pdf>.

31 See Daisy Dunne, "Explorer: Six ideas to limit global warming with solar geoengineering" (*Carbon Brief* 9 May 2018) <www.carbonbrief.org/explainer-six-ideas-to-limit-global-warming-with-solar-geoengineering>.

The price taken into account in a calculation of overall consumer welfare therefore equals Market Price + SCC, and:

$$\text{Overall Consumer Surplus} =$$
$$(\text{WTP} - \text{Market Price} - \text{SCC}) \times \text{Quantity Consumed}$$

If the SCC decrease is more than the market price increase, consumers still benefit overall.[32] But do private actors have sufficient incentive to lower the SCC, and can this adequately compensate consumers who care little about sustainability (or cannot afford to pay more[33])?[34] The more consumers who attach little value to sustainability, the more difficult it is to compensate them for a price increase.

Whether a sustainability agreement that raises prices should be allowed depends on whether consumers must be fully compensated for the price increase in quality or monetary terms, and whether that compensation must be in the same product market. As explained below, that is current EU policy, but is not required by EU law – and violates the "polluter pays" principle under Article 191(2) TFEU. But even apart from that:

– Whether consumers are adequately compensated should not be assessed just on the basis of consumption in market goods – goods that have an observable monetary value. Models assuming that consumer welfare is directly proportional to consumption of market goods are inadequate. Consumers derive utility from non-market goods, too, including clean air, water, an enjoyable natural and biodiverse environment, health, and the prospect of a sustainable and just future. Models based on purely rational, selfish, consumption-maximising consumers and profit-maximising producers do not fully reflect human reality. Humans may attach a real value to non-market resources even if they do not (or not yet) consume these themselves – and that value increases the scarcer the non-market goods are. Informative economic models should at least build in a choice for non-market goods, so as to allow for trade-off between consumption of market goods and access to non-market goods.[35]

– When valuing the utility of non-market goods, WTP is usually assessed based on stated preferences (surveys), or revealed preference studies.[36]

32 Some might argue that consumer surplus should be determined at an individual level, in part because individual consumers do not pay for externalities. (That is equivalent to saying a shoplifter should be allowed the surplus from not paying for his shopping.) See discussion below on non-market goods and how consumers benefit also from benefits accruing to fellow citizens.
33 The solution is a proper social safety net and provision of affordable sustainable alternatives, not ignoring sustainability at the expense of everyone losing out.
34 Schinkel and Spiegel (n 11).
35 See also Maurice E Stucke, "Should Competition Policy Promote Happiness" (2013) 81 Fordham L Rev <https://papers.ssrn.com/sol3/papers.cfm?abstract_id=2203533>.
36 See, for instance, Rick Baker and Brad Ruting, "Environmental Policy Analysis: A Guide to Non-Market Valuation" Australian Government Productivity Commission Staff Working Paper (2014) <www.pc.gov.

It is important, though, not to fall for demand-side market failures, as mentioned above. Many consumers underestimate the future cost of climate change, or the effects that imposing costs on others may have for themselves in the long run. A proper WTP study therefore needs to explain the social costs of GHG to survey participants and the benefits of abatement (to reduce imperfect information, confirmation bias and hyperbolic discounting), neutralise free rider concerns, and give the option of sacrificing consumption as an alternative to just paying more. Where future costs of current consumption can be objectively calculated, it is better to rely on that than on surveys reflecting subjective judgments. This may be considered paternalistic but, given the risks at stake, we cannot afford to ignore known cognitive biases and irrational behaviour.

II. A Model For a "Polluter Pays" Agreement

For the reasons explained above, especially in markets where WTP < True Price, competition policy should enable cooperation between market players, to overcome market failures and compensate for government failures, or to create a minimum efficient scale. An example would be an agreement between truck makers to phase out combustion engines by 2040 and invest in clean propulsion.[37] Actual and potential examples are found elsewhere in this book.[38]

Opponents of integrating sustainability in competition policy occasionally denigrate sustainability agreements as "cartels", and argue that one should not try to justify the price increase inherent in any cartel on the ground of reduced emissions, because that would just create a windfall for the cartelists without adequate sustainability effort, failing the "fair share to consumers" test. This argument does not invalidate real sustainability agreements.

Consider the following thought experiment, involving a model for a "polluter pays agreement" within an industry sector (say, airlines flying a particular route). Participants could agree to each calculate the SCC of their individual GHG emissions, and each commit to spend that amount (minus the cost of

---

au/research/supporting/non-market-valuation/non-market-valuation.pdf>. See also Bengt Kriström and Per-Olov Johansson, "Economic Valuation Methods for Non-market Goods or Services" (*Oxford Bibliographies in Environmental Science* 2019) <www.oxfordbibliographies.com/view/document/obo-9780199363445/obo-9780199363445-0044.xml>.

37 ACEA, "All new trucks sold must be fossil free by 2040, agree truck makers and climate researchers" Press release (15 December 2021) <www.acea.be/press-releases/article/all-new-trucks-sold-must-be-fossil-free-by-2040-agree-truck-makers-and-clim>.

38 The ACM Draft Guidelines mention codes of conduct for environmentally or climate-conscious market behaviour; agreements to stop polluting production; initiatives that create new products or markets or that require a joint initiative to achieve sufficient scale; and agreements to respect laws. See also Dirk Middelschulte, "Sustainability cooperations between competitors & Art 101 TFEU: Unilever submission to DG COMP" (2020).

any GHG taxation or emission trading rights) for a period of time on effective GHG offset,[39] or on **R&D** to eliminate **GHG** emissions (e.g., carbon-neutral jet fuel[40]). They could engage in joint **R&D** to the extent permitted under the joint **R&D** Block Exemption Regulation and the Guidelines on Horizontal Agreements. Each participant may pass all or some of its costs on to customers, but need not do so – and they should avoid any understanding or information exchange to that effect. They are free, for instance, to lower their margins and absorb these costs. This way, they retain an incentive to reduce their individual emissions as much as they can through innovation. To avoid cheating, they certify compliance with a green label, and charge an independent auditor to monitor and verify compliance (with an efficient penalty going to joint **R&D** or carbon offset).[41]

This is just a model. The agreement can take various forms, such as a commitment to achieve some standard to abate emissions or pollutions. Nowag and Teorell posit the idea of an online platform connecting buyers willing to pay a True Price and sellers selling at a True Price.[42] They point out that the platform model offers vast opportunities, but entails high risks. These risks could be eliminated by structuring the platform in accordance with this model.

1. Restriction of competition and consumer harm?

The "polluter pays agreement" does not qualify as a hard core cartel or a by object restriction, in that the parties do not agree to "fix prices or output or to share markets".[43] It could be argued that it "enables the parties to maintain, gain or increase market power", since it addresses a market failure that makes it difficult to make the investment independently, but query whether this is "likely to give rise to negative market effects with respect to prices, output, product quality, product variety or innovation"?[44] That depends on whether the effect is, on balance, "negative".

On the one hand, the effect on price is desirable in that that it restores a True Price, solving a coordination problem and eliminating a market failure – which the parties

---

39 See Myles Allen and others, *The Oxford Principles for Net Zero Aligned Carbon Offsetting* (University of Oxford 2020) <www.smithschool.ox.ac.uk/publications/reports/Oxford-Offsetting-Principles-2020.pdf>.
40 Stephen Beard, "A new jet fuel offers the prospect of no-carbon, "guilt-free" flying" (*Marketplace* 2019) <www.marketplace.org/2019/10/10/anew-jet-fuel-offers-the-prospect-of-no-carbon-guilt-free-flying/>.
41 For the penalty to be efficient and effective, it should be calculated by reference to the profits that the firm expected to obtain from the infringement, divided by the probability of detection. Gary S Becker, "Crime and punishment: an economic approach" (1968) 76(2) J Political Econ 169.
42 Julian Nowag and Alexandra Teorell, "Beyond Balancing: Sustainability and Competition Law" in Guy Canivet and others, *Sustainability and competition law* (2020) Concurrences N° 4–2020, Art N° 97390. The concept already exists offline <https://trueprice.org/true-price-store-opening/>.
43 Commission, "Guidelines on the applicability of Article 101 of the Treaty on the Functioning of the European Union to horizontal co-operation agreements" [2011] OJ C11/1 (Horizontal Guidelines), [3] and [25].
44 Horizontal Guidelines, [3]. A restriction by effect requires "an appreciable adverse impact on at least one of the parameters of competition on the market, such as price, output, product quality, product variety or innovation" ([27]).

could not do independently[45] – while enabling green innovation or carbon offset, and maintaining price competition. On the other hand, since marginal costs increase for all participants, there is a good chance that market prices will increase (and output will decrease). Whether that happens depends on whether cost commonalities are significant, margins are enough to absorb the cost of paying for the SCC, and the market remains sufficiently competitive. Innovation may in time lead to lower production costs. If prices increase, that may be offset by price decreases for complementary products, immediately or at a later stage. Even if there is no such offset, the effect may still be positive if consumers perceive the arrangement as a quality increase. A WTP study could provide insight, provided that the study is organised and questions are phrased in a way that avoids demand-side market failures as discussed above. If the average WTP is equal to or greater than the expected market price increase, the agreement should pass.

2. Ancillary restraints, proportionality and constitutional principles

If prices increase and sustainability benefits arise, the current Guidelines on Horizontal Agreements provide that "the balancing of restrictive and pro-competitive effects is conducted exclusively within the framework laid down by Article 101(3)".[46] The reason so to limit the analysis seems to be administrative convenience, yet CJEU case law also permits a balancing test as part of an ancillary restraints analysis under Article 101(1) TFEU.

In *Albany*, for instance, collective labour agreements fell outside Article 101(1) TFEU.[47] The CJEU reviewed "the objectives to be pursued by the Community and the Member States" set out in Article 2 EC (now Article 3 TEU), and other provisions on social policy. It "follows from an interpretation of the provisions of the Treaty as a whole which is both effective and consistent that agreements concluded in the context of collective negotiations between management and labour in pursuit of such objectives must, by virtue of their nature and purpose, be regarded as falling outside the scope of Article [101](1)".[48] The keys were the "nature" of the agreement (a multi-stakeholder arrangement), and its "purpose" (an EU goal of constitutional importance).

In *Wouters,* a prohibition of partnerships of lawyers and accountants fell outside Article 101 TFEU.[49] The prohibition restricted competition, but Article 101 did not apply in view of its "overall context" and "objectives". The former included

---

45 Horizontal Guidelines, [30].
46 See Commission, "Guidelines on the application of Article 81(3) of the Treaty" [2004] OJ C101/97 (Exemption Guidelines), [20] and [43]. Article 101(3) TFEU does not mention "pro-competitive effects".
47 Case C–7/96 *Albany International BV v Stichting Bedrijfspensioenfonds Textielindustrie* [1999] ECR I-5751.
48 ibid [60].
49 Case C–309/99 *Wouters v Algemene Raad van de Nederlandse Orde van Advocaten* [2002] ECR I-1577, [86] ff.

"the need to make rules relating to organisation, qualifications, professional ethics, supervision and liability", and the latter was a public policy interest "to ensure... integrity and experience". The court analysed whether the restrictions were "inherent" in or "necessary" for the public policy interest. It concluded that the measure passed muster because it could "reasonably be considered to be necessary in order to ensure the proper practice of the legal profession".

Finally, in *Meca-Medina,* restrictions on athletes to penalise them for doping escaped Article 101 TFEU.[50] The court again referred to the "overall context" and "objectives", and "whether the consequential effects restrictive of competition are inherent in the pursuit of those objectives... and are proportionate to them".[51] Anti-doping rules were permissible as "inherent in the organisation and proper conduct of competitive sport and its very purpose is to ensure healthy rivalry between athletes".

These cases have in common a restriction of competition that was inherent[52] in, and proportionate to, an objective not merely of commercial nature or efficiency-related, but reflecting important public policy. This same could apply to agreements pursuing environmental goals and climate change mitigation, because these are core EU objectives.

- Article 3(3) TEU states that the Union shall work for "the sustainable development of Europe based on... a high level of protection and improvement of the quality of the environment". The word "improvement" means mere stability is not enough, and "shall" indicates a mandatory goal. Article 3(5) TEU clarifies this is not limited to EU territory, stating that the EU "shall contribute to... the sustainable development of the Earth".

- Article 7 TFEU confirms that these are not isolated objectives, but that "the Union shall ensure consistency between its policies and activities, taking all of its objectives into account..." Article 11 TFEU reiterates that "environmental protection requirements *must* be integrated into the definition and implementation of the Union's policies and activities, in particular with a view to promoting sustainable development".[53] Article 37

---

50 Case C–519/04 P *Meca-Medina and Majcen v Commission* [2006] ECR I-6991; Marc van der Woude, "Antidoping rules: The ECJ holds that the CFI gave a too narrow definition of the scope of the competition rules, but rejects the application in view of the legitimate objective pursued by the contested rules (*Meca-Medina*)" (2006) Concurrences N° 4–2006, Art N° 12548, 68.
51 ibid [42].
52 On ancillary restraints, see also Case C–382/12 P *Mastercard v Commission* EU:C:2014:2201, [91]; Irene Fraile, "The EU Court of Justice dismisses the final appeal in a case regarding inter-bank card fees *(MasterCard)*" (2014) e-Competitions Art N° 68929.
53 See also Case T–210/02 *British Aggregates v Commission*, EU:T:2012:110, [117] ("the principle whereby all Community measures must satisfy the requirements of environmental protection"); Bruno Stromsky, "Advantage – Selectivity: The General Court reduces State's freedom to grant exemptions from an environmental levy, since every exemption has to be justified taking into account the objective pursued by this levy (*British Aggregates/Commission*)" (2012) Concurrences N° 2–2012, Art N° 45780; and Case C–62/88 *Greece v Council* [1990] ECR I-1527, [20].

of the EU Charter of Fundamental Rights repeats that a "high level of environmental protection and the *improvement* of the quality of the environment *must* be integrated into the policies of the Union and ensured in accordance with the principle of sustainable development".[54]

– Article 191(2) TFEU, finally, provides that "Union policy on the environment shall aim at a high level of protection… It shall be based on the precautionary principle and on the principles that preventive action should be taken, that environmental damage should as a priority be rectified at source and that the polluter should pay." This means that, in case of doubt, environmental protection takes precedence over economic interests.[55]

The "polluter pays agreement" above pursues objectives consistent with these provisions. An obligation on producers to invest an amount equal to their individual SCC is "inherent" in the principle of "polluter pays" under Article 191(2) TFEU. The agreement would clearly fall under *Albany* if it resulted from multi-stakeholder negotiations including suppliers, consumer associations and environmental groups.[56] It can be argued, however, that *Albany* is broader and applies to other agreements that are justified – i.e., reasonably necessary and proportionate – to achieve goals of constitutional importance. After all, *Wouters* and *Meca-Medina* did not involve multi-stakeholder arrangements, yet were cleared.

The proportionality test, finally, would require proof that (a) the agreement is capable of achieving the objective; (b) there are no less restrictive and equally efficient and effective ways of doing so; and (c) a balancing of interests of all stakeholders militates in favour of the agreement.[57] In balancing these interests, it should be kept in mind that competition (contrary to sustainability) is no longer an EU objective of constitutional importance, but a mere tool, since the Treaty of Lisbon relegated the text of Article 3(1)(g) EC to a mere recital in Protocol (No 27).

3. Article 101(3) TFEU (ad hoc exemption analysis)

Even if the *Albany* and *Wouters* exception does not apply, a "polluter pays agreement" should pass the conditions of Article 101(3) TFEU.

---

54 Emphasis added. As the Dutch Supreme Court held in *Urgenda*, Articles 2 and 8 ECHR mandate a "positive obligation" for governments "to take appropriate steps to safeguard the lives of those within its jurisdiction" in view of a "real and immediate risk" from climate change via "reasonable and appropriate measures." Dutch Supreme Court Case 19/00135 *Netherlands v Urgenda* NL:HR:2019:2007. See also Article 2(1) of the EU Charter of Fundamental Rights, which protects "the fundamental right to life".

55 Joined Cases T–74/00 *Artegodan v Commission* [2002] ECR II-4945, [184].

56 Giorgio Monti, "Four Options for a Greener Competition Law" (2020) 11(3–4) JECLAP 124 (arguing the *Albany* exception requires "discussion among a range of stakeholders that are affected by the policy (e.g. producers of the polluting product, its employees, consumers and non-governmental organisations representing relevant environmental interests)").

57 See C–331/88 *Fedesa and others* [1990] ECR I-4023, [13].

To qualify for exemption under Article 101(3), the agreement must "contribute to improving the production *or* distribution of goods *or* to promoting technical *or* economic progress" (emphasis added), (2) "[allow] consumers a fair share of the resulting benefit", (3) "not... impose... restrictions which are not indispensable to the attainment of these objectives", and (4) "not... afford such undertakings the possibility of eliminating competition in respect of a substantial part of the products in question."

Benefits. The goals of Article 101(3) TFEU are exhaustive, but stated in the alternative. They include sustainability.[58] "Improving production" includes a better allocation of resources resulting from internalisation of environmental and climate costs, and circular economy practices. "Improving distribution" includes lowering the ecological footprint of transport. "Technical progress" includes development and implementation of new sustainability technology. "Economic progress" is anything that provides a higher standard of living[59] – including access to both market and non-market goods.

A fair share to consumers. To determine if consumers get "a fair share", the Exemption Guidelines suggest that "the assessment under Article [101](3) of benefits flowing from restrictive agreements is in principle made within the confines of each relevant market to which the agreement relates".[60] So the Commission would ignore environmental efficiencies in a different market from the one in which the restrictions arise, even if they benefit the same consumers who suffer the disadvantage. The words "in principle" leave room for exceptions, but even so, the Guidelines are too strict (and the hypothetical "polluter pays agreement" should be allowed), for the following reasons.

 – *Out-of-market benefits should count.* Other than administrative convenience, there is no reason to limit efficiencies to the same market, or to market goods. Consumers derive real (and quantifiable) utility from non-market goods, too.

 – Under Article 101(3), benefits such as emission cuts can justify a restrictive agreement so long as it "allow[s] consumers a fair share of the resulting benefit." Whatever the Guidelines say, Article 101(3) itself does not limit benefits within the "relevant market". A literal interpretation does not exclude that the "fair share" may accrue to the same consumers in a different market, and even to different consumers. For instance, an agreement to reduce pollution may increase prices for some consumers, but should qualify

---

58 Commission, "On environmental agreements" (Communication) COM (96) 561 final. See Christopher Townley, "Is There (Still) Room for Non-Economic Arguments in Article 101 TFEU Cases?" (17 October 2012) <https://ssrn.com/abstract=2162864>. See also *CECED* (Case IV.F.1/36.718) [2000] OJ L187/47, [47] – [57]; *Exxon/Shell* (Case IV/33.640) [1994] OJ L144/20, [71].
59 cf. Ludwig Von Mises, *Theory and History* (Mises Institute 1957) <https://mises.org/library/definition-economic-progress>.
60 Exemption Guidelines, [43].

for exemption if it reduces all consumers' healthcare costs and increases their life expectancy and quality of life by more – overall – than the extra amount consumers in the relevant market pay for the cleaner products.[61]

- The Exemption Guidelines suggest that the Court of First Instance held in *Shaw* that "the assessment under Article 81(3) had to be made within the same analytical framework as that used for assessing the restrictive effects."[62] But *Shaw* was not about whether out-of-market benefits could count, but about whether the Commission should have verified whether users each individually and fully enjoyed the benefits that justified the exemption. The court rejected that, because the "assessment... had to be made within the same analytical framework, that of the effect of the notified agreements on the functioning of the market, and hence on the situation of the tied lessees taken as a whole, not on each lessee considered in isolation". Moreover, "it is not material that the benefits produced by the notified agreements do not entirely compensate the price differential suffered by a particular tied lessee if the average lessee does enjoy that compensation". So the case does not mean that the Commission cannot consider out-of-market benefits; it means merely that an exemption can be based on the benefits received by the "consumers as a whole". Out-of-market benefits were not even mentioned, and the case does not say that they cannot be considered even when it makes sense to do so. With *Shaw* falling away, the limitation in the Exemption Guidelines lacks legal basis.

- Other cases support this. In the foundational case *Consten and Grundig*, the Court of Justice required "appreciable objective advantages of such a character as to compensate for the disadvantages... in the field of competition".[63] The court did not say that the net effect should be positive, that the consumers should be fully compensated, that this should be assessed within the same market as where the restriction occurs, or that this should benefit the same consumers. Environmental and climate change abatement benefits based on a "polluter pays" principle could qualify as "appreciable objective advantages".

- In *Compagnie Générale Maritime v Commission*, the court said that:

  "for the purposes of examining the merits of the Commission's findings as to the various requirements of Article 85(3) of the Treaty... regard should naturally be had to the advantages arising from the agreement in question, not only for the relevant market... but also, in appropriate cases, for every other market on which the agreement in question might have

---

61 See also *CECED* (n 57), [52].
62 Case T–131/99 *Shaw v Commission* [2002] ECR II-2023.
63 Cases C–56 & 58/64 *Consten and Grundig v Commission* [1966] ECR 429.

beneficial effects, and even, in a more general sense, for any service the quality or efficiency of which might be improved by the existence of that agreement... without requiring a specific link with the relevant market."[64]

While the customers of the services were essentially the same group on the different sea transport markets, the court could not be clearer that out-of-market efficiencies count.

– Finally, in *Mastercard*, the CJEU held that:

"it is necessary to take into account... all the objective advantages flowing from that measure not only on the market in respect of which the restriction has been established, but also on the market which includes the other group of consumers associated with that system... it is necessary to assess, where appropriate, whether such advantages are of such a character as to compensate for the disadvantages which that measure entails for competition."[65]

This, too, indicates that out-of-market benefits can count, and the word "character" in the last sentence suggests that this assessment can be qualitative and need not be quantitative. The CJEU added that:

"the General Court was, in principle, required, when examining the first condition laid down in Article 81(3) EC, to take into account all the objective advantages flowing from the MIF, not only on the relevant market, namely the acquiring market, but also on the separate but connected issuing market. It follows from this that, should the General Court have found that there were appreciable objective advantages flowing from the MIF for merchants, *even if those advantages did not in themselves prove sufficient to compensate for the restrictive effects* identified pursuant to Article 81(1) EC, all the advantages on *both* consumer markets in the Mastercard scheme, including therefore on the cardholders' market, could, if necessary, have justified the MIF if, taken together, those advantages were of such a character as to compensate for the restrictive effects of those fees."[66]

In the end, the CJEU rejected the appeal in the absence of *any* appreciable objective advantages for merchants. This confirms that out-of-market benefits can count, and even benefits to other categories of consumers,

---

64 Case T–86/95 *Compagnie Générale Maritime v Commission* [2002] ECR II-1011, [343].
65 Case C–382/12 P *Mastercard v Commission* EU:C:2014:2201, [237]; Fraile (n 52).
66 ibid [240] – [241], emphasis added.

"taken together", so long as the consumers who bear the costs share at least some of the benefits.[67] Indeed, in the light of the finding in *Compagnie Générale Maritime* and *Mastercard*, the Exemption Guidelines violate the rule that "it is necessary to take into account all the objective advantages," and impose impermissible limits on assessment of out-of-market benefits, benefits to other consumers, and benefits that do not exceed the disadvantages in terms of market goods, but still qualify as "appreciable objective advantages".

– The Exemption Guidelines keep the door open where they say that "the condition that consumers must receive a fair share of the benefits implies *in general* that efficiencies generated by the restrictive agreement within a relevant market must be sufficient to outweigh the anticompetitive effects produced by the agreement within that same relevant market" (emphasis added). That allows for exceptions. Agreements to address climate change, environment and biodiversity should be such an exception, even if they involve non-market goods, because a climate disaster looms at the horizon.

– *No need for full compensation.* The traditional approach to determine the "fair share" is to calculate the costs and benefits for the customers of the parties to the agreement (excluding benefits accruing to other consumers), and approve the agreement only if the benefits exceed the costs *for those specific customers* in monetary terms.[68] This is stricter than required by the Treaty and the case law mentioned above. Article 101(3) demands a "fair share", not a "full share".

– The share allowed to consumers can be "fair", where even a small reduction of a risk with potentially large consequences could significantly improve – indeed preserve – the customer's life and home and that of their offspring, and thus outweigh the economic cost of a price increase.[69] Even if discounted, the value of avoiding a climate cataclysm is significant. As the Dutch Supreme Court found in *Urgenda*, "The possibility exists that even a smaller warming of the earth and a lower [increase of the] concentration of hothouse gases causes a dangerous climate change, for instance because a tipping point is reached… The precautionary principle means that more rather than fewer far-reaching measures have to be adopted to reduce the emission of hothouse gases".[70]

---

67 For a more limited reading, see Peeperkorn (n 3), [35] ff.
68 Exemption Guidelines [80]. Case C–23/14 *Post Danmark v Konkurrencerådet* EU:C:2015:651, [49] appears to impose a less strict text ("counteract") for Article 102 TFEU; Anne-Lise Sibony, "Exclusionary abuse: The Court of Justice of the European Union refuses to make the 'as efficient competitor' test mandatory for fidelity rebates (*Post Danmark*)" (2015) Concurrences N° 1–2016, Art N° 77419, 94–98 https://www.concurrences.com/en/review/issues/no-1-2016/case-comments/Exclusionary-abuse-The-EU-Court-of.
69 Article 101(3) TFEU recognises future benefits. Exemption Guidelines, [87] – [88].
70 *Urgenda* (n 54), [7.2.10].

  – Even apart from this, benefits to other consumers are relevant. Fairness is not inherently individualistic or selfish. Fairness is a social norm based on reciprocal altruism.[71] A consumer benefits when their society benefits, especially if the stake is as significant as avoidance of a calamity affecting everyone.[72] *All* consumers, *including* the companies' customers, benefit from emission cuts and pollution reduction. An appreciable collective benefit should qualify, as the Commission held in *CECED*:

  > "The Community pursues the objective of a rational utili-
  > sation of natural resources, taking into account the potential
  > benefits and costs of action. Agreements… must yield
  > economic benefits outweighing their costs and be compatible
  > with competition rules…. the benefits to society brought about
  > by the CECED agreement appear to be more than seven times
  > greater than the increased purchase costs of more energy-
  > efficient washing machines. Such environmental results for
  > society would adequately allow consumers a fair share of the
  > benefits *even if no [economic] benefits accrued to individual
  > purchasers of machines.*"[73] (emphasis added).

  – *Fairness should reflect the "polluter pays" principle.* It is not "fair" for consumers to benefit from consumption while imposing costs (exter-nalities) on others (who moreover have no say in the decision). In the words of the ACM, "their demand for the products in question essen-tially creates the problem for which society needs to find solutions."[74] Restoring the balance by eliminating the costs on others is mandated by Article 191(2) TFEU that EU policy "shall be based on the… prin-ciples… that environmental damage should as a priority be rectified at source and that the polluter should pay." For this reason alone, envi-ronmental and GHG emission abatement benefits can and should be included in the calculation under Article 101(3) TFEU.

The Dutch ACM proposes to count benefits to others only if "the agreement must contribute to a policy objective that has been laid down in an international or national standard to which the Dutch government is bound… In other cases… users still need to be fully compensated… Think of product standards or environmental standards that are more ambitious than the existing, binding

---

71 See Ken Binmore, *Natural Justice* (OUP 2005), 14ff, and "Bargaining and fairness" (2014) 111 (Supplement 3) PNAS 10785–10788 <www.pnas.org/content/111/Supplement_3/10785.full>.

72 Adam Smith (yes, the man who wrote about the invisible hand), *The Theory of Moral Sentiments* (first published 1759, Gutenberg 2011) ("How selfish soever man may be supposed, there are evidently some principles in his nature, which interest him in the fortune of others, and render their happiness necessary to him, though he derives nothing from it except the pleasure of seeing it."). See also Elias Khalil, "Adam Smith and the Three Theories of Altruism" (2001) 4(67) Recherches économiques de Louvain 435.

73 *CECED* (n 57), [56]. For a more limited reading, see Peeperkorn (n 3) [34].

74 ACM Draft Guidelines, [41].

standard for the government."[75] The idea was perhaps to ensure that the ACM proposals would be limited to sustainable development goals of greatest importance, such as climate change. But this falls in the trap of "government failure", discussed above. It is precisely where government targets are too low, or a government fails to set targets at all, that private initiative is needed.

Necessity, and remaining competition. Article 101(3) TFEU finally requires that agreements should "not… impose… restrictions which are not indispensable to the attainment of these objectives" and "not… afford such undertakings the possibility of eliminating competition in respect of a substantial part of the products in question". There should not be less restrictive and equally effective alternatives to reach the goals. In theory, effective regulation, taxation or carbon trading rights are the best answer to market failure. If *fully* effective regulation existed, cooperative agreements may not be necessary. But government failure means that in practice, existing regulation remains inadequate. Free market competition is not the answer either, in markets where consumers are insufficiently willing to pay for sustainability, or where individual firms cannot achieve sufficient scale. In such markets, we need private cooperation to complement regulation.[76]

The "polluter pays agreement" model described above should meet the "indispensability" and "no elimination of competition" conditions. The agreement is limited to spending an amount equal to the SCC on reducing or offsetting GHG emissions, in accordance with the "polluter pays" principle. Parties are left free to decide how to spend these funds, so long as they use them for sustainability. They are free to pass on these costs or absorb them. Finally, effective competition is preserved by avoiding spillover, and monitoring compliance is done independently. The parties retain an incentive to compete by reducing the SCC as much as they can.

Less restrictive alternatives are probably not as effective. For instance, leaving buyers the option to make a voluntary payment for carbon offset suffers from market failures, including information deficiency, and free-rider concerns. Merely providing information on carbon emissions may reduce demand somewhat to the extent that enlightened thinking or guilt dissuades some consumers, but demand may well switch to equally polluting products that do not advertise their carbon costs.

III. Conclusion

The climate crisis has become an emergency. We need permanent sequestration of GHG to get back to the level of 50 years ago. Market failures and government failures mean that we cannot rely only on free market competition, regulation,

---

75   ACM Draft Guidelines, [41].
76   For a further discussion of "necessity" and the Dutch *Chicken of Tomorrow* case, see Dolmans, "Sustainable Competition",

taxation and carbon trading as a solution. Competition between firms drives innovation in sustainable technology, and we are making technological progress as showcased by "Project Drawdown". But we have no certainty that innovation will provide a timely and complete solution. We need a coherent and consistent programme of regulation, innovation, taxation, education, reforestation and private cooperation. Competition law should enable this cooperation, including by enabling agreements reflecting the "polluter pays" principle. This means recognising that (a) environmental benefits "contribute to improving the production or distribution of goods or to promoting technical or economic progress", (b) consumers benefit from these even if they are compensated by better access to non-market goods or out-of-market benefits, and (c) consumers enjoy "a fair share" if the arrangements eliminate costs imposed on others (negative externalities) in accordance with the "polluter pays" principle, or reduce environmental or climate change harm to *all* consumers.

Article 101(3) TFEU: the Roadmap for Sustainable Cooperation

ELLA VAN DEN BRINK AND JORDAN ELLISON*

Google | Slaughter and May

I. Introduction

We believe that the current application of EU competition law can be improved and streamlined to help competing firms cooperate on sustainability goals. Competition agencies could promote a lot more beneficial cooperation without any new legislation and provide firms with legal certainty around their opportunities to cooperate. In places, the current application of the law is not based on legislation or on clear judicial precedent.

We recognise the need to protect consumers from nefarious or misguided cooperation that harms competition without providing any substantial sustainability benefits. We also recognise that competition agencies are not well placed to make controversial political value-judgments as to whether consumers can be expected to endure higher prices in order to advance nebulous social objectives.

However, a specific implementation of Article 101(3) TFEU[1] could be a practical way to promote cooperation between firms without placing an undue burden on consumers or an impossible task on competition agencies:

   – As a first step, we propose that well-established carbon (and other greenhouse gas (GHG)) prices are used to assess whether any consumer

---

*   Ella van den Brink is a competition lawyer at Google and Jordan Ellison is a competition lawyer at Slaughter and May. All views expressed in this paper are entirely personal. Thanks to Charlotte McLean, Sophia Real and Joel Marsden for their invaluable input on this paper. All mistakes are those of the authors.
1   Consolidated version of the Treaty on the Functioning of the European Union [2012] OJ C326/47.

harm caused by competition cooperation is outweighed by benefits to *society as a whole*. We call this approach the "carbon defence".[2]

– As a second step, competition authorities could explore similar methodologies for other sustainable efficiency gains.[3]

Several competition agencies across Europe have shown an increased interest in changing practice to provide more scope for cooperation. The leading example so far (the Dutch Authority for Consumers and Markets (ACM)) has done so in part using a similar interpretation of Article 101(3) TFEU to that proposed in this paper, and others appear keen to follow suit.

II. Legal Framework for Cooperation

1. A failure of incentives

EU competition law permits significant cooperation between competing firms pursuing sustainability goals. There are several legal routes to concluding that cooperation does not breach Article 101 TFEU:

– Some cooperation falls outside Article 101(1) TFEU entirely;

– Some cooperation benefits from the "ancillary restraints" doctrine; and

– Some cooperation infringes Article 101(1) TFEU but is justified by efficiencies under Article 101(3) TFEU.

In this section we give some examples of how these doctrines can be used with confidence for competitors to cooperate. But we also contend that, in practice, the legal safe ground has been scoped too narrowly. This has the result that beneficial cooperation is being discouraged even where there is no strong legal or economic reason to prevent cooperation.

The precise scope of the "safe ground" under the rules above is unclear. Lack of clarity is common to many legal rules. But this is a more acute problem where firms are considering cooperating for non-commercial motives, such as improving their sustainability profile, and do not stand to make a short-run profit from the cooperation.[4] Where firms want to cooperate for commercial motives, they have

---

2   This paper in part builds on a previous article on the carbon defence, see Jordan Ellison, "A Fair Share: Time for the Carbon Defence" (18 March 2020) <https://papers.ssrn.com/sol3/papers.cfm?abstract_id=3542186>.

3   These could include, for example, reductions in the use of harmful substances or emission of air pollutants. There are established methodologies based on e.g. damage costs or impact pathway approaches to assess the monetary impacts associated with sustainable efficiency gains. See Theon van Dijk, "A New Approach to Assess Certain Sustainability Agreements under Competition Law", in this book.

4   Sustainability agreements are not necessarily unattractive commercially, but they are more likely than other types of cooperation to have a long-term rather than a short-term benefit (which inherently is more uncertain) for the firms involved.

an incentive to take calculated risks with legal grey areas. Competition agencies and courts adjudicate on these cases and that process helps define the law. The situation is different with sustainability cooperation. The benefits of cooperation (e.g. reducing GHG emissions) are usually not captured by the cooperating firms but by society as a whole.

This means firms do not have a direct commercial incentive to take any risk. The firm will often be willing to proceed with cooperation, but it will not be willing to risk breaking the law in order to do so. This chilling effect means there have been very few adjudicated cases to clarify the legal limits of cooperation – which only reinforces the problem.

At the same time, competition agencies are understandably fearful of encouraging anticompetitive cooperation, or stepping outside their remit as provided to them by legislators. Agencies have therefore been reluctant to give guidance that might help firms or advisers take a broader view of the safe ground. Until recently competition law has therefore been stuck in a feedback loop where both agencies and firms lack the incentives to take the risks inherent in exploring the boundaries of the law. We believe that the demands of climate change in particular mean this loop needs to be broken.

2. Where is the safe ground today?

A. *Agreements outside Article 101(1) TFEU for lack of effect on competition*

In practice, the safe ground today is mainly limited to cooperation that falls outside Article 101(1) TFEU because it is obvious that there is no appreciable effect on competition. This permits some types of environmental cooperation. For example:

- Loose environmental commitments where no firm is subject to a specific commitment;

- Firms making commitments to achieve a general outcome but with no specifics as to how;

- Firms making commitments on specific actions but those actions do not relate to material parameters of competition; or

- Firms cooperating to create new markets.[5]

---

5 Commission Notice, "Guidelines on the applicability of Article 81 of the EC Treaty to horizontal cooperation agreements" [2001] OJ C3/2, [184] – [187] (no longer in force); Commission Notice, "Guidelines on the applicability of Article 101 of the Treaty on the Functioning of the European Union to horizontal co-operation agreements" [2011] OJ C11/1, [27], [163], [277] – [282], fn 14 (the Horizontal Guidelines).

While these forms of cooperation can be beneficial to the environment,[6] they also have inherent limits. Almost by definition, if cooperation falls outside the scope of Article 101(1) TFEU because it does not materially impact competition, there are limits to how much such cooperation can change firms' behaviour, or their willingness and ability to be a "first-mover". For example, firms might agree to take an energy-intensive product off the market or agree to use low-carbon (but more expensive) energy in their production processes. This type of cooperation might be hugely beneficial for the environment but it will usually be difficult to argue that it falls outside Article 101(1) TFEU.

B. *Agreements justified by ancillary restraints doctrine*

The European Courts have found that certain agreements restrict competition but that this restriction is ancillary to a "legitimate objective" such that Article 101(1) TFEU is not infringed. This doctrine has been used to exempt from antitrust scrutiny professional rules to ensure the integrity of the legal profession, anti-doping rules to ensure the integrity of sporting competitions and collective bargaining by workers to advance objectives of economic justice.[7] In principle, agreements to reduce GHG emissions could be seen as pursuing "legitimate objectives" such that any accompanying restriction on competition can be permitted as merely ancillary to a bigger objective. Support for this could be drawn from the European treaty provisions that enshrine environmental protection as a key objective of EU law.[8] However, there is little or no direct precedent from competition authorities or courts taking this approach. Therefore, in practice, the ancillary restraints doctrine does not provide much comfort to firms wanting to avoid legal risk.

C. *Agreements justified under Article 101(3) TFEU*

Article 101(3) TFEU provides that cooperation that restricts competition can nonetheless be justified if four conditions are satisfied:

- – The agreement results in an objective benefit;

- – A fair share of the benefit goes to consumers;

- – The restriction on competition is essential to achieve the benefit; and

- – The agreement does not eliminate competition.

---

6 For example, a lot of benefit has come from industry certification schemes that create visibility as to the environmental performance of firms without including specific binding commitments to compete in a specific manner.

7 Case C–309/99 *Wouters v Algemene Raad van de Nederlandse Orde van Advocaten* [2002] ECR I–1577; Case C–519/04 P *Meca-Medina and Majcen v Commission* [2006] ECR I–6991; Marc van der Woude, "Antidoping rules: The ECJ holds that the CFI gave a too narrow definition of the scope of the competition rules, but rejects the application in view of the legitimate objective pursued by the contested rules (*Meca-Medina*)" (2006) Concurrences N° 4–2006, Art N° 12548, 68; Case C–67/96 *Albany International BV v Stichting Bedrijfspensioenfonds Textielindustrie* [1999] ECR–5751.

8 TFEU, arts 11 and 191.

It is generally recognised that GHG emissions reductions can be treated as an objective benefit capable of justifying an agreement between competitors under the first condition of Article 101(3) TFEU.[9] But, crucially, several competition authorities take the view that a reduction in competition can only be justified under the second condition of Article 101(3) TFEU if consumers are fully compensated for any loss of competition so that they are left no worse off by the agreement. We call this the "no worse off" interpretation.

The type of agreements that can be justified under current practice are those where either:

– The consumer is made better off in a direct financial sense as a result of the agreement, for example prices are lowered; or

– The consumer is made better off in "quality-adjusted" pricing as a result of the agreement. In this situation any price increase has to be at least equal to the extra value that consumers attribute to the improved product resulting from the agreement. For example, the Dutch competition authority rejected an application to approve an agreement between supermarkets to sell only chicken produced to higher welfare standards. The decision was partly based on consumer surveys that showed Dutch consumers did not value the higher-welfare chicken as much as the price increases that would be caused by the agreement.[10]

As currently applied, Article 101(3) TFEU cannot be used with confidence to justify agreements unless direct benefits to the consumers of the relevant product outweigh competitive harm such as price rises, in particular because Article 101(3) TFEU requires firms to carry out a self-assessment. This is the key limiting factor on the usefulness of Article 101(3) TFEU: environmental benefits like reduced GHG emissions are, by definition, shared amongst billions of current and future global citizens who may not be in scope of the definition of "consumers".[11] In contrast, the costs of price rises are concentrated on the consumers of a product or service. This means that an agreement to reduce GHG emissions will rarely satisfy Article 101(3) TFEU under the "no worse off" interpretation.

3. Extending the safe ground through the "carbon defence"

Other papers in this book contain several creative ideas for extending the safe ground for sustainability cooperation. These include, for example, a tighter

---

9   For example, reduced GHG emissions were recognised by the European Commission as a potential efficiency benefit in *CECED* (Case IV.F.1/36.718) Commission Decision 2000/475/EC [2000] OJ L187/47, [48] and by the Dutch ACM in *ACM analysis of closing down 5 coal power plants as part of SER Energieakkoord* (ACM analysis of 26 September 2013) (Coal Power Plants), 4.

10 *Chickens of Tomorrow* (ACM/DM/2014/206028) (ACM analysis of 26 January 2015) <www.acm.nl/ sites/default/files/old_publication/publicaties/13789_analysis-chicken-of-tomorrow-acm-2015-01-26. pdf.pdf>.

11 Commission Notice, "Guidelines on the application of Article 81(3) of the Treaty" [2004] OJ C101/97, [86] (Article 101(3) TFEU Guidelines).

interpretation of what is caught by Article 101(1) TFEU in the first place and a more expansive interpretation of what cooperation can benefit from the ancillary restraints doctrine. In this paper we argue that the easiest way to extend the safe ground is a better understanding of Article 101(3) TFEU, initially through the "carbon defence".

A. *The carbon defence*

The carbon defence gives firms more freedom to make binding agreements to reduce their GHG emissions without breaking competition law. The exact nature of the agreements could vary sector by sector but they might include, for example:

- Agreements for firms to eliminate or reduce their use of energy from fossil fuels;

- Agreements for firms to invest in robust off-setting measures for their GHG emissions; or

- Agreements for firms to sell only products that meet specific emissions standards.

The carbon defence would permit agreements that result in higher prices for consumers – but *only if* the price rise is less than the total savings to society of the emissions reduction.

At the core therefore is a comparison between the estimated price rise to consumers on one hand and the estimated cost saving to society on the other. Both these data points are obtainable. First, competition authorities are well versed in estimating the price effects of restrictive agreements and in any event are required to do so under the current approach.

Second, there are authoritative independent estimates of the economic cost to emitting a tonne of carbon dioxide (including from European and US government agencies).[12] There are estimates that focus on the economic impact of global warming (for example, destruction of infrastructure or loss of crops), as opposed to non-economic impacts (for example, loss of human life). Implementing the carbon defence would require the relevant competition authority to use a benchmark cost of saved emissions against which the estimated price rise from any agreement would be tested.[13]

For example, imagine a market with three competing metal smelters, A, B and C. Each of the three smelters emits two million tonnes of carbon dioxide per year through their electricity consumption. A, B and C want to agree that by

---

12 The European Commission estimated the damage caused by GHG emissions in *CECED* (n 9), [48]. The ACM used a couple of valuation methods for emissions savings in Coal Power Plants (n 9), [4] – [5].
13 See van Dijk (n 3).

2025 they will source at least half of their electricity from renewable sources. Assume that this will increase A, B and C's variable cost base (their energy bills) and result in higher metal prices for their customers. For easy maths, let's assume the European Commission has stipulated a benchmark of €100/tonne of carbon dioxide emitted. The three smelters mentioned above are effectively agreeing to each eliminate one million tonnes of annual emissions by 2025, so three million tonnes in total. The benchmark counts that as a €300m/year saving to society in 2025. But in order to achieve this by 2025 the smelters are going to be using energy from renewable sources, which they expect to be more expensive than conventional energy, and it is likely that much of the increased cost will be passed on to their customers.

If the expected price rise to consumers is less than €300m/year, the agreement is socially valuable because the benefits are greater than the costs. The carbon defence would be available and the agreement between the smelters would be legal. If the expected price rise is more than €300m/year, the economic costs are greater than the benefits. The carbon defence would not be available and the agreement between the smelters would risk breaking competition law.

The carbon defence would only apply to the emissions reduction obligation – the firms would have to continue to compete in all other respects. So, in our example, the defence would only allow the smelters to agree to the obligation to reduce emissions by 2025. The defence would not allow the smelters to make any other agreement, for example on:

- How they meet the emissions obligation – each would compete independently to find the cheapest alternative energy sources; or

- Whether and how they pass on any increased costs to their customers – each would compete independently on downstream pricing.

B. *The carbon defence is justifiable under current law*

The carbon defence requires a departure from the "no worse off" interpretation when assessing whether cooperation results in a "fair share" of benefits for "consumers". We believe that this is possible because the "no worse off" standard currently used by some competition authorities when applying Article 101(3) TFEU has no sound basis in law, and other policy arguments support a new approach.

First, there are no obvious legal blocks for taking this approach. The text of Article 101(3) TFEU does not require that consumers are "no worse off" because of an agreement. Article 101(3) TFEU chooses the more open standard of a "fair share" for consumers. The EU case law cited in the Article 101(3) TFEU Guidelines on this point does not clearly mandate the "no worse off" interpretation. Neither do the Horizontal Guidelines cite any case law in support of the "no worse off" interpretation. Instead, the "no worse off" standard mainly seems to come from the guidance and decisional practice of competition authorities – and so could also be changed by competition authorities. In fact, before it adopted its current guidelines, the European Commission itself adopted an approach very similar to that suggested here in at least one case.[14] These guidelines are not binding on national competition authorities and, of course, the European Commission can change the guidelines in its forthcoming 10-year review.

Second, the "no worse off" standard may not be equally appropriate in all circumstances. It might be a good standard for most situations in which Article 101(3) TFEU is used – but still be the wrong standard for assessing agreements to reduce GHG emissions. It seems like the "no worse off" standard was primarily developed to regulate the distribution of benefits between *firms and consumers*. It makes sure that firms pass on enough of a benefit to consumers who are suffering the harm of reduced competition caused by their agreement. That makes sense: firms are required to compete and they should not be allowed to make consumers worse off simply to benefit themselves. But with agreements to reduce GHG emissions (or other sustainability agreements) a different distribution of benefits is at stake: the distribution of benefits between *citizens and consumers*. Where the benefit is reduced GHG emissions, there is no question of an out-sized share of that benefit being withheld to the benefit of the firms involved. The benefits of the reduction in GHG emissions are inevitably and by their nature enjoyed by all citizens. A "fair share" in the citizen/consumer context could be quite different from a "fair share" in the firm/consumer context. This provides a basis to distinguish agreements to reduce GHG emissions from other agreements.

Third, when we think about a "fair share" as between the consumer and their fellow citizens we are really asking who should bear the costs of the GHG emissions caused by the consumer's consumption (or the cost of avoiding those emissions). This is a value judgment where reasonable people might differ.[15] The carbon defence approach means that the costs of avoiding GHG emissions are borne by the consumer. This seems defensible given that the consumer is the person who (i) will usually have most benefit from the emissions; and (ii) will often be better-placed to avoid or reduce the relevant consumption. Critically, the current "no worse off" standard does not get rid of the costs of GHG emissions – it just means they are spread across a lot of people who (i) usually do not get any benefit from the consumption; and (ii) are in no position to reduce or control the emissions. These two elements, (i) enjoyment of the

---

14 In *CECED* (n 9), the European Commission approved an agreement between competitors to phase out energy-intensive washing machines and replace them with more efficient models, under Article 101(3) TFEU. As part of its assessment the European Commission sought to value the benefits of lower emissions to consumers.

15 A different question is, of course, whether the main responsibility for sustainable choices lies with citizens or consumers as opposed to governments or firms. While the answer to that question is outside of the scope of this paper, we believe that a combination of public and private action is needed to tackle global warming and other sustainability challenges.

benefit; and (ii) control over the consumption, together seem to be the strongest argument that it is fair for the consumer rather than their fellow citizens to bear the costs.

C. *Why the carbon defence?*

Using Article 101(3) TFEU to implement the carbon defence is a realistic and promising route to real change in the near future.

First, competition authorities may (rightly) have concerns about changing doctrine in any way that has the potential to harm consumers. Any competition authority that was not at least prima facie sceptical of agreements that might increase prices for consumers would be asleep on the job. Authorities may therefore be resistant to broad unsubstantiated arguments. Regardless of the legal merits, in practice, authorities may worry that this approach cedes too much control and limits their ability to intervene, for example, where cooperation has big costs to competition and only small environmental benefits. The carbon defence allows competition authorities more control and a clear framework for enforcement: the balancing exercise that Article 101(3) TFEU requires means that environmental cooperation could only be justified where the environmental benefits clearly outweigh any harm to competition.

Second, competition authorities may (rightly) have concerns about being drawn into quasi-political judgments where they are required to trade-off financial harm to consumers against non-financial benefits to citizens. How much extra can consumers be asked to pay for energy in order to reduce GHG emissions is a political question and the answer depends on many variables and perspectives. Of course, these trade-offs are unavoidable. But unelected officials such as competition authorities need a clear roadmap to help make these trade-offs. Article 101(3) TFEU provides a roadmap for this type of balancing and the quantitative €/tonne methodology provides a proxy that can help competition author[2]ities take an objective and consistent approach across cases.

Third, for the same reasons, the carbon defence has the potential to provide a good level of legal certainty to firms. Firms need a clear roadmap to be able to assess *ex ante* whether a specific cooperation proposal will be legal. The carbon defence obviously requires judgment and leaves room for discretion – but it at least provides a clear structure for firms and their advisers to assess cooperation proposals.

Fourth, Article 101(3) TFEU provides a framework for thinking about other sustainable defences in addition to the "carbon defence". While we have selected agreements on GHGs as a starting point (especially given the availability of price data), Article 101(3) TFEU can provide a useful framework for structuring the approach to other forms of cooperation.

III. Practical Guidance from European National Competition Authorities (NCAs)

For firms, legal certainty is an important incentive to consider when entering into sustainability agreements. Harmonised European standards are particularly important for firms that act across borders, but also for measuring relevant outcomes such as reduced GHG emissions consistently.

The European Commission acknowledges that in order to succeed with the European Green Deal, "everyone in Europe will have to play their part – every individual, every business, every public authority. And that includes competition enforcers."[16] It has put out a call for contributions[17] as to how competition policy can support the European Green Deal. We call on the European Commission to adopt the "carbon defence" and include it in its guidance for firms and NCAs, in particular given the interest from various NCAs in supporting firms better with their sustainability initiatives. In the meantime, we provide an overview of the practical guidance from European NCAs that may support firms in their decision-making process.[18]

1. ACM (the Netherlands)

On 9 July 2020, the Dutch ACM published its draft "Sustainability agreements" guidelines (the Guidelines).[19] In the Guidelines, ACM acknowledges the need for sustainability agreements between undertakings in order to hit any of the climate goals included in international agreements.[20]

ACM defines sustainability agreements as those "aimed at the identification, prevention, restriction or mitigation of the negative impact of economic activities on people (including their working conditions), animals, the environment, or nature".[21]

---

16 Margrethe Vestager, "The Green Deal and competition policy" (Renew Webinar, 20 September 2020) <https://ec.europa.eu/commission/commissioners/2019-2024/vestager/announcements/green-deal-and-competition-policy_en>.

17 Commission, "Competition Policy supporting the Green Deal: Call for contributions" <https://ec.europa.eu/competition/information/green_deal/call_for_contributions_en.pdf> accessed 1 January 2021.

18 Other competition authorities, like the French Autorité de la Concurrence (<www.autoritedelaconcurrence.fr/en/press-release/autorite-de-la-concurrence-announces-its-priorities-2020>) and the UK Competition and Markets Authority (<https://assets.publishing.service.gov.uk/government/uploads/system/uploads/attachment_data/file/873689/Annual_Plan_2020-21.pdf>, 17–18), have announced that sustainability is one of their priorities for 2020. DG COMP has also announced in its 2020 Management Plan that it will focus its antitrust enforcement on behaviour that may be restricting competition in sustainable initiatives (such as clean technologies and infrastructures for the circular economy), <https://ec.europa.eu/info/system/files/management-plan-comp-2020_en.pdf>, 6–7.

19 ACM, "Draft Guidelines: Sustainability agreements" (9 July 2020) <www.acm.nl/sites/default/files/documents/2020-07/sustainability-agreements%5B1%5D.pdf> (Guidelines). Press release <www.acm.nl/en/publications/draft-guidelines-sustainability-agreements>.

20 Guidelines, [3] – [4].

21 Guidelines, [6].

ACM's guidance is rooted in three main principles:

– Guidance. ACM publishes guidance which should help companies to carry out a self-assessment to determine whether their agreement might infringe competition law.[22]

– Feedback. Companies that are unsure can discuss their sustainability agreements with ACM and solicit feedback from ACM in advance of the agreement entering into force.[23]

– No fines. If those agreements eventually turn out to be incompatible with competition law, and the companies involved have followed the correct process, no fines will be imposed.[24]

In applying Article 101(3) TFEU or the Dutch equivalent, ACM will use the European Commission's guidance,[25] European and Dutch precedents and the 2016 Policy Rule[26] on Competition and Sustainability.[27]

The Guidelines provide companies that wish to rely on Article 101(3) TFEU for sustainability agreements with the following guidance:

a) **Objective benefits.** The Guidelines give companies an idea of the type of *objective* benefits that may follow from sustainability agreements, such as the reduction of negative externalities, reducing operational costs, increased innovation or quality, and a greater variety of products (including, for example, products that are animal-friendly or that assure a fair income).[28] In substantiating these benefits, companies may use quantitative tools (e.g., through data on reduction of emissions), and/or qualitative tools, and firms should keep in mind that the ACM is particularly interested in the *likelihood* of the benefits actually materialising.[29]

b) **A fair share of benefits for consumers.** In line with (and even broader than) the proposed "carbon defence", the Guidelines distinguish between (i) environmental-damage agreements (those that "aim to improve production processes that cause harm to humans, the environment, and

---

22 Guidelines, [60].
23 Guidelines, [60] – [61]. If market participants publish their agreements the same principles apply, as long as, upon finding out that their agreements are incompatible with competition law, the companies adjust them in accordance with ACM's individual guidance, and the guidance that has been published (see Guidelines, [62]).
24 Guidelines, [62].
25 Article 101(3) TFEU Guidelines.
26 Beleidsregel mededinging en duurzaamheid 2016, nr. WJZ/16145098, <https://wetten.overheid.nl/BWBR0038583/2016-10-06/0/Artikel5> (in Dutch).
27 Guidelines, [25]. The Guidelines also identify categories of sustainability agreements that typically fall outside of Article 101(1) TFEU. These are discussed by Maurits Dolmans in this book.
28 Guidelines, [30].
29 Guidelines, [31] – [33].

nature"); and (ii) other sustainability agreements (e.g., those that focus on labour conditions or animal welfare):[30]

i. For environmental-damage agreements, ACM will take into account benefits for others than just the consumers (e.g., society as a whole, including people who are not considered "consumers"), thereby deviating from the European Commission's principle that consumers should be fully compensated for the harm caused by the restriction of competition to them. In order to qualify, the agreement must meet two criteria:

(1) It aims "to prevent or limit any obvious environmental damage" (e.g., an agreement to use carbon-neutral energy only); and

(2) It contributes efficiently to a policy objective captured in international or national standards that the Netherlands is bound to.[31]

ii. In other situations (including other sustainability agreements), consumers (as a group) will need to be fully compensated for any harm caused by any restriction of competition – this will also be required where the agreement is more ambitious than current standards the Netherlands is bound to.[32]

c) **Indispensability.** The parties to an agreement will need to make a credible case that no other, less restrictive alternatives are available to realise the same objective. They will need to show that: (i) an agreement is necessary (i.e., no other undertaking can afford to be the first mover unilaterally); and (ii) the agreement does not contain any unnecessary restrictions of competition.[33]

d) **No elimination of competition.** The Guidelines note that even in the case of a market-wide agreement, this criterion is met if there is still sufficient competition on key parameters (which are not further defined, but may include e.g., price, quality, etc.).[34]

The Guidelines provide some guidance to companies about how to best substantiate their claims under Article 101(3) TFEU.[35] In particular, there is no quantification needed of the pros and cons of a sustainability agreement if:

–   The firms involved have a combined market share of 30% or less. In addition, they will have to show (i) that their agreement is "specifically aimed

---

30 Guidelines, [38] – [39].
31 Guidelines, [38] – [41].
32 Guidelines, [42] – [44].
33 Guidelines, [56] – [57].
34 Guidelines, [59].
35 Although this guidance appears under condition (b) in the Guidelines, it seems to apply to the complete Article 101(3) TFEU assessment.

at certain sustainability objectives"; and (ii) that "real benefits can reasonably be expected".[36]

– The benefits of the agreement are "obviously" more significant than the harms, and it is immediately clear that consumers will get their share of the benefits (the Guidelines give the example of an agreement to reuse packaging which leads to a modest, and temporary, price increase for consumers).[37]

2. Hellenic Competition Commission's (HCC) Staff Discussion Paper

On 17 September 2020, HCC issued a Staff Discussion Paper (the Discussion Paper) on competition law and sustainability. The HCC is very clear about the need for competition law to rethink its stake in sustainability initiatives: "Competition authorities should facilitate this transition to a green economy",[38] and provides the following recommendations for consideration:

– **A "methodological upgrade" of competition law.** HCC argues for competition law to include "long-term sustainability effects and… intergenerational equality" in assessments of competitive harm.[39]

– **Legal certainty.** HCC proposes to provide undertakings with legal certainty through a "clear set of rules". That way, it argues, undertakings can be encouraged to make the "necessary investments" in sustainable business practices.[40]

– **Cooperation between regulators.** The Discussion Paper recommends closer cooperation between regulators (competition, sector-specific and others), through the formation of an "Advice Unit" to "enable more direct communication between firms, the government and other stakeholders".[41]

– **Sustainability sandbox.** This would entail a safe space for industries and companies (even competing ones) to experiment with "new business formats" or "more permanent changes in market structure" that aim to reach sustainability goals. There would not be any fines or sanctions, even if those arrangements had anticompetitive effects.[42]

---

36 Guidelines, [47].
37 Guidelines, [46] and [48].
38 Discussion Paper, [110].
39 Discussion Paper, [111].
40 Discussion Paper, [112].
41 Discussion Paper, [113].
42 Discussion Paper, [114]. However, the HCC can impose other remedies. We assume they may include an order to stop the conduct.

- **Regular reviews.** The Discussion Paper proposes to systematically review merger and antitrust infringement cases from both a competition and a sustainability perspective.[43]

- **Guidance.** HCC envisages adopting guidelines for companies that are considering collective sustainability initiatives (along similar lines to ACM's Guidelines). There will be a public consultation of the guidelines.[44]

- **Case-law.** HCC suggests that cases with an effect on EU trade could be considered by European Courts.[45]

The Discussion Paper provides companies that wish to rely on Article 101(3) TFEU for sustainability agreements with the following guidance:

a) **Objective benefits.** The Discussion Paper holds that the agreement's total benefits to all consumers should be considered in an antitrust analysis: "it's not a question of what types of sustainability benefits and costs should be taken into account, but how it is possible to monetise these with the tools provided by, for example, environmental and ecological economics as well as the weight we should place on each of these."[46]

b) **A fair share of benefits for consumers.** The Discussion Paper considers that this is a "flexible concept", that can take account of various sustainability benefits, and that there is no need to limit the analysis here to "narrow financial considerations" only:[47] "it is not required that the same consumers benefit from each and every improvement and economic progress identified under the first condition. It suffices that sufficient benefits are passed on to the broader sociological category of consumers so as to compensate, overall, for the negative effects of the restrictive agreement."[48]

c) **Indispensability.** Like ACM's Guidelines, the Discussion Paper sets out that companies will need to show (i) the necessity of the agreement, and (ii) the necessity of the specific restrictions in the agreement.[49]

d) **No elimination of competition.** The Discussion Paper notes that for industry-wide agreements, the firms subject to the agreement continue to compete on key parameters and, "in case this is not possible, envisage the imposition of some state-mandated conduct that would enable the companies to argue state compulsion."[50]

---

43 Discussion Paper, [115].
44 Discussion Paper, [116].
45 Discussion Paper, [117].
46 Discussion Paper, [67].
47 Discussion Paper, [80].
48 Discussion Paper, [77].
49 Discussion Paper, [81] – [82].
50 Discussion Paper, [83].

3. Bundeskartellamt (BKa)

In 2020, the BKa dedicated its annual Working Group on Competition Law to "Open markets and sustainable economic activity – public interest objectives as a challenge for competition law *practice*".[51] In anticipation of the meeting, the BKa published a working paper (the Working Paper). Like other competition authorities, the BKa recognises in its Working Paper that private cooperation may be an alternative to legislation to achieve public welfare (including sustainability) goals.[52] It also observes that an increasing number of competition authorities feel the need to take sustainability into account in their antitrust assessments. So far, in some cases the BKa has relied on its discretion not to investigate certain practices in cases that concern sustainability issues. In other instances, agreements might have fallen outside of Article 101(1) TFEU altogether, without the BKa having to assess the sustainability issues in detail. The Working Paper asks whether that is the right call given the increased call for official guidance,[53] and the need for legal certainty for companies.[54]

The Working Paper provides companies that wish to rely on Article 101(3) TFEU with the following guidance about its two first conditions:

a) **Objective benefits.** The Working Paper holds that it has not yet been clarified to what extent cooperation with the aim to achieve public welfare goals (such as environmental protection or animal welfare) can be seen as efficiency gains as meant in Article 101(3) TFEU.[55] It notes that, in this respect, it is particularly difficult to quantify those benefits appropriately. Even though there are a few alternative methods available, they often lead to different outcomes.[56] In addition, the Working Paper notes that there may be moral reasons why one would not want to express these benefits in monetary terms (such as reducing child labour, or avoiding health issues from measures to protect the environment).[57]

b) **A fair share of benefits for consumers.** While the Working Paper questions whether (positive) external effects can at all be taken into account in the Article 101(3) TFEU assessment, it concludes that NCAs might be able to be more flexible than the European Commission, given the lack of a binding effect of Commission guidance on them.[58]

---

51 Bundeskartellamt, "Sustainability initiatives and competition law practice – virtual meeting of the Working Group on Competition Law" (5 October 2020) <www.bundeskartellamt.de/SharedDocs/Meldung/EN/Pressemitteilungen/2020/05_10_2020_AKK_2 020.html>.
52 Working Paper, [44].
53 Working Paper, [45], and Bka, "Report of the Federal Cartel Office on its activities in 2015/2016" (18/12760, 15 June 2017), 54.
54 Working Paper, [40].
55 Working Paper, [22], [45].
56 Working Paper, [23–26]. These methods are discussed in more detail in van Dijk (n 3).
57 Working Paper, [26].
58 Working Paper, [27].

IV. Conclusion

We are encouraged by the thinking coming out of NCAs like the ACM, the HCC and the BKa. The guidance and discussion papers produced show a diligent focus on finding ways to facilitate beneficial cooperation without neglecting the authority's primary responsibility to protect consumers. We believe that Article 101(3) TFEU provides the legal justification for a new approach and provides the decision-making roadmap for the carbon defence and other sustainable efficiency gains.

A New Approach to Assess Certain Sustainability Agreements under Competition Law

THEON VAN DIJK[*]

Netherlands Authority for Consumers and Markets

I. Introduction

Under competition law in the European Union and in most Member States, a restriction of competition in the form of cooperation between competitors is not prohibited if consumers receive a fair share of any benefits resulting from that cooperation.[1] Which "consumers" are considered in this "fair-share-to-consumers" condition? And what share is a "fair" share?

The short and traditional answer to these questions is as follows. Only the consumers in the same relevant market as the cooperating competitors are considered when accounting for the benefits, because they are the ones that are exposed to any negative effects due to the restriction of competition. And a fair share means that these consumers should be fully compensated for any negative effects. The net effect of the cooperation for them should at least be neutral.

---

[*]   Theon van Dijk is chief economist, Authority for Consumers & Markets (ACM) in the Netherlands and has over 20 years' experience as an expert on the economics of competition law.
I would like to thank Eric van Damme, Simon Holmes, Erik Kloosterhuis, Rob van der Noll, Luc Peeperkorn and Martijn Snoep for comments on an earlier draft. The views expressed are not necessarily those of ACM.
1   This is one of four cumulative conditions for countervailing benefits under the Dutch Competition Act, art 6(3), or the Treaty on the Functioning of the European Union (TFEU) [2012] OJ C326/47, art 101.

This paper proposes an alternative interpretation of "consumers" and "fair share", in specific and well-defined circumstances, in order to facilitate sustainability agreements that reduce negative external effects and increase total consumer surplus (more precisely: total surplus of citizens, including consumers and non-consumers). This proposal is set out in the new draft sustainability agreement guidelines that were published recently by the Dutch Authority for Consumers and Markets (ACM).[2] Out of a sense of urgency to make a competition policy contribution (or at the very least not to be perceived as an obstacle), ACM's draft guidelines have the objective to facilitate efficient joint private initiatives in the Netherlands to reduce environmental damage caused by overuse of common resources, such as damage due to greenhouse gas and air pollutant emissions, to complement public action in this area.

II. The Same Test For Different Categories of Cooperation?

As a starting point it is useful to note that, from a consumer surplus point of view, the traditional fair-share-to-consumers condition for exceptions to the cartel prohibition makes sense in many but not all cases. The reason is that the condition works out differently for different categories of cooperation.

Clearly, cooperation between competitors in the form of, for example, price cartels is prohibited. They only increase prices without resulting in any benefits for consumers – and therefore also not a fair share of benefits. Here there are no exceptions, and this is naturally captured by the fair-share-to-consumers test.

The second category of agreements is aimed at generating benefits for the group of consumers of the product in question. An example are R&D cooperation agreements that result in improved products or lower production costs, or in faster ways to achieve these. Although there can be positive R&D spill-overs that benefit others than those direct consumers, in the development phase the main beneficiaries are typically the consumers that purchase the improved products and pay lower prices.

The traditional fair-share-to-consumers condition is expected to work reasonably well for this category of cooperation agreement, in the sense that most effects on consumer surplus are taken into account, as this is the very object of the cooperation. The consumers that suffer from the restriction of competition – in this example in the form of reduced individual R&D incentives or an increased risk of product market collusion – must at least be compensated by any benefits that are passed on to them. Since, by and large, the consumers that are exposed

---

2   ACM, "Draft Guidelines: Sustainability Agreements" (first published for consultation on 9 July 2020. Second Draft Guidelines published 26 January 2021).

to the negative effects of the R&D cooperation are the same ones that benefit most from it, the fair-share-to-consumers test is naturally confined to the same relevant market. Out-of-market benefits are typically expected to be small or not present.

This is different for a third category of horizontal cooperation agreements. There are areas of cooperation where the main object of the cooperation and the resulting benefits are not confined to the cooperating firms or to the consumers of the product in question. Think for example of products or production processes that emit large volumes of greenhouse gases or air pollutants. The negative effects of these emissions go far beyond the consumers of these products. More importantly, these negative effects imposed on others are usually not accounted for in the prices that consumers pay for the products. In other words, there are negative external effects at play that suppress total surplus of consumers and non-consumers (citizens). Consequently, when competing producers of such products cooperate with the object of reducing emissions, the benefits end up not only with the consumers of these products but with a wider group of beneficiaries.

What would the fair-share-to-consumers test look like if such out-of-market benefits are important? One could take the traditional view and only count within-the-market benefits as relevant for the fair-share-to-consumers test. However, that would completely miss the point – a large proportion of the benefit does not end up with present or even future consumers in the relevant market, and that is not the object of the cooperation. That would in principle make the argument for taking out-of-market efficiencies into account.[3] However, there can be good reasons to stick to the traditional approach, even in these cases. This is explored in the next section.

III. Arguments For and Against a New Approach For Certain Sustainability Agreements

1. Arguments in favour of a new approach

What are the considerations in favour of deviating from the traditional interpretation of the fair-share-to-consumers test to justify cartel prohibition exceptions for sustainability agreements?

First of all, in the Netherlands and elsewhere in Europe, there is a sense of urgency to reduce the emission of greenhouse gases, including mainly but not exclusively carbon dioxide (CO_2), and to battle climate change and its negative effects on

---

3   Note that out-of-market efficiencies do not refer here to one or more specific other markets but to improvements in consumer surplus more broadly. In fact, the efficiencies are social benefits that result from solving the coordination problem that causes overuse of common resources.

social welfare. Other substantial environmental damage (in the Netherlands, even more so than greenhouse gas emissions) is caused by the emission of air pollutants, in particular by nitrogen oxides (NO_x) and ammonia (NH_3) emissions, and also this has substantial negative effects on social welfare, in particular in terms of health and biodiversity.

Admittedly, this urgency is not immediate, since the most damaging effects of, for example, CO_2 emissions do not materialise in the very short term. But that makes it an even harder problem to tackle. Measures are required now but the full benefits follow only generations later. The problem is not always perceived as immediately pressing enough to overcome political differences. It may be for this reason that public measures do not sufficiently come off the ground and governments and NGOs frequently call upon the business community to take responsibility for their own role in climate change. Perhaps more so than with other policy problems, all hands are needed on deck, and the sooner the better. Initiatives from the private sector are needed to complement public measures (in particular if the public sector fails to deliver).

Against this background, and with the appropriate modesty about the role of competition policy in the larger scheme in mind, the question is how competition policy can encourage joint private initiatives to reduce environmental damage – or at the very least not discourage them. The traditional fair-share-to-consumers test does not take the crucial broader social benefits of environmental agreements into account. It is therefore inadequate to facilitate certain efficient private cooperation initiatives to reduce environmental damage. That is the second consideration in favour of a new approach.

Besides urgency, in combination with the inability of the traditional approach to take the key aspect into account, a third reason to make an exception is that sustainability is increasingly a dimension over which firms compete with each other. Many consumers value sustainability and are prepared to pay a premium for sustainable products. Thus, just like competition in dimensions such as quality, R&D and innovation, competition in sustainability is in some sectors at the heart of the competitive process. Sustainability is therefore not just any public interest that is unrelated to competition policy (just like the quality, R&D and innovation dimensions). However, in some circumstances competition hinders sustainability initiatives or results in less efficient outcomes (as may happen for those other competition dimensions). Restriction of competition in the form of agreements to jointly improve sustainability, through new or improved production processes or products, or through withdrawing the most polluting processes or products, may then be positive.

Finally, there are arguments for a new and more open approach that follow from economic reasoning. According to the polluter-pays-principle, it is fair (as well as more efficient from a social welfare perspective) that consumers of polluting products are the ones that pay a higher price for the reduction of the negative external effects they are causing with their consumption. By comparing the negative price-increasing effects paid for by the consumers with the benefits that occur both inside and outside the market, this is exactly what happens.

A more abstract economic reasoning goes as follows. In a way, the "non-consumers" of a polluting product are essentially "consumers" of the negative external effects. These "consumers" derive a negative utility from their forced consumption of pollution. Even though this is, of course, not a market in the traditional sense, with a stretch it could be seen as one: there is supply of, say, greenhouse gases; there is demand, which is forced and inevitable; and the virtual price paid is a negative utility. In this interpretation, the reduction of negative external effects benefits the "consumers" in the market of pollution. Hence all benefits are within the affected "markets" and the traditional fair-share-to-consumers test can be applied.

2. Arguments against a new approach

What are possible reasons for not taking out-of-market efficiencies into account when assessing cooperation agreements that reduce negative external effects?

One reason is that such an approach could open the floodgates for other agreements, meant to reduce negative external effects in other areas. This is the "slippery slope" argument. Cooperation agreements between competitors, for example, that genuinely boost employment may reduce the negative external effects associated with unemployment. Or agreements to create national champions, which might generate positive external effects beyond the direct and possibly negative effects, might also be argued to deserve a special treatment.

Another consideration for not having a more open competition law treatment of certain sustainability agreements, is that it could "crowd out" public measures to reduce environmental damage. With more private initiatives, there is arguably less need for public measures, and it may even be used as an excuse for not taking public measures. However, under the traditional approach to out-of-market-benefits (that is, without any crowding-out effect), public measures have insufficiently come off the ground. Moreover, important to note is that this crowding-out is only problematic if the public measures that otherwise would be taken come at a lower social cost than the negative effects of cooperation agreements that restrict competition.

To some extent weighing the arguments in favour and against the new approach is a matter of personal preference or belief. The crowding-out argument is, however, not very convincing if one places much weight on the large negative effects for social welfare that are associated with even a small risk of public inaction. The slippery slope consideration can to a large extent be dealt with by applying the new approach to very specific circumstances, as in the next section. Admittedly, the question remains why environmental and no other external effect-reducing agreements deserve a new approach. The answer lies in a combination of the close relationship between competition and sustainability, and the urgent need to make a competition law contribution toward solving common-resource problems (rather than abusing the exemption provision for competition-reducing agreements that serve national interests in competition between countries).

IV. "Isolating" Sustainability Agreements With Substantial

Out-of-Market Benefits

The key to keeping the benefits while reducing the risks, is to "isolate" the new approach to specific sustainability agreements and under specific circumstances (and only to those). The draft ACM guidelines formulate the following limiting conditions:

1. The agreement under consideration should be related to environmental damage with substantial negative external effects caused by overuse of common resources. Agreements between competitors to reduce the emission of *greenhouse gases or air pollutants* are examples in point.

By defining the specific group of agreements to which it applies, the new approach is clearly limited. This limit is economically substantiated: the external effects of greenhouse and air pollutant emissions are caused by overuse of common resources, known in public economics as the common-pool problem.[4] At its heart this a coordination problem, the solution of which results in social benefits. Some other environmental sustainability agreements or social sustainability agreements (such as animal welfare or fair trade) are not or are much more distantly related to negative externalities – or in any case not to externalities caused by overuse of common resources.

2. There should be a *concrete policy goal set* by the government or another public institution for the reduction of the emission of the substance in question in the Netherlands. This can be a set policy target that is not binding for government. Another possibility is that there is a legal requirement based on a treaty ratified by parliament that binds the government to such goal. This goal is not (yet) binding for firms or industries.

This limiting condition serves two goals. First, it provides the democratic legitimacy for a competition authority to redistribute consumer surplus from consumers to

---

4 In public economic terms, common resources are the category of goods that are non-excludable (restricting access to use is not possible) and rival (use by one affects the use by another). See Richard Cornes and Todd Sandler, *The Theory of Externalities, Public Goods and Club Goods* (CUP 2003) for the distinguishing characteristics of private goods (excludable and rival), public goods (non-excludable and non-rival), club goods (excludable and non-rival) and common resources (non-excludable and rival). See Mancur Olson, *The Logic of Collective Action* (2nd edn, Harvard UP 1974) and Garrett Hardin, "The Tragedy of the Commons" (1968) 162 *Science* 1243, for more on common-pool resources.

non-consumers (which is in fact what happens under the new approach). Second, it allows the use of the abatement method from environmental economics, which as set out below has a number of advantages for the practical assessment. Additionally, the reason for the goal not (yet) being binding for firms is that if the goal were binding for firms, encouragement of sustainability initiatives would not (no longer) be needed. In the latter case, cooperation might still be beneficial to achieve certain efficiencies but those do not concern out-of-market efficiencies.

3. The measure to reduce the emissions that cause environmental damage, as foreseen in the cooperation agreement, should result in an *efficient contribution* towards achieving the set goal. This includes an assessment of whether the measure is cost-efficient.

The new approach does not apply to instances in which the set policy or legally binding goal has already been achieved. As far as measures are concerned that are more costly than the lower-ranking-in-cost measure that is just needed to achieve the set goal: these do not meet this efficient contribution test. This will be explained in the brief exposition of the abatement cost approach below.

An additional point to note is that a sustainability agreement could propose a measure that results in an efficient contribution towards emission reduction, but not the most efficient measure possible. Still, under the abatement cost approach this would count as an efficient contribution and is not problematic as long as it does not stand in the way of more efficient measures being implemented (which is indeed the case as emissions are still far off the set goal).

4. The *total benefits* that are passed on to all persons that suffer from the negative external effects – that is, to consumers of the product plus out-of-market benefits to non-consumers, or indeed social or citizens' benefits more generally – should outweigh any negative effects for consumers that are due to the restriction of competition. In other words, there should be a net positive effect on the total consumer surplus.

These limiting conditions narrow down the novel interpretation of the fair-share-to-consumers test to specific circumstances. As long as each of the above conditions are met, consumers are considered to have a "fair" share of the net social benefits resulting from the sustainability agreement.

V. Methods From Environmental Economics to Value the Benefits

1. Environmental cost – benefit analysis

A qualitative assessment of the fair-share-to-consumers condition can suffice in some cases. For example, when it is obvious that the total benefits are much larger than the costs, or when reliable estimates of the benefits are not available.

The fair-share assessment of most environmental damage agreements, however, is expected to require at least some quantification.

It is important to note that the new approach conceptually boils down to an environmental social cost – benefit analysis (SCBA). Total benefits for consumers and non-consumers are balanced against the total costs, which are the negative effects of the restriction of competition due to the agreement (often a price increase and reduced demand). SCBAs are routinely carried out by governments in various areas to assess the impact of policies or interventions. The Dutch government has published SCBA guidelines with instructions how such analyses should be carried out.[5] In an international context, the OECD has published SCBA guidelines specifically for environmental projects.[6] Similarly, the European Commission carries out impact assessments before specific measures are taken or new policies are implemented.[7]

A key concept in environmental SCBAs is the so-called "shadow price": the social value of environmental damage caused by one unit of emission. For example, the shadow price of CO_2 has been estimated (central estimate with large range) to be €57/tonne in 2017 in the Netherlands.[8] This implies that, by and large, a reduction in CO_2 emissions of 5.000 kilotons is centrally estimated to represent a value of €285 million.

Below, the two main methods to estimate shadow prices are first briefly explained. Next it is discussed how shadow prices can be used in a practical assessment of the effects of environmental agreements.

2. Methods to estimate shadow prices[9]

In order to quantity the total social benefits of an agreement that reduces environmental damage, insights from environmental economics are needed. In monetary terms the total environmental damage of the emission of a greenhouse gas or air pollutant in a specific geographic space is, by and large: (1) the quantity of emissions × (2) the cost per unit of emission. The cost per unit of emission is the monetary social welfare loss due to the environmental damage caused by one unit of emission – in other words: the shadow price.

The cost per unit of emission cannot be valued using market prices, since the damage caused by emissions is an external effect for which by definition there are no market

---

5   CPB Netherlands Bureau for Economic Policy Analysis and PBL Netherlands Environmental Assessment Agency, "Algemene leidraad voor maatschappelijke kosten – batenanalyse" (2013).
6   OECD, *Cost-Benefit Analysis and the Environment: Further Developments and Policy Use* (OECD 2018) <www.oecd.org/governance/costbenefit-analysis-and-the-environment-9789264085169-en.htm>
7   See documents related to the European Commission's Environmental Impact Assessment (EIA) Directive: European Commission, "Nature Protection and Environmental Impact Assessment" <https://ec.europa.eu/environment/legal/law/2/module_3_1.htm> accessed 2 January 2021.
8   Sander de Bruyn and others, *Environmental Prices Handbook 2017* (CE Delft 2018).
9   This section is based on E Drissen and H Vollebergh, "Monetaire milieuschade in Nederland, een verkenning" (PBL Netherlands Environmental Assessment Agency, 15 June 2018).

prices. Therefore, a shadow price, which is a virtual price, needs to be determined. Generally, there are two main methods to do this: (1) the damage cost method; and (2) the abatement cost method. Each is explained in further detail below.[10]

A. *Damage cost method*

In the damage cost method, the valuation of the environmental damage caused by emissions depends on valuations by individuals. These can be estimated or constructed in various ways.

One possible way is hedonic pricing or contingent valuation, which identifies external factors that affect prices. An illustration: the difference in average housing prices in the same area between houses close to a park and houses close to a highway can be used to estimate the shadow price of unattractive views and noise disturbance (for example, expressed as the housing price difference per kilometre closer to the park). As well as methods based on revealed preferences, stated preference methods such as conjoint analysis can be used to value or determine the willingness-to-pay of individuals for specific environmental aspects.

Another way is to construct shadow prices more broadly across individuals by deconstructing the total environmental damage into different components. Each component can then be valued. To get a flavour, a damage cost method to value the damage caused by greenhouse gas and air pollutant emissions could look as follows. This example uses nitrogen oxides (NO_x), which are gases produced during combustion.

- Step 1 is to express the substance into a concentration or a deposition per geographic unit, for example, 365 ppm (parts per million) NO_x, equivalent to 748 mg NO_x per m³.

- Step 2 is to determine how this concentration is related to damage components such as damage to health, climate, ecosystems and buildings.

- Step 3 is to express each damage component in monetary units.

  - For health damage, the monetary valuation of a quality-adjusted life year (QALY) in the Netherlands can be used to assess the monetary value of a reduction in expected QALYs due to the relevant NO_x concentration.

  - For damage to the ecosystem, the value of biodiversity can be expressed as PDF (potentially disappeared fraction of species) per square metre per year. The monetary value of a unit of PDF can be based on valuation studies for specific species.

---

10   For a more elaborate overview of economic measurement methods, see Roman Inderst, Eftichios Sartzetakis and Anastasios Xepapadeas, "Technical Report on Sustainability and Competition", jointly commissioned by the ACM and the Hellenic Competition Commission (forthcoming).

- Finally, the value of environmental damage to buildings, including corrosion and damage to stones or paints due to acidification, can be based on maintenance and repair costs.

– Step 4 is to sum up these damage valuations for components to form the shadow price for a unit of NO_x emission, which has been estimated €34,700 per kiloton of NO_x.

B. *The abatement cost method*

Abatement costs are the costs associated with reducing environmental damage. When applied to public policy and social valuation of damages, the abatement cost method requires a specific environmental objective. Objectives can be set by government in law or in policies.[11] The method then estimates the costs that are needed to achieve that objective. To that end a supply curve is constructed, ranking possible measures to prevent damage according to their costs (from low to high). This curve represents the marginal abatement costs at different levels of emission reduction. The shadow price for the emission of a specific substance is equal to the costs associated with the costliest measure on the supply curve that is just needed to achieve the government objective. This price reflects the highest cost society is prepared to pay, as determined by the public policy goal, for environmental damage reduction.

The advantage of the abatement cost method compared with the damage cost method is that no valuation of the damage by individuals is necessary to estimate the shadow price. This is an advantage because these valuations can be complex and have large error margins. A governmental or other formal objective, as defined by a target emission level of a specific substance, and the supply curve for emission-reducing measures for that substance, are all that is needed to determine the shadow price.

VI. How Can the Assessment Be Carried Out in Practice?

After this short detour to get a flavour of methods to estimate shadow prices, how can the assessment of the benefits and costs of a specific environmental damage agreement take place in practice?

1. Benefits

To calculate the benefits, first it needs to be established which substances (greenhouse gases and air pollutants) are affected by the agreement. In the Netherlands, the quantities of physical emissions of a large number of greenhouse gases, air pollutants and other environmentally damaging substances to land, water and

---

11 Or, exceptionally, determined in court as in the *Urgenda* judgment in which the Dutch Supreme Court ruled that greenhouse gas emissions in the Netherlands should be 25% lower by the end of 2020 compared with 1990.

air are centrally registered in the Emissions Register ("Emissieregistratie"). The Emissions Register uses a bottom-up approach, measuring emissions at installations of companies. Reports of emissions are available per company.[12] Similarly, at European level, the European Environment Agency maintains an EU Registry on Industrial Sites.[13]

Next, for each of these substances the reduction in emission volumes that is foreseen by the parties under the agreement needs to be scrutinised, and the plausibility substantiated.

Once the actual emission volume reductions due to the agreement are determined for each substance, these need to be multiplied by the shadow price per substance. In the Netherlands, shadow prices are estimated and periodically published by environmental thinktank CE Delft in its Environmental Prices Handbook.[14] This Handbook sets out the methodology that is used and provides an overview of estimated shadow prices (with lower, upper and central estimates) for hundreds of substance emissions that damage air, water and soil.[15] In an international context, for example, the OECD has estimated shadow prices for a number of greenhouse gases and air pollutants for selected countries.[16]

In the simplest possible and crude way, the total benefits are estimated by the reductions in emissions of substances due to the agreement (which also includes a demand-reduction effect due to the price increase) × the shadow price per unit of the substance. These benefits constitute the benefits for consumers and for the non-consumers that suffered from the negative external effects.

2. Costs

The costs are any negative effects that are due to the restriction of competition resulting from the agreement. In practice, these will typically take the form of a price increases and demand reduction, due to more costly production processes or to withdrawing cheaper product varieties. More precisely, the expected price increase of a specific agreement is based on: (1) the costs of adjusting the product or production process in order to be able to generate lower emissions × (2) the degree of passing-on of these additional cost to consumers through higher retail prices.[17]

---

12   See Emissieregistratie <www.emissieregistratie.nl/erpubliek/erpub/facility.aspx>.
13   See European Environment Agency, Eionet Reporting Obligations Database <https://rod.eionet.europa.eu/obligations/721>.
14   n 8, English version <www.cedelft.eu/en/publications/2113/envionmental-prices-handbook-2017>.
15   CE Delft uses the abatement cost method for the CO_2 shadow price, and the damage cost approach for the valuation of other substances.
16   T Dang and A Mourougane, "Estimating Shadow Prices of Pollution in OECD Economies" (2014) OECD Green Growth Papers, No 2014-02.
17   This assumes that the additional costs that are absorbed (not passed on) in the vertical supply chain should not be part of the cost – benefit analysis.

According to the new approach, consumers receive a fair share of the benefits as long as the total benefits are larger than the additional costs that are passed on (and the other conditions are met as well). If all households in the Netherlands are consumers, as is for example the case for energy consumption, then the cost – benefit analysis boils down to comparing the post-agreement retail price increase to the reduction in environmental damage per unit of produced energy, based on the shadow price. If consumers are only a subset of those affected by negative external effects, then the difference in volumes on the cost side (only consumers) and benefit side (all affected) needs to be accounted for.

VII. Indispensability of Cooperation

The fair-share-to-consumers condition is one out of four conditions that must cumulatively hold for an exception to the cartel prohibition under TFEU, Articles 101(3) and (1), respectively. The other conditions are that there should be efficiency benefits, that the competition restrictions should be necessary to achieve the objective and, finally, that competition should not be eliminated for a substantial part of the products in question.

The necessity condition can be applied at two levels, what could be called "absolute necessity" and "relative necessity". Whether or not cooperation is necessary to achieve emission reductions in the first place is a question of absolute necessity. Whether or not all provisions or all parties in the agreement are needed (for example, it remains to be seen whether a provision on joint pricing would be necessary) is a question of relative necessity of the agreement.

As far as absolute necessity is concerned, there are general circumstances in which cooperation between competitors is needed and in which it is not needed. Cooperation is not needed if the willingness-to-pay for sustainable products is sufficiently high to cover the additional costs for individual companies. Competition can then take place in the dimension of sustainability, in very much the same way as on product quality or on innovation. Some consumers are prepared to pay a premium for sustainability, and some are not (depending perhaps on income). Sustainable (high-quality) products as well as non-sustainable (low-quality) products coexist in the market.

However, there are also circumstances in which unilateral sustainability initiatives do not come off the ground, and cooperation is necessary.

First, there may be first-mover disadvantages associated with introducing sustainable products. Consumers may switch away in large numbers from more expensive sustainable products to cheaper non-sustainable products, reducing the incentive to be the first to introduce them. Consumers may switch away because their willingness-to-pay for sustainable products is simply too small – in which case cooperation does not help either. But consumers may also switch away from sustainable products because of free-riding behaviour. They may prefer others to buy sustainable products but still appreciate and enjoy the resulting benefits. In that case the willingness-to-pay can be sufficiently large but not as long as there are cheaper varieties around that allow for free-riding. Yet another possibility is a combination of both motives, and is a more behavioural-economic outcome: the willingness-to-pay can be large if there is some assurance that others also purchase sustainable products and thus contribute to the sustainability improvement.[18] All these possibilities, including the free-rider aspect, can be investigated in a willingness-to-pay consumer survey.

Second, there may be fixed costs associated with making products or production processes more sustainable. If the demand for a sustainable product of an individual company is insufficient to recover those fixed costs, then cooperation to share the fixed costs between more companies may establish the absolute necessity for the agreement.

Once the absolute necessity for cooperation to achieve sustainability improvements is shown, from a relative necessity perspective it should be established whether all restrictions in the agreement are necessary. For example, if the agreement is motivated by fixed-cost sharing, then it is not necessary to have pricing restrictions as part of the agreement.

VIII. Conclusion

The key aspect of the proposed new approach is to include in the competition law assessment of certain sustainability agreements the benefits to the non-consumers who suffer from the negative external effects caused (eventually) by consumption. Consumers obtain a fair share if the total benefits to consumers and affected non-consumers are larger than the price increase due to restricted competition.

Although the implementation of this new approach is considered practically doable (and this paper has set out in broad and simplified terms how it can be done), there are complicating circumstances which have not been discussed. For example, shadow prices are dynamic and can change over time, depending on what private and public measures to reduce emissions are taken or planned and on whether policy goals are adjusted. In these eventualities further reflections are needed to select the correct shadow prices for the assessment.

Finally, besides the proposed new approach in ACM's draft guidelines, there are other ways to facilitate joint private initiatives that are more in line with

---

18 See, for example, U Fischbacher, S Gächter and E Fehr, "Are people conditionally cooperative? Evidence from a public goods experiment" (2001) 71(3) Economics Letters 397.

the full compensation principle of Article 101(3) TFEU. A recent paper by Thomas and Inderst[19] proposes an interesting way, which is to take account of the likelihood that the willingness-to-pay for sustainability improvements may be higher for future consumers than for current consumers. That could also provide an opening under competition law to be more facilitating to private sustainability initiatives.

---

19 Stefan Thomas and Roman Inderst, "Prospective Welfare Analysis – Extending Willingness-to-Pay Assessment to Embrace Sustainability" (25 September 2020) <https://papers.ssrn.com/sol3/papers.cfm?abstract_id=3699693>.

Green Antitrust: Friendly Fire in the Fight Against Climate Change

MAARTEN PIETER SCHINKEL* AND LEONARD TREUREN**

University of Amsterdam

> People of the same trade seldom meet together, even for merriment and diversion, but the conversation ends in a conspiracy against the public, or in some contrivance to raise prices... But though the law cannot hinder people of the same trade from sometimes assembling together, it ought to do nothing to facilitate such assemblies; much less to render them necessary.
>
> Adam Smith, *An Inquiry into the Nature and Causes of the Wealth of Nations* (first published 1776), Book I, Chapter 10.

I. Introduction

The urgency of the climate crisis and the apparent failure of many governments to meet the Paris Agreement objectives have led inspired competition law scholars to push for "green antitrust policy".[1] The idea behind this movement is to revise the competition rules, as far as they may stand in the way of companies

---

* Professor of Economics, University of Amsterdam: m.p.schinkel@uva.nl. His research interests and teaching are in industrial organisation, competition policy and regulation, in particular cartel behaviour and enforcement.
** PhD candidate, University of Amsterdam: l.m.treuren@uva.nl. He works in industrial organisation, with a focus on competition policy, in particular investigating product and labour market effects of cartels and mergers. Parts of this paper were previously published in Dutch as one of the KVS Preadviezen titled "Beter geen mededingingsbeperkingen voor duurzaamheid." In MA Haan and MP Schinkel (eds), KVS Preadviezen 2020 Mededingingsbeleid (Koninklijke Vereniging voor de Staathuishoudkunde 2020).
1 See Christopher Townley, *Article 81 EC and Public Policy* (Hart Publishing 2009); Suzanne Kingston, *Greening EU Competition Law and Policy* (CUP 2011); Giorgio Monti, "Four options for a greener competition law" (2020) 11(3) – (4) JECL & Pract.

contributing to sustainability factors and a climate-neutral economy.[2] Corporate lobbies claim to want to take more social responsibility for a better world, but that this is impossible without collectively restricting competition first. Acting alone while competing, no company would be able to hurdle the so-called "first-mover disadvantage". Whereas in cooperation, the argument is, competitors would be able to make the transition to more sustainable ways of production. The transferred concern is that with restrictions of competition potentially being illegal, companies are restricted from taking joint sustainability initiatives through fear of competition law interventions and liabilities. In response, several European competition authorities are already considering to allow anticompetitive conduct that would be forbidden under the current interpretation of competition law, in return for sustainability benefits. Proposals on how to implement such exemptions of the cartel prohibition, the rules to prevent abuse of dominance, and merger control are being avidly put forward and discussed.[3] They are well received by corporates, politicians and lawyers. The European Commission considers how competition policy can best support the Green Deal.[4] Green antitrust clearly is gaining momentum across Europe.[5]

The central idea behind the green antitrust movement is that conflicts between market and environment could be resolved by the build-up of market power. Most concrete are proposals to exempt sustainability agreements restrictive of competition from the cartel law, under Article 101(3) of the Treaty on the Functioning of the European Union (TFEU). In essence, these proposals interpret the advance of sustainability factors as "economic progress", and an anticompetitive agreement contributing such progress can be allowed if it gives consumers a "fair share" of the benefits that compensates them for the anticompetitive effects of the agreement. The European Commission set a precedent with *CECED*, in which avoided emissions of carbon dioxide, sulphur dioxide and nitrous oxide were taken into consideration to allow a collective of washing machine producers to take their

---

2   See CPI, "EU: MEPs demand fundamental overhaul of competition policy" (*CPI*, 4 February 2019); Panel on "Sustainability and EU competition law" (Competition and Consumer Day, Helsinki, 25–26 September 2019); Council of the European Union, "External Dimension of European Competitiveness" 14055/1/19 (19 November 2019). The Dutch Competition Authority (ACM) has been a forerunner with its 2014 "Vision Document on Competition and Sustainability".

3   Panel at the 2019 Competition and Consumer Day (n 2); GCLC conference "Sustainability and competition policy: Bridging two worlds to enable a fairer economy" (Brussels, 24 October 2019); Hellenic Competition Commission, "Competition Law and Sustainability" (28 September 2020); OECD, "Sustainability and competition" (1 December 2020). The subject of green state aid control, which is also part of the green antitrust discussion, is outside the scope of this paper.

4   CPI, "EU: MEPs demands fundamental overhaul of competition policy" (*CPI*, 4 February 2019); European Commission, "Competition Policy supporting the Green Deal: Call for Contributions" (22 September 2020) <https://ec.europa.eu/competition/information/green_deal/> accessed 3 January 2021.

5   In US antitrust, wider public policy arguments on welfare merits traditionally have had little traction, see Gregory J Werden, "Antitrust's Rule of Reason: Only Competition Matters" [2014] Antitrust LJ 713. However, the idea that agreements amongst competitors would be necessary for impactful corporate sustainability efforts is gaining popularity there too. See, for example, Rebecca Henderson, *Reimagining Capitalism in a World on Fire* (Public Affairs 2020).

least energy-efficient models off the market.[6] Importantly, *CECED* was not *decided* on the projected environmental benefits. The Commission concluded that a typical consumer would be compensated for the increased purchase costs of more energy-efficient washing machines by saving more on electricity bills in use alone. While the sustainability benefits for all of Europe were valued at more than seven times the higher product price, these were additional collective benefits for which the Commission did not assess the appreciation of consumers.[7]

The green antitrust movement, however, seeks to exempt collaborating companies on decisive compensatory sustainability benefits. From allowing such "green cartels", it seems a small step to condoning other forms of market power – based conduct on the companies' promise to switch to more sustainable production methods. A merger, for example, that leads to appreciable market power accumulation yet also promises to shift all production to low-emissions plants. Performing the trade-off of expected cost synergies against the anticompetitive effects of a merger quantitatively is standard application in assessing the efficiency-defence in merger control. Already is the Commission considering methods for measuring "green merger efficiencies" in this context.[8] Also, in enforcement against abuse of dominance there is discretion to take sustainability benefits into account.[9] For example, a dominant firm that excludes a polluting rival from the market may in the same spirit be able to count on a friendly review. The ever more widely felt need that climate change requires immediate action to improve sustainability has created a strong urge also with competition authorities to do their bit.

The Dutch Authority for Consumers and Markets (ACM) is a forerunner of re-orienting competition policy this way. In spring 2014, the ACM was obliged by the Dutch Ministry of Economic Affairs to take "sustainability" into account in its application of the Dutch cartel law exemption clause, which is practically identical to Article 101(3) TFEU.[10] To this day very few qualifying sustainability initiatives have come forward. The two cases the ACM has publicly dealt with so far are the *National Energy Agreement* – hereafter *Coal* – and *Chicken of Tomorrow* – hereafter *Chicken*.[11] Both initiatives were denied an exemption.

---

6   *CECED* (Case IV.F.1/36.718) Commission Decision C(1999) 5064 [2000] OJ L187/47.
7   ibid, recital 56.
8   MLEX, "Green merger efficiencies to be looked at by the EU 'discussion group', Régibeau says" (*MLEX*, 18 November 2020). See, on assessing cost efficiencies in merger control, Marie Goppelsroeder, Maarten Pieter Schinkel and Jan Tuinstra, "Quantifying the Scope for Efficiency Defense in Merger Control: The Werden-Froeb-Index" (2008) 56(4) J Industrial Economics 778.
9   See, for instance, Massimiliano Kadar, "Article 102 TFEU and Efficiency Pleas: A 'Fact-Check'" in Nicolas Charbit and Sonia Ahmad (eds), *Richard Whish QC (Hon) Liber Amicorum, "Taking Competition Law Outside the Box"* (Concurrences 2020).
10 Conceptually, the idea is akin to the efficiency defence in horizontal mergers, which in essence requires merger-specific marginal cost reductions that offset the unilateral effects of the merger, so that consumer prices do not increase. See Article 6(3) Mededingingswet. The policy rule is Beleidsregel Mededinging en Duurzaamheid, WJZ/14052830 (6 May 2014).
11 ACM, "Analysis of the sustainability arrangements concerning the 'Chicken of Tomorrow'" (26 January 2015); ACM, "Analysis of the planned agreement on closing down coal power plants from the 1980s as part of the Social and Economic Council of the Netherlands' SER Energieakkoord" (26 September 2013).

After extensive investigation, the ACM concluded that they provided too few sustainability benefits for the respective consumers. Subsequently, the Ministry insisted that "the benefits for society as a whole" must be considered – even though it also remained required that consumers be compensated.[12] Hoping to be able to welcome more initiatives, in July 2020 the ACM published draft "Guidelines: Sustainability Agreements". The requirements for an exemption are clarified by various hypothetical examples of agreements that ACM would not see in conflict with the cartel prohibition.[13] More importantly, the draft Guidelines make a landmark proposal to lower the threshold for exempting sustainability agreements: consumers of the product no longer need to be fully compensated if others benefit sufficiently.

Green antitrust appears very sympathetic: a fast transition to more sustainable production and consumption is essential to the future of our planet, and corporations must certainly take some responsibility for it too. Where government coordination fails to nudge the balance from grey to green equilibria – because of lack of information, legal options, political will or otherwise – perhaps private coordination can come to the rescue. After all, polluting companies will typically know best how to reduce their own externalities. And indeed, green CEOs increasingly stand up for good causes. For some time now, passionate competition law scholars have been hammering home the importance of sustainability.[14] But is contributing to the fight against climate change truly a nail in this case? Or is it rather a screw? Deciding this first is essential when selecting the right tool to use to fix the problem – all the more so when it is urgent. The central question here, therefore, is whether it can be expected that undertakings will take more corporate social responsibility when they compete less. The key premise of the green antitrust movement is that tensions between competition and sustainability can be eased with less competition. But is that premise true?

In this paper we review the available economic literature to find that it provides little-to-no ground for believing that restrictions of competition would incentivise companies to take more sustainability initiatives. On the contrary, it appears that *competition* induces companies to produce more sustainably, as well as if they are in part intrinsically motivated to do so. Even if first-mover disadvantage, a concept to which the proponents of green antitrust policy point, would lead to a deadlock

---

12 Letter from the Minister of Economic Affairs of the Netherlands to the Dutch Parliament, "Duurzame ontwikkeling en beleid" (23 June 2016). Beleidsregel Mededinging en Duurzaamheid, WJZ/16145098 (30 September 2016), [3.3]. The strict compensation requirement was insisted on in a letter from the European Commission, DG COMP Johannes Laitenberger to the Ministry of Economic Affairs of the Netherlands, concerning the "Beleidsregels mededinging en duurzaamheid" (26 February 2016).

13 ACM, "Draft Guidelines: Sustainability Agreements" (9 July 2020). A revision has been announced for January 2021.

14 See Simon Holmes, "Climate change, sustainability, and competition law" (2020) 8(2) J Antitrust Enforcement 354; Maurits Dolmans, "Sustainable competition policy" (2020) 5(4) Competition Law and Policy Debate; Nicole Kar, Emma Cochrane and Bella Spring, "Environmental Sustainability and EU Merger Control: EU Competition Policy's Dark Horse to Support Green Investment" (2021), in this book.

preventing more sustainable production, sustainability agreements create no incentive to break that impasse. The rare genuine sustainability agreement cannot justify relaxing general competition rules. It seems proper, therefore, to regard the corporate cheers for green antitrust policy with some scepticism and suspicion. That is also the attitude that we should expect our competition agencies to have. After all, they are tasked first and foremost with the protection of competition.

We warn against two major risks of green antitrust policy. One risk is cartel green-washing. Competitors who are allowed to coordinate their trade have an incentive to provide minimal sustainability benefits for maximum price increases. The more accommodating the competition authority, the less "green" will be delivered. Competition authorities will have to strictly demand sufficient compensatory sustainability benefits, and then constantly monitor exempted agreements. This task requires a staggering amount of information that these agencies cannot reasonably be expected to have. It will tie up a lot of their resources at the expense of other enforcement and advocacy priorities. The second risk is that being able to point to corporate self-regulation gives the part of government that should promote sustainability further excuse to shun their responsibility for designing proper regulation. The green antitrust movement may thus exacerbate the very government failure it seeks to correct.

II. Conditions for Exempting Sustainability Agreements

A horizontal sustainability agreement in restriction of competition can be exempted from the cartel prohibition if four cumulative conditions specified in Article 101(3) TFEU are satisfied. Together they provide an assessment framework that can be applied using standard economic methods of analysis. The first requirement is that the agreement indeed generates concrete and objectively measurable sustainability benefits. It is well known that people typically have an appreciation for greener products that generate fewer or less-damaging side-effects, such as environmental pollution, and are manufactured under fairer conditions, such as no child labour, good safety at the workplace, no cruelty to farm animals, and above-subsistence-level wages.[15] These values can be identified and quantified, for example by marketing econometrics or techniques from environmental economics.[16]

The second requirement is that consumers of the products concerned receive a "fair share" of the sustainability benefits. For operationalisation of this condition, micro- and welfare economics provide a firm conceptual and practical framework.[17] In essence, the appreciation of buyers for a more sustainably manufactured product

---

15 See Markus Kitzmüller and Jay Shimshack, "Economic perspectives on corporate social responsibility" (2012) 50(1) J Econ Literature 51.
16 See, for instance, Nick Hanley and Edward Barbier, *Pricing Nature: Cost – Benefit Analysis and Environmental Policy* (Edward Elgar 2009).
17 A particularly accessible textbook is Joseph E Stiglitz and Jay K Rosengard, *Economics of the Public Sector* (Norton 2015).

– be it derived directly from consuming a higher quality good or from appreciation of its positive or less negative externalities – needs to be balanced against the downsides of the anticompetitive agreement made to obtain it, which typically are higher product prices. Not each and every buyer is to be compensated, but the "overall impact on consumers of the products within the relevant market" on average.[18] This introduces the need for interpersonal utility comparison, which is somewhat tricky to do, but nevertheless a balancing that economics can help make concrete. The policy has some leeway, because no strict Pareto-criterion is applied – which would give each consumer veto-power. The working interpretation of "fair share" is a share large enough to fully compensate the representative consumer of the product, who should not be worse off with the agreement in place.

The third condition in Article 101(3) TFEU is that the restriction of competition must be necessary for reaping the sustainability benefits. While this may suggest a broad duty of the competition authority to consider and give priority to alternative ways in which the projected sustainability benefits could be achieved – in particular government regulation – in practice the interpretation is narrow. The agreement must not go beyond what is necessary to generate the projected sustainability increase compared with competition. The actual improvement only needs to be marginal to pass this third condition. Government failure has been called on as a justification for green antitrust policy, including by the competition authorities advocating the policy. Yet it does not seem to be the case that the giving of an exemption from cartel law is seen by its proponents as a measure of last resort, that is only to be taken after all the different ways to push government to take regulatory responsibility have been probed. For doing that, competition authorities also lack the mandate and instruments. Whether narrowly or widely interpreted, economic analysis can help assess the necessity condition.

The fourth requirement is that the agreement to be exempted does not "eliminate" all competition around the product concerned. Competition must remain on dimensions such as price, brand image or technological development, with which the European Commission was content in *CECED*. It does not seem too difficult to argue some dimensions of remaining competition in any case in practice. In particular, a sustainability agreement may involve only the larger companies, excluding small or less efficient producers also active in the relevant market. Such a competitive fringe may be interpreted as remaining competition sufficient for meeting the fourth condition. Economic analysis of oligopoly models in industrial organisation can bring out the anticompetitive effects of partial collusion, which can be harmful.[19]

---

18 European Commission, "Guidelines on the Application of Article 81(3) of the Treaty" [2004] OJ C101/97, recital 85.

19 See Iwan Bos and Joseph E Harrington Jr, "Endogenous cartel formation with heterogeneous firms" (2010) 41(1) RAND J Econ 92; Roman Inderst, Frank Maier-Rigaud and Ulrich Schwalbe, "Umbrella Effects" (2014) 10(3) J Competition L & Econ 739.

Only agreements on sustainability parameters are meant to be considered for an exemption, the ACM insists in its proposal: coordination should not also extend to prices or production. Yet since a transition to more sustainable ways of manufacturing typically implies higher production costs, prices will have to increase with them. It should not be necessary to make price agreements for this, since those costs can be passed through in competition on prices. Yet, under cover of the inevitable price increases, allowing competitors to make sustainability agreements also provides them with opportunity to raise prices by more than what is necessary. They certainly have the incentive for this. It is well known that meeting can easily tempt competitors to talk about prices as well. Frequently, perfectly legitimate coordination between competitors, for example over the implementation of antiterrorism regulation, product quality standards or R&D, has led to malignant collusion.[20] It is questionable whether a competition authority will be able to enforce that agreements are limited to sustainability factors alone – however firmly it is stated that exemptions can only be given the latter. Ultimately, the balance will have to be between the green advance supplied and the total price increase demanded for it.

III. *Coal* and *Chicken* fell short

The effective application of the assessment framework by the Dutch competition authority in *Coal* and *Chicken* is insightful. *Coal* was an agreement among electricity producers to close five coal-fired electricity plants five years ahead of the regulated schedule. This meant a reduction of approximately 10% of total electricity production capacity in the Netherlands. The ACM calculated that the resulting price increases would give the Dutch, all consumers of electricity, higher electricity costs totalling €75 million a year. The benefit would be reductions of emissions. Using quite sophisticated environmental economics, ACM valued these at €30 million a year.[21] The benefits were much lower than the harm, mostly because ACM recognised that the prominently claimed CO_2 emissions reductions were not actually there. The reason was that the parties did not intend to take their unused CO_2 emissions rights out of the EU Emissions Trading System, so that the emissions were merely relocated, presenting no benefit to the Dutch. Offered the option to take a compensating amount of emission rights off the market and burn it, the electricity companies refused, claiming that this would make the deal too expensive for them. The closures were later brought forward by regulation.

---

20 See Tomaso Duso, Lars-Henrik Röller and Jo Seldeslachts, "Collusion Through Joint R&D: An Empirical Assessment" (2013) 96(2) Rev Econ & Statistics 349; Cento Veljanovski, "Collusion as Environmental Protection – An Economic Assessment" SSRN working paper (2020).
21 ACM, "Analysis of the planned agreement on closing down coal power plants" (n 10). See also Erik Kloosterhuis and Machiel Mulder, "Competition Law and Environmental Protection: The Dutch Agreement on Coal-fired Power Plants" (2015) 11(4) J Competition L & Econ 855.

In *Chicken*, the ACM also concluded that the sustainability benefits were too small compared with the anticompetitive harm. In this initiative, poultry farmers and supermarkets responded jointly to protests of animal rights activists against the poor living conditions of so-called "plofkippen" – "exploding chicken". Farmers promised to improve the welfare of broiler chicken kept for this cheapest type of chicken meat for the Dutch market – only about 30%: the rest of poultry in the Netherlands was bred for export. The supermarkets pledged not to import competitive cheap chicken substitutes. The ACM investigation showed that prices would increase by €1.46/kg of chicken on average, while Dutch consumers valued the better living conditions for chicken at only €0.82/kg.[22] The insufficient willingness to pay reflected that the proposed agreement would achieve only a minimal increase in cage space, and only for a minority of chicken reared for the domestic market. The ACM disallowed the agreement. In 2020, ACM's own follow-up research found that the restriction of competition had not been necessary: "plofkip" has virtually disappeared from the supermarkets without.[23]

IV. Not Less but More Competition
Leads to Greater Sustainability

The central question of whether it should be expected that firms will produce more sustainably in an anticompetitive agreement than in competition squarely falls on economics to answer. It is reasonable to base the analysis on two standard premises. The first is that (potential) consumers care about sustainability. Eichholtz, Kok and Quigley document a higher willingness to pay for office buildings with sustainability labels.[24] Casadesus-Masanell, Crooke and Reinhardt report a higher willingness to pay for T-shirts made with organic cotton.[25] In a survey of the literature, Kitzmüller and Shimshack conclude that willingness to pay in general positively depends on the degree of corporate social responsibility a firm engages in.[26] More recently, Aghion, Bénabou, Martin and Roulet find that green innovation is positively correlated with consumers' stated sustainability preferences.[27]

---

22 ACM, "Analysis of the sustainability arrangements concerning the 'Chicken of Tomorrow'" (n 10).

23 ACM, "Welfare of today's chicken and that of the 'Chicken of Tomorrow'" (1 September 2020). See also ACM, "Vision Document on Competition and Sustainability (2014). These conditions are similar to the requirements for mounting an efficiency defence in merger control in Commission, "Guidelines on the assessment of horizontal mergers under the Council Regulation on the control of concentrations between undertakings" [2004] OJ C31/5. ACM, "Analysis of the planned agreement on closing down coal power plants" (n 10), the approval of the ACM, which was open to valuing the CO_2 reduction higher than the prevailing market price per tonne, hinged on this point. See Section II for references.

24 Piet Eichholtz, Nils Kok, and John M Quigley, "Doing Well By Doing Good? Green Office Buildings" (2010) 100(5) American Econ Rev 2492.

25 Ramon Casadesus-Masanell and others, "Households' willingness to pay for 'green' goods: evidence from Patagonia's introduction of organic cotton sportswear" (2009) 18(1) J Econ & Management Strategy 203.

26 Kitzmüller and Shimshack (n 14).

27 Phillippe Aghion and others, "Environmental Preferences and Technological Choices: Is Market Competition Clean or Dirty?" (2020) NBER working paper 26921.

A second premise is that, no matter how noble the proposed initiatives may appear, firms are ultimately driven by profit motives. Rate of return incentives can certainly lead to intricate and forward-looking firm behaviour, for instance investing in a good public image in order to attract more consumers. Running up short-term losses with a CEO passionate about corporate social responsibility can therefore still be consistent with long-term profit maximisation. Yet under pressure of shareholders and investors, firms are interested in sustainability initiatives first and foremost to increase their profitability, in particular through buyers' higher willingness to pay.[28] The latter are the revenue returns to sustainability investments, which are costs. Therefore, companies will strive for profit-maximising price increases and sustainability advances, for which cost-minimisation is a necessary condition. That these incentives lead to little green is reflected in the literature on greenwashing. Firms certainly like to have a "green" public image, but when consumers cannot assess the true extent of their sustainability investments, they only undertake the minimum.[29] In general, we should expect no less, and no more, from for-profit enterprises, both in competition and in coordination.

The relationship between competition and sustainability is studied in a limited but recently growing literature. The current consensus is that competition increases investments in sustainability, with firms investing in sustainability because it lowers their costs or allows them to stand out to consumers. Green, in other words, is a dimension of product differentiation. Porter and Kramer and Roulet and Bothello point out that corporate social responsibility (CSR) can be a strong competitive advantage.[30] Simon and Prince show that a reduction in industrial concentration in the United States is associated with a reduction in toxic releases at factory level.[31] Fernández-Kranz and Santaló and Flammer show that competition has a positive effect on CSR at business level, in studies of variations in import duties and concentration.[32] Aghion and co-authors show that the positive relation between consumers' stated sustainability preferences

---

28 In addition to the presence of regulatory failure, firms may benefit from reducing environmental externalities through workers' willingness to accept a lower wage. See Jean-Etienne de Bettignies, Hua Fang Liu and David T Robinson, "Corporate Social Responsibility and Imperfect Regulatory Oversight: Theory and Evidence from Greenhouse Gas Emissions Disclosures" (2020) NBER working paper 28159.

29 See Catherine A Ramus and Ivan Montiel, "When Are Corporate Environmental Policies a Form of Greenwashing?" (2005) 44(4) Business & Society 377; Magali A Delmas and Maria J Montes-Sancho, "Voluntary Agreements to Improve Environmental Quality: Symbolic and Substantive Cooperation" (2010) 31(6) Strategic Management J 575.

30 Michael E Porter and Mark R Kramer, "Strategy and Society: The Link Between Competitive Advantage and Corporate Social Responsibility" Harvard Business Review (December 2006); Thomas Roulet and Joel Bothello, "Why 'De-growth' Shouldn't Scare Businesses" Harvard Business Review (24 February 2020).

31 Daniel H Simon and Jeffrey T Prince, "The effect of competition on toxic pollution releases" (2016) 79 J Environmental Econ & Management 40.

32 Daniel Fernández-Kranz and Juan Santaló, "When necessity becomes a virtue: The effect of product market competition on corporate social responsibility" (2010) 19(2) J Econ & Management Strategy 453; Caroline Flammer "Does product market competition foster corporate social responsibility? Evidence from trade liberalization" (2015) 36(10) Strategic Management J 1469.

and the probability that a firm engages in green innovation increases with the degree of product market competition.[33] This suggest that as pro-environment attitudes become more common over time, the role of competition in fostering green innovation will only increase. Ding, Levine, Lin and Xie link antitrust policy to sustainability by showing that stricter competition law regimes are positively associated with CSR, and that this link is stronger in countries where consumers indicate stronger pro-environment attitudes.[34]

Few papers study the relationship between horizontal agreements and sustainability directly. They relate to the literature on exempting research joint ventures, which can increase R&D investments above competitive levels if spill-overs of innovations are so large that unilateral investments are discouraged.[35] For this reason, there is a broad exemption clause available for R&D joint ventures, including for research into more sustainable production methods. However, with limited spill-overs, competition is the stronger driver of R&D. There is concern, therefore, that mergers reduce innovation.[36] Importantly, sustainability initiatives of the kind considered for exemption, such as investments in cleaner technology or better quality of life for farm animals, have little or no spill-over from one company to another. These cases are more about implementation than innovation.

Schinkel and Spiegel analyse the link between anticompetitive agreements and sustainability in a two-stage duopoly model where firms first select investments in sustainability and subsequently compete on the product market.[37] They find that allowing the firms to coordinate their sustainability levels leads to the lowest sustainability levels. Sustainability is a product attribute that consumers care about, and hence is used by firms to compete and attract each other's customers. Allowing firms to coordinate their sustainability levels allows them to cut the costs associated with this business-stealing by reducing their sustainability investments. The analysis reveals a policy paradox: if price collusion is allowed, and not agreements on sustainability, sustainability investments are highest. The reason is that the increased margins due to price coordination make it extra attractive to poach customers by differentiation through sustainability. The higher willingness to pay can subsequently be extracted with high collusive prices. We noted above that a risk of allowing firms to agree on sustainability is that they also manage to coordinate prices. However, when firms coordinate both dimensions of competition, sustainability investments are lower still than in competition, which goes to show the power of competition in advancing green. Treuren and Schinkel

33 Aghion and others (n 26).
34 Wenzhi Ding and others, "Competition laws, norms and corporate social responsibility" (2020) NBER working paper 27493.
35 Claude d'Aspremont and Alexis Jacquemin, "Cooperative and Noncooperative R&D in Duopoly with Spillovers" (1988) 78(5) American Econ Rev 1133.
36 Giulio Federico, Gregor Langus and Tommaso Valletti, "Horizontal mergers and product innovation" (2018) 61(C) Intl J Industrial Organization 590.
37 Maarten Pieter Schinkel and Yossi Spiegel, "Can collusion promote sustainable consumption and production?" (2017) 53(C) Intl J Industrial Organization 371.

generalise these findings to more firms and remaining competition.[38] Note that when firms coordinate prices and sustainability investments, sustainability levels are still lower than in competition. This means that also if coordinating their sustainability investments allows the companies to collude on prices as well, a risk we noted above, sustainability does not benefit from coordination.

Proponents of green antitrust policy point out that today's corporate leadership increasingly pledges allegiance to take responsibility for stakeholders more widely, including their environment.[39] They view profit-driven firm analysis as outdated, and Friedman's appeal to it as an ancient belief.[40] Green CEO's may not even be controllable by shareholders anymore if they wanted to. Importantly, however, if firms operate with an intrinsic motivation to produce more sustainably too, investments typically remain higher in competition than with sustainability agreements, and the difference may even become larger. In Schinkel and Treuren, the level of sustainability investments features directly in each firm's objective function, besides in the profits part.[41] Since intrinsically motivated investments are independent of the competitive regime, they are higher in absolute value in both competition and coordination. Moreover, coordination reduces the additional intrinsically motivated green investments, since the loss of profit due to increasing sustainability beyond the normal profit-maximising level is larger for firms who jointly decide on sustainability. That an intrinsic motivation to do green makes anticompetitive agreements not more, but rather even less suitable to promote sustainability investments underlines our warning not to lean too far in sympathies for initiatives to take corporate social responsibility jointly.

V. First-mover Disadvantage Is A Rare Phenomenon

With the evidence pointing towards more, not less, competition increasing sustainability, on what basis does the ACM build its trust of coordinated sustainability initiatives? A term that is often used in this context is "first-mover disadvantage": no single firm would be able to make investments in sustainability because they come with cost increases that necessitate price increases, and consumers would not be willing to pay such price increases.[42] Unilateral initiatives would (temporarily) worsen a firm's competitive position and profitability. This is

---

38 See Leonard Treuren and Maarten Pieter Schinkel, "Can collusion promote sustainable consumption and production? Not beneficially beyond duopoly" (2018) Amsterdam Center for Law and Economics working paper 2018-01.

39 See, for example, the reception of the initiative Business Roundtable, "Statement on the Purpose of a Corporation" (*Business Roundtable*, 19 August 2019) <https://opportunity.businessroundtable.org/ourcommitment/> accessed 19 January 2021. Henderson (n 4) contains many other examples.

40 See Milton Friedman, "A Friedman Doctrine: The Social Responsibility of Business is to Increase Its Profits" *New York Times* (New York, 13 September 1970).

41 See Maarten Pieter Schinkel and Leonard Treuren, "On Corporate Social Responsibility by Joint Agreement" (2021) Amsterdam Center for Law and Economics working paper 2021-01.

42 ACM Draft Guidelines (n 12), 15.

seen as an obstacle that only the whole sector could manage to overcome together with coordinated sustainability investments.

We note that the first-mover disadvantage argument assumes that either (potential) consumers have no willingness to pay for sustainable products, that consumers fully free ride on the sustainable consumption of others, or that firms cannot credibly signal that their products are sustainable – or a combination of such conditions. As the empirical literature shows, however, firms *can* differentiate their products as more sustainable, and consumers *do*, in general and increasingly, have a willingness to pay for them that is great enough to make unilateral sustainability investments profitable. The first-mover disadvantage therefore seems a rather special case. If, nonetheless, going alone would be loss-making, it is unclear why firms would increase sustainability investments when acting jointly. After all, in that case their joint profitability would still be higher with lower investments. In order to increase sustainability above competitive levels, joint sustainability initiatives will therefore require price increases above and beyond mere cost recoupment in order for their profitability not to decline – while price agreements are explicitly *not* the aim of green antitrust policy.

It seems that agreements on sustainability in response to a first-mover disadvantage are only likely to increase sustainability if willingness to pay for more sustainable products increases *as a result of the agreement*. This requires consumers to be willing to pay for sustainability, but *only* if sustainability is delivered by coordinated sustainability agreements. It is unclear why this would be the case in general. Two possibilities come to mind, both rather peculiar. One is the case of full free-riding, in which no consumer would buy the greener product, despite having a willingness to pay for it, as long as a grey substitute remains available. This case seems extreme and, where it does exist, government regulation would be the appropriate to coordinate.. The other possibility is that a green corporate cooperative can "educate" consumers on their preferences by forcing them to consume more sustainably manufactured products. That idea may imply a theory of "green experience good". If made to consume more sustainably produced goods really helps to cultivate a willingness to buy them, the paternalism required would be more appropriately provided by the government, acting on democratic mandate, than by a cooperative of corporate interests.

The rare occurrence of first-mover disadvantage appears to be a weak foundation on which to base a general revision of competition law. In fact, the common term in the literature is first-mover *advantage*.[43] If a good or service can truly only be developed in coordination, an assessment as joint venture seems the more obvious route for progress, avoiding Article 101(1) TFEU altogether. After

---

43 See, for example, Wojciech Przychodzen, Dante I Leyva-de la Hiz and Justyna Przychodzen, "First-mover advantages in green innovation – Opportunities and threats for financial performance: A longitudinal analysis" (2020) 27(1) Corporate Social Responsibility & Environmental Management 339.

all, if green really cannot be a dimension of competition, and no firm would provide a more sustainable manufactured product on its own, competition may not be restricted by an agreement to offer it, and so cartel law not apply at all. All the complexities and stretches of law to obtain exemption possibilities may then be avoided. If not, we note that consumers must have at least some willingness to pay for more sustainably produced commodities in order to be able to enjoy any sustainability benefit at all, let alone receive a "fair share" of those benefits. Without it, the compensation criterion for exemption under Article 101(3) TFEU cannot be met. All-in-all, it seems that even if the first-mover disadvantage would hold up sustainability initiatives in rare extreme cases, cartel exemptions are not the way to break the impasse.

VI. Green Antitrust Requires Permanent Surveillance Against Cartel Greenwashing

In view of the incentives that companies face, competition authorities are advised not to put too much trust in the coordinated green promises of corporates. They are likely to fall short in their efforts in competition, so that the consumer compensation condition needs to be strictly monitored and enforced, which in turn reduces incentives to invest – as in *Coal*. Since coordination creates a deadweight loss, full compensation of consumers typically leaves the firms with a loss.[44] By their decision to purchase the original unsustainable product, consumers reveal a low willingness to pay for the sustainability benefits, which makes compensating them particularly expensive – as in *Chicken*.[45] Also with competition remaining in some dimension, as required by the fourth exemption condition, these pessimistic findings continue to hold.[46] Maybe this explains why green initiatives are rarely proposed: there simply are few, if any, that can create a welfare increase for consumers while not be loss-making for the businesses. A competition authority that is able to enforce consumer compensation, therefore, will deter most initiatives.

Companies that still do apply for exemption with a sustainability agreement, despite the unattractive conditions, have all the incentives to establish the largest possible price increase for the lowest possible sustainability benefits required to compensate their consumers. They may be rare exceptions, or they may count on being able to pass the exemption test of an imperfectly informed competition authority with less-than-full consumer compensation. In any case, competition authorities will need to bargain with corporate cooperatives for sufficient sustainability efforts on behalf of consumers. The initiative will seek to choose a sustainability – price

---

44 See Schinkel and Spiegel (n 36).
45 See Maarten Pieter Schinkel and Lukáš Tóth, "Compensatory public goods provision by a private cartel" (2020) Amsterdam Law School research Paper 2016-05.
46 See Treuren and Schinkel (n 37).

combination on the representative consumer's indifference curve in order to meet the compensation requirement. As long as the sustainability level is higher than in competition – and the agreement at least does not explicitly appear to be on prices – this will satisfy the competition authority in its narrow interpretation of the necessity condition. Importantly, however, after exempting such a sustainability agreement in restriction of competition, the welfare objective of the competition authority remains permanently opposed to the profit-objective of the cooperative. The competition authority must therefore strictly and constantly supervise the agreement to ensure that sustainability is in fact being delivered, and that price increases do not exceed what is needed to cover the cost of the sustainability increase.

Proper assessment and surveillance require a staggering amount of knowledge and resources for a competition authority. Even though the burden of proof lies with the firms, the competition authority will need to verify the firms' claims, which essentially requires information about the preferences of all consumers (or even all citizens – see section VIII) – not only on the willingness to pay for private goods, but also for public goods and broader environmental concerns such as clean air and biodiversity.[47] Acquiring this information, keeping it constantly up-to-date and processing it appears to be a near-impossible task for any competition authority. Green antitrust policy will therefore be extremely demanding on time and budget, crowding out other important competition enforcement objectives. Any information asymmetry in these market oversight games presents a high risk of abuse of the green antitrust policy for cartel greenwashing. Competition authorities' resources could be better spent than on permanently and imperfectly controlling sustainability agreements to do enough green, when the firms involved would have almost always done more in competition.

VII. Green Antitrust Excuses
Government Failure to Regulate

In the classical economic approach, damaging side-effects of market interactions are seen as externalities. The solution is to force market participants to internalise these externalities. The social costs of pollution, for example, then become part of the production costs to be expressed in the product prices. Higher prices decrease demand and thereby environmental damage, while higher costs incentivise firms to look for more sustainable production methods. This way, market forces are harnessed to benefit the environment. Through competition, an optimal allocation of production and consumption will result, based on a society's preferences for the climate relative to consumption goods. The efficient allocation of scarce resources over alternative means then remains firmly based on consumer

---

47   See Schinkel and Tóth (n 44) and Luc Peeperkorn, "Competition and Sustainability: What can competition policy do?" in Guy Canivet and others, *Sustainability and competition law* (2020) Concurrences N° 4–2020 Art N° 97390.

sovereignty, i.e. the preferences of the people.[48] Care for the future has a prominent place in this framework. Welfare of future generations is taken into account, for instance through the intergenerational altruism and bequest motives of the current population.[49] This is also how the future can consistently enter into competition authorities' assessments of green efficiencies.

It is first and foremost a government task to ensure that the social costs of production are reflected in the private costs of manufacturers. This can be done through taxation, or by ensuring that private property rights for climate-related issues are well defined, such that private parties will ensure that the costs of their use will be priced in. Where this is hard to achieve, for instance because the source of pollution remains disputed, governments can use direct regulation to force firms to produce in a more sustainable way. Unsustainable production, like under-provision of public goods, is a well-understood market failure, but it is a government failure that well-known solutions have only been used sparingly in the last several decades. Trying to remedy this government failure by creating market failure – market power – seems a response that is itself doomed to fail.

To begin with, trying to have private market powers advance public interests is orthogonal to key lessons of classical public economic theory. One way of seeing this green antitrust policy is as mandating private companies to increase their prices by an overcharge, i.e. "tax" a private good, and to use that money to finance a compensating public good, sustainability. Samuelson's rule prescribes that public good provision should be increasing with the utility that people derive from the public good. But for an anticompetitive sustainability agreement, the higher the willingness to pay for sustainable products, the *less* sustainability the corporate cooperative needs to deliver to compensate consumers for a given product price increase. After all, consumers with a high appreciation for green can be made indifferent with less of it, compared with consumers that appreciate green little. There is no reason for a green corporate cooperative to invest more of its extra revenue in sustainability than it is minimally required to do: the rest it can pocket as profit. Government, though certainly imperfect, at least strives for optimal taxation and break-even public good provision. Companies with market power instead have an incentive to maximise their margin.

In addition, green antitrust policy runs the risk of exacerbating government failure. That governments keep failing to live up to their mandate to guarantee the public interest has many reasons, including public choice incentives ranging from regulatory laziness to outright corruption. Being able to point to industry self-regulation, in the form of sustainability agreements in restriction of competition, is another perfect excuse for governments not to take up their regulatory

---

48 See, on a related legal argument, Edith Loozen, "Strict Competition Enforcement and Welfare: A Constitutional Perspective based on Article 101 TFEU and Sustainability" (2019) 56(5) Common Market L Rev 1265.
49 See, for instance, Simone Galperti and Bruno Strulovici, "A Theory of Intergenerational Altruism" (2017) 85(4) Econometrica 1175.

responsibility. Why the effort to regulate, after all, if government officials can simply rely on private initiatives to help meet sustainability goals? This is exactly how *Chicken* entered the stage: the Dutch cabinet did not want to improve by regulation the abysmal circumstances in which poultry is reared, because it would apply to all chicken, including the vast majority bred for export purposes. Yet there was strong public pressure to act. The problem was conveniently redirected towards the ACM, which was subsequently reproached for refusing to exempt the meagre initiative. The green antitrust movement therefore insists on a turn that, once taken, risks leading us down a path where competition authorities are accused of standing in the way of sustainability initiatives, behind which accusations firms can hide as an excuse for not becoming more sustainable. That is barking up the wrong tree: where there is a true need for coordinated implementation of more sustainable production, government should regulate it, and firms with such green initiatives should lobby the designated public authority for effective regulation, rather than competition authorities for protection from competition.

VIII. A Citizens' Welfare Standard Weakens Competition Authorities' Ability to Bargain for Green

Even though, after careful investigation, the ACM said, "no: too little sustain-ability" to the initiatives *Coal* and *Chicken*, the Dutch competition authority seems keen to exempt one sometime. The ACM is leading the way in green antitrust with its recent Draft Guidelines. They importantly relax the compensation requirement by proposing that it can be satisfied if the harm to consumers is exceeded by sustainability benefits for *all* Dutch citizens, consumers *and* non-consumers. This implies a fundamental change in the interpretation of the exemption conditions under Article 101(3) TFEU. The ACM interprets "a fair share" as not having to be a fully compensating share for actual consumers.[50] With this interpretation of the European Treaty, the Dutch competition authority single-handedly proposes to replace the common consumer welfare standard in European competition policy by a "citizens' welfare standard". The consequence that consumers may end up worse off, ACM justifies by opining that: "their demand for the products in question essentially creates the problem for which society needs to find a solution."[51] ACM disposes; the polluter pays.

At first sight, this may appear reasonable. After all, the "polluter pays" principle is well-established and appropriate for internalising externalities – even though it is certainly not implied by the Coase Theorem. Also, reductions in negative externalities as a result of more sustainable production will typically be appreciated more broadly by more than just the buyers of the product. As said, consumers of a polluting product, by their very choice of buying it, typically value the

---

50 ACM Draft Guidelines (n 12), recital 38.
51 ibid, recital 41.

sustainability benefits least. The full consumer compensation requirement can therefore be seen as discriminating against externality benefits. By no longer requiring full consumer compensation, it becomes possible to exempt more sustainability agreements, which carry lower compensation costs for the corporate cooperative, so may be profitable and thus proposed more. In *Coal*, all Dutch citizens were already taken into account as electricity consumers, so the ACM decision in that case should be the same under the stretched compensation requirement. Yet *Chicken* probably could have been exempted under the citizens' welfare standard: counting on the benefit-side vegetarians' appreciation for improvements in living conditions of industrial broiler chicken as well should make it easily weigh up against the price increases paid by actual consumers of chicken.

The ACM tries to avoid having to revise its decision in *Chicken* by distancing itself in the Guidelines from sustainability gains other than environmental externalities. It focuses on the prevention of environmental damages, in particular the reductions in CO_2 emissions that the Netherlands is bound to by the Paris Agreement, presumably to be on firmer ground for valuing benefits and legitimising its role as redistributor of wealth. Yet such a distinction between externalities related to environment and other sustainability factors is conceptually weak. Just like air pollution or rising sea levels, cruelty to animals or antibiotic resistance are negative externalities that affect many. Without a good conceptual reason to allow the reduction of the one but not the other to count as sustainability benefits, stretching the compensation criterion is bound to have wide implications for many types of external effects and corporate agreements. Moreover, by merely giving greater weight on the benefit side to the projected sustainability efforts, the stretch of the compensation criterion does not increase sustainability investments. On the contrary: the citizens' welfare standard just makes more agreements with *the same or fewer* sustainability advances eligible for a cartel law exemption, while allowing the companies involved to charge consumers larger price increases. In addition, the proposal increases the information required by the competition authority to properly assess sustainability agreements by necessitating knowledge of the preferences of all citizens, rather than just the consumers – which, as said, is a tall order already.

There is a political side to the proposal too.[52] The citizens' welfare standard implies that the competition authority makes political decisions on redistribution. This is not the case, under the common compensation requirement that consumers cannot be worse off. Any benefits beyond that minimum standard are welcome welfare surplus. Under the citizens' welfare standard, however, the competition authority needs to make value judgments in each and every specific case about the net harm to consumers that the authority finds acceptable in exchange for achieving the

---

52 See also Luc Peeperkorn, "Competition and Sustainability: Which test do we want competition policy to apply?" (2021) in this book.

benefits for non-buyers: "How much more is it reasonable for the Dursleys to pay for their chicken breast fillet, to the wellbeing of all pescatarians?" Moreover, this redistribution that competition authorities would engage in is broadly from the poor to the rich, because of the nature of the products that are particularly eligible for a cartel law exemption: primarily cheap and unsustainably produced goods, such as grey electricity, battery chicken and low-end washing machines. Affluent non-consumers, with the means already to be self-sufficient with solar-panels, eat free-range chicken and own an A-label washer, will obtain the environmental benefits from forcing more expensive sustainable consumption on others for free. In between are the cooperating firms trying to retain a profit margin for their shareholders.

The stretched compensation criterion substantially lowers the standard for justifying an anticompetitive sustainability agreement. After all, a few non-consumers who are sufficiently passionate about the benefits of a sustainability agreement can easily tip the balance against any net harm to consumers. The consumer compensation criterion is typically a high bar, for it would take quite a lot of green to compensate consumers with a low willingness to pay for it. The citizen compensation criterion, on the other hand, can be met with a little bit of green for enough non-buyers against a high price increase. Less ambitious in demanding green, the proposal aggravates the risk of abuse by cartel greenwashing. The stretched compensation criterion weakens a competition authority's bargaining position to ask for more green. After all, the more people with an appreciation for a given increase in sustainability are counted on the benefit size, the smaller the required compensating increase in sustainability can be. The result is a less strict test, for which much more information is required, that is only imperfectly available, making it that much harder to spot the greenwasher. Easier exemptions also further facilitate government shirking. All-in-all, there appears to be a lot of collateral damage for welcoming corporate agreements that are unlikely to lead to greater sustainability than they would achieve in competition.

IX. Concluding Remarks

The task of competition authorities is to protect competition. There is strong indication that competition also is the main force to induce firms to deliver more sustainably produced goods – along with other desired properties, high quality of service, efficient production, low prices and an optimal allocation of scarce resources. Whenever consumers have at least some willingness to pay for more sustainably manufactured products, corporations are incentivised to deliver them in competition more than when they are allowed to conclude sustainability agreements. The drive to green can be expected to be stronger in competition than in collusion still when firms have some intrinsic motivation to promote sustainability in addition to their profit motive. The crucial insight is that the *difference* in sustainability investments between competition and cooperation is positive. That competition, and therefore competition authorities, would somehow be in the way of a more sustainable future is an idée-fixe – a false self-image.

We are not claiming, of course, that the sustainability level in competition is likely to be socially optimal: when there are externalities it typically is not. This is exactly why there is a clear role for government. The much-needed environmental protection requires a strong government that assigns property rights, levies taxes, grants subsidies and regulates. But it is a mistake to think that market power would make firms internalise externalities. The trust put by the green antitrust movement in anticompetitive agreements is also peculiar in light of several important cartel cases in which the objective of the colluding firms was in fact to eliminate competition in the sustainability dimension. These cases range from the *Phoebus* conspiracy in the 1920s to reduce the design life of light bulbs, to the recent collusive hindering of car battery recycling and the *Trucks* cartel members, as well as German car manufacturers, jointly delaying the introduction of lower-emission technology.[53]

Conceptually, the green antitrust movement attempts to solve one market distortion – due to the persistence of externalities – by creating another market distortion – market power. In the general theory of second best, two or more market distortions may counteract each other and so improve upon the efficiency of the situation with only the original distortion.[54] It implies that if there exists an uncorrectable market failure, the optimal government intervention may be in another direction than the first best solution. In the case of competition policy, allowing anticompetitive conduct may be welfare enhancing if regulation is not feasible. A straightforward example would be allowing a merger or a cartel that increases prices that do not reflect the full social costs of production, thereby reducing negative externalities.[55] The benefits do not

53 On the Phoebus cartel, see Markus Krajewski, "The Great Lighbulb Conspiracy: The Phoebus cartel engineered a shorter-lived lightbulb and gave birth to planned obsolescence" (2014) 51(10) IEEE spectrum 56. *Car Battery Recycling* (Case AT.40018) Commission decision C(2017) 2223 [2017] OJ C396/7; European Commission, *The EU Commission fines three car battery recycling companies for cartel (Campine)*, 8 February 2017, e-Competitions Art N° 83539. *Trucks* (Case AT.39824) Commission decision C(2017) 6467 [2020] OJ C216/9; Martin Favart, "The Regional Court of Munich dismisses follow-on damages claims totalling €600 million against participants in a truck cartel *(Trucks cartel)*" (2020) e-Competitions Art N° 94018. On the Commission's ongoing investigation into German car manufacturers, see Commission, "Antitrust: Commission sends Statement of Objections to BMW, Daimler and VW for restricting competition on emission cleaning technology (Press release IP/19/2008, 5 April 2019).
54 See Richard G Lipsey and Kelvin Lancaster, "The General Theory of Second Best" (1956) 24(1) Rev Econ Studies 11.
55 The example is given in Peter J Hammer, "Antitrust beyond Competition: Market Failures, Total Welfare, and the Challenge of Intramarket Second-Best Tradeoffs" (2000) 98(4) Michigan L Rev 849, 860, as a "provocative" illustration of the "second best" principle. Hammer advocates a "second best-defence" for anticompetitive conduct within individual markets in isolation – which is the standard partial equilibrium approach in competition policy – to be based on a total welfare standard. Richard A Posner, *Antitrust Law* (2nd edn, University of Chicago Press 2001), 13 fn 5, disapproves of the idea, based on his classic argument that rent-seeking cost should be included in the social cost of market power and his assessment that it would make antitrust enforcement "completely unworkable". The "second best"

go beyond a mere volume-effect, however. As we have shown, more market power does not counteract too little investments in more sustainable production technologies – which the green cartel policy aims to stimulate. Furthermore, second best theory reinforces our warnings. It reveals the staggering amount of information required to determine the second best. The social engineering involved in balancing anticompetitive conduct against externalities would overwhelm any competition authority – as well as being at odds with the nature of their task, which is to protect the competitive processes. Done imperfectly, the supposedly counteracting market powers can easily lower welfare and create further inefficiencies. Moreover, the problem of externalities is not an uncorrectable market imperfection, but one that can be directly addressed with far superior solutions.

Green antitrust is a sympathetic but counterproductive attempt to solve the global climate crisis. Fighting one market failure – environmental externalities – with another – market power – will mostly make matters worse. There is huge potential for welfare improvement by preventing negative externalities and pursuing the positive, public goods. Giving firms market power does not create incentives to tap into that potential, however. Relaxing the strict competition law enforcement criteria in order to better accommodate such ineffective sustainability agreements in restriction of competition is not, therefore a good policy. Instead, governments should be held accountable for their failure to adequately address damaging production externalities. The right response of competition authorities to a corporate cartel exemption request for its sustainability initiative is referral to the part of government best placed to assess the idea and possibly implement it through proper regulation – rather than stepping in and become an excuse for government failure. However well intended, the green antitrust movement risks doing damage to both competition and sustainability.

---

approach was recently called upon by Paul Krugman, "The Big Green Test" *New York Times* (New York, 22 June 2014) to be creative about environmental public policies in the face of politically infeasible better solutions – without suggesting private market power build-up.

Chapter 2
Abuse of Dominance

Radical For Whom? Unsustainable Business Practices as Abuses of Dominance

Marios C Iacovides[*] and Christos Vrettos[**]

University of Oxford | Stockholm University

I. Time for Action

The Paris Agreement marked its fifth anniversary on 12 December 2020. To date, the Agreement's most important goal, i.e. to maintain global temperature increase up to 1.5–2°C by the end of this century,[1] remains largely out of reach. The newly released 2020 United Nations Environment Programme (UNEP) Emissions Gap Report shows how current efforts at tackling the climate crisis remain woefully inadequate, while atmospheric greenhouse gas concentrations keep rising.[2] Meanwhile, the COVID-19 pandemic has exposed the fragility of the global socioeconomic system by supercharging existing inequalities and pre-existing overlapping crises.

It is becoming all the more clear that our socioeconomic system's method and goals, i.e. ruthless competition and profit for the sake of profit, are defined by the narrow boundaries of capitalist rationality, thus failing to appreciate the holistic

---

[*] Dr Marios C Iacovides (marios.iacovides@law.ox.ac.uk) is a research fellow at the University of Oxford's Institute for European and Comparative Law and legal counsel (on leave) at the Swedish Competition Authority.
[**] Chris Vrettos is a masters student in social-ecological resilience for sustainable development at Stockholm University's Resilience Centre, a scholar of the Onassis Foundation, and a co-founder of the Climate Collective.
All links in the footnotes were last accessed 31 December 2020.
[1] Paris Agreement under the United Nations Framework Convention on Climate Change FCCC/CP/2015/L.9/Rev.1 (12 December 2015), art 2(1)(a).
[2] UNEP, *Emissions Gap Report 2020* (UNEP December 2020).

nature of sustainability. Unfortunately, not even the global COVID-19 – induced reductions in economic activity are expected to have any significant long-term effect on climate change. Efforts to "Build Back Better" have largely fallen on deaf ears, with astronomically large fiscal recovery packages being earmarked to bail out carbon intensive industries like aviation, fossil fuels and Big Agriculture.[3]

The climate crisis is not, as is often argued, a "tragedy of the commons", attributed to humanity's greed and collective inability to manage its shared resources.[4] It is a logical consequence of a system built on extreme material and carbon inequality.[5] As the UNEP report asserts, emissions of "the richest 1 per cent of the global population account for more than twice the combined share of the poorest 50 per cent".[6] Similarly, just 100 companies are responsible for 71% of global industrial greenhouse gas emissions since 1988.[7]

To limit global temperature rise and ensure that environmental conditions remain conducive to the maintenance of an organised human society will require an enormous effort.[8] To achieve this rapid decarbonisation, every economic sector and every part of society will need to adapt. As a step in that direction, an increasing number of states and cities are declaring climate emergencies, passing "Green Deal" – style policy packages and setting targets of net-zero greenhouse gas emissions within the next couple of decades.[9]

Nevertheless, to even begin to address these systemic issues, we must first acknowledge the extent to which society is embedded within ecological systems. Only then can we commence the urgent work towards finding solutions that promote both socioeconomic equity and environmental stewardship. The existential threat of the climate crisis requires a radical reconfiguration of societal relations. In practice, this means that business models and the societal institutions that guide them, such as law, will have to evolve to do their part.[10]

---

3   Simon Evans and Josh Gabbatiss, "Coronavirus: Tracking how the world's 'green recovery' plans aim to cut emissions" (*Carbon Brief*, 16 June 2020) <www.carbonbrief.org/coronavirus-tracking-how-the-worlds-green-recovery-plans-aim-to-cut-emissions>; for the implications of this regarding the democratic legitimacy of state aid, see Julian Nowag and Marios Iacovides, "Covid-19 and the transformative power of State Aid: a framework for a democratically legitimate recovery" op-ed for blog of the European Competition and Regulatory Law Review (*Lexxion*, 2020) <www.lexxion.eu/en/coreblogpost/covid-19-and-the-transformative-power-of-state-aid-a-framework-for-a-democratically-legitimate-recovery/>.

4   Garrett Hardin, "The Tragedy of the Commons" (1968) 162(3859) Science 1243.

5   Tim Gore, "Confronting Carbon Inequality: Putting climate justice at the heart of the COVID-19 recovery" Oxfam media briefing (*Oxfam*, 21 September 2020) <www.oxfam.org/en/research/confronting-carbon-inequality>; T Wiedmann and others, "Scientists' warning on affluence" (2020) 11 Nature Communications 3107 <https://doi.org/10.1038/s41467-020-16941-y>.

6   UNEP (n 2), XV.

7   Paul Griffin, "The Carbon Majors Database – CDP Carbon Majors Report 2017" (*CDP*, July 2017) <www.cdp.net/en/articles/media/new-report-shows-just-100-companies-are-source-of-over-70-of-emissions>.

8   Will Steffen and others, "Trajectories of the Earth System in the Anthropocene" (2018) 115(33) Proceedings of the National Academy of Sciences 8252.

9   These include major economies like China, the EU, Japan, South Korea and the UK.

10   Notable examples illustrating how law can be used as a vehicle for socio-ecological sustainability include a successful civil society lawsuit against the government of the Netherlands (Dutch Supreme Court Case

Competition law can be no exception. Research shows how powerful transnational corporations precipitate ecological and climate breakdown, but they can also leverage their market power and influence to enhance stewardship of the Earth system.[11] Yet, the discussion about how EU competition law can support sustainability goals, such as those of the European Green Deal, entirely neglects the role Article 102 TFEU can play.[12] Equally absent is a discussion of the role competition law enforcement can play to strike down unsustainable business practices. Instead, the debate is mostly dominated by how competition law can facilitate (otherwise anticompetitive) agreements between undertakings through the application of Article 101(3) TFEU, essentially, offering less competition in exchange for sustainability initiatives.

Our research addresses the Article 102 TFEU gap in the debate and in the enforcement of EU competition law by looking at why and how the prohibition can be used as a sword to strike down unsustainable business practices. In this paper, we present our research on the nexus between dominance and unsustainable business practices (section II), examine briefly Article 102's purpose and how it informs the concept of "abuse" (section III), and introduce our coming research project on unsustainable business practices as "abuses" of a dominant position (section IV).

II. Dominance and Unsustainable Business Practices

Realising that the apparent enforcement and research gap as to the role Article 102 TFEU can play as a cause of action against unsustainable business practices might exist because such practices and market power are unrelated, we decided to test the hypothesis that there is a nexus between the two. The method we used to test that hypothesis is unique in competition law research, as it regards competition law through a socio-ecological lens.[13] That means that we understand "sustainability" in a way that is much more in tune with contemporary research in other fields than law.

Our definition of sustainability assumes the "planetary boundaries" framework as a departure point. The framework has been fundamentally influential for global sustainability research, paving the way for understanding the Earth as a globally interconnected, complex living system. This system is defined by ecological

---

19/00135 *Netherlands v Urgenda* NL:HR:2019:2007) as well as a successful lawsuit by Colombian youth to grant the Amazon rainforest additional protections (Case STC4360-2018 Colombian Supreme Court Opinion of 5 April 2018).

11 Victor Galaz and others, "Finance and the Earth system – Exploring the links between financial actors and non-linear changes in the climate system" (2018) 53 Global Environmental Change 296; Henrik Österblom and others, "Transnational Corporations as 'Keystone Actors' in Marine Ecosystems" (2015) 10:5 PLoS ONE e0127533.

12 E.g. the Commission's public consultation "Competition Policy supporting the Green Deal" (13 October 2020), which only asked for contributions regarding state aid, Article 101 TFEU, and merger control.

13 Jan Dick and others, "What is socio-ecological research delivering? A literature survey across 25 international LTSER platforms" (2018) Science of the Total Environment 1225.

thresholds and tipping points that should not be transgressed in order to maintain humanity within a safe operating space. Four of the boundaries have already been pushed beyond what is considered a safe limit, namely climate change, biodiversity loss, biochemical flows of nitrogen and phosphorus, and land system change.[14]

With "planetary boundaries" as departure point and drawing from socio-ecological studies, which consider society and the environment as inextricably linked and mutually embedded systems,[15] for the purposes of our research we define as "sustainable" any action that both respects ecological boundaries (do no harm) and delivers societal benefits (do well). To concretise this holistic definition of sustainability, we use a heuristic tool by ecological economist Kate Raworth, the "Doughnut Framework", that combines the planetary boundaries with the 17 UN Sustainable Development Goals.[16] The Doughnut thereby delineates a *safe* and *just* operating space where every person's minimum societal needs are met (e.g. healthcare, housing, decent work, access to water, food and energy, justice, equality, social equity), within the planet's carrying capacity (i.e. without exacerbating the climate and environmental emergency). Accordingly, we define as "unsustainable" any practice that contributes to the transgression of the planetary boundaries and/or contravenes the SDGs, in other words, any action that pushes the world towards a more *unsafe* and *unjust* space.

To further operationalise this definition within the scope of our research we use the ten principles of the UN Global Compact for corporate sustainability, which relate to human rights, labour, the environment and anti-corruption.[17] Without aiming to establish a causal relationship, as this is beyond the scope of this research and unnecessary for the application of Article 102 TFEU,[18] we demonstrate empirically how market power facilitates undertakings engaging in unsustainable business practices.

We begin with a review of the rich socio-ecological literature examining the connection between consolidation and unsustainable business practices. We find there is a tendency for transnational corporations to grow so large that they effectively control critical functions of the biosphere.[19] This is not a sector-specific issue; it is observed across most economic sectors, such as agriculture, forestry, seafood, cement, minerals and fossil fuels. Beyond their supply chain – wide range of impacts on society and the environment, large undertakings tend to leverage their market position to influence political processes, which in turn grant them additional competitive

---

14 Will Steffen and others, "Planetary boundaries: Guiding changing planet" (2015) 347 Science 6223.
15 We have relied in particular on the work of the Stockholm Resilience Centre, see "Planetary boundaries" <www.stockholmresilience.org/research/planetary-boundaries.html>.
16 UN General Assembly Resolution on 25 September 2015, "Transforming our world: the 2030 Agenda for Sustainable Development" UN document A/RES/70/1 (21 October 2015), 14.
17 UN, "The Ten Principles of the UN Global Compact" <www.unglobalcompact.org/what-is-gc/mission/principles>.
18 Case 6/72 *Europemballage Corporation and Continental Can Company Inc. v Commission* [1973] ECR 00215, [27].
19 Carl Folke and others, "Transnational corporations and the challenge of biosphere stewardship" (2019) 3:10 Nature Ecology and Evolution 1396.

advantages, such as watered-down regulations for harmful toxins or waste management.[20]

To test the veracity of the nexus identified in the reviewed literature and to be in line with EU competition law's definition of dominance, we then shifted our attention to individual companies. We examined whether undertakings that have already featured in DG COMP's enforcement of Article 102 TFEU as dominant undertakings have also engaged in unsustainable business practices. We identified 86 unique dominant undertakings in the decisional practice and have categorised them in six sectors. We cross-checked how many of these feature on the Environmental Justice Atlas (EJAtlas). The EJAtlas systematically collects and maps socio-ecological conflicts from across the world, analysing the actors behind each conflict, as well as the relevant impacts on society and the environment. The key findings of this exercise are summarised in Figure 1.

Figure 1: Key results from the matching exercise between the DG COMP list and the EJAtlas

- We found 27 undertakings (31% of the total 86) on the EJAtlas, featuring in a total of 176 cases.
- Cases of socio-ecological conflict are observed across all six surveyed sectors.
- Nearly half of the undertakings (13) and most relevant cases (149) are in the energy and mining sector.
- 154 cases (87.5%) involve environmental damage.
- In 142 (92.2%) of the 154 cases of environmental damage, there is also a breach of human rights, disregard for basic labour standards or corruption.
- Of the 51 cases where corruption is documented, 45 cases (88.2%) overlap with human rights violations.
- Of those same 51 cases, 41 cases (80.4%) overlap with breaches of environmental principles.
- We found cases of dominant undertakings engaging in unsustainable business practices both within and outside the EU.

We can deduce some key conclusions from our results. First, there are indeed dominant undertakings engaging in unsustainable business practices. Second, this is not a sector-specific phenomenon, but instead it seems to be characteristic of all economic sectors. Third, there is a wide prevalence of breaches of environmental protection, indicating that dominant undertakings systematically contribute to ecological breakdown. Fourth, the significant overlap between environmental damage, corruption, and human and labour rights violations empirically backs our theoretical stand, i.e. that environmental and social sustainability should be viewed

---

20 Jennifer Clapp, "Mega-Mergers on the Menu: Corporate Concentration and the Politics of Sustainability in the Global Food System" (2018) 18(6) Global Environmental Politics 12; Pat Mooney, *Too big to feed: Exploring the impacts of mega-mergers, consolidation and concentration of power in the agri-food sector* Report of the International Panel of Experts on Sustainable Food Systems (IPES-Food 2017).

as inextricably related. Fifth, the pervasiveness of corruption and rent-seeking lobbying shows that competition law may have a significant role to play, even in the presence of regulation. Sixth, unsustainable business practices by dominant undertakings is not exclusively a problem for jurisdictions outside the EU.[21]

III. "Abuse" in Light of Article 102's True Purpose

The nexus we identify between market power and unsustainable business practices is significant, as it shows that addressing such practices through the enforcement of Article 102 TFEU is not only a theoretical possibility, it is a real opportunity to tackle environmental and social injustices and thereby contribute to addressing the most important existential threat currently facing humanity; climate change. To be caught by Article 102 TFEU, such practices have to be "abuses". In this section, we look at the meaning of "abuse".[22]

Abuse is "the conduct of a dominant undertaking that, through recourse to methods different from those governing normal competition on the basis of the performance of commercial operators, has the effect, to the detriment of consumers, of hindering the maintenance of the degree of competition still existing in the market or the growth of that competition".[23] Abuse is "an objective concept"[24] and, thus, does not depend on the dominant undertaking's intentions.

Unsurprisingly, the breadth of the definition has led to a proliferation of ways to show "abuse" in practice, and several tests have been proposed.[25] In EU competition law, the predominant understanding of "abuse" revolves around the idea of competition on the merits.[26] The antithesis of competing on the merits, and therefore "abuse", is to compete by recourse to methods other than those that condition normal competition.

---

21 For the full results, a more detailed method, and implications, see Marios C Iacovides and Chris Vrettos, "Falling Through the Cracks No More? Article 102 TFEU and Sustainability I – The Nexus Between Dominance Environmental Degradation and Social Injustice" (2020) Faculty of Law, Stockholm University Research Paper No 79.

22 This is part of an ongoing project, provisionally titled Marios C Iacovides and Chris Vrettos, "Falling through the cracks no more? Article 102 TFEU and sustainability II – Environmental degradation and social injustice as abuses of dominance" (forthcoming, 2021).

23 Case C–209/10 *Post Danmark I* EU:C:2012:172, [24]; Anne-Lise Sibony, "Selective rebates – Universal service obligations: The Court of Justice, Grand Chamber, rules that selective rebates targeting clients of a competitor are not abusive when prices are below incremental cost but cover marginal cost and when no intent to eliminate competitor has been established (*Post Danmark*)" Concurrences N° 2–2012 Art N° 45619, 64–68.

24 Case 85/76 *Hoffmann-La Roche v Commission* [1979] ECR 00461, [91].

25 See the tests suggested by various jurisdictions in OECD Report, *Competition on the Merits* DAF/COMP(2005)27. Many tests are circular and empty of content: Konstantinos Stylianou, "Can Common Business Practices Ever Be Anticompetitive? Redefining Monopolization" (2020) 57(1) American Business LJ 169, 170–171. This further reinforces the point that the concept is flexible enough to encompass unsustainable business practices.

26 E.g. *Hoffmann-La Roche* (n 24), [91]; Case C–95/04 P *British Airways v Commission* [2007] ECR I-2331, [66]; Catherine Prieto, "Fidelity rebates: The ECJ holds abusive the discounts system granted

The Court of Justice of the EU (CJEU) has on numerous occasions stressed that the list of examples of abuse contained in Article 102 TFEU is non-exhaustive.[27] Thus, the case law and decisional practice are abundant with "atypical" abuses,[28] and new categories form as the case law develops and new economic activities and practices emerge.[29] Moreover, "abuse" in any given case can emerge from a series of diverse events and may consist of a collection of different types of abusive conduct.[30]

We can deduce that from the outset there is nothing in the way the CJEU has interpreted "abuse" that would preclude unsustainable business practices from constituting abuses of dominance within the meaning of Article 102 TFEU. Why, then, is it perceived as a radical position to suggest that unsustainable business practices can be abuses of a dominant position when subsumed in other abuses[31] and even more so independently?[32]

We think that this is because of a misconception, namely that the "more economic approach" requires us to focus on a narrowly construed "consumer welfare" standard, with the result of losing sight of what Article 102 TFEU is supposed to and is able to achieve. In our view, there can be no way of knowing what constitutes "abuse" within the meaning of Article 102, while being agnostic as to the true purpose of the prohibition.

not only for tickets sold once the sales target is achieved, but also for tickets sold before (*British Airways/ Virgin*)" (2007) Concurrences N° 2–2007 Art N° 13492, 115–116; *Post Danmark* (n 23), [24]; Case C–413/14 P *Intel v Commission* EU:C:2017:632 [136] and the case law cited there.

27 *Continental Can* (n 18), [26]; Case C–333/94 P *Tetra Pak v Commission* [1996] ECR I-5951, [37]; Joined Cases C–395 and 396/96 P *Compagnie Maritime Belge Transports v Commission* [2000] ECR I-1365, [112]; *British Airways* (n 26), [57] – [58]; Case T–201/04 *Microsoft v Commission* [2007] II-3601, [860] – [861]; Catherine Prieto, "The Microsoft Saga: The Court of First Instance upholds the Commission's finding that Microsoft had abused its dominant position in the PC operating system market (*Microsoft*)" (2007) Concurrences N° 4–2007 Art N° 14478, 78–83 ; Case C–280/08 *Deutsche Telekom v Commission* [2010] ECR I-9555, [173]; Anne-Lise Sibony, "Margin squeeze: The European Court of Justice rules for the first time on a margin squeeze case and confirms that partly regulated tarifs by a dominant operator may be abusive (*Deutsche Telekom*)" (2010) Concurrences N° 1–2011 Art N° 34039, 91–95 .

28 E.g. Case C–457/10 P *AstraZeneca v Commission* EU:C:2012:770; Anne Wachsmann and Nicolas Zacharie, "Market definition – Abusive use of regulatory procedures: The Court of Justice sanctions definitively the abusive use of regulatory procedures to prevent or delay the arrival of generic drugs on the market (*AstraZeneca*)" (2012) Concurrences N° 1–2013 Art N° 50455, 78–81 ; Case T–814/17 *Lietuvos geležinkeliai AB v Commission* EU:T:2020:545; Samuel Hall, "The EU General Court maintains Commission decision finding that a Lithuanian railway company abused its dominant position on the national rail freight sector (*Lietuvos geležinkeliai*)" (2020) e-Competitions Art N° 98217 .

29 E.g. "self-preferencing": *Google (Shopping)* (Case AT.39740) Commission decision C(2017) 4444 final.; Frédéric Marty, "Anticompetitive leverage: EU Commission sanctions the dominant operator of the online search market on the basis of an anticompetitive leverage strategy oriented toward the online price compactors market (*Google Shopping*)" (2017) Concurrences N° 1–2018 Art N° 86088, 87–93 .

30 *Irish Sugar* (Case IV/34.621, 35.059/F-3) Commission Decision 97/624/EC [1997] OJ L258/1.

31 Simon Holmes, "Climate Change, Sustainability, and Competition Law" (2020) 8(2) JAE 354, 385 and 387.

32 These are the kinds of comments we have received while presenting our research at conferences and seminars. See also the Hellenic Competition Commission, "Draft Staff Discussion Paper on 'Sustainability Issues and Competition Law'" (September 2020) <www.epant.gr/enimerosi/ygiis-antagonismos-viosimi-anaptyksi.html>, 37.

It may sound trite but Article 102 TFEU is part of the EU's system of competition law. That law is a tool to achieve the goals of the EU's competition policy. The significance of that is that ultimately the prohibition must serve the purposes of EU competition policy.

What are, then, the goals of EU competition law? The extensive literature providing answers to that question has recently been reviewed and summarised by Stylianou and Iacovides.[33] On the basis of that, the authors identified seven overarching goals for EU competition law: efficiency, welfare, freedom to compete, market structure, fairness, single market and competition process. Furthermore, they conducted comprehensive empirical research, searching for 74 different keywords and phrases giving expression to the seven goals in 3,749 Commission decisions, CJEU judgments, advocate general opinions and Commissioner for Competition speeches.[34] They found references to all seven goals and no goal emerged as being predominant, although they observed that EU competition law prioritises process (e.g. fairness, equality of opportunity, level playing field), over outcome (e.g. efficiency, welfare).[35]

That the practice of EU competition law – when we regard it as a whole rather than choosing to focus on a few cases – reveals the pursuit of a variety of goals, should come as no surprise. We have made elsewhere the argument that this is mandated by the EU treaties,[36] and others are of the same opinion.[37] This is, we submit, the correct interpretation of the rules of EU competition law and the only one compatible with the specific EU law method of interpretation. It is also congruous with treaty provisions having horizontal application, in particular Article 7 TFEU (consistency) and several mainstreaming obligations regarding, for instance, environmental protection,[38] equality, and the protection of workers.[39]

Consequently, EU competition law is not and does not have to be focused on a Chicago school – inspired narrow "consumer welfare" standard.[40] That it is

---

33 Konstantinos Stylianou and Marios C Iacovides, "Goals of EU Competition Law – A Comprehensive Empirical Investigation" (December 2020) <https://ssrn.com/abstract=3735795>, s 2 and Table 1.
34 ibid, s 3.
35 ibid, 26–30. The full database is available at <www.db-comp.eu>.
36 Iacovides and Vrettos, "Article 102 TFEU and Sustainability I" (n 21).
37 E.g. Holmes (n 31).
38 Art 11 TFEU and Charter of Fundamental Rights of the European Union [2012] OJ C326/2, art 37. On environmental protection and EU competition law see further Julian Nowag, *Environmental Integration in Competition and Free-Movement Laws* (OUP 2016), 31–48. For a recent application in state aid law, see Case C–594/18 P *Austria v Commission* EU:C:2020:742, [42] – [45]; Bruno Stromsky, "Compatible aid: The Court of Justice of the European Union confirms the legality of a decision authorizing aid for the promotion of nuclear energy and finds that the compatibility of aid under Article 107(3)(c) is not conditional on the pursuit of an objective of common interest (*Hinkley Point C*)" (2020) Concurrences N° 4–2020 Art N° 97650, 179–181.
39 Arts 8–10 TFEU; Charter of Fundamental Rights, Title IV.
40 Michelle Meagher, "Powerless Antitrust" (*CPI Antitrust Chronicle*, 7 November 2019), 5; Lina M Khan, "The Ideological Roots of America's Market Power Problem" (2018) 127 Yale Legal Journal Forum 960, 967–970. For the roots of this standard see Robert H Bork, *The Antitrust Paradox: A Policy at War with Itself* (Basic Books 1978), 50 and 110–112.

predominantly seen as being so[41] is a product of the Commission's conscious move towards a "more economic approach".[42] This is notable as, in effect, the Commission has been furthering a policy choice (consumer welfare with a specific content) through the application of primary EU law (Articles 101 and 102 TFEU).[43] That choice, made in the 1990s, goes hand-in-hand with an ideology (neoliberal, laissez-faire, trickle-down economics) and a model of competition, between companies just as among states, that was prevalent at *that* time. That ideology and model of competition has not only failed to deliver on its promises,[44] it has catapulted our social, economic and ecological systems into perpetuating and mutually reinforcing crises.[45] Either naively or because that policy choice has become so entrenched[46] that it is now thought to be the only truth, competition lawyers are unable to think outside its narrow market logic confines.

Yet, obviously, policy *can* and *does* change and – to be aligned with the Commission's overarching Green Deal goals of decarbonising the economy through a socially fair and just transition path[47] and the European Parliament's call on the Commission to "urgently take the concrete action needed in order to fight and contain the threat of climate and environmental catastrophe before it is too late"[48] – it *must* change.

IV. Unsustainable Business Practices as "Abuses"

If certain conduct is prohibited as abusive because it runs counter to what Article 102 TFEU is supposed to protect and, if we understand the latter correctly, which we can only do by reading Article 102 through the EU constitutional law lens, then we will see that "abuse" must be construed as including unsustainable business

---

41   Giuliano Amato, *Antitrust and the Bounds of Power: The Dilemma of Liberal Democracy in the History of the Market* (Hart 1997), 95–129; Massimo Motta, *Competition Policy: Theory and Practice* (CUP 2004), 21–22; Roger Van den Bergh and Peter D Camesasca, *European Competition Law and Economics: A Comparative Perspective* (2nd edn. Sweet & Maxwell 2006), 18; Okeoghene Odudu, "The wider concerns of competition law" (2010) 30(3) OJLS 559, 605–612; Renato Nazzini, *The Foundations of European Union Competition Law: The Objective and Principles of Article 102* (OUP 2011), 107–154; Pinar Akman, *The Concept of Abuse in EU Competition Law: Law and Economic Approaches* (Hart 2012), 182–184; A Douglas Melamed and Nicolas Petit, "The Misguided Assault on the Consumer Welfare Standard in the Age of Platform Markets" (2019) 54 Rev Industrial Organization 741; Edith Loozen, "Strict Competition Enforcement and Welfare: a Constitutional Perspective Based on Article 101 TFEU and Sustainability'" (2019) 56(5) CMLR 1265.
42   White Paper on the Modernisation of the Rules Implementing Articles 85 and 86 of the EC Treaty [1999] OJ C132/1; Bill Bishop, "The Modernisation of DGIV" (1997) 18(8) ECLR 481.
43   Usually, the executive branch of government does not implement its policy choices through the application of constitutional provisions of primary law but rather through regulation and secondary legislation.
44   Era Dabla-Norris and others, "Causes and Consequences of Income Inequality: A Global Perspective" (IMF 2015), 7; Owen M Zidar, "Tax Cuts for Whom? Heterogeneous Effects of Income Tax Changes on Growth and Employment" (2015) NBER Working Paper No 21035.
45   Steffen and others, "Trajectories of the Earth System' (n 8), 8252.
46   This has happened with a time lag, as policy choices of the Commissioner for Competition take years to materialise in cases and to seep through the system of competition law and enforcement.
47   Commission, "The European Green Deal" (Communication) COM(2019) 640 final.
48   European Parliament Resolution on the climate and environment emergency (2019/2930(RSP)).

practices. In this section, we explore how unsustainable business practices could be shown to breach Article 102 and we suggest – on the basis of our empirical research into such practices[49] – how such practices lead to distortions of competition.[50]

Let us begin by looking at the kind of conduct we found dominant undertakings engaging in in the EJAtlas. Dominant undertakings are documented as violating human rights or being complicit in human rights violations, undermining the right to work, not upholding freedom of association or not recognising the right to collective bargaining, discriminating in respect of employment and occupation, producing under hazardous working conditions, undertaking activities that push the planet beyond the planetary boundaries, discouraging greater environmental responsibility and engaging in corruption and rent-seeking lobbying.

In terms of impact, such conduct is documented in the EJAtlas as leading, inter alia, to deaths, land dispossession, loss of livelihoods, chronic illnesses, increase in violence and crime, militarisation and increased police presence, repression, criminalisation of activists, lack of work security, occupational disease and accidents, unfair treatment of migrant labourers, biodiversity loss, pollution, large-scale disturbance of hydro and geological systems, deforestation, global warming, desertification, fires, drought, loss of indigenous knowledge and cultures, and increase in corruption and clientelism. Those effects may not immediately be identifiable as relevant for competition law, but in fact they have a lot to do with a model of toxic competition to which competition law has hitherto wilfully turned a blind eye.

There are two ways in which unsustainable business practices and their impacts can be shown to be more relevant for competition law and be shown to be abuses within the meaning of Article 102 TFEU. First, they can be subsumed in existing and well-established types of abuse. Second, they can be shown to lead to distortions of competition in their own right, if they harm the competitive process, distort the level playing field, lead to consumer harm, can be considered "unfair", lead to reductions of welfare or, more broadly, to reductions in citizens'[51] wellbeing.[52] Which approach will be most appropriate in each case will depend on the individual circumstances and whether they indeed fit existing types of abuse, just like with every other conduct that is examined under Article 102.

Irrespective of approach, successfully proving the abuse will depend on satisfying the relevant test, which, as mentioned above, relates to competition on the merits. Unsustainable business practices may be relevant to several typical

---

49   See section III.
50   We develop our ideas on unsustainable business practices as abuses of dominant position in "Article 102 TFEU and Sustainability II" (n 22).
51   Ioannis Lianos, "Polycentric Competition Law" (2018) 71(1) CLP 161, 173.
52   Matthew Agarwala and others, "Assessing the Relationship Between Human Well-Being and Ecosystem Services: A Review of Frameworks" (2014) 12(4) Conservation and Society 437, describing multidimensional wellbeing.

elements of the test, for example anticompetitive effects, barriers to entry and theories of harm, and econometric tests such as the as-efficient-competitor test (AEC test). To appreciate how our two suggested approaches could be operationalised requires consideration of how such elements are affected in practice.

What such practices have in common is that they push the planet beyond a safe and just operating space. In terms of effects, they result in making production inputs, such as raw materials, labour and energy, cheaper than they ought to be.[53] A prime example is meat production. Meat has become cheap because large meat producers have succeeded in controlling the market and its rules; they secure subsidies, clear forest for grazing and avoid higher labour standards by getting exceptions for low-paid immigrant workers. Lower standards cheapen every aspect of production, resulting in lower production costs. Although the practices may also entail certain costs (e.g. reputational costs, litigation, fines), those are often too low to offset the increased profit made by engaging in them. These practices also have externalities, since the market prices of the products or services offered do not reflect the true costs.

Moreover, as a consequence of reduced costs, an undertaking engaging in unsustainable business practices gains a competitive advantage over any competitor that does not engage in them, even more so over competitors that sacrifice profit to actively pursue sustainable practices or innovate in order to be sustainable.[54] This is unfair competition, as the competitive advantage cannot truly be attributed to normal competition on the merits. There can be nothing "normal" and "meritorious" in toxic competition through bribery, extortion, human rights violations, destruction of habitats and livelihoods, offering exploitative salaries and working conditions; EU competition law cannot pretend such competition is fair and on terms reflecting a level playing field, while being consistent with EU law. It may also enable the dominant undertaking to engage in all sorts of conduct that is typically abusive, such as cross-subsidies, loyalty-inducing rebates or margin squeeze.

Furthermore, unsustainable business practices may result in raising barriers to entry for competing undertakings. For instance, through bribery, a dominant undertaking may be able to secure a licence to extract a raw material needed for the production of a product, to the detriment of actual or potential competitors. Through rent-seeking lobbying, a dominant undertaking could put pressure to bring about regulatory changes in its favour, which act as barriers to entry for other undertakings. This may also be part of a strategy of raising rivals' costs,

---

53   Raj Patel and Jason W Moore, *A History of the World in Seven Cheap Things: A Guide to Capitalism, Nature, and the Future of the Planet* (Verso 2018).
54   Tommy Lundgren, Lammertjan Dam and Bert Scholtens, "Sustainable Business Practices – An Environmental Economics Perspective" in Suzanne Arvidsson (ed), *Challenges in Managing Sustainable Business Reporting, Taxation, Ethics and Governance* (Palgrave Macmillan 2019), 217–218.

for example by forcing them to source inputs more expensively, or to spend more on marketing to counter unfair advantages enjoyed by the dominant undertaking.

All this may result in both exclusion of competitors and exploitation of customers or consumers. Unsustainable business practices may exclude efficient competitors, at least if the chosen cost benchmarks are not those of the dominant undertaking, which will reflect the dominant undertaking's market power and of the abuse itself. It seems absurd (and counterproductive) to rely on costs that are the result of unsustainable business practices in order to conduct the AEC test.[55] Unsustainable business practices could also be exploitative, as they might allow the dominant undertaking to benefit from unfair purchase prices or impose other unfair trading conditions on its customers or consumers.[56]

Additionally, unsustainable business practices may reduce incentives to innovate, as an undertaking engaging in such practices does not need to stay on top of the game in order to maintain or enlarge its market power. Even assuming such undertakings could be punished by consumers willing to pay for more sustainable alternatives, to the extent such alternatives exist and consumers behave rationally, this disregards the fact that market choices may themselves reflect market failures, such as lack of transparency and information or unincorporated externalities. Picking up our example of meat production again, how are alternatives, from slowly grown organic meat alternatives to vegan replacements, going to compete and get the necessary scale if not enough consumers are willing to pay for what they consider to be "expensive" and "elitist" sustainable choices?

Finally, a question we consider important to address is whether it makes any difference if unsustainable business practices are subsumed in existing abuses or if they are seen as standalone new abuses. Conceptually, it seems to us that it is much easier to argue convincingly for the former approach and it will be more palatable to competition lawyers, economists and authorities that are used to doing things in certain ways. Such an approach would also avoid any arguments about unsustainable business practices being new types of abuse and, thus, that finding a breach of Article 102 TFEU on the basis of one should carry no fine.[57]

At the same time, we consider it important to also advocate for the latter approach. Accepting that unsustainable business practices can be abuses of a dominant position, regardless of whether they can be easily "translated" into our existing categories, makes sure that we focus on what we as a society and

---

55 Based on the same logic, it is nowadays accepted that prices that are the result of market power cannot be a proper baseline for the conduct of a SSNIP test, in order to avoid the "cellophane fallacy": Commission notice on the definition of relevant market for the purposes of Community competition law [1997] OJ C372/5, [19].

56 Holmes (n 31), 384–386.

57 "Novel" abuses have carried fines before, where the undertakings engaging in them could not have been unaware of the highly anticompetitive nature of their conduct: *AstraZeneca* (n 28), [164].

Article 102 TFEU care about. It ensures that competition law takes a stance against such ways to compete, something that carries significant normative force for undertakings. It creates fertile ground for the development of abuses that have hitherto been largely in the shadows, especially exploitative ones. It also ensures that cases can be brought and won on the basis of the kind of evidence that will be available (e.g. documented violations of labour rules or environmental damage), instead of having to procure or produce other evidence and analyses (e.g. econometric evidence). A market logic may work, but do we really want everything to be filtered through that logic, if that is only possible because we contort concepts (e.g. consumer welfare) and tests that were devised in a different time and on the basis of discredited assumptions and failed ideologies?

V. Radical for Whom?

In this short paper, we presented our research on the nexus between dominance and unsustainable business practices and, considering abuse in light of Article 102 TFEU's purpose, introduced our coming research project on unsustainable business practices as abuses of a dominant position.

Our ideas for using Article 102 TFEU as a sword to strike down dominant firms' conduct that harms people and planet will, probably, be dismissed by some as too radical. Undoubtedly, our approach is a departure from how Article 102 is currently enforced and will seem chimeric for competition lawyers and economists who espouse an economic approach to EU competition law that is obsessed with efficiency instead of fairness and level playing field, that understands competition as a race to the bottom to reward undertakings that care only about profit, that is disjointed from the acute problems our societies currently face, and that is based on a blind belief that markets will solve those problems. Yet, that approach has failed and there is nothing normal, logical or inevitable about the kind of competition it has enabled. We realised long ago that common standards (e.g. harmonisation), offsetting charges (e.g. tariffs, anti-dumping measures, countervailing duties for subsidies) or exceptions on public policy grounds are needed in order to ensure states do not compete unfairly with low regulation. Why is it radical to suggest that powerful market players should be constrained from doing the same?[58]

Our approach is about more competition, just not the toxic kind. It is a call for refocusing competition policy and reconnecting concepts such as "abuse" with the goals of the system of EU competition law. Our proposals are activist, but they are certainly not radical.

---

58 The constitutionalisation of private law is certainly not a new phenomenon.

Exploring the Sustainability
of Article 102

CHRISTOPHER THOMAS[*]

Hogan Lovells

Article 102 TFEU is many years older than the United Nations' Sustainable Development Goals – or indeed the European Commission's Green New Deal. Originally conceived as Article 86 of the EEC Treaty in the 1950s, it dates from another age, when society was more concerned about sustaining economic recovery in Europe than, as now, about the sustainability of the planet itself. But competition law is not a rigid code of conduct. Rather, it is an expression of principles and objectives. This paper explores whether the principles and objectives of Article 102 support or inhibit undertakings as they seek to play their part in slowing climate change and achieving environmental sustainability.

I. Abuse of Dominance Allegations
Against Sustainability Schemes

Industry-wide schemes set up to advance sustainability objectives are not exempt from Article 102 TFEU by virtue of the good intentions underlying the scheme. Indeed, given their objective of changing market behaviour across an entire sector it is perhaps surprising that there have not been more cases challenging the activities of such schemes.

An illustration of the potential concerns is provided by the European Commission's intervention against DSD in relation to the details of its packaging waste

---

[*]   Christopher Thomas is a partner in the competition law practice of Hogan Lovells, based in Brussels.

recovery scheme.[1] The background was German legislation requiring manufacturers and distributors of packaging to take back and recover used sales packaging outside the public waste disposal system.[2] The legislation exempted manufacturers from this obligation where they participated in a system that guaranteed the regular collection of used sales packaging from the final consumer or in the vicinity of the final consumer's home in order for it to be recovered.

That is where DSD (Der Grüne Punkt – Duales System Deutschland GmbH) came in. DSD operated an exemption system throughout Germany with approvals from all the relevant Länder authorities. Specifically, it operated a network of local collection undertakings to which it outsourced the collection of packaging, and it arranged for the waste to be transported to a recycling centre to be recovered. DSD was highly successful in pursuing these laudable sustainability activities. Indeed, it was the only undertaking to offer an exemption system throughout Germany, collecting around 70% of sales packaging in Germany, and 82% of sales packaging collected from final consumers in Germany. In other words, from the perspective of Article 102 TFEU, DSD was dominant.

Obviously, all this good work needed to be paid for. DSD came up with a simple, practical solution. Manufacturers participating in DSD's recovery scheme would place its logo – the now famous Green Dot mark – on packaging that they wanted to be recovered by DSD, and pay a licence fee calculated by reference to the amount of packaging on which they placed the Green Dot. That arrangement earned DSD a formal condemnation for abuse of dominance.[3]

So where did DSD go wrong?

The antitrust concerns all arose from the practicalities involved when a manufacturer sought to have some of its sales packaging for a product in Germany disposed of using a self-management solution or a competing exemption system (while using DSD for the remainder), or to have all of the sales packaging of a product in Germany disposed of using a self-management solution or a competing exemption system (while participating in a system using the Green Dot mark in other EU Member States). The Commission made a number of factual findings in this respect:[4]

- To avoid the DSD licence fee on packaging that would be recovered using a self-management solution or a competing exemption system, the manufacturer would need to mark some of its packaging with the Green Dot mark and some not. This would lead to "considerable additional costs"

1 *DSD* (Case COMP D3/34493) Commission decision C(2001) 1106 [2001] OJ L166/1; upheld in Case C–385/07 P *Der Grüne Punkt – Duales System Deutschland v Commission* EU:C:2009:456; Anne-Lise Sibony, "Exploitative abuse : The ECJ confirms CFI judgement in relation to excessive licencing fees by the operator of the major recycling scheme in Germany"(*Der Grüne Punkt*), 16 August 2009, Concurrences N° 4-2009, Art. N° 29258, pp. 105-106.
2 For simplicity, only manufacturers are mentioned in the following explanations.
3 The Commission did not seek to impose a fine, although of course it has extensive powers to do so.
4 See *DSD* decision (n 1), recitals 104–108.

where the manufacturer wished to use one form of packaging for several countries (e.g. common German-language packaging for Germany and Austria) or common multilingual packaging for Europe. A similar problem would arise where uniformly designed packaging was to be distributed via different channels (e.g. self-service department stores and local supermarkets), with different arrangements being made for each channel.

– Manufacturers would also need to ensure that packaging marked with the Green Dot ended up only at outlets serviced by a DSD collection system, and that packaging not marked with the Green Dot mark only ended up at outlets serviced by the competing system. The Commission found that this would "often be outside the organisational and coordinating power of a manufacturer", and indeed that would "probably always be the case where a manufacturer makes use of independent intermediaries (e.g. the wholesale trade)".

– Finally, the final consumer would often not decide until after buying the packaged product, and sometimes after consuming the product, whether to dispose of the packaging close to their home or to bring it back to the place where they bought it. It was therefore impossible to determine correctly which quantities should be marked with the Green Dot mark and which not.

On the basis of these facts, the Commission concluded that it was "economically unrealistic" for a manufacturer marking some of its packaging in Germany with the Green Dot to avoid DSD's licence fee on other packaging intended to be recovered using a self-management scheme or a competing exemption system.[5]

From this, a number of consequences followed under Article 102 TFEU, in the view of the Commission and, ultimately, the Court of Justice of the European Union. First, DSD infringed Article 102(a) by charging unfair prices, in that it charged fees that were disproportionate to the economic value of the service provided. This was the consequence, given the circumstances set out above, of DSD requiring payment of a fee for all packaging carrying the Green Dot and put into circulation in Germany, even where customers showed that they did not use DSD's system for some or all of that packaging.[6] Second, DSD committed an exclusionary abuse because, in their actual effect, DSD's terms were very close to being an exclusivity requirement. In the Commission's view, they made it much more difficult for competitors to enter the market, they strengthened DSD's dominant position and they further weakened competition.

What lessons can be drawn for industry-wide schemes aiming to achieve sustainability objectives? At its simplest, the main point is that any activity that can

---

5   ibid, recital 103.
6   *Der Grüne Punkt – Duales System Deutschland v Commission* (n 1), [143]; *DSD* decision (n 1), recital 113.

properly be viewed as a service provided in a market is subject to the normal rules of Article 102 TFEU. Where the scheme is likely to be held dominant, the same concern to avoid conduct that exploits customers or excludes competitors that would inform the design of the business strategies of any dominant firm should inform the design of the scheme as well.

Within that framework, it is normal to advise a dominant firm that arrangements that might sound simple and practical from the perspective of the dominant firm need to be considered in light of their real-world implications for customers, and their likely effect on the ability of rivals to compete. The promoters of sustainability schemes need to exercise the same diligence, and not just assume that "we're the good guys".

In *DSD*, the Commission held that unfair commercial terms exist "where an undertaking in a dominant position fails to comply with the principle of proportionality". It explained that, in balancing the various interests in the case, DSD did not appear to have any reasonable interest in linking the fee payable by its contractual partners not to the exemption service actually used but to the extent to which the mark was used.[7] Those two concepts – proportionality and the reasonable interests of the scheme – are key to avoiding exploitative abuses in the design of schemes to achieve sustainability goals. As for exclusionary abuses, the Commission's final remark makes explicit the concern that schemes need to address: "There is no equality of opportunity for competitors".[8]

Further lessons can be drawn from the Commission's intervention in the structure of the German Fountain Cooperative, the Genossenschaft Deutscher Brunnen (GDB).[9] That case also began with German waste management legislation. The rules in Germany had already removed plastic one-way bottles from the market, and new rules then prohibited disposable glass bottles (one-way glass) and other one-way packaging without a system for its recycling.

At that time, GDB operated a pool of standardised refillable glass bottles and crates in Germany, for use by German water producers. The benefits of this scheme for sustainability are obvious. And yet it ended up on the receiving end of a Commission investigation, and had to change its rules to avoid a more painful outcome to that investigation. Why?

A formal complaint by the Belgian water producer SPA led to the adoption of a statement of objections requiring GDB to open its pool to mineral water producers from elsewhere in the EU. The Commission's preliminary finding was that starting a new pool of refillable glass bottles was not "a realistic proposition" since most water wholesalers and supermarkets in Germany did not wish to introduce a second

---

7   *DSD* decision (n 1), [112].
8   ibid, recital 115.
9   *Spa Monopole/GDB* (1993) 23rd Comp Rep EC, [240].

pool besides GDB. This would have involved "considerable additional handling and stocking costs". Theoretical alternatives such as disposable glass bottles and other one-way packaging were not feasible in practice given the new German legislation. Accordingly, in the Commission's preliminary view, the only way for non-German producers to be competitive in the German market was to bottle their products in GDB bottles, and thus access to the GDB pool was essential.

Again, it is striking that the illegality identified by the Commission was not evident simply from the contractual language of the arrangements established by GDB. It required an examination of actual market conditions, in light of the evolving legislation in the field. Another common element with *DSD* is that GDB no doubt considered that dealing only with German producers made everything simpler and more convenient. In today's antitrust vocabulary, *GDB* shows that customer preferences and legislative changes may transform an arrangement set up by private parties to advance sustainability goals into an "essential facility". When that happens, all the normal rules applicable to essential facilities must be respected – especially where the facility is nationwide, and the exclusion of outsiders would isolate the national market from the remainder of the EU internal market.

II. Abuse of Dominance Allegations Against Individual Firms Pursuing Sustainability Objectives

It is not only the promoters of industry-wide sustainability schemes that need to be conscious of Article 102 TFEU. Individual undertakings wishing to assume their responsibilities in the framework of sustainability also need to be aware of the limits on their conduct imposed by Article 102. The "special responsibility" of a dominant firm not to allow its behaviour to impair genuine, undistorted competition on the internal market does not disappear simply because it is pursuing worthy environmental objectives.

In particular, leading companies may come under considerable pressure not to deal with those considered to have a poor record in terms of sustainability, or to offer favourable terms or other rewards to partners that engage in beneficial environmental efforts. It might even be thought that a particular supplier or customer is acting contrary to sustainability legislation and that, as a result, they should be denied access to some product or other resource under the company's control.

The case law of the EU courts is not favourable to such initiatives.

In *Hilti*, a firm later held to be dominant in the supply of nail guns and Hilti-compatible cartridge strips (for loading nails into the gun) took various measures that tended to foreclose the nails of certain competitors.[10] These included, in

---

10 *Eurofix-Bauco v Hilti* (Cases IV.30.787 and 31.488) Commission decision 88/138/EEC [1988] OJ L65/19; upheld in Case T–30/89 *Hilti v Commission* EU:T:1991:70 (upheld on unrelated issues in Case C–53/92

particular, tying its own nails to its dominant cartridge strips. Hilti argued that its conduct was objectively justified, given its concerns that the competing nails in question were substandard and dangerous.

The General Court of the EU (at that time, the Court of First Instance) rejected this purported justification as a matter of principle. The Court underlined that Hilti had not approached the competent national authorities for a ruling that the use of the competitors' nails in Hilti tools was dangerous. It explained that the legitimate rights of those competitors would not have been impaired had the national authorities acceded to Hilti's request for a ban on the use in its tools of their nails and, where appropriate, of all misleading advertisements issued by them.[11] Finally, in words that could easily be transferred to legislation advancing sustainability goals, the Court warned:

> As the Commission has established, there are laws in the United Kingdom attaching penalties to the sale of dangerous products and to the use of misleading claims as to the characteristics of any product. There are also authorities vested with powers to enforce those laws. In those circumstances it is clearly not the task of an undertaking in a dominant position to take steps on its own initiative to eliminate products which, rightly or wrongly, it regards as dangerous or at least as inferior in quality to its own products.[12]

The same court issued a similar and indeed more extensive warning in *TetraPak*.[13] In that case, a supplier of cartons intended for the packaging of liquid foods, and of machines used for this purpose, was found to have tied its cartons to its machines. TetraPak was held by the Commission in principle to have abused dominant positions in various markets, and the question arose whether the conduct could be objectively justified on the basis of public health.[14]

When rejecting TetraPak's invocation of public health as a justification for its actions, the Court did not rely merely on the availability of public authorities to enforce existing laws. It specifically held that it is not for dominant firms to unilaterally adopt their own rules, and that the remedy for such public health concerns must be sought instead through legislation or regulations:

> In those circumstances, whatever the complexity in this case of aseptic filling processes, the protection of public health may be guaranteed by other means, in particular by notifying machine

---

P *Hilti v Commission* EU:C:1994:77).

11 *Hilti* (General Court) (n 10), [115] – [117].

12 ibid, [118].

13 *Tetra Pak II* (Case IV/31043) Commission decision 92/163/EEC [1992] OJ L72/1; upheld in Case T–83/91 *Tetra Pak International v Commission* EU:T:1994:246 (upheld in Case C–333/94 P *Tetra Pak International v Commission* EU:C:1996:436).

14 This is of course the case in which it was held, in the circumstances of the case, that TetraPak's conduct in the non-aseptic markets could constitute an abuse of its dominant positions held in the aseptic markets.

users of the technical specifications with which cartons must comply in order to be compatible with those machines, without infringing manufacturers' intellectual property rights. Moreover, even on the assumption, shared by the applicant, that machinery and cartons from various sources cannot be used together without the characteristics of the system being affected thereby, the remedy must lie in appropriate legislation or regulations, and not in rules adopted unilaterally by manufacturers, which would amount to prohibiting independent manufacturers from conducting the essential part of their business."[15]

In light of this, firms liable to be found dominant should be cautious with proposals that they act commercially in such a way as to incentivise others to abandon unsustainable products or practices. Pointing to sustainability goals, however important for society, is unlikely in itself to justify the exclusion of competitors by means of unilateral refusals to deal or tying.

But that does not mean that dominant firms may not take into account sustainability objectives when designing their *own* products and services. Normally, of course, such decisions are recognised as an integral aspect of competition on the merits. But as the General Court warned in *Baltic Rail*, "as a general rule, any conduct by an undertaking in a dominant position which is capable of restricting competition on a market may be categorised as abusive".[16] In theory, choices made in the design of an undertaking's products and services might therefore be challenged under Article 102 TFEU on the basis of perceived adverse effects on competitors.

A comparison with the courts' approach to "unfair" trading conditions – as exemplified by *DSD* – may help illustrate the issues likely to be in play in such a challenge. Whether articulated as an aspect of the "unfairness" analysis, or in terms of objective justification, the issues are likely to revolve around the legitimacy of the interests pursued, and determining whether those interests should prevail over the perceived impact on competitors.

As to legitimacy, it might be noted that the EU courts have previously recognised enhancing stability in the provision of employment as an objective benefit capable of excusing a restriction of competition under Article 101(3) TFEU.[17] More generally, and albeit with some caution, the Court of Justice has recognised that "in the context of an overall assessment, the Commission is entitled to base itself on considerations connected with the pursuit of the public interest" in order to

---

15 *TetraPak* (General Court) (n 13), [84]. The Court of Justice upheld the General Court's findings on the existence of an unlawful tie, albeit without specifically addressing paragraph 84 (see the Court of Justice's judgment (n 13), [36]).
16 Case T–814/17 *Lietuvos geležinkeliai v Commission* EU:T:2020:545, [85].
17 Case 26/76 *Metro SB-Großmärkte v Commission* EU:C:1977:167, [42].

grant an exemption under Article 101(3) TFEU.[18] It thus seems plausible that the courts would recognise the achievement of sustainability goals as likewise capable of being taken into account in the context of Article 102 TFEU.

The dominant firm would thus be arguing that its conduct is "proportionate" when compared with any adverse effect it is likely to have on competition. The model for that assessment is likely to be the Court of Justice's guidance in *United Brands*, where it held that even dominant firms are entitled to take reasonable and proportionate steps to protect their commercial interests if they are attacked.[19] Similarly, in *DSD*, the underlying issue was expressly one of the proportionality of DSD's arrangements in light of their impact on competing solutions. Respect for the principle of proportionality will mean that the greater the impact on the competitive activities of third parties, the greater the sustainability benefits will need to be. Likewise, there must not be alternative means to achieve the same objectives with less damage to competition.

If sustainability were recognised as an "efficiency", then the dominant firm might also be able to call on the efficiency defence established in *Post Danmark I*. In that case, the Court of Justice held that there is a defence where the dominant undertaking shows that the efficiency gains likely to result from its conduct counteract any likely negative effects on competition and consumer welfare in the affected markets, that those gains have been, or are likely to be, brought about as a result of that conduct, that such conduct is necessary for the achievement of those gains in efficiency, and that it does not eliminate effective competition by removing all or most existing sources of actual or potential competition.[20]

Of course, recognising sustainability as an efficiency for the purposes of EU competition law would be an act of judicial policy on the part of the EU courts. The Article 101(3) cases cited earlier may be pertinent in this respect. Likewise, it is surely relevant that the Treaty on European Union calls at Article 3 for the Union to "work for the sustainable development of Europe based on balanced economic growth and price stability" and, in its relations with the wider world, to "contribute to the sustainable development of the Earth, solidarity and mutual respect among peoples, free and fair trade, eradication of poverty and the protection of human rights". Article 11 TFEU provides that environmental protection requirements "must be integrated into the definition and implementation of the Union's policies and activities, in particular with a view to promoting sustainable development". There would thus appear to be scope for the courts to recognise sustainability as an efficiency, should they wish to do so.

---

18 Cases T–528/93, T–542/93, T–543/93 and T–546/93 *Métropole Télévision and others v Commission* EU:T:1996:99, [118].
19 Case 27/76 *United Brands v Commission* EU:C:1978:22, [189] – [190].
20 Case C–209/10 *Post Danmark v Konkurrencerådet* EU:C:2012:172, [42]; Lucas Peeperkorn, "The EU Court of Justice affirms the application of a consumer-oriented effects-based approach to exclusionary pricing practices of dominant undertakings and the "as efficient competitor test"" (*Post Danmark*), 27 March 2012, e-Competitions March 2012, Art. N° 48816.

In theory, these considerations would apply whatever the alleged abuse. That said, it is easiest to contemplate their application to an allegation relating to the dominant firm's product design. In the case of more "classic" abuses, it may be harder to persuade the courts. One could imagine defending an allegation of charging unfair prices (that have no reasonable relation to the economic value of the product) on the basis that the environmental benefits deriving from the product need to be considered as part of its value. But where a product is priced below average variable costs, will it really be enough to say that the risk of foreclosing competitors should be accepted in light of the sustainability virtues of the dominant firm's product? Finally, the *Hilti* precedent teaches us that tying consumables or spare parts is unlikely to be justified by the argument that the dominant firm's products have superior environmental credentials than those of its rivals.

III. A Sustainability Abuse?

An obvious question is whether Article 102 TFEU could be used directly to challenge practices viewed as non-sustainable.

In relation to contractual provisions, there must be at least some prospect in this regard. Contracts with business partners are undoubtedly market conduct falling within the scope of Article 102, and the notions of "unfair purchase or selling prices" and "unfair trading conditions" in Article 102(a) have yet to be fully explored. But outside this context it is harder to speculate. The established understanding of Article 102 is that it covers practices that cause harm to consumers, whether "directly" or through their impact on competition.[21] Where the perceived harm is to the climate, or to the environment more generally, it is far from obvious that this test is satisfied. While individuals will undoubtedly be prejudiced as a consequence of damage to the climate or the environment, it is arguable whether they are affected as "consumers", and almost by definition they are not harmed "directly".

In short, while it may well be that certain forms of conduct viewed as non-sustainable will also amount to abuses of Article 102 TFEU, it seems unlikely that Article 102 can be stretched to create a sustainability abuse as such.

---

21   ibid, [20].

Chapter 3
EU Merger Control

Environmental Sustainability and EU Merger Control: EU Competition Policy's Dark Horse to Support Green Investment

NICOLE KAR, EMMA COCHRANE AND BELLA SPRING[*]

Linklaters

I. Introduction

While the current debate in relation to competition law and sustainability focuses largely on competitor cooperation,[1] merger control and other legal instruments such as state aid have an important role to play in fostering green investment.

Social and political pressure to tackle the impact of climate change is growing. The European Commission (the Commission) has made the transition to carbon

[*] Nicole Kar is head of Linklaters' London Competition Practice, co-head of Linklaters' Global Banking Sector Group and Trade Law Practice and is vice chair of the City of London Solicitors' Competition Committee. Emma Cochrane is a practice development lawyer in the Linklaters Competition/Antitrust group and works closely with clients to provide updates on market trends, legal and regulatory developments and considers how they may impact their business. Bella Spring is a senior professional support lawyer in Linklaters' London office, advising on all areas of EU and UK competition law.

The authors would like to thank Dr. Matthew Bennett, a Vice President at Charles River Associates, Christian Ahlborn, Sara Feijao, Gerwin van Gerven, William Huynh, Annamaria Mangiaracina, Simon Pritchard, Amarveer Randhawa and Hayley Tennant for their useful comments on the draft. All errors remain those of the authors.

[1] Linklaters, "Competition law needs to cooperate: companies want clarity to enable climate change initiatives to be pursued" (Linklaters-commissioned Censuswide survey of 200 corporate sustainability leaders, April 2020) <https://lpscdn.linklaters.com/-/media/files/document-store/pdf/uk/2020/april/linklaters_competition-law-needs-to-cooperate_april-2020.ashx?rev=2c2c8c7d-91a8-496f-99fb-92a799c55cb2&extension=pdf&hash=6641BEDB36EC877CA43C7D995BD6EEDA>.

net-zero by 2050 via the European Green Deal (Green Transition) its top policy priority,[2] including by ensuring a "green recovery" from the pandemic. Treating efforts to mitigate climate change as a relevant merger consideration is part of a broader move in Europe towards consideration of the wider effects of a merger on issues like innovation competition, long-term investment incentives and impact on small businesses. This stems in part from a growing awareness of competition policy in a wider framework of social and economic inequality. The traditional narrow, price-focused interpretation of the consumer welfare standard in competition law is becoming somewhat outdated. In a number of contexts, the Commission is being asked to look at out-of-market efficiencies whereby transactions may bring benefits to consumers more generally: beyond the agreement or merger in question and encompassing present and future generations.

There is, however, no guidance on how the Commission may factor environmental objectives into its merger reviews. Of course, a transaction which is harmful to both competition and the environment can be dealt with under existing tools. But more difficult questions arise in at least two scenarios:

   i.   a transaction that harms competition but has a positive effect on the environment and that would require account to be taken of environmental efficiencies resulting from the deal; and

   ii. a transaction that does not harm competition (or at least not sufficiently to require a remedy or prohibition decision) but does have a negative environmental effect.

Commission officials have commented that there are significant legal obstacles, in the form of Article 2 of the European Merger Regulation (EUMR),[3] to considering environmental efficiencies within the mergers framework. As a result, at present, consideration of environmental factors in merger cases tends to be asymmetric: it is more likely that a reduction of competition in terms of sustainability parameters or restricting "sustainability innovation" would be considered by agencies as an additional reason for *blocking* an anticompetitive merger rather than sustainability benefits being a reason for clearing it.[4] This reflects a broader asymmetry at play in

---

2   Commission, "A European Green Deal" <https://ec.europa.eu/info/strategy/priorities-2019-2024/european-green-deal_en> accessed 30 December 2020; Commission, "European industrial strategy" <https://ec.europa.eu/info/strategy/priorities-2019-2024/europe-fit-digitalage/european-industrial-strategy_en> accessed 30 December 2020.

3   Council Regulation (EC) 139/2004 on the control of concentrations between undertakings (EC Merger Regulation) [2004] OJ L24/1, art 2.

4   A current exception to this framework is the design of the German merger control legislation and the possibility of ministerial override as demonstrated by the German Economics Ministry decision in August 2019 to allow the Miba/Zollern joint venture that had previously been blocked by the German Federal Cartel Office. The minister ruled that the positive effects of the deal for the environment and climate protection (such as noise reduction, reduced fuel consumption and, more generally, climate protection and a sustainable environment policy) outweighed the competitive disadvantages of the merger. *Miba/Zollern* [2019] Az.: IB2 – 20302/14-02, subsequently rejected on appeal by the Düsseldorf Court of Appeal (Oberlandesgericht) in August 2020 (VI-Kart 4/19 (V)

merger control where factors restricting competition are generally subject to a lower standard of proof than efficiencies. However, there are some early signs that sustainability considerations are becoming part of the merger control analysis.

In this paper we will consider[5] how the Commission currently approaches environmental factors within the EU merger control process, what is legally possible within the existing framework, and some ways in which the merger control framework could incorporate sustainability considerations. There are few merger cases in which sustainability grounds have been argued before agencies so far. But the regime does not in principle prevent progress in this area, including by allowing intervention by Member State governments on public interest grounds and potentially through a revised approach to efficiencies. Beyond the EU merger control framework, EU state aid rules and to some extent foreign investment control powers form part of the policy tools available to the Commission and Member States to further progress towards achieving Green Deal objectives.

To play their part in the Green Transition, European competition agencies are currently focusing on using their antitrust and state aid tools.[6] Merger control policy may be, on its face, a less flexible tool to support environmental progress and would require the Commission to fundamentally change the way it assesses efficiencies.[7] But it could and should – from a system coherence point of view, at a minimum – play a role, not least by enabling the creation of (private) environmental champions, without (further) depleting stretched public funds.

To achieve this, the onus will be firmly on dealmakers (and their advisers) to bring forward mergers motivated by sustainability objectives or that will generate sustainability benefits. Business rationales need to be clearly articulated and efficiency analyses well grounded. Could this be an important and timely opportunity to create a virtuous circle? More merger cases will push the Commission to conclude on key issues such as its approach to the efficiencies assessment and, crucially, to articulate that conclusion in merger decisions. This will in turn

---

<www.justiz.nrw.de/nrwe/olgs/duesseldorf/j2020/Kart_4_19_V_Beschluss_20200826.html> accessed 1 October 2020); Laura Lehoczky-Deckers, "The Higher Regional Court of Düsseldorf dismisses an appeal brought by two producers of hydrodynamic slide bearings against a decision of the Competition Authority prohibiting them to create a joint venture (*Miba/Zollern*)" (2020) e-Competitions Art N° 97129.

5   In this paper we tackle the legal framework for consideration of sustainability factors in merger control reviews in Europe. We appreciate there are many important elements from an economic perspective which inform the required analysis, including that environmental benefits will generally run in the opposite direction to standard cost efficiencies: lower cost and more output is a general efficiency, but higher output will always lead to higher pollution etc. However, these are beyond the scope or purpose of this paper.

6   It is noteworthy that Commissioner Vestager omitted the role of merger control policy from her speech on 22 September 2020 ("The Green Deal and competition policy" (Renew Webinar, 22 September 2020) <https://ec.europa.eu/commission/commissioners/2019-2024/vestager/announcements/green-deal-and-competition-policy_en>).

7   As discussed further below, such a change would, arguably, need to apply more generally to the merger control assessment rather than being limited to the realisation of environmental efficiencies.

provide much-needed certainty over the assessment framework to other merging parties keen to pursue green agendas. With the revised horizontal guidelines potentially still some way off, and with "technical and economic progress" finding common expression in Article 101(3) TFEU[8] and in Article 2 EUMR, it could even shape the Commission's thinking on wider issues, including sustainability cooperation.

II. The M&A Climate: Sustainable Investment as a Corporate Imperative

Social and political pressure to meaningfully tackle climate change has grown dramatically. This is best demonstrated by the ambitious European Green Deal[9] – a set of far-reaching policy initiatives designed to stimulate green investments by public and private players in order to reduce the bloc's greenhouse gas emissions to net-zero by 2050. The Commission has made clear that the Green Transition is its top policy priority.[10]

The global pandemic and the Black Lives Matter movement have sparked further, urgent reflection amid a heightened awareness of social and racial inequality and environmental harm. Any concerns that the climate crisis would be side-lined as the pandemic spread were quickly dispelled when the Commission took the opportunity to further EU environmental policy goals by overseeing the extraction of sustainability commitments from recipients of COVID-19 state aid packages (so-called "green strings"). For example, Renault's €5 billion guarantee from France was made conditional[11] upon Renault joining the batteries IPCEI,[12] while the Dutch government imposed sustainability conditions on its €3.4 billion support to airline KLM.[13] Further, the Commission subsequently announced

---

8   Treaty on the Functioning of the European Union.
9   Commission, "The European Green Deal" (Communication) COM(2019) 640 final <https://ec.europa.eu/info/sites/info/files/european-green-deal-communication_en.pdf>.
10 Commission, "European industrial strategy" (n 2).
11 Commission, "State aid: Commission approves €5 billion loan guarantee by France to the Renault group to mitigate economic impact of coronavirus outbreak" Press Release (IP/20/779, 29 April 2020) <https://ec.europa.eu/commission/presscorner/detail/en/IP_20_779> and Sam Morgan, "Macron demands carmakers turn to 'Made in France' for €8bn virus aid" (*Euractiv*, 27 May 2020) <www.euractiv.com/section/electric-cars/news/macron-demands-carmakers-turn-to-made-in-france-for-e8bn-virus-aid/>.
12 Commission, "Criteria for the analysis of the compatibility with the internal market of State aid to promote the execution of important projects of common European interest" (Communication) (2014/C 188/02) <https://eur-lex.europa.eu/legal-content/EN/TXT/PDF/?uri=CELEX:52014XC0620(01)&from=EN>. Commission, "State aid: Commission approves €3.2 billion public support by seven Member States for a pan-European research and innovation project in all segments of the battery value chain" Press Release (IP/19/6705, 9 December 2019) <https://ec.europa.eu/commission/presscorner/detail/en/ip_19_6705>.
13 Commission, "State aid: Commission approves Dutch plans to provide €3.4 billion in urgent liquidity support to KLM" Press Release (IP/20/1333, 13 July 2020) <https://ec.europa.eu/commission/presscorner/detail/en/ip_20_1333>.

that 37% of the Next Generation EU fund (the EU's COVID-19 recovery fund) will be spent directly on European Green Deal objectives.[14]

Private investors are themselves recognising the role they can (and must) play in the green recovery from the COVID-19 crisis. After growth potential, sustainability credentials and transparency are the joint-second most important factors when managing fund portfolios.[15] The financial incentives for this seem clear: ESG (environmental, social and governance) funds have significantly outperformed non-ESG funds in recent years, with markedly higher survivability rates.[16] It follows that upgrading environmental credentials and reducing exposure to environmental risks across investment portfolios are now integral features of investment strategies and business models to ensure not only long-term resilience to withstand market shocks, but also profitability.[17]

EU-regulated funds will also be encouraged by upcoming EU regulations that explicitly entrench ESG considerations into investment decision-making, such as the Sustainable Finance Disclosure Regulation,[18] Taxonomy Regulation[19] and Low-Carbon Benchmarks Regulation.[20] Against this backdrop, we can expect many more acquisitions (and divestments[21]) for which a core driver is sustainability. Unlike the self-assessment regime which governs cooperation agreements

---

14 Ursula von der Leyen, "State of the Union 2020" (speech to the European Parliament, 16 September 2020) <https://ec.europa.eu/commission/presscorner/detail/en/speech_20_1655>. This forms part of some wider European reflection about the importance of tackling the climate crisis. The European Central Bank, for example, is questioning whether its traditional market neutrality is the appropriate benchmark for central bank asset purchase programmes in the face of climate change (Ella Milburn and Khalid Azizuddin, "'Market neutrality may not be the appropriate benchmark' says ECB as it mulls exclusion of climate-risky bonds" (*Responsible Investor* 29 September 2020) <www.responsible-investor.com/articles/market-neutrality-may-not-be-the-appropriate-benchmark-says-ecb-as-it-mulls-exclusion-of-climate-risky-bonds>).

15 Linklaters, "Green recovery in sight as one in four infrastructure funds expect to grow green assets more than a fifth by 2022" (Linklaters-commissioned Censuswide online survey of 302 fund and portfolio managers who invest in the energy & utilities or infrastructure/transport sectors in the UK, France, Germany, Italy, Spain, Belgium, the Netherlands and Luxembourg, 28 July 2020) <www.linklaters.com/en/insights/blogs/linkingesg/2020/july/green-recovery-in-sight-as-1-in-4-infra-funds-expect-to-grow-green-assets-more-than-a-fifth-by-2022>.

16 Morning Star Manager Research, "How Does European Sustainable Funds' Performance Measure Up?" (June 2020). However, some market commentators have suggested that this "outperformance" is because the price of oil crashed and ESG funds rely less on oil investments, rather than because they are a better investment choice overall.

17 It is likely that private recapitalisations from investors and banks will also be increasingly conditional upon raising environmental standards in accordance with the Principles for Responsible Investment and Principles for Responsible Banking, which include setting and implementing targets to align with sustainability goals.

18 Under which, from March 2021, EU-regulated funds will be required to disclose their approach to taking positive and adverse ESG impacts into account in investment decision-making (EU Regulation 2019/2088 on sustainability-related disclosures in the financial services sector [2019] OJ L317/1).

19 Proposal for an EU Regulation on the establishment of a framework to facilitate sustainable investment (COM/2018/353 final).

20 Regulation (EU) 2019/2089 amending Regulation (EU) 2016/1011 as regards EU Climate Transition Benchmarks, EU Paris-aligned Benchmarks and sustainability-related disclosures for benchmarks [2019] OJ L317/17.

21 Especially of thermal coal assets as well as other polluting business divisions.

under Article 101 TFEU, transactions that satisfy the EU merger thresholds[22] must be notified to the Commission. Therefore, dealmakers will largely drive the merger control agenda based on the deals they do in pursuit of their investment strategies. The onus will be on them (and their advisers) to bring forward green deals with clearly articulated business rationales and well-evidenced efficiency analyses to the Commission for its review.

The more merger cases there are with clear-cut conclusions on environmental efficiencies, the more dealmakers will be encouraged to pursue their green investment strategies with certainty. And while we await clearer guidance in the cooperation context (with revised horizontal guidelines currently expected in 2022,[23] although the Commission has intimated[24] that it may take specific action in the environmental context sooner, based on the findings of its recent consultation[25]), the Commission's approach to merger efficiencies could provide crucial insight into its broader thinking in this space within a much shorter timeframe – as long as relevant cases are brought to it.

III. Potential Procedural Impact on the EUMR Referrals Process

Because the EU merger control regime is mandatory, transactions meeting the applicable jurisdictional thresholds must be notified to the Commission for approval prior to completion, regardless of whether they raise competition concerns.[26]

However, given the Commission's keen focus on delivering the Green Transition, we can expect much more scrutiny of deals with an environmental impact. The Commission may be particularly alive to the risk that an established market player with a polluting business model may seek to remove a smaller innovator selling a more sustainable product (so-called "sustainability-killer" acquisitions)[27] and there is no question that the existing framework is sufficient to deal with this situation.

---

22 EUMR (n 3), art 5.
23 Commission, "Review of the two Horizontal Block Exemption Regulations" consultation available at: <https://ec.europa.eu/competition/consultations/2019_hbers/index_en.html> accessed 30 December 2020.
24 Vestager, "The Green Deal and competition policy" (n 6).
25 Commission, "Competition Policy supporting the Green Deal: Call for contributions" (1 November 2020) <https://ec.europa.eu/competition/information/green_deal/call_for_contributions_en.pdf>.
26 Compare the voluntary UK regime, under which the Competition and Markets Authority has a broad discretion to "call in" transactions meeting the UK thresholds that it thinks may harm competition. Given the increasing political importance placed on sustainability, it is possible that in future we would see the CMA being more likely to call in a transaction e.g. involving green tech.
27 The concept of the "killer acquisition" theory of harm is relatively well established in the pharmaceutical sector, where a dominant incumbent acquires an innovative challenger for an inflated purchase price in order to eliminate future competition from a pipeline product. This theory of harm was later applied in the digital merger context, with competition authorities starting to actively scrutinise so-called "killer acquisitions" by Big Tech designed to remove potentially disruptive technology or competitors. Sustainability killer acquisitions are likely to be the next frontier, especially in the energy sector, as the sustainability profile of a supplier and its product becomes an increasingly important parameter of competition.

At a procedural level, this heightened Commission interest may impact the approach to referrals for green deals, with the Commission potentially refusing to accept requests by Member States to review mergers meeting the EU thresholds.[28] Such refusals have been prevalent, for example, in the telecoms sector, based on the Commission's "particular interest in the sector" (i.e. the desire to have cross-border telecoms operators) and/or "the need for consistency in the sector across the EEA".[29]

IV. Consideration of Environmental Factors as Part of the Substantive Merger Assessment

1. Framework for the debate

Article 2 EUMR requires the Commission to determine whether a transaction would result in a significant impediment to effective competition (SIEC) in the internal market or a substantial part of it.[30] Article 2(1)(b) sets out factors which the Commission must take into account when assessing a transaction, including the market position of the parties, alternatives for suppliers and customers, barriers to entry, supply and demand trends and, crucially, the "the development of technical and economic progress provided that it is to consumers' advantage and does not form an obstacle to competition".

A key question, therefore, is whether sustainability considerations can be included in a merger control analysis because they represent "technical and economic progress". Opinions are divided on this.

A narrow view against this proposition is certainly consistent with the economic approach to competition law reflected in the Commission's focus, in particular, on short-term price effects when assessing a merger: will the merging parties have the ability and incentive to raise prices (or to lower quality, choice or innovation)?[31]

---

28 Under EUMR, art 9.
29 Examples include *Vodafone/Liberty Global* (Case M.7978) Commission Decision [2016] OJ C225/4; Sergio Sorinas and Marie Louvet, "Remedies: The European Commission clears the creation of a joint venture between two telecom companies in Netherlands, subject to conditions (*Vodafone/Liberty Global*)" (2016) Concurrences N° 3–2017 Art N° 84521, 103–105; *Hutchinson 3G/Telefonica UK* (Case M.7612) Commission Decision [2015] OJ C357/15; *Altice/PT Portugal* (Case M.7499) Commission Decision [2015] OJ C238/2; *Orange/Jazztel* (Case M.742) Commission Decision [2014] OJ C376/10; Ianis Girgenson, "Phase II decision: The European Commission conditionally clears an acquisition reducing the number of suppliers from four to three on the market for fixed broadband in Spain (*Orange/Jazztel*)" (2015) Concurrences N° 1–2016 Art N° 77683, 133–136 and *Liberty Global/Virgin Media* (Case M.6880) Commission Decision [2013] OJ C162/8; Ianis Girgenson, "Unconditional clearance: The European Commission clears the acquisition of Virgin Media by Liberty Global (*Liberty Global/Virgin Media*)" (2013) Concurrences N° 3–2013 Art N° 53936, 120.
30 With effect from 1 December 2009, the TFEU introduced certain changes, such as the replacement of "Community" by "Union" and "common market" by "internal market". We adopt the terminology of the TFEU in this paper.
31 Guidelines on the assessment of horizontal mergers under the Council Regulation on the control of concentrations between undertakings (Horizontal Merger Guidelines) [2004] OJ C31/5, para 8.

Some previous cases would also suggest a narrow interpretation by the Commission. In 2017, in the context of the Commission's review of the *Bayer/Monsanto* transaction, Commissioner Vestager expressly commented that negative effects of mergers related to human health, food safety, consumer protection and the environment and climate, although of great importance, "do not form the basis of a merger assessment".[32]

However, fast-forwarding to 2020 and beyond, the competition law orthodoxy is under challenge and the legal framework is being called upon to respond.[33] Climate change is a challenge of such proportions that urgent action is required by public and private players alike. And, crucially, legislative legitimacy to push the environmental agenda already exists both through the EU treaties as well as more recent developments such as the European Green Deal. The Commission is required to "place its appraisal within the general framework of the achievement of the fundamental objectives" of the EU when assessing a merger.[34] This includes, notably, "the sustainable development of economic activities and a high level of protection and improvement of the quality of the environment".[35] While not yet law, the draft EU Climate Law arguably gives greater and more immediate scope to the Commission to take active steps to support the Green Transition, stating that: "The relevant Union institutions and the Member States shall take the necessary measures at Union and national level respectively, to enable the collective achievement of the climate-neutrality objective."[36]

As for the EUMR itself, article 2 does not limit the Commission to an analysis of price effects. It asks the Commission to determine whether a transaction would significantly impede effective competition in the internal market. In our view, the meaning of "technical and economic progress" is sufficiently broad to capture sustainability objectives as a parameter of competition, as suggested by the Hellenic Competition Commission in its Draft Staff Discussion Paper, which states that it is possible to take into account environmental and sustainability issues "under the broad umbrella of 'economic progress'".[37]

The other important question relating to Article 2 EUMR is how to interpret what constitutes "competition in the internal market". Specifically, does it require only considering the relevant market(s) affected by the merger? Director General

---

32 Letter from Commissioner Vestager to petitioners in the Bayer/Monsanto case (22 August 2017) <https://ec.europa.eu/competition/mergers/cases/additional_data/m8084_4719_6.pdf>.

33 See, for example, the Hellenic Competition Commission "Draft Staff Discussion Paper on Sustainability Issues and Competition Law" (17 September 2020), paras 97–108.

34 EUMR, recital 23.

35 Treaty establishing the European Community (Consolidated version 2002), art 2; Treaty on European Union (TEU), art 3(3); and EU Charter of Fundamental Rights, art 37. See also TEU, arts 7, 9 and 11.

36 Proposal for a Regulation of the European Parliament and of the Council establishing the framework for achieving climate neutrality and amending Regulation (EU) 2018/1999 (European Climate Law) COM(2020) 80 final, art 2(2).

37 Hellenic Competition Commission, "Draft Staff Discussion Paper on Sustainability Issues and Competition Law" (n 34), para 100 .

Guersent in September 2020 stated his view[38] that Article 2 EUMR requires the strictest interpretation of "competition" and does not allow the Commission to consider fundamentally out-of-market environmental efficiencies; i.e. those flowing to a wider group of consumers beyond those impacted by the merger. In his view, efficiencies will count only if they accrue to the customers of the merged firm (in-market efficiencies) and the consideration of out-of-market efficiencies would require an amendment to Article 2 EUMR.[39] However, Commission chief economist Pierre Régibeau has subsequently raised the possibility of capturing out-of-market green efficiencies as part of the merger analysis and has asked his team to develop the requisite analytical tools.[40] This is in line with evolving European attitudes, for example that of the Dutch competition authority (ACM) (as endorsed by the Commission), to capture some out-of-market benefits in the context of sustainability agreements.[41] Of course green efficiencies are not exclusively out-of-market. They will benefit consumers in the relevant market in the same way as they benefit consumers outside the relevant market. But there may be reasons why consumers in the market do not value sustainability or do not consider the entire wider value to others when making a purchasing decision (see below).

For these reasons, in our view, there is scope within the existing legal framework to factor environmental and other sustainability goals into the substantive analysis of mergers. The remainder of this paper will focus on how this is already happening in practice and the areas where more could be done.

2. Environmental factors are already shaping market definition

As a fundamental part of any merger assessment, the Commission must first define the product and geographic market(s) in which the merging parties operate.

---

38 Olivier Guersent, "Sustainability goals and Antitrust: Finding the common ground" (Concurrences Law & Economics webinar, 14 September 2020).

39 A working group of the German Bundeskartellamt (*Arbeitskreis Kartellrechthas*) has expressed a similar view that Article 2 EUMR cannot – and indeed should not – accommodate "non-competition" factors like effects on the environment (Bundeskartellamt, "Open markets and sustainable management: public welfare goals as a challenge for antitrust law practice" (1 October 2020), 42–43. Available (in German) at: <www.bundeskartellamt.de/SharedDocs/Publikation/DE/Diskussions_Hintergrundpapier/AK_Kartel-lrecht_2020_Hintergrundpapier.pdf;jsessionid=B1F60C9F1746298D6D5A6BF361EC51A6.2_cid362?__blob=publicationFile&v=2>.

40 Hellenic Competition Commission, "Sustainable development and competition law: Towards a Green Growth regulatory osmosis" (28 September 2020). A "group of volunteers" in his team are looking at how claims that mergers would help sustainability could be assessed in "concrete cases". (EU Competition and Sustainability, Episode 3 (Dentons round table series, 18 November 2020)).

41 ACM, "Draft Guidelines: Sustainability Agreements" (9 July 2020) <www.acm.nl/sites/default/files/documents/2020-07/sustainability-agreements%5B1%5D.pdf>. The guidelines take the position that for agreements that aim to prevent or limit any obvious environmental damage and efficiently promote compliance with a binding international or national standard ("environmental damage agreements"), it should be possible to take into account benefits for others, not just the customers in the relevant market. This is because those customers (as a group) already sufficiently benefit from the agreement as members of society. For other sustainability agreements, any benefits must "fully compensate" relevant customers for the anticompetitive harm they suffer as a result of the sustainability agreement. This means that such agreements will have to attach sufficient value to the benefits to offset the harm (paras 40–44).

This frames its SIEC assessment and provides the reference point for market shares and calculation of concentration levels.[42]

Existing case law already shows environmental factors at play when it comes to market definition, because sustainability features are becoming more important to consumers. For example, although it did not need to conclude on market definition, in *DEMB/Mondelez/Charger OPCO*, the Commission considered a market segment for non-conventional coffee (organic, fair trade and other certified coffees) v conventional coffee.[43] Evidence submitted to the Commission indicated that some consumers did not view the two as substitutable given that non-conventional coffee fulfilled different needs, including the need for an environmentally sustainable coffee or one that contributed to sustainable development. In *Aleris/Novelis*, the Commission was concerned that the combined entity would have very high market shares and control a very significant proportion of the manufacturing capacity for aluminium automotive body sheets in the EEA, meaning higher prices and reduced choice for customers. Of particular relevance to its conclusion on a separate product market was that these sheets were used in the production of lighter, more fuel-efficient cars.[44]

The Commission concludes many merger investigations, sometimes even in phase 2, without making a finding on market definition. This gives it significant scope to drill down into market segments that are sustainability related even if they do not (yet) form a properly defined antitrust market and to assess potential competitive harm in these segments if required.

3. Blocking "dirty" deals – establishing an SIEC

Beyond market definition, existing Commission practice makes it hard for sustainability concerns to be given much weight (as discussed above). Recent deals

---

42 Horizontal Merger Guidelines (n 32), para 11.
43 *DEMB/Mondelez/Charger OPCO* (Case M.7292) Commission Decision notified under document C(2015) 3000, [2015] OJ C376/7, para 7.3.
44 *Aleris/Novelis* (Case M.9076) Commission Decision [2019] OJ C121/1. [The US Department of Justice explained that the arbitrator in *Novelis/Aleris* found that "there are substantial differences in the physical properties of aluminum (as compared to steel), such that an automotive engineer designing a car with particular weight, performance, safety specifications, and target retail price is unlikely to view steel and other materials as full functional substitutes for aluminum for the various car parts being designed." *United States of America v Novelis, Inc. and Aleris Corporation*, Competitive Impact Statement No: 1:19-cv-02033-CAB (12 May 2020) <www.justice.gov/atr/case-document/file/1276101/download>. The US agencies have also considered other product characteristics, such organic v conventional, as part of product market definition, e.g. *In the Matter of Post Holdings, Inc.*, Complaint, FTC Docket No 9388 (19 December 2019), <www.ftc.gov/system/files/documents/cases/d09388posttreehousecomplaint.pdf> and *United States of America v Danone SA and The WhiteWave Foods Company*, Competitive Impact Statement No: 1:17-cv-0592-KBJ (13 April 2017) <www.justice.gov/atr/case-document/file/957591/download>. See Eric Paroche and Céline Verney, "Commitments: The European Commission clears a merger, subject to several commitments, between two global manufacturers of aluminium flat rolled products (*Novelis/Aleris*)" (2019) Concurrences N° 1–2020 Art N° 93342, 118.

including *Bayer/Monsanto*,[45] *Siemens/Alstom*[46] and *Dow/Dupont*[47] have demonstrated the Commission's unwillingness to block a deal where (sufficient) harm to the competitive process cannot be established, but where there are (arguably) wider harms to society (taking into account broader social factors such as the impact on the environment or jobs). Changing the existing approach to recognise that harm to the environment that will not be addressed by the market should be recognised as a type of competitive harm would be a significant step. But it is arguably in line with the European Green Deal agenda as well as with evolving attitudes to consumer harm in the antitrust context to include broader social goods like data privacy[48] and employment.[49]

Take the following examples:

i. Two firms plan to merge. Internal documents indicate that they anticipate realising economies of scale that will allow them to expand production and reduce cost per unit. This will enable them to lower prices to their customers, but the expansion will result in a significant increase in their combined emissions. The evidence suggests that "cleaner" rivals will not have scope to reduce their own prices because their greener technology is more expensive than that used by the merged entity. The externality (carbon cost of increased emissions) is higher overall than the reduction in price offered to customers of the merged entity and "clean" rivals may not be able to match the lower prices (which do not fully reflect the environmental cost).

ii. A "sustainability killer acquisition" scenario: A and T compete to produce widgets. A has a traditional (polluting) production facility, T has developed green technology, ensuring its production facilities are carbon neutral. T does not yet compete with A on price because the green tech is more expensive than A's "dirty" tech. A plans to acquire T and maintain a niche presence in green tech, but will not roll out the

---

45 *Bayer/Monsanto* (Case M.8084) Commission Decision [2018] OJ C459/8.
46 *Siemens/Alstom* (Case M.8677) Commission Decision [2019] OJ C300/5; Jean-Mathieu Cot, "Prohibition: The European Competition prohibits a merger between the two main European players in the railway signalling systems and very high-speed train industries (*Siemens/Alstom*)" (2019) Concurrences N° 4–2019, Art N° 92344, 125–128.
47 *Dow/DuPont* (Case M.7932) Commission Decision [2017] OJ C353/9; Jean-François Bellis and Valérie Lefever, "Commitments: The European Commission, following an in-depth review, clears a merger between two American groups active in crop protection and seeds, subject to structural commitments aiming at maintaining price competition and innovation for pesticides (*Dow/DuPont*)" (2017) Concurrences N° 1–2018 Art N° 86220, 121–123.
48 See the German Bundeskartellamt's decision that Facebook is abusing its dominant position on the social networks market by not providing users with a choice about how it uses data generated outside of Facebook (Decision of 23 June 2020 – KVR 69/19 – No 080/2020).
49 See the Commission's plans to introduce regulations or guidance to ensure that competition rules do not prevent self-employed platform workers from collectively bargaining with their employers ("Competition: The European Commission launches a process to address the issue of collective bargaining for the self-employed" Press Release (IP/20/1237, 30 June 2020) https://ec.europa.eu/commission/presscorner/detail/en/IP_20_1237).

green tech to the rest of A's production facilities nor will it licence the tech more widely in the market. This effectively prevents the expansion of T's innovative technology to the detriment of consumers and the Commission could (and should) prohibit the transaction.

These are scenarios where it is possible that cleaner rivals will be able to persuade enough consumers who care sufficiently about the negative impacts of the merged entity's product to switch away from it. If so, then there is no need to block the merger because competition (on sustainability parameters) will work effectively (although of course a government may take a more interventionist stance, discussed further below). But we know that consumers may not perceive future costs to be as large as they actually are (hyperbolic discounting), have status quo biases which make them reluctant to try new products or may believe that choices made at an individual level cannot make a difference.[50] And this means that where sustainability factors come into play, consumers may be less effective at curbing harmful effects. In these circumstances, it may be appropriate for a competition authority to consider environmental impact as a negative, weighed against the possible benefits of short-run lower costs and, where appropriate, impose remedies that address the competitive harm.

4. Clearing green deals – efficiencies and beyond

In this section we discuss transactions that may result in harm to the competitive process, but which have environmental benefits that could potentially outweigh that harm.

A. *Building an effective efficiencies argument*

Under the Horizontal Merger Guidelines, efficiencies brought about by a merger may "counteract the effects on competition and in particular the potential harm to consumers that it might otherwise have". Thus, the Commission can take into account the factors mentioned in Article 2(1)(b) EUMR, including the "development of technical and economic progress provided that it is to the consumers' advantage and does not form an obstacle to competition".

To be accepted, efficiency claims must satisfy three conditions.[51] They must: benefit consumers, be merger-specific and be verifiable.

Benefit to consumers

The first criterion (the need to benefit consumers) goes to the heart of the debate about competition policy and sustainability: which consumers must benefit from the efficiencies, how and when?

---

50 NYU Institute of Policy Integrity, "Experts on the economics of climate change expressed higher levels of concern about climate change impacts than the general public, when asked identical survey questions" (Expert Consensus Report 2015) <www.edf.org/sites/default/files/expertconsensusreport.pdf>.

51 Horizontal Merger Guidelines (n 32), paras 78–88.

To date, efficiency claims in general in merger cases have been met with deep scepticism by the Commission[52] (and other competition authorities[53]).

Indeed, at the time of writing there has been *no* case where the Commission has approved an otherwise problematic transaction on the basis of efficiencies offsetting the alleged harm and no merger case where the Commission has attempted to quantify environmental efficiencies.[54] This is significant: factoring in environmental factors into an efficiency analysis will require the Commission to reconsider its historical approach to efficiencies in general. In our view, recognition of a functional efficiency defence in the merger control context could not be confined only to sustainability efficiencies, but would need to apply across the board. The overriding importance of the environmental agenda could provide the catalyst for wider reform.[55]

That said, there are a few (rather old) cases in the context of horizontal cooperation agreements. These have seen the Commission and national competition authorities employ relatively narrow methodologies to quantify environmental benefits, focusing on attributing monetary values to short-term environmental effects[56] (which at the very least may fail to take into account benefits to be realised over time) or the willingness to pay of direct consumers within the relevant affected markets only, notwithstanding the reality that many more consumers (outside of the relevant markets) would likely benefit.

And, similarly, the focus in the Horizontal Merger Guidelines (albeit with an emerging set of cases on innovation competition) is on lower prices achieved through cost savings in production or distribution, which are then passed on to purchasers of that product.[57] Accordingly, reductions in variable costs are more

---

52 For example, in *Dow/DuPont* (n 48), the Commission rejected the claimed efficiencies on the basis that they "... depend[ed] on future strategic decisions by the companies and on detailed knowledge of companies' assets and capabilities and of the function of the industry and its dynamics". More recently, in *Siemens/Alstom* (n 47), the Commission rejected the parties' claimed synergies as they were not provable nor merger-specific.

53 For example, the German Bundeskartellamt's rejection of efficiency claims in *Miba/Zollern* (January 2019). The appeal by the parties was subsequently rejected by the *Oberlandesgericht*, the Düsseldorf Court of Appeal, in August 2020 (n 4).

54 In *Aurubis/Metallo* (Case M.9409) Commission Decision [2019] OJ C356/7, the parties claimed efficiencies relating to additional metal recovery and environmental benefits. The Commission found ([844] ff) that, while some of the efficiencies claimed by the parties were "at least a possibility", the evidence to substantiate those claims was not sufficiently strong to dispel the Commission's concerns and, further, that the claims were not verifiable or likely to arise in a timely fashion.

55 In particular, if the CJEU upholds the General Court's finding in *Hutchison/O2* (Case T-399/16 *CK Telecoms UK Investments v Commission* EU:T:2020:217).

56 See, for example the Commission's approach in *CECED* (Case IV.F.1/36.718) Commission Decision [1999] OJ L187/47, where it compared the increased price of energy efficient washing machines against the benefits of lower electricity consumption; or the ACM's analysis of higher electricity prices from closing coal plants against the benefits of lower emissions: <www.acm.nl/sites/default/files/old_publication/publicaties/12082_acm-analysis-of-closing-down-5-coal-power-plants-as-part-of-ser-energieakkoord.pdf>.

57 Horizontal Merger Guidelines (n 32), para 79.

---

likely to be relevant to the assessment of efficiencies than fixed costs because they are more likely to be passed on to consumers.

But a merger where the deal rationale is environmental may not result in any cost saving at all. In fact, quite the opposite. Take the following example. Acquirer (A) intends to acquire Target (T), a competitor which has developed technology that has enabled T to reduce its emissions by 15%. At least in the short term, A's cost base will increase as it incurs the costs of modifying its existing production facilities to integrate T's technology, and possibly in the longer term if the new technology has higher running costs.

Even if A were able to achieve some cost-saving as a result of the merger (perhaps the technology makes the operation of its plants more efficient, as well as reducing emissions), this is a reduction in A's fixed cost, not its variable cost.[58] Under the approach in the Horizontal Merger Guidelines, this is less likely to be passed on to consumers (and therefore given less weight in the assessment of efficiencies).

This example demonstrates that if the Commission focuses on whether the transaction will raise prices to A's or T's customers, there may be no benefit from the merger for the customers of the merged firm. But whether consumers overall are better or worse off as a result of the merger requires the Commission to look at the broader context.

As argued elsewhere, and in particular by Simon Holmes,[59] the notion of consumer benefit can be interpreted broadly to encompass the interest of all consumers in the environment and in reversing the damaging effects of climate change.[60] Increased consideration of benefits not directly related to price is an area that the authorities already emphasise in relation to, for example, effects on innovation – an issue highly relevant in the sustainability context. If authorities are willing to consider changes in quality-adjusted prices (to account for changes in quality), why should they not also consider changes in social-cost – adjusted prices (improvement in environmental quality being an improvement in social cost).

---

58 That said, it would be wrong to assume that an environmental cost would never be "priced in". There are schemes which are intended to internalise the environmental social cost, for example, through emission rights. If a merger were to lead to significant reductions in carbon emissions and as a result the merged firm would need fewer carbon emission rights, that represents a reduction in variable cost which should be considered.

59 Simon Holmes, "Climate Change is an Existential Threat: Competition Law must be part of the solution and not part of the problem" (26 September 2019), draft available at <www.law.ox.ac.uk/sites/files/oxlaw/simon_holmes.pdf>.

60 In the UK, merger control law uses the concept of "Relevant Customer Benefits" and under the Enterprise Act 2002, s 30(4), the CMA is able to take into account benefits to consumers in markets other than where the SLC (substantial lessening of competition) is found as well as benefits to future consumers. See further Simon Holmes, "Climate Change, Sustainability and Competition Law in the UK" (University of Oxford working paper CCLP(L)51) <www.law.ox.ac.uk/sites/files/oxlaw/cclp_working_paper_cclpl51.pdf>.

As mentioned above, this follows the very welcome approach proposed by the ACM, and endorsed by the Commission,[61] in the context of sustainability cooperation agreements to explicitly acknowledge that the relevant benefits to be considered are those accruing to the whole of society and not only to consumers of the specific product.[62]

And indeed, quantification of environmental costs and benefits has developed over recent years, for example in Europe through the EU carbon emissions permit scheme or the Taxonomy Regulation, which sets out an EU-wide classification system to identify those economic activities which are considered "environmentally sustainable", and to provide technical benchmarks against which dealmakers and authorities can more clearly measure the impact of sustainability projects.[63] The EU is also considering introducing its own ESG disclosure requirements. While there is still much more work to be done to improve the comprehensiveness, reliability and comparability of the data being provided, efforts to develop appropriate and usable metrics are certainly headed in the right direction. A challenge, of course, is to ascertain where benefits might be felt and, importantly, to ensure that polluting activities are not merely shifted out of the EU to somewhere else in the world.

While a detailed consideration of how the quantification of environmental benefits could be done is beyond the scope of this paper, it is undeniably possible, and the Commission should be (and is[64]) considering how this could be done in practice. Once developed, it will be essential to give clear guidance on its methodology.

Merger specificity

For efficiencies to be recognised they must be a "direct consequence" of the merger and cannot be achieved through less anticompetitive alternatives (for example via a non-structural change to the market, like a commercial arrangement).[65] This is similar to the requirement in Article 101(3) TFEU that restrictions on competition must be "no more restrictive than necessary". In practice, it requires the Commission to conduct a proportionality assessment, for example, whether

---

61 Commission, "Statement on ACM public consultation on sustainability guidelines" (Antitrust News, 9 July 2020) <https://ec.europa.eu/competition/antitrust/news.html>.

62 ACM, "Draft Guidelines: Sustainability Agreements" (n 42).

63 From 1 January 2022, the Taxonomy Regulation will apply to its first two environmental objectives which focus on emissions (climate change adaptation and climate change mitigation). From 1 January 2023, it will have a wider remit and apply to its remaining four environmental objectives (sustainable use and protection of water and marine resources, transition to a circular economy, pollution prevention and control, and protection and restoration of biodiversity and ecosystems), once the relevant technical screening criteria have been developed. For more detail see Linklaters, "EU Taxonomy Regulation: What does it do and what happens next?" (*Linklaters*, 22 September 2020) <www.linklaters.com/en/insights/blogs/linkingesg/2020/september/eu-taxonomy-regulation-what-does-it-do-and-what-happens-next>.

64 Hellenic Competition Commission "Sustainable development and competition law: Towards a Green Growth regulatory osmosis" (n 41).

65 Horizontal Merger Guidelines (n 32), para 85.

licensing emissions-reducing technology would result in a less restrictive outcome than the acquisition of a company developing such technology.

Verifiability

The ability to verify efficiency claims is also clearly required – merging parties cannot simply assert that a transaction will have sustainability benefits without providing evidence to support their claims. As the sustainability agenda hits the mainstream, corporate reporting on sustainability factors is becoming more common and, therefore, easier for competition authorities to properly judge whether a transaction will offer meaningful progress on the environment that cannot be achieved through other means.[66] However, as there is still no single EU or global mandatory standard for reporting on environmental and other sustainability data, comparability and inconsistency are still an issue – one that the asset management world is only too aware of as they prepare to comply with the requirements in the Sustainable Finance Disclosure Regulation.

For both merger specificity and verifiability, the balancing exercise should be aligned with the approach in Article 101(3) TFEU for consistency. Moreover, the standard of proof should be consistent with the standard of proof for establishing competitive harm (rather than as currently, requiring a much higher standard).

B. *Employing a dynamic assessment*

Although an efficiency argument may seem to be the natural home for sustainability arguments in the merger control context, it is not the only way to factor them into the analysis. In contrast to Article 101 TFEU, Article 2 EUMR does not require a two-step analysis that first assesses the extent of any competitive harm resulting from the merger and then assesses whether this harm is outweighed by the benefits of the merger. Rather, sustainability benefits can be taken into account in concluding that there is no SIEC in the first place as part of the "overall assessment of the foreseeable impact of the merger in the light of the relevant factors and conditions".[67] This is why it is so important for merging parties to articulate clearly and credibly sustainability arguments as part of the deal rationale, as supported by their internal business documents (see next section).

Taking into account changes in consumer preferences, even if there is a price effect as a result of the merger, such price increases would arguably not constitute a cognisable anticompetitive harm if customers are willing to pay more for "cleaner" products.[68] Surveys of customer groups may be required to establish whether this is the case.

---

66 See, for example, the World Economic Forum's Consultation Draft of proposed common standards for corporate disclosure of ESG factors (January 2020) <www.wlrk.com/docs/WEFIBCESGMetricsDiscussionPaper.pdf>.
67 Horizontal Merger Guidelines (n 32), para 13.
68 Recent research by IBM found that 77% of consumers seek products that are sustainable and environmentally responsible. 72% of consumers that consider sustainability/environmentally responsible products

5. The important role of internal documents

As with all arguments that are put before merger authorities, in order to run a successful sustainability argument to achieve a merger clearance (or a prohibition for complainants), internal business documents are key.

Arguing that the deal rationale is based on rolling out clean technology to existing plants is doomed to failure when senior executives have had email discussions about killing off that same technology because it is a competitive threat. And arguing that the key rationale for your deal is to reduce emissions through closing down non-essential facilities will not take you far if your deal documents only talk about rationalising capacity in the hands of a few players and not the environmental benefits.

A company's existing ESG record could also be scrutinised. A deal that will allow a company to reduce packaging waste by 1% could be a substantial efficiency. But such claims will likely be met with scepticism that they will be realised where that same company has not yet rolled out basic recycling facilities at its headquarters, which could allow it to reduce waste by 3% (without an associated competition restriction). The increased levels of ESG reporting will provide important context.

V. Acceptability of Sustainability Remedies

Where the Commission finds that a merger will result in an SIEC, the parties may offer remedies which resolve the Commission's concerns and allow the merger to be cleared.[69] Remedies must "eliminate the competition concerns entirely" and be "capable of being implemented effectively within a short period of time".[70] In principle, a remedy aimed at eliminating an environmental harm should be possible where that environmental harm forms part of the competition concern and remedying the competitive harm will also address the environmental harm.

Sustainability concerns played into the remedies package offered in *Novelis/Aleris*.[71] As noted above, the Commission was concerned that the merger would result in reduced choice of suppliers and higher prices for aluminium automotive body sheets, a particular concern because of the use of that product to develop more fuel-efficient cars. This traditional competitive analysis was resolved through

---

to be very important are willing to pay a premium of 35% (Karl Haller, Jim Lee and Jane Cheung, "Meet the 2020 consumers driving change" (IBM Research Insights 2020) <www.ibm.com/downloads/cas/EXK4XKX8>, figs 3–4).

69 EUMR, arts 6(2) and 8(2).
70 Commission notice on remedies acceptable under Council Regulation (EC) No 139/2004 and under Commission Regulation (EC) No 802/2004 (2008/C 267/01), [9].
71 *Novelis/Aleris* (Case M.9076) Commission Decision [2019] OJ C70/12.

a traditional remedy: divestment of Aleris' entire aluminium automotive body sheet business in Europe.[72]

However, where the Commission adopts a less traditional competition analysis, for example by factoring in the cost of carbon and/or considering a broader concept of consumer welfare, the legal framework still requires the remedy to eliminate the "competition concerns" (and not any harm – environmental or otherwise – that may result from the deal). The prerequisite for reflecting a sustainability agenda into a remedies strategy is, therefore, that the Commission can articulate sustainability harms within the competition framework. As explained above, this is possible. For example, if the Commission were to take into account the carbon "price" when assessing the competitive effect, then a remedy that would reduce emissions or counter any negative effects (e.g. carbon off-setting) could be appropriate. Where the Commission is concerned about competition problems relating to a particular category of customers (perhaps those involved in the development of more environmentally friendly products) a remedy to supply those customers on no less favourable terms than other customers or on fair, reasonable and non-discriminatory terms could be a potential remedy.

Sustainability remedies are more likely to fall into the category of behavioural remedies. The Commission has stated that structural commitments are preferable, but nevertheless will accept behavioural commitments where they are capable of addressing the SIEC.[73]

What would be more controversial, and arguably outside the scope of the legal framework, would be for the Commission to accept a "green remedy" that overall makes a merger less damaging to the environment, but without articulating how this resolves an identified competition concern.[74] This limitation means that it

---

72 At the time of writing the full text decision is unavailable, so it is not possible to assess whether the fact that this case was relevant to sustainability resulted in special treatment, although it is notable that the use of the body sheets for fuel-efficient cars was specifically highlighted in the press release.

73 Remedies Notice, para 15. See e.g. *Dentsply/Sirona* (Case M.7822) Commission Decision [2016] OJ C12/5, where the Commission required the parties to extend their existing licensing agreements with competing block suppliers until 2026. In *Qualcomm/NXP Semiconductors* (Case M.8306) Commission Decision [2018] OJ C143/6, the Commission imposed behavioural remedies relating to the interoperability of the merged companies' products with competitors and access to patents under fair and reasonable terms. See also Margrethe Vestager, "Competition and the Digital Economy" (speech at OECD/G7 conference, Paris, 3 June 2019) <https://wayback.archive-it.org/12090/20191129200956/https://ec.europa.eu/commission/commissioners/2014-2019/vestager/announcements/competition-and-digital-economy_en>.

74 Although a very extensive remedy that addresses environmental concerns could potentially be offered by parties if they wanted to avoid their transaction being referred for a more extensive Phase 2 investigation. At Phase 1, the Commission can decide under EUMR, art 6(2) that the remedy has removed "serious doubts" as to whether the concentration is compatible with the internal market. This means that remedies offered to avoid a Phase 2 investigation can be more extensive than those that would be required at the end of a Phase 2 investigation.
Arguably there may be more scope to use remedies under UK law where the CMA is "required to decide whether action should be taken to remedy, mitigate or prevent the SLC *or any adverse effects resulting from the SLC*" (emphasis added). See further, Simon Holmes, "Climate Change, Sustainability and Competition Law in the UK" (n 61).

may not always be possible to design a remedy that will counter negative environmental effects of a merger. Similarly, limitations as to jurisdiction (given the global nature of environmental harms) may mean that an effective remedy cannot be identified.

VI. Sustainability as a Public Policy Objective

1. Greater state interventionism as part of the green recovery

This paper does not contend that any environmental harm caused by a merger can or should result in the Commission prohibiting the transaction (or extracting a green remedy). Indeed, we would expect this to be rare (indeed prohibition decisions are generally rare[75]). There will be circumstances where environmental harm cannot be expressed in terms of a harm to competition (or at least there is enough uncertainty about what will happen that the relevant standard of proof cannot be reached). In these circumstances, the appropriate role of a competition authority would be to approve the merger. Similarly, the authors consider that there are limitations on the extent to which merger reviews can (and should) be used as a means of ensuring that M&A has an environmental upside. However, between these two extremes sustainability considerations can play a role in merger review.

Beyond the merger control framework, environmental protection becomes a public policy question. State interventionism in M&A is increasing generally and, given the unprecedented scale of state support granted to address the impact of COVID-19, we expect this to continue. There are several potential ways for governments to intervene in the M&A process on sustainability grounds.

A. Blocking "dirty" deals to protect legitimate public interests under Article 21(4) EUMR

When a merger falls for review by the Commission, Article 21(4) EUMR allows Member States to take appropriate measures to protect specific "legitimate public interests" besides competition, provided that they are compatible with the general principles and other provisions of EU law.

There is no explicit reference to sustainability or environmental protection as a legitimate interest under Article 21(4),[76] although it might be possible (albeit rather a stretch) to construe them as falling within one of the three existing public interests – most likely public security (e.g. security of sustainable energy supplies).

In order to achieve greater clarity, Article 21(4) could be amended to provide environmental protection as a fourth express legitimate interest. Alternatively,

---

75 As at the time of writing, the Commission has prohibited a total of six mergers in the last five years.

76 Three types of public interests are expressly specified in EUMR, art 21(4): public security (including interests related to defence policy), plurality of the media and prudential rules.

a Member State could apply to the Commission to recognise environmental protection as a legitimate interest.

However, Article 21(4) has important limitations. It can only be used as an instrument to block "dirty" deals which have been approved (conditionally or unconditionally) by the Commission on competition grounds. It does not enable governments to push through deals which have otherwise been prohibited, but which would result in significant environmental benefits (e.g. the *Miba/Zollern* fact pattern) although arguably this situation could be addressed by reforming the approach to efficiencies.

B. *Public interest considerations as part of national merger reviews*

To the extent that a merger falls outside the EUMR, it may fall for review by one or more Member States. Many national regimes allow for government intervention on public interest grounds in a much wider range of scenarios than (currently) at EU level.

As discussed above, the most striking example of intervention on environmental grounds is the approval in August 2019 by the German Minister of Economy of *Miba/Zollern*,[77] a deal which had been blocked by the Federal Cartel Office on competition grounds, but which was approved on the basis that "know-how and potential for innovation for the energy turnaround and sustainability" are paramount public interests.

Public interest criteria have been introduced in an increasing number of competition regimes, most notably in South Africa, where several public interest factors are now central to the merger assessment.[78]

We also note here the UK's approach regarding *Lloyds/HBOS*[79] at the height of the 2008 global financial crisis to create a new "stability of the UK financial system" public interest under the UK merger control regime which permitted the secretary of state to override the UK competition authorities' objection to the merger.[80] While clearly rare, this could similarly – and relatively straightforwardly – be done to address the climate crisis.

C. *Complementary policy tools*

It is beyond the reach of this paper to consider in detail complementary policy tools, including state aid policy, to achieve Green Deal objectives. However, one recent policy trend is notable in this context. One far-reaching consequence of the global pandemic has been to turbocharge moves by governments to introduce

---

77   *Miba/Zollern*, subsequently rejected on appeal by the Düsseldorf Court of Appeal in August 2020 (n 4).
78   Competition Act 89 of 1998 (as amended), No. 1392 of 1998.
79   Anticipated acquisition of HBOS plc by Lloyds TSB Group plc (31 October 2008).
80   The UK Secretary of State can modify section 58 of the Enterprise Act 2002. Previously, it had only specified national security and newspaper and media public interest considerations.

or strengthen foreign investment (FI) controls to protect vulnerable strategic assets from opportunistic (predatory) foreign takeovers.[81]

For its part, the Commission has urged Member States without existing FI controls to introduce them.[82] As for portfolio investments which do not constitute FI (and therefore cannot be screened using Member State FI controls), the Commission has advised Member States to screen them instead for compliance with the Treaty provisions on free movement of capital – citing the most relevant exception as "public policy or public security" under Article 65 TFEU to ensure, for example, security of supply "in the energy field".[83] It is not a huge leap to think (similar to the above logic regarding Article 21(4) EUMR) that a Member State could impose restrictions upon a foreign investment that risks security of supply of a sustainable energy source. Although the focus to date has been on technological sovereignty and domestic government protecting public health and essential goods and services providers, similar motivations may yet emerge in relation to domestic sustainability innovators, given the growing driver of sustainability as a competitive parameter.

VII. Conclusion

Merger reviews tend to be asymmetric, with innovation effects and other non-price factors being taken into account as (additional) reasons for the Commission to block a deal or to require remedies (for example in the context of perceived killer acquisitions), but not as reasons to clear an otherwise problematic deal.

We do not expect the outcome of a merger review to turn on environmental considerations alone. Conventional factors like concentration measures and barriers to entry will of course continue to be important. But we do expect environmental factors to play an increasingly important role in the analysis – both by the Commission and by Member States on public policy grounds – in line with ambitious net-zero targets and green policy objectives, the reality that

---

81 For example, procedural thresholds have been lowered to capture a wider range of investments via recent reforms in France, Germany, Italy, the UK and Spain. Their focus has been predominantly on technology and protective equipment. The UK government introduced immediate changes to its foreign investment regime in June 2020 to capture transactions involving UK companies involved in the pandemic response (e.g. vaccine development, PPE production, internet services and food supply chain) (Enterprise Act 2002 (Specification of Additional Section 58 Consideration) Order 2020). As a second step, the government intends to bring three additional technology sectors (AI, cryptographic authentication technology and advanced materials) within the purview of the reduced jurisdictional thresholds introduced in June 2018 for the military/dual-use, computer processing and quantum technology sectors (Enterprise Act 2002 (Share of Supply Test) (Amendment) Order 2020 and Enterprise Act 2002 (Turnover Test) (Amendment) Order 2020 (which will be subject to the negative procedure)).

82 Commission, "Guidance to the Member States concerning foreign direct investment and free movement of capital from third countries, and the protection of Europe's strategic assets, ahead of the application of Regulation (EU) 2019/452 [2020] (FDI Screening Regulation)" (C(2020) 1981 final) <https://trade.ec.europa.eu/doclib/docs/2020/march/tradoc_158676.pdf>.

83 FDI Screening Regulation, 3.

in many markets players will increasingly compete on sustainability factors, and the evolving concept of consumer welfare to capture wider, longer-term benefits. Beyond the merger control process, in appropriate cases Member States may decide to use their FI control powers to intervene

Ultimately, the driver of any expansion of merger review criteria will be dealmakers bringing more green deals for review by the Commission, testing its approach on critical aspects like quantification of environmental efficiencies and, hopefully, providing clearly articulated guidance in published merger decisions. This is vital to give much-needed clarity about its assessment framework which, assuming it is supportive, will provide encouragement to merging parties to pursue their own green investment agendas.

Can Environmental Interests Trump
An EUMR Decision?

Alec Burnside, Marjolein De Backer and Delphine Strohl[*]
Dechert LLP

Sustainability[1] has seen a surge in interest from the antitrust circuit in the last couple of years.[2] However, the focus has been primarily on issues of industrial cooperation. Sustainability in merger control has been much less debated, and indeed at first sight seems less fertile ground than Article 101 of the Treaty on the Functioning of the European Union (TFEU), since it lacks any counterpart to Article 101(3) TFEU under which restrictions of competition may be outweighed by other considerations: the operative provisions of the European Merger Regulation[3] (EUMR) focus narrowly on a transaction's impact on the competitive dynamics of the internal market.[4]

---

[*] Alec Burnside is a partner, Marjolein De Backer a senior associate and Delphine Strohl an associate, all at Dechert LLP in Brussels. They act as pro bono advisers to the Fair Trade Advocacy Office in Brussels, in particular in relation to issues of sustainability and antitrust.

1 United Nations (UN) Resolution 66/288, "The future we want" A/RES/66/288 (27 July 2012), para 4, defines sustainable development as encompassing the following overarching objectives and essential requirements: "poverty eradication, changing unsustainable and promoting sustainable patterns of consumption and production and protecting and managing the natural resource base of economic and social development" Full text: <www.un.org/ga/search/view_doc.asp?symbol=A/RES/66/288&Lang=E>.

2 See, notably, Margrethe Vestager, "Competition and sustainability" (GCLC/Fairtrade Conference on Sustainability and Competition Policy, Brussels, 24 October 2019) <https://wayback.archive-it. org/12090/20191129200524/https://ec.europa.eu/commission/commissioners/2014-2019/vestager/ announcements/competition-and-sustainability_en>; see also Margrethe Vestager, "The Green Deal and competition policy" (Renew Webinar, 22 September 2020) <https://ec.europa.eu/commission/commis-sioners/2019-2024/vestager/announcements/green-deal-and-competition-policy_en>.

3 Council Regulation (EC) 139/2004 of 20 January 2004 on the control of concentrations between undertakings (the EC Merger Regulation) [2004] OJ L24/1 (EUMR).

4 EUMR, art 2.

The European Commission's (Commission) mandate is indeed limited to preserving undistorted competition. Published guidance and decisional practice confirms the Commission's exclusive focus on the significant impediment to effective competition (SIEC) test, and that a transaction's positive or negative contribution to wider environmental and social goals is irrelevant for purposes of the EUMR (see section I).

It happens of course that the Commission encounters environmentally friendly or sustainable products in the course of merger reviews. For instance, it previously recognised a separate market for organic and/or Fairtrade bananas as opposed to conventional bananas.[5] This is however purely a function of the economic test set out in the EUMR, reflecting the fact that sustainable products may sometimes be seen as distinct from conventional products from a consumer or supplier standpoint. Aside though from specific cases where there is indeed a separate market for sustainable products, we will explore whether it would be possible to infuse more sustainability into the SIEC test (see Section 2).

Complementing that discussion, we will explore whether Member States could rely on other bases to act upon sustainability concerns within the framework of the EUMR. Notwithstanding the Commission's exclusive jurisdiction over transactions with an EU dimension, some very narrowly circumscribed circumstances – so called "legitimate interests" – can be invoked by Member States to impose conditions on, or even block, a transaction otherwise under the Commission's sole jurisdiction. We explore whether Member States could invoke sustainability as a "legitimate interest" (see section III). We address in particular the EU's increased awareness of the risks posed to the Union and the security of its citizens by climate and environmental challenges, and lessons learned from merger control in other jurisdictions. Notably we explore whether the setting up of an EU framework for the screening of foreign direct investments could influence in time the notion of legitimate interest.

I. The EUMR's Standard of Review – SIEC Test

Although DG COMP's assessment of mergers must take place "within the general framework of the achievement of the fundamental objectives referred to in Article 2 of the Treaty establishing the European Community and Article 2 of the Treaty on European Union",[6] which include e.g. the respect for human rights, the substantive test is strictly focused on competition.[7] The EUMR's objective is to ensure that competition in the EU internal market is not distorted and

---

5   See e.g. *Chiquita brands international/Fyffes* (Case COMP/M.7220) Commission decision C(2014) 7268 final [2015] OJ C33/1, [73].
6   EUMR, recital 23.
7   OECD, "Note by the European Union: Public interest considerations in merger control" DAF/COMP/WP3/WD(2016)11 (14 – 15 June 2016) <www.oecd.org/officialdocuments/publicdisplaydocumentpdf/?cote=DAF/COMP/WP3/WD(2016)11&docLanguage=En>, [4].

reflects a policy based on an "open market economy with free competition".[8] The substantive test is an economic one and assesses whether a proposed transaction would significantly impede effective competition in the internal market or a substantial part thereof, in particular as a result of the creation or strengthening of a dominant position, the so-called SIEC test.[9]

Indeed it is worth recalling that the original Merger Regulation from 1989 more explicitly required the Commission to "place its appraisal within the general framework of the achievement of the fundamental objectives referred to in Article 2 of the Treaty, *including that of strengthening the Community's economic and social cohesion*, referred to in Article 130a".[10] The highlighted words were a nod in the direction of Member States which had wanted to soften the sole pursuit of ensuring competition. They were though no more than a nod: the recital had no corresponding operative articles in the Regulation. Nothing in the original or amended Regulation empowers the Commission to take account of non-competition aspects such as climate change, the environment, employment, human rights or sustainable development goals, for example.

Despite the recent debates about "industrial policy",[11] European Champions and the foreign subsidies consultation paper,[12] the EUMR's conception is purely economic, without regard to any social values, certainly not to sustainability or more narrowly environmental or climate challenges. DG COMP indeed strongly rejected the notion of basing itself on non-competition grounds in its *Bayer/Monsanto* decision.[13]

The SIEC test is admittedly not directed solely at price, but includes "the interests of the intermediate and ultimate consumers, and the development of technical and economic progress", i.e. notions of product quality, product choice and innovation. In particular the notion of "technical and economic progress" is a deliberate echo of Article 101(3) TFEU, as emphasised in declaratory notes adopted together with the original 1989 Regulation:[14] "The Commission considers that the concept of technical and economic progress

---

8   EUMR, recitals 2 – 6 and 24.
9   EUMR, art 2(2) and 2(3).
10 Council Regulation (EEC) 4064/89 on the control of concentration between undertakings [1989] OJ L395/1 (emphasis added).
11 See e.g. Commission, "A New Industrial Strategy for Europe" (Communication) COM/2020/102 final; see also Council of the European Union, "A recovery advancing the transition towards a more dynamic, resilient and competitive European industry" (Council conclusions, 16 November 2020) <https://data.consilium.europa.eu/doc/document/ST-13004-2020-INIT/en/pdf>.
12 Commission, *White paper on levelling the playing field as regards foreign subsidies* (COM(2020) 253 final) <https://ec.europa.eu/competition/international/overview/foreign_subsidies_white_paper.pdf>.
13 See *Bayer/Monsanto* (Case COMP/M.8084) Commission decision C(2018) 1709 final [2018] OJ C459/10, [3010].
14 See "Notes on Council Regulation (EEC) 4064/89" in Commission, *Merger control law in the European Union* (Commission 1998) <https://ec.europa.eu/competition/mergers/legislation/notes_reg4064_89_en.pdf>.

must be understood in the light of the principles enshrined in Article 85(3) of the Treaty, as interpreted by the case law of the Court of Justice." But whereas Article 85 EEC (now 101 TFEU) explicitly allowed such progress to protect the agreement in question from nullity, there is no equivalent in the EUMR. It will be recalled that, at the time of the adoption of the original Merger Regulation in 1989, the Commission still exercised the power of individual exemption under (then) Article 85(3) EEC and Regulation 17. The omission of any corresponding power under the Merger Regulation was very much deliberate, as is the absence of any political override equivalent to the German *Ministererlaubnis*.

So there is no option for **DG COMP** to adopt a decision purely on the basis of non-competition law considerations, nor any explicit mechanism allowing a SIEC to be disregarded in the name of the Treaty objectives invoked in recital 23. The only remaining hope would be for sustainability to be weighed within the assessment as to whether any SIEC would arise.

II. Sustainability as a Parameter of the SIEC Test?

As mentioned above, in specific circumstances the environmental or sustainable characteristics of some products could allow for the definition of a separate market for such products, and the assessment of the merger's impact on different relevant markets.[15] However, such markets are likely to be adjacent and to influence each other. The more vital question is whether sustainability could be taken into account in the SIEC test when there is only one relevant product market, encompassing both sustainable and non-sustainable products.

We consider that sustainability could be taken into account as a parameter of product quality, both when assessing the impact of the merger on competition and when assessing potential efficiencies from the merger. However it is hard to imagine a case in which it is likely to be decisive for the outcome, at either stage.

1. Less sustainable products – a decrease in product quality?

Current concerns surrounding the environment in particular, and sustainability more generally, make it easier to recognise the environmentally-friendly or sustainable nature of a product as a parameter of product quality. As such, if a merger were expected to result in reduced supply of (for example) environmentally friendly products, or prevalence of "unfriendly" products, this could be assessed as a reduction of product quality or product choice and thus

---

15 See e.g. *Aurubis/Metallo Group Holding* (Case COMP/M.9409) Commission decision C(2020) 2752 final, where DG COMP assessed whether the merger would negatively impact the copper recycling sector by lowering the incentives for recyclers to collect and sort copper scrap.

contribute to SIEC concerns.[16] It seems though unlikely that the outcome could turn on this.

First, the existence of EU environmental standards and regulations would likely make it more difficult to find a significant decrease in product quality, as a merger could not cause products to go below such standards. The Commission previously found that the probability of a merger between HVAC producers resulting in a race to the bottom, in terms of the products' environmental friendliness, was "limited or even non-existent", referring inter alia to the fact that "environmental standards [were] framed by European Directives".[17] Absent any relevant EU or international standard, the Commission might more readily be able to substantiate a significant decrease in the sustainable nature of the product.

Second, even assuming that the Commission were able to substantiate an argument that the merger would result in prevalence of products with poorer sustainability characteristics, it would still have to balance such a decrease against other parameters of competition, notably price. In many cases, environmentally-friendly or sustainable products may be more expensive than their non-sustainable counterparts, and the increase in quality may not outweigh the price increase.

2. Increased sustainability – a merger-specific efficiency?

Sustainability could also come into play in assessing the efficiencies that would result from a merger. Parties have already claimed that their merger would result in more environmentally friendly products, and the Commission appears to have been open to the idea when market investigations supported the importance of more environmentally friendly products for customers.[18]

However, as in the previous section, it is hard to see that the promotion of more environmentally friendly or sustainable products may fully offset the impact of a merger on other parameters of competition, in particular the likely price increase.[19]

Furthermore, efficiencies must be merger-specific, and it would take a very particular set of facts to establish that it is only by means of the merger that the parties could commit themselves to sustainable policies, products or

---

16 Product quality and choice form part of the benefits derived from effective competition. See Commission, Guidelines on the assessment of non-horizontal mergers under the Council Regulation on the control of concentrations between undertakings [2008] OJ C265/6, [10], and *Dow/DuPont* (Case COMP/M.7932) Commission decision C(2017) 1946 final [2017] OJ C353/9, [1990]: "the merger control system established by the regulation aims at preventing mergers which would be likely to deprive customers of a number of benefits of effective competition, which are not only low prices, but also high quality products, a wide selection of goods and services and innovation."

17 See *Daikin/Oyl* (Case COMP/M.4271) S-G Greffe(2006) D/205482, [27].

18 See e.g. *Metso/Aker Kvaerner* (Case COMP/M.4187) Commission decision C(2006)6513 final [2008] OJ C6/11, [103] *et seq.*; John Gatti, Mary Loughran, *The European Commission conditionally clears a merger in the development and production of equipment for pulp mills (Metso/Aker)*, 12 December 2006, e-Competitions December 2006, Art. N° 38257.

19 ibid., [108] – [109].

practices. Nevertheless the Commission has signalled interest in the topic of sustainability efficiencies within merger control, and its Chief Economist recently announced that DG COMP has set up a team of volunteers to look further into so-called "green efficiencies", i.e. out-of-market efficiencies, and better understand what kind of efficiencies could be taken into account and how to measure them.[20]

The recently updated merger assessment guidelines published for consultation by the UK Competition and Markets Authority confirm that sustainability can indeed be included in the assessment of efficiencies. They state that "[w]hat constitutes higher quality, greater choice or greater innovation will depend on the facts of individual cases. It might be, for example, that benefits in the form of environmental sustainability and supporting the transition to a low carbon economy are relevant customer benefits in some circumstances."[21]

For all these reasons, although environmental friendliness and sustainability can indeed form part of the assessment within the current EUMR framework, we consider that a decrease of sustainability is unlikely in practice to be viewed as sufficient to serve as a basis for prohibition or remedies, and that pure sustainability efficiencies are unlikely to be viewed as sufficient to outweigh a merger's anticompetitive effects. Of course we may hope for enlightened guidance to shine a different light, but the recent vigilance of the General Court must surely cause the Commission to hesitate before venturing far in this direction.[22]

If sustainability is to play a stronger role in merger control without any EU-level policy reforms, this may more likely be via a different mechanism, for instance as a legitimate interest. As examined further below, though, this route offers only scope to impede deals otherwise permitted by the Commission – not a means to override adverse action by the Commission under the EUMR.

---

20 "Green merger efficiencies to be looked at by EU 'discussion group', Régibeau says" (*MLex Market Insight*, 18 November 2020); PaRR, "EC economists team looking at how sustainability criteria can fit into competition assessments" (Informa conference, 24 November 2020).

21 CMA, "Merger Assessment Guidelines" (CMA129 CON, November 2020), [8.18], <https://assets. publishing.service.gov.uk/government/uploads/system/uploads/attachment_data/file/935593/Revised_ MAGs_Nov_2020.pdf>.

22 See e.g. Case T – –399/16 *CK Telecoms UK Investments v Commission (Hutchison)* EU:T:2020:217; Olivier Billard, Guillaume Fabre, Solène Hamon, "Annulment: The General Court of the European Union annuls a decision prohibiting a merger in an oligopolistic market, recalling the scope of the notion of significant impediment to effective competition as well as the standard of proof applicable for the European Commission to conclude that there is a risk of non-coordinated effects" (*CK Telecoms UK*), 28 May 2020, Concurrences N° 4-2020, Art. N° 97596, pp. 159-165; Cases T – 778/16 and T – 892/16 *Ireland and Others v European Commission (Apple)* EU:T:2020:217; Jacques Derenne, Caterina Romagnuolo, "Tax ruling: The General Court of the European Union annuls a decision of the European Commission on Irish tax rulings for lack of evidence of an advantage" *(Apple)*, 15 July 2020, Concurrences N° 4-2020, Art. N° 97653, pp. 184-189.

III. Sustainability as a Legitimate Interest?

Despite the Commission's exclusive jurisdiction over mergers with an EU dimension, the EUMR provides a limited scope for Member States to intervene to protect other policy considerations.

1. Member States' legitimate interests under the EUMR

Article 21(4) EUMR allows Member States to take appropriate measures to protect interests other than competition, as long as the measures are necessary and proportionate to their aim and compatible with all aspects of EU law. The article allows Member States to block mergers cleared at EU level or to impose additional conditions, but Member States cannot allow a merger that was blocked by the Commission to proceed, nor waive commitments imposed by the Commission.[23]

These so-called "legitimate interests" are grouped into two categories.

The first category covers legitimate interests that are "recognised" and named in the EUMR itself: public security, plurality of the media and prudential rules.[24] Member States can take measures to protect any of these three interests without prior notification or approval by the Commission.[25] But the measures must genuinely aim to protect one of the recognised interests, be proportionate and non-discriminatory.[26]

The second category comprises all other candidate legitimate interests. Any measures intended by a Member State based on such a claimed legitimate interest must be communicated to the Commission before they can be implemented.[27] The Commission has 25 working days to examine whether the measures are necessary and proportionate for the protection of an interest that is compatible with EU law, and that they do not constitute a breach of general principles or other provisions of EU law, e.g. a means of arbitrary discrimination or a disguised restriction on the freedom of establishment or of the free movement of capital.[28] A Member State has, for example, successfully invoked

---

23 Note to the OECD (n 7), [9].
24 EUMR, art 21(4), para 2.
25 See e.g. *Enel/Acciona/Endesa* (Case COMP/M.4685) Commission decision C(2007)5913 final, [23].
26 Note to the OECD (n 7), [11].
27 The ECJ confirmed that the Commission can still assess the validity of such an interest and its compatibility with EU law even absent any communication by the Member State. See Case C – 42/01 *Portugal v Commission* [2004] ECR I-06079; Stanislas Martin, "Commission's jurisdiction: The ECJ rules that Article 21-4 Regulation (CE) 139/2004 gives the Commission a decisional power to protect its exclusive jurisdiction vis-à-vis the Member States" (*Portugal/Commission*), 22 June 2004, Concurrences N° 1-2004, Art. N° 12040, pp. 72-73.
28 See e.g. *Enel/Acciona/Endesa* (n 25), [24].

the need to safeguard regulatory provisions governing water and electricity industries.[29]

The question then is whether sustainability, inter alia environmental protection, could be a legitimate interest.

2. Could sustainability be a legitimate interest consideration under the EUMR?

A. *A novelty with some prospects of success*

Of the three recognised legitimate interest grounds in EUMR, article 21(4), the only one that could potentially cover sustainability grounds is "public security". The concept of public security has, however, consistently been interpreted strictly by the European Court of Justice (ECJ) because any derogations from EU law on this basis restrict the fundamental free movement principles.[30] Any exceptions based on public security are therefore limited to situations where there is "a genuine and sufficiently serious threat to a fundamental interest of society".[31] This would apply, for example, to a Member State's involvement in cases of military security.[32] In a merger context this could relate to concentrations concerning the production of or trade in arms, munitions and war material.[33]

But there is support for application of the "public security" ground beyond military matters. Notably, when assessing restrictions on free movements, the ECJ has ruled that the corresponding exceptions can be invoked for reasons of security of supply of products that are of vital importance to a Member State. More concretely this has involved situations in relation to energy sources (oil,[34] gas,[35] electricity[36]) as well as telecommunication services.[37] The Commission echoes this cautiously wider approach, beyond the purely military, referring to situations where "supplies to the country in question of a product or service [are] considered of vital or essential interest for the protection of the population's

---

29 *Water Industry Act* Commission decision of 29 March 1995 [1995] OJ C94/2; *Lyonnaise Des Eaux/Northumbrian Water* (Case COMP/M.567) Commission decision of 21 December 1995 [1996] OJ C11/3; *EdF/London Electricity* (Case COMP/1346) Commission decision of 27 January 1999 [1999] OJ C92/10.

30 See e.g. Case C – 78/18 *European Commission v Hungary* EU:C:2020:476, [91]: "it is settled case-law of the Court that where the grounds of public policy and public security mentioned in Article 65(1)(b) TFEU allow a derogation from a fundamental freedom provided for by the EU Treaty they must be interpreted strictly, so that their scope cannot be determined unilaterally by each Member State without any control by the EU institutions."

31 See, e.g. Case C – 463/00 *Commission v Spain* [2003] ECR I-4581, [72].

32 Subject to specific rules for mergers in the defence sector, see Article 346 TFEU.

33 Note to the OECD (n 7).

34 See e.g. Case C – 72/83 *Campus Oil and Others v Ministry for Industry and Energy and other* [1984] ECR I-2727, [34]: "petroleum products, because of their exceptional importance as an energy source in the modern economy, are of fundamental importance for a country's existence since not only its economy but above all its institutions, its essential public services and even the survival of its inhabitants depend upon them."

35 See e.g. Case C – 503/99, *Commission v Belgium* [2002] ECR I-4809.

36 See e.g. Case C – 463/00, *Commission v Spain* [2003] ECR I-4581, [71].

37 ibid.

health."[38] The original notes accompanying the adoption of the 1989 Regulation indeed stated that there:[39]

> may be wider considerations of public security, both in the sense of Article 224 [now Article 347 TFEU] and in that of Article 36 [now Article 36 TFEU[40]], in addition to defence interests in the strict sense. Thus the requirement for public security, as interpreted by the Court of Justice, could cover security of supplies to the country in question of a product or service considered of vital or essential interest for the protection of the population's health.

As noted, support for the recognition of a broader notion of public order or public interest, as opposed to military security, can be found in the exceptions provided by the EU Treaties with regard to the four freedoms of movement,[41] and ECJ case law in relation to reasons of overriding public interest.[42] Previously recognised reasons of overriding public interest already include, for instance, the protection of the environment – recognised even as one of "the essential objectives of the European Union"[43] – or social policy objectives.[44] If such objectives can allow a Member State to derogate from EU primary law, there is obvious scope for similar derogation from secondary law.

Experiences of other jurisdictions also argue in favour of the inclusion of a wider public interest notion within the recognised legitimate interests, which could in turn include sustainability and/or environmental protection. Various Member States allow intervention in mergers for the protection of wider public interests,[45] including macroeconomic advantages, protection of employment, industrial

---

38 Note to the OECD (n 7).
39 Notes on Council Regulation 4064/89 (n 14).
40 Article 347 TFEU provides for consultation between Member States when adopting measures that may affect the functioning of the internal market "in the event of serious internal disturbances affecting the maintenance of law and order, in the event of war, serious international tension constituting a threat of war, or in order to carry out obligations it has accepted for the purpose of maintaining peace and international security" while Article 36 TFEU concerns permitted exceptions to the principle of the free movement of goods, i.e. "on grounds of public morality, public policy or public security; the protection of health and life of humans, animals or plants; the protection of national treasures possessing artistic, historic or archaeological value; or the protection of industrial and commercial property".
41 See e.g. Article 53(1) TFEU: "The provisions of this Chapter and measures taken in pursuance thereof shall not prejudice the applicability of provisions laid down by law, regulation or administrative action providing for special treatment for foreign nationals on grounds of public policy, public security or public health." See also article 36 TFEU quoted in n 41.
42 See e.g. Directive 2006/123/EC on services in the internal market [2006] OJ L376/36, recital 40, summarising grounds recognised as overriding reasons relating to the public interest by the ECJ, including public health, the maintenance of order in society; social policy objectives; the protection of workers, including the social protection of workers; animal welfare; the protection of the environment and the urban environment, including town and country planning; cultural policy objectives.
43 See e.g. Case C – 524/07 *Commission v Austria* [2008] ECR I-187, [58].
44 See e.g. Case C – 724/18 and C – 727/18, *Cali Apartments Sci and HX v Procureur général près la cour d'appel de Paris and Ville de Paris* EU:C:2020:743, [67], relating to social housing policy.
45 This is the case for instance in France, Germany, Hungary, Italy, the Netherlands, Portugal and Spain.

development, and international competitiveness. Spain already provides for intervention by the Council of Minister on grounds of environmental protection.[46]

Sustainability, environmental protection and threats to the climate have never been raised as a "legitimate public interest" in the context of the EUMR. The lack of precedent should not in itself be decisive, because public interest and public security must be evolving concepts as societal interests and security threats develop over time.[47] Sustainability, both within the European market[48] and worldwide,[49] is one of the goals of the EU, so there is support in primary law for such objectives. Recent EU policy initiatives also recognise climate and environmental challenges as a source of public insecurity ranging from political instability to concerns regarding sustainable food supplies. The European Green Deal describes tackling these climate and environmental challenges as "the defining task for this generation" so as to ensure Europe's security regarding a number of factors.[50]

First, access to resources must be preserved, especially to safeguard "the supply of sustainable raw materials, in particular of critical raw materials necessary for clean technologies, digital space and defence applications".[51] Resource security and reliable access to strategic raw materials are identified as important EU goals[52] and appear to include, for example, food security. The European "Farm to Fork Strategy" explicitly states that the effects on food security from climate change and biodiversity loss must be addressed to make sure that everyone in the EU has access to sufficient, nutritious, sustainable food.[53]

Second, climate and environmental challenges are seen as a significant source of instability and the EU's policies must prevent them from becoming a source of conflict or food insecurity: "Climate policy implications should become an integral part of the EU's thinking and action on external issues, including in the context of the Common Security and Defence Policy."[54]

When presented with a transaction that will be cleared under the EUMR but which poses a significant threat to the environment in a particular Member State

---

46 Article 10(4) of the Spanish Competition Act allows the Council of Ministers to assess economic concentrations in light of criteria of general interest other than protecting competition, including environmental protection.

47 See e.g. Commission "EU Security Union Strategy" COM/2020/605 final, II: "Both vulnerabilities and threats are in a state of constant evolution, and the EU needs to adapt."

48 Article 3(3) TFEU: "It shall work for the sustainable development of Europe based on balanced economic growth and price stability, a highly competitive social market economy, aiming at full employment and social progress, and a high level of protection and improvement of the quality of the environment."

49 Article 3(5) TFEU: "In its relations with the wider world, the Union shall uphold and promote its values and interests and contribute to … the sustainable development of the Earth, … free and fair trade, eradication of poverty and the protection of human rights, in particular the rights of the child …"

50 Commission, "The European Green Deal" COM/2019/640 final, 2.

51 ibid, 8.

52 ibid, 22.

53 Commission, "A Farm to Fork Strategy for a fair, healthy and environmentally-friendly food system" COM/2020/381 final, 4.

54 European Green Deal (n 51), 21.

or Member States, national governments might be persuaded to invoke a legitimate interest under article 21(4) EUMR. The *Urgenda* ruling from the Dutch Supreme Court may be relevant here, stating that "Articles 2 and 8 ECHR relating to the risk of climate change should be interpreted in such a way that these provisions oblige the contracting states to do 'their part' to counter that danger".[55] We await seeing whether other Member States follow this lead and, indeed, the European Court of Human Rights itself.

Regardless of whether it would be invoked as a "public security" interest or a new category of legitimate interest, notification of the measure to the Commission must be a prudent course of action given the novel nature of this claim. The Commission has indeed already stated that notification is appropriate where an interest may appear to be legitimate under the recognised categories written into article 21 EUMR but where the application is new.[56] In cases of a new "legitimate interest", the Member State must show that the interest is a public one as opposed to a private one[57] – this would seem to be the case for any environmental or other sustainability threat. Further, the Member State will need to show that the measures are in line with the general principles and other provisions of EU law. The EU Green Deal would arguably be a basis to claim that the elimination of environmental threats to security is in line with the EU's acquis, as well as previous recognition of environmental protection as an essential objective of the EU.[58] Finally, the Member State invoking the legitimate interest will also need to show that blocking the transaction or applying conditions is necessary and proportionate to eliminate the threat arising from the merger.

It remains to be seen whether a proposed merger would ever be so threatening to a sustainability concern that there is an overriding interest from one Member State – or several – to block the transaction or impose additional measures. It is difficult to identify a particular situation that may give rise to such circumstances relating to the environment or climate change. Maybe a plausible scenario would be a threat to the security of medical or food supply in a Member State if, for example, the merged entity might discontinue local production or impede national supply channels.

B. *FDI regimes may be of assistance*

The recent spate of legislation to screen foreign direct investments (FDI) is relevant here. Concentrations within the meaning of the EUMR will likely meet the investment thresholds triggering national FDI regimes relevant to the deal in question, indeed FDI laws often apply at levels of investment even below EUMR "control".

---

55 *Netherlands v Stichting Urgenda* Dutch Supreme Court No 19/00135, 19 December 2019, [5.8].
56 *E. ON/Endesa* (Case COMP/M.4197) Commssion decision C(2006) 7039 final, [56].
57 EUMR, art 21(4), refers to "any other *public* interest" (emphasis added).
58 Case C – 524/07 *Commission v Austria* [2008] ECR I-187, [58].

For some time FDI screening mechanisms in Europe, where they existed, focused narrowly on sectors that would often fall within the notion of recognised legitimate interests. The recent adoption of the EU regulation establishing a framework for the screening of FDIs into the Union (EU FDI Regulation)[59] preceded, coincidentally, the COVID-19 pandemic during which many countries adopted[60] and extended screening mechanisms,[61] indeed under encouragement[62] from the Commission. The EU FDI Regulation sets up a cooperation mechanism between Member States when screening FDI and gives the Commission a role in which it may often encourage the use of national FDI powers.

If then the Commission is encouraging national opposition to certain acquisitions, with its FDI hat on, how may this affect its traditionally restrictive stance in relation to the notion of EUMR legitimate interests? And if there is a new permissive approach to national interventionism, might sustainability become an FDI screening ground?

Interplay of FDI screening and merger control

The EU FDI Regulation provides but limited guidance as to how it will interact with the EUMR. It merely asserts the need to interpret coherently the notion of legitimate interest in the EUMR and the screening grounds provided for in the EU FDI Regulation, i.e. security or public order.[63] This leaves a significant margin of appreciation, and legal uncertainty. One possibility would be to consider that the notification of new or amended FDI screening mechanisms required by the EU FDI Regulation, article 3(7), should be treated de facto as recognition of the screening grounds as legitimate interests within the meaning of the EUMR.[64] However, despite the need for coherent interpretation,[65] in

---

59   Regulation (EU) 2019/452 establishing a framework for the screening of foreign direct investments into the Union [2019] OJ L79I /1.
60   E.g. Slovenia introduced a screening mechanism in May 2020 and Malta set up a "National Foreign Direct Investment Screening Office", explicitly to "implement the provisions of Regulation (EU) 2019/452 establishing a framework for the screening of foreign direct investments into the Union." See also pending proposals in e.g. Belgium, the Netherlands and Sweden.
61   See e.g. France, Spain, or Germany, which extended their screening mechanisms; some countries also overhauled their screening mechanisms, e.g. Poland or Hungary.
62   Commission, "Guidance to the Member States concerning foreign direct investment and free movement of capital from third countries, and the protection of Europe's strategic assets, ahead of the application of Regulation (EU) 2019/452 (FDI Screening Regulation)" C(2020) 1981 final [2020] OJ C991/1: "the Commission calls upon ... Member States that currently do not have a screening mechanism, or whose screening mechanisms do not cover all relevant transactions, to set up a full-fledged screening mechanism".
63   EU FDI Regulation, recital 36: "To the extent that the respective scope of application of those two regulations overlap, the grounds for screening set out in Article 1 of this Regulation and the notion of legitimate interests within the meaning of the third paragraph of Article 21(4) of Regulation (EC) No 139/2004 should be interpreted in a coherent manner, without prejudice to the assessment of the compatibility of the national measures aimed at protecting those interests with the general principles and other provisions of Union law."
64   See EUMR, art 21(4).
65   Cf. the German principle of *Einheit der Rechtsordnung*, i.e. the need for all laws forming part of the same legal system to be interpreted coherently.

formal terms the two regulations will inevitably be viewed as separate instruments by the Commission. So Member States, in addition to notifying DG TRADE of their screening mechanisms under the EU FDI Regulation, would be required to apply to DG COMP for recognition of the relevant screening ground as an EUMR legitimate interest, if the FDI intervention goes beyond the recognised EUMR legitimate interests. The dialogue with DG COMP would be needed at the latest before applying measures to a specific EUMR-notifiable concentration.

The obvious interest in coherent application of the two regulations may be expected to entail a de facto widening of the notion of legitimate interest under the EUMR. Otherwise we might enjoy the spectacle of a Member State being urged to intervene for purposes of the EU FDI Regulation, for transactions impacting an EU project,[66] but prevented from doing so under the EUMR.

Our expectation, therefore, is that the growing use of FDI screening will likely lead to the widening of the notion of legitimate interest, to include at least the factors listed in the EU FDI Regulation, article 4. It is less clear whether *all* national FDI screening grounds would be construed as legitimate interests from the EUMR standpoint. Certain national regimes are notably broad, e.g. Hungary, where the law may apply to wholesale and retail, for example. As regards sustainability, the question arising is whether sustainability goals could emerge as an FDI screening ground.

Sustainability as an FDI screening ground

There appears to be ready scope for sustainability objectives (at least certain of them) to be invoked within national FDI screening mechanisms – and for these to qualify as EUMR legitimate interests.

The EU FDI Regulation provides for the possibility of screening on grounds of security and public order,[67] and when setting out the factors that can be taken into account when screening an FDI, the EU FDI Regulation includes, for example, "supply of critical inputs, including energy or raw materials, as well as food security".[68] These provisions are in substance consistent with the interpretations of the EUMR notion of "public security" discussed earlier. Such factors could very easily allow for intervention in transactions which would have an impact on the environment or the sustainability of supply chains, where they impact the supply of critical inputs. At national level, various countries already provide for relevant screening grounds, for instance the

---

66   Article 8 of the EU FDI Regulation provides that when an FDI is likely to affect projects or programmes of Union interest, the screening Member State must take the "utmost account of the Commission's opinion and provide an explanation to the Commission if its opinion is not followed."

67   EU FDI Regulation, art 1(1). See above for discussion of possible interpretation of legitimate interests in these areas.

68   EU FDI Regulation, art 4(1)(c).

security of food supply is included as a screening ground in France, Austria, and Slovenia.

Moreover, although public health is not included as such in the list of factors – which includes only the protection of critical health infrastructure – it is commonly included in the notion of public order in many Member States, and listed as a specific screening ground in some Member States, e.g. France and Spain. Therefore, we expect that a deal which may have significantly detrimental effects on public health could incur an adverse outcome following an FDI screening. It will be for discussion as to how far *environmental* concerns may, in a given case and on its facts, be treated as akin to a matter of public health.

Overall, relevant FDI interventions may readily come within the existing EUMR notion of public security – failing which the Member State could in any event seek to have it recognised as a new legitimate interest, relying for that purpose on consistency with the EU FDI Regulation and associated Commission guidance.

IV. Conclusion

As outlined above, although the environmentally friendly and sustainable nature of products can form part of an EUMR assessment, we consider that a decrease in such quality parameters alone is unlikely to be sufficient to be decisive for the outcome of a case; and equally that pure sustainability efficiencies would be unlikely to suffice to outweigh other anticompetitive effects of a merger. There is however scope – albeit limited – for Member States to intervene in merger cases on the basis of a legitimate interest. This concept may be interpreted more broadly in the future under the influence of the increasing FDI screening regimes in Europe.

In fact, legitimate interests and FDI screening mechanisms may by their nature be more suited to take sustainability and environmental protection into account than merger control: FDI – and by extension legitimate interests claimed by Member States under the EUMR – are more policy-driven decisions, as opposed to the rather objective SIEC test of the EUMR.

In addition, sustainability is not a homogeneous notion, but encompasses many different and sometimes divergent interests. For instance, a transaction could have at one and the same time both a positive impact on the environment and a negative impact on European employment. The more social goals are added into the equation, the more complex the balancing act required. This would seem to go beyond the legitimate scope of EUMR review. It may also fairly be remarked that governments better enjoy the democratic legitimacy to arbitrate between such goals, as compared to competition agencies.

Chapter 4
State Aid

State Aid and Sustainability

JAMES WEBBER[*]

Shearman & Sterling

I. Background to EU State Aid Control

The EU is unique in having a legal system of multilateral subsidy control. There are no equivalent systems in other countries or trading blocs.[1] As a form of competition law it is idiosyncratically European and quite different from antitrust and merger control.

Unlike Articles 101 and 102 TFEU, which are addressed to undertakings, the prohibition in Article 107 is directed at Member States. The Treaty itself created no rights or obligations for undertakings in respect of state aid. It is Member States that are prohibited from granting aid that distorted the single market – not undertakings for receiving it. Indeed, until the Court of Justice judgment in *Commission v Germany* in 1973,[2] there were no legal consequences for undertakings from unlawful aid. State aid therefore was originally – and is still in large part – best understood as a system to control competition between Member States rather than between companies. Many of the procedural issues that are discussed in this paper stem from a tension between this characteristic and the ECJ's decision in 1973 to superimpose legal consequences for undertakings.

The Treaty provisions work by first defining and prohibiting state aid. The Commission is then entrusted to permit otherwise prohibited aid that it deems

---

[*] James Webber is a partner in the antitrust practice of Shearman & Sterling in Brussels and London. The author would like to thank Mark Steenson for his help in researching this chapter.

[1] See Thomas Pope and Alex Stojanovic, *Beyond state aid: The future of subsidy control in the UK* (Institute for Government 2020) for discussion of subsidy control outside the EU.

[2] Case 70/72 *Commission v Germany* [1973] ECR 813, [13].

compatible with the single market. The definition of state aid is a substantial topic outside the scope of this paper; however, the basic criteria are:

- an advantage not available under market conditions;
- that is granted by or through state resources;
- via a measure that is imputable to the state;
- favouring certain undertakings (selectivity);
- that threatens to distort competition within the EU; and
- affects trade between Member States.

The last two criteria have long been merged by the Court of Justice of the European Union (CJEU) and Commission and are for practical purposes irrelevant for aid sums above the Commission's *de minimis* threshold.[3,4] The other four criteria are readily established for state measures that are targeted to incentivise behaviour that companies would not undertake in normal market conditions. Given that such measures are central to government and European policy to accelerate the transition to a sustainable European economy, we can address this paper to the interventions by governments that are considered state aid.

Once a measure falls within the definition of aid, it is prohibited unless the Commission approves it. The approval process either occurs via block exemption or an individual basis following notification.

The general block exemption regulation (GBER)[5] has energy and environmental provisions that can permit smaller projects to proceed without notification, provided the terms of the GBER are complied with.[6]

For large aid projects – for example energy infrastructure projects where the aid required exceeds €50 million – individual notification is required. These are assessed on the basis of policy guidance published by the Commission. The Commission is largely free to define the policy objectives that it wishes to pursue in approving such aid. The current guidance for environmental aid is found in the « Guidelines on State aid for environmental protection and energy 2014 – 2020 »

---

3   Currently €200,000 over three years – subject to a time limited increase to €800,000 under the Temporary Framework for COVID-19.
4   This became a particularly controversial feature of the UK's FTA negotiation, where the EU sought to impose its state aid rules on the UK. See for example evidence of George Peretz QC to the House of Lords EU Sub-Committee (5 March 2020): Mr Peretz noted that analysis of [this] effect on trade « takes place "at an astonishingly superficial level". The UK and EU have now agreed to a comprehensive Trade and Cooperation Agreement which contains some subsidy provisions, although these are substantively and procedurally very different from EU state aid rules and outside the scope of this paper.
5   Commission Regulation (EU) 651/2014 declaring certain categories of aid compatible with the internal market in application of Articles 107 and 108 of the Treaty [2014] OJ L187/1.
6   In 2018 around €15 billion of state aid spending for environment and energy measures was block-exempted under the GBER. Commission, "State Aid Scoreboard 2019", 38.

(EEAG),[7] which were designed to facilitate attainment of the EU's 2020 climate targets. The policy choices embedded in the EEAG and fitness for purpose in attaining the European Green Deal are discussed at the end of this paper.

This structure – a low threshold for what counts as aid together with freedom for the Commission to determine its own policy for assessing compatibility with the single market – grants the Commission direct and legally enforceable executive authority over Member States' tax and spending decisions. This is unusual and not a power the Commission has to the same extent in almost any other field of EU law, such as tax harmonisation, Eurozone governance, environmental, R&D, regional or energy policy.

The cumulative effect of significant power in respect of state aid approval, but much weaker powers in many other areas, is that the Commission uses state aid as a tool to pursue lots of different policy objectives: regional development, industrial policy, tax harmonisation, environmental and energy goals, financial stability via bank resolution and restructuring, etc. These objectives are often – but not always – consistent with each other. Moreover, even where there is no conflict, assessing consistency of (say) an environmental aid project with industrial or regional policy goals adds to the weight of the approval process in time and resources.

Across these policies, the Commission has made significant efforts to make its assessment criteria coherent – including «common assessment criteria» for aid. These criteria are with a view to:

> strengthening the internal market, promoting more effectiveness in public spending through a better contribution of State aid to the objectives of common interest, greater scrutiny of the incentive effect, ... limiting the aid to the minimum necessary, and ... avoiding the potential negative effects of the aid on competition and trade.[8]

These common assessment criteria themselves embed policy choices – for example greater scrutiny of incentive effect and limiting aid to the minimum necessary requires evidence and investigation and affects the design of aid measures. This adds to the time and resources required to get approval and hence delays when the aid can be delivered to the beneficiaries. The cost of this is real, as the COVID-19 crisis illustrates. We have seen €3 trillion of aid authorised since March 2020[9] with speed of approval and maintenance of economic capacity (no doubt rightly) prioritised over careful investigation of incentive effect or whether the aid is limited to the minimum necessary.

---

7   [2014] OJ C200/1. Recently extended to the end of 2021 to give the Commission time to prepare revised guidelines – in particular to replace the EEAG.
8   EEAG, recital 12.
9   Commission, «Coronavirus: Commission Statement on consulting Member States on proposal to prolong and adjust State aid Temporary Framework»(Statement/20/1805, 2 October 2020).

II. European Green Deal

The European Green Deal (Green Deal) is the EU's ambitious long-term environmental strategy, launched by the Commission in December 2019. The Commission communication says the Green Deal «resets the Commission's commitment to tackling climate and environmental-related challenges that is this generation's defining task».[10] The headline goal is to reduce greenhouse gas emissions by 55% (compared with 1990) by 2030 and to make Europe the first climate-neutral continent by 2050.[11]

Achieving this target will require an overhaul of certain industries. Most obviously, a focus of the Green Deal is supporting the transition to clean energy, as the EU's current energy profile accounts for 75% of the EU's greenhouse emissions.[12]

In 2018, 55% of total EU spend on state aid, amounting to €66.5 billion, was attributed to environmental and energy savings.[13] This was a massive increase on the previous 10 years, where of the total state aid spent on environmental protection and energy-saving measures, only around 2.4% (€8.2 billion) concerned energy-saving measures, and only 0.2% (€0.7 billion) renewable energy.

But achieving the energy transition will require a step change. The level of investment required to innovate and deploy, at speed, new and green technologies at scale will be vast. The Commission recognises that the private sector is unlikely to provide capital on this scale and will need «the catalyst of public spending to make it happen fast enough».[14]

State aid measures can either be aimed at the demand or supply side of the energy transition. Aid measures on the supply side are typically aimed at investment or operating aid (such as via contracts for difference for renewable or nuclear energy). These measures are aimed at increasing the supply of green energy above the level the market would produce on its own. Aid measures on the demand side are aimed at increasing demand for green energy above the level the market would produce on its own. Demand-side measures do not usually target specific beneficiaries and may include tax exemptions for users of green energy or hydrogen – or compensation to energy intensive industry from carbon price floor policies.

---

10 Commission, "The European Green Deal»(Communication) COM(2019) 640 final.
11 Ursula von der Leyen, « State of the Union Address »(speech at the European Parliament Plenary, 16 September 2020).
12 Commission, "Powering a climate-neutral economy: Commission sets out plans for the energy system of the future and clean hydrogen» press release (IP/20/1259, 8 July 2020).
13 State Aid Scoreboard 2019 (n 6), 4. The State aid Scoreboard 2019 also notes that average spending [by Member States] in 2018 for notified energy and environmental measures was around €354 million, due in large part to the German EEG 2014 aid scheme, while for GBER measures it was around €25.7 million.
14 Margrethe Vestager, « The Green Deal and competition policy »(Renew webinar, 22 September 2020).

Supply-side measures are more popular among Member States,[15] probably because they are politically easier to implement. Public money is being used to provoke domestic investment and hence jobs and regional development goals. As such, we should consider the extent to which state aid procedure – especially for supply-side investment or operating aid schemes – either facilitates or acts as a brake to such investments.

III. State Aid Procedural Concerns

The current state aid procedural rules are complex and fraught with pitfalls – especially for investment aid. These stem from the tension noted at the beginning of this paper, where the Treaty is directed at Member States but case law subsequently created significant legal consequences for business. Procedural issues are not specific to environmental aid, but insofar as they operate to increase investors' legal uncertainty – creating administrative and procedural friction – they risk undermining the role of state aid in achieving the EU's sustainability goals.

1. GBER v individual notification

The EU's efforts over the last decade to increase green energy and environmental aid projects have presented very differently in the two main procedural routes to aid clearance. The number of individually notified aid cases under the EEAG remained flat from 2014 – 2018 – although the aid distributed under such cases has increased significantly this is distorted by a single large scheme in Germany which accounts for almost 20% of total state aid spending in this area.[16] GBER cases increased by 116% during the same period.[17] We are seeing a flat number of individually notified cases – with larger budgets – and a growing number of GBER cases. The main difference between notified and GBER projects is scale. GBER projects are subject to the caps listed in GBER, article 4, on the amount of aid that can be paid either in the scheme as a whole or to specific beneficiaries. The large discrepancy in case numbers between environmental aid authorised under GBER and environmental aid via individually notified projects could be due to a number of factors, e.g. Member States' unwillingness to allocate budget over the GBER thresholds. However, it is also consistent with procedural disincentives for individual or scheme notification for investment aid.

---

15 For instance, only one carbon price floor aid scheme has been approved : *United Kingdom – Aid for indirect Carbon Price Floor costs* (SA.35449).
16 State aid Scoreboard 2019 (n 6), 38, (Figure 27).
17 State Aid Scoreboard 2019 (n 6), 38, (Figure 28).

2. Lack of speed and legal certainty

Approval timescales for individual or scheme notifications are highly variable but can be slow. For example, Hinkley Point C nuclear power station took a year from notification to approval,[18] but that excludes pre-notification, which is likely to have been significant.

Supply-side investment projects for energy transition (e.g. hydrogen infrastructure or new nuclear electricity generation) of the scale required to achieve the objectives of the Green Deal require huge long-term investments. The Green Deal objectives also imply a high degree of urgency – a year is 10% of the time available to achieve the interim goal of a 55% reduction in greenhouse gas emissions by 2030. It is imperative for private parties making such large investments that approval of a state aid component occurs quickly so as to allow final investment decisions and large capital commitments to be made. Recall that although the EU wishes to be the first climate-neutral continent, it is also the only continent with a state aid regime. The Commission has acknowledged this in a recent speech, saying that environmental measures will benefit from an increased block exemption thresholds and prioritisation once notified.[19]

Once Commission approval has been obtained, parties (and their financial backers) also require legal certainty that the state aid component of a project will not be withdrawn further down the line when the project is in operation and financing has been syndicated. Litigation before the CJEU concerning the GBER is very unusual,[20] but common for notified investment aid, especially if a project or scheme faces domestic or international political opposition or faces a competing technology. Litigation injects fresh delay and uncertainty.

A recent example is the successful action brought by Tempus Energy for the annulment of the Commission's 2014 decision not to open a formal investigation into the UK electricity capacity scheme.[21] The UK electricity capacity scheme

---

18 See Commission Decision on the aid measure SA.34947 (2013/C) (ex 2013/N) which the United Kingdom is planning to implement for support to the Hinkley Point C nuclear power station [2015] OJ L109/44, recital 1.

19 Margrethe Vestager, "State aid" (speech at event organised by the Berliner Gesprachskreis zum Europaischen Beihilfenrecht, 30 October 2020).

20 The author is aware of only two such examples: BMW's appeal regarding aid to its Leipzig factory in Case T – 793/13 *Bayerische Motoren Werke v Commission* EU:T:2017:599 (plus ECJ appeal); and Case C – 493/14 *Dilly's Wellnesshotel GmbH* via preliminary reference; Bruno Stromsky, "Exemption by category: The Court of Justice of the European Union confirms the mandatory nature of the conditions for exemption set by a regulation, which exempts Member States from the obligation to notify certain categories of aid, even if the violated condition is limited to a lack of express reference to this regulation by the aid scheme" *(Dilly's Wellnesshotel)*, 21 July 2016, Concurrences N° 4-2016, Art. N° 82081, pp. 146-147.

21 Case T – 793/14 *Tempus Energy v Commission* EU:T:2018:790; Bruno Stromsky, "Proportionality: The General Court of the European Union annuls a decision not to raise any objection against a State aid scheme granted to the energy capacity market" *(Tempus Energy, Tempus Energy Technology)*, 15 November 2018, Concurrences N° 1-2019, Art. N° 89299, pp. 137-140.

covers the period 2014 – 2024 and is intended to enhance energy security by subsidising plants to be on standby for generation when energy demand peaks and additional supply is required. Tempus Energy sells demand-side-response (DSR) electricity consumption management technology, and argued that the scheme, which involves remunerating electricity capacity providers in exchange for their commitment to provide electricity or to reduce or delay their electricity consumption during times of system stress, privileges generation over DSR in a discriminatory and disproportionate manner, which should have raised doubts as to its compatibility with the internal market. As a result of the General Court's judgment, the scheme was suspended in 2018.

In 2019, after a full investigation, the Commission decided that the UK scheme was compatible. Throughout this period of at least five years, companies and their financial backers had allocated capital to UK electricity capacity – without legal certainty that the subsidy scheme that underpins the investment case would be upheld.

While by no means a state aid issue specifically, the reality is that current CJEU procedure with no active case management, no summary judgment or trial of a preliminary issue, no leave requirement for appeals – together with an inability in state aid cases for the court itself to make a substantive finding on compatibility – means that investors can be left in limbo for many years as to the legal status of the aid measures on which their investment was predicated.

3. Change of political priorities

The state aid regime also injects uncertainty by giving Member States a route to change their political priorities and avoid Bilateral Investment Treaty or Energy Charter Treaty (ECT) obligations to investors under the measures of a previous government. A noteworthy example of this is the lowering of renewable energy support in Spain. In 2007, Spain introduced incentives to support electricity generation from renewable energy sources, cogeneration and waste, known as the "premium economic scheme". The incentives attracted tens of billions of euros of investment in renewable assets. However, following the Eurozone debt crisis and under pressure from the Commission and European Central Bank to reduce public spending, the Spanish government began to reduce the subsidy incentives that had attracted the investment, and in 2013 the premium economic scheme was repealed and replaced with the – significantly less generous – "specific remuneration scheme", which was approved by the Commission.[22]

When the investors sued Spain under the ECT, the Commission took the view that any arbitral award for payments expected under the prior scheme would be

---

22 *Spain – Support for electricity generation from renewable energy sources, cogeneration and waste* SA.40348 [2017] OJ C442/1. The premium economic scheme was never notified to the Commission.

additional, incompatible, state aid.[23] In this way Spain was prohibited under EU law from paying any award granted to investors by the arbitral tribunal.

This is part of a wider conflict between international investment treaty protections and the Commission's approach to the EU state aid regime.[24] The Commission takes the view that insofar as arbitral awards constitute aid, they require the approval of the Commission before they can be paid. This significantly undermines the benefit of investment treaty protection and creates a risk for investors that simply does not exist in jurisdictions outside the EU.

4. Lack of procedural rights for aid beneficiaries

Added to this is the lack of any effective procedural rights for beneficiaries during the Commission procedure. The aid beneficiary has no formal right to be heard – save a right to make written comments on the opening of the formal investigation procedure. This is despite the fact that the consequences of an adverse decision fall exclusively on the aid beneficiary and can be very significant. Coupled with the legal uncertainty inherent in the EU state aid regime, this presents a significant risk to beneficiaries.

The Commission's process is also necessarily political. State aid is primarily directed at competition between Member States: the Commission must balance one Member State's interests against the whole and in doing so is empowered to control Member States' fiscal decision-making.

The political dimension can manifest itself at a micro as well as macro level within a case. For example, the Commission's approach to the treatment of evidence can vary in practice, depending on how enthusiastic the Commission is in supporting the project. The Commission has significant discretion over the weight it attributes to the evidence before it – this discretion is rarely subject to judicial supervision by the court as most appeals concern a decision not to open proceedings or the definition of aid.[25] This can allow the Commission to be selective with how it uses and attributes weight to evidence in order to find (or not find) sufficient evidence. This can also be a feature of merger investigations,

---

23 *Ibid.*, recitals (159) and (165).
24 See, in particular, Commission Decision 2015/1470 on State aid SA.38517 (2014/C) (ex 2014/NN) implemented by Romania – Arbitral award *Micula v Romania* of 11 December 2013 [2015] OJ L232/43, in which the Commission decided that the payment of compensation pursuant to an ICSID arbitral award, which had the effect of reinstating a revoked aid regime, did constitute, in and of itself, state aid. The Commission's *Micula* decision was subsequently annulled by the General Court (joined Cases T – 624/15, T – 694/15 and T – 704/15 *European Food v Commission* EU:T:2019:423), and is now on appeal to the ECJ (Case C – 638/19 P *Commission v European Food*); Athanase Popov, "The EU General Court annuls the Commission's State aid decision on the basis that it lacked jurisdiction to implement relevant law in situation where all relevant facts have taken place before Romania's accession to the EU" *(Micula)*, 18 juin 2019, e-Competitions June 2019, Art. N° 94141.
25 The General Court's judgment in Case T – 356/15 *Austria v Commission* (Hinkley Point C) EU:T:2018:439 is a notable exception; Bruno Stromsky, "Public interest objective: The General Court of the European Union upholds a European Commission's decision authorizing an aid for the promotion of nuclear energy

but in state aid there is no disciplined timetable nor any of the internal checks and balances that are present in merger review.

It should be recalled that not all the checks and balances come from the Commission's review. Beneficiaries involved in the state aid approval process typically only receive aid for less than 50% of the total eligible cost, meaning that, notwithstanding the intrusive process, most of the risk is still with the private sector.

Conversely, the route the Commission and CJEU have taken to mitigate the uncertainty and lack of rights of defence for beneficiaries is to restrict standing for third parties seeking to challenge aid approvals. The standing rules before the Commission are tightly drawn to "interested parties"[26] – which in practice usually means competitors. Before the court it is even more difficult – especially if seeking to challenge a decision adopted after the formal investigation procedure. There it would be necessary to show *Plaumann* standing – i.e. that «persons other than those to whom a decision is addressed may only claim [standing] if that decision affects them by reason of certain attributes which are peculiar to them or by reason of circumstances in which they are differentiated from all other persons»[27]. The way this test has been interpreted by the CJEU in a State aid context represents an almost insurmountable hurdle in most cases requiring a third party to demonstrate that its competitive position has been affected by the aid – in a different way to other competitors.[28]

The system does not serve anyone well – beneficiaries, competitors or civil society organisations seeking to challenge aid approval that may harm transition objectives.

It is also likely that these procedural issues contribute towards the relative attractiveness of the GBER compared with individual notification. One solution to this is to dramatically increase the thresholds under GBER – which would bypass the great majority of these issues. But the level of investment required to support the Green Deal cannot all be block exempted – the sums are too large and the risks of distortion too great. For larger projects – especially investment or operating aid projects – these procedural challenges will continue to act as a brake on the ability of state aid to support energy transition.

and clarifies how the objectives of the *Euratom* treaty match together with Treaty on the Functioning of the European Union objectives" (*Austria / Commission*), 12 July 2018, Concurrences N° 4-2018, Art. N° 88249, pp. 159 – 162.

26 Article 108(2) TFEU.
27 Plaumann & Co v Commission, (1963) C-25/62 ECLI:EU:C:1963:17
28 For example, see Case T – 118/3 *Whirlpool Europe v Commission* EU:T:2016:365, [47]; Pascal Cardonnel, "State aids: The General Court of the European Union holds inadmissible the action brought by a competitor of the beneficiary of a State aid decision amended in order to comply with a prior GC ruling in its favor" (*Whirlpool Europe*), 22 June 2016, Concurrences N° 3-2016, Art. N° 80971, pp. 145 – 146.

IV. State Aid – Fairness Between Member States in Tension with Environmental Effectiveness

In the last 10 years, almost 80% of total nominal state aid spending for environmental protection and energy projects has come from five Member States – the third largest of which was the UK.[29] This reflects the large differences in the fiscal strength of the Member States and gives rise to two concerns: first, cohesion issues if only wealthier Member States are able to benefit from the opportunities that energy transition represents; second, that important projects that would contribute to EU policy objectives never materialise due to the difficulties associated with cross-border projects.

This is something the Commission has tried to address in its 2014 state aid rules regarding Important Projects of Common European Interest (IPCEIs) (the IPCEI Communication).[30] The IPCEI Communication sets out criteria for projects to satisfy in order to be compatible with state aid rules. The stated aim of this is to encourage Member States to channel their public spending to large projects that make a clear contribution to economic growth, jobs and the competitiveness of Europe, in line with the Europe 2020 objectives.[31]

The ambitious targets set by the Green Deal mean such projects will increasingly be geared towards sustainable energy and environmentally friendly/green technologies. The latest project, approved under the IPCEI Communication in December 2019, was related to lithium battery technology – an important part of industrial strategy for the automotive supply chain, where the EU currently lags behind China and the US. The project involved seven Member States and up to €3.2 billion of state aid in the coming years.

However, there have only been two such IPCEI projects – partly because they are so difficult to put together. Member States have called to simplify the rules to allow for quicker approval. Political pressure has come from France and Germany, who have stated that "the IPCEI is a useful tool for financing large scale innovative projects, but it is very complex to implement and that consequently "it may be appropriate to revise the implementing conditions to ensure that the IPCEI is easier and more effective to implement".[32] However, the Commission's fitness check, published on 30 October 2020, suggests movement, if any, will be in the opposite direction, increasing the number of Member States that need to participate, requiring the participation of SMEs, and further rules

---

29 State Aid Scoreboard 2019 (n 6).
30 Commission, Criteria for the analysis of the compatibility with the internal market of State aid to promote the execution of important projects of common European interest [2014] OJ C188/4.
31 Commission, "State aid: Commission adopts new rules to support important projects of common European interest, Press release (IP/14/673, 13 June 2014).
32 See "Franco-German manifesto for a European industrial policy fit for the 21st Century" (19 February 2019).

on aid being used to provoke relocation of activities from a country to EEA.[33] These incremental requirements all add to the investigative load of a case, requiring more time, evidence and effort to design aid schemes that comply. It will be interesting to see how quickly and effectively the green hydrogen IPCEI announced in December 2020 with 22 member States plus Norway can be implemented.[34]

Prioritising other policy objectives – such as spreading investment among the largest possible group of Member States – may not create optimal conditions to achieve the goals of the Green Deal. Difficult engineering and technical challenges may be made more so by political imperatives to see jobs and prestige divided between states – rather than allocated to where they are likely to deliver the fastest and greatest environmental dividend.

V. State Aid – Reform to the EEAG

The Commission acknowledges that changes to the EEAG and GBER are necessary and it has launched a call for contributions on what those changes should be.[35] Those changes should consider creating a hierarchy of objectives, with environmental goals placed higher than other EU policy objectives. This would be a major change for the Commission's compatibility assessment, which has not previously created an explicit hierarchy between policy objectives but has rather attempted to cohere all objectives together.

Competition policy has historically had the accepted primary goal of enhancing consumer welfare. While there is currently debate as to whether this is still appropriate, state aid has long been used as a tool to achieve a far wider range of EU policy goals – regional development, cohesion policy, industrial strategy, remedying socially unacceptable market failures etc. This is in part because state aid concerns public spending decisions and must therefore cohere with how democratic governments wish to spend their taxpayers' money; and in part because the Commission lacks tools as potent as state aid to pursue such goals. This means that a state aid measure for environmental purposes must be assessed against industrial, regional, SME development policies etc. Similarly, the Commission uses common assessment criteria to achieve a degree of coherence across its state aid policymaking. This requires evidence of incentive effect and that the aid is limited to the minimum necessary to reduce the competitive distortion created by the aid.

The EEAG guidelines reflect this balancing – and that is to be expected. It is of the essence of the Commission's role in assessing compatibility with the single

---

33 Commission Staff Working Document, "Fitness Check of the 2012 State aid modernisation package, railways guidelines and short-term export credit insurance»(30 October 2020).
34 See <www.hydrogen4climateaction.eu/ipcei-on-hydrogen>.
35 Commission, "Competition Policy supporting the Green Deal: Call for contributions»(13 October 2020).

market. Nevertheless, there are reasons to believe that the balance is not correctly drawn. Diedrik Samsom, Chef de Cabinet to Commissioner Timmermans, has said recently that "we need to overhaul our state aid strategy as a whole, and especially its regulations for energy and environment".[36]

Some candidate areas for this overhaul are:

Large companies

The EEAG, like state aid policy generally, favours SMEs over large enterprises. Aid intensities for large companies are lower than for small or medium sized enterprises. Evidentiary burdens placed on large enterprises are also greater. Yet large companies (those with over €50m in revenue or over 250 employees) are much more likely to be able to make investments operate at efficient scale and be able to access the capital required to make investments in energy transition.

Existing standards

The EEAG rules out any aid for complying with existing EU standards. Aid is only possible for going beyond EU standards or achieving them ahead of time. As EU standards tighten, this may be unduly restrictive – not all Member States are starting with industry that is in reality fully compliant with existing standards – and many gains could be made by permitting aid to comply with existing standards. Permitting aid to achieve compliance with EU emissions standards allows those standards to be met sooner – and thus rise faster.

Nuclear

The EEAG did not address nuclear energy at all – the deeply held differences between those supporting nuclear power and those opposed could not be reconciled in 2014. Now, however, the Hinkley Point C decision and CJEU judgments upholding it have established the basis on which state aid can be used to support nuclear, so there is no reason not to include nuclear power support in the next iteration.

Use of counterfactual for assessment of incentive effect

The EEAG, at recitals 51 and 52, requires the incentive effect of aid (i.e. that the aid *caused* the subsidised investment to proceed) to be proved against a counterfactual. Large companies must submit documentary evidence proving what they would have done without the aid. This in practice requires a financial model demonstrating an alternative – more profitable (but less green) – investment scenario. The maximum permissible aid is the delta between the eligible costs of the actual project and the counterfactual – subject to the aid intensity ceilings in EEAG Annex 1.

---

36 Diedrik Samson, "Speech» (launch of WindEurope Flagship report: Wind energy and economic recovery in Europe, WindEurope, online, 16 October 2020).

This requirement can be difficult to fulfil and can result in close examination of the assumptions used to create the counterfactual as well as extensive documentary disclosure to support its robustness. The counterfactual may also be somewhat artificial where there is no meaningful alternative project, as may be the case for new technologies such as hydrogen.

The Commission has helpfully already suggested that this could be replaced by the use of a funding gap approach.[37] This would involve looking at the proposed project alone and providing aid to bridge the gap between expected cash flows and those required to justify the investment against the beneficiaries' hurdle rate. This approach creates a greater risk of overcompensation.

However – as the response to COVID-19 has shown – it is necessary in a crisis to move quickly and define your priorities. If state aid is to reach energy transition projects more quickly and in larger volumes than it has up to now, it is likely that both the procedure and substance of the Commission's review need to be reorientated to place environmental sustainability ahead of the many other policy goals that the state aid regime is currently asked to serve.

---

37 Commission, "Sustainable Europe Investment Plan European Green Deal Investment Plan" (Communication) COM/2020/21 final, 13.

The Role of State Aid in Promoting Environmental Sustainability

NICOLE ROBINS, ANTON BURGER AND LAURA PUGLISI[*]

Oxera

I. Introduction

The European Union has embarked on an ambitious journey by recently setting itself a target of reducing greenhouse gas emissions to at least 55% by 2030 (compared with 1990 levels) and reaching climate neutrality by 2050 – and is the first continent worldwide to commit to such targets.[1] The Green Deal, proposed by the European Commission in December 2019, is at the core of the EU's climate policy and sets out a roadmap to achieve these climate targets. The green transition cuts across all sectors of the economy and will trigger significant changes in the energy sector in Europe.

As part of the Green Deal, the Commission will review, and revise where necessary, all climate-related policy instruments within the next few years, including the relevant state aid rules.[2] The revision of the Emission Trading

---

[*] Nicole is a partner at Oxera and heads Oxera's Brussels office and state aid practice. She leads Oxera's advice to clients on economic and financial issues associated with a diverse range of state aid matters across sectors including energy, financial services, health, post and telecoms, transport and sports infrastructure. Nicole also teaches the state aid module on the postgraduate diploma in Economics for Competition Law at King's College London, and provides training for EU judges on the economics of state aid. Anton is a senior consultant at Oxera, specialising in the economics of the energy sector. Based in Oxera's Berlin office, Anton leads Oxera's energy practice in Austria, Germany and Switzerland, advising clients on a range of competition, regulation and state aid matters. Laura is an experienced consultant at Oxera, specialising in economic and financial analysis in the state aid context, based in Oxera's Brussels office.

[1] Commission, "State of the Union Address 2020" (16 September 2020) <https://ec.europa.eu/info/sites/info/files/soteu_2020_en.pdf> accessed 25 October 2020.

[2] Commission, "State of the Union: Commission raises climate ambition and proposes 55% cut in emissions by 2030" (Press release IP/20/1599, 17 September 2020) <https://ec.europa.eu/commission/presscorner/detail/en/IP_20_1599> accessed 26 October 2020.

System (ETS) state aid guidelines marks the first climate-related update to the state aid framework since the publication of the Green Deal.[3] This is supplemented by the Commission's ongoing evaluation of other climate-relevant state aid rules – in particular, the Guidelines on State Aid for Environmental Protection and Energy (EEAG).[4] Furthermore, the Commission is reviewing the state aid framework for research, development and innovation (R&D&I) and the state aid framework for important projects of common European interest (IPCEI), which will be key in developing new, environmentally friendly technologies.

The state aid framework is a central pillar of the internal market and ensures a level playing field between Member States. As highlighted by the Commission, regulation is likely to be key to bringing about the energy transition.[5] However, state aid rules play a vital role in ensuring that the transformation can be implemented in an economically and socially viable way.

The magnitude of the investment challenge to achieve the climate and energy targets requires significant funding to be mobilised, from both the public and private sector.[6] The Commission estimates that approximately €260 billion of additional investment will be needed each year over the period 2020–30.[7] This funding will be used to foster research and innovation, and to support the deployment of new, climate-friendly, technology at market scale, while also phasing out fossil fuels.

This paper focuses on two areas that will be necessary to achieve a climate-neutral economy and which are likely to involve significant amounts of state aid: namely, the deployment of renewable hydrogen and the phase-out of electricity generated from coal and lignite plants. In particular, we discuss the role of economic and financial analysis within the state aid framework to support a cost-effective transition to carbon neutrality in these two areas.

---

3   ETS state aid provisions enable Member States to compensate certain heavy industries for higher electricity prices resulting from the carbon price signals created by the EU ETS. The new state aid rules reduce the number of sectors that can receive compensation and the amount of aid allowed (the aid intensity). In addition, aid is conditional on additional decarbonisation efforts by the companies concerned. See Commission, "State of the Union: Commission adopts revised EU Emission Trading System State Aid Guidelines" (Press release IP/20/1712, 21 September 2020) <https://ec.europa.eu/commission/presscorner/detail/en/ip_20_1712> accessed 25 October 2020.

4   On 13 October 2020, the Commission published a call for contributions about how competition rules, including state aid rules, and sustainability policies work together. See Commission, "Competition policy and the Green Deal" (13 October 2020) <https://ec.europa.eu/competition/information/green_deal/index_en.html> accessed 25 October 2020

5   Commission, "The Green Deal and competition policy" (Renew webinar, 22 September 2020) <https://ec.europa.eu/commission/commissioners/2019-2024/vestager/announcements/green-deal-and-competition-policy_en> accessed 27 October 2020.

6   ibid.

7   Commission, "Sustainable Europe Investment Plan European Green Deal Investment Plan" (Communication) COM (2020) 21 final, 1.

II. The Role of Hydrogen in Achieving the Green Deal Objectives

As at the time of writing this paper, almost all hydrogen produced in the EU is from natural gas and coal.[8] Central to the Commission's strategy of reaching the zero net emission target is therefore the widespread use of renewable hydrogen (i.e. hydrogen produced using renewable energy sources, such as solar and wind). During the transitional period, the Commission also sees an important role for low-carbon hydrogen (e.g. fossil-based hydrogen with carbon capture).

To develop renewable forms of hydrogen, it is estimated that total investment of up to €458 billion will be required by 2030.[9] As renewable and low-carbon forms of hydrogen[10] are not yet cost-competitive compared with fossil-based hydrogen, public intervention will be needed to close the significant cost gap and to incentivise the large-scale production of hydrogen technologies.[11]

1. What is the Commission's Hydrogen Strategy and what is the role of state aid therein?

The Commission's Hydrogen Strategy sets the strategic objective to install 40GW of renewable hydrogen electrolysers in the EU by 2030, and identifies three phases to reach this objective.[12]

1. Between 2020 and 2024, the focus will be on scaling up production capacity – in particular, the manufacturing of (large) electrolysers[13] and the retrofitting of existing hydrogen production plants.

2. Between 2025 and 30, the Commission expects an EU-wide logistics infrastructure to be developed, including a network of refuelling and

---

8   ibid.
9   The majority of the funding is likely to be required for the installation of new solar and wind generation capacity. See Michael Liebreich, "Separating Hype from Hydrogen – Part One: The Supply Side" (*BloombergNEF*, 8 October 2020) <https://about.bnef.com/blog/liebreich-separating-hype-from-hydrogen-part-one-the-supply-side/> accessed 27 October 2020.
10   Low-carbon hydrogen includes fossil-based hydrogen with carbon capture and electricity-based hydrogen, with significantly reduced full-life cycle greenhouse gas emissions compared with existing hydrogen production.
11   Carbon prices in the range of €55–€90/tonne of CO_2 would be needed to make fossil-based hydrogen with carbon capture competitive with fossil-based hydrogen today. Latest carbon pricing forecasts predict that the average carbon price in the EU throughout the 2020s will be €32/tonne of CO_2 equivalent. Commission, "A hydrogen strategy for a climate-neutral Europe" (Communication) COM (2020) 301 final, 4; Sarah George, "EU carbon price to reach €32 by 2030, short of required price for UK's net-zero target" (*Edie*, 29 June 2020) <www.edie.net/news/6/EU-carbon-price-set-to-rise-to-EUR32-by-2030--but-experts-say-EUR81-necessary-to-achieve-net-zero-in-the-UK/> accessed 27 October 2020.
12   Commission, "A hydrogen strategy for a climate-neutral Europe" (n 11), 2.
13   Electrolysers enable the separation of water into hydrogen and oxygen. For the production of renewable hydrogen, renewable energy is used in this process.

storage stations to transport hydrogen from renewable-energy – rich areas to serve demand in other Member States. Most of the hydrogen is likely to be transported via pipelines, which may require investment aid for the repurposing of existing gas pipelines.

3.   From 2030 onwards until 2050, the Commission expects that renewable hydrogen technologies will have reached maturity and will be deployed at large scale to reach all hard-to-decarbonise sectors.

In light of the scale of the changes required, state aid for investment in hydrogen production and network infrastructure will be crucial in making hydrogen commercially viable within the timescales targeted. For example, France and Germany have recently announced €2 billion and €9 billion of aid respectively for the development of hydrogen.[14]

In light of the significant price differential between conventional and renewable hydrogen, operating aid is also likely to be needed alongside investment aid.[15] In particular, in order to scale up renewable and low-carbon hydrogen production before it becomes cost-competitive, the Commission is likely to allow tendering systems for carbon contracts for difference (CfDs), where aid would be granted as a premium to the market price of renewable or low-carbon hydrogen.[16]

In order to make renewable hydrogen cost-competitive, Member States are also likely to allocate significant funding to R&D&I initiatives, including initiatives to intra-EU cooperation of Member States in the context of IPCEIs. For example, France, Germany, Portugal and the Netherlands have already expressed their intention to coordinate efforts on the development of renewable hydrogen under an IPCEI.[17]

Lastly, policymakers are also likely to consider the implementation of demand-side measures, such as green certificates and quota obligations, in order to stimulate investments in hydrogen. The economic and political aspects of the available policy tools to support hydrogen are set out in Table 1 and described below.

---

14 Arezki Yaïche, "France's EUR 2 billion hydrogen support package to be notified soon to EU, minister says" (*MLex*, 8 September 2020); Giulia Bedini, "Hydrogen sees boost in new EU industry alliance, Franco-German push for common projects" (*MLex*, 8 July 2020); Andreas Franke, "France cranks up hydrogen plans with 6.5-GW, 2030 target, plays down new nuclear" (*S&P Global*, 8 September 2020) <www.spglobal.com/platts/en/market-insights/latest-news/electric-power/090820-france-cranks-up-hydrogen-plans-with-65-gw-2030-target-plays-down-new-nuclear> accessed 27 October 2020; Federal Government of Germany (2020), "The National Hydrogen Strategy" (June 2020) <www.bmbf.de/files/bmwi_Nationale%20Wasserstoffstrategie_Eng_s01.pdf> accessed 27 October 2020, 5.

15 In the German government's National Hydrogen Strategy (n14), exemptions from taxies and levies for electricity used in the production of green hydrogen are highlighted.

16 Commission, "A hydrogen strategy for a climate-neutral Europe", (n 11), 13.

17 MLex, "EU green hydrogen project sees boost in Portuguese – Dutch cooperation" (*MLex*, 23 September 2020); Yaïche (n 14); Bedini (n 14). Germany has called for steelmakers aiming to use renewable-based hydrogen to be supported by an IPCEI. See Giulia Bedini, "Clean steelmaking should feature in EU-backed hydrogen project, Altmaier says" (*MLex*, 5 October 2020).

Table 1: Economic and Political Aspects of Hydrogen Support Measures

	Investment aid	Operating aid (i.e. CfD)	Demand support	
			Hydrogen-specific: tax exemptions, quotas	Not hydrogen-specific: carbon price mechanism
Economic aspects				
Technology neutrality	By definition, technology-specific	Typically technology-specific	Typically open for various market-driven solutions to produce hydrogen	Open for various market-driven solutions to reduce CO_2 emissions
Effect on future wholesale hydrogen price	Lowers hydrogen price as the supply of hydrogen is supported		Raises hydrogen price (as demand for renewable and low-carbon hydrogen is supported), triggering a market-driven increase in hydrogen supply	
Political aspects				
Economic or industrial policy	Aid can be targeted to specific companies, thereby promoting specific industry and employment objectives	Large degree of control over which technologies are used to produce hydrogen	Market will supply hydrogen in cheapest way possible	Politically challenging to implement, and risk of carbon leakage

Note: The table excludes R&D&I aid. It is assumed that demand support schemes will be granted for green or low-carbon hydrogen only, and that the necessary certification systems will be put in place.
Source: Oxera

Hydrogen-specific demand support and carbon prices both have the objective of increasing demand for hydrogen, and thus the price, for renewable and low-carbon hydrogen.[18] The market will then supply the hydrogen as economically as possible, by producing it from renewable energy or natural gas in combination with carbon capture and storage, or through imports from international carbon-free sources. Investment and operating aid for hydrogen will help to increase the supply of hydrogen and to balance out the increase in hydrogen prices resulting from the demand-side measures. Investment aid and operating aid work differently, in that certain ways of producing hydrogen are financially supported, which will increase the production of hydrogen and, all else being equal, reduce the market price for hydrogen.

From a political point of view, an increase in carbon prices might be challenging to implement due to the social consequences of higher energy prices.[19] In addition, an effective carbon border tax should be put in place to avoid carbon leakage. Therefore, there might be a tendency to prefer more direct measures such as investment and operating aid, as these tools offer more control over the effects of the measure.

---

18 It is expected that only relatively high carbon prices would influence hydrogen demand.
19 Giulia Bedini, "Carbon pricing works but is politically tough, EIB official says" (*MLex*, 19 February 2020).

These design choices could have implications for the assessment of the incentive effects and the appropriateness of aid. Putting greater emphasis on the *ex ante* assessment of design choices and their effects when developing state aid rules for hydrogen and assessing large aid measures can help to ensure that aid is indeed needed, appropriate and does not unduly distort competition and trade.

2. How might the role for economic and financial analysis in assessing the compatibility of aid change?

In line with the common principles for assessing the compatibility of state aid, the application of economic and financial analysis will be important to ensure that public funding for investment and operating aid is limited to the minimum necessary (i.e. ensuring the proportionality of the aid), while minimising any adverse impact on competition and trade.

In relation to operating aid in form of CfDs, auctioning or competitive bidding processes to select the beneficiaries should normally help ensure that any aid is limited to a minimum. However, depending on the design of the tender, the proportionality of the aid may still need to be considered.[20] For example, if CfDs are tendered out under a predetermined strike price (i.e. a price set by the administration that determines the amount of aid as top-up in relation to the market price), economic and financial analysis should be applied to assess, on an individual basis, that the aid is the minimum needed for each of the selected operators. This typically requires the expected profitability of the investment for each operator to be calculated and for this to be compared to a benchmark return that would be required by a private investor.

In relation to investment aid, the Commission has suggested that, for investments that are compatible with the transition to climate neutrality, including hydrogen projects/investments, the requirement to assess eligible costs against a counter-factual (a less environmentally friendly) investment could be replaced by the use of a funding gap approach.[21] This approach would provide greater flexibility for "green" projects. The funding gap is calculated as the net present value of the difference between the positive and negative expected cash flows from the project, including investment costs, over the lifetime of the investment. Given the potentially long time horizon of investments in hydrogen infrastructure, particular

---

20 This would be in line with the approach followed by the Commission in the case of aid provided by the UK government for the conversion of RWE's coal power plant to biomass. Although the project was selected via a tender, the Commission still analysed the proportionality of the aid. See *SA.38758 (2014/N), SA.38759 (2014/N), SA.38761 (2014/N), SA.38763 (2014/N) & SA.38812 (2014/N) – United Kingdom, Support for five Offshore Wind Farms: Walney, Dudgeon, Hornsea, Burbo Bank and Beatrice* Commission decision C(2014) 5074 final; *State aid for Lynemouth Power Station Biomass Conversion SA.38762 (2015/C) which the United Kingdom is planning to implement* Commission decision C(2015) 8441 final [2017] OJ L205/70.

21 Commission, "Sustainable Europe Investment Plan European Green Deal Investment Plan" (n 7), 13.

attention should be paid to the robustness of the results in order to avoid the risk of overcompensation.

To incentivise the necessary investment in hydrogen technologies, specific eligibility and compatibility criteria, including the determination of maximum aid intensities for hydrogen investments, could be included in the revised EEAG. However, one of the challenges in setting the maximum aid intensities will be to avoid crowding out private investment, which could occur if the thresholds are set too high. In this respect, a regular review – based, for example, on *ex post* evaluations of large individual aid measures and aid schemes – could be used to inform adjustments to the applicable thresholds. In addition, thresholds should differentiate between the type of support needed for renewable hydrogen and that required for low-carbon hydrogen, including provisions for a phase-out of such aid when the technologies reach market maturity.

In terms of incentivising the necessary R&D&I in hydrogen, it is possible that Member States will continue to use the General Block Exemption Regulation (GBER) as a main tool to grant R&D&I aid.[22] The Commission has recently announced the introduction of a "green bonus", which would allow Member States to use more state aid for projects that make a genuine contribution to the EU's green goals, and could also be applied for R&D&I aid.[23] While in certain areas, such as the level of allowed aid intensities, there could be arguments to allow more flexibility for "green" projects under state aid rules, any significant relaxing of the existing rules carries risks. It would be important to ensure that the usual safeguards are not eroded, to mitigate the risk of crowding out private investment and causing distortions to competition. Since the upcoming aid schemes for "green" investments, including hydrogen, may be very large in terms of volume, certain aspects of the compatibility assessment, such as the assessment of the incentive effects and proportionality of the aid, and the evaluation of the impact of aid on competition and trade, should be applied more rather than less rigorously.

III. Assessment of the Compatibility of Aid with the Phase-out of Coal

The Commission has recently announced that state aid rules will be revised to facilitate the phasing-out of fossil fuels.[24] The assessment of the compatibility of aid with the closure of coal-fired power plants, while not covered under the

---

22 Since the entry into force of the R&D&I Framework in 2014, the Commission has assessed four individual state aid measures to date, compared with 55 individual ad hoc measures notified under the previous R&D&I Framework, in place 2007–2014. While only 19% of R&D&I aid was assessed under the GBER between 2007 and 2014, this share had increased to 85% in 2018. Based on information provided in the Commission's state aid case register and from the Commission's state aid scoreboard.
23 Commission, "The Green Deal and competition policy" (n 5).
24 Commission, "Sustainable Europe Investment Plan, European Green Deal Investment Plan" (n 7), 12.

current EEAG, mirrors the principles of these guidelines. The Commission has recently emphasised that, where compensation for the (early) closure of coal-fired plants is granted, particular focus will be placed on the assessment of the proportionality of the aid (i.e. to ensure that aid is limited to the minimum necessary), as well as the impact of the aid on competition.[25]

1. How has the Commission assessed the compatibility of aid with the phase-out of coal power plants?

The Commission has already approved aid for the phase-out of coal power plants in a number of EU Member States. The approach adopted in the past by the Commission to assessing measures for the closure of coal power plants in Germany and the Netherlands is described in Box 1 below.

**Box 1: Assessing the compatibility of aid
with the phase-out of coal- and lignite-fired power plants**

Aid for the closure of lignite-fired power plants in Germany[26]

In 2015, Germany decided to gradually shut down eight lignite-fired power plants, representing 2.5% of the country's total generation capacity at the time. Before being decommissioned, the power plants were to be kept on standby for four years as an emergency reserve. Germany provided a compensation scheme with a total budget of €1.6 billion to be granted to the operators during the four-year standby period.

Before turning to the compatibility assessment, the Commission considered the existence of aid. The German authorities argued that the compensation would not confer a selective economic advantage to the operator since it constituted a compensation for damages resulting from an act of the state. However, as the Commission could not conclude with certainty that under German law there would be a claim for compensation of this amount, it could not rule out the existence of aid, and proceeded with the compatibility assessment.

The compensation was calculated as the profits that the plants would have made if they had continued operating commercially, i.e. by selling electricity as well as providing services to the transmission system operators, such as redispatch or balancing. In order to calculate the plants' forgone profits, the expected costs, such as fuel costs and the costs of purchasing emission allowances, were subtracted from the expected revenues. In addition to the forgone profits, the remuneration included compensation for the plants' costs of preparing the initial mothballing and the fixed costs of remaining in standby for four years, excluding any avoidable costs.

The German authorities also presented a scenario analysis to assess the impact of higher prices for emission allowances and lower wholesale electricity prices on the operators' profitability. The scenario analysis showed that during the four-year standby period operators were expected to remain price-competitive, and would therefore continue to operate if they were not required to close. While the scenario analysis evidenced the need for aid and the incentive effects of the aid, it was not used to inform the level of compensation in the proportionality assessment. In particular, the expected

---

25   ibid, 14.
26   *Closure of German lignite-fired power plants* Commission decision SA.42536 (27 May 2016) [2016] OJ C258/1.

revenues from selling electricity during the four-year standby period were assumed to be constant, based on forward electricity prices in the years 2012–14. While the Commission highlights that using outturn data on forward prices does not allow expected changes in electricity prices over the period in which the aid will be granted to be taken into account, it considered this approach as suitable, given that the operators would be provided with certainty upfront about the amount of compensation.

The Commission approved the aid on the basis that, overall, the positive effects of the aid in terms of reducing CO_2 emissions would outweigh any distortions to competition and trade.

Aid for the prohibition of coal-based production of electricity in the Netherlands[27]

In 2019, the Dutch government adopted a law for the phase-out of coal-based electricity production by 2030. While most of the power plants affected by the law were granted a transition period of 5–10 years, one plant was required to close shortly after the adoption of the law due to its age and low levels of efficiency. The Dutch government granted compensation of €52.5 million to the owner of this plant. As in the German case, the compensation was calculated as the plant's expected forgone profits based on projections of future costs and revenues that the plant would have incurred if it had continued operating.

As in the German case, the Commission could not provide a definitive answer to the question of the existence of aid, but concluded that the compensation was compatible.

Regarding the proportionality of the aid, the compensation was also calculated on a forgone profit approach. While the Commission did not provide a detailed assessment of the calculations submitted, it noted that the assumptions underlying the calculation were reasonable. Based on the public version of the Commission's decision, it is not clear whether sensitivity analysis was undertaken to assess expected profitability under different price scenarios. Overall, however, the Commission concluded that the compensation was proportionate. As the other compatibility criteria were also found to be met, the Commission approved the compensation as compatible aid. A number of Member States have already decided to phase out of coal over the coming years.[28] Some of the planned schemes phasing out coal are much wider in scope compared with the measures approved so far. For example, under the German Coal Exit Act, all coal-based electricity generation (40 GW) is planned to be phased out by 2038.[29] In general,

---

27 *Prohibition of coal for the production of electricity in the Netherlands* Commission decision SA.54537 (2020/NN) 12 May 2020 [2020] OJ C220/1.

28 As at the time of writing (October 2020), Denmark, Finland, France, the Netherlands, Portugal, Slovakia and Spain are expected to phase out coal by 2030, without a significant increase in fossil fuel gas. Greece, Hungary, Ireland and Italy are also expected to phase out coal, but with an increase in fossil fuel gas. See Climate Action Network Europe, "The EU Member States which are set to receive most of the Just Transition Fund plan to stick with coal" (Press release, 9 September 2020) <www.caneurope.org/publications/press-releases/1989-report-the-eu-member-states-which-are-set-to-receive-most-of-the-just-transition-fund-plan-to-stick-with-coal> accessed 26 October 2020.

29 See Federal Ministry for Economic Affairs and Energy, "Final decision to launch the coal-phase out – a project for a generation" (Press release, 3 July 2020) <www.bmwi.de/Redaktion/EN/Pressemitteilungen/2020/20200703-

if compensation for the early closure of coal plants is envisaged, it should balance the merits of protecting property rights against the public interest of reducing carbon emissions, while ensuring compliance with state aid rules.

2. How might the role for economic and financial analysis change going forward?

In light of the Commission's announcements in its Green Deal investment plan, and given the number of Member States that plan to phase out coal, it is likely that the Commission will put more emphasis on the proportionality assessment in future cases. Such an approach would be beneficial to reduce the risk of overcompensation and to avoid inconsistency in the application of the compatibility assessment.

In relation to the proportionality of the aid, this would require more detailed scrutiny of the calculation of coal plants' forgone profits in order to ensure that compensation does not go beyond the plants' expected loss of profits due to the closure. The energy market is likely to change substantially over the next few years, given the various measures aimed at supporting the green transition. For example, greater consideration might need to be given to examining the impact of CO_2 prices and subsidies for competing technologies on the forgone profits of coal power operators.

Furthermore, even if tender procedures or auctions are used, where plant operators bid the amount of compensation at which they would be willing to close, the risk of overcompensation cannot always be ruled out – for example, due to strategic bidding. Economic analysis can be applied to assess the implications of auction design for the level of compensation payments and to help ensure the appropriate auction design to reduce the risk of overcompensation.

In its Green Deal guidance, the Commission has highlighted that compensation for the closure of coal power plants should be structured in a way to limit any distortions to competition.[30] In the case of the German Coal Exit Act, for example, in light of the volume of the scheme, the measure is likely to have implications for the European electricity market that will persist for several years. Economic analysis might therefore also play a more prominent role going forward in assessing the impact of large-scale phase-out schemes on competition and trade – for example, in relation to market barriers to entry for renewable and other low-carbon technologies.

While it remains to be seen whether the Commission will include specific rules for the phase-out of coal in the revised EEAG, the application of economic and financial analysis should be made more central to compatibility assessments for

---

final-decision-to-launch-the-coal-phase-out.html> accessed 26 October 2020.

30   Commission, "Sustainable Europe Investment Plan, European Green Deal Investment Plan" (n 7), 14.

the phase-out of coal, as it can help to ensure that the decarbonisation targets are reached while minimising distortions and any unintended side effects of large scale phase-out programmes.

IV. Conclusion

Alongside regulation, state aid will play a vital role in supporting the green transition. The large-scale deployment of hydrogen and the phase-out of coal are two areas that are fundamental to achieving the objectives of the Green Deal. Neither is yet covered under the energy-related state aid framework, which is currently being reviewed by the Commission.[31] While it is possible that specific criteria for investment and production aid for hydrogen will be included in the revised state aid framework, the assessment of the compatibility of compensation for the phase-out of coal remains open.

In light of the broader market reforms being contemplated as part of the European Green Deal and their implications for the European energy market, certain aspects of the state aid framework will be central for assessing the compatibility of aid – in particular, the assessment of the need for aid, its proportionality and the expected impact on competition and trade. As highlighted in this paper, based on the examples of hydrogen and the phase-out of coal, the application of sound economic and financial analysis is likely to be key in ensuring that the green transition is implemented in a cost-efficient way, does not crowd out private investments and limits distortions to competition and trade.

31 The Commission has announced that the EEAG will be revised to be consistent with the Green Deal objectives. See Commission, "The Green Deal and competition policy" (n 5).

Chapter 5
Public Procurement

Environmental and Climate Sustainability in Public Procurement

PATRICK THIEFFRY[*]

The outreach of environmental problems is striking when it questions well-established market practices, and this extends to climate concerns that were initially not at the forefront of that discussion, but which now weave through the whole environmental discourse.

The "European Green Deal" was proposed by the European Commission in a communication of 11 December 2019,[1] the day before the European Council endorsed "the objective of achieving a climate-neutral EU by 2050, in line with the objectives of the Paris Agreement"[2] and announced new "Nationally Determined Contributions" (NDCs) to that effect.[3] A "roadmap for making the EU's economy sustainable by turning climate and environmental challenges into opportunities across all policy areas and making the transition just and inclusive for all",[4] the "Green Deal" is at the same time an anticipated announcement of these new NDCs, a prefiguration of the EU's forthcoming Eighth Environmental Action Programme for 2030, and part of the EU strategy to implement the UN 2030 Agenda and Sustainable Development Goals.[5]

---

[*] Patrick Thieffry is an independent arbitrator and a member of the Paris and New York Bars. He specialises in competition law and environmental law.
1   Commission, "The European Green Deal" (Communication) COM(2019) 640 final.
2   Conclusions of the meeting of the European Council of 12 December 2019, EUCO 29/19.
3   Council of the European Union, "Long-term low greenhouse gas emission development strategy of the European Union and its Member States – Submission to the UNFCCC on behalf of the European Union and its Member States" (5 March 2020, no 6612/20).
4   Commission, "The European Green Deal sets out how to make Europe the first climate-neutral continent by 2050, boosting the economy, improving people's health and quality of life, caring for nature, and leaving no one behind" (Press release IP/19/6691, 11 December 2019).
5   See UN Resolution "Transforming our world: the 2030 Agenda for Sustainable Development" A/RES/70/1* (25 September 2015).

To that end, the EU must "rethink policies" for clean energy supply across the economy, industry, production and consumption, large-scale infrastructure, transport, food and agriculture, construction, and taxation and social benefits, which may require delicate "potential trade-offs between economic, environmental and social objectives". Quite unsurprisingly in such a context, the European Green Deal makes the case that "public authorities, including the EU institutions, should lead by example and ensure that their procurement is green". The Commission's communication thus announces that it will propose "further legislation and guidance on green public purchasing",[6] noting that the EU's trade policy "facilitates trade and investment in green goods and services and promotes climate-friendly public procurement".[7] Perhaps more significantly for further legislative and administrative developments, it calls for policy reforms to help to ensure "effective carbon pricing throughout the economy" that would "… facilitate an increase in sustainable public and private investment".[8] The potential market impact of the European Green Deal through public procurement appears potentially considerable when it claims that "national budgets play a key role in the transition", and that "a greater use of green budgeting tools will help to redirect public investment, consumption and taxation to green priorities and away from harmful subsidies".[9] Yet, the "roadmap" annexed to the Commission's communication does not envision a review of the current EU public procurement legislation among the many legislative actions listed, and this may lead some to wonder whether the Commission considers that such legislation as it currently stands already sufficiently addresses the matter.

The Court of Justice applied for the first time in 2002 the so-called "integration principle" – that according to which the requirements of environmental protection must be taken into account in other policies and actions of the EU – in the context of EU rules on public procurement. At the time, secondary EU law on public procurement[10] was still silent on environmental protection, just as the EC Treaty had been itself until not so many years before that. The court then held in the much-remarked *Concordia Bus* case that, when a contracting authority awards a contract to the tenderer that presented the most economically advantageous tender, it may take ecological criteria into consideration.[11] In this case, the city of Helsinki, the contracting authority, had adopted a system of points linked to a number of criteria, including inter alia NO_x emissions and external noise levels of the buses that would be used for the operation of public transportation routes. While it referred expressly to Article 6 TEEC (now Article 11 TFEU) which had transcribed the

---

6 Commission, "The European Green Deal" (n 1), [2.1.3].
7 ibid, section 3.
8 ibid, [2.1.1].
9 ibid, [2.1.2].
10 Directive 92/50 relating to the coordination of procedures for the award of public service contracts [1992] OJ L209/1; Directive 93/38/EEC coordinating the procurement procedures of entities operating in the water, energy, transport and telecommunications sectors [1993] OJ L199/84.
11 Case C–513/99 *Concordia Bus Finland Oy Ab v Helsingin kaupunki* [2002] ECR I-7213.

integration principle in the Treaty, the court interpreted public procurement in a way favourable to the environment. However, this should not have come as a surprise, since the integration principle is first and foremost a legislative action principle. Barely one year later, in *EVN AG*, the court accepted that the use of energy produced from renewable energy sources could be considered in a public procurement contract.[12]

Public procurement rules were thereafter revised so as to allow a compromise between market integration and protection of the environment. By reference to the solutions given in *Concordia Bus* and *EVN AG*, the directives on public procurement positively recognised the principle of integration as early as 2004.[13] These directives referred directly to Article 6 TEEC. Quite remarkably, the co-legislators explained at length and at the forefront of their introductory considerations that they acted in the aftermath of ECJ case law "... which clarifies the possibilities for the environmental protection requirements... to be integrated into the definition and implementation, in particular with a view to promoting sustainable development..., including in the environmental and/or social area".[14] Just as prominently, they explained that they purported to clarify "how the contracting entities may contribute to the protection of the environment and the promotion of sustainable development, while ensuring the possibility of obtaining the best value for money for their contracts".[15] These statements signalled a significant departure from the preceding normative vacuum.

Since then, yet another step was made with the adoption of the three directives on 26 February 2014: Directive 2014/24 on public procurement,[16] Directive 2014/25 on procurement by entities operating in the water, energy, transport and postal services sectors[17] and Directive 2014/23 on the award of concession contracts.[18]

Upon further analysis, the high degree of integration of environmental require-ments in the public procurement legislation in the 2014 directives' substantive provisions, which remain in force as of today, is unquestionable (see section I, below). However, further legislative action which was meant to ensure the effec-tiveness of those provisions by setting forth methods to quantify – the more illustrative neologism "monetising" is sometimes used – has faltered, which leaves open the question of the balance between environmental and climate considerations, on the one hand, and purely economic ones, on the other, in the EU's future legislative actions (see section II, below).

---

12 Case C–448/01 *EVN AG* [2003] ECR I-14527
13 Directive 2004/17 coordinating the procurement procedures of entities operating in the water, energy, transport and postal services sectors [2004] OJ L134/1; Directive 2004/18 on the coordination of procedures for the award of public works contracts, public supply contracts and public service contracts [2004] OJ L134/114.
14 Directive 2004/17 (n 13), recital 1; Directive 2004/18 (n 13), recital 1.
15 Directive 2004/17 (n 13), recital 12; Directive 2004/18 (n 13), recital 5.
16 Directive 2014/24 on public procurement and repealing Directive 2004/18/EC [2014] OJ L94/65.
17 Directive 2014/25 on procurement by entities operating in the water, energy, transport and postal services sectors and repealing Directive 2004/17/EC [2014] OJ L94/243.
18 Directive 2014/23 on the award of concession contracts [2014] OJ L94/1.

V. The Unquestionably High Degree of Integration of Environmental and Climate Requirements in EU Public Procurement Legislation

Just as remarkably as in 2004, and perhaps somewhat curiously, the 2014 co-legislators again described their reasoning with respect to the integration of the requirements of environmental protection in public procurement, albeit in a much less dramatic fashion than their 2004 predecessors, as far as the priori-tisation of the stated underlying considerations to their action is concerned. It is only at a much later stage in the 2014 directives' introductory recitals that the legislature stresses the importance of complying with the environmental obliga-tions that apply at the place where the works are executed or the services provided[19] at the relevant stages of the procurement procedure.[20]

It should not be inferred from that formal "repositioning" of considerations pertaining to the environment, or more broadly to sustainable development, that they would have faded away in the EU institutions' determination or that this would involve some kind of a downgrading. If only one sign that these institu-tions remain serious about such concerns were to be offered, it could be their further announcement that operators which commit serious or repeated violations of environmental law may be excluded from obtaining such contracts,[21] a threat that cannot be ignored by the many such operators for which public procurement is a vital part of their business, especially on environmental services markets, such as in the water and waste sectors. Indeed, public purchasers are encouraged to take into account "all costs over the life-cycle of works, supplies or services" including those "imputed to environmental externalities". The legislature stresses that "control of the observance of the environmental, social and labour law provisions should be performed at the relevant stages of the procurement procedure, when applying the general principles governing the choice of participants and the award of contracts, when applying the exclusion criteria and when applying the provisions concerning abnormally low tenders".[22] These comprise factors involved in the specific process of production, provision or trading and during a later stage of their life cycle, "even where such factors do not form part of their material substance".[23]

Environmental requirements may thus have to be taken into account at the various stages of the public procurement process. For instance, the conditions

---

19 Directive 2014/23 (n 18), recital 55; Directive 2014/24 (n 16), recital 37; Directive 2014/25 (n 17), recital 52.
20 Directive 2014/23 (n 18), recital 58; Directive 2014/24 (n 16), recital 40; Directive 2014/25 (n 17), recital 55.
21 Directive 2014/23 (n 18), recital 70; Directive 2014/24 (n 16), recital 101; Directive 2014/25 (n 17), recital 106.
22 Directive 2014/25 (n 17), recital 40.
23 Directive 2014/24 (n 16), recitals 96–97; see also Directive 2014/23 (n 18), recital 64, and Directive 2014/25 (n 17), recitals 83 & 101.

under which a contract must be performed may be set forth by laying down "special conditions… including environmental considerations, provided that they are linked to the subject-matter of the contract and indicated in the call for competition or in the procurement documents". However, the stages at which most legal issues should be expected to arise are those of the definition of technical specifications and of the selection criteria.

1. Technical specifications

Technical specifications are most important in public procurement since they are an essential instrument to guarantee equality between bidders, and thus the smooth operation of competition and markets. Technical specifications may include environmental characteristics with respect to expected performance or functional requirements of the contemplated goods or services, provided that "the parameters are sufficiently precise to allow tenderers to determine the subject-matter of the contract and to allow contracting authorities to award the contract".[24] The remarkable new provision in this respect is that "those characteristics may also refer to the specific process or methods of production or provision of the requested works, supplies or services or to a specific process for another stage of its life cycle even where such factors do not form part of their material substance".[25]

Contracting authorities may require a specific label "as means of proof that the works, services or supplies correspond to the required characteristics." They are only obliged to accept another label with different requirements where an economic operator had demonstrably no possibility of obtaining the specific label indicated or an equivalent label while under prior law they were required to accept any other means of proof, such as a producer's technical file or a recognised body's test report. However, in order to avoid any risks of discrimination, label requirements must meet a few conditions such as, classically, being "linked to the subject-matter of the contract" and "appropriate to define characteristics of the works, supplies or services that are the subject-matter of the contract", being based on objectively verifiable and non-discriminatory criteria, established in an open and transparent procedure in which all relevant stakeholders may participate, accessible to all interested parties, etc.[26] The Directive thus takes on board the findings of the ECJ in the important matter *Max Havelaar*. In its judgment in that matter, the ECJ had found that contracting authorities had "the option to use the detailed specifications of an eco-label, but not the eco-label as such".[27]

---

24 Directive 2014/24 (n 16), art 42(3)(a); Directive 2014/25 (n 17), arts 60(1) and 60(3)(a).
25 Subject to the traditional requirement that "they are linked to the subject-matter of the contract and proportionate to its value and objectives" (Directive 2014/24 (n 16), art 42(1); Directive 2014/25 (n 17), art 60(1)).
26 Directive 2014/24 (n 16), art 43 and Directive 2014/25 (n 17), art 61.
27 Case C–368/10 *Commission v Netherlands* EU:C:2012:284; Laurens Ankersmit, "The EU Court of Justice establishes that public authorities can use fair trade criteria as criteria to award public supply contracts of products (Netherlands Max Havelaar)" (2012) e-Competitions Art N° 64145.

Such new provisions are not all present in Directive 2014/23 on concession contracts. In particular, while technical and functional requirements may refer to the "specific process of production or provision of the requested works or services", the life-cycle approach is not included, and even less the material contents of the performance.[28] Likewise, eco-labels are not provided for in that Directive, perhaps as a result of the concession contractor's freedom of organisation as to the way it performs the public service.

2. Award criteria

Contract award criteria are now limited – and this is not specific to environmental considerations – to those which make it possible to determine the offer that is the "most economically advantageous from the point of view of the contracting authority",[29] which is more likely to take into account environmental and climate considerations than the traditional "lowest price".[30] In this respect, in *Concordia Bus*, additional points had been given on the basis of the emissions of NO_x emissions of the buses that would be used and of their noise emissions.[31] According to the court, in the context of a public contract for the provision of urban bus transport services, the contracting authority "may take into consideration ecological criteria such as the level of nitrogen oxide emissions or the noise level of the buses, provided that they are linked to the subject-matter of the contract, do not confer an unrestricted freedom of choice on the authority, are expressly mentioned in the contract documents or the tender notice, and comply with all the fundamental principles of Community law, in particular the principle of non-discrimination".[32] In *EVN AG*, a weighting of 45% pertaining to the use of energy produced from renewable energy sources was accepted.[33] By contrast, however, the court ruled out such a criterion where it is not accompanied by requirements that permit the accuracy of the information contained in the tenders to be effectively verified.[34]

Not only is the most economically advantageous tender now to be chosen under the 2014 directives, such tender is determined "using a cost-effectiveness approach, such as life-cycle costing… and (it) may include the best price-quality ratio, which shall be assessed on the basis of criteria, including qualitative, environmental and or social aspects".[35]

Again, Directive 2014/23 on concession contracts does not go as far as its two siblings on procurement: the taking into account of environmental impacts in

28 Directive 2014/23 (n 18), art 36(1).
29 Directive 2014/24 (n 16), art 67(1) – (2); Directive 2014/25 (n 17), art 82(1) – (2).
30 See, e.g., Directive 2004/17 (n 13), art 55(1)(b).
31 *Concordia Bus* (n 11).
32 ibid, [69].
33 *EVN AG* (n 12).
34 ibid, [72].
35 Directive 2014/24, art 67 and directive 2014/25, art 82.

the selection of the tender is not provided for, much less that of the life-cycle costing. The award criteria may just "include, inter alia, environmental… criteria".[36] Developments below shall thus focus on Directives 2014/24 and 2014/25. As in all aspects of public procurement, the criteria used must be "linked to the subject-matter of the public contract in question". This may clearly play as a limitation factor in the integration of environmental requirements. Yet, such criteria are deemed to be linked to the subject matter of a public contract "where they relate to the works, supplies or services to be provided under that contract in any respect and at any stage of their life cycle", including the specific process of production, provision or trading of those works, supplies or services, "even where such factors do not form part of their material substance".[37]

The life-cycle costing covers, "to the extent relevant", end-of-life costs and, more importantly, "costs imputed to environmental externalities linked to the product, service or work during its life cycle, provided their monetary value can be determined and verified", in particular those of greenhouse gas emissions and other climate change mitigation costs.[38] The legislature further comments that this means "internal costs, such as research to be carried out, development, production, transport, use, maintenance and end-of-life disposal costs but can also include costs imputed to environmental externalities, such as pollution caused by extraction of the raw materials used in the product or caused by the product itself or its manufacturing, provided they can be monetised and monitored".[39]

VI. The Questionable Valuation of Environmental and Climate Externalities in EU Public Procurement Legislation

Under the 2014 directives, public purchasers are thus encouraged to take into account "all costs over the life-cycle of works, supplies or services". Such costs include those "imputed to environmental externalities" which comprise factors involved in the specific process of production, provision or trading, and during a later stage of their life cycle. More strikingly, "even where such factors do not form part of their material substance", they should be taken into account. Thus, the notion of "life-cycle costing", as used in the directives, raises the question of "valuing" or "monetising" costs "such as pollution caused by extraction of the raw materials used in the product or caused by the product itself or its manufacturing".

---

36   Directive 2014/23 (n 18), art 41(1) – (2).
37   Directive 2014/24 (n 16), art 67; Directive 2014/25 (n 17), art 82.
38   Directive 2014/24 (n 16), art 67; Directive 2014/25 (n 17), art 83.
39   Directive 2014/24 (n 16), art 96.

While the 2014 directives provide little guidance as to such "valuation" or "monetisation" of life-cycle costs to be used for public procurement at large, significant expectations developed in the area of road transport vehicles as a possible model for other sectors – albeit in vain.

1. Monetisation of life-cycle costs in public procurement at large

When they decided that the most economically advantageous tender to be chosen is determined "using a cost-effectiveness approach, such as life-cycle costing", the EU institutions did not ignore the underlying issues. They could not be clearer in this respect: "… methods which contracting authorities use for assessing costs imputed to environmental externalities should be established in advance in an objective and non-discriminatory manner and be accessible to all interested parties. Such methods can be established at national, regional or local level, but they should, to avoid distortions of competition through tailor-made methodologies, remain general in the sense that they should not be set up specifically for a particular public procurement procedure."[40]

These prescriptions led to the question of the "valuation" or "monetisation" of such external costs, a recurring issue in the attempts to implement the "polluter pays" principle.[41]

Beyond "traditional" internal costs, such as research, development, production, transport, use, maintenance and end-of-life disposal costs, this approach can also now include costs imputed to environmental externalities, such as pollution caused by extraction of the raw materials used in the product, manufacture or the product itself, provided they can be monetised and monitored.

Common methodologies should be developed at EU level for the calculation of life-cycle costs for specific categories of supplies or services. Where such common methodologies are developed, their use should be made compulsory.[42] Article 68 of Directive 2014/24 provides for methods to valorise externalities and article 68(3) states that when such methods are adopted they are listed in Annex XIII.

However, Annex XIII only lists Directive 2009/33 on the promotion of clean and energy-efficient road transport vehicles.[43] This initially led to expectations that other such methods would be added to Annex XIII for other products and services.

---

40 ibid.
41 See, e.g., Patrick Thieffry, *Traité de droit européen de l'environnement et du climat* (4th edn, 2020 Bruylant), 357 *et seq.*
42 Directive 2014/24 (n 16), recital 96.
43 [2009] OJ L120/5.

2. Monetisation of life-cycle costs
of road transport vehicles

Directive 2009/33, a remarkable and rare binding legislation strongly influenced by the "polluter pays" principle and the externalities theory, aimed to "influence the market… by ensuring a level of demand for clean and energy-efficient road transport vehicles which is sufficiently substantial to encourage manufacturers and the industry to invest in and further develop" such vehicles.[44] It relied on the consideration that, while clean and energy-efficient vehicles initially have a higher price than conventional ones, "creating sufficient demand for such vehicles could ensure that economies of scale lead to cost reduction".[45] To this end, it required contracting authorities, contracting entities and certain operators to "take into account lifetime energy and environmental impacts" when purchasing road transport vehicles.[46]

The "operational energy and environmental impacts" to be taken into account included "at least" energy consumption, emissions of CO_2, and emissions of NOx, NMHC and particulate matter.[47] The Directive provided a set of options for taking into account energy and environmental impacts that enabled purchasers that had already developed relevant methods to continue applying these methods.[48] This could be fulfilled either by setting technical specifications on each of the impacts considered, or by including energy and environmental impacts in the purchasing decision, using these impacts as award criteria and monetising them for inclusion in the purchasing decision.[49]

The latter option, based on a schedule, required the assessment of operational lifetime costs, respectively, for energy consumption, for CO_2 emissions and for emissions of NOx, NMHC and particulate matters.[50] Thus, for example, a bus was deemed to travel 1 million km during its existence, CO_2 was deemed to cost €0.03/kg, and NOx €0.0044/kg, etc. All well, considered this was a unique effort to apply the "polluter pays" principle in an area where no such application could be done on its own, without such presumptions.

However, instead of deploying such an approach in other sectors than road transport, it is Directive 2009/33 that was recently amended to a very great extent by Directive 2019/1161.[51] As a sign of the radical change of direction for the integration of environmental and climate requirements in EU public procurement law, Directive 2019/1161 went as far as to replace the title of the initial legislation

---

44 ibid, recital 11.
45 ibid, recital 13.
46 ibid, art 1.
47 ibid, art 5(1).
48 ibid, recital 19.
49 ibid, art 5(2).
50 ibid, art 6.
51 Directive 2019/1161 amending Directive 2009/33/EC on the promotion of clean and energy-efficient road transport vehicles [2019] OJ L188/116.

with the following: "Directive 2009/33 of 23 April 2009 on the promotion of clean road transport vehicles in support of low-emission mobility". The shift of that measure's aim from "clean and energy-efficient road transport vehicles" to "clean road transport vehicles in support of low-emission mobility" is significant in more than one respect. From an institutional point of view, it should be recalled that Directive 2009/33 was adopted on the basis of the EU's environmental competence (Article 175 TEC, now Article 192 TFEU) but that the Lisbon Treaty introduced the energy policy at Article 194 TFEU, effective on 1 December 2009, just a few months later. Yet, Directive 2009/33 as amended by Directive 2019/1161 remains based on Article 192 TFEU and it would be awkward for its purpose as stated in its title to keep pursuing "… energy-efficient…" purposes.

Directive 2019/1161 states that the Commission made an assessment of the implementation of Directive 2009/33 and concluded that that approach "did not trigger a market uptake of clean vehicles across the Union", that the impact "has been very limited in reducing greenhouse gas and air pollutant emissions and in promoting industry competitiveness", and that there would be "benefits of changing the overall governance approach to clean vehicle procurement at Union level".[52]

The change was most important: Directive 2019/1161 plainly suppressed articles 6 and 7 which used to set forth the methodology for the calculation of operational lifetime costs described above. Member States are no longer required to take the life-cycle internal and external costs into account in public procurement. Instead, Member States must set minimum procurement targets in an attempt to effectively help reach the objective of promoting and stimulating the market uptake of clean vehicles rather than relying on the internalisation of external cost into overall procurement decisions. In short, instead of valorising externalities and adding them the bidding price, purchasing authorities are now free to proceed as they wish, provided that their purchases reach certain targets of "clean" vehicles.

Thus it is a creative and fierce attempt to allow market instruments to assist in furthering the integration of environmental and climate requirements into public procurement that had previously failed. Not only did it fail, it deterred the spread of similar approaches in other sectors, as contemplated by the 2014 legislation for public procurement at large. In other words, while public purchasers remain instructed to take account of life-cycle environmental externalities (in purchases other than road vehicles), the EU leaves them with very limited guidance as to the way to cope with what may be the most complex issue in the area.

---

52   Directive 2009/33 as amended by Directive 2019/1161, recital 11.

Procuring a Greener Future

FIONA M BEATTIE[*]

Macfarlanes

I. Introduction

As may be expected, the European Commission's (the Commission) 2019 announcement on the European Green Deal[1] growth strategy for a sustainable EU economy identified the public procurement regime as playing an important role in furthering these environmental objectives and called for public authorities to lead by example and ensure their procurement is green.[2] The Commission also signalled an intention to bring forward further legislation and guidance on green purchasing.[3] Although such statements are to be welcomed, they do give rise to a distinct sense of déjà vu, given the earlier policy objectives contained in, for example, the Lisbon Strategy of 2000 and the Europe 2020 strategy of 2010,[4] raising the question as to what will be different this time around.

Public procurement related spending across the EU accounts for around €2 trillion (approx. 14% of GDP) per annum[5] and the ability to harness such spending power to promote wider EU policy objectives has long been recognised.[6] There has of

---

[*]   Fiona M Beattie is a senior counsel at Macfarlanes LLP. Fiona is based in London and regularly advises a variety of clients in both the public and private sector on a range of competition, procurement and state aid issues. The views expressed here are the author's own. Thanks are due to Anne Todd and Jim Murrell of Macfarlanes for their assistance with the preparation of this article.
1   Commission "The European Green Deal" (Communication) COM (2019) 640 final.
2   ibid, 8.
3   ibid.
4   See for example the comments in Peter Kunzlik, "From suspect practice to market-based instrument: policy alignment and the evolution of EU law's approach to green public procurement" (2013) 3 PPLR 97.
5   Commission, "Internal Market, Industry, Entrepreneurship and SMEs: Public Procurement" <https://ec.europa.eu/growth/single-market/public-procurement_en> accessed 7 October 2020.
6   See, for example, Directive 2004/18/EC, recital 2 and the comments in para 3 of Proposal for a Directive of the European Parliament and of the Council on public procurement (Classical Directive) (First reading) – Approval of the final compromise text – 11745/13 LIMITE – 12 July 2013.

course been progress, both in terms of the development of case law recognising the lawfulness of taking environmental considerations into account in certain circumstances[7] and through changes to the public procurement directives themselves.[8] However, in a post-COVID era, where public spending is expected to be constrained, the willingness to voluntarily take account of longer-term environmental and life-cycle costing benefits may be reduced in the favour of short-term cost savings. Consequently, proposals for more ambitious and stringent legal obligations regarding the approach to environmental considerations may be at greater risk of being watered down as the legislative process progresses. This paper briefly summarises the approach of the current public procurement regime, identifies some of the barriers to progress and considers potential solutions.

I. Brief Overview of Key Public Procurement Principles

The EU public procurement regime is designed to ensure that contracting authorities conduct open, fair, transparent and non-discriminatory tender processes before awarding any contracts for works, service or supplies, or appointing concessionaires where the value exceed certain specified thresholds.[9]

The EU public procurement rules are contained in various directives which are then transposed into national law by each Member State.[10] The legislation is supplemented by a significant body of case law from both the EU and national courts, which provides further details as to how key principles should be applied in practice. This is often supplemented by "soft" guidance from the European Commission and from Member States on key topics. A remedies regime enables actual or potential bidders to challenge breaches of the procurement rules.

It is important to recognise at the outset that the procurement regime was originally introduced to facilitate the creation of the EU single market by ensuring that fair and transparent processes were used by "public bodies" to prevent such bodies

---

7   See for example Case C–513/99 *Concordia* [2002] ECR I-07213; and Case C–368/10 *Commission v Netherlands (Dutch Coffee)* EU:C:2012.284; Laurens Ankersmit, "The EU Court of Justice establishes that public authorities can use fair trade criteria as criteria to award public supply contracts of products *(Netherlands Max Havelaar)*" (2012) e-Competitions Art N° 64145.

8   See for example article 43 (Labels) and article 68 (Life-cycle costing) of the Public Contracts Directive (Directive 2014/24/EU).

9   The key thresholds for 2020–2022 are €5,548,000 for works and concession contracts; €144,000 for services and supplies contracts awarded by central government bodies; and €221,000 for services and supplies contracts awarded by all other contracting authorities.

10   The key legislation is contained in the Public Contracts Directive (Directive 2014/24/EU on public procurement), the Concessions Contracts Directive (Directive 2014/23/EU on the award of concession contracts) and the Remedies Directive (Directive 89/665/EEC on the coordination of the laws, regulations and administrative provisions relating to the application of review procedures to the award of public supply and public works contracts). The Public Contracts Directive will be the main focus of this paper. The Utilities Directive (Directive 2014/25/EU) provides for a lighter touch and more flexible regime for utilities, although in practice many utilities have been exempted from these obligations on the basis that the appropriate utilities market in the relevant Member State has been adequately liberalised.

favouring bidders from their home Member State. Accordingly, the procurement rules are designed to ensure that bidders' rights to fair treatment are protected. In certain circumstances, this can constrain the ability of contracting authorities' freedom to act. For example, the fact that a direct award without a tender may be perceived as more efficient, less costly and/or bring environmental benefits will not typically, in and of itself, be sufficient reason to avoid a tender process.

It is not uncommon for arguments to be made that the procurement legislation acts as a barrier and/or prevents the acquisition of environmentally friendly solutions. However, as explained below, there is already significant flexibility within the regime to enable environmental considerations to be taken into account.

1. When do the procurement rules apply?

The obligations contained in the Public Contracts Directive and the Concessions Directive apply to "Contracting Authorities".[11] This definition includes not only central and regional/local government bodies but also "bodies governed by public law" (essentially bodies that are effectively owned, controlled or financed by other Contracting Authorities). Except in very limited circumstances, a Contracting Authority is normally obliged to advertise the tender opportunity for works, services or supplies that exceed the specified financial thresholds in the Official Journal of the EU and to conduct the subsequent tender in accordance with certain procedures.

2. Need for a flexible approach

As the obligations contained in the procurement regime apply to a wide range of organisations and to the purchase of a very wide variety of works, services and supplies, the provisions of the directives are deliberately based on high-level principles that Contracting Authorities can adapt as necessary, to reflect the individual circumstances of their procurement process. Due to the broad scope of the public procurement regime, there has traditionally been considerable reluctance from Member States and others to adopt more detailed rules that could limit the discretion of Contacting Authorities to tailor their procurement processes to best fit the needs of their communities.

There are two key stages of the tender process which provide Contracting Authorities with the flexibility and opportunity to take into account environmental considerations:

- Setting the technical specifications that the works, goods or services to be procured must meet; and

- Selecting the individual award criteria that will be used to evaluate which of the tenders received is the most economically advantageous.

---

11 Public Contracts Directive, art 2.1(1) and (4).

3. Setting technical standards

The Public Contracts Directive sets out a number of rules as to how Contracting Authorities can set technical standards which the goods/services must satisfy[12] and enables Contracting Authorities to set technical specifications by reference to environmental characteristics, should the Contracting Authority wish to do so. Technical specifications or environmental requirements can also be included in the resulting contract as conditions which the successful bidder must satisfy. There are certain general principles that must be taken into account when setting the technical specifications. For example they:

–   Must not create unjustifiable barriers to opening the tender opportunity up to competition;

–   Must be sufficiently precise to enable the award of the contract (i.e. enabling the Contracting Authority to verify compliance);

–   Can be set by reference to performance or functional requirements; and

–   Can be set by reference to relevant standards (or their equivalent).

The procurement regime requires that only those tenders that satisfy the technical standards set for that particular tender will be compliant. Although it is ultimately for the bidders to prove that their tender does satisfy the relevant specifications, Contracting Authorities have a duty to ensure that they are able to verify that the relevant technical specifications have been satisfied.[13] Accordingly, when designing technical specifications Contracting Authorities must be confident that they can appropriately assess compliance at tender stage, particularly if more ambitious standards are used. In a similar fashion, where environmental objectives are included as a condition of contract, careful thought will be required about how such requirements are monitored and enforced to ensure, for example, that the works are in practice as energy efficient as the tender submission indicated.

4. Tender evaluation

Most procurement processes involves two distinct stages of evaluation. The first, initial, stage relates to assessing the credentials and appropriateness of the bidder (often referred to as prequalification or selection) and the second (the award stage) to assessing which of the bids represents the best or "most economically

---

12   See for example the Public Contracts Directive, art 42 on technical specifications, art 43 labelling requirements (e.g. eco labels etc) and art 44 (test reports and certification requirements to establish minimum standards are met. Art 70 enables conditions relating to the performance of the contract to be applied.

13   Thus for example, in Case C–448/01 *EVN & Wienstrom* [2003] ECR I-14527 the award of the contract to the bidder who agreed to provide the highest volume of renewable electricity was successfully challenged on the basis that there was no way for the contracting authority to verify how much of the electricity was in fact generated from renewable sources.

advantageous" tender when considered in light of the Contracting Authority's chosen award criteria. Although, bidders can be excluded from a tender process if they can be shown to have violated certain environmental obligations,[14] the greater potential to positively influence the environmental impact of any public contract will be through the award criteria.

The Public Contracts Directive enables Contracting Authorities to tailor the award criteria they wish to apply to the needs of the particular tender. Although article 67(2) states that Contracting Authorities must select the most economically advantageous tender "which shall be identified on the basis of price or cost, using a cost-effectiveness approach", it is clear that Contracting Authorities have the discretion to take into account a large number of factors such as price, quality and delivery, as well as environmental factors that are linked to the subject matter of the contract.[15] Price itself can be determined in a variety of ways including by applying a life-cycle costing methodology.[16] Whenever a common methodology for the calculation of life-cycle costing has been made mandatory by EU law, that method shall be applied.[17] The relevant criteria and their respective weightings (e.g. that price will account for 40% of the marks) must be disclosed to bidders in the tender documents, together with any relevant sub-criteria. Contracting Authorities must also ensure that they are able to effectively verify how well the individual tenders meet the award criteria.[18]

It is therefore clear that the current procurement regime provides the flexibility to take environmental considerations into account, should Contracting Authorities wish to do so. Member States have also taken steps to encourage Contracting Authorities to take wider social and environmental objectives into account. For example in England and Wales, the Public Services (Social Value) Act 2012 requires Contracting Authorities to consider how the procurement process could improve social, economic and environmental wellbeing of a relevant

---

14 See, for example, Public Contracts Directive, art 57(4)(a) and C–395/18 *Tim SpA* EU:C:2020:58.
15 Art 67(3) clarifies that award criteria are linked to the subject-matter of the contract "where they relate to the works, services or supplies to be provided under the contract in any respect and at any stage in their life cycle, including factors involved in a) the specific process of production, provision or trading of those works, services or supplies; or b) a specific process for another stage of their life cycle even where such factors do not form part of their material substance".
16 Art 68 sets out specific rules for the use of life-cycle costing and, in summary, it provides that it can take account of costs borne by the Contracting Authority or other users, such as the costs relating to acquisition, use (e.g. energy consumption), maintenance costs and/or end-of-life cost, as well as costs imputed to environmental externalities (such as emissions of greenhouse gases and other pollutants and climate change mitigation costs) linked to the product, service or works during the life cycle, provided their monetary value can be determined and verified. Where life-cycle costing is used, the procurement documents must contain the data to be provided by bidders and the method to be used to calculate the life-cycle costs.
17 Public Contracts Directive, art 68(3), which cross-refers to the mandatory life-cycle costing for clean and energy efficient road transport vehicles. Life-cycle costing methodologies are now available for imaging equipment, outdoor and indoor lighting, vending machines and computers and monitors: Commission, "Environment" <https://ec.europa.eu/environment/gpp/lcc.htm> accessed 4 January 2021.
18 Case C–448/01 *EVN & Wienstrom* (n 13).

area at the pre-procurement stage. Further practical advice on promoting social and environmental considerations was provided in, amongst other things, the UK's Crown Commercial Service's 2016 guidance on Procuring for Growth: Balanced Scorecard.[19] Given that the incentive effects of a greener public procurement policy have been recognised for some time, it raises the question as to why, in practice, it does not seem to be driving environmental change to the extent anticipated.

II. Slow Progress

The question as to why public procurement has not embraced the environmental objectives as fully as may be wished, is of course not a new one. In his 2013 article, Professor Kunzlik referred to five key obstacles: cost; lack of knowledge about the green options; lack of political leadership; fragmented demand given the large number of Contracting Authorities; and restrictive procurement legislation.[20] As noted above, the current procurement directives have remedied many of the previous concerns surrounding legislative barriers. Although some progress has been made, it nonetheless appears that obstacles remain.

Lack of awareness surrounding the availability of "green" options remains a problem, particularly for some smaller Contracting Authorities. As the procurement rules render it very difficult for a Contracting Authority to change its technical standards after a tender process has begun, Contracting Authorities are often nervous about including requirements that may prove to be undeliverable by the market or otherwise unaffordable. Changes introduced via the Public Contracts Directive, article 40, which confirm that Contracting Authorities can now undertake a degree of "market testing" prior to launching their tender process, could be used to greater effect to address such concerns. The market testing enables Contracting Authorities to seek feedback from a variety of market participants and independent experts on issues such as the solutions that may be available to satisfy technical requirements and potentially to gain some insight into potential costs.

The Commission's Green Public Procurement initiative[21] (which is a voluntary initiative for Contracting Authorities to use if they wish) does seek to address this knowledge gap by providing some guidance on technical criteria that could be used for different types of tenders. Guidance is available in relation to a number of areas including office building design, construction and management, food, catering services and vending machines, public space maintenance, data centres, server rooms and cloud services, and most recently for imaging equipment,

---

19 Procurement Policy Note 09/16 (14 October 2016).
20 Kunzlik (n 4).
21 Commission, "Environment: Green Public Procurement" <https://ec.europa.eu/environment/gpp/index_en.htm> accessed 4 January 2021.

consumables and print services. It is not immediately clear how much awareness of such initiatives there is amongst Contracting Authorities and the extent to which this has increased the use of environmentally friendly specifications, particularly given that use is voluntary.

1. Advancing the Green New Deal or artificially narrowing competition?

When setting the technical specifications, Contracting Authorities must, however, be mindful of the new provisions introduced by the Public Contracts Directive in articles 18(2) and (3), which require that the design of the procurement must not "artificially narrow competition". This can occur where "the design of the procurement is made with the intention of unduly favouring or disadvantaging certain economic operators". This raises an interesting question as to whether setting "green" technical standards can, in certain circumstances, breach the article 18 obligations. It has long been recognised that promoting environmental standards may result in some economic operators being disadvantaged and finding it harder or more costly to compete, although it is also recognised that this can generate procompetitive benefits over the longer term by raising environmental standards to the benefit of the public as a whole.[22]

Clearly in many cases, the interaction with the article 18 obligations are unlikely to be more than a theoretical issue, given the obligation is not to "unduly favour" particular providers. Where there is adequate competition amongst providers meeting such environmental standards and the standards themselves are relatively common in the relevant industry, it is unlikely that their use could give rise to concerns.[23] However, in circumstances where Contracting Authorities have chosen to aim high when setting such standards with the result that only a very small number of potential providers (or possibly even one) can meet the standards, the question as to whether this has artificially narrowed competition may well arise.

The focus would of course be on whether the standards "unduly" favour or disadvantage certain operators. This is likely to require an assessment as to whether the environmental objectives of the Contracting Authority can outweigh the negative implications from a perceived lack of competition. For example, the more a specification or standard focuses on key characteristics or descriptions that closely resemble a specific provider's goods or services, (which may be the

---

22 See, for example, Commission, "Guidelines on the applicability of Art 101 Treating on the Functioning of the European Union to horizontal co-operation agreements" [2011] OJ C11/1, [329].

23 See, for example, the Public Contracts Directive, recital 74: "The technical specifications drawn up by public purchasers need to allow public procurement to be open to competition as well as to achieve objectives of sustainability. To that end, it should be possible to submit tenders that reflect the diversity of technical solutions standards and technical specifications in the marketplace, including those drawn up on the basis of performance criteria linked to the life cycle and the sustainability of the production process of the works, supplies and services."

case if the proposal relates to new or emerging technical solutions), the greater the risk that it contradicts article 18(2). At this point it is worth recalling an important distinction between competition law and the public procurement regime. To the frustration of many Contracting Authorities (and some bidders) there is no express equivalent of article 101(3) TFEU that enables you to balance wider benefits against any negative effects associated with a restriction of competition. As noted above, the public procurement regime is instead very much designed to ensure equality of opportunity between bidders in fair and transparent processes, rather than necessarily to promote the policy objectives of the Contracting Authority. In that context, the European courts have consistently made clear that proportionality is a key principle that lies at the heart of the procurement regime, including in respect of requirements contained in the tender documents.[24]

Although the courts typically recognise that Contracting Authorities should be given a degree of discretion, the extent to which the Contracting Authority has considered all the relevant factors before setting the standards is likely to undergo some scrutiny. It cannot necessarily be assumed that high-level environmental policy objectives alone would be considered sufficient to rebut allegations that the competition has been artificially narrowed. If the issue were to arise, much would depend upon the circumstances of the case in question. For example, could similar environmental objectives be achieved through a slightly less rigorous technical standard that would allow for greater competition, and to what extent did the Contracting Authority consider this? How significant are the environmental gains compared with a less restrictive approach? To what extent could those additional gains be taken into account through the setting of the award criteria? How many eligible bidders/solutions can meet the higher standards? It is also likely that any challenger would look to the holistic environmental impact – for example if the proposed technical standards drive the Contracting Authority towards a solution that has other, less positive, environmental impacts, questions could arise as to the overall proportionality. Accordingly, the article 84 procurement case file detailing the internal decision-making is likely to be particularly relevant to any assessment here. Similar issues could also arise in any challenge to an attempt to justify a direct award of a contract (i.e. without first holding a tender process) on the basis that there was only one possible provider in accordance with article 32(2)(b).

---

24 See, for example, Case C–413/17 *Roche Lietuva UAB* EU:C:2018:865, [40] – [41]:
   In the light of the above factors, it is for the referring court to determine if, taking into account the contracting authority's margin of appreciation in laying down the technical specifications according to the qualitative requirements related to the subject matter of the procurement contract at issue, the particularly detailed character of the technical specifications at issue does not indirectly favour a tenderer. It is also necessary that the level of detail of the technical specifications complies with the principle of proportionality, which implies, in particular, an examination of the question establishing whether that level of detail is necessary to achieve the desired objectives.
   See also C–395/18 *Tim SpA* (n 14) and C–76/16 *Ingsteel* EU:C:2017:549.

2. Identifying the greenest bid

As noted above, Contracting Authorities can also be discouraged by the perceived cost implications of environmentally friendly products/standards. Most Contracting Authorities will have a clear budget set aside for particular projects and will place a considerable degree of emphasis on price in any most economically advantageous tender calculation, with environmental considerations (insofar as they are expressly included at all) typically accounting for a far lower percentage of marks. Tenders can sometimes be abandoned if all bids received are above a predetermined affordability criteria.

Accordingly, during the preliminary stages of tender preparation, Contracting Authorities may revise and refine their proposed requirements to take account of affordability concerns. The Commission's Green Public Procurement initiative, referred to above, includes some suggested award criteria reflecting common procurements that Contracting Authorities could consider including although, as above, it is unclear to what extent Contracting Authorities and their advisers are aware of this guidance and/or consider it common/good practice. Although life-cycle costing is expressly recognised in the Public Contracts Directive as a permissible mechanism for assessing the price of a bid, it is unclear to what extent Contracting Authorities (particularly those that are not central government bodies) and/or their advisers consider they have sufficient information or knowledge to design a methodology to assess environmental externalities. Contracting Authorities will always be concerned about the delays and legal costs associated with procurement challenges to their tender processes. Concerns about the vulnerability of such environmental methodologies to successful procurement challenge are likely to discourage Contracting Authorities from taking the initiative in the absence of (or awareness of) any reputable common methodologies that may exist. In that regard, the recent work by the Commission relating to life-cycle costing is to be welcomed.

It is already the case that tender processes, particularly for larger works and services contracts are already considered to be complex, costly and burdensome, with bidders required to devote significant time and resources to any tenders. Contracting Authorities may be nervous of placing further information requirements on bidders, particularly if the information is not easily accessible (e.g. if it is required from further down the supply chain when subcontractors may not yet have been chosen). Any affordability discussions within a Contracting Authority could potentially be affected, particularly if the longer-term benefits of lower emissions etc. are not always represented in a comparable way (i.e. quantifying the monetary benefits), which could in turn give rise to a potential risk of challenge to any eventual award decision. Again, the recent work by the Commission relating to life-cycle costing, referred to above, is likely to be helpful.

III. A Greener Future?

Just as the issues hampering the deployment of green public purchasing power are not new, the potential solutions do not necessarily have to be revolutionary. They do, however, need commitment to ensure they are actually followed through. It is hoped that the Commission's proposed legislative package, once details are made available, will play an important step in moving the environmental agenda forward.

The current procurement regime focuses on enabling Contracting Authorities to take account of environmental considerations in their procurements, however, for real change to occur it may be time to go further and actively require such considerations to be taken into account. For example, new guidance has been issued to central government bodies in England and Wales requiring that a minimum of 10% of the award criteria scores are allocated to "social value considerations".[25] Although this is clearly a positive step forward and should be welcomed, given these marks can encompass not simply environmental considerations, but wider social value issues such as helping local communities recover from COVID-19, supporting SMEs, increasing supply chain resilience and capacity, and promoting equal opportunities, among others, it is perhaps questionable whether the marks accorded to environmental considerations will be sufficient to genuinely drive change by having a material impact on the overall evaluation process.

In a similar fashion, using technical standards or other conditions of contract to deliver environmental objectives has been possible for some time under the procurement rules, and greater use of this flexibility will be important if the policy objectives of the New Green Deal policy objectives are to be met. However, the challenge remains as to how to drive the use of these provisions in a manner that ensures that the standards set create a meaningful incentive for change. The one-size-fits-all nature of the public procurement regime, which applies the same principles to the creation of new infrastructure as it does to the purchase of personal protective equipment, creates the risk that any generic obligations to apply appropriate environmental standards could be seen as little more than greenwashing, with Contracting Authorities setting a low bar to tick the environmental box, as opposed to applying the more ambitious stretch targets that would be required to drive meaningful change.

One helpful starting point could be to consider what additional clarity can be provided to ensure that setting ambitious environmental standards or demanding specifications will not be vulnerable to challenge on the basis that such requirements artificially narrow competition contrary to article 18. It will also be

---

25   UK Cabinet Office, "Procurement Policy Note 06/20 – taking account of social value in the award of central government contracts" (September 2020).

important to ensure that post-contractual monitoring is in place to ensure that any ongoing environmental commitments continue to be met and conditions of contract enforced. That is likely to require the Contracting Authority to consider a number of issues when preparing the contract documents. This may include what ongoing resources it may need to allocate to monitor compliance, whether it has the necessary expertise to carry out the exercise, or would it need third-party expertise (if so who pays for that), and what information and audit rights should be included to be able to conduct the monitoring? Just as important, consideration should be given to what remedy will be applied for any failure to comply. The Commission's Green Public Procurement initiative guidance documents contain some draft clauses, which may prove a helpful starting point in considering what contractual conditions could be applied. The Commission's consultation on proposals requiring companies to substantiate claims they make about the environmental footprint of their products/services by using standard methods for quantifying them should, in due course, also provide assistance.[26] Ensuring the delivery is in fact as "green" as promised in the bid will play an important role in ensuring the Green New Deal is a success.

As noted above, the procurement regime has long been seen as a mechanism to drive wider social change, including by creating greater opportunities for SMEs to compete for public contracts. Accordingly, any desire to introduce changes requiring the use of more challenging environmental standards is likely to need to be balanced against the potential for negative impacts on other objectives, including the desire to widen SME participation. These potentially competing objectives could, however, be balanced by limiting such changes to high value contracts, at least initially.

In each case, given the disparate knowledge, skills and resources available to Contracting Authorities, access to information and best practice will play an important, practical role in promoting greener procurement and therefore continuing the initiatives relating to life-cycle costing etc. for different types of works and services. Raising the profile of these initiatives will be of great assistance in building the confidence of Contracting Authorities to adopt more sophisticated and nuanced evaluations. If there is clearer information on the long- and short-term cost and benefits of the various environmental requirements, this can help counter possible reservations as to the affordability of "going green", particularly in a post-COVID environment where budgets of many public sector organisations are expected to be very stretched. It will also be worth considering whether more can be done to promote common methodologies for calculating the environmental externalities that form part of any consideration of the longer-term environmental benefits, and identifying the type of information

---

26 Commission, "Consultation: Environmental performance of products & businesses – substantiating claims" (27 August – 3 December 2020) <https://ec.europa.eu/info/law/better-regulation/have-your-say/initiatives/12511-Environmental-claims-based-on-environmental-footprint-methods/public-consultation>.

that may be required from bidders to conduct such analysis, taking account of the extent to which such information is likely to be readily available to bidders or Contracting Authorities.

In conclusion, there are a number of potential measures that can be considered to support the Green New Deal, however, the extent to which the procurement regime can be used to drive a greener future will ultimately depend upon the willingness of Member States and Contracting Authorities not only to enact the policies but also to make the necessary financial investments to deliver a greener vision.

PART II
Industry Perspectives

Preface:
Competition Policy as an Enabler
of a Sustainable Economy
– A View Across Sectors

DIRK MIDDELSCHULTE[*]

Unilever

This part of the book brings together a particularly wide range of perspectives. They are hugely diverse in terms of the organisations with which the authors are affiliated, their geographic, industry or academic backgrounds, and their confidence (nor not) in both the environmental and social merits and the legal feasibility of business efforts to drive sustainability.[1]

I will try to distil what I feel is the essence of the 15 contributions, sometimes highlighting links to pieces included in the other two Parts of this volume. Needless to say, my takeaways are subjective and no replacement for reading the individual articles, which speak much better for themselves.

---

[*] Dirk Middelschulte is global general counsel competition at Unilever, based in Brussels.
[1] Most authors are European-based and focus on EU competition law, although most of their reflections can probably be applied more widely.

I. Is Industry Cooperation Necessary
– or Even Desirable – to Pursue Sustainability Goals?

Let's first take a look at industry cooperation and Article 101 TFEU, as this is the topic on which most authors have chosen to focus.[2] Observations on how Article 102 TFEU can deter or even fight anti-sustainable practices are covered in section V.

1. Competitors should join forces where they cannot achieve sustainability targets alone …

The contributors working for companies or their associations, all in-house lawyers, echo Commissioner Vestager's call for "everyone in Europe … to play their part – every individual, every business, every public authority"[3] – to achieve the Green Deal objectives. They unequivocally agree that business contribution requires cooperation across value chains and sectors, but also between competitors.

Views are, however, very nuanced when it comes to joining forces with industry rivals: As Andreas Gayk (Markenverband) vividly depicts for the consumer goods industry, brands will always want to distinguish themselves from competing offerings on the market, and the sustainability of a product becomes an ever more powerful differentiator in that sense. In other words, companies have every reason to focus their sustainability efforts on winning a competitive advantage over their peers.

Collective action has a complementary role to play where first-mover disadvantages and/or lack of scale threaten to render unilateral efforts unviable or ineffective. As Martyn Chu (Danone) puts it, the "more deep-rooted structural issues … require … collective action" as the "more ambitious and game-changing ideas … would otherwise take longer to achieve or never even materialise". The most transformational sustainability improvements may make products too expensive to remain competitive against conventional alternatives. Moreover, consumers may be uncomfortable embracing a more sustainable but unfamiliar product feature unless adopted across competing brands, an experience Unilever has in fact had with compressed deodorants in the UK.[4]

---

2   Embedded in the section on horizontal cooperation, state aid and public procurement law are touched on under section IV below, given their possible role model function in respect of some aspects of Article 101(3) TFEU.

3   See Margrethe Vestager, "The Green Deal and Competition Policy" (Renew webinar, 22 September 2020) <https://ec.europa.eu/commission/commissioners/2019-2024/vestager/announcements/green-deal-and-competition-policy_en>.

4   A new compression technology for aerosol deodorants enabled the production of smaller cans with the same amount of product while saving packaging and reducing emissions from production and transportation. Unilever was first to market the innovation and made the science available to everyone to use in the hope that others would follow. However, no one did and since the products were smaller, they were

Gayk points at how sluggish change can be if not coordinated. He invokes the slow penetration of organic foods in Germany where the first "Bio-Supermarkt" opened almost 35 years ago, but the market share of organic food still simmers around 6%.[5] As much as unilateral solutions remain the default option when pursuing their sustainability agendas, companies stretching their targets will need more cooperation to attain their own growing ambitions, as Angélique de Brousse (Johnson & Johnson) points out. Like several other business contributors, she considers regulation to be insufficient, in that it is often slow, subject to political compromise, sometimes only half-hearted or even absent. Hugh Mullan, Marc Braithwaite and Rosy Cheetham-West (UK Payment Systems Regulator/Financial Conduct Authority) illustrate these concerns very pointedly when flagging the lack of regulation for investments qualifying as sustainable from an environmental, social and governance (ESG) perspective – UK regulatory standards don't ban oil and gas assets from featuring as green financial investments.

Part of the answer to such shortcomings can be hybrid models, where governments moderate a process in which market players agree on standards taking the place of legislation or complementing it. Boris Kasten and Hendrik Reffken (Schindler) highlight a voluntary agreement between retailers and the German environment minister in 2016 to substantially reduce the provision of plastics bags in supermarkets.[6]

2. … or *not?*

Looking at competitor collaborations, Michelle Meagher (University College London) and Simon Roberts (University of Johannesburg) disagree with the contributors working for businesses and sector regulators on almost every count: "Enabling cooperative agreements amongst multinational corporations may lead to marginal benefits but also risks perverse outcomes."

Although they approach the issue from a very distinct economic policy standpoint, Meagher and Roberts arrive at conclusions similar to those of Maarten Pieter Schinkel and Leonard Treuren in Part I (Legal Themes). They are aligned in their belief that businesses strive to maximise profits but have no genuine interest in environmental and social progress. This makes the authors assume an overarching risk that sustainability collaborations would be aimed at the

---

perceived by consumers as being of lower value. Sales were poor and the compressed cans were eventually delisted.

5   See also GfK market analysis, "German market for organic products again grows significantly in 2019" (18 February 2020) <www.freshplaza.com/article/9189807/german-market-for-organic-products-again-grows-significantly-in-2019/>.

6   In a similar vein, in 2019 car manufacturers agreed with the Californian state government to introduce emissions standards stricter than the ones envisaged by the federal administration; see Coral Davenport, "Justice Department Drops Antitrust Probe Against Automakers That Sided With California on Emissions" *New York Times* (New York, 7 February 2020) <www.nytimes.com/2020/02/07/climate/trump-california-automakers-antitrust.html>.

entrenchment of "existing power structures" (Meagher and Roberts) or the establishment of "green cartels" (Schinkel and Treuren).

Meagher and Roberts' and Schinkel and Treuren's points of view are interesting in that they deviate eloquently from more mainstream positions. But they didn't convince me. As more and more companies stretch their environmental and social targets aggressively, way beyond what is legally required, it is hard to argue that businesses don't care about a purpose greater than top and bottom line numbers. What is more, the economic incentives to engage in sustainable business practices are just too compelling – for the sake of meeting evolving customer demands,[7] ensuring long-term value and growth, reducing liability risks, retaining talent and meeting expectations of investors and societal stakeholders.[8]

In that sense, collective action is another means for companies to pursue environmental and social objectives where unilateral initiatives are not viable. For the purposes of a competition policy debate, however, there is probably little harm in agreeing to disagree on the ultimate underlying motivations of businesses: when it comes to actual industry collaborations, competition authorities are supposed to assess every case rigorously on its merits, consider the relevant facts and see for themselves what prompts a particular cooperation and, most importantly, which results it promises to deliver.

To be sure, within the appraisal of industry collaborations, enforcers should intervene against any "expansion of private standards organised by leading firms [which] risks raising obstacles for smaller rivals and imposing the majority of adjustment costs on smaller input suppliers", as Meagher and Roberts suspect would happen. They rightly argue that "sustainability is meaningless without fairness, equality and justice". There are grounds to be confident that the EU competition legal framework is capable of integrating these elements (see section IV).

II. Practical Examples – and the Questions They Trigger for the Application of EU Competition Law

Sustainability collaborations between competing firms are, of course, already a reality. Many of the existing, and many contemplated cooperations are likely to

---

7   There is comprehensive evidence of sustainable brands and companies outperforming conventional products; see Nielson, "The Sustainability Imperative" (October 2015): <www.nielsen.com/wp-content/uploads.pdf>. See also Randi Kronthal-Sacco and Tensie Whelan, "Research on IRI Purchasing Data (2013–2018)" (NYU Stern, 11 March 2019) <www.stern.nyu.edu/sites/default/files/assets/documents/NYU%20Stern%20CSB%20Sustainable%20Share%20Index™%202019.pdf>.

8   "Special Report: Business and climate change" *The Economist* (19 September 2020). See also Rebecca Henderson, *Reimagining Capitalism in a World on Fire* (Penguin 2020), a thoroughly researched analysis and emphatic plea for sustainable capitalism and self-regulation, building on the (individual and collective) efforts of companies across industries.

fall outside Article 101(1) TFEU.[9] Others will qualify for a straightforward exemption under Article 101(3) TFEU. However, the authors of this Part III have collated a rich body of examples of desirable cooperations where they feel EU case law, the Commission's horizontal guidelines and other reference points are *not* sufficiently clear. I hope I am not alone in finding these longer or shorter descriptions of actual and possible scenarios particularly inspiring:

–   Morgan Frontczak's (Shell) contribution deals with the systematic changes that are necessary to switch from heavy fuel oil to zero or net zero carbon fuels in the shipping industry – and the urgency to initiate these changes given asset lifespans of up to 50 years. She argues that sectoral collaboration is imperative to identify and operationalize zero carbon solutions in the form of R&D collaborations, joint emission reduction commitments or agreements between ship owners and charterers on sustainable procurement criteria. Such co-operations would also give energy suppliers more certainty as to demand for alternative fuels, thus enabling targeted investments into R&D and fuel production, and similarly for green energy requirements in other hard-to-abate sectors such as chemicals, cement, iron and stell, aviation and road transportation.

–   Starting from the late 1990s *ACEA, JAMA* and *KAMA* decisions, Ian Rose (Volvo Trucks) asks how far automotive companies can go collaboratively when striving to achieve environmental targets that they loosely commit to collectively, as they did, with the Commission's endorsement, in those precedents. Rose's concern is that a prudent interpretation of the law will constrain businesses to light-touch initiatives with little impact, as he illustrates with the (otherwise aptly named) "Drive Sustainability" forum of automotive manufacturers. How can they define mandatory requirements for suppliers without qualifying as collective boycott? Rose also raises recent examples of industry collaborations in the quest for emission-neutral technologies.

–   Jérôme Cloarec (Michelin) describes the evolution of the once highly secretive tyre industry into a sector where competing companies share R&D efforts and collaborate in open labs and incubators. He asks how far agreements on measuring and indicating the long-term performance of tyres – which account for 20% of a vehicle's energy consumption – would be legally feasible; currently labels only specify the performance of tyres for as long as they are new. Cloarec also touches on the benefits of logistics collaborations on the "last mile" to avoid "armies of half-empty lorries", while acknowledging the potential information-sharing risks. He also wonders how far carbon reductions can be considered for an exemption under Article 101(3) TFEU.

---

9   See Unilever, "Sustainability cooperations between competitors & Art. 101 TFEU" (May 2020) <www.unilever.com/Images/unilever_submission_sustainability_competition_law_tcm244-551751_en.pdf> accessed 11 February 2021, 3–8.

- With an estimated investment of €6.2 trillion needed by 2030 to limit global warming to 2°C,[10] it is difficult to overstate the importance of green finance. But few are the professional and retail investors that have managed to make sense of the divergent approaches financial institutions have chosen to qualify investments as sustainable. Mullan, Braithwaite and Cheetham-West encourage the industry to agree on relevant definitions and on how to assess a company's ESG credentials. Standards would have to be demanding to mitigate greenwashing risks, and they may have to be mandatory to be effective. The authors also look at climate-related disclosures that will soon be legally mandated in the UK. How financial institutions can ensure the required detail of disclosures while avoiding illicit information exchanges is a particularly intricate question, as the authors demonstrate.

- Stephan Bredt (Hessian Ministry of Economics), representing the regulator of the Frankfurt stock exchange, adds another intriguing perspective as to how recent government- and industry-driven responses to climate change upend the financial sector. He describes collective self-commitments by financial institutions to structure their lending and investment portfolios in line with the targets of the Paris Agreement, and explains how the European Securities and Markets Authority and national financial services regulators incentivise investors and asset managers to exercise shareholder rights jointly, in compliance with takeover rules, as stewards of good corporate governance and green standards. Bredt finally looks at large-scale efforts to create data pools that help financial institutions improve environmental risk modelling and management, rather than continuing to under-price climate risk. He is optimistic as to the legal viability of the initiatives he recounts but notes that "there remains space for the finance industry to engage with more far-reaching activities to contribute via more qualified and self-binding activities."

- Gianni de Stefano (AkzoNobel) raises a very pertinent practical question for companies in their capacity as suppliers – how can they agree with their peers on criteria for green certification to meet common customer demands? Similar to de Stefano's reflections on non-price exchanges in trade associations, Kasten and Reffken flag the unclear limits of permissible information exchange, especially in technical collaborations.

- Ben Graham (ABInBev) shows that the brewing industry already shares insights into corruption risks to better vet suppliers. He commends cooperation to propel supplier sustainability and green logistics, the sharing of innovations between competitors and more stringent collective

---

10 Green Finance Platform, "Explore Green Finance: Overview" <www.greenfinanceplatform.org/page/explore-green-finance> accessed 11 February 2021.

plastics commitments "with closer monitoring, stricter targets and tangible consequences".

– Providing another consumer goods industry viewpoint, de Brousse agrees with Graham that non-mandatory standardisation may be less effective than binding agreements to outsource non-recyclable packaging materials or certain types of plastics. At the same time, she is worried that such initiatives, however desirable, could be deemed to be collective boycotts under current enforcement standards, and has similar concerns in relation to other social obligations (living wages, human rights standards) that companies may want to impose collectively on suppliers.

III. Considering Sustainability Benefits in Article 101 (and 102) TFEU

Most in-house lawyers contributing their industry perspectives touch on the controversial question as to whether Article 101(3) TFEU provides enough leeway for sustainability cooperations between competitors. In what circumstances do sustainability benefits outweigh anticompetitive effects (an issue also relevant to Article 102 TFEU)? Closely related is the question as to the extent to which consumers need to receive a "fair share" of any such benefits, notably when they only materialise in the future or in other markets – reductions of greenhouse gas emissions are an instructive example.

1. Uncharted quality and innovation dimensions of the consumer welfare standard

Several authors make the argument that current enforcement practice overemphasises price effects, leaving the quality and innovation dimensions of Article 101(3) TFEU underexplored. Cloarec pointedly remarks that qualitative arguments risk being reduced to "ornament" – "good material for a press release, but are they always seriously considered?". Kasten and Reffken analyse the consumer welfare standard that frames the Commission's reading of Article 101 TFEU. They invoke Justice Scalia's famous remark in the US Supreme Court's groundbreaking *Leegin* case: "So the mere fact that it would increase prices doesn't prove anything."[11] In that sense, US law, rarely a reference in the competition policy debate about sustainability, is a useful reminder that consumer welfare is a very heterogeneous concept.

Examining the quality aspect of Article 101(3) TFEU, Graham argues "that – unlike on price – the consumer is not always right". He mentions a common

---

11   Leegin Creative Leather Products, Inc v PSKS Inc., 551 US 877 (2007), transcript of oral argument (26 March 2007), 15 line 11–12.

consumer perception that products made from glass are more environmentally friendly, arguing that there are instances where plastic packaging may have a better environmental footprint since it is lighter to transport, preserves the product longer and is recyclable: relying on competitive markets to promote sustainability risks companies substituting real pro-sustainability decisions, for focus on the preferences of partially-informed customers. A thought, certainly contentious, that deserves discussion.

2. Recognising sustainability benefits – how far?

Recent DG COMP statements suggest that the Commission might more readily embrace the quality and innovation dimensions of the consumer welfare standard when scrutinising sustainability collaborations between industry peers.[12] Within (or beyond), such (re-)interpretation of the efficiencies test, there are ample grounds to side with Christopher Thomas (in Part I: Legal Themes): he argues that the sustainable development and environmental protection objectives of Article 3 TEU and Article 11 TFEU respectively are "surely relevant" and identifies "scope for the courts to recognise sustainability as an efficiency, should they wish to do so".[13]

But how exactly to strike the balance with cost (and, consequently, often price) increases and other restrictive outcomes remains the million-dollar question. Not surprisingly, the authors' views differ in *how far* they feel a "sustainable" reading of Article 101 (and 102) TFEU goes.

Echoing other contributors, Chu notes that "consumers are … first and foremost citizens and people, whose prosperity and longevity is inextricably linked to the preservation of the planet and the maintenance of healthy, well-functioning societies". Similar to the approach outlined by Chu, Gayk promotes a balancing exercise, inspired by the principle of *Praktische Konkordanz* anchored in German constitutional law, to factor into the Article 101 TFEU analysis the EU treaties' sustainability objectives, thus remedying "limitations of a [social and economic] model … that values wealth over wellbeing".

Kasten and Reffken agree that many sustainability collaborations could be qualified as efficiency-enhancing without revolutionising the analytical framework – provided that enforcers adopt a less restrictive approach. However, they fear that a general recognition of public interests as efficiencies risks being too "wobbly" and provoking arbitrary outcomes. Depending on circumstances,

---

12 "Green wave to hit EU competition policy in 2021" (*MLex*, 22 December 2020). See also DG COMP Director General Olivier Guersent, "Closing Remarks" (EU Competition Policy and the Green Deal conference, 4 February 2021) <https://ec.europa.eu/competition/information/green_deal/index_en.html>.

13 A finding supported by Stylianou and Iacovides' empirical analysis of overreaching goals in more than 3,700 Commission decisions, CJEU judgments, advocate general opinions and competition commissioner speeches, Konstantinos Stylianou and Marios Iacovidis, "The Goals of EU Competition Law – A Comprehensive Empirical Investigation" (4 December 2020) <https://ssrn.com/abstract=3735795>.

designated legislation might be better suited.[14] The jury is still out on where to draw the line between sustainability benefits that constitute benefits under Article 101(3) (and 102) TFEU and those that don't.

IV. Taking Inspiration from European State Aid Policy and Public Procurement Law

Benjamin Linke and Udo Woll (Deutsche Bahn) provide inspiration for antitrust policy from neighbouring domains of competition law.[15] In its state aid and public procurement framework for the transportation sector, notably Regulation 1370/2007 and the 2008 State Aid Railway Guidelines, the Commission has prioritised the modal shift from road to rail or inland waterway transport. Recognising that negative externalities brought about by road transport are not captured in prices, the Railway Guidelines endorse subsidies of up to 50% of external costs for railways as less-polluting mode of transport.

Similarly, the EU public procurement directives require contracting authorities to reflect lifetime energy and environmental impacts when procuring road transport vehicles. Some Member States expressly require contracting bodies to include environmental and other sustainability criteria in their tender decisions. Linke and Woll see room for improvement, such as additional incentives for operators to make sustainability investments not imposed by the contracting authority, or abolishing the 50% cap on railway aid intensity which, as they feel, inhibits a meaningful modal shift away from road. Overall, however, they believe the legal framework is "equipped for the application of sustainability goals".

State aid and public procurement rules differ from antitrust law in a number of ways, as they primarily aim to regulate market participation and intervention of public bodies or sectoral contractors. That said, it is striking to see the extent to which state aid and public procurement legislation and enforcement practice have not only integrated the market failure rationale and a long-term view, but also how this has been translated into detailed rules for the analysis, including the quantification, of negative externalities – a possible blueprint for the appraisal of sustainability benefits in Articles 101 and 102 TFEU?

---

14 Kasten and Reffken and Gayk point at the example of the *Minstererlaubnis* in section 42 of the German Act against Restraints of Competition, which in case of a prohibition by the Bundeskartellamt empowers the Minister of Economics to clear mergers on public interest grounds.
15 On this aspect see also Patrick Thieffry, "Environmental and Climate Sustainability in Public Procurement" in Part I: Legal Themes.

V. Antitrust Law as a Shield, or Sword, Against Anti-sustainable Conduct

Several authors examine where and how competition law should be employed to bar non- or anti-sustainable business practices.

De Stefano analyses the relevant Commission case practice on horizontal cartels. It ranges from the older *Detergents* case, where a legal industry initiative to reduce dosage and weight of detergent powders and its packaging transmuted into an illegal price-fixing agreement, and the more recent *Trucks* cartel's coordinated delay of the implementation of mandatory emissions technologies, to the ongoing *Car Emissions* investigation with allegations around delayed technology roll-out that look similar to those in *Trucks*. It appears that the existing competition law framework is fit for purpose in capturing the types of restrictive behaviour identified in *Detergents* and *Trucks* – and, more generally, confirms that there is no room for "greenwashing" or "mission creep".

Eleni Diamantopoulou (ClientEarth) examines the Commission's 2018 *DE/DK Interconnector* decision to illustrate how Article 102 TFEU can be employed against unsustainable practices. The remedies accepted by the Commission reflect the minimum capacity requirements for electricity transmission network operators foreseen under the (at the time) draft Clean Energy package. In essence, the draft legislation's new mechanism to ensure that renewable energy providers receive more network access inspired antitrust enforcement – an original approach which, however, the Commission disregarded in another decision rendered around the same time. Further, Diamantopoulou argues that the remedies should have adopted a more stringent reading of the minimum capacity requirement, preventing the dominant network operator from an allocation of the remaining capacity which would run contrary to the decarbonisation rationale of the Clean Energy package.

The application of antitrust law to structural weaknesses in the food supply chain is relatively unchartered territory in EU decisional practice. The three contributors dealing with this topic concur that the conventional food system is in poor shape. It "poses a major threat to the long-term sustainability of our planet" (Chu) and is incapable of "guaranteeing [everyone's] access to healthy, culturally appropriate, adequate and affordable food while regenerating the planet and preserving it for the future generations" (Claudio Lombardi and Tomaso Ferrando).

As to the relevant legal framework, Lombardi and Ferrando see in Articles 39 and 42 TFEU a "potential safe harbour" for cooperation between small-scale agricultural producers while the Unfair Trading Practices (UTP) Directive responds to power imbalances between suppliers and retailers absent market dominance but within a relatively narrow scope of application. This leads to the question that is at the heart of the theses of Lombardi and Ferrando and Meagher and Roberts: how can and should Article 101 and, in particular, Article 102 TFEU be applied as a sword to remedy supply-chain imbalances?

Both pairs, similar to Iacovides and Vrettos (in Part I: Legal Themes) advocate for an extended reading of Article 102 (and Article 101) TFEU. Meagher and Roberts and Lombardi and Ferrando aim to capture more practices under the umbrella of exploitative abuses. But it seems that Article 102 TFEU case law provides little encouragement for more interventionist approaches: Thomas concludes that "it seems unlikely that Article 102 can be stretched to create a sustainability abuse as such." It would in fact be useful to better understand *how* Article 102 TFEU should be applied "to strike down unsustainable business practices" (Iacovides and Vrettos),[16] where the established analytical framework would have to be revisited with regard to which particular practices and to what effect.[17] Simon Holmes' reflections on abusive purchase prices for agricultural products might give food for further thought.[18]

Ultimately, as Lombardi and Ferrando acknowledge, "issues are deeper and wider than simply improving enforcement and subordinating competition law to public objectives". Even with a progressive reading, EU competition law may conceptionally just not be the right tool to accommodate the bigger agenda around the "unequal distribution of power across the food chain" (Lombardi and Ferrando) or even the "historic harms inflicted by the Global North" (Meagher and Roberts).

As Tembinkosi Bonakele shows (Part III: Agency Outlook) with his impressive account of South African competition law and practice, competition legislation that effectively addresses broader and deeper societal ills does exist.[19] But as Bonakele explains, the South African example must be understood with the backdrop of the breakdown of the apartheid regime that had skewed economic development in favour of the white minority. A similarly stringent overhaul of EU competition law is hardly conceivable in the foreseeable future. Other designated instruments promise to be better suited. For the food supply chain, the EU's Farm-to-Fork strategy, a pillar of the Green Deal roadmap, makes a good starting point.

---

16 Though conceptionally very intriguing, I have doubts as to the methodological soundness of Iacovides and Vrettos' underlying assumption that dominant companies are more likely to engage in unsustainable practices: they draw this conclusion from a set of 176 Commission decisions – 85% of cases relate to the mining/energy sector, which leaves a mere 27 cases for all other industries, a weak basis for statistically significant conclusions that "it seems to be characteristic of all economic sectors" and that "dominant undertakings systematically contribute to ecological breakdown".

17 See also Hellenic Competition Commission, "Draft Staff Discussion Paper on Sustainability Issues and Competition Law" (17 September 2020), [91] – [93].

18 Simon Holmes, "Climate Change, Sustainability, and Competition Law" (2020) 8(2) JAE 354, 384.

19 Regarding the new abuse of dominance provisions in the South African Competition Act following the 2018 amendments, see also Fox, "Competition Law and Equality: Restoring Equity by Antitrust in a Land where Markets were Brutally Skewed" (2019) CPI.

VI. Making It Happen – Mitigating Legal Uncertainty and Galvanising Support for Collective Action

All in-house lawyers call on the Commission to provide designated guidance for sustainability cooperation between competitors to address the chilling effect of legal uncertainty. Together with takeaways from other contributions, these requests can be translated into several **suggestions directed at the Commission**:

–   It would be most valuable if the revised Horizontal Guidelines give detailed designated guidance on the assessment of sustainability collaborations under Article 101 TFEU (including Article 101(3) TFEU).[20] The Commission can (and should) draw on:

  • The rich input it has received from 189 stakeholders in its consultation on the Green Deal and competition policy; some contributions very precisely set out the areas that their authors believe are in need of clarification.[21]

  • The *acquis* of Commission decisions issued under the notification system prior to Regulation 1/2003.[22]

  • The relevant case law of the European Courts, especially on the recognition of certain public interests within Article 101(1) TFEU[23] and the relationship of competition policy with other provisions and objectives of the treaties.[24]

–   Clear guidance in relation to the following *questions* would be particularly useful:

  • In which circumstances would *mandatory standardisation* agreements be admissible under Article 101 TFEU?

  • Under which conditions can companies, without engaging in collective boycott, agree to *exclude abstractly defined groups of suppliers that do not meet defined sustainability requirements*?

---

20   Similarly, it would be helpful if the Commission's new Vertical Guidelines lay out how sustainability considerations play out in vertical agreements.
21   See, for instance, the comprehensive "catalogue" of questions in the contribution from FoodDrinkEurope, "Competition Policy supporting the Green Deal" (20 November 2020) <www.fooddrinkeurope.eu/publication/green-deal-and-competition-policy/>.
22   Relevant Commission decisions include *ACEA* (Case COMP/37.231); *JAMA* (Case COMP/37.634); *KAMA* (Case COMP/37.612); *CEMEP* (Case COMP/F1–37.775) [2000] OJ C74/5; *DSD* (Case COMP D3/34493) Commission decision C(2001) 1106 [2001] OJ L166/1; *Eucar* (Case No IV/35.742 – F/2) [1997] OJ C185/12; and CECED (Case IV.F.1/36.718) Commission Decision C(1999) 5064 [2000] OJ L187/47.
23   See Case C–309/99 *Wouters v Algemene Raad van de Nederlandse Orde van Advocaten* [2002] ECR I-1577; Case C–519/04 P *Meca-Medina and Majcen v Commission* [2006] ECR I-6991; Case C–1/12 *Ordem dos Técnicos Oficiais de Contas v Autoridade da Concorrencia* EU:C:2013:127; Case C–67/96 *Albany International BV v Stichting Bedrijfspensioenfonds Textielindustrie* [1999] ECR I-5751.
24   See Case C–283/81 *CILFIT Srl v Ministry of Health* [1982] ECR 3415, [20]; Case T–210/02 *British Aggregates v Commission* EU:T:2012:110, [117]; Case C–62/88 *Greece v Council* [1990] ECR I-1527, [20].

- In how far can *sustainability benefits* qualify as quality improvements under Article 101(3) TFEU, notably if they reduce negative externalities and/or materialise "out-of-market"?

– The Commission should make use of comfort letters,[25], and findings-of-inapplicability decisions under Regulation 1/2003, article 10.

The more the Commission and other agencies put forward guidance for sustainability collaborations, the more they will "blow away a smoke screen behind which businesses could hide", as Martijn Snoep described the aspiration of the Dutch competition authority's sustainability guidelines.[26] A very practical consideration, as Mullan, Braithwaite and Cheetham-West show when identifying the risk of financial firms using antitrust law as a pretext to refrain from granular sustainability disclosures or rigorous industry-wide standard-setting for ESG investments.

This leads to a *recommendation for companies and, primarily, their internal lawyers*: The increasing openness of competition enforcers, spearheaded by the Dutch and Greek agencies, creates cooperation opportunities that businesses should seize to advance their sustainability agendas. In-house practitioners have a decisive role to play in bringing the relevant evolutions of the enforcement environment to the attention of their internal stakeholders, encouraging them to explore collaboration in areas where individual action does not deliver the necessary sustainability results. This is a chance to make an impact in a space that is nowadays at the heart of many company strategies – in-house lawyers should not miss out on it.

---

25 A recently rediscovered instrument,: Commission, "Guidelines on the optimal and rational supply of medicines to avoid shortages during the COVID-19 outbreak" [2020] OJ C116I/1.
26 Martijn Snoep, "Panel: Competition law and sustainability" (IBA Conference, 9 September 2020) <www.ibanet.org/conf1124-Wednesday-9-Sept.aspx>.

Chapter 1
Automotive and Transportation

Sustainability in the Automotive Industry, a Quest for Certainty in Troubled Times?

JÉRÔME CLOAREC*

Michelin

I. Background

There is a great momentum for sustainability, as environment has become one of the major topics on the political agenda, from the Paris Agreement to the EU Green Deal. This push has been widely praised by many players in the automotive industry, at least in the EU, where the incentives are high for companies: green solutions are consistent with brand value and a high-end market approach. It favours premium brands who believe that greenwashing does not lead far, but true investments for sustainable solutions attract not only customers but investors. In addition, for some companies, sustainability is also a matter of internal consistency, as employees are also citizens, and relations with communities where the company is integrated are key to success.

The rush for sustainability solutions should be considered against the background of the demands faced by the automotive industry: the evolution of the century-old system of propulsion (from combustion to electric), the move from mostly industrial production to service providers (as part of digitalisation), potential disruptions

---

* Jérôme Cloarec is head of antitrust for the Michelin Group (which as well as tyre manufacturing covers diversified areas such as publishing and high-tech materials). Jérôme started his career in Brussels at the French Representation to the EU before starting his legal career and becoming a competition law specialist. Jérôme has worked in law firms and at the European Commission (DG COMP), where he spent several years mostly in the merger network, but also in antitrust and state aids. All views expressed are personal.

as a global market for mobility emerges (including through in-vehicle data services) and high targets for reductions of carbon emissions. Having in mind this complex environment, sustainability goals also require a radical change of mindset.

II. How to Make Enforcement Operationally Fit for Sustainability?

The aim of this section is not to make an in-depth assessment of the impact of sustainability as regards competition enforcement. This has been done in other parts of this book. The aim is, rather, to consider the potential impact of sustainability on competition assessment, based on the experiences of business support.

1. Competition enforcement as one among many other public policies?

Competition enforcers have traditionally separated themselves from other public bodies and policies. This is not just a matter of administrative organisation due to "silos" existing between, for example, Directorates of the European Commission: it is common that in big structures, whether private or public, entities tend to fight for their independence. In fact, competition practitioners themselves tend to approach their field of expertise as being remote from other policy considerations, which has fuelled criticism.[1]

Competition enforcement now faces increasing pressure from stakeholders, including elected politicians, to accept that (i) competition is one among many other public policies, and (ii) it is only democratic that, whatever the importance of competition law, it cannot be excluded from public policies and priorities of elected bodies and their administrations.

As for competition policy itself, the widely-used but less-often-defined notion of "consumer welfare" seems to have reached its limits, as the benefits of consumers may not always be aligned with those of citizens who are targeted by sustainability. One can, of course, argue that consumers and citizens may be the same people in the end. However, the way that consumer welfare is addressed, in effect, is mainly price driven, and does not answer the fundamental question of negative externalities that sustainability tries to address.[2] Faced with a business

---

1   See, for instance, the criticism raised by merger control policy and enforcement such as the EU prohibition in *Siemens/Alstom* (Case M.8677) final report of the hearing officer [2019] C300/12; Jean-Mathieu Cot, "Prohibition: The European Competition prohibits a merger between the two main European players in the railway signalling systems and very high-speed train industries (*Siemens/Alstom*)" (2019) Concurrences N° 4–2019 Art N° 92344, 125–128.
2   Even if consumers are ready to pay more for greener options, in so much as it can be quantified, public debates such as that on carbon pricing show that consumers might not be ready to pay the full cost, i.e. the cost of externalities.

decision to push for a sustainability initiative that exposes a potential competition risk, beyond a potential gain in efficiencies, legal departments will find it difficult to make out arguments based on overall environmental gains before the authorities. Consequently, it will be equally difficult for legal departments to offer guarantees to operational business teams that the way ahead is safe.

2. Regulatory versus market-driven approach

Sustainability goals can be addressed either by public intervention (regulatory constraints and/or subsidies) or by market approach (where players are incentivised to address market inefficiencies through unilateral behaviour as well as cooperation).

Competition authorities tend to consider their task strictly limited to enforcement of competition rules, and that general policy issues, such as sustainability, should be addressed by regulation and not by market players on their own initiative.[3] It is understandable that competition authorities do not wish to widen the scope of enforcement too far. However, in the long term, the minimalistic approach does not seem appropriate.

First, political and stakeholder pressure on the one hand, together with companies asking for more guidance from authorities as a prerequisite for action on the other, should favour enforcement evolution. Second, as shown during the first months of the COVID-19 crisis, when authorities had to enact temporary measures, one can wonder whether competition enforcement should not favour market-based initiatives instead of public intervention, including by means of state aid, which could have a much more detrimental effect on competition. It is a question of a pragmatic approach, as well as consistency with the very nature of competition law.[4] The Dutch Competition Authority (ACM)'s innovative views on considering negative externalities is an encouraging step in the right direction.[5]

III. How to Make Business Operations Safe Enough for Sustainability?

So, what might practitioners need if we want to achieve the legal certainty needed for enabling sustainability solutions?

---

[3]   See for instance, Olivier Guersent (EU Commission): "sustainability goals are better pursued and achieved through regulations rather than company initiatives" (Concurrences webinar "Sustainability goals and antitrust: Finding the common ground", 14 September 2020)

[4]   For a stimulating assessment on merits of market initiatives compare to state support/aid, see on the COVID-19 crisis, Lademann & Associates and Norton Rose Fulbright, "To save competition: Rethinking exceptions to the ban on cartels" (May 2020) <www.nortonrosefulbright.com/en-de/knowledge/publications/f54767ee/erwagungen-fur-freistellungen-in-anwendung-von-art-101-abs-3-aeuv> accessed 10 January 2020.

[5]   On 9 July 2020, the Netherlands Competition Authority (ACM) published its draft revised Guidelines on Sustainability Agreements.

1. Collaborative approach must not be bad per se

In recent decades, through regulatory push (reduction of carbon emissions), companies have heavily invested in environmentally-friendly ways of doing business, from production to client service. Huge progress has been made, but this progress remains insufficient for two reasons: first, ambitious goals require more innovation and second, sustainability can only be achieved if solutions are adopted industry-wide.

In the good old days, companies would, on their own, develop innovations that could be a game-changer, and it would be for competitors to take up the challenge. In the tyre industry, when Michelin developed the radial tyre after the Second World War (technology now widely used, in everything from motorcycles to airplanes), it allowed the company decades of growth, from its roots as a manufacturer based in Auvergne, France, to its present status as a global player. The key word was secrecy, as R&D was a matter of keeping the technology for a company's own products.

Today, companies in the tyre industry, like elsewhere, have opened up. R&D efforts have kept part of the secrecy, but efforts have also been shared with other companies to expand development opportunities and discoveries. Open labs and incubators, for example, have grown significantly, and it is sometimes hard to distinguish between non- and current, or potential, competitors. Reaching sustainability goals will require competition law, as well as other areas of the law, to accept that the limits of a once clearly-defined legal entity are more and more blurred within increasingly complex ecosystems.

A traditional answer from regulators is to consider a safe harbour (such as the typical 30% threshold in the vertical restrictions guidelines of the EU Commission) or a level of market power under which cooperation would be safe. This might be impossible, as it is sometimes increasingly challenging to determine what is the relevant market and what the market power of participants, and sometimes whether they are even part of the same market. In that regard, we can only hope that the current review by the European Commission of the relevant market definition will broaden the perspective.[6] In addition, efficient sustainability solutions require that they be spread across the whole industry, which goes against the threshold principle.

Of course, the usual self-assessment by counsel or in-house advisers would help, but clearly general guidelines will not be enough to address the point. Case-by-case guidance, based on an effects assessment, will be needed to avoid self-assessment meaning self-censorship, which often seems to be the case.[7]

---

6   Commission, "Consultation: Evaluation of the Commission Notice on the definition of relevant market for the purposes of Community competition law" (26 June–9 October 2020) <https://ec.europa.eu/competition/consultations/2020_market_definition_notice/index_en.html> accessed 10 January 2020.

7   See a recent survey by Linklaters of 200 sustainability leaders in the UK, USA, France, Germany and the Netherlands: "57% of sustainability leaders say that there are concrete examples of sustainability

2. Qualitative arguments should not be an ornament

Companies willing to push for innovative projects, including mergers and acquisitions, are sometimes faced with a conservative approach from authorities: qualitative arguments are often accepted as general principles, which hardly mitigate quantitative elements such as an impact on prices or market power of the companies being considered. Qualitative elements are good material for a press release, but are they always seriously considered? Innovation boost, product quality and long-term benefits are highly regarded by authorities, but they are sometimes used only to confirm that a given project/transaction is harmless, competition-wise.

If authorities are serious about sustainability, they will have to consider qualitative elements not as fancy ornaments but as matters of real substance. But this implies that, in a way, they take their share of the risk assessment, as qualitative arguments are less tangible than quantitative ones.

3. Quantitative aspects and market inefficiencies

Sustainability in the tyre industry might be closely related to the question of how to address market inefficiencies that one manufacturer, on its own, cannot tackle. Let's take the example of logistics. It is commonly said that manufacturers struggle for the so-called "last mile". There is a lack of reactivity, the availability of tyres can be poor and customers can be left with a more limited choice than they should have. One consequence is that armies of half-empty lorries circulate to deliver to points of sale. It is not just cost-inefficient, but it also significantly increases the carbon footprint of each company.

It is unlikely that manufacturers will be able to address this point without cooperation. This is a typical example of quantitative gains proving decisive when conducting a competition assessment.

A first challenge is obviously to evaluate the efficiency gain, another is to demonstrate that all benefits will be transferred to the end customer. On this latter aspect, the ACM Guidelines provide a significant step forward by considering that not all efficiency gains need to be passed on to the end customer. It significantly lowers the standard usually required for a competition test, and one can only hope that it will be followed by other authorities.[8]

However, the question remains half-answered. Efficiency gains refer to cost and price, but they also refer to reduction of carbon emission. Without a proper consideration of carbon gains from fewer vehicles on the road for the same amount of tyres delivered, sustainability solutions might remain theoretical. This shows the limits of the traditional price-driven approach.

---

projects that they have not pursued because the legal risk was too high".

8   ACM Guidelines (n 6).

Sustainability has become a decisive point for the long-term consideration of competition. That will have to be considered in the competition assessment, if not, incentives for innovative solutions will be passed over due to the risks associated with them, and players indifferent to sustainability will prevail, to the detriment of sustainability goals.

4. CSR, a dangerous game?

Virtuous manufacturers wishing to push for green solutions to be spread among their industry face a grey zone. In the tyre industry, premium players usually favour improved testing and other solutions for promoting environmentally friendly solutions. However, the capacity to act, as with industry associations, is limited, and anything that would be too close for business operations (and thus effective) will be avoided by members.

One can see at least two main obstacles that would require innovative views from the authorities. First, labelling and standardisation are absolutely needed to create the right incentives. In the tyre industry, self-assessment is usually used for performance, including its impact on consumption (a tyre, due to rolling resistance, accounts for 20% of a vehicle's petrol consumption). Performances are poorly considered if one considers their long-lasting effect, and it happens that consumers might be deceived by label indications on a tyre that would be irrelevant after a few thousand kilometres on the road. That clearly favours players that are indifferent to sustainability. More stringent labelling requires regulatory intervention. Labelling by pro-sustainability manufacturers would significantly accelerate industry transformation. However, especially in the US, the risk is high that labelling or its standardisation would be considered as a way to exclude competitors by the main players.

Second, CSR projects might be impacted and limited by merger control constraints. When solutions are jointly adopted among competitors, even without a commercial purpose, affecting a dimension of the industry such as a key input, companies are faced with unclear situations. For example, tyre manufacturers wishing to improve farmers' conditions and the environmental conditions of natural rubber plantations are faced with the risk that any structured project could be seen as a transaction that would require merger notification. Indeed, among the 200 components of a tyre, natural rubber is still an important one. To exclude this type of agreement, with precautions and criteria about the effective purpose, from the scope of merger control would be of great value to manufacturers looking for sustainability goals.

IV. Conclusion

While there is much enthusiasm among the automotive and tyre industries for sustainability, the legal environment remains unclear.

Beyond guidelines and the usual self-assessments by manufacturers, direct guidance on a case-by-case basis would be welcome, as traditional tools of assessment (such as thresholds of market shares or *de minimis*) cannot reflect the inherent complexity of the matter. This obviously implies a more risk-based approach by authorities, as *ex ante* guidance might not prevent anticompetitive effects from happening. It would surely enhance the existing trend for an effects-based approach.

Finally, current discussions on sustainability are mainly of EU focus. There are already innovative legal frameworks in other regions, especially in Asia, but specific enforcement is still missing or limited in scope. The automotive and tyre industries being worldwide in scope, the issue arises on at least two levels. First, cooperation (coordination?) between authorities is much-needed, and absent a consistent approach between them, manufacturers will be exposed to the risk that projects that are safe in the EU could be prohibited elsewhere due to extraterritorial legislation. Second, as for the current thinking on reforming competition law in Europe, sustainability might also be linked to trade law as, in the end, it is also a matter of creating a level playing field where manufacturers are not disadvantaged by less virtuous competitors.[9]

In a nutshell, implications of sustainability go beyond the mere implementations of dedicated projects, but impact competition enforcement as a whole.

---

9   In that regard, the thinking of the economist and climate change specialist Professor William Nordhaus on carbon pricing and how to create consistency within a given economic zone or group of countries (including through border tax for those not incurring the same cost) is food for thought.

Right on Track – The Legal Framework as a Locomotive for Sustainability in Transportation

BENJAMIN LINKE AND UDO WOLL[*]

Deutsche Bahn AG

I. Reaching Sustainability in the Transport Sector

Sustainability is not only an important topic for the transport sector. The transport sector is also important for sustainability. The overall achievement of environmental goals is fundamentally linked to an environmentally focused transport sector. Hence, the European Commission has declared 2021 the "European year of rail" – to reach the objectives of the Commission's European Green Deal.[1] Why? While transport is responsible for a quarter of the EU's greenhouse gas emissions,[2] railways only account for 0.5 % of all greenhouse gas emissions from transport.

---

[*]   The authors work as lawyers in the legal department of Deutsche Bahn AG (DB). DB is a leading supplier of mobility and logistical services with a clear focus on rail and bus transport in Germany. By integrating transport and rail infrastructure, as well as through the economically and environmentally intelligent linking of all modes of transport, DB moves both people and goods.

1   Commission, "2021: The European Year of Rail" (FS/20/363, March 2020) <https://ec.europa.eu/commission/presscorner/detail/en/FS_20_363> accessed 12 November 2020; see also: Commission, "Proposal for a Decision of the European Parliament and the Council on a European Year of Rail (2021)" COM(2020) 78 final. The Council and European Parliament already reached a provisional agreement on designating 2021 as the European Year of Rail: Council of the European Union, "European Year of Rail 2021 – informal agreement with the European Parliament" (Press release, 12 November 2020) <www.consilium.europa.eu/en/press/press-releases/2020/11/12/european-year-of-rail-2021-informal-agreement-with-the-european-parliament/> accessed 13 November 2020.

2   Commission, "The European Green Deal" (Communication) COM(2019) 640 final, [2.1.5].

In its "Green New Deal" the European Commission identifies the transport sector as a particularly important area in order to accomplish future climate targets: to achieve climate neutrality, a 90% reduction in transport emissions would be needed by 2050, and all transport modes must contribute.[3] Such a modal shift will have to start with a change in user behaviour. According to the Commission, this means specifically prioritising a shift from road to rail or inland waterway transport (a so-called "modal shift").[4] Such an approach has to go along with reaching – or at least working towards – a level playing field between transport modes.[5] Since road transport accounts for 72% of global emissions from transport,[6] the approach is sensible. A further key objective is to encourage the uptake of clean vehicles and alternative fuels.

So far, "there is no standard way in which sustainable transportation is being considered".[7] It is commonly measured by the effectiveness and efficiency of a transport system concerning directly transportation-related aspects (e.g. safety) as well as economic, environmental and socio-cultural/equity-related indicators.[8] Not all transport modes contribute equally to reaching environmental goals. Although, it is advisable to focus on a variety of transport modes in order to make them more environmentally compatible, some modes of transport are *per se* more sustainable than others. In the passenger transport sector, generally bus and rail transport are considered to have a better environmental balance than motorised individual transport.[9] In the freight transport sector, railways and are much more eco-friendly than road freight transport.[10] In 2017, railways accounted for only 0.5% of greenhouse gas emissions from transport in the EU while having 7.6% of the passenger share and 17.4% of the freight share

---

3   ibid.
4   See also Intergovernmental Panel on Climate Change (IPCC), *Fifth Assessment Report (AR5)* (IPCC 2014), 603.
5   Udo Woll, "Putting transport policy on track or off the track? An analysis of the European Commission's State aid decisions in the railway sector" in Carola Pagliarin, Christoph Perathoner and Simon Laimer, *Per un'Europa più unita: Le nuove sfide del diritto del trasporto nazionale ed internazionale* (Giuffrè Francis Lefebvre 2020), 43 *et seq.*
6   Shiying Wang and Mengpin Ge, "Everything You Need to Know About the Fastest-Growing Source of Global Emissions: Transport" (World Resources Institute, 16 October 2019) <www.wri.org/blog/2019/10/everything-you-need-know-about-fastest-growing-source-global-emissions-transport> accessed 12 November 2020.
7   Christy Mihyeon Jeon and Adjo Amekudz, "Addressing Sustainability in Transportation Systems: Definitions, Indicators, and Metrics" [2005] J Infrastructure Systems 31, 33.
8   ibid, 41 *et seq.*
9   See Communauté européenne du rail (CER), "The journey to sustainable and smart mobility begins with rail" (July 2020) <www.cer.be/sites/default/files/publication/200710_CER%20input%20to%20the%20EU%20SSSM_Summary_The%20journey%20to%20smart%20and%20sustainable%20mobility%20begins%20with%20rail.pdf> accessed 12 November 2020.
10   German rail freight transport only emits approx. 19 grams of CO_2 per ton-km, i.e. 82 % less than motorised trucks (103 g/ton-km), cf. Verband Deutscher Verkehrsunternehmen (VDV), "Mit Bahnen und Bussen in die Zukunft – Input zur EU-Strategie für eine nachhaltige und intelligente Mobilität" (September 2020) <www.vdv.de/zur-eu-strategie-fuer-eine-nachhaltige-mobilitaet.aspx> accessed 13 November 2020, 7.

(2011–2016).[11] In addition to a modal shift, sustainability includes the use of ecological production components. Such components can be vehicles, energy or infrastructure. Sustainability also relates to reducing the consumption of energy, space and manufacturing materials. According to the Commission, automated and connected multimodal mobility will also play an increasing role, together with smart traffic management systems enabled by digitalisation.[12]

In passenger transport, bus and rail services in the EU mostly rely on public funding.[13] For example, the average cost coverage rate in German local public passenger transportation was 75.6% in 2017.[14] However, one needs to bear in mind that public passenger transportation saves many external costs, not only for the environment, but also with regard to traffic intensity, the use of public space etc. Therefore, fostering public passenger transport through public subsidies and keeping it as a reliable and affordable alternative to individual transport is in the common interest. Since public funding might interfere with European competition law, a modern and suitable legal framework allows for a sensible allocation of public funds in order to further strengthen sustainable transport modes.

II. Sustainability in the Current Legal Framework

The goal of achieving a modal shift must be reflected in the relevant legal framework. In this respect, two very important areas of law are European state aid law and public procurement law.

1. Sustainable transport in state aid law

State aid law plays an important role in the transport sector in general,[15] and for the railway sector in particular. According to DG COMP's state aid scoreboard, state aid for the railway sector in the EU amounted to over €43.5 billion in 2017; €22 billion for public service compensation and pensions; €21 billion for infrastructure and other aid.[16] Public co-financing and funding in transport may constitute state aid in the sense of Article 107(1) TFEU. Since state aid threatens to distort competition and (potentially) affects trade between Member States, it must be notified to

---

11 Commission, "2021: The European Year of Rail" (n 1). See also IPCC (n 4), 606.
12 Commission Communication (n 2), [2.1.5].
13 Michael Fehling and Benjamin Linke, "Einleitung" in Benjamin Linke, *VO (EG) 1370/2007 – Kommentar* (2nd edn, CH Beck 2019), [81]; Commission, "Sixth report on monitoring development of the rail market" COM/2019/51 final, 11.
14 Verband Deutscher Verkehrsunternehmen (VDV), "Kostendeckungsgrad" <www.mobi-wissen.de/Finanzierung/Kostendeckungsgrad> accessed 12 November 2020.
15 See for example Udo Woll and Andrew Meaney, "Transport aid" in Philipp Werner and Vincent Verouden, *EU State Aid Control: Law and Economics* (Wolters Kluwer 2016), 605 *et seq.*
16 See Commission, "State Aid Scoreboard 2018: Subsidies to the railway sector" (2018) <https://ec.europa.eu/competition/state_aid/scoreboard/scoreboard_2018.html> accessed 12 November 2020 (website contains a specific link that leads to "Subsidies to the railway sector").

and be declared compatible with the internal (European) market by the European Commission.[17] An exemption is (partly) made for the funding of railway infrastructure since it does not distort competition nor affect trade between Member States.[18] Any state aid not approved by the Commission is only admissible if a block exemption declares it compatible with the internal market by law.

In public passenger transport (including tram and metro) a special block exemption regulation exists with Regulation (EC) No 1370/2007 (Reg 1370).[19] However, not all cases in public transport fall within the framework of Reg 1370. Some cases might also be exempted from prior notification on basis of the General Block Exemption Regulation.[20] With this regulation the Commission declared specific categories of state aid – applicable to various industry sectors – compatible with the Treaty if they fulfil certain conditions.[21] If none of the block exemption regulations apply,[22] state aid has to be approved by the Commission in order to be admissible.

According to Article 93 TFEU, aid measures granted to the transport sector "shall be compatible with the Treaties if they meet the needs of coordination of transport or if they represent reimbursement for the discharge of certain obligations inherent in the concept of a public service". Article 93 TFEU is directly applicable as the legal basis for establishing the compatibility of aid not covered by Reg 1370 or other block exemptions regulations, concerning, in particular, the different needs of coordination (e.g. in the context of multimodal transport systems).

2. In particular: sustainability aspects under the Railway Guidelines

In 2008 the Commission released guidelines on state aid for railway undertakings that clarify the conditions under which the Commission approves state aid on

---

17 Cf. art. 108(3) TFEU.
18 According to the Commission this is the case, if "(i) an infrastructure typically faces no direct competition, (ii) private financing is insignificant in the sector and Member State concerned and (iii) the infrastructure is not designed to selectively favour a specific undertaking or sector but provides benefits for society at large", see Commission, "Infrastructure Analytical Grid for Railway, Metro and Local Transport Infrastructure" (2016-2017) <https://ec.europa.eu/competition/state_aid/modernisation/grid_rail_metro_en.pdf> accessed 12 November 2020, [7]. In older decisions the Commission displayed an even less strict approach with no further conditions to fulfil (see Woll (n 5)).
19 Council Regulation (EC) No 1370/2007 on public passenger transport services by rail and by road and repealing Council Regulations (EEC) 1191/69 and 1107/70 [2007] OJ L315/1. See also Reg 1370, art 9(1).
20 Commission Regulation (EU) No 651/2014 declaring certain categories of aid compatible with the internal market in application of Articles 107 and 108 of the Treaty [2014] OJ L187/1; see art 3.
21 For example, section 4 (aid for research and development and innovation), section 5 (training aid), section 6 (aid for disadvantaged workers and for workers with disabilities), specifically section 7 (aid for environmental protection). Section 9 (social aid for transport for residents of remote regions), section 14 (aid for regional airports) and section 15 (aid for ports) relate to other transport modes.
22 The applicable *de minimis* regulations may also be relevant: Commission Regulation (EU) No 1407/2013 on the application of Articles 107 and 108 of the Treaty on the Functioning of the European Union to de minimis aid [2013] OJ L352/1; Commission Regulation (EU) No 360/2012 on the application of Articles 107 and 108 of the Treaty on the Functioning of the European Union to de minimis aid granted to undertakings providing services of general economic interest [2012] OJ L114/8.

basis of Article 93 TFEU (the Railway Guidelines).[23] The Railway Guidelines cover the public financing of railway companies by means of railway infra-structure funding, aid for the purchase and renewal of rolling stock, debt cancellation and aid for restructuring railway companies, aid for the coordination of transport, and state guarantees for railway companies.

The broadest category of aid covered by the Railway Guidelines concerns aid for the coordination of transport.[24] This category is also explicitly mentioned in Article 93 TFEU. While many parts of the Railway Guidelines refer to the general state aid rules and allow for some deviations, the chapter on the coordination of transport provides specific guidance for the direct application of Article 93 TFEU. It plays an important role for sustainability. It is ultimately based on a market failure rational: of negative externalities and coordination failure. The Railway Guidelines recognise that certain modes of transport, in particular road transport, do not bear the costs of the negative externalities that they impose on society in the form of air pollution, climate change, traffic congestion or accidents.[25] These measures of coordination of transport are particularly justified due to the lower external costs of railway transport, as other modes of transport do not bear the costs of the negative externalities which they impose on society. In its decisional practice on the Railway Guidelines, the Commission also refers to the environmental objectives in Articles 3, 6 and 191 TFEU through the Common Transport Policy.[26] Programmes aiming at a modal shift from road to other, more environmentally friendly, modes of transport are therefore considered compatible. The eligible costs may be subsidised by up to 50% and are calculated on basis of the external costs for rail transport and competing transport modes (with regard to aid for reducing external costs). For example, to assess the environmental benefits of a scheme to generate a modal shift of freight transport from road to rail, the benefits are calculated by the net unpaid external costs of road transport in comparison with rail transport with regard to congestion, accidents, noise, pollution, climate change etc.

There have been many Commission decisions that recognise this policy objective and have therefore authorised support schemes in different Member States for rail freight transport in general,[27] for new rail freight transport services,[28] for exempting electric rail transport from a climate change levy[29] or for grants to

---

23 Commission, "Community guidelines on State aid for railway undertakings" [2008] OJ C184/13.
24 Railway Guidelines, [85] *et seq.* and fn 31.
25 See, e.g., *SA NN 29/2008 – Hungary: Excise duty exemptions for railway transportation* Commission Decision C(2009) 10493 final, [18] *et seq.*
26 See, e.g., *SA.33417 – Hungary: Promotion of single wagon traffic* Commission decision C(2011) 347 final, [19].
27 *SA.36758 – Denmark: Environmental scheme for the transport of goods by rail* (2013/N) Commission decision C(2013) 9867 final.
28 *SA.38152 – Italy: Emilia Romagna region* (2014/N) Commission decision C(2014) 4025 final.
29 *SA.31348 and SA.32614 – United Kingdom: exemption from the climate change levy for electrified rail* (2011/N) Commission decision C(2011) 2613 final.

retrofit existing rail freight wagons with less noisy, composite brake blocks.[30] Germany, Italy and Austria, in particular, have introduced funding schemes to contribute to a modal shift in the freight transport sector from road to rail.[31]

It should be noted that, currently, the Railway Guidelines are assessed under the European Commission's "fitness check". On 7 January 2019 the Commission launched the evaluation of certain state aid rules in line with the Commission's "Better Regulation Guidelines", inter alia the Railway Guidelines. The aim of the fitness check is to analyse the relevance, effectiveness, efficiency, coherence and EU-added value of these state aid rules. The Commission also wants to evaluate and assess their contribution to achieving EU 2020 policy objectives. A Commission Staff Working Document on the results of the fitness check was published on 30 October 2020.[32] The Commission concludes from the public consultation of the fitness check that, according to respondents, the Railway Guidelines somewhat failed to provide the incentives necessary to encourage a modal shift from road to rail.[33] However, the Commission also acknowledges that since the adoption of the Railway Guidelines, the Commission has received many notifications based on schemes for the coordination of transport, totalling 64 decisions.[34] The Commission decisions and the underlying documentation of the Member States, in particular with regard to decisions for the prolonging of schemes, in the Commission's view also provided "evidence of the positive impact on society not only in terms of freight volumes shifted from road to rail, but also in terms of avoided external costs to the benefit of the environment".[35]

3. Sustainable transport in public procurement law

As already mentioned, public passenger transport on land is highly dependent on public subsidies. Bus and rail passenger services in Europe are, therefore, procured by the public sector in many Member States. The award of contracts is regulated by European public procurement law.[36] In addition to general European public procurement law, Reg 1370 applies as a *lex specialis* for the sector.[37]

---

30 *SA.34156 – Germany: Funding Guidelines for noise reduction measures on freight wagons* (2012/N) Commission decision C(2012) 9467 final.

31 See Woll (n 5), for analysis of Commission decisions concerning funding schemes in the transport sector.

32 "Commission Staff Working Document: Fitness Check of the 2012 State aid modernisation package, railways guidelines and short-term export credit insurance" SWD(2020) 257 final.

33 ibid, 132 (Annex 8).

34 The leading Member States to notify for the coordination of transport were Italy (17), Austria and Germany (10 each) and, to a lesser extent, the Netherlands (6).

35 Commission Staff Working Document (n 34), 137.

36 Contract values are regularly above the threshold values for the application of public procurement law.

37 For the general requirements set by Reg 1370, see section 4, below. For the priority relationship between Reg 1370 and general public procurement law, see Reg 1370, art 5(1). For this, see Benjamin Linke and Hans-Joachim Prieß in Linke (n 13), Article 5 [29] *et seq.*

General public procurement law already offers various opportunities to reflect sustainability aspects in public passenger transport. The legal framework consists mainly of EU directives from 2014.[38] These directives do not contain mandatory provisions to consider environmental aspects. However, Directive 2009/33/EC, which also applies requires contracting authorities to consider lifetime energy and environmental impacts, including energy consumption and emissions of CO_2 and certain pollutants, when procuring certain road transport vehicles.[39] An obligation to apply environmental aspects in tender documents can also be found in national legislation. For example, German public procurement law (§ 97(3) GWB[40]) calls for environmental protection to be considered when awarding contracts. Even before the procurement directives of 2014 were adopted, the ECJ recognised that European procurement law does not preclude the possibility of taking sustainability criteria into account.[41]

Under current (2014) procurement law, sustainability requirements can be found in certain individual provisions. Particularly, it is made clear that sustainability criteria may be set as contract award criteria. According to Directive 2014/24/EU, art 67, contract award criteria might include qualitative, environmental and/or social aspects, linked to the subject matter of the public contract in question. That allows consideration of award criteria – aside from the price – such as energy consumption, greenhouse gas emissions, share of recycled material etc. The most economically advantageous tender can also be identified based on life-cycle costing according to Directive 2014/24/EU, art 68. Additionally, procurement criteria can be introduced as minimum criteria that a procured service must meet so that it is not excluded from competition.[42] Sustainability requirements can also be made as special obligations the contractor must adhere to. Above that, Directive 2014/24/EU, art 18(2), requires Member States to "take appropriate measures to ensure that in the performance of public contracts economic operators comply with applicable obligations in the fields of environmental, social and labour law established by Union law, national law, collective agreements or by the international environmental, social and labour law provisions listed in Annex X" of the Directive.

4. Sustainable transport in the framework of Regulation (EC) 1370/2007

If a competent authority wants to award (financial) compensation to an undertaking for the fulfilment of public service obligations in public passenger

---

38   Directives 2014/23/EU, 2014/24/EU and 2014/25/EU [2014] OJ L94/1–374.
39   Directive 2009/33/EC on the promotion of clean and energy-efficient road transport vehicles [2009] OJ L120/5, amended by Directive (EU) 2019/1161 [2019] OJ L188/116.
40   See also § 13(2) Bundes-KlimaschutzG.
41   Case C-448/01 *EVN AG, Wienstrom GmbH v Republik Österreich* [2003] ECR I-14558, [34]. See also "Interpretative communication of the Commission on the Community law applicable to public procurement and the possibilities for integrating environmental considerations into public procurement" [2001] OJ C333/12.
42   Examples are the amount of CO_2 emissions during transport, fulfilment of Euro standard, level of noise emission or a certain longevity.

transport, it must do so in accordance with Reg 1370, art 3(1), as part of a public service contract. Granting benefits under state aid law for services of general economic interest in public passenger transport is therefore primarily based on Reg 1370. This applies to both the state aid law – relevant aspects of public service contracts as well as their award from a public procurement perspective. If the requirements of Reg 1370 are met, such measures do not need to be notified to the Commission in accordance with Article 108(3) TFEU (cf. Reg 1370, art 9(1)). The latter is important since the exemption from prior approval by the Commission enables the smooth and swift granting of compensation payments that is usually required in public passenger transport.

Granting compensation for public service obligations in passenger transport includes the option of financing particularly sustainable services. Specifically, Reg 1370 addresses the possibility of financing environmentally friendly quality standards. Additional financial burdens of the implementation of such requirements can be offset as part of its net financial effect formula. Reg 1370 enables full cost compensation. However, the Regulation requires special sustainability requirements to be defined in the public service contract (entrustment act) as part of the public service obligations under Reg 1370, arts 2a(1) and 4(6).[43] Such quality standards could concern the use of specific types of vehicles (e.g. E-buses or hybrids). It is also possible to incentivise a provider to reach sustainability targets through bonuses, e.g. usage of less energy. Specifically, Reg 1370, Annex, para 7, requires the method of compensation to promote the maintenance or development of a sufficiently high service standard. Such standards can concern sustainability goals as well. Furthermore, it is not excluded that quality standards (regarding sustainability) are established in so-called General Rules according to Reg 1370, art 3(2).[44]

In conclusion, it is possible to require service providers to make environmentally friendly business decisions and indemnify the operator for additional costs incurred by following sustainability goals. However, Reg 1370 requires a competent authority to set additional sustainability goals itself, as public service operators can only receive compensation payments within the framework of a public service contract. Any environmental efforts the provider makes that are not part of the remit may not be compensated by the contracting authority. Reg 1370, art 4(1) requires the clear definition of the public service obligations and establishment of the parameters on the basis of which the compensation payment is calculated in advance, i.e. before the operator starts to perform the services (no so-called "mission creep").[45] Consequently, the problem remains that the

---

43   Reg 1370, art 4(6) requires competent authorities to include certain quality standards in tender documents and public service contracts. Such quality standards also comprise possible environmental aspects of the services. Regarding legal consequences in case of a missing specification of public service obligations, see Benjamin Linke in Linke (n 13), Article 2a [21].
44   It is legally disputed whether it is possible to set standards other than a "maximum tariff" in General Rules. See Marcel Kaufmann and Benjamin Linke in Linke (n 13), Article 2 [61b].
45   Benjamin Linke and Thomas Lübbig in Linke (n 13), Article 4 [17].

operator is only incentivised to comply with sustainability standards or goals stemming from the competent authority. He will refrain from implementing any additional (and maybe feasible) improvements regarding sustainability since such endeavours could result in financial disadvantage. It is instead an invitation to the tendering authorities to leave enough leeway in entrustment acts as to allow an operator to implement self-imposed sustainability goals without having to fear financial loss.[46]

III. Strengthening Sustainability in the Legal Framework

So far, the current legal framework shows that it is equipped for the application of sustainability goals. However, in order to even further prioritise sustainability objectives in the transport sector, it is suggested that the legal framework should be adapted, and additional measures introduced.

1. Railway Guidelines

The Railway Guidelines are currently under revision. And indeed, there is room for improvement and further alignment of the Railway Guidelines with the sustainability goals of the European Commission's Green Deal and the necessary modal shift. Dating from 2008, the Railway Guidelines clearly need an update. They should reflect the growing need for speeding up the modal shift in the passenger as well as the freight transport sector, from road towards the more environmentally friendly railways. Though, this was already the underlying principle of the current guidelines, the experience of more than 12 years of Commission decisions and the future challenges resulting from climate change and the need for digitalisation clearly underline the need for further development. Fortunately, the Commission seems to share this view. In its analysis of the Railway Guidelines' impact the Commission concludes that the rules on the coordination of transport have helped Member States "to shift road transport away from road to more sustainable modes of transport like rail and has thereby reduced the external costs to society".[47]

Considering the still low modal share of railways, more needs to be done. This becomes evident, for example, regarding aid intensity on funding schemes for the coordination of transport. The current Railway Guidelines rightly recognise that funding is proportionate if it addresses the gap between the different external costs caused by different modes of transport. As a 2019 study on the external costs of transport prepared for the European Commission shows: road transport is still predominant, causing by far the most external costs (83% of total costs), with rail

---

46 E.g. the establishment of innovation budgets within a service contract for the performance of greener services.
47 Commission Staff Working Document (n 34), 145.

accounting only for 1.8%.[48] These include accident costs, congestion costs, climate change and air pollution costs, noise costs and habitat damage. As long as the high external costs of other modes of transport are not internalised, at least the difference should be compensable for the transport mode that does not cause such external costs – inter alia, railways. However, the incentive for a modal shift might not be enough, if the aid intensity of such funding schemes is limited to 50% of the external cost difference. Greater flexibility on these thresholds is therefore needed. A presumption of compatibility for aid up to 100% of the eligible costs would seem suitable. In other words: funding schemes should be allowed to compensate the full difference of external costs. This should include the possibility to indemnify for any additional, consequential costs stemming from a measure (e.g. higher fuel costs from vehicle alterations). Such an approach might attract even more Member States to introduce such funding schemes and encourage the already-acting Member States to expand their schemes accordingly. Moreover, it should result in an actual level playing field for the different modes of transport, reflecting the external costs for society caused by the more polluting types.[49] It would contribute to the overarching EU transport policy objective for reducing transport externalities and sustainable growth, and a resource efficient and low-carbon economy.

2. Public procurement law

The approach of the 2014 directives on public procurement to allow for consideration of environmental aspects is overall consistent, since according to Article 3(3) TEU, the EU shall work for the sustainable development of Europe. However, to reach sustainability more rapidly, a more mandatory approach might be desired.[50] Tendering authorities are not always inclined to change their procurement approach, i.e. introduce environmental aspects in tender documents. This might be due to financial aspects but also because there is a procurement history regarding specific services, with tender documents and award criteria being slightly adapted but not significantly changed. One must bear in mind that, according to Article 11 TFEU, environmental protection requirements must be integrated into the definition and implementation of the Union's policies and activities, in particular with a view to promoting sustainable development.[51] Consequently, higher incentives to actually include environmental aspects regarding the procurement of transport are implied.

3. Regulation (EC) 1370/2007

A practical working way of financing public (passenger) transport – and therefore also sustainable aspects of a services – is within the framework of Reg 1370. However, Reg 1370 is not necessarily applicable to all funding schemes in

---

48 CE Delft, *Handbook on the external costs of transport* (European Commission 2019).
49 VDV (n 14), 6.
50 E.g. the mandatory use of vehicles with alternative engine technologies in tenders.
51 According to Article 7 TFEU the EU shall ensure consistency between its policies and activities, taking all of its objectives into account, including environmental goals.

transport. This is the case, for example, if funding relates solely to infrastructure (e.g. installation of charging areas for electric buses) or other transport assets (e.g. vehicles, ETCS-technology), which are isolated from public service obligations as Reg 1370 always requires a connection to a service that is running under public service obligations.[52] Consequently, also the funding of purely commercially running services (without public funding and exclusive rights) does not fall in the framework of Reg 1370, even if an authority wants to grant financial means (only) for certain sustainable aspects (for example technical installations improving the ecological balance of the used vehicles).

Additional investment costs in additional ecological assets are high and, consequently, often avoided. (e.g. alternative engines, refuelling infrastructure for hydrogen trains, vehicle alterations). Therefore, it would be useful to widen the scope of Reg 1370 in order to include public funding of sustainability aspects in public (passenger) transport independently of whether it benefits a service operating under public service obligations.[53] As railway transport is much more sustainable than other transport modes, further exempting schemes from prior notification to the Commission might be justified. Reg 1370 already provides the mechanics in order to assess the compatibility with the common market regarding funding for sustainability (especially with view to the Reg 1370, Annex). These mechanics should be used (*de lege ferenda*). With view to No 6 (reasonable profit) and No 7 (incentive mechanism) of the Reg 1370 Annex, the legislator could also consider allowing for the introduction of an additional "Green Bonus" for reaching sustainability goals within the remuneration calculation.

---

52 See for example *SA. 26763 Région Île-de-France* (2014/C (ex 2012/NN)) Commission Decision C(2017) 439 final. See also Kaufmann and Linke (n 47), Article 2 [5a]. Not all services run under public service obligations and it is not always possible to connect the sustainability objectives of a funding scheme to already existing public service obligations.
53 Public service compensation paid on basis of Reg 1370 does not need to be notified to the Commission. This reduces the administrative burden for Member States, specifically when lower authorities responsible for the scheme are hesitant to take a measure to federal ministries for notification.

·

The Role of Competition Law in Shaping the Future of Road Transportation

IAN ROSE[*]

Volvo Truck Corporation

I. Introduction

Road transport is considered to be a major source of greenhouse gas emissions, reportedly producing around 15% of the EU's CO_2 emissions.[1] Accordingly, the automotive sector has a highly significant role to play in achieving climate objectives.

Experience from previous cooperation and recent initiatives in the automotive sector show that with some "thinking outside the box", environmental sustainability objectives can be pursued by companies working together, while keeping them vigorously in the "competitive game".

The following are some examples of horizontal commitments, sustainability partnerships and collaboration projects. These show that, despite the efforts already taken, caution around going further persists. The examples illustrate that companies would greatly benefit from guidance, workable safe harbours and enhancements

[*] Vice President, Compliance, Volvo Truck Corporation. The views expressed in this article are personal. The author would like to thank the following for their valuable input in the preparation of the article: Patrik Hemberg (General Counsel, Volvo Bus Corporation); Eva Bennis (Director Responsible Purchasing, Volvo Group Purchasing); Magnus Prick (Corporate Legal Counsel, AB Volvo (publ.)); and Frank Wijckmans and Herlinde Burez (Partners, Contrast).
1   Commission, "Environmental aspects of the automotive industry" <https://ec.europa.eu/growth/sectors/automotive/environment-protection_en>.

to investigation processes in managing their competition law risk by engaging in cooperation. Such guidance, safe harbours and process enhancements would enable companies to take even bolder steps and to contribute further to Europe's climate goals and to satisfying the pressing needs of the planet.

II. Horizontal Commitments

The 2001 version of the guidelines on the applicability of Article 81 of the EC Treaty to horizontal cooperation agreements contained a specific chapter on "environmental agreements".[2]

The guidelines identified environmental agreements as generally not falling within the prohibition of anticompetitive agreements contained in what is now Article 101(1) TFEU, where no precise individual obligation was placed on the parties, or if the parties "loosely committed" to contributing to the attainment of a sector-wide environmental target.

In the case of such a "loose commitment", the competition law assessment would focus on the discretion left to the parties as to the means that were technically and economically available in order to achieve the agreed environmental objectives. The more varied such means, the less appreciable would be the potential restrictive effects.

Prior to the 2001 guidelines, the Commission had considered, in three cases concerning, respectively, European, Japanese and Korean car manufacturing companies, the application of "loose commitments" by industry players, to achieve an industry-wide target. In each case, the trade association representing its members, ACEA for Europe, JAMA for Japan and KAMA for Korea, entered into commitments to reduce CO_2 emissions from new passenger cars in place of legislative measures.[3]

In the case of ACEA, the commitments were aimed to achieve an *average target* of 140g CO_2/km for new passenger cars by 2008, representing a reduction of 25% from 1995 levels. This would be monitored by the Commission and the Member States using publicly available data, and the Commission would consider binding legislation if the target was not achieved. Notably, the commitments did not impose *individual targets* on any manufacturer. Each ACEA member was free to apply more stringent or less stringent emissions levels, and they would develop new CO_2-efficient technologies independently and in competition with each other. It was only if the average target were not met that legislation would be considered.

---

2   Guidelines on the applicability of Article 81 of the EC Treaty to horizontal co-operation agreements [2001] OJ C3/2.
3   *ACEA* (Case COMP/37.231); *JAMA* (Case 37.634); *KAMA* (Case 37.612).

The Commission found that the ACEA commitments satisfied the Community's strategy on CO_2 emissions from cars, but that the Commission could not take a final position until the commitments had been notified under Article 85 of the Treaty (as it then was). It was only after notification by ACEA and review by the DG COMP that the Commission stated its view that the commitments did not restrict competition under Article 85(1). Accordingly, the Commission reported that it had sent a "comfort letter" to ACEA, stating that the Commission would not take any further action.

In *JAMA* and *KAMA*, the commitments were similar, aiming to achieve an *average* target of 140g CO_2/km for new passenger cars sold in the EU by 2009. The monitoring would be undertaken by the Commission and by JAMA and KAMA, rather than by the Member States as in *ACEA*. As in *ACEA*, the manufacturers would seek to achieve the average target in competition with each other, but it was added that the monitoring reports would not refer to individual companies' achievements, "in order not to distort competition between the members". As in *ACEA*, the Commission took the view that the commitments did not restrict competition under Article 81(1) of the EC Treaty (as the prohibition had become), and the Commission reported that it had sent "comfort letters" to JAMA and KAMA accordingly.

The commitments were accompanied by other activities to reduce CO_2 emissions from passenger cars, including raising consumer awareness through publication of information on fuel efficiency and fiscal measures such as relating car taxes to emissions. The success of such measures depended, respectively, on consumer sensitivity to the environmental impact of their purchasing decisions and on how Member States applied the discretion they have in tax matters.

ACEA, *JAMA* and *KAMA* show that industry commitments on environmental targets can be agreed, using the good offices of industry trade associations, which complement activities such as fiscal measures and consumer information campaigns, without infringing the prohibition of anticompetitive agreements under competition law. The cases show that there is a need to ensure that individual companies remain free to choose the means by which they contribute to the achievement of the targets, and that exchange of information to monitor achievement does not create a market transparency that could have an anticompetitive effect. Pressure on each manufacturer to "do its bit" in the affected market, and therefore avoid "free riding", comes from the threat of legislation if the average target is not achieved.

It is, however, important also to ensure that commitments are entered into on a global level, to avoid distortions of competition in world markets, but that is a matter for international diplomatic efforts.

In the event, the Commission found only limited success of the measures, reporting, "between 1995 and 2004 average emissions from new cars sold in the EU-15 fell by 12.4%, from 186g CO_2/km to 163g CO_2/km. Over the same period new cars sold in the EU became significantly bigger and more powerful… the voluntary approach has delivered a solid CO_2 reduction but has not been as successful as hoped."[4] As a result, and since the Commission found that the 120g CO_2/km target would not be met by 2012 without additional measures, legislation to reduce emissions was proposed, alongside further financial and consumer-information measures.

The question then arises, should the trade associations and their members have been allowed to go further in collaborating to reach the targets? Would manufacturers have been able more easily to reach the targets, if they had been able to develop new CO_2-efficient technologies together and to exchange more information?

The commitments certainly seem to err on the side of caution, choosing to fall outside the prohibition of anticompetitive agreements altogether, rather than allowing for any potential restriction of competition that did not eliminate competition and that was manifestly outweighed by the environmental and, therefore consumer, benefits. The then-existing notification and "comfort letter" procedure would have enabled the Commission to reach such a conclusion, and the manufacturers thereby to have certainty. However, it seems that even with such a notification and comfort letter procedure, bolder steps were difficult to take.

The notification-and-comfort-letter procedure was consigned to history on 1 May 2004, with the coming-into-force of Regulation 1/2003.[5] Companies were left to self-assess their agreements, with only a limited ability to obtain "informal guidance" from the Commission in cases of "genuine uncertainty" because of "novel or unresolved questions" for the application of EU competition rules.

The concept of the comfort letter was, however, revived on a temporary basis by way of a Commission Communication in relation to the COVID-19 pandemic.[6] This allowed, for example, pharmaceutical manufacturers to share, under conditions, certain information on the availability of medicines, which might normally be considered an exchange of commercially sensitive information contrary to competition law. The Communication stated, in its first paragraph, "the COVID-19 outbreak is a severe public health emergency for citizens and societies. It is also a major and unprecedented shock to the global and Union economies."

Short of a comfort letter, it was reported that ACEA had requested informal guidance in June 2020 from the Commission about ways in which manufacturers could support suppliers in a cooperative way, in order to safeguard the future

---

4   Commission, "Questions and answers on the proposed regulation to reduce CO_2 emissions from cars" (Memo 07/597, 19 December 2007).
5   Council Regulation (EC) 1/2003 on the implementation of the rules on competition laid down in Articles 81 and 82 of the Treaty [2003] OJ L1/1.
6   Temporary Framework for assessing antitrust issues related to business cooperation in response to situations of urgency stemming from the current COVID-19 outbreak [2020] OJ C116/1.

of suppliers hit by the pandemic.[7] The Commission provided such guidance in September, although this could have taken longer if ACEA had sought a full comfort letter rather than informal guidance.

It was reported that the guidance confirmed that the envisaged cooperation would raise competition law compliance concerns in "normal times", and that the Commission had made various recommendations to mitigate the risks. These included open access to the discussions and maintaining the participants' freedom to act independently, as well as a suggestion that "clean teams" should be put together to have access to information about suppliers, which would not include those who would take part in commercial negotiations in the future. In any event, commercially sensitive information such as prices and volumes should not be shared, and an independent third party should be used to aggregate data.

Some might argue that the climate crisis represents a similar emergency to the pandemic and should be viewed as a similar shock. If that is the case, then the argument in favour of a similar system of comfort letters, even a system that addresses only the path to achieving industry commitments, rather than individual agreements between specific manufacturers, could be compelling. Even informal guidance of the type that it is reported ACEA received from the Commission would be helpful.

III. Sustainability Partnerships

For the last 10 years, the major international automotive manufacturers have been working together in an association, "Drive Sustainability", moderated by CSR Europe, which is a European business network for Corporate Sustainability and Responsibility.[8] Lead partners include the major global automotive manufacturers, with a "common strategy for a circular and sustainable automotive supply chain".

The automotive manufacturing industry is characterised by its highly complex and diverse supply chain. Suppliers consist of businesses from major component manufacturers supplying a range of products, to small, specialist manufacturers supplying a limited but essential range. The businesses are located throughout the world and, where suppliers sit below the "Tier 1" suppliers who engage directly with the automotive manufacturers, they may have very limited contact with the manufacturers.

Automotive manufacturers may find it difficult to establish and forge direct relationships throughout the supply chain, while the achievement of sustainability

---

7   "Carmakers benefit from 'soft' EU cooperation guidance to weather Covid-19" (*MLex Comment*, 11 November 2020).

8   Drive Sustainability <www.drivesustainability.org/>; CRS Europe <www.csreurope.org/>.

goals requires the engagement of all players in the chain and support of them by the manufacturers. Sharing knowledge, capacity-building and supporting suppliers with a consistent approach in areas such as monitoring and reporting might be said to be important elements of such engagement.

The Drive Sustainability partners believe that in order to enhance supplier sustainability and to put in place the measures necessary to achieve sustainability, it is essential that they collaborate. This is echoed by the US organisation, the Automotive Industry Action Group (AIAG).[9]

Achieving carbon neutrality is part of the Drive Sustainability Action Plan, in addition to other activities within "sustainability", including business ethics and human rights. Activities in the period 2020–2025 to achieve carbon neutrality are centred around standardisation. The aim is to agree on and promote the use of a common standardised method and tool, to measure and reduce emissions in the supply chain, and "impact key projects", with the aim to reduce such emissions.

The competition law compliance issues around standardisation are tried and tested, and they are subject to case law and guidance. The indicators to ensure that standardisation agreements do not, as a starting point, infringe competition law are that participation should be unrestricted; the procedure for adopting the standard should be transparent; there should be no obligation to comply with the standard; and access to the standard should be provided on fair, reasonable and non-discriminatory (FRAND) terms.[10] While these indicators are not the definitive rules for compliant standardisation, any different approach to the standardisation process and access to the standard creates legal uncertainty.

How "impact key projects" fit within competition law compliance requirements is, however, not as clear. Nonetheless, they are a very important element of the range of activities, which together can contribute to tackling the climate crisis. Standardisation on its own will not solve all of the issues, and legislation, tax incentives and subsidies bring their own challenges around global competitiveness and enforcement.

It is perhaps an indication of the difficulties around implementing projects within a forum such as Drive Sustainability, while ensuring competition law compliance, that activities have not gone further than supporting suppliers with information events, common reporting standards and guidelines. However impactful these are, it seems that they could be more effective if they were complemented by mandatory requirements. Such requirements could, however, carry the risk of being qualified as a collective boycott, contrary to competition law.

Drive Sustainability has published Global Automotive Sustainability Practical Guidance, which outlines the expectations of automotive manufacturers towards

---

9   AIAG <www.aiag.org/>.
10   Guidelines on the applicability of Article 101 of the Treaty on the Functioning of the European Union to horizontal co-operation agreements [2011] OJ C11/1, [280].

suppliers on sustainability issues, based on the Drive Sustainability published Principles, which do not impose mandatory requirements.[11] The guidance is basic and does not contain specific targets. Suppliers are expected, for example, to track and document "greenhouse gas" emissions, and to have an energy management strategy and programme.

Guidance is published also by the AIAG, which perhaps goes further than Drive Sustainability by stating that not only does the guidance describe minimum expectations from suppliers, and their subcontractors and suppliers, but also that it is expected that the standards will be upheld and cascaded down the suppliers' supply chain.[12]

Nonetheless, both Drive Sustainability and the AIAG could not be clearer in their commitment to competition law compliance. Both organisations emphasise their commitment and publish their antitrust policy.[13] The policies naturally exclude the possibility of any kind of collective boycott of a supplier, as well as any other anticompetitive behaviour.

No policy could, however, exclude that an authority might object to an activity which fell into a grey zone. Even if ultimately the activity were found not to infringe competition law, this could be only after a time-consuming, expensive and disruptive investigation.

The conclusion which can be reached in the case of organisations such as Drive Sustainability is that the projects that the organisation wishes to develop and implement could be bolder and more impactful if they could benefit from detailed guidance. Giving the projects regulatory legitimacy would help in incentivising the suppliers to participate, and there could even be the possibility of including mandatory requirements within a competition law – compliant framework.

The guidance could outline not only where projects did not have any restrictive effects on competition, but also what restrictive effects could be permitted as the restrictions were outweighed by the benefits arising from the contribution the projects would make to tackling the climate crisis and achieving environmental sustainability goals. The guidance would usefully have global application, endorsed by multiple regulators. It would establish "safe harbours" within which companies could proceed with certainty. Such safe harbours would not usefully be based on market shares, as the establishment of a correct market definition would be difficult since markets would have novel features or could be completely new. Moreover,

11   Drive Sustainability, "Global Automotive Sustainability Practical Guidance" (*Drive Sustainability*, 12 May 2017) <www.drivesustainability.org/wp-content/uploads/2020/07/Practical-Guidance.pdf> accessed 7 January 2021.
12   AIAG, "Corporate Responsibility" <www.aiag.org/corporate-responsibility> accessed 7 January 2021.
13   Drive Sustainability, "Anti-trust Statement" <https://drivesustainability.org/wp-content/uploads/2020/04/Anti-trust-policy-1.pdf> accessed 7 January 2021, AIAG, "Antitrust Compliance Policy" <www.aiag.org/about/antitrust-compliance-policy> accessed 7 January 2021.

market shares in such novel or emerging markets are seldom an appropriate proxy for market power. The guidance would need to be specific and targeted, in order to provide the right level of comfort to the participants. If such guidance could not be provided, then a system of informal guidance or comfort letters would need to fill the gap.

IV. Collaboration Projects

The final area which this paper considers is collaboration projects in the quest for emission-neutral technologies. One of the greatest challenges facing automotive manufacturers is finding an energy source as an alternative to diesel. Several possibilities exist, notably electricity, but electricity has drawbacks in particular in terms of the weight, volume and capacity of batteries. Alternative technology needs to be developed, based on alternative fuels.

In the case of long-distance heavy transport in particular, power demands, and the weight of batteries and the space they take up mean that it is necessary to consider alternatives to electricity. Other fuels, in particular hydrogen, and the related "fuel cell" solutions, have been identified as viable alternatives.

However, the level of technological innovation and the investment required should not be underestimated. The development work itself is highly complex and challenging, involving cutting-edge science, as well as multiple sophisticated interacting technologies; but this is only part of the story. In addition, manufacturers, together with their suppliers, need to develop the components and the software that can run the systems. Moreover, the owners of the trucks need to be sure that there is, and that there will continue to be, reliable production of the fuel at competitive prices, as well as the distribution networks and infrastructure to deliver the fuel to the truck.

The following are three examples of reported horizontal collaborations between automotive manufacturers, in relation to alternative fuels and fuel cell technology.

First, on 28 October 2020, Traton SE, the subsidiary of the Volkswagen Group which includes the truck brands MAN and Scania, and Hino Motors, Ltd a subsidiary of Toyota Motor Corporation active in truck manufacturing, announced that they had entered into an "e-mobility" joint venture.

The companies said that they would combine to develop electric vehicles including battery electric vehicles, fuel cell vehicles and relevant components, as well as creating common electric vehicle platforms including software and interfaces. They would form a team of specialists from both companies and launch activities first in Sweden and then in Japan, teaming up to shorten lead times for future products with battery and fuel cell technology, having been convinced that both technologies would be needed in the future.

The joint venture followed the signing between the parties of a strategic long-term partnership in 2018 and a procurement joint venture in 2019, and the parties would explore each other's capabilities and investigate further possibilities to collaborate in other future fields of technology.

Second, on 2 November 2020, the truck manufacturers Volvo Group and Daimler Truck AG announced that they had signed a binding agreement for a joint venture to develop, produce and commercialise fuel-cell systems for use in heavy-duty trucks as the primary focus, as well as other applications.

The parties stated that it was their ambition to make the new company a leading global manufacturer of fuel cells, and thus help the world take a major step towards climate-neutral and sustainable transportation by 2050. The transaction was expected to close during the first half of 2021, subject to merger control review by relevant authorities as well as other approvals. The Volvo Group and Daimler Truck AG would own equal interests in the joint venture, but they would continue to be competitors in all other areas such as vehicle technology and fuel-cell integration in trucks.

Third, in the USA, Kenworth Truck Company, a truck manufacturer within the PACCAR group (which also includes the DAF brand), and Toyota North America, announced in January 2019 that they were collaborating to develop ten zero-emission Kenworth T680s models, powered by Toyota hydrogen fuel cell electric powertrains.

The collaboration came within a grant-funded project administered by the California Air Resources Board, which was part of a larger programme to put fuel-cell electric tractors, hydrogen fuelling infrastructure and zero-emissions cargo-handling equipment into operation in the ports and Los Angeles basin in 2020. The programme also includes support for the establishment of hydrogen fuel infrastructure, including fuel stations.

The above examples illustrate that there are many different ways in which competitors might collaborate to achieve emission-neutral solutions, not only using electricity but also finding other energy sources. The complexities of the science and the technologies, and the need to ensure reliable production and distribution networks and infrastructure, mean that multiple specialists need to work together, and the investments are immense.

V. Conclusions

In addition to legislation, tax incentives and subsidies, cooperation between industry players has its part to play in working towards environmental sustainability goals to deal with the climate crisis. Indeed, such cooperation is often essential in order to achieve the objectives.

It can be seen from the discussion above on horizontal commitments, sustainability partnerships and collaboration projects that companies are ready and willing to engage. However, given the uncertainties around competition law compliance, and the consequences of taking a wrong step, companies need guidance and support from competition authorities when engaging with each other. The more supportive the authorities can be, the bolder companies can be in bringing about the changes which are so urgently required.

Chapter 2
Banking and Finance

Competition Law as an Obstacle for Financing a Sustainable Economy?

STEPHAN BREDT[*]

Ministry of Economics, Energy, Transport
and Housing of the State of Hessen

I. The Rise of Sustainable Finance

1. Introduction

Sustainable finance as a topic in market action and regulation has risen exponentially in the last couple of years. Sustainable finance requires that financial institutions such as issuers, or products such as portfolios or securities support concrete ESG-targets (environmental, social and corporate governance). The funding raised by sustainable bonds, for example, must be invested in projects that positively contribute to projects in ESG areas, e.g. wind parks or social housing.[1]

Particularly following policy accords on the problem of climate change, a policy framework with increasingly more clearly formulated targets – Paris Agreement, UN Sustainable Development Goals – has evolved in the past years. Underpinning this, new market players like specialised rating agencies or banks have entered the

---

* Dr Stephan Bredt is Director General, responsibilities economic sector, financial services and exchanges at the Ministry of Economics, Energy, Transport and Housing in the State of Hessen. His duties comprise – among others – the development of the Financial Center Frankfurt, the supervision of the Frankfurt exchanges and the public banks, in particular the savings banks, the state bank and the development bank. He is chairman of the Green and Sustainable Finance Cluster Germany, an association of numerous financial, academic and public institutions to support the development of sustainable finance. He previously worked for Deutsche Bahn and at the German parliament. This article expresses his personal views.
1 Lena Liebich and others, "Current Developments In Green Finance" (2020) German Council of Economic Experts Working Paper 5/2020 <www.sachverstaendigenrat-wirtschaft.de/fileadmin/dateiablage/Arbeitspapiere/Arbeitspapier_05_2020.pdf>, 3.

market. One of the characteristics of rising sustainable finance in the past, and still today, were the evolving voluntary market standards – green bond principles, lending principles, principles for responsible banking, principles for responsible investment, principles for sustainable insurance, PRI standards or Task Force on Climate-related Financial Disclosures (TCFD) disclosure rules.[2] The latest step in the rise of sustainable finance are regulatory initiatives in the EU and globally.[3]

The focus of the following assessment will be on three very topical and partly new kinds of voluntary market cooperation for sustainable finance that demonstrate that financial institutions can influence sustainable investments in different roles:

    a.   Horizontal collective self-commitments of financial institutions;

    b.   Shareholder and asset manager cooperation, acting in concert;

    c.   Collaboration on collection and exchange of sustainable finance data.

The three diverse topics address different sections of the finance industry, banking, insurance, investors and risk management. They represent different approaches to foster efforts in sustainable finance: by management commitment, by shareholder engagement and by setting up a cooperative entity. Finally they reflect that there are diverse opportunities for the finance industry to engage with sustainable finance and enhance companies outside the financial sector.

It will be examined whether these collective voluntary actions accord with Article 101(1) TFEU, which prohibits agreements with the object or effect of restricting competition and, if they do, whether Article 101(3) can be invoked as a defence for an agreement which enhances efficiency gains, so that economic progress, for example, is indispensable, benefits consumers and does not eliminate competition in important areas. The agreements are first presented, then analysed under competition law.

2. Collective self-commitments of financial institutions

In several European countries, the Netherlands, Spain and Germany, market participants have entered into collective action and cooperation.[4]

---

2   Bundesanstalt für Finanzdienstleistungsaufischt (BaFin), "Guidance Notice on Dealing with Sustainability Risks" (15 January 2020) <www.bafin.de/SharedDocs/Downloads/EN/Merkblatt/dl_mb_Nachhaltig-keitsrisiken_en.html?nn=9866146>, 19.

3   For overviews seen Liebich and others (n 1), 24; and Deutsche Bundesbank, "Sustainable finance market: A stocktake" (monthly report, October 2019_ <www.bundesbank.de/resource/blob/811962/78ce97c46 96b5a252429cd1b557f2164/mL/2019-10-nachhaltige-finanzanlage-data.pdf>.

4   See "German financial sector's collective commitment to climate action" Press release (30 June 2020) <https://cdn.website-editor.net/8475c96237754ffc80b1a6b6961f9bcb/files/uploaded/Press%2520release-German%2520Collective%2520Commitment%2520to%2520Climate%2520action_eng.pdf>; Nederlandse Vereniging van Banken, "50 financial institutions sign up for climate goals" (10 July 2019) <www.nvb.nl/ english/50-financial-institutions-sign-up-for-climate-goals/>; Sebastian Rink and others, "FINANCE-FIT-FOR PARIS (3FP) – BANKS: Technical handbook on aligning commercial banks with the Paris Agreement"

The German financial sector started a collective commitment to climate action including joint measures and objectives to meet climate targets agreed by politics. On 30 June 2020, 16 German financial sector players, with combined assets of over €5.5 trillion and more than 46 million customers in Germany, signed a voluntary commitment to structure their lending and investment portfolios in line with the targets of the Paris Agreement on Climate Change. The German commitment states:

> … To this end, we agree in particular to align our products and services and our commitments in our networks accordingly, and also to directly or jointly work with our customers to facilitate and support the economic transition required to achieve climate neutrality by 2050. We will support each other in collecting the necessary emission data to develop the methodologies for measuring climate impact and approaches to managing business activities in line with the targets.[5]

3. Shareholder cooperation and stewardship

The cooperation of shareholders and (especially) investment managers highlights the cross-industry function of the financial sector for the economic development and therefore the variety of instruments with which financial institutions may exercise influence for good corporate governance. Such cooperation might consist of discussing issues that could be raised with the board, making representations to the board on those issues, or tabling or voting together on a particular resolution. The issues on which shareholders or asset managers might cooperate could include matters relating to corporate social responsibility (such as environmental policy or compliance with recognised standards or codes of conduct).[6] Such activity, or "stewardship", comprises the responsible allocation and active management of assets with the aim of sustainable value creation and consideration of ESG criteria. Instruments are dialogue with portfolio companies, the use of shareholders rights and the exchange with other asset managers.[7]

(Frankfurt School – UNEP Collaborating Centre for Climate & Sustainable Energy Finance, 28 September 2020) <www.fs-unep-centre.org/wp-content/uploads/2020/09/3fP-Banks-Discussion-Paper.pdf>, 23.

5   Triodos Bank N.V. Deutschland, "The collective commitment of the German financial sector to achieve the targets of the Paris Agreement on Climate Change" <https://cdn.website-editor.net/8475c96237754 ffc80b1a6b6961f9bcb/files/uploaded/German%2520collective%2520commitment%2520to%2520clim ate%2520action%2520of%2520finacial%2520sector.pdf>. For more information, see <www.klima-selbstverpflichtung-finanzsektor.de>.

6   European Securities and Markets Authority (ESMA), "Information on shareholder cooperation and acting in concert under the Takeover Bids Directive" (20 June 2014, last updated 8 January 2019) <www.esma. europa.eu/sites/default/files/library/esma-2014-677-rev_public_statement_concerning_shareholder_ cooperation_and_acting_in_concert.pdf>, 3.

7   DVFA Kommission Governance and Sterwardship, DVFA Stewardship-Leitlinien, (March 2020) <www. dvfa.de/fileadmin/downloads/Verband/Kommissionen/Governance_Stewardship/DVFA_Stewardship_ Leitlinien.pdf>, 1.

Financial market national authorities agree that national takeover rules should not be applied in such a way as to inhibit such cooperation. Therefore, a "White List" of certain activities in which shareholders might wish to engage in order to exercise good corporate governance (but without seeking to acquire or exercise control over the company) has been identified by ESMA, based on existing laws, regulations and practices in Member States. When shareholders cooperate to engage in any activity included on the ESMA White List, insofar as that activity is available to them under national company law, that cooperation, in and of itself, will not lead to a conclusion that the shareholders are acting in concert, and thus the risk of those shareholders making a mandatory bid.[8]

The White List includes sustainability issues: "… agreeing to vote the same way on a particular resolution put to a general meeting, in order, for example: … to approve or reject: … the company's policy in relation to the environment or any other matter relating to social responsibility or compliance with recognised standards or codes of conduct."[9]

The question is whether there could be an overarching understanding of cooperation, acting in concert and horizontal cooperation in competition law, and whether it could provide security and enable cooperation when such a white list is developed for sustainable finance purposes or more sustainable finance issues are included in the European Commission's Guidelines on Horizontal Co-operation Agreements (EU Guidelines).[10]

4. Data-sharing and aggregation

Sufficient data forms the basis for a correct pricing of climate-related risks and an implementation of sustainable finance in banks' risk models. However, limited data availability and a lack of consistency among data sources pose an additional substantial obstacle to adequate risk assessment.[11]

Market agents therefore lack necessary information. As a consequence, there is empirical evidence of under-pricing of climate risk in financial markets.[12] Consequently, different initiatives such as the G20 Green Finance Study Group, the United Nations Environment Programme (UNEP) and the Network for

---

8   ESMA (n 6), 4.
9   ibid, 6.
10 European Commission, Guidelines on the applicability of Article 101 of the Treaty on the Functioning of the European Union to horizontal co-operation agreements [2011] C11/1.
11 See Liebich and others (n 1), 23; Sustainable Finance-Committee of the German Federal Government, *Interim Report: The Significance of Sustainable Finance to the Great Transformation* (FC4S, 2020) <www.fc4s.org/publication/interim-report-the-significance-of-sustainable-finance-to-the-great-transformation/>, 17; Rink and others (n 4), 12.
12 Morgan Despres and Paul Hiebert (eds), *Positively green: Measuring climate change risks to financial stability* (ESRB 2020) <www.esrb.europa.eu/pub/pdf/reports/esrb.report200608_on_Positively_green_-_Measuring_climate_change_risks_to_financial_stability~d903a83690.en.pdf?c5d033aa3c648ca0623f5 a2306931e26>, 3; Liebich and others (n 1), 23, with an overview.

Greening the Financial System (NGFS) have repeatedly recommended that public authorities make data that is relevant for climate risk assessment publicly available.[13] The national German Interim Report by the advisory committee to the federal government recommends the creation of a "raw-data-bank".

The initiative "Financial Big Data Cluster" (FBDC) established by more than 20 international financial institutions, public institutions and technology providers aims at setting up a financial big data space created by private undertakings that offers access to public and regulatory restricted financial data under the standards of the EU Data Protection Regulation and Financial Market Regulation. It is the financial sector part of the Gaia-X initiative of the EU, French and German governments.[14]

The project includes a workstream on sustainable finance. This workstream aims to offer solutions for gaps in the current data situation and associated obstacles to risk management processes. Also, the platform is planned to be designed to support the transfer of the findings into users' operational risk modelling. Users can, while keeping their data sovereignty, use their own data, combine it with data from other sources in the platform and train AI algorithms on this combined data space. The FBDC platform aims to develop as a potential central sustainable finance data space that could help to overcome the short-comings of information in sustainable finance data. It aims to provide, under the legal framework, data from regulatory disclosure processes of financial institutions.

II. Sustainable Finance Horizontal Cooperation and Competition Law

1. Collective self-commitments and competition law

The self-commitments comprise (1) "alignments of products and services" and joint work with customers, (2) agreement on standard-setting of certain processes ("develop methodologies for measuring") and (3) the exchange of data ("support each other in collecting the necessary emission data").

Concerning the standardisation aspect of the commitment (2), it can be said that standardisation agreements usually produce significant positive economic effects, for example by promoting economic interpenetration on the internal market and encouraging the development of new and improved products or

---

13 Liebich and others (n 1), 23.
14 Gaia-X, "Financial Big Data Cluster (FBDC)" <www.data-infrastructure.eu/GAIAX/Redaktion/EN/Artikel/UseCases/financial-big-data-cluster-fbdc.html> accessed 4 February 2021.

markets and improved supply conditions.[15] In the case of the three commitments, the exchange and development of standards will be helpful for the development of new processes, markets and products.

The alignments of products and services as well as the joint work with customers (3) will require more specification in the execution of the commitment. This target probably has potential for restrictive effects on competition, depending on its execution. However, it is probable that the alignment will focus on standards for products and the application of the latter to the work of self-commitment participants with customers.

Participation in the commitments is unrestricted and the procedure for adopting the standard in question is transparent, the commitments contain no legally binding obligation to comply with the standard and provide access to the standard on fair, reasonable and non-discriminatory terms, so they will normally not restrict competition within the meaning of Article 101(1) TFEU.

The risk for the participants emanating from a breach of the self-commitment could be reputational risk, which could be seen as a corporate, regulatory and supervisory mismanagement. The German financial supervisor BaFin has expressed its expectation that financial institutions deal with the risk emerging from climate change and transition of the economy. BaFin states that if the decision is taken to comply with voluntary sustainability standards, their application across the entire group is encouraged. That means that if entities have voluntarily agreed to abide by external sustainability standards or to implement recommendations, these should be reflected in in-house strategies and organisational guidelines. It may create reputational risk if some group entities apply non-binding sustainability standards that are violated by other entities in the group.[16] Therefore, an indirect self-binding commitment creates two consequences in case of non-compliance: a reputational risk and a potential violation of supervisory requirements. Therefore the non-binding commitment potentially influences the market conduct of at least one of the parties by causing a change in its incentives. The ECB Guidelines do mention voluntary standard-setting but do not elaborate on potential regulatory risks in that context.[17] However, as the process for participation in these self-commitments is open to further participants and is transparent, there should be no restrictive effects on competition under Article 101(1) TFEU in the understanding of the EU Guidelines.

The collaboration concerning the collection of emission data, e.g. for reporting processes or risk management, could be seen as an exchange between competitors of strategic data (data that reduces strategic uncertainty in the market), and

---

15 EU Guidelines, [263].
16 BaFin (n 2), 38.
17 European Central Bank, "Guide on climate-related and environmental risks: Supervisory expectations relating to risk management and disclosure" (November 2020) <www.bankingsupervision.europa.eu/ecb/pub/pdf/ssm.202011finalguideonclimate-relatedandenvironmentalrisks~58213f6564.en.pdf>, 14–15.

would therefore more likely to be caught by Article 101(1) TFEU than exchanges of other types of information. Sharing strategic data can give rise to restrictive effects on competition because it reduces parties' decision-making independence by decreasing their incentives to compete. Strategic information can be related to risks, investments, technologies and R&D programmes and their results.[18]

As for a potential restrictive effects on competition, it must be considered that sustainable finance is a market and marketing strategy for the financial institutions. According to the UNCTAD World Investment Report (2014), attaining the sustainable development goals by 2030 will require annual global investment of $5–7 trillion, of which $3.3–4.5 trillion will need to be allotted to developing countries.[19] Self-commitments and the sharing of standards, processes and methods can help establish this market, which could be profitable for the institutions active in it. This new market is perceived in this way by market participants, even if there are studies with divergent findings on the market's profitability.[20] However, the economic interest of market participants demonstrates that this new market is evolving and that the exchange of information and processes can help it build on further competition within it.

2. Cooperation under ESMA's White List and acting in concert as horizontal cooperation

Shareholder agreements agreed upon by asset management firms can be classified as agreements with the object or effect of restricting competition, as they aim to influence market behaviour of the companies concerned, such as product variety, and to leave fewer decision-making capacities with the parties.

The cooperations and agreements included the White List itself, however, are also non-binding for asset management firms. Moreover there is no supervisory or reputational risk evolving from non-compliance with such agreements.

The White List exempts actions taken and included in the list from specific legal consequences as do the EU Guidelines. Rules on concerted action are applicable in all Member States at different levels: in the majority of Member States, the percentage of voting rights that confers control of the company under the Takeover Bids Directive, article 5.1 (the "primary threshold"), has been set at around 30%. Some have set the primary threshold at higher or lower levels than 30% and some have an alternative primary threshold.[21]

Shareholder cooperation under the White List could be justified under Article 101(3) TFEU, as it aims to create efficiency gains for the companies

---

18   EU Guidelines, [86].
19   Liebich and others (n 1), 6.
20   ibid, 7.
21   ESMA (n 6), 11.

concerned. The cooperations at stake aim at enforcing compliance with ESG standards and considering the risks associated with climate change in their companies' respective business strategies.

The question is whether the stipulations on cooperation as included in the White List to strengthen companies efforts in sustainable finance could or should be incorporated in the EU Guidelines. Such an addition could mobilise capital and market participants to more easily exert their influence for the development of sustainable finance.

3. Shared data aggregation in sustainable finance and competition law

Data relevant for sustainable finance is and will be collected by supervisory authorities through mandatory regulatory disclosure rules from financial institutions and beyond. For example, supervisory institutions are informed of the physical, transitory and financial instability risks of financial institutions concerning climate change. The problem is that this data is then isolated in supervisory institutions and cannot, or can only in a limited way, be used to improve financial institutions' individual analysis that would be important for business strategy or product development. The question is whether such regulatory data could be used in full compliance with regulatory and data protection law by an undertaking, set up in a horizontal cooperation for the specific purposes of improving the use of sustainable finance data. The above-mentioned FBDC is such a horizontal cooperation. As the collection, interoperability and use of data for a successful development of sustainable is indispensable, clarity on the legality of horizontal cooperation in this field would be beneficial.

A. *Exchange of sustainable finance data on the FBDC platform*

Exchange of genuinely aggregated data, where the recognition of individualised company-level information is sufficiently difficult, is much less likely to lead to restrictive effects on competition than exchanges of company-level data. Such data collection and publication may allow market participants to make better-informed individual choices in order to adapt efficiently their strategy to the market conditions.[22]

In view of the intended function of the FBDC, it should be assumed that Article 101(1) TFEU must be observed. The exchange of data and collusion for the purpose of analysis and artificial intelligence applications of actors competing on the financial market is one of the objectives of cooperation. In this context, precautions must be taken to check which information of a competitor may be used by another competitor, or what technical or

---

22 EU Guidelines, [89].

organisational measures must be taken before processing, to prevent competitors from gaining unauthorised access.

B. *Sustainable finance data space as a horizontal cooperation and undertaking*

Data Spaces like the FBDC are supposed to operate as a joint venture of undertakings and public institutions. It will be providing its services at market conditions, so could therefore be seen as a horizontal production agreement. Production agreements can lead to a direct limitation of competition between the parties. In the case of the FBDC, however, the aim is to make sustainable data, that would otherwise not be accessible, accessible and exchangeable for customers. It therefore creates a whole new opportunity for sustainable finance market participants to base their decisions on new data and corresponding IT instruments, such as artificial intelligence. Moreover, the data provision market on sustainable finance is developing strongly, globally, and competition will not be significantly restricted by such an initiative even if it can provide a certain product that other data providers might be not be able to provide.

The FBDC concept on sustainable finance holds also elements of R&D cooperation, as it is aiming at developing and improving the access and usability of sustainable finance data with artificial intelligence. Most R&D agreements do not fall under Article 101(1) TFEU. In the case of the FBDC, the use case is supported by the German national government as R&D. After completion of the set-up of the sustainable finance use case, the application of the methods developed are assumed and will be applied and offered to market participants within the FBDC. It can be seen as R&D at a rather early stage, far removed from the exploitation of possible results.[23] Finally, the data space project could, under Article 101(3) TFEU and like many R&D agreements – with or without joint exploitation of possible results – bring about efficiency gains by combining complementary skills and assets, thus resulting in improved or new products and technologies being developed and marketed more rapidly than would otherwise be the case.

III. Conclusion

The analysed financial sector commitments, shareholder cooperation and data exchange – based entities probably remain unproblematic under European competition law regime, depending, of course, on the handling of their execution. That indicates that to the contrary there remains space for the finance industry to engage with more far-reaching activities to contribute via more qualified and self-binding activities. As all three levels of cooperation

---

23   ibid, [129].

discussed – collective binding commitments, agreements of shareholders and asset managers and the collection and aggregation of data and its use in horizontal cooperation – seems essential to enhance the development of sustainable finance by further horizontal cooperation, competition law guidelines could be adapted to this specific field to make such an development more secure and possible.

Potential Competition Concerns as the Banking and Finance Industry Responds to Climate Change

HUGH MULLAN, MARC BRAITHWAITE
AND ROSY CHEETHAM-WEST[*]

UK Payment Systems Regulator | UK Financial Conduct Authority

I. Introduction

Other papers in this book examine how competition law might apply to sustainability agreements. This article instead discusses where those rules might need careful consideration in relation to financial services.

It may not initially be obvious that there is a substantial overlap between banking and finance, competition law, and climate change. We therefore start by highlighting key interactions between the banking and finance industry and environmental issues before considering potential competition law questions.

1. The direct impact of banking on environmental sustainability

As a service industry, banking and finance is unlikely to be a major contributor to carbon emissions compared with, for example, basic industries or the travel industry.

---

[*] Hugh Mullan is a technical specialist and economist at the Payment Systems Regulator in the UK, and has previously worked as assistant director at the Competition and Markets Authority (CMA); Marc Braithwaite is a manager and lawyer in the competition enforcement team at the UK's Financial Conduct Authority (FCA), and previously worked as an assistant director at the CMA; Rosy Cheetham-West is a senior associate and lawyer in the competition enforcement team at the FCA, and was previously in private practice at Slaughter and May. The views expressed are those of the authors and do not necessarily represent the views of the institutions where they work.

That said, one obvious direct contribution is the physical distribution of cash and coin throughout the economy (though that will reduce over time as usage diminishes). A 2018 study by the Central Bank of the Netherlands[1] looked at the environmental impact of the Dutch cash payment system and debit card payment chain. It found that:

– Cash transport had the largest environmental impact, with copper ore extraction (for coin production) and ATM power consumption also significant.

– In the debit card payment chain, point-of-sale terminals had the largest environmental impact, followed by debit card payment processing centres and plastic card production.

The study proposed several changes, such as reducing ATM numbers and transporting cash using hybrid trucks. The Bank of England (BoE) has similarly considered carbon emissions generated by the cash system and made various improvements, such as introducing polymer £5 and £10 notes. Still, as identified by the Dutch study, there remain several other emission-cutting measures that could be applied.

Worse than plastic cards or cold hard cash, however, is an entirely virtual currency: Bitcoin. Bitcoin appears to share an astonishingly high carbon consumption with other cryptocurrencies validated via blockchain technology, but is at the top end of the scale, with a carbon footprint estimated to sit between those of the nations of Jordan and Sri Lanka.[2]

While improving environmental sustainability is crucial, we note that doing so may affect competition and innovation. Indeed, a BoE consultation on consolidating wholesale cash infrastructure included that impact among its evaluation criteria.[3] Evidently, there may be trade-offs; this book is largely about how competition law should handle such potential trade-offs.

Finally, as well as the systemic industry issues this article focuses on, tackling sustainability issues requires firms and individuals to take responsibility. The finance sector is a large-scale employer with a high proportion of wealthy firms and individuals; it may, therefore, have more to ask itself in this regard than other industries. Do we really need to fly to New York for that meeting rather than speaking on Zoom? Could the firm recycle more and use renewable energy sources? And so on…

---

1   De Nederlandsche Bank, "Life cycle assessment of cash payments" DNB working paper 610 (9 October 2018) <www.dnb.nl/en/news/dnb-publications/dnb-working-papers-series/dnb-working-papers/Workingpapers2018/dnb379444.jsp>.

2   Christian Stoll, Lena Klaaßen and Ulrich Gallersdörfer, "The Carbon Footprint of Bitcoin" (2019) 3(7) Joule 1647 <www.sciencedirect.com/science/article/pii/S2542435119302557>.

3   BoE, "Consultation on the Future of the UK's Wholesale Cash Distribution Model" WDSG Consultation paper (24 June 2020) <www.bankofengland.co.uk/-/media/boe/files/paper/2020/consultation-on-the-future-of-the-uks-wholesale-cash-distribution-model.pdf?la=en&hash=D9B4FB7B6CA6FD3F846E5C277A E3BB8D20F2B928>.

2. The indirect impact of banking and finance on environmental sustainability

Notwithstanding the above, the major environmental impact of banking and finance is indirect, lending them a critical role in helping to address the significant challenges of limiting climate change.

One report found that 33 global banks have financed fossil fuels with $1.9 trillion since the Paris Agreement was adopted (2016–2018), and that this amount has risen each year.[4] At the same time, €6.2 trillion of investment will be required by 2030 to limit global warming to 2°C. Some of this will come from public actors, but the transition to a low-carbon economy requires substantial investment, which, realistically, can only be financed with private sector involvement.[5]

The financial sector also plays a key role in pricing the risks of climate change, and in transmitting the pricing effects, should these risks crystallise. Both physical and transitional risks of climate change may impact the position of financial firms. In relation to physical risks, damage to homes and businesses from climate change, including storm impacts, may increase the risk of defaults on loans and the viability of insurance products. Similarly, the transition to a more sustainable economy is likely to entail significant changes in asset prices in response to changes in technology, policy and the law.

It is not in principle obvious that competition law should significantly impede the pro-environment measures needed to tackle these issues. However, we identify two related areas where the banking and finance sector needs to make improvements and discuss how competition law concerns could arise: standard-setting and disclosures.

II. Standard-Setting

Increasing flows of capital are being directed to "ESG" funds – those sold as having strong environmental, social and corporate governance credentials.[6] However, terms such as "green", "ethical" and "sustainable" are not clearly defined in the context of investing and, inevitably, fund managers and investment platforms use them in very different ways. Such ambiguity may exacerbate the

---

4   Alison Kirsch and others, "Banking on Climate Change, Fossil Fuel Finance Report Card 2019" (20 March 2019) <www.banktrack.org/download/banking_on_climate_change_2019_fossil_fuel_finance_report_card/banking_on_climate_change_2019.pdf>.
5   "Explore Green Finance" (*Green Finance Platform*) <https://greenfinanceplatform.org/page/explore-green-finance> accessed 27 January 2021.
6   Investors continued to pour money into sustainable funds in the first three months of 2020, even as the coronavirus pandemic unfolded. Investors across the globe put $45.6 billion into funds focused on ESG in the first quarter of the year. This compares with global outflows of $384.7 billion for the overall fund universe. Hortense Bioy, "Investors Back ESG in the Crisis" (*Morningstar News*, 12 May 2020) <www.morningstar.co.uk/uk/news/202274/investors-back-esg-in-the-crisis.aspx>.

problem of "greenwashing".[7] For example, there are no UK regulatory standards on whether firms can feature oil and gas assets within "green" financial products.

Even if there were agreed definitions, assessments of businesses and investment opportunities against these criteria are likely to differ. In the absence of well-defined terms, it can be difficult for investors to know what they are investing in, and to compare what is on offer.[8]

By way of illustration, Credit Suisse found in one study that "there is little relationship between the ESG appraisals for a given stock by different agencies. The correlations are astonishingly low. At best, ESG ratings are a starting point, and investors need to understand them and supplement them with their own scrutiny."[9] Even in the long term, it is unrealistic to expect that a sufficient number of investors will have the ability or inclination to take on such a challenging task.

It is therefore arguable that a common set of minimum standards on green finance is essential:

> Most importantly, a harmonised definition of "green" and a taxonomy of green activities are needed to help investors and financial institutions efficiently allocate capital and make well-informed decisions. The definition of green finance needs to be more transparent to prevent "greenwashing". And a common set of minimum standards on green finance is essential... Voluntary principles and guidelines for green finance, complemented with regulatory incentives, need to be implemented and monitored for all asset classes.[10]

One specific problematic area of standard-setting arises in relation to disclosures by financial institutions about how climate change risks may affect the valuation of their assets and their businesses overall. Currently, disclosures by banks are typically more advanced than those by insurers or asset managers, with the most advanced describing the methodologies used for scenario analysis and lending exposure to high carbon sectors.[11] However, there appears to be limited comparability between banks – primarily because here, too, there are no standardised methodologies or metrics in place.[12]

---

7   The CMA has recently opened an investigation into greenwashing across a range of sectors, although its focus does not currently appear to include banking and finance: CMA, "CMA to examine if 'eco-friendly' claims are misleading" Press release (*Gov.uk*, 2 November 2020) <www.gov.uk/government/news/cma-to-examine-if-eco-friendly-claims-are-misleading>.

8   Climate Financial Risk Forum, "Climate Financial Risk Forum Guide 2020: Disclosures Chapter" (June 2020) <www.fca.org.uk/publication/corporate/climate-financial-risk-forum-guide-2020-disclosures-chapter.pdf> (CFRF Guide), 12.

9   Elroy Dimson, Paul Marsh and Mike Staunton, *The Global Investment Returns Yearbook* (Credit Suisse Research Institute 2020).

10 Green Finance Platform (n 5).

11 CFRF Guide (n 8), 27.

12 ibid.

Considering these challenges, there would be merit in the finance industry coming together to agree on the interpretation and definition of terms relevant to sustainable investments, and how to assess the ESG credentials of a company.[13] It remains to be seen if this will need to involve mandatory definitions, or whether a clear set of principles will suffice.

1. Potential competition concerns

In some circumstances, standardisation risks harming competition. For example, investment platforms and fund managers may compete based on their own assessment of a firm's ESG credentials, or by creating their own ESG funds and definitions. This might provide more options for investors to choose between. Indeed, investors are likely to differ in the weighting they give to the different elements that may be included within ESG – i.e. environmental factors may be paramount to one investor while social and corporate governance is crucial to another. It may be that ESG has gained popularity in part because it is open to different approaches.

In addition, more demanding standards may increase compliance costs for firms, and enhanced rigour could lead to products formerly marketed as "ESG" exiting the market if they fail to meet classification requirements. There may be, therefore, a reduced range of sustainable funds for consumers in the short term. However, this should be seen as competition working effectively, because it would reflect the higher quality of the retained products' credentials.

Demanding standards are likely to be necessary if they are to mitigate green-washing risks. If terms like "green" can apply to investments with little or no positive environmental impact, those seeking a competitive advantage by offering better sustainability credentials are at risk of being undermined. On the other hand, some will argue that setting the bar particularly high will unfairly exclude products that have legitimate claims to being sustainable.

Setting standards will therefore likely affect competition and choosing a particular standard will not suit everyone. Indeed, concerns have already been raised in this context, as indicated in responses to a recent FCA discussion paper, including on:[14]

- The narrow scope of the EU taxonomy and its focus on so-called "dark green" activities, which could limit sustainable investments to the exclusion of other positive-impact projects; and

---

13 The EU is progressing a Sustainable Finance Action Plan to encourage investments in sustainable activities. One part of this plan is to create a common language on sustainable activities that everyone in the financial system can use. A new EU regulation, published in draft form in May 2018, proposes to introduce criteria to establish, in the first instance, what can be considered an environmentally sustainable activity. A technical expert group published a draft of the taxonomy in June 2019. FCA, "Climate Change and Green Finance: summary of responses and next steps. Feedback to DP18/8" (October 2019) <www.fca.org.uk/publication/feedback/fs19-6.pdf>, [3.34].
14 FCA (n 13), [3.37] – [3.39].

- The emerging definitions: questioning their prescriptiveness and the potential inflexibility of a legislative approach, and the possibility it could stifle innovation.

There is undeniably merit in some standardisation of the meaning of terms and approaches to business appraisal. Cooperation between firms should aim to create common standards in sustainable finance that are in the interests of consumers. We want consumers to be able to understand and compare the products they are offered, and to eliminate "greenwashing".

While the concerns above remind us of the need to be wary that standardisation does not eliminate valuable competition, it should be possible to produce standards that ensure sufficient competition on environmental factors while providing better information on where to invest, and confidence that green investments are just that. Competition law – compatible standards in other areas could provide useful lessons in assessing exactly where that balance should be struck.

III. Information Sharing/Disclosure

Climate change is important when assessing the financial risks faced by financial institutions; indeed, 70% of UK banks now consider climate change to be a financial risk. However, only 10% of UK banks are taking a long-term strategic approach to managing the financial risks of climate change, and the total global and domestic value of outstanding green bonds is only a fraction of the financing required.[15]

The UK's Prudential Regulation Authority (PRA) has described the financial risks from such physical and transition risk factors as relevant to multiple business lines, sectors and geographies, meaning their full impact on the financial system may be larger than for other types of risks, and these risks are potentially non-linear, correlated and irreversible.[16] Arguably this identifies climate change as a material risk, implying that disclosures should be made in supervised firms' annual reports and accounts.

In addition, the UK government's Green Finance Strategy set out an expectation for all listed companies and large asset owners to provide, by 2022, disclosures in line with the recommendations of the Taskforce for Climate-related Financial Disclosures (TCFD). More recently, the government announced its intention to make TCFD-aligned disclosures mandatory across the economy by 2025, with

---

15 HM Government, "Green Finance Strategy Transforming Finance for a Greener Future" (July 2019). <https://assets.publishing.service.gov.uk/government/uploads/system/uploads/attachment_data/file/820284/190716_BEIS_Green_Finance_Strategy_Accessible_Final.pdf>, 6.
16 PRA, "Supervisory Statement: Enhancing banks' and insurers' approaches to managing the financial risks from climate change" SS3/19 (April 2019).

a significant portion in place by 2023.[17] The FCA has indicated its desire to see similar disclosures by security issuers and regulated firms.[18]

Given all this, there will likely be greater climate-related disclosure by banks and other financial institutions going forward. But what should such disclosure look like?

1. Potential competition concerns

The TCFD identifies seven principles that effective disclosures should meet:[19]

- Represent relevant information;
- Be specific and complete;
- Be clear, balanced, and understandable;
- Be consistent over time;
- Be comparable among companies within a sector, industry, or portfolio;
- Be reliable, verifiable and objective; and
- Be provided on a timely basis.

Detailed, transparent, comparable, and up-to-date disclosures could get competition lawyers very hot under the collar if they reveal information about competing companies that could lead to a distortion of competition. While it is not obvious that financial disclosures would do so, it is certainly possible. To be most useful, disclosures would provide a lot of detail on, for example, banks' loans; asset managers' investments; insurers' risks; and climate change risk mitigation strategies. At what point might competitors disclosing such detailed information lead to competition concerns?

The CFRF Guide states that: "Firms are unlikely to make disclosures at a level of granularity that would cause competition concerns [while] minimum expectations around disclosures could (i) help provide comfort to firms, since many disclosing at the same time are likely to be in a similar position and (ii) enable those that have invested ahead of time and are well positioned to gain market visibility and reward for their efforts."[20]

Whether competition authorities are worried or not, firms may themselves have concerns about potential competition law implications, which may lead them to

---

17 See HM Treasury, "UK joint regulator and government TCFD Taskforce: Interim Report and Roadmap" (*Gov.uk*, 9 November 2020) <www.gov.uk/government/publications/uk-joint-regulator-and-government-tcfd-taskforce-interim-report-and-roadmap>.

18 FCA (n 13).

19 CFRF Guide (n 8), 8.

20 CFRF Guide (n 8), 45, The CFRF Guide has been written by industry, for industry. Although the CFRF discussions were convened and facilitated by the PRA and the FCA, the views expressed in the guide do not necessarily represent the view of the regulators.

limit the extent of their disclosure – even when no genuine harm to competition may arise. In this context, there has been some criticism of the harshness of the approach of competition authorities to instances of information exchange that do not directly impact on prices.[21]

The risk of revealing competitively sensitive information could be heightened due to the different perspectives of the disclosing companies and their audiences. For example, some investors (with ESG concerns) might want to know more about the climate change implications of investments while disclosing firms may not see these as having a material impact on their business. Thus, investors or users may want more commercially sensitive information to be revealed.[22]

The CFRF Guide provides an example whereby:[23]

- The user of the disclosure wants information on the scenarios and assumptions used, as well as the financial impact of climate-related issues on the organisation; but

- The disclosing business considers it difficult to disclose scenario analysis assumptions, as they include confidential business information.[24]

It considers how commercially sensitive information might be revealed as a by-product of disclosure, and how this could either harm competition or be used as an excuse not to engage in proper disclosure. Ultimately, as with any standard-setting for "green" terminology, a balance will need to be struck between providing disclosures that are sufficient to inform investment decisions but which do not unduly distort competition. We consider that the benefits of achieving such a balance outweigh the risks of trying to do so.

2. The risks of collusion over disclosure

Might there also be a risk of collusive behaviour over financial disclosures?

The CFRF Guide states that "High-quality disclosures can be viewed as a competitive advantage for firms," and that "Investors, regulators and consumers should... value high quality disclosure...".[25] However, it is recognised that, conversely, a barrier to financial institutions disclosing climate-related financial

---

21 Alfonso Lamadrid, "Bananas – Case C–286/13 P, Dole v Commission" (*Chillin'Competition*, 28 April 2015) <https://chillingcompetition.com/2015/04/28/bananas-case-c-28613-p-dole-v-commission>; Martine Behar-Touchais, "Exchange of information: The Court of Justice of the European Union confirms that strategic information exchange is a restriction of competition by object (*Dole Food, Dole Fresh Fruit Europe*)" (2015) Concurrences N° 2–2015 Art. N° 72738, 81–82.
22 See CFRF Guide (n 8), 8.
23 CFRF Guide (n 8), 9 (Fig 1).
24 In this context, the CFRF Guide notes "the possibility that the firm's competitors could benefit from the information the firm discloses" (n 8), 11.
25 CFRF Guide (n 8), 5.

information is the potential competitive disadvantage that may arise if such disclosure more clearly highlights a firm's position vis-à-vis its competitors.[26]

Might firms compete over the quality of their financial disclosures, if investors value this quality? If so, is there also an incentive to collude? Businesses would have less incentive to reduce climate-change financial risk if they did not need to disclose these risks in detail; and businesses may not feel the need to do so if they think their competitors will take the same approach. There may therefore be incentives to collude (even tacitly) to reduce the quality of disclosures.

We are not aware of any past instances of financial institutions colluding over the quality of disclosures; and one might not expect issues to arise specifically in relation to climate-change related-financial risks. However, the possibility illustrates how the standard-setting discussed earlier could lead to practical competition law risks. We might hope that the financial sector, particularly with a push from regulators and legislators, will introduce minimum standards of disclosure, and for these to become more demanding over time; but conversations about minimum standards risk effectively setting a maximum standard.

IV. Conclusions

The banking and finance industry has a critical role in allocating capital towards more sustainable technologies. To achieve this, firms will need to work together, as well as following the lead of regulators and government.

It will be important to ensure that cooperation does not lead to competition concerns. For example, standard-setting, while playing a valuable role in supporting the development of an orderly and trustworthy market and reducing greenwashing, could also lead to unintended consequences such as limiting incentives to innovate or compete on ESG credentials, harming competition and reducing customer choice. Standards need to be designed carefully to avoid inadvertently reaching such outcomes.

Banks and other financial institutions will face increased pressure for greater transparency about how climate change risks may impact on their assets and business models. Investors may need considerable detail to make these assessments. Greater detail creates a risk that the information-sharing, intentionally or otherwise, leads to a softening of competition, since uncertainty about the strategies and actions of one's competitors is an essential element of effective competition. However, this uncertainty may also undermine investors' ability to assess the environmental sustainability of businesses in which they are considering investing. Disclosures will need to strike the right balance between the two considerations.

---

26   CFRF Guide (n 8), 45.

Of course, banks and financial institutions will need to consider the risks of competition law enforcement action by authorities when cooperating with competitors. However, we believe that it is possible both to increase the consistency and transparency of ESG definitions in a competition law – compatible way, and to improve the quality of financial disclosures in this area; competition law should not be a barrier to progress. The greater risk may be that the actors in this industry use competition law as a reason not to act, whether to avoid setting demanding standards in how terms are defined, or to avoid disclosing how their businesses and assets affect, or would be affected by, climate change.

Ultimately, if the reality of driving sustainability objectives forward creates significant tension with competition law, government may need to decide between competing public policy goals, for example by amending competition law to take greater account of the need for sustainability.[27]

---

27   The Dutch ACM is for example exploring such an approach. See ACM, "Draft Guidelines: Sustainability agreements" (9 July 2020) <www.acm.nl/en/publications/draft-guidelines-sustainability-agreements>.

Chapter 3
Consumer Goods

Competition Law and Sustainability: an Industry Perspective

ANGÉLIQUE DE BROUSSE[*]

Johnson & Johnson

I. Introduction

Sustainability has been the subject of broad debate around the role of competition law in contributing to the von der Leyen Commission's agenda, in particular the Green Deal. A lot has been said (and written) about whether competition rules are adequate or should be amended to cater for sustainability objectives. The author is of the view that competition law is part of the solution, not the problem.[1]

Johnson & Johnson, a 134-year-old company, has been committed to sustainability since its very early days. This is reflected as a key priority in "Our Credo",[2] a nearly 80-year-old statement summarising the company values, which are part of the company's DNA and drive decision-making at all levels of the company to this day. It states inter alia that "We must maintain in good order the property we are privileged to use, protecting the environment and natural resources".[3]

---

[*] The author is senior legal counsel, Head of Competition Law & Policy Group EMEA at Johnson & Johnson, responsible for all aspects of competition law and all business sectors. She is a founding member and vice-president of l'Entente (asbl), the association of French competition practitioners based in Brussels, as well as a founding member and board member of Women@ CompetitionFR, a platform for female competition practitioners in France. The author writes in her own personal capacity, and none of the statements or opinions are to be attributed to Johnson & Johnson or any of its affiliates.

1 Quoting from Simon Holmes, "Climate Change is an Existential Threat: Competition Law Must be Part of the Solution and not Part of the Problem" *CPI Antitrust Chronicle* (July 2020).
2 Johnson & Johnson, "Our Credo" <www.jnj.com/credo/> accessed 24 January 2021.
3 Johnson & Johnson, "Health for Humanity: 2020 Goals" <www.jnj.com/_document/johnson-johnson-health-for-humanity-2020-goals?id=0000015c-adde-d4cb-a5fd-efdef8110000> accessed 24 January 2021.

Individual efforts are key to achieving sustainability goals. Collective efforts, however, can make initiatives more powerful and efficient, faster and less costly. And competition law should not stand in the way of either individual or collective efforts – if they are genuine and made in good faith.

This paper contains an in-house practitioner's perspective, aiming to contribute to the debate from a business perspective. It is meant to provide a practical approach to a number of questions, focusing on antitrust and mergers. It addresses the specific needs of companies in terms of clarity and legal certainty (1). It also sets out the reasons why the current rules are sufficient to cater for the need of companies in their sustainability efforts (2). It then explains the kind of guidance that would help address uncertainties (3) and the specific issues that such guidance would need to cover (4).

II. Companies Need Clarity and Legal Certainty

Many aspects of the interplay between sustainability and competition law have already been addressed elsewhere, including whether sustainability objectives (environment, climate change, workers' working conditions and wages, inequalities, etc) should be part of competition authorities' assessment in deciding on mergers or agreements between competitors. A number of questions still remain to be answered, but at this point, already, the mere existence of the debate – and the large number of articles and conferences dedicated to the topic – is testimony that there is a need for more guidance and clarity.

Executive Vice-President Margrethe Vestager has already acknowledged that competition authorities have a role to play in contributing to the Green Deal objectives,[4] and national authorities have already contributed to this debate, in particular the ACM, the Dutch Competition Authority, by issuing Draft Sustainability Agreements Guidelines,[5] as well the Greek[6] and German competition authorities.[7]

From a Fast Moving Consumer Goods (FMCG) industry's perspective, sustainability, and in particular the need for greener, more sustainable products, has become a key topic. In the consumer health sector, in particular, Johnson & Johnson

---

4   See, for example, Margrethe Vestager, "The Green Deal and competition policy" (Renew Webinar, 22 September 2020) <https://ec.europa.eu/commission/commissioners/2019-2024/vestager/announcements/green-deal-and-competition-policy_en>.

5   ACM, "Draft Guidelines: Sustainability agreements" (9 July 2020) <www.acm.nl/en/publications/draft-guidelines-sustainability-agreements> (ACM Draft Guidelines).

6   Hellenic Competition Commission, "Draft Staff Discussion Paper on 'Sustainability Issues and Competition Law'" (September 2020) <www.epant.gr/en/enimerosi/competition-law-sustainability.html>.

7   Bundeskartellamt, "Sustainability initiatives and competition law practice – Virtual meeting of the Working Group on Competition Law" (5 October 2020) <www.bundeskartellamt.de/SharedDocs/Meldung/EN/Pressemitteilungen/2020/05_10_2020_AKK_2020.html>.

has been involved in sustainability for many years,[8] and has set a target of 100% of consumer health plastic packaging being recyclable by 2025, by design, partnership or innovation.[9] Changes are triggered by regulations and taxes, but also by pressure from consumers, who are progressively becoming conscious of the impact of their consumption habits on the planet, and calling for companies to adapt their offer. Companies are reacting and adapting their production and distribution processes, but there is a consensus that some initiatives would not take place if not collectively, or would be more costly and/or take much longer to materialise if undertaken by companies individually. These obstacles are well understood, in particular, the need for scale or the first-mover disadvantage and corresponding risk of free-riding by competitors. These can constitute serious disincentives and nip a number of initiatives in the bud. Smaller companies may not have the necessary economic, financial and human resources required to change their production or distribution practices, and may only switch – if they still can – once market forces have eventually led to the disappearance of less sustainable products.

Moreover, competition rules may have a chilling effect on companies wanting to reach out to their competitors to develop joint initiatives or actions. In this author's view, competition rules may prevent companies from getting together on sustainable projects, and there are indeed examples of agreements with a genuine sustainability objective that would likely be seen as restrictive of competition:

- Agreements or collective decisions (including via trade associations) to stop sourcing certain input due to environmental considerations or other sustainability reasons.[10] In the FMCG industry, this includes agreements to stop developing products with non-recyclable packaging or using certain types of plastics. This could be seen as collective boycott;[11]

- Agreements to require certain standards of their suppliers in relation to working conditions, such as level of wages, child labour, etc (including outside the EU), which may also be seen as a de facto boycott;

---

8   Today, 75% of its consumer health products are recyclable, and the company runs numerous initiatives to increase sustainability efforts.

9   J&J has announced a $800 million investment in making consumer products more sustainable, including by moving away from single-use plastic to reusable, recyclable or compostable packaging, and offering more refill options. Hallie Levine, "Johnson & Johnson Consumer Health Commits $800 Million Through 2030 to Make Its Products More Sustainable for a Healthier Planet" (*Johnson & Johnson news*, 8 September 2020) <www.jnj.com/latest-news/johnson-johnson-commits-800-million-to-making-more-sustainable-products>.

10 See, for example, the French competition authority has decided not to open an infringement procedure against candy manufacturers that agreed to ban the use of titanium dioxide in the production of candy, Interview with Isabelle de Silva, President of the French authority (4th Annual W@Competition Conference, November 2020) <www.youtube.com/watch?v=OfYo53ld15Q>, at 26.15.

11 Although non-mandatory standards adopted by industries – whereby industry players may would remain free to source more polluting products – may have a less restrictive effect from a competition law perspective, their efficacy in reaching the Green Deal objectives would be significantly smaller than a binding undertaking to stop sourcing such more polluting products.

- Agreements or collective decisions to stop producing certain more polluting products, or to close more polluting production facilities, which could lead to a reduction in output and be considered as restricting competition;

- Agreements to develop new, greener standards for certain products, that would de facto exclude certain suppliers' products;

- Agreements to focus production on greener products, and discontinue other, more polluting products – including with a view to avoid first-mover disadvantage – which could lead to price increases if additional costs are not entirely absorbed by the companies.

Similarly, unilateral decisions by a dominant company to stop sourcing more polluting raw material or to discontinue the production of non-sustainable products may also be considered an abuse in some circumstances and be sanctioned under Article 102 of the Treaty on the Functioning of the European Union (TFEU).

Even for less restrictive projects, competition rules can stand in the way because of a perception that such discussions may raise concerns in the first place.[12] In situations where sustainability, despite gaining importance in board discussions as well as for shareholders and investors, remains peripheral to most companies' day-to-day businesses (and has potentially a negative impact on their profit and loss due to increased costs), any compliance risks – even if only perceived ones – may put to bed the best-intentioned projects. Requiring companies to invest significant amounts in lawyers and economists in order to assess whether a proposed cooperation or merger, the main objective of which is to decrease their carbon impact, may effectively kill a project due to the effort, cost and time that the exercise entails. This is particularly true for medium-sized companies, whose resources and priorities may not translate – yet – in sustainability advancement, and even more valid in challenging economic times where savings and even, for some, staying afloat has become the main concern in day-to-day business.

The author has, therefore, no doubt that a strong signal from competition authorities is called for to reinforce much-needed private sector efforts in accelerating the greening of industrial activity. There is also a great need for a consistent approach at EU level, and for the EU DG COMP to step up, while we see a growing number of initiatives at national level, however laudable, which may jeopardise a clear and intelligible message for companies.

---

12 See, for example, Margrethe Vestager: "it is important that companies know about the opportunities which they already have to work together for sustainability. There is a certain level of conservatism in the advisory industry" (Sustainability and Competition Policy Conference, 23 October 2019) (phrase added at delivery, see <www.youtube.com/watch?reload=9&v=7mpWAOhkQbY>, at 58.09).

III. Current Rules Are Sufficient To Take Account of Sustainability in Antitrust and Merger Assessment, Provided Enforcement is Flexible

There are suggestions to create exceptions or new rules for sustainability agreements, such as expressly adding sustainability as an objective of competition law, alongside consumer welfare, or developing specific block exemption regulations. Although such considerations may be interesting, they do raise a significant number of concerns.[13]

At the same time, standing by is not an option, and competition law can accelerate the impact of other initiatives, like regulation, which may not be sufficient in and of itself for several reasons. Regulation takes time, is often the result of compromise and may not be aggressive enough to reach the very ambitious goals of the Green Deal.[14] As mentioned, DG COMP and national competition authorities (NCAs) have understood that they have a role to play, and current rules already allow for a broad range of agreements and practices to be developed in compliance with competition rules:

- – Sustainability agreements that have no or limited effects competition would fall outside Article 101(1) TFEU;
- – Provided they create clear benefits, they may benefit from an Article 101(3) TFEU exemption;
- – In the case of mergers, sustainability efforts can be assessed under efficiencies.

Recent practice, especially in the context of the COVID-19 pandemic, has also shown that additional tools can be used, such as informal guidance and the use of comfort letters. DG COMP officials have publicly expressed the willingness to use Regulation 1/2003, Article 10, a provision never previously used so far. Finally, although limited, there are precedents both under Article 101 TFEU and the merger rules, where sustainability has been considered and taken into account in general terms.[15] This paper considers the flexibility already embedded in existing legislation and guidelines and that already today would allow for much-needed flexibility in competition enforcement.

---

13 See, among many pertinent contributions and diverging views, Christina A Volpin, "Sustainability as a Quality Dimension of Competition: Protecting our Future (Selves)" *CPI Antitrust Chronicle* (July 2020); Luc Peeperkorn, "Competition and Sustainability: What Can Competition Policy Do?" in Guy Canivet and others, *Sustainability and competition law* (2020) Concurrences N° 4–2020 Art N° 97390, 26–65.

14 See Dirk Middelschulte, "Sustainability Cooperation Between Competitors & Art. 101 TFEU" (Unilever submission to DG COMP) <www.unilever.com/Images/unilever_submission_sustainability_competition_law_tcm244-551751_en.pdf> accessed 24 January 2021.

15 See, for example, Julien Nowag, "Sustainability & Competition Law and Policy – Background Note" DAF/COMP(2020)3 (OECD, 1 December 2020) <www.oecd.org/officialdocuments/publicdisplaydocumentpdf/?cote=DAF/COMP(2020)3&docLanguage=En>; Middelschulte (n 14); Volpin (n 13).

IV. The Need for Clarification and Guidance, as Precedents Are Either Old or Not Adapted to Current Issues

The significant ongoing debate around competition law and sustainability shows that there is a certain level of uncertainty – justified or not – which warrants more clarity. As mentioned before, not all companies are equipped with competition law specialists nor willing to invest time, effort and significant legal and economic support to assess sustainability agreements, especially if these are not core to their business and may potentially raise competition questions.

Therefore, clarification of existing rules, as well as enforcement priorities, are essential to bring much-needed comfort for companies willing to engage in sustainability projects. Obviously, there is no space for greenwashing, and this must also be made clear to companies and their advisers. But, similar to what the Commission and the ECN have done to cater for the COVID-19 emergency, they have the flexibility to address pro-sustainability initiatives, and should express – as for COVID-19 – their willingness to use this flexibility. As already explained, they have the tools, and communication is key to deliver such comfort. The director general of DG COMP has stated publicly that DG COMP would be prepared to issue Article 10 decisions if parties bring forward the right cases. Confirmation that DG COMP would also be prepared to continue using the revived tool of comfort letters for sustainability projects should also be made loud and clear.

But ad hoc guidance on a case-by-case basis, useful as it can be, will not be sufficient. Guidelines as to what is possible may help address a broader range of potential cooperation agreements, mergers or projects, especially since there is little precedent of what can be done with respect to sustainability. Previous EU clearance letters that dealt with such projects are rare and may not address the more novel questions arising in the present context. More recent cases tend to give guidance about what cannot be done, rather than what is authorised. Rules must be clear so that they can be assessed by in-house counsel without a systematic need for outside counsel and economists, though such assistance may remain necessary for the most complex or critical projects.

Obviously, the revisions of the horizontal and vertical block exemption regulations are the perfect occasion to include such guidance. A specific, dedicated notice for sustainability agreements could also be foreseen, based on the public consultation carried out by DG COMP and the many examples gathered or communicated by NCAs.

V. Guidance Will Need to Address Open Questions

The next few months will be critical in addressing this need for clarity and legal certainty, and to answer the remaining questions raised by the competition community at large, in particular as to whether competition authorities are prepared to be flexible in the application of competition rules. Below are a few of these questions:

1. Sustainability as an objective of competition policy

One of the key issues raised is that competition rules are not designed to cater for objectives other than consumer welfare, and that there are other policies and tools, regulation and taxation in particular, better placed to do so. However, as has been argued, sustainability does not need to be a goal of competition policy, but should rather be considered a factor of competition in and of itself. Sustainability requires innovation, improves quality of goods for consumers and increases choice by bringing new, less polluting products to the market. There is, therefore, a strong argument to say that more sustainable products contribute to consumer welfare – without the need to add sustainability as an objective to competition policy.[16] And although such characteristics – quality, choice, innovation – are probably more difficult to quantify than a price increase, competition authorities should not shy away from taking such considerations into account when assessing an agreement under Article 101(3) TFEU, a unilateral practice under Article 102 TFEU or a merger under the EU Merger Regulation (and their national equivalents).

2. Consideration of a broader "consumer welfare" concept

Another consideration is that benefits to consumers, both under Articles 101 and 102 TFEU as well as merger rules, is supposed to relate to the very consumers that may suffer from the specific agreement, practice or merger.[17] In order to reconcile that requirement with sustainability objectives – which may benefit a broader group of consumers, or even society, but may not necessarily address the harm suffered by the specific consumers as a result of the agreement, practice or merger – some are arguing to expand the notion of consumer welfare to a broader category of customers. This would mean including "out-of-market" customer benefits, including even society as a whole, as a wider group would benefit from, say, a less polluted planet. The debate on this is in full swing[18] and, as much as we have seen a recent move towards a "fairer" competition policy, we could see a trend towards a more "sustainable" competition policy, which could

---

16   See, for example, Volpin (n 13).
17   See, for example, Peeperkorn (n 13).
18   See, for example, the ACM Draft Guidelines and Luc Pepperkorn for diverging views on the question.

include "out-of-market" customers in the equation of an Article 101(3) analysis, or an efficiency argument under merger control rules. Such a new approach seems possible under the current rules without the need to change the legislation.

The ACM Draft Guidelines advocate for such a change of approach.[19] Just as the Commission and NCAs have shown flexibility in the application of competition rules in times of COVID-19, they should display similar flexibility in relation to sustainability. The current guidelines do allow for such flexibility, in particular the ones on Article 101(3) TFEU which state that benefits to consumers occur "through increased quality or other benefits",[20] or the horizontal merger guidelines, providing that efficiencies can be taken into account, including "the development of technical and economic progress"[21] and "should, in principle (emphasis added), benefit consumers in those relevant markets where it is otherwise likely that competition concerns would occur", thereby allowing for exceptions to such "principle".[22]

3. Timing considerations: long-term benefits and faster innovation

Traditionally, competition authorities assess efficiencies and the impact of a transaction or merger in the short-to-medium term, e.g. a three-year timeframe. Although assessing the effects of a transaction beyond this horizon may prove difficult, long-term sustainability effects of a transaction should not be excluded from the equation as simply irrelevant.

Here again, the competition assessment should not be based only on the immediate effect on prices. Indeed, competition authorities are able to assess the impact of a transaction on "output, product quality, product variety and innovation".[23] And short-term price increases may be outweighed by longer-term benefits, typically if some products are initially priced at a higher level but become cheaper over time, as the market evolves and the offer develops (as we have seen for bio-labelled products, the price of which has significantly decreased as demand and offer have increased).

Another consideration in this context is whether a restriction of competition is strictly necessary if the same outcome can take place over a longer period of time, without a given cooperation or initiative. The *Chicken of Tomorrow* case[24] provides a concrete example. In this case, an agreement between producers and retailers to

---

19   See also Martijn Snoep, President of the ACM, "Interview" *CPI Antitrust Chronicle* (July 2020).
20   Commission, Guidelines on the application of Article 81(3) (now 101(3)) of the Treaty [2004] OJ C101/97, [86].
21   Guidelines on the assessment of horizontal mergers [2004] OJ C31/5, [76].
22   ibid, [79].
23   Commission Guidelines (n 23), [16].
24   ACM, "ACM's analysis of the sustainability arrangements concerning the 'Chicken of Tomorrow'" (26 January 2015) <www.acm.nl/en/publications/publication/13789/ACMs-analysis-of-the-sustainability-arrangements-concerning-the-Chicken-of-Tomorrow>.

encourage more sustainable chicken in the Netherlands was considered anticompetitive. Years later, it appeared that, even without the agreement, more sustainable chickens were largely promoted and distributed by retailers. The ACM therefore considered that the agreement was actually not only restrictive but also not necessary to reach its sustainable objectives, as eventually, supermarkets increased their offer of "more sustainable" chicken unilaterally, without the need of the proposed – and prohibited – cooperation. One should, however, put the Article 101(3) criteria in time-sensitive perspective. The Green Deal objectives are very ambitious and, although individual initiatives may eventually lead to desirable changes, cooperation agreements may contribute to bringing these needed changes much faster. As a consequence, timing must also be taken into account in assessing whether a sustainability cooperation is necessary under Article 101(3) TFEU.

4. Quantification of sustainable benefits/efficiencies

One of the key challenges in order to be able to balance pros and cons within a competition law assessment, be it under Article 101(3), Article 102 or a merger review, is to be able to compare apples with apples. When sustainability benefits can be quantified in terms of price or cost, the impact on consumers can be measured. This is what the ACM has attempted to do in the *Chicken of Tomorrow*, whereby it considered that customers were not prepared to bear the additional costs triggered by a cooperation agreement to promote more sustainable chicken.

However, impact on sustainability, such as CO_2 or noise reduction, animal welfare, workers' conditions, may not always be quantifiable or easily expressed in monetary terms – and even if it can, such quantification may be subject to many variable parameters that can make the assessment uncertain or unreliable.[25] This is why guidance is needed to allow companies to assess whether the benefits of a project in terms of sustainability will outweigh the potential restriction of competition of their agreement. The Commission recognises that non-quantitative benefits can be taken into account, by "providing estimates and other data to the extent reasonably possible, taking into account of the circumstances of the individual case".[26] For example, discontinuing the use of a polluting component, which may increase production costs, should not automatically be prohibited just because it leads to a price increase for consumers, or a price increase that consumers are not – yet – prepared to bear (as in the *Chicken of Tomorrow*).

5. "Benefit of the doubt" to good-faith sustainable projects

Finally, in times of uncertainty, companies need not only guidance but also to feel confident that their practices, if pursued in good faith and with a clear

---

25 See, for example, Peeperkorn (n 13).
26 Commission Guidelines (n 23), [104]. See also Gianni de Stefano, "EU Competition Law and the Green Deal: the Consistency Road" *CPI Antitrust Chronicle* (July 2020).

sustainable objective, will not be sanctioned at a later stage if the specific initiative leads to unforeseen restriction of competition. Seeking formal or informal guidance at the time of designing the project may mitigate the risk of sanctions at a later stage. However, as previously stated, not all companies may be able to seek such guidance, for lack of support or budget. Provided they have been acting in good faith and have relied on public guidance existing at the time of their cooperation, a message from competition authorities – such as the one in the ACM Draft Guidelines – that sanctions would not be imposed would send the right signal and encourage companies to engage more, or more quickly, in sustainable projects.

VI. Conclusion

There is a strong call from businesses and competition law practitioners for a pragmatic approach to the application of the competition rules, in order to create a favourable environment for companies to take their part in supporting the Green Deal. Clarity over the types of agreements, practices or mergers that should be allowed, in view of their benefits or efficiencies, is therefore needed from competition authorities. Obviously, this must not lead to a blank check for companies, and guidelines are therefore needed to help companies to stay on the right side of the line. Although the current toolbox of the Commission (and most NCAs) should allow them to be flexible in their enforcement and cater for sustainability goals, a clear message to businesses is also needed to unlock the potential for greater cooperation and for more sustainability projects to see the light of day.

Brands, Competition and Sustainability

ANDREAS GAYK[*]

Markenverband e.V. (German Brands Association)

Competition and sustainability are both elements in the DNA of brands. They can interact positively with each other. In certain situations, however, it is assumed that there is a conflict of objectives between competition protection and sustainability matters.

For branded companies it is of great importance to resolve such conflict and to give effect to both competition and sustainability to the maximum extent possible. Here we try to show a way to achieve this.

I. Sustainability in Competition Policy

The question as to how relevant sustainability objectives are for the application of the European Union's competition rules is twofold. First, it must be determined whether sustainability objectives can be taken into account at all without changing primary law. Secondly, it must be asked whether such consideration is desirable.

1. The possibility

The Brundtland Commission's definition, also used in the EU, considers sustainability to be a "development that meets the needs of the present without

---

[*] Andreas Gayk is member of the executive board of the German Brands Association and has been responsible (with others) for competition and distribution policy for more than 10 years. Previously he was in private practice in the same field and, as in-house counsel, advised Coca-Cola on competition issues.

compromising the ability of future generations to meet their own needs" and adds, in a less frequently cited passage:

> Development involves a progressive transformation of economy and society... Physical sustainability cannot be secured unless development policies pay attention to such considerations as changes in access to resources and in the distribution of costs and benefits. Even the narrow notion of physical sustainability implies a concern for social equity between generations, a concern that must logically be extended to equity within each generation.[1]

The European Union's Green Deal takes up this idea of change. It aims to overcome limitations of a model of society that values wealth above wellbeing.[2] At the same time, the Green Deal requires completion of the transformation by 2050 at the latest. This calls for rapid and effective change.

A modified understanding of market and competition becomes obvious; wealth creation is being supplemented by elements of a liberalism of fear. But can this process of change have an impact on the application of the EU's unchanged competition rules; would there not be a need for a revision in the procedure under Article 48 TEU?[3]

A change of meaning without a change of wording, especially at constitutional level,[4] is often viewed with suspicion. According to this view, it is necessary to prevent basic legal norms from becoming ingratiated with the spirit of the times: the original will of the (constitutional) legislator must be brought to the fore.

Even if basic fundamental rules, such as EU competition rules, also have a preservative function, two arguments must be made against their resistance to change. First, the will of the original legislator is also the result of interpretation, since he is neither a concrete person nor present in the decision-making process. Second, an interpretation could only be avoided by assuming that language itself is unambiguous. The opposite is true for terms such as "competition", "improvement" or "progress" in Article 101 TFEU. They are open to different meanings. Solidified changes in ideas over time can and must be taken into account if they are relevant from a legal perspective. Orator uses the example

---

1   UN, "Report of the World Commission on Environment and Development: Our Common Future" (Annex to document A/42/427: "Development and International Co-operation: Environment", 4 August 1987) <www.un-documents.net/wced-ocf.htm> accessed 6 November 2020.

2   Ursula von der Leyen, "State of the Union 2020" (speech to the European Parliament, 16 September 2020) <https://ec.europa.eu/commission/presscorner/detail/en/SPEECH_20_1655> accessed 6 November 2020.

3   See Andreas Voßkuhle, "Verfassungsinterpretation und Verfassungswandel: Die Rolle des Bundesverfassungsgerichts" (Konrad Adenauer Foundation: Legal Policy Congress, Berlin, 29 November 2018) <www.kas.de/documents/252038/3346186/Verfassungsinterpretation+und+Verfassungswandel-Festvortrag+KAS+Berlin.pdf/2779c5a1-f31e-2d45-e900-0ce4db789456?version=1.0&t=1543847127152> accessed 6 November 2020.

4   Cf. Case 294/83 *Les Verts v European Parliament* [1986] ECR 1339, [23]; Case Avis 1/17 *Opinion of the full court pursuant to Article 218(11)* TFEU re CETA EU:2019:341, [110].

of Article 114 TFEU to show that the EU also follows this path in the cooperation between the ECJ and EU legislators.[5]

The changes brought about by sustainability requirements are fundamental and permanent. Reproducing them in the application of competition rules does not mean chasing a short-term trend. The EU's competition rules can therefore also be part of the process of change at the level of primary law.

2. The desirable

This does not answer the question of whether and how non-competitive aspects of the public interest should be integrated into decision-making in competition law. It arises in the context of sustainability considerations as well as other aspects of the common good.

A. *Assignment of competences in German law*

The question was explicitly clarified in the German Act against Restraints of Competition (ARC) by rules of competences. Considerations of the common good were the sole responsibility of the policymakers: the Minister of Economics can approve a prohibited merger if it is justified by an overriding public interest, i.e. by non-competitive considerations (s42 ARC). The same applied to cartels until 2005. The Bundeskartellamt (FCO) is therefore limited exclusively to competition issues.

Whether this will continue to apply to antitrust law is not certain. The 10th amendment to the ARC facilitates interim measures by the FCO in a way that calls into question the separation of competences between policymakers and the FCO. According to the new s. 32a(1) ARC, interim measures are excluded if they represent undue hardship for the companies concerned only if they are not required by "overriding public interests". It is up to the FCO to examine these conditions. The clear assignment of competition considerations to the FCO on the one hand and public interests to policymakers on the other is broken, and the argument of "policy-free" competition law is less convincing.

B. *The principle of the legal exception as a stumbling block in European law?*

European competition law does not provide for a comparable attribution of competence. However, by way of argument against the taking into account of non-competitive aspects in the application of Article 101 TFEU, and following Regulation 1/2003 and the introduction of a legal exception from Article 101(1) TFEU, it is suggested there is no authority responsible for an authentic

---

5   Andreas Orator, "*Änderung und Wandlung der Unionsverfassung seit dem Vertrag von Lissabon*" in Philipp B Donath and others (eds), *Verfassungen – ihre Rolle im Wandel der Zeit* (Nomos 2019), 329 ff (342 f).

determination and weighing of the public interests of the EU in the application of competition rules.[6] This understanding overlooks the fact that Article 7 TFEU requires each and every activity of the EU to take account of all Union objectives. The horizontal clause of Article 11 TFEU therefore cannot be ignored when applying competition rules.[7] Because of the uncertainties involved, assistance from the Commission in the form of guidelines, recommendations etc. would be desirable.

C. *Development of understanding of the market and competition*

The Commission continues to apply the traditional standard of consumer welfare as the sole objective of competition and competition rules.[8]

The ECJ, however, seems to follow a different approach. It has stated on several occasions that harm to consumers in the sense of a reduction in consumer welfare is neither a necessary nor a sufficient condition for a restriction of competition.[9] Therefore it is more obvious to accept the concept of markets as a social phenomenon and to understand competition as a legal principle governed by the ideas of freedom and equality of all legal persons, interdependent and complementary with private autonomy.[10] In this understanding, and in accordance with Article 7 TFEU, non-competitive objectives of the Union can more easily be taken into account in the interpretation of competition rules. This is achieved by ensuring that the criteria for the (legal) assessment of the behaviour of companies in the market are not reduced to questions of economic efficiency. Instead, a "practical concordance" must be established between the protection

---

6   Ernst Mestmäcker and Heike Schweitzer, *Europäisches Wettbewerbsrecht* (3rd edn, Beck 2014), s14 [86]; Edith Loozen, "Strict Competition Enforcement and Welfare: A Constitutional Perspective Based on Art. 101 TFEU and Sustainability" (2019) 56 CMLRev 1265.
7   Case T–451/08 *Föreningen Svenska Tonsättares Internationella Musikbyrå (Stim) v Commission* EU:T:2013:189, [73].
8   Commission, "Guidelines on the application of Article 81(3) of EC Treaty" [2004] OJ C101/97, [13]; most recently Commission, "Competition Policy supporting the Green Deal: call for contributions" (DG COMP, 13 October 2020) <https://ec.europa.eu/competition/information/green_deal/call_for_contributions_en.pdf> accessed 25 November 2020.
9   Case C–95/04 P *British Airways v Commission* [2007] ECT I-2331, [106]; Catherine Prieto, "Fidelity rebates: The ECJ holds abusive the discounts system granted not only for tickets sold once the sales target is achieved, but also for tickets sold before (*British Airways/Virgin*)" (2007)_ Concurrences N° 2–2007, Art N° 13492, 115–116; Case C–8/08 *T-Mobile Netherlands v Raad van bestuur van de Nederlandse Mededingingsautoriteit* [2009] ECR I-4529, [36] – [38]; Dominique Ferré, "Anticompetitive object: The ECJ decides on the criterions to assess the anticompetitive object of an exchange of informations (*T-Mobile Netherlands*)" (2009) Concurrences N° 3–2009 Art N° 29662; Case C–501/06 *GlaxoSmithKline Services v Commission* [2009] ECR I-9291, [63]; Cyril Sarrazin, "Exemption: The ECJ upholds the analysis of the CFI on restrictions of parallel trades in medicines and restriction of competition by object (*GlaxoSmithKline*)" (2009) Concurrences N° 1–2010 Art. N° 30307, 89–90; Karine Biancone, "Exemption: The ECJ rules that in determining whether a restraint on parallel trade contributes to technical or economic progress within the meaning of Art. 101§3 of the EU Treaty, 'efficiency losses' must be weighed against 'efficiency gains' (*GlaxoSmithKline*)" (2009) Concurrences N° 1–2010, Art N° 30618; Case C-286/13 *Dole v Commission* EU:C:2015:184, [125].
10 Meinrad Dreher and Michael Kulka, *Wettbewerbs- und Kartellrecht* (10th edn, Müller 2018), [610].

---

of competition and sustainability objectives.[11] The concept of "practical concordance" has been developed in German constitutional law to resolve conflicts between legal interests. It does not require the balancing of interests, which carries the risk of one prevailing at the expense of the other. Instead, both interests must be limited to ensure both are put into effect to the maximum extent possible. The limits can only be established on a case-by case basis. They must be proportionate and not go further than necessary to achieve concordance.

II. Differentiation and Cooperation

Based on the self-perception of brands, the example of the detergent cartel and the "Chicken of Tomorrow" initiative can show how competition rules can contribute to the Green Deal.

1. Brands, driver of sustainability

According to modern understanding, a brand is more than an IP right. Rather, the latter is only the starting point for the process of creating a brand. Only when the mark has established itself in the hearts and minds of consumers and has formed a firm image of the promised benefits, does a brand come into being. It is a construct of trust and a sign of the bond between consumers and brands. This bond must be constantly strengthened, otherwise it erodes. First and foremost, this requires the brand to continuously deliver on its promises. Brand promises should be individual and different from others. The criteria for differentiation are manifold: in addition to rational attributes, they include emotions, images and perceptions, as well as aspects such as health, sustainability, political positioning, regionality and tradition. The importance of the individual aspects follows the change in social ideas. Therefore sustainability today is of great impact on the differentiation of brands.

Wherever possible, it is in the interest of brands to approach sustainability initiatives unilaterally and to use them to strengthen the bond with consumers. Initiatives in cooperation, especially with close competitors, are only the second best option. Competition will lead to copycats and force brands to develop further and to strive for ever new sustainability goals.

2. Cooperation to overcome first-mover disadvantage

However, unilateral pursuit of sustainability goals by brands reaches its limits when coordination problems arise. If there is a risk that a company is the only

---

11 Cf. Juliane Kokott and Daniel Dittert, "Die Pflicht zur Berücksichtigung außerwettbewerblicher Belange im Rahmen von Art. 101 AEUV und ihre praktische Umsetzung" in Monopolkommission (ed), *Politischer Einfluss auf Wettbewerbsentscheidungen* (Nomos 2015), 15–20.

one pursuing a certain sustainability goal and therefore may suffer considerable competitive disadvantages, desirable efforts may be omitted or delayed. Cooperation can help in these cases.

A. *Detergent cartel*

The Commission decision in the detergent cartel case shows both the need to jointly overcome first-mover disadvantage and the dangers and the limitations involved.[12] It illustrates that industry-wide sustainability initiatives can only be allowed if the dangers of restrictions by object are eliminated.

The industry initiative was aimed at promoting sustainable use of detergents and had been approved by the Commission in a recommendation.[13] It aimed to reduce the dosage and weight of detergent powder and packaging material in four successive steps. The simultaneous introduction of each step across the industry had to be ensured.

The necessity for this synchronicity is due to the specific nature of purchasing fast-moving consumer goods. Consumers trust that the self-similar appearance of a brand signals to them that the expectations placed in it will continue to be fulfilled. Market research regularly shows that the product portfolio relevant to the consumer's immediate purchase decision at the point of sale consists not only of one brand, but often of three. They are often referred to as the "relevant set". In a fraction of a second, the decision for one of them is made at the shelf. Therefore the slightest uncertainty, e.g. due to clearly recognisable weight or size deviations, leads one to expect that consumers may switch to alternative products from the relevant set if those remain unchanged. A one-off decision may well perpetuate itself into a permanent shift of preference. The innovative first-mover is permanently disadvantaged.

An industry agreement can compensate for this disadvantage. While timing of the market introduction of products with improved environmental characteristics certainly is an important competitive factor, competition in this case is shifted to the innovative products. If it cannot be established that, without industry agreement, an earlier market entry of improved products would have been likely, the agreement should not constitute a restriction of competition.[14]

---

12 *Consumer Detergents* (Case COMP/39579) Commission decision [2011] OJ C193/14; Elina Laurinen, "The European Commission adopts a cartel settlement decision prohibition decision against three major detergent manufacturers (*Henkel, Unilever and Procter & Gamble*)" (2011) e-Competitions April 2011 Art N° 48005.

13 Commission Recommendation concerning good environmental practice for household laundry detergents [1998] OJ L215/73.

14 See C–307/18 *Generics (UK) and others v CMA* EU:C:2020:52; Michel Debroux, "Restriction by object: The Court of Justice of the European Union clarifies the conditions for a pay-for-delay agreement to be qualified as a restriction of competition by object following a preliminary ruling request of the Competition Appeal Tribunal (*Generics – UK, GlaxoSmithKline, Xellia Pharmaceuticals ...*)" (2020) Concurrences N° 2–2020 Art N° 94728, 72–74.

Recourse to the doctrine developed by the ECJ since Wouters supports this.[15] The doctrine would exempt coordination by undertakings from the prohibition of Article 101(1) TFEU if the restrictions imposed are proportionate to a legitimate (antitrust neutral) objective and do not go beyond what is necessary. Even if the meaning of "legitimate objective" remains unclear, the promotion of sustainability will certainly be covered.[16] Because the Commission approved the sector initiative, the objection that the Wouters doctrine should be limited to cases of state delegation to private parties is not valid; approval by the Commission is equivalent.

In the reported case, however, the companies also aimed to achieve market stabilisation as well as to coordinate prices at European level. These restrictions by object were not necessary to achieve legitimate objectives and cannot be justified by means of practical concordance.[17]

B. *Chicken of Tomorrow*

The Dutch Autoriteit Consument & Markt (ACM) took a different path in its *Chicken of Tomorrow* decision.[18] As part of a broader initiative, the *Chicken of Tomorrow* arrangement was launched by organisations from the poultry sector, covering almost the entire market. The aim was to ensure that by 2020 only chicken meat that met the initiative's criteria beyond the legal requirements would be sold in Dutch supermarkets. The ACM concluded that the agreement infringed national and European antitrust law by regulating the purchasing behaviour of the participating supermarkets and limiting consumer choice by depriving them of standard chicken meat. This finding appears questionable.[19] The ACM also concluded that the conditions of Article 101(3) TFEU are not met. According to the ACM, a contribution to improving the production or distribution of goods, or to promoting technical or economic progress can only be assumed if consumers attach a (monetary) value to the effects of the agreement that exceeds the costs likely to be passed on to them. According to the results of the "willingness to pay" analyses, however, this was not the case.

"Improving" and "progress" within the meaning of Article 101(3) TFEU certainly require more than just any change. It requires a comparison of the advantages

---

15 C–309/99 Wouters v Algemene Raad van de Nederlandse Orde van Advocaten [2002] ECR I-1577; C-519/04 P Meca-Medina and Majcen v Commission [2006] I-6991; C–1/12 Ordem dos Técnicos Oficiais de Contas v Autoridade da Concorrencia EU:C:2013:127; Cyril Sarrazin, "Association of chartered accountants: The Court of Justice rules that the Portuguese association of chartered accountants is an association of undertakings and that a regulation relating to a system of compulsory training may restrict competition (*Ordem dos Técnicos Oficiais de Contas/Autorisade de Concorrência*)" (2013) Concurrences N° 2–2013 Art N° 52245, 63–6; C–136/12 Consiglio nationale dei geologi v Autorità garante della concorrenza e del mercato EU:C:2013:489.

16 Giorgio Monti and Jotte Mulder, "Escaping the Clutches of EU Competition Law" (2017) 42 ELRev 635, 646.

17 Kokott and Dittert (n 11), 15, 20.

18 ACM assessment of the sustainability agreements "*Chicken of Tomorrow*" ACM/DM/2014/206028 (26 January 2015).

19 See Monti and Mulder (n 16), 650.

and disadvantages resulting from the restriction of competition.[20] But monetisation and simple arithmetic cannot do justice to sustainability objectives. For logical reasons, the monetary value of sustainability cannot be quantified, despite all the efforts of economists.[21] Beyond the (arbitrary) setting of a price for an intact environment by state, supranational or international authorities, the pricing would require a transaction that cannot exist.[22] First, nobody has power of disposal over the goods in question. Second, the contracting parties must be able to face each other on the market at the same time. In the case of intergenerational interests such as sustainability, therefore, present and future generations would have to negotiate,[23] which is impossible because they cannot meet each other in their lifetime. An analysis of the willingness of today's consumers to pay as a basis for a comparison of advantages and disadvantages resulting therefore falls short in environmental aspects. It assumes that future generations have no claim to the environmental goods or do not value them.

In addition, animal welfare aspects are not anthropocentric but rather based on ethical judgments. Their monetisation and thus quantification are opposed by fundamental concerns. Although ethical judgments may be put into perspective and, in cases of conflict, weighed against each other, this is not a matter of quantification but of establishing a practical concordance. This is even more so when human rights are involved. In Germany, the Federal Constitutional Court has consistently ruled that any quantification of human dignity is categorically prohibited by the Constitution.[24]

However, this does not imply a per se rule that the pursuit of sustainability objectives in applying Article 101(3) TFEU always prevails over adverse effects on competition. Nor can the conclusion be drawn that they are excluded from the outset because no assessment of the weight of the objectives could be made. As the Commission notes, the protection of the environment might be considered as an element that contributes to improving the production or distribution of goods and to promoting technical and economic progress,[25] and the use of cleaner facilities will result in less air pollution, and consequently direct and indirect benefits for consumers within the meaning of Article 101(3) TFEU.[26] However, no mathematical comparison of costs and benefits can lead to this result. Rather a situation-specific value judgment is required.

---

20   Case T–168/01 *GlaxoSmithKline Services v Commission* [2006] ECR II-2969, [247]; Karine Biancone (n 9).
21   On the different approaches see Bundeskartellamt, "Offene Märkte und nachhaltiges Wirtschaften: Gemeinwohlziele als Herausforderung für die Kartellrechtspraxis" (Background paper: Antitrust law working group conference, 1 October 2020), 24 ff <www.bundeskartellamt.de/SharedDocs/Publikation/DE/Diskussions_Hintergrundpapier/AK_Kartellrecht_2020_Hintergrundpapier.pdf?__blob=publicationFile&v=2> accessed 25 November 2020.
22   Ronald Coase, "The Problem of Social Cost" (1960) 3 JL Econ 1.
23   UN report (n 1).
24   See BVerfG – 1BvL 7/16 *Sanktionen im Sozialrecht* DE:BVerfG:2019:ls20191105.1bvl000716 (judgment of 5 November 2019) [119] f.
25   Commission, "On Environmental Agreements" (Communication) COM(96) 561 final, [28].
26   *Philips-Osram* (Case IV/34.252) Commission decision 94/986/EC [1994] L378/37 [27].

The fact that this led to an exemption of the agreement in the specific case of *Chicken of Tomorrow* is not refuted by the *ex post* evaluation of the ACM.[27] The ACM notes that despite the prohibition of the initiative, it has now become clear that (1) even without a restrictive agreement, the objectives of the initiative have been exceeded and (2) consumers have shown a much higher willingness to pay for animal welfare gains than was expected at the time. The ACM attributes this in particular to the importance of an independent label for animal welfare and improvement in consumer education to create confidence in more sustainable production methods. However, while the ACM had addressed the issue of first-mover disadvantage in its decision and argued that the market dynamics at the time pointed towards a trend of differentiation with regard to animal welfare and/or sustainability,[28] the *ex post* evaluation does not discuss this question. It cannot be excluded that the fact that the *Chicken of Tomorrow* initiative had been launched in public turned the expected first-mover disadvantage into an advantage. Each company was well aware of the willingness of others to invest actively in animal welfare. The participation of the individual companies was communicated to the public, so the credibility of the companies would have been in question if they had abandoned the basic idea of the initiative.

III. Conclusion

The two cases not only show that sectoral agreements promoting sustainability initiatives must be examined carefully. They also illustrate the risk of clear restrictions of competition on the occasion of a sustainability initiative.

Above all they demonstrate the power of private initiatives to promote sustainability in cooperation with companies faster and more extensively than is prescribed by law or unilateral action in specific cases. They can and must actively accompany consumers on their way from a green conscience to a green decision. They can help to overcome the legislator's fear of international competitive and local disadvantages arising from more ambitious sustainability requirements. What will help is an interpretation of EU competition rules that breaks away from the implementation of economic models and understands competition as a legal principle also able to take account of societal change and new requirements arising from the transformation towards sustainability.

In order to not only shrug off but to actively support the political and soon to be legal goals of the Green Deal, it is no longer enough to trust that distant indicators point towards a trend by which individual companies want to differentiate themselves from others through sustainability initiatives in the distant

---

27 ACM, "Welfare of today's chicken and that of the 'Chicken of Tomorrow'" (Memo, 13 August 2020) <www.acm.nl/sites/default/files/documents/2020-08/welfare-of-todays-chicken-and-that-of-the-chicken-of-tomorrow.pdf> accessed 22 November 2020.
28 ACM assessment (n 18), 7.

future. There is simply not enough time. The development of the organic food sector in Germany illustrates this: the first supermarket for organic food in Germany opened in Mannheim in 1987. For almost 20 years, the development of the sector had been bogged down in statistically insignificant numbers. It was not until the financial crisis of 2008 that a certain dynamic of development began, which 12 years later led to a total market share of about 6% for organic food. In order to accelerate such a slow development, it is necessary to actively initiate market dynamics either together or alone, as the case may be. Article 101(1) and (3) TFEU gives us the opportunity to do so, as we develop the established case law of the European courts. We should make use of it.

What Role Does Antitrust Play in How FMCG Companies Choose to Pursue Sustainability Goals?

BEN GRAHAM*

AB InBev

FMCG (fast-moving consumer goods) companies across the globe are increasingly focusing on – and investing in – sustainability. There are many drivers pushing companies into these efforts, including their own sense of responsibility and desire to do business sustainably, consumer demand, pressure from activist organisations, and national and supra-national regulation.

When weighing up how to respond to these varying demands, and how to achieve the best, most efficient and most effective results, companies have a range of options, only some of which touch on antitrust. To properly frame and understand the antitrust debate in this area, it is important to understand those corporate choices.

The purpose of this paper is to deep-dive into the different options FMCG companies can take to pursue their sustainability goals and how antitrust can impinge on these. Fundamentally, companies can act: alone through unilateral moves; vertically through influencing their supply chain (and to a lesser extent, their distribution partners); in partnerships with other organisations; or horizontally with competing companies.

Different options are appropriate for different goals, and trigger differing levels of antitrust sensitivity. Where antitrust is a factor, companies would benefit

---

* Ben Graham is Europe Legal Director at Anheuser-Busch InBev in Leuven, Belgium. He is qualified as a UK solicitor, and works on diverse legal topics across the European business.

from simple, clear and low-cost access to guidance on what is and is not permitted. In the absence of such guidance, it is to be expected that lower risk options will typically be taken, whether or not they represent the optimal outcome for sustainability.

The intention is that this background will assist authorities, academics, lawyers and others in understanding how companies think and, in turn, where reassuring against antitrust concerns could have the biggest impact. This context should assist in fertilising ideas on where to focus attention and resources in the evolving debate around antitrust and sustainability.

I. What is Sustainability?

The Green Deal states that "Europe needs a new growth strategy that will transform the Union into a modern, resource-efficient and competitive economy… by turning climate and environmental challenges into opportunities".[1] The prioritisation of environmental considerations is also clear from Article 11 TFEU, which insists that "environmental protection requirements must be integrated into the definition and implementation of the Union's policies and activities, in particular with a view to promoting sustainable development". Countless references by EU leaders to the criticality of a "green recovery" demonstrate that this intention is taken in earnest.

While the focus of this paper will be on the environment, sustainability is a much broader topic. The United Nations Sustainable Development Goals include wider ambitions around food security, nutrition, alleviation of poverty, sustainable agriculture, health, inequality, peace and justice. Many companies – including AB InBev – place a deliberate focus on contributing to progress towards all of those sustainability goals.[2]

II. Approaches to Sustainability in Corporate Decision-making

As mentioned above, the core purpose of this paper is to set out how FMCG companies work to pursue sustainability goals, giving examples along the way of how this works in practice in my own company, AB InBev. The different approaches are presented in turn below.

---

1   Commission, "A European Green Deal" <https://ec.europa.eu/info/strategy/priorities-2019-2024/european-green-deal_en> accessed 17 January 2021.
2   Specifically, AB InBev divides its initiatives into Smart Agriculture, Water Stewardship, Circular Packaging, Climate Action and Smart Drinking. More information on these initiatives and how they link to the UN SDG is available here: <www.ab-inbev.com/sustainability/2025-sustainability-goals.html> accessed 17 January 2021.

1. Companies acting alone

Companies can choose to act alone. This approach is generally uncontroversial under antitrust rules, and is the right option for some initiatives. Fundamentally, sustainability and antitrust are aligned on the positive impact of corporate efficiency. Moreover, the bigger a company is, the more its efficiency and scale can drive meaningful positive change. And the more competitors see a company leading the way, the more likely they are to adapt and evolve too. Efficient stewardship of water, efficient production methods, efficient transport and so on are all uncontroversial positive goals.

Companies can unilaterally pursue sustainability in many ways, including through production innovation that prioritises sustainability, more sustainable logistics choices and investigating circularity options. Below are examples of each from AB InBev's own operations.

Sustainable *production innovations* for AB InBev relate to the brewing process. For example, the recent "simmer and strip" innovation allows a 5% reduction in the carbon footprint of brewing beer. As the company has scale, the innovation can be implemented across 200 breweries worldwide, saving annual energy consumption equivalent to a small city.

Sustainable *logistics choices* made by AB InBev include leading in the adoption of e-trucks across the globe, where again larger scale allows the company to build and drive demand for the technology.

Sustainable *production circularity* includes, in particular, packaging circularity and rethinking how to handle biproducts from beer production (such as creating a high-fibre and high-protein beverage called "Nana" for undernourished Mozambicans, which again can be scaled).

2. Companies focusing on their supply chain

Companies can increase their sustainability by developing sustainable supply chains. Sustainability initiatives may be proactive programmes to support and improve environmental impact, but also working conditions and – ultimately – lives along the supply chain. Many such supply chain initiatives have low antitrust sensitivity and serve primarily to drive improvement in efficiency and working conditions.

For example, in its "Smart Barley" programme, AB InBev partners with barley growers around the world to collaboratively produce high-quality malt barley. AB InBev also uses blockchain for supply chain payments transparency, allowing the company to connect with last mile farmers and ensure they earn their keep while also providing them with an economic identity – some for the very first time.

However, some supply chain sustainability possibilities would require joint action by competitors – or at least by competing buyers – which could trigger antitrust concerns. This is particularly the case for pushing for changes in supplier sustainability levels and for driving supplier compliance.

On *pushing supplier sustainability*, purchasers might want more transparency over sources of raw materials, or more sustainable production techniques. However, many upstream markets are rather consolidated: they may have incumbents with very strong market positions, or production supply investments so tightly aligned with demand that purchasers have few alternatives and so limited opportunity to impose real competitive pressure. In such circumstances, purchasers are even less able to bring desirable sustainability matters into negotiations, let alone secure strong commitments.

However, purchasers might be able to secure such supplier actions if they could act jointly. Current antitrust rules limit purchasers' ability and willingness to consider such collaborative, pro-sustainability moves. Clarity on the boundaries of what would be permitted, or even a relaxation of the rules in that area, could unblock sustainability barriers.

On *driving supplier compliance*, companies can introduce internal systems to monitor the sustainability of their operations, such as deep focus on working conditions or intensive supply chain checks on labour standards. Avoiding or rooting out corruption can in many instances also be an important way to advance sustainability. Companies mostly work alone in this area.

AB InBev tackles corruption in large part through our BrewRight data analytics platform, but to improve results we are establishing a BrewRight consortium with other large companies. The ultimate goal of this consortium is to give multiple companies insight into corruption risks in different geographies, to better be able to analyse suppliers (especially as in many cases publicly available information is limited) and fundamentally to improve the sustainability of the supply chain.

Antitrust clarity on how such supplier information can be shared, and the boundaries, would assist in driving adoption and consequent impact of this and similar initiatives. This could have a profound impact on supply chain sustainability.

3. Companies engaging in multi-sectoral partnerships

To maximise impact deep into communities and across supply chains, multi-sectoral partnerships may be the best approach. Such partnerships may involve private sector, civil society and governments working together to scale viable solutions.

For AB InBev, the critical example is water stewardship, where the company actively engages with multiple stakeholders across many countries. The scale of the global water challenge is bigger than any one company alone. AB InBev works together with local authorities, other water users, and partners, such as the World Wide Fund for Nature and The Nature Conservancy, to invest financial and technical resources into green infrastructure initiatives, conservation and reforestation projects, habitat restoration efforts and improved water infrastructure.

Often, such partnerships will not give rise to antitrust sensitivities on their own, or the sensitivities will be the same as for supply chain or inter-competitor cooperation. Nonetheless, they are often an important approach to improving sustainability.

4. Companies working with competitors

Consumers are increasingly conscious of sustainability concerns, and increasingly act accordingly, either by preferring sustainable products or – conversely – by boycotting products or companies perceived as environmentally or socially harmful. Consequently, the sustainability of products unquestionably has become a competitive differentiator between competitors and competing products.

In the case of AB InBev, our global beer brands each have an identity linked to a sustainability concern: Budweiser to renewable energy, Corona to protecting the oceans from plastic pollution and Stella Artois to clean water access. AB InBev is far from unique, many brands in large and small companies have sustainability goals embedded in their identity.

Given that sustainability is a competitive differentiator, and that horizontal cooperation is highly antitrust sensitive, it is understandable that this is where analysis and commentary on antitrust and sustainability have focused hardest.

Nonetheless, it is most likely also where many of the greatest sustainability rewards are to be won: in order for an industry to change, it may need to overcome "first-mover disadvantage"; competing suppliers would be more efficient if each could access the other's efficiency innovations; commitments to better supply chains could benefit consumers. Antitrust rules choose where the balance is set, and the antitrust community must assume this burden.

Below are several examples where AB InBev either has taken actions with competitors, has considered such actions but not taken them or could have gone further but chose not to due to antitrust concerns.

Collaboration with competing alcoholic and non-alcoholic beverage producers to *preserve natural resources.* Specifically, AB InBev and five competitors championed a project to ensure broad, long-term watershed sustainability of a water basin in Mexico. All of the competitors had an interest in the sustainability of the water basin, and developed a project encompassing environmental education and studies, reforestation, repairing water filtration and reservoirs, and habitat conservation.

Packaging goals with other companies, such as "plastic pacts" to reduce the levels of plastic in packaging. Such pacts are typically coordinated through trade associations or federations of businesses, allowing the development of such joint commitments. Through these "plastic pacts" businesses reduce the overall use of plastic in packaging through elimination, innovation or circulation. More stringent commitments, with closer monitoring, stricter targets and tangible consequences would be possible with a clearer antitrust greenlight.

Potential *logistics collaborations*, or even data sharing, with other beverage or FMCG companies, to facilitate more efficient logistics provision. Such collaboration could serve to reduce the overall kilometres travelled by logistics companies, and so reduce environmental impact. However, this data sharing can also lead to antitrust concerns, and so is either handled very delicately through third parties, or simply left as an unaddressed sustainability opportunity.

With regard to *innovation*, there is a delicate balance to be set between competition stimulating innovation for more efficient and sustainable production, and sharing of innovation to benefit an industry more broadly. For AB InBev, let us take the example of "simmer and strip", mentioned above, where the company has chosen to make the related IP available to all brewers to purchase at fair market value, and to small brewers for free. Antitrust rules could help clarify how and when innovations could and should be shared.

5. The way forward for antitrust and sustainability

Every business, consumer and activist has particular sustainability priorities. Especially when considering this topic from an antitrust standpoint, it is worth considering that – unlike on price – the consumer is not always right. Consumers make a huge number of consumption decisions, which are necessarily partially informed. Consumers may therefore prefer a product that is, for example, made from glass rather than plastic, when in fact for that particular product, plastic packaging has a much lower environmental impact as it is lighter to transport, preserves the product longer and is recyclable. Antitrust authorities have a real responsibility to ensure that the true, rounded sustainability interests of society are taken into account in their enforcement decisions, over and above protecting the interests of the immediate consumer.

Additionally, antitrust authorities wield enormous power, can shift how companies do business and impose very large fines. Consequently, companies rightly have very low tolerance for antitrust risk. While companies give high priority to sustainability and related investments and innovations, their business is normally much broader. As such, if any particular initiative risks triggering antitrust consequences, there is a real possibility that companies will opt for the option with the lowest antitrust risk, even if that does not give the best sustainability outcome. If an option requires significant investment in antitrust legal advice before moving forward, this will count against it and may push it off the table altogether – even more so if such legal advice comes coupled with significant delay while an authority is consulted.

Consequently, antitrust authorities can promote sustainability, and foster collaborative and highly impactful initiatives by:

–   Providing clear guidance on how sustainability initiatives will be assessed, including technical aspects. In that way, both advice from external law firms and decisions taken by in-house legal teams can be clear and confident, not inhibited by uncertainty or disclaimers.

–   A true open door and show of trust, to be open to optimistic and productive consultations with companies. Such cooperation would be strengthened if the process was fast (and did not involve extensive information requests) and use of any information received was strictly limited (in particular, that it would not be used for any other purpose than the current review).

Especially where antitrust is concerned, companies need swift clarity and certainty to act with confidence. In the absence of this, companies could limit or avoid entirely antitrust-sensitive collaborations, to the detriment of sustainability and, ultimately, the Green Deal itself.

Chapter 4
Energy

Abuse of Dominant Position and Sustainability – How to Use Article 102 TFEU as a Sword to Promote Sustainability: Lessons Learnt From DE/DK Interconnector

Eleni Diamantopoulou[*]

ClientEarth

Interconnectors are a vital element for the achievement of the EU's decarbonisation targets and for the transition to a sustainable, well-integrated energy market. Physically, they are the cables that connect different electricity grids and systems between Member States, allowing cross-border exchanges of electricity flows. Through these exchanges, interconnectors facilitate the integration of renewables (RES) and efficient energy management, while guaranteeing security of supply, leading to environmental and climate benefits, including achievement

[*] Eleni Diamantopoulou is a senior lawyer at ClientEarth. She is a dual-qualified lawyer (Greece and England & Wales). She has a litigation background in energy, environmental and public law. She has been working with ClientEarth's Energy Programme since April 2017. Since September 2019, she has led the legal interventions in energy systems. Eleni holds an interdisciplinary diploma in European studies from the University of Strasbourg III; an LLM in international law from the National and Kapodistrian University of Athens; and a joint LLM in energy law from the Universities of Groningen, Oslo, Aberdeen and Copenhagen. All views in this paper are strictly personal and should not be construed as reflecting the opinion of ClientEarth. Comments are welcome at ediamantopoulou@clientearth.org.

I am grateful to Simon Holmes for the opportunity to contribute to this publication, for his valuable comments and for his inspiring views on sustainability and competition.

of the 50% EU target of RES generation.[1] Moreover, they promote competitiveness by reducing the cost of electricity.[2]

Interconnectors are part of the electricity transmission network, which constitutes a natural monopoly exclusively operated by Transmission System Operators (TSOs). TSOs' exclusive rights have been early[3] and repeatedly[4] identified as one of the main barriers to effective competition in cross-border trade, for example by misusing or underusing existing interconnection capacity; or by underinvesting in new capacity.[5] Regulatory changes introduced through the Energy Packages sought to remedy these behaviours.[6] Yet, the rules adopted have not always been properly applied, making it necessary from time to time to use antitrust rules to remedy anticompetitive behaviours: a recent example is *DE/DK Interconnector*,[7] the subject of the present analysis. The innovation of the case is that the Commission uses Article 102 as a sword to promote sustainability by applying a priori the draft energy market rules of the Clean Energy for all Europeans Package (Clean Energy Package).

I. DE/DK Interconnector

TenneT is a transmission system operator that owns and operates approximately 40% of Germany's transmission network, including the DE/DK interconnector, which connects the northern German and the western Danish borders. The interconnector is situated in the Schleswig-Holstein region, where the network is congested during peak hours of wind generation.[8] The net transfer capacity of the interconnector is currently 1780 MW, and it is expected to reach 3500 MW by the end of 2025 with the addition of two lines.[9] The interconnector is of paramount importance for the internal market integration; almost 40% of the

---

1   Commission Expert Group on electricity interconnection targets, "Towards sustainable and integrated Europe" (November 2017) <https://ec.europa.eu/info/news/moving-10-15-final-report-commission-expert-group-2030-electricity-interconnection-targets-2017-nov-09_en> accessed 2 February 2021.
2   Commission, "Energy prices and costs in Europe" (Communication) COM (2020) 951 final.
3   Commission, "The Internal Energy Market" (Communication) COM (88) 238 final.
4   Commission, "DG Competition report on energy sector inquiry" SEC(2006) 1724; Commission, "Staff working document Impact Assessment Accompanying the document Proposal for a Directive on common rules for the internal market in electricity" SWD(2016) 410 final.
5   Staff working document, (n 4).
6   The Third Energy Package introduced the most important changes through Regulation (EC) 714/2009 on conditions for access to the network for cross-border exchanges in electricity [2009] OJ L 211/15 and the delegating act Commission Regulation (EU) 2015/1222 establishing a guideline on capacity allocation and congestion management [2015] OJ L 197/24 (CACM).
7   *DE/DK Interconnector* (Case COMP/AT.40461) Commission decision C(2018) 8132 final [2019] OJ C 58/7 <https://ec.europa.eu/competition/elojade/isef/case_details.cfm?proc_code=1_40461> accessed 2 February 2021 (the Decision); Tim Kasten, "The EU Commission accepts commitments from a company to settle an investigation into conduct affecting the German and Danish electricity markets (*TenneT)*" (2018) e-Competitions December 2018 Art N° 88822. The Decision annexes the Final Commitments offered by TenneT on 12 November 2018 (the Commitments) <https://ec.europa.eu/competition/antitrust/cases/dec_docs/40461/40461_462_3.pdf> accessed 2 February 2021.
8   Decision (n 7), recital 14.
9   Decision (n 7), recital 26

total transmission capacity between the Nordic countries and continental Europe flows through DE/DK, making Denmark a transit country for electricity trade.[10] As most of the electricity traded is of RES origin[11] the interconnector is equally important for promoting sustainability.

II. Alleged Infringement of Article 102 TFEU

In March 2018, the European Commission initiated an investigation into TenneT[12] for potential breach of Article 102 TFEU and Article 54 EEA. In its preliminary assessment the Commission found that TenneT might have abused its dominant position in operating DE/DK by systematically limiting (even to 0) the import commercial capacity of the interconnector since at least 2011.[13] TenneT's behaviour also had potential anticompetitive effects as it introduced a residence-based discrimination between different system users, thus leading to a partitioning of the market. More specifically, the restriction has put electricity producers from Denmark and Nordic countries at a competitive disadvantage vis-à-vis German producers. The former could not export cheap electricity to Germany, Austria and Luxembourg.[14] As a result, in the short term consumers in those countries paid artificially higher prices, while in the long term the distorted market signals hindered efficient network investment, including in RES.[15]

The Commission rejected TenneT's arguments that import restrictions were objectively justified as a congestion management measure during peak wind generation. Regulation 714/2009, art 16 and annex I, along with CACM,[16] in principle prohibit resolving congestion on a discriminatory basis; instead, they prioritise solutions like countertrading and redispatch, solutions that were not explored or properly exploited by TenneT.[17]

TenneT did not accept the Commission's preliminary findings of Article 102 infringement. Nevertheless, it agreed to offer commitments to address the

---

10 Decision (n 7), recital 17.
11 See Maria E Leoz Martin-Casallo and Elaine O'Connell, "Making electricity flow in Europe – strengthening regional system operation" in Christopher Jones and Florian Ermacora (eds), *EU Energy Law Volume XII: Electricity Market Design in the European Union* (Claeys & Casteels 2020), [5.102].
12 Commission, "Antitrust: Commission opens investigation into German grid operator TenneT for limiting cross border electricity capacity with Denmark" Press release (IP/18/2122 19 March 2018). The investigation was open on the basis of Council Regulation (EC) 1/2003 on the implementation of the rules on competition laid down in Articles 81 and 82 of the Treaty [2003] OJ L1/1), art 9.
13 Decision (n 7), recitals 74 (duration) and 31–33, table 1 and figure 2 (intensity). Commercial or trading capacity is the capacity made available for trade to the market, see definition in Commitments (n 7), [35].
14 Germany, Austria and Luxembourg form a single bidding zone, Decision (n 7), recital 10.
15 See preliminary assessment. It is worth mentioning that a similar case was brought in 2009 against the Swedish TSO, Svenska Kraftnät, who was limiting the export transmission capacity of Swedish interconnectors to neighbouring interconnected Member States, *Swedish Interconnectors* Case (Case COMP/AT.39351) Commission decision C(2010) 142/08 [2010] OJ C142/28. The main solution adopted in this case was to split the Swedish Market in bidding zones.
16 See n 6.
17 Decision (n 7), recitals 37–39.

Commission's competition concerns (Initial Commitments).[18] Following a market test,[19] on 8 December 2018 the Commission adopted the Decision and the Commitments.

III. Remedies

To remedy the limitation on cross-border electricity flows, the Decision establishes a minimum guaranteed commercial capacity in the interconnector of approximately 75%. According to the Decision, this capacity is sufficient to guarantee the much-needed increase of cross-border trade. At the same time, the Commission assumes the remaining margin of 25% will allow TenneT to operate the network securely when needed.[20] In addition to the safety net of 25%, the Decision recognises two exemptions from the minimum guaranteed threshold of 75%: in case of planned/unplanned outages;[21] and in cases of emergency or technical lack of redispatch or counter-trading.[22] Both exemptions operate under the caveat of the proportionality principle.[23]

The 75% threshold applies to the existing infrastructure, where the alleged infringement took place; and to the planned new lines, when commissioned.[24] For the existing line, the 75% should have been reached gradually by June 2019 through a phase-in period of six months.[25] The increase in the new lines follows a linear trajectory principle; it will be implemented until 2026 in equal steps in the calendar years following the commissioning of each line.[26] The decision is valid for nine years,[27] but it may be reviewed for specific reasons.[28] A monitoring trustee will oversee the implementation of the Commitments.[29]

---

18   Commitments offered by TenneT on 19 March 2018 <https://ec.europa.eu/competition/antitrust/cases/dec_docs/40461/40461_187_3.pdf> accessed 2 February 2021, and Annex 1 <https://ec.europa.eu/competition/antitrust/cases/dec_docs/40461/40461_188_6.pdf> accessed 2 February 2021.

19   "Communication from the Commission published pursuant to Article 27(4) of Council Regulation (EC) No 1/2003 in Case AT.40461 – DE-DK Interconnector" C/2018/2015 [2018] OJ C118/20.

20   Decision (n 7), recital 84.

21   However, the lowest minimum available capacity should not fall below 500 MW. The principle of the linear trajectory applies equally to the 500 MW threshold for the new lines: Decision (n 7), recital 87; Commitments (n 7), [46(i)] and Annex 2.

22   The Decision prohibits the use of the exemption for economic considerations. Moreover, it limits the technical lack of redispatch and countertrading to specific circumstances as prescribed i:n CACM (n 6), arts 26 and 30; Decision (n 7), recital 87; Commitments (n 7), [46(ii)] and Annex 3.

23   Commitments (n 7), [46].

24   Decision (n 7), recital 86. TenneT's Initial Commitments were identical to the final Commitments with regards to the phase-in period, but they made no provision on the future reinforcement of the interconnector capacity with the addition of extra lines. Also, they took a volumetric approach to the increase of the capacity, rather than a percentage. The volumetric approach is maintained in the Commitments, in which no reference to 75% is made.

25   In fact, for the existing cable the final capacity will reach 73% (1300 MW out of 1780 MW).

26   Commitments (n 7), Annex I, provides for different scenarios based on different timelines of the commissioned capacity. If the lines are commissioned in 2025 or 2026, TenneT will proceed to one-off increase of the guaranteed capacity for each line.

27   With effect from notification to TenneT: Decision (n 7), art 1; Commitments (n 7), [62].

28   Commitments (n 7), [63] – [67].

29   Decision (n 7), recital 95; Commitments (n 7), [47] – [61].

IV. Decision and the Clean Energy Package

In its reasoning the Decision makes reference to compliance with the Third Energy Package rules of Regulation 714/2009 and the CACM. However, the chosen remedies are de facto aligned with the Clean Energy Package and the draft recast Electricity Market Regulation.[30] At the time the commitments were outlined, the European Parliament and the Council amended the initial Commission proposal, which strengthened the principles of maximising use of interconnectors' capacity and cross-border trade in a cost-efficient way, and prohibited limitations as a congestion management measure. The amendment introduced the linear trajectory principle and the 75% threshold, the latter being further reduced to 70% in the final text.[31] As with the remedies, the remaining margin of 30% serves as a safety valve for the secure operation of the network.[32] Although the minimum threshold is legally binding as of 1 January 2020, the introduction of several grace periods for compliance with this rule[33] has delayed the increase of the available capacity for cross-border trade at least until 2025.[34]

According to recital 96 of the Decision, TenneT has to comply with both the Commitments and the existing or future applicable regulatory framework, especially in the case of more stringent rules. Conflicts with (i) EU and national implementation of the capacity allocation and congestion management methodologies and principles; or (ii) future European legislation, may trigger further reviews of the Decision.[35]

---

30   Regulation (EU) 2019/943 on the internal market for electricity [2019] OJ L158/54 (EMR).
31   The 75% minimum cross-border trade capacity was introduced as proposed article 14(7), and the linear trajectory as article 13(3) (amendments 76 and 68 respectively, see Committee on Industry, Research and Energy, "Report on the proposal for a regulation of the European Parliament and of the Council on the internal market for electricity (recast)" COM(2016)0861 – C8-0492/2016 – 2016/0379(COD) (A8-0042/2018)). For the initial Commission proposal see "Proposal for a Regulation on the internal market for electricity (recast)" COM(2016)861 final. Several market stakeholders criticised the amendment, fearing that the minimum threshold would become the default maximum capacity, for example see EFET, Eurelectric, MPP and Nordenergi, "Joint statement: The CEP should foster – not threaten – the availability of cross-border transmission capacity" (February 2018) <www.eurelectric.org/media/2345/joint_statement_on_art__14_feb2018-2018-030-0099-01-e-h-5D07B33B.pdf>. The proposal was also inconsistent with ACER's benchmark recommendation of 85%, ACER/CEER, *Annual Report of the Results of Monitoring the Internal Electricity and Gas Markets in 2016* (October 2017) <https://acer.europa.eu/Official_documents/Acts_of_the_Agency/Publication/ACER%20Market%20Monitoring%20Report%202016%20-%20ELECTRICITY.pdf> accessed 2 February 2021, Annex 2. Indeed, the wording of the draft and the final version of EMR, art 16(8) and 15(2)(7), clearly state that the obligation to maximise the use of interconnector capacity has been complied with if the minimum threshold of 70% is met.
32   EMR (n 33), recitals 27–28.
33   Germany and Poland opted for an action plan (linear trajectory principle until 2025, EMR, art 15(2)); while the majority of Member States sought derogations until 2021 on the basis of EMR, art 16(9). The German action plan includes transmission infrastructure but does not affect the DE-DK interconnector and the Decision. However, it still remains unclear whether the lowering of the minimum threshold can trigger an amendment of the Commitments.
34   ACER, *ACER Report on the Result of Monitoring the Margin Available for Cross-Zonal Electricity Trade in the EU in the First Semester of 2020*, (18 December 2020).
35   The latter does not seem to include the Clean Energy Package rules, which constitute a separate reason for review after 2025 (Commitments (n 7), [67]), so after the end of the German Action Plan. This is

V. Why the Decision Matters for Sustainability

The Commission enjoys different levels of discretion when applying antitrust rules[36] and "it is responsible for defining and implementing the orientation of Community competition policy".[37] *DE/DK Interconnector* highlights an interesting and promising example of that discretion: the application in antitrust proceedings of draft rules designed to implement a more ambitious climate and energy policy.

As opposed to pre-existing EU energy legislation, the Clean Energy Package has elevated sustainability from mere and scattered references, to the subject matter and scope of the recast energy rules establishing a clear connection between energy markets and environment/climate protection.[38] This is further confirmed in the recent consultation on "Competition Policy contributing to the Green Deal", which clearly states that antitrust rules already play a role in achieving the decarbonisation targets of the Green Deal amongst other by "facilitating energy flowing freely across border".[39] But even before the Clean Energy Package or the Green Deal, the EU Treaties imposed an obligation to develop the internal market in line with the principle of sustainable development (Article 3(3) TEU) and to integrate environmental protection in EU policies and activities (the so-called integration principle, Article 11 TFEU).[40] Following that obligation, the Commission must carry out an environmental protection and sustainability compatibility check when enforcing competition law.[41]

---

rather confusing considering that the implementation of the Clean Energy Package brings significant material changes to the substance of CACM (n 6). Therefore, a revision of the Commitments on the basis of the new minimum threshold cannot be excluded.

36　The specific procedure of an article 9 decision entails a high level of discretion, for example, in initiating an investigation, accepting the offered commitments, reopening the case.

37　Case C–344/98 *Masterfoods v HB Ice Cream* [2000] ECR I-11369, [46].

38　See EMR, art 1(a); Directive (EU) 2019/944 on common rules for the internal market for electricity [2019] OJ L158/125, art 1.

39　See Commission, "Competition Policy contributing to the Green Deal: Call for contributions" (13 October 2020) <https://ec.europa.eu/competition/information/green_deal/call_for_contributions_en.pdf> accessed 2 February 2021, 3.

40　The integration principle is reiterated in Article 37 of the Charter on Fundamental Rights of the European Union (CFEU), which by virtue of Article 6(1) TEU has the "same legal value" as the EU Treaties. As a result, policies and measures adopted by the EU (and Member States) must not contradict the provisions of the CFEU, including the sustainable development principle. For analysis of the principle in the context of competition/state aid rules see Simon Holmes, "Climate change, sustainability, and competition law" (2020) 8(2) JAE 354; ClientEarth, Agora Energiewende, "A State Aid Framework for a Green Recovery: Mainstreaming Climate Protection in EU State aid law" (September 2020) <www.clientearth.org/media/c45naoms/2020-09-30-a-state-aid-framework-for-a-green-recovery-coll-en.pdf> accessed 2 February 2021; ClientEarth, "Competition policy supporting the Green Deal: Our call for a sustainable competition policy" (20 November 2020) <www.clientearth.org/media/kthkuhb4/clientearth-reply-to-call-competition-policy-and-green-deal_20-11-2020.pdf> accessed 2 February 2021.

41　The recent *Hinkley Point C* judgment confirmed the obligation to check the compatibility of state aid decisions with environmental laws, in line with Article 11 TFEU and Article 37 CFEU. However, non-compliance with those principles does not in all circumstances preclude the grant of state aid: Case C–594/18 P *Austria v Commission* EU:C:2020:742, [44 – 45], [100] and [49]; Bruno Stromsky, "Compatible aid: The Court of Justice of the European Union confirms the legality of a decision authorizing aid for the promotion of nuclear energy and finds that the compatibility of aid under

The choice of the Commission to apply the draft Clean Energy Package rules sets an important precedent on how Article 102 TFEU can be used as a sword to promote sustainability. Yet, in light of the above analysis, it would have been useful if the Commission had integrated in the Decision's reasoning clear reference to the Commitments' compatibility check with the integration, environmental protection and sustainable development principles. The lack of this reference potentially weakens the impact of the Decision on similar proceedings, or even the intention of the Commission to contribute to sustainability goals through the application of policies and draft legislation designed to achieve the decarbonisation objectives of the EU, for example through the upcoming changes of the Green Deal.

That said, the Commission has not been consistent with *DE/DK Interconnector* when settling antitrust proceedings during the drafting of the Clean Energy Package. For example, *Greek Lignite*, which was also settled in spring 2018, completely disregards the draft rules and even harms its future implementation.[42] The Commission's final decision in *Greek Lignite* had a potential adverse impact on sustainability: through a divestment procedure, it extended the use of lignite in the Greek energy mix to the detriment of cleaner alternatives.[43] Despite the eventual lignite phase-out, national measures taken in 2019 to boost the repeatedly failed divestment sealed the negative impact of the *Greek Lignite* on the RES sector and sustainability.[44]

Finally, the integration of a sustainability reasoning in the Decision would have minimised the risk of the 70% (at the time of the Decision: 75%) threshold being used by dominant system operators in a detrimental way for EU decarbonisation objectives, by lowering the ambition to maximise interconnection capacity. TSOs could argue that they cannot be said to be abusing that position when they operate at or below that level, even in circumstances where there is no good reason (or "objective justification") not to operate at a higher level. They will try to rely on the regulatory argument that the remaining 30% capacity is a safety net necessary for the operational security of the network. Even if these thresholds were necessary for the existing capacity of interconnectors as the electricity network adjusted to a new (decentralised) model, the application of the 70%

Article 107(3)(c) is not conditional on the pursuit of an objective of common interest (*Hinkley Point C*)" (2020) Concurrences N° 4–2020 Art N° 97650, 179–181. Nevertheless, it might still be possible for the Commission to exercise a degree of discretion when assessing sustainability in antitrust proceedings within the limits of existing legislation, guidelines and case law.

42 *Greek Lignite* (Case AT.38700) Commission decision C(2018) 2104 final [2018] OJ C93/3

43 Simon Holmes and Eleni Diamantopoulou, "End of the Road for the Sale of Greece's dirty fuel of the past" (*Energy Post*, 31 January 2019), <https://energypost.eu/end-of-the-road-for-the-sale-of-greeces-dirty-fuel-of-the-past/> accessed 10 November 2020.

44 As of 1 January 2019 PPC enjoyed a cut of its contribution to a levy that funded the special account for RES in Greece. This measure was one of the main contributors to a huge deficit in the special account which makes RES investment in Greece difficult, "Surcharge cut, unnecessary for PPC, has sunk RES account" (Energypress, 14 October 2020) <https://energypress.eu/spef-surcharge-cut-unnecessary-for-ppc-rebound-has-sunk-res-special-account/> accessed 2 February 2021. For the deficit of RES account see Commission, "Enhanced Surveillance Report – Greece, November 2020" (Institutional Paper 137, 18 November 2020) <https://ec.europa.eu/info/publications/enhanced-surveillance-report-greece-november-2020_en> accessed 2 February 2021.

rule on the new lines does not seem justified. With this approach, the Clean Energy Package ambition to increase interconnection capacity in Europe by 15% is watered down.[45] Even so, the Commission can still step in and enforce competition law rules, for example, in case exemptions are abused to disguise anticompetitive behaviours. Constant delays to reach the minimum threshold should mobilise the Commission to investigate the real reasons of the TSOs' behaviour.

VI. Conclusion

Just a few months after the adoption of the Clean Energy Package, the declaration of a climate emergency by the European Parliament in November 2019, the announcement of the Green Deal in December 2019 and the Green Recovery package in May 2020 signalled amendments to existing legislation or adoption of new legislation in order to increase the EU's climate and sustainability ambition. Several changes impact or aim to affect the application of competition law, including antitrust and state aid rules. Irrespective of the final regulatory changes, the Commission should be inspired by *DE/DK Interconnector* and approach the investigation of cases with the same wide discretion: if not applying, where possible, draft rules that promote sustainability, then by taking into account the spirit and objective of the upcoming changes and integrating a sustainability reasoning in its decisions. This practice may contribute to greening competition law and policy by establishing several good examples and eventually bringing consistency in the treatment of competition cases, and with the fundamental objective of sustainable development, as required by the EU Treaties.

---

45   According to Regulation (EU) 2018/1999 on the Governance of the Energy Union and Climate Action [2018] OJ L 328/1, art 2(11).

Setting the Course – Removing Competition Law Obstacles to Industry Sustainability Collaborations

MORGAN F FRONTCZAK[*]

Shell International BV

I. Introduction

The time to act to solve the climate challenge is now. To do this, industry and governments must come together to find solutions for the difficult task of decarbonising a world reluctant to change patterns of consumption and energy usage. And this wide-ranging industry – government collaboration must happen now if we are to limit rising average global temperatures below 2°C. The challenge is far too big for any single government agency, organisation, industry player, or consumer to solve. Industries and governments must work together to incentivise the change necessary to reach this goal. One important partnership, that I discuss in this paper, is that of industry competition law counsel and competition law authorities. Together, we must remove competition law obstacles, whether real or perceived, that may prevent the fast-moving collaboration needed for rapid, large-scale decarbonisation. We simply do not have time to wait.

In this paper, I introduce some of the challenges industry faces to decarbonise hard-to-abate industrial and transportation sectors as an example of why the

---

[*] Morgan Frontczak is a senior antitrust counsel at Shell International BV. The views expressed her are her own and do not necessarily reflect those of Shell International BV or other companies of the Shell group.

solution to the climate challenge cannot rest with governments alone, why collective industry action is often necessary, and why industry must act now. The more it is understood how complex and critical solutions to the climate change challenge are, the better the debate can be as to how competition law enforcement could be a blocker to or enabler of those solutions. I also advocate for competition law authorities and industry to overcome potential scepticism of the other side and work together on solutions to prevent overly narrow interpretations of competition law standing in the way of the collaborative industry action that is needed to help solve the climate challenge.

II. Sustainability in the Energy Context

Sustainability can mean many things, even within the energy industry context. For purposes of this paper, though, I refer to sustainable agreements as those aimed at decarbonisation and the reduction of greenhouse gases (GHG). Decarbonisation efforts include those aimed at reducing consumers' emissions from the use of energy products as well as the emissions from the production of energy towards the goal of net-zero emissions.[1] Examples of potential sustainability agreements in the energy context range from the relatively easy to achieve and implement to transformational changes to the types of and ways in which energy is used.

In order to drive substantial decarbonisation across industry, significant changes must occur in the demand for energy types and the supply of those new energies. Energy users will need to know, for example, what fuels can be supplied in order to determine how to use that zero- or net-zero carbon energy in the future. And energy suppliers need certainty that if investments are made into alternative zero- or net-zero carbon fuels, there will be demand for those fuels. This connectedness between energy supply and energy demand has created the need for a sectoral approach to decarbonisation pathways, especially for certain hard-to-abate industrial (chemicals, cement, and iron and steel) and transportation (shipping, aviation, and road freight) sectors.[2] Thus, sustainability agreements in the energy and related sectors often involve sectoral or industry-wide

---

1   Net-zero emissions is the balance between the amount of GHG produced and the amount removed from the atmosphere. Net-zero emissions will likely need to come from a combination of removing and offsetting man-made emissions as well as dramatically reducing new emissions created. V Masson-Delmotte and others, "IPCC Special Report on the impacts of global warming of 1.5°C above pre-industrial levels and related global greenhouse gas emission pathways, in the context of strengthening the global response to the threat of climate change, sustainable development, and efforts to eradicate poverty" (IPCC 2018).

2   The challenge to decarbonise is particularly pronounced in six harder-to-abate sectors that, according to the International Energy Agency, currently account for around 30% of global CO_2 emissions. Shell and Deloitte, "Decarbonising Shipping: All Hands on Deck" (Shell 2020) <www.shell.com/promos/energy-and-innovation/decarbonising-shipping-all-hands-on-deck/_jcr_content.stream/1594141914406/b4878 c899602611f78d36655ebff06307e49d0f8/ decarbonising-shipping-report.pdf> accessed 20 September 2020 (Decarbonising Shipping Report).

collaboration as energy users and suppliers work together through sectoral approaches to create rapid and realistic decarbonisation pathways across the hardest to abate sectors.

III. All Hands on Deck
– the Shipping Decarbonisation Example

The shipping industry is one hard-to-abate sector that helps to illustrate the need for private industry to work together, in addition to and possibly in lieu of government regulation, to solve the decarbonisation challenges.

The nature of the shipping industry and the world's reliance on shipping as a means of transporting freight create a sizeable decarbonisation challenge. Around two-thirds of the world's freight is transported by international shipping, leading to an estimated 2% of global CO_2 emissions.[3] The shipping industry operates via large, long-life assets and a dependence on a global supply of high-carbon fuel. And since shipping is also a capital-intensive industry with historically thin margins, decarbonisation of the shipping industry will be complex as well as expensive.[4]

Within the shipping industry, most of the sector's emissions come from large, deep-sea ships.[5] The life cycle of ships creates additional hurdles to decarbonisation and requires urgency for industry consensus on future fuels. Most of today's ships are large, complex assets that require major capital and several years to build. They are also costly to modify. Deep-sea ships frequently also have a lifespan over 20 years, meaning ships entering the water in 2030 will still be in use by 2050.[6] Thus, zero-emission vessels need to enter the global fleet by 2030. Due to stringent operational safety requirements, new ship technology can take a long time to enter the market, so new ship designs should be in the works now. However, shipowners are reluctant to invest in building net-zero vessels due to risks resulting from lack of clarity regarding future fuels, lack of global regulatory framework and limited customer demand for lower-emission shipping.[7]

---

3   IEA (2020), "International Shipping" (IEA 2020) <www.iea.org/reports/international-shipping> accessed 11 September 2020.

4   One study estimated the total costs of decarbonising the shipping industry as over USD1 trillion by 2050. Johannah Christensen, "How decarbonizing shipping could unlock a global energy transition" (World Economic Forum, 22 January 2020) <www.weforum.org/agenda/2020/01/decarbonizing-shipping-global-energy-transition/> accessed on 11 September 2020.

5   Decarbonising Shipping Report, 6.

6   In 2018, the International Maritime Organization (IMO) announced its initial strategy to reduce GHG emissions. The strategy outlines an ambition to at least halve international shipping emissions by 2050, whilst reducing CO_2 emissions intensity by at least 40% by 2030, and pursuing efforts towards 70% by 2050 compared with a 2008 baseline. IMO "Adoption of the initial IMO strategy on reduction of GHG emissions from ships and existing IMO activity related to reducing GHG emissions in the shipping sector" (April 2018) <https://unfccc.int/sites/default/files/resource/250_IMO%20submission_Talanoa%20Dialogue_April%202018.pdf> accessed 11 September 2020 (IMO Initial Strategy).

7   Decarbonising Shipping Report, 6.

The desire to meet the IMO 2030 and 2050 targets creates significant pressure to identify fuel alternatives as soon as possible.[8] Switching the primary fuel source away from heavy fuel oil (HFO) will not be easy. Fuels have changed dramatically over the history of shipping, but not significantly in recent times.[9] Reconfiguring shipping supply-chain infrastructure to new fuels will also be a challenge. Some infrastructure associated with fuel supply chains can have an economic lifespan of up to 50 years.[10] And given the vast quantities of energy consumed by the industry, transitioning the world's fleet to new energy sources will take a sizeable effort to build out the necessary fuel production and bunkering infrastructure.[11] However, there is no agreed alternative fuel pathway. Potential alternative fuels such as ammonia, hydrogen, methanol or biofuel all currently appear to have technical limitations, need further development, or are not yet perceived as safe.[12] And it is widely assumed that any new fuel will likely cost more, at least initially, than HFO.[13]

Timely, systematic changes, like the required switch from HFO to zero- or net-zero carbon fuels, will not be possible without broad collective action by industry and governments. Governments will need to play a significant role in creating long-term demand signals through investment incentives, consumption or emissions-based tariffs, or sectoral decarbonisation roadmaps[14] that will help drive demand for lower carbon fuels, level the playing field and create incentives for first movers. But, as discussed, there is little time to wait for government action. In the absence of government intervention, to fill legislative gaps or to otherwise correct market failures where consumers have not yet expressed a willingness to pay for more sustainable products or services, industry will need to collaborate.

Thus, sectoral collaboration in the shipping industry is imperative to identify and ultimately operationalise zero-carbon fuel solutions and to put zero- or net-zero-emitting ships in the water by 2030. But in what form will that sectoral collaboration take? One could think of numerous ways the shipping sector could collaborate to speed the switch to zero- or net-zero carbon fuels. Possibilities could include joint industry R&D collaborations, industry agreements on targets that limit emissions from shipping to a certain level, or agreements between shipowners and charterers on sustainable procurement criteria. Another possibility includes joint lobbying to governments and international regulatory bodies

---

8   Decarbonising Shipping Report, 23.
9   Decarbonising Shipping Report, 19.
10 Global Maritime Forum, "Ambition Statement" <www.globalmaritimeforum.org/getting-to-zero-coalition/ambition-statement> accessed 10 September 2020.
11 Decarbonising Shipping Report, 24.
12 Decarbonising Shipping Report, 19.
13 Decarbonising Shipping Report, 6.
14 European legislators appear to be headed in the right direction as amendments to the pending Climate Law adopted in October 2020 call for an issuance of sectoral decarbonisation roadmaps. Amendments adopted by the European Parliament on 8 October 2020 on the proposal for a regulation of the European Parliament and of the Council establishing the framework for achieving climate neutrality and amending Regulation (EU) 2018/1999 (European Climate Law) (COM(2020)0080 – COM(2020)0563 – C9-0077/2020 – 2020/0036(COD)) (8 October 2020).

like the IMO to mandate tariffs on carbon emissions in the sector. Yet another option to reduce future fuel uncertainty could involve joint commitments of shipping companies and fuel providers to agree on the likely alternative fuel pathways.[15] Any such sectoral collaboration initiative will need sign-off from industry competition counsel. Thus, clarity on competition law compliance for sustainability agreements is key to enabling much-needed industry collaboration.

IV. Know the Ropes – Clarifying Legal Uncertainties Regarding Sustainability Agreements

The shipping decarbonisation challenge helps to illustrate both the enormity and complexity of the climate crisis, but also the dilemmas with which industry competition law counsel may increasingly be presented. At this time, it is not always clear how various potential industry agreements aimed at decarbonisation would be assessed by competition authorities. Differing political and economic priorities have already created an unlevel playing field of global regulation and enforcement priorities. And while European authorities are taking the lead in discussing the intersection of competition law and sustainability agreements,[16] there is not yet agreement even among European competition law authorities on the interpretation and application of competition law to sustainability agreements.[17] Additionally, while there are helpful earlier precedents from the European Commission in decisions like *CECED* and in the 2001 Horizontal Guidelines,[18] guidance on environmental agreements was notably absent from the 2010 Horizontal Guidelines and the Article 101(3) guidelines.[19] It is hardly surprising then, that many questions remain as to how competition authorities would view sectoral sustainability agreements aimed at decarbonisation where competition may be affected but where the benefits of the agreement likely outweigh any potential harm.

The first point of needed clarification is the question of when sustainability agreements fall outside the scope of Article 101(1) TFEU. There are certainly many

---

15 While such sectoral decarbonisation pathways or roadmaps appear to be garnering support at the legislative level in Europe, it remains to be seen whether there will be widespread government adoption of such sectoral mandates. It also remains unclear whether competition authorities will oversee or participate in the sectoral roadmap process to ensure competition law compliance.

16 An effort which is much applauded by private industry. Note, whilst I have limited this paper to a European perspective, this is by no means a European-only problem. Similar considerations apply in regimes throughout the globe.

17 Jay Modrall, "Sustainability and Antitrust – Advocates, Sceptics and Technocrats" (*Kluwer Competition Blog*, 15 February 2021).

18 *CECED* (Case IV.F.1/36.718) [2000] OJ L187/47; see also 2001 Horizontal Guidelines inclusion of guidance on environmental agreements: Commission, "Guidelines on the applicability of Article 81 of the EC Treaty to horizontal co-operation agreements" [2001] OJ C3/02, [179] – [198] (2001 Horizontal Guidelines).

19 Commission, "Guidelines on the applicability of Article 101 of the Treaty on the Functioning of the European Union to horizontal co-operation agreements" [2011] OJ C 11/01) (2010 Horizontal Guidelines); Guidelines on the application of Article 101(3) TFEU (formerly Article 81(3) TEC) [2004] OJ C101/97.

sectoral agreements that fit into a category of agreement that the Commission has stated do not fall under Article 101(1),[20] such as where agreements do not impose precise obligations on individual companies,[21] where the agreement specifies environmental performance but has no appreciable effect on product and production diversity, or where the agreement gives rise to "genuine market creation".[22] Additionally, precedents exist from the European Court of Justice that agreements can fall outside the scope of Article 101(1) if the restrictions in question are necessary for the pursuit of a legitimate public policy objective or are aimed at other objectives of the European treaties.[23] Treaty environmental goals[24] require environmental consideration to be taken into account when implementing all of the EU's policies and activities.[25] Finally, agreements may not fall under Article 101(1) if the agreement involves pre-competitive[26] or early-stage R&D[27] – though clarity is necessary to understand when sustainability R&D efforts are at such pre-competitive stages.

To be clear, there will likely be many proposed sustainability initiatives that could have the potential to create appreciable effects on competition due to the scope of the arrangement or the number of industry players who participate. Examples of such initiatives include where scale is key to achieving the decarbonisation or other sustainability goal, where mandatory standards are necessary to achieve meaningful progress on a sustainability target and where legislation to create the mandate is lagging, or where transformational changes to a method of production, input or product will result in additional costs initially that create both first-mover disadvantages and disincentives for individual companies who lack certainty over consumer demand for the new, sustainable products.[28] These collaborations might then fall under Article 101(1) and will need to be analysed on a case-by-case basis.

Another area of needed clarification relates to when industry can meet the requirements of an Article 101(3) TFEU exemption. Further guidance is needed for industry to understand competition authorities' willingness to build on and develop existing

---

20 2001 Horizontal Guidelines.
21 ibid; see also *JAMA* (Case COMP/37.634) and *KAMA* (Case COMP/37.612) (1999); Commission, "Commitments by Japanese and Korean Car Manufacturers to reduce CO_2 emissions comply with EC Competition rules" Press release (IP/99/922, 1 December 1999).
22 2001 Horizontal Guidelines; see also *DSD* (Case COMP D3/34493) Commission decision C (2001) 1106 [2001] OJ L166/1.
23 Case C–309/99 *Wouters v Algemene Raad van de Nederlandse Orde van Advocaten* [2002] ECR I-1577; Case C–519/04 P *Meca-Medina and Majcen v Commission* [2006] ECR I-6991; Marc van der Woude, "Antidoping rules: The ECJ holds that the CFI gave a too narrow definition of the scope of the competition rules, but rejects the application in view of the legitimate objective pursued by the contested rules (Meca-Medina*)*", 18 July 2006, Concurrences N° 4-2006, Art. N° 12548, p. 68.
24 Consolidated versions of the Treaty on European Union and the Treaty on the Functioning of the European Union (TFEU) [2016] OJ C202/53.
25 Simon Holmes, "Climate change, sustainability, and competition law" (2020) 8(2) JAE 354.
26 *Eucar* (Case No IV/35.742 – F/2) [1997] OJ C185/05.
27 2010 Horizontal Guidelines.
28 Dirk Middelschulte, "Sustainability Cooperation Between Competitors & Art. 101 TFEU" (Unilever submission to DG COMP) <www.unilever.com/Images/unilever_submission_sustainability_competition_law_tcm244-551751_en.pdf> accessed 10 September 2020.

precedent that acknowledges that the harm caused to competition should be weighed against the benefits, including environmental benefits, brought to wider society and to move away from a narrow assessment that only takes account of the benefits that accrue specifically to consumers in the market where the cooperation is taking place.[29] Clarification is needed for industry to understand when and how the potential benefits of sustainability agreements to further technical progress can be accounted for, when environmental results for society would adequately allow consumers a fair share of the benefits, and how such benefits should be measured, including what qualitative criteria will be relevant under this assessment.

The Netherlands Authority for Consumers and Markets (ACM) has recently demonstrated how competition authorities can appropriately support decarbonisation initiatives through the provision of guidance on sustainability agreements. The ACM's guidelines on sustainability agreements (ACM Sustainability Guidelines)[30] provide welcome clarity on how the ACM will evaluate section 6.3 requirements.[31] According to the ACM Sustainability Guidelines, efficiency gains include sustainability benefits that reduce negative externalities like pollution as well as increased innovation and quality improvements.[32] Interpreting the fair share to consumers requirement, the ACM Sustainability Guidelines state that if an agreement is aimed at preventing or limiting environmental damage, companies can take into account benefits of that agreement, such as the reduction of GHG, that extend to wider society.[33] Industry awaits further information on the European Commission's approach following its consultation and it is to be hoped that the Commission's guidance will also make it clear that wider, societal benefits of decarbonisation initiatives can be accounted for in an Article 101(3) analysis.

While each potential sectoral collaboration or agreement will need to be analysed on a case-by-case basis, the above clarifications will help give industry the required comfort to move forward with legitimate, collaborative action that could help to solve the climate crisis.

V. In the Same Boat – the Role of Competition Law Authorities

Time is of the essence for global competition law authorities to weigh in on the dilemmas posed by the need for industries to take collective decisions to help solve the climate crisis. Given the need for immediate action, new competition law regulation in the form of exemptions for certain types of agreements or

---

29 *CECED* (n 19).
30 ACM, "Sustainability Agreements – Opportunities within competition law" (26 January 2021) (ACM Sustainability Guidelines).
31 Section 6.3 is the Dutch Competition Act corollary to Article 101(3) TFEU.
32 ACM Sustainability Guidelines, 6.
33 ACM Sustainability Guidelines, 14.

legislation that otherwise more explicitly sets out how the environmental benefits are to be weighed is unlikely to come quickly enough, especially on a global basis. And while it may be argued that greater certainty will come through cases being brought through the relevant judicial systems, there is a risk that the prospect of potentially intrusive investigation will result in companies adopting an overly conservative approach to collaborations. In any event, if that certainty does come through the courts, it will take time. The urgency of the climate crisis does not allow that time. It is imperative that authorities, in consultation with industry and its advisers, provide new guidance on how to interpret existing law in the area of sustainability agreements. Competition authorities have a vital role to play in their competition law enforcement activities – as a solutions-oriented complement to legislative action that seeks to solve the climate crisis.

Competition law authorities can provide industries with clarity and comfort through a number of actions. First, authorities should consider ways to set enforcement priorities that make clear that authorities will not actively pursue investigations and enforcement actions of legitimate efforts to create sustainability solutions, even if such agreements create some restriction on competition. Without such a step, the fear of investigations and enforcement actions,[34] which create significant reputational issues and uncertainty for industry – often for very long periods – will continue to have a chilling effect on potentially vital industry collaboration. No one is asking competition law authorities to look askance at cartel behaviour operating under the guise of sustainability. However, industries must feel free to pursue collaborative thinking, exchange of information and, potentially, collaborative decision-making on how to decarbonise or otherwise help to solve the climate crisis. The ACM commitment to seek solutions not fines[35] is a welcome example of such enforcement priorities. This type of commitment helps to change the tone of the conversation and goes a long way towards reducing the concerns and fears of practitioners by demonstrating a willingness to collaborate that is much-needed if competition law is not to be interpreted in a way that creates a block to vital industry initiatives. Time will tell if other authorities are willing to follow suit.

Second, authorities should consider ways to provide detailed and practical guidance to industry as to what is and is not a sustainable agreement that violates competition law. Again, the ACM has come forward with guidance in this regard. And more European authorities, like the Hellenic Competition Commission, are joining the ACM.[36] Industry awaits similar guidance from the European Commission, with the hope that European competition authorities will become aligned in their approach. Whether this guidance comes in the form of specific

---

34 Nicole Kar, "Competition rules stymie co-operation on climate goals" *Financial Times* (London, 30 January 2020).
35 ACM Sustainability Guidelines.
36 Hellenic Competition Commission, "Draft Staff Discussion Paper on 'Sustainability Issues and Competition Law'" (September 2020).

sustainability guidelines or in the form of revised horizontal guidelines or block exemption regulations that address sustainability agreements, the Commission must also rise to the challenge of giving guidance and building on existing precedents to give more clarity as to how sustainability agreements will be assessed, including on how the benefits of those agreements are to be measured in the balance.

Third, authorities should consider ways to provide a path for timely reviews of specific sustainability agreements that could result in greater certainty in the form of comfort letters or other approvals. Companies fear that attempts to seek guidance and clarity through a review could result in open-ended, resource-intensive processes. This fear could act as a deterrent to many who would otherwise welcome certainty over sustainable agreements. Thus clarity on the scope and timing of regulatory reviews will act as incentive for companies to engage. Additionally, publication of the outcome of reviews (subject to confidentiality concerns being worked out) will help give additional guidance and transparency to industry.[37]

VI. Do Not Swing the Lead – the Role of Industry

If authorities show willingness to articulate their interpretation of competition law, take bold steps in setting enforcement priorities, or to give guidance on what does and does not violate competition law, their industry counterparts must also be willing to act. Private practitioners must commit to finding solutions that allow collective action where necessary to address the climate challenge.

Lack of legal certainty on competition law threatens to be a significant bar to legitimate industry action. When faced with uncertainty over a collaboration's competition law compliance (coupled with fear of open-ended investigations or aggressive enforcement agendas), industry is often understandably reluctant to push forward on action that poses any competition law risk.[38] Thus, achieving industry consensus to proceed with legitimate, but less straightforward, sustainability collaborations may still be difficult. Armed with clear statements on

---

37 While comfort letters had not been part of regular agency practice, the European Commission as well as the US Department of Justice, returned to comfort letters to give industry guidance during the COVID-19 pandemic. Commission, "Antitrust: Commission provides guidance on allowing limited cooperation among businesses, especially for critical hospital medicines during the coronavirus outbreak" Press release (IP/20/618, 8 April 2020); US DOJ, "Department of Justice Issues Business Review Letter to Medical Supplies Distributors Supporting Project Airbridge Under Expedited Procedure for COVID-19 Pandemic Response" Press release (20-360, 4 April 2020).

38 A survey conducted by law firm Linklaters found that "nearly 6 in 10 (57%) businesses have had to walk away from cross-industry environmental initiatives because the legal risk was too high." "This is despite an overwhelming number of businesses (93%) wanting to work closely with peers in responding to climate change." Linklaters, "92 percent of businesses call for changes to competition rules to boost climate change collaboration" (30 April 2020).

enforcement priorities, guidelines and review processes, advisers and industry may feel able to be a little less conservative.[39]

Industry counsel must then be willing to provide guidance that helps their clients manage competition law sensitivities, even if the guidance can only come in the form of a path for finding answers if no answers currently exist. Many initiatives can be approved through self-assessments, especially once industry counsel are equipped with clear and detailed guidance, and industry counsel must be brave enough to make those self-assessments. Some initiatives may present tricky questions or may be high stakes enough that thorough reviews and help from advisers will be necessary as part of a self- assessment. And for some initiatives, industry must be willing to avail themselves of the opportunities to seek clarification or comfort on competition law interpretation and to seek solutions. In order to be effective, engagement with authorities may require parties to potential collaborations to come prepared – having conducted analysis into the likely impacts on competition and the potential benefits of the collaboration to consumers and citizens. Such evidence and data should enable a dialogue that helps alleviate scepticism on both sides.

VII. Conclusion

Competition law need not be a deterrent to industry collaboration on solutions to help fight the climate crisis. Together, competition authorities and industry counsel can help remove competition law obstacles that threaten industry action that will help transform and dramatically decarbonise even the most difficult to decarbonise sectors.

---

39 "And I agree there is a certain level of conservatism in the advisory industry." Margarthe Vestager, "Keynote Address" (Sustainability and Competition Policy: Bridging two Worlds to Enable a Fairer Economy, Brussels, 24 October 2019).

Chapter 5
Food Supply Chain

Competition Policy
for a Sustainable Food Sector:
An In-House Counsel Perspective

MARTYN CHU*

Danone

> *The greatest threat to our planet is the belief*
> *that someone else will save it.*
>
> Robert Swan, explorer

I. Introduction

There is growing recognition that the global food system in its present form poses a major threat to the long-term sustainability of our planet, society and human health.[1] A model predicated on maximising output while minimising cost has surpassed its natural limits.

This threat manifests itself in multiple ways, all of which are interconnected. These range from well-documented environmental concerns like climate change, pollution, biodiversity loss and food waste, to social issues such as inequality, labour rights and poor health outcomes linked to food security, food safety or nutritional quality.[2]

---

* Martyn Chu is the head of antitrust and competition law at Danone. All views are expressed in a personal capacity, and do not necessarily reflect the position of Danone.
1 See, e.g., Food and Agriculture Organization of the United Nations, "Sustainable Food Systems: Concept and Framework" (2018) <www.fao.org/3/ca2079en/CA2079EN.pdf>; EAT-Lancet Commission, "Summary Report: Healthy Diets from Sustainable Food Systems" (2020) <https://ec.europa.eu/knowledge4policy/publication/eat-lancet-commission-summary-report_en>; and Tim G Benton and others, "Food System Impacts on Biodiversity Loss" (Chatham House 2021) <www.chathamhouse.org/sites/default/files/2021-02/2021-02-03-food-system-biodiversity-loss-benton-et-al_0.pdf>.
2 In Europe: the food sector constitutes the largest manufacturing sector; agriculture is responsible for over 10% of greenhouse gas emissions; around 20% of food produced is lost or wasted; 33 million people

In order to play its part in breaking this vicious circle of existential risks, the food sector must undergo a fundamental transformation. This need is confirmed by the European Commission's comprehensive "Green Deal" roadmap for sustainable growth, which includes a pillar – the Farm-to-Fork Strategy – dedicated to reforming the end-to-end food supply chain.[3]

At the same time, the food sector and companies operating in it have long been subject to close scrutiny by competition authorities across Europe.[4] This is largely because food is an essential daily requirement, which represents a significant proportion of the average household budget,[5] meaning that its accessibility and affordability to consumers is (quite rightly) considered to be of high priority.[6]

The combination of these two industry characteristics – sustainability enabler and competition law magnet – places an onus on policymakers, enforcers and practitioners to examine the extent to which competition rules can be applied in a manner that (further) enhances progress towards a sustainable food sector, without jeopardising consumers' right to quality food at a fair price.

In this new paradigm, such policy questions are not merely theoretical, but rather have important practical implications for food companies' capacity to effect positive change, and ultimately the extent to which the global food system can be harnessed as a positive driver of environmental and social sustainability.

With the aim of examining how the food industry and the competition community should respond to these challenges, this paper will cover:

- The role of businesses in driving sustainability (section II);

- Why and how competition policy should facilitate the pursuit of sustainability goals (section III);

---

are suffering from food insecurity; more than 20% of adults are obese.

3   See Commission, "Reinforcing Europe's resilience: halting biodiversity loss and building a healthy and sustainable food system" Press release (IP/20/884, 20 May 2020). Other pillars of the Green Deal are also of direct relevance to the food sector, most notably the Biodiversity Strategy (*ibid.*) and the Circular Economy Action Plan (Commission, "Changing how we produce and consume: New Circular Economy Action Plan shows the way to a climate-neutral, competitive economy of empowered consumers" Press release (IP/20/420, 11 March 2020)).

4   From January 2012 to June 2017, competition authorities in Europe conducted 167 investigations and 16 sector inquiries in the food sector: Commission, "Commission Staff Working Document: Document accompanying the report on the application of the Union competition rules to the agricultural sector" SWD(2018) 450 final.

5   Spending on food and non-alcoholic beverages represented approximately 13.8% of the average EU household budget in 2017: Commission, "Agriculture, food and fisheries: overview" <https://ec.europa.eu/competition/sectors/agriculture/overview_en.html> accessed 25 January 2021.

6   Of course, competition law enforcement is not the only available means of safeguarding (or improving) the accessibility and affordability of food. It is just one tool for addressing what is a highly complex and multi-dimensional issue: see, e.g., Food and Agriculture Organization of the United Nations, "The State of Food Security and Nutrition in the World 2020: Transforming Food Systems for Affordable Healthy Diets" (2020) <www.fao.org/3/ca9692en/CA9692EN.pdf>.

– The ability of in-house counsel to boost companies' sustainability programmes (section IV); and

– Conclusions and a call to action (section V).

II. The Role of Business

European Commission Executive Vice-President, Margrethe Vestager, has said of the Green Deal, "To succeed, everyone in Europe will have to play their part – every individual, *every business*, every public authority".[7]

Within the food sector, the European Commission has especially highlighted the power of food processors and retailers to put food production and consumption on a sustainable path.[8] And, in that light, it is encouraging that manufacturers are making and executing ever-stronger sustainability commitments across a wide range of areas.[9]

Of course, such actions are not entirely altruistic. While they are motivated by a moral and social duty to "do the right thing", they also make economic and business sense. More specifically, an authentic and robust sustainability strategy creates long-term value and reduces financial risk for a company by:

– Addressing consumers' growing demand for sustainable products (and their related scrutiny of companies' sustainability credentials);[10]

– Driving product innovation and competitive differentiation;

– Enhancing employee engagement and loyalty;

– Meeting the expectations of shareholders and investors;[11] and/or

– Future-proofing the natural resources and supply chain on which revenue streams depend.

---

7   Margrethe Vestager, "The Green Deal and competition policy" (Renew webinar, 22 September 2020) (emphasis added).
8   Commission, "Questions and Answers: Farm to Fork Strategy – building a healthy and fully sustainable food system" (QUANDA/20/885, 20 May 2020).
9   See, e.g., FoodDrinkEurope, "The path of the food and drink industry towards Sustainable Food Systems" (2019) <www.fooddrinkeurope.eu/uploads/publications_documents/FoodDrinkEurope_-_The_path_towards_Sustainable_Food_Systems.pdf>.
10 79% of consumers say they are changing their purchase preferences based on sustainability factors, according to Capgemini, "How Sustainability is Fundamentally Changing Consumer Preferences" (2020) <www.capgemini.com/wp-content/uploads/2020/07/20-06_9880_Sustainability-in-CPR_Final_Web-1.pdf>. And 81% of consumers say it is "extremely" or "very important" that companies implement programmes to improve the environment (that figure rising to 85% among millennials aged 21–34): see Nielsen "Sustainable Shoppers Buy the Change they Wish to See in the World" (16 November 2018) <www.nielsen.com/eu/en/insights/report/2018/sustainable-shoppers-buy-the-change-they-wish-to-see-in-the-world/#>.
11 See, e.g., Riccardo Boffo and Robert Patalano, "ESG Investing: Practices, Progress and Challenges" (OECD 2020) <www.oecd.org/finance/ESG-Investing-Practices-Progress-Challenges.pdf>.

Even if the full commercial benefits of sustainability initiatives may not materialise until quite some time after a company has made the necessary up-front (and often substantial) investments, the long-term survival and resiliency of food businesses will almost certainly depend on their ability to get this delicate balancing act right.[12] In short, the economic incentives could not be clearer or more compelling – and the question facing each company is how to make the transition, rather than whether to make it at all.

The efforts and advances made to date by the most progressive companies have shown the way forward. But, given the scale and urgency of the transformation required, even more needs to be done to accelerate the journey, to bring others on board and to trigger the necessary systemic changes.

Accordingly, it is incumbent on everyone, within their respective fields of activity, to identify any hurdles that lie in the way of further and faster progress, and to assess how these can be overcome. The competition community is no exception.

III. The Role of Competition Policy

1. The status quo

Primary EU legislation makes clear that competition policy, and by extension the authorities who enforce it, must take the EU's objective of "sustainable development" into account, whose dimensions expressly include "environmental protection", "social protection" and "protection of human health".[13]

Moreover, in the context of the food sector, the legislation states that competition rules must take account of the objectives of the EU's Common Agricultural Policy (CAP) – and some of those objectives clearly embody specific sustainability-related goals, such as "to ensure a fair standard of living for the agricultural community" and "to assure the availability of supplies" (which must presumably include a requirement to configure today's production processes and supply chains in ways that will remain viable in the long-term).[14]

It is true that, by its very nature, competition law indirectly promotes sustainability to some degree – for example, by driving innovation and the efficient

---

12 According to Mark Carney, the then-governor of the Bank of England, "firms that align their business models to the transition to a net zero world will be rewarded handsomely. Those that fail to adapt will cease to exist", "TCFD: strengthening the foundations of sustainable finance" (TCFD summit, Tokyo, 8 October 2019) <www.bankofengland.co.uk/-/media/boe/files/speech/2019/tcfd-strengthening-the-foundations-of-sustainable-finance-speech-by-mark-carney.pdf>.
13 See Article 3 of the Treaty on European Union, and Articles 7, 9, 11 of the Treaty on the Functioning of the European Union (TFEU).
14 Articles 39(b) and (d) TFEU and Article 42 TFEU. Indeed, the European Court of Justice has declared that the CAP objectives take precedence over competition law: Case C–671/15 *APVE and others* EU:C:2017:860, [37] and [48].

allocation of resources. However, when reviewing the application of competition policy and enforcement in recent times, there is very little evidence that sustainability factors are being given the requisite level of *direct* consideration, either systematically or in individual cases.

To understand why this is the case – and, therefore, to identify what may need to be changed – it is instructive to examine the notion of "consumer welfare", which has emerged as the main touchstone used by many competition authorities as a basis for intervention.[15]

In the competition law field, consumer welfare is generally assessed according to the parameters of price, quality, innovation and choice. This list appears to offer some hope, as the three non-price elements should, in principle, enable sustainability factors to come into play – for instance, in the form of perceived environmental or personal health benefits (e.g. organic foods), new product types (e.g. "plant-based" alternatives) and new, sustainability-led brands.

In reality, though, competition authorities have shown a tendency to default to a narrow interpretation of consumer welfare that focuses primarily on short-term economic impact, as measured by reference to consumer price. And such an approach unfortunately leaves virtually no room for non-economic sustainability considerations, notwithstanding the clear legal requirement to the contrary.

2. A new approach

In order to address the competition policy gaps outlined above, the scope and application of the consumer welfare concept needs to be reset in a way that allows sustainability to be integrated into the competitive assessment process[16] – ideally as a standalone factor, or at minimum under the parameters of quality, innovation and choice.[17]

This view is supported by the growing evidence that a significant proportion of consumers are willing to pay more for sustainable products, thereby demonstrating that they recognise and value sustainability's welfare-enhancing benefits.[18] And,

15 According to the International Competition Network's report "Competition Enforcement and Consumer Welfare – Setting the Agenda" (2011), fig 1.2, 89% of competition authorities globally consider "consumer welfare" as a goal, or the goal, of competition law enforcement: <www.internationalcompetitionnetwork.org/wp-content/uploads/2019/11/SP_CWelfare2011.pdf>.

16 Leading competition lawyers have advocated strongly for this approach: see Maurits Dolmans, "Sustainable Competition Policy" (2020) 5(4) and 6(1) CLPD, s 3; and Simon Holmes, "Climate Change, Sustainability, and Competition Law" (2020) 8(2) Oxford Journal of Antitrust Enforcement, s IV.

17 In the pending EU *Car Emissions* case (AT.40178), the parties' agreement to limit the development and roll-out of emission cleaning technology has been characterised by the Commission as a restriction of competition on quality and innovation: Commission, "Antitrust: Commission sends Statement of Objections to BMW, Daimler and VW for restricting competition on emission cleaning technology" Press release (IP/19/2008, 5 April 2019).

18 According to a survey conducted on behalf of the European Commission, 66% of European citizens are prepared to pay 10% more for agricultural products that are produced in a way that limits their carbon

in any event, consumers are not merely economic units that purchase goods and services, but first and foremost citizens and people, whose prosperity and longevity is inextricably linked to the preservation of the planet and the maintenance of healthy, well-functioning societies.

Such an approach does not necessarily require that more (or even equal) weight be given to sustainability relative to other aspects of consumer welfare, nor that a precise economic analysis be conducted on a case-by-case basis. Rather, in cases where there is a potential conflict between sustainability on the one hand, and price (or other consumer welfare goals) on the other, a fact-based balancing exercise between the different impacts could be performed based on their respective magnitude, probability and timing. The key point is that sustainability should always be part of the equation.

In the food sector context, support for the notion of such a balancing exercise can be found in another of the CAP objectives, namely "to ensure that supplies reach consumers at *reasonable* prices" (rather than the lowest possible prices).[19] When interpreted alongside the CAP's own extensive sustainability aims,[20] it must follow that a price rise which is proportionate to (and a necessary consequence of) a corresponding sustainability benefit could qualify as "reasonable" for these purposes, and therefore satisfy the objective.

Indeed, in relation to proposals for future reform of the CAP, the European Parliament has stated that competition rules should not apply to "vertical agreements and concerted practices aimed at applying higher environmental, animal health or animal welfare standards than the ones prescribed by EU or national laws … if the advantages to the public outweigh the disadvantages".[21]

There is, of course, recent precedent for a similar resetting of competition law boundaries, albeit on a temporary basis. In response to the COVID-19 crisis, many governments and competition authorities around the world decided to relax restrictions on competitor collaboration, to the extent necessary to secure consumers' continued access to scarce or essential goods, including food.[22]

---

footprint: see Kantar, "Special Eurobarometer 504: Europeans, Agriculture and the CAP" (2020) <https://ec.europa.eu/commfrontoffice/publicopinion/index.cfm/survey/getsurveydetail/instruments/special/surveyky/2229>, p 16. Similarly, a study by IPSOS and the Innovation Forum found that 68–71% of consumers overall are willing to pay more for products that address their environmental, social or governance concerns: "Sustainability: The Next Generation of Consumers" (2019).

19 Article 39(e) TFEU (emphasis added).

20 The European Commission states that "the CAP aims to ensure that agriculture and forestry in the EU is socially, economically and environmentally sustainable": see Commission, "Sustainable agriculture in the EU" <https://ec.europa.eu/info/food-farming-fisheries/sustainability_en> accessed 29 January 2021. And the Commission aims to further reinforce such aims as part of the upcoming CAP reforms: see Commission, "Future of the common agricultural policy", section on "Higher green ambitions" <https://ec.europa.eu/info/food-farming-fisheries/key-policies/common-agricultural-policy/future-cap_en> accessed 29 January 2021.

21 "How to help farmers deal with risks and crises" (23 October 2020) -to-help-farmers-deal-with-risks-and-crises>.

22 See, e.g., the joint statement issued by the European Competition Network, <https://ec.europa.eu/competition/ecn/202003_jointstatement_ecn_corona-crisis.pdf>; the UK's exemption of certain types of collaboration among food retailers, suppliers and logistics providers, <www.legislation.gov.uk/uksi/2020/369/

This echoes the "availability of supplies" CAP objective, and the same logic should also justify a more permanent adjustment of competition policy to accommodate the environmental and social risks outlined in section I. After all, even if these dangers seem less tangible and immediate than those created by the global pandemic, their potential consequences threaten to be even more lasting and harmful.[23]

In short: when companies are having to reconcile short-term economic drivers with the need to future-proof their business models, and consumers are adapting their purchasing behaviour to support environmental and social causes, it is no longer viable for authorities to omit sustainability-related impacts from the scope of competition policy on the basis that they are too remote, irrelevant or difficult to assess.

3. Practical implications

How would this new approach contribute to progress in real terms? Put simply, it would enable competition policy to reinforce and accelerate sustainability goals by ensuring that, within its jurisdiction, businesses are not unduly deterred from engaging in activities that genuinely enhance sustainability.

Within the competition community, much of the debate concerning the relationship between sustainability and competition law has focused to date on whether competition policy and enforcement in their present form unduly inhibit sustainability-enhancing collaborations between competitors. The level of priority given to this question by many advocates implies that such risk does indeed exist, and that its removal would represent the most significant contribution that competition policy could make to advancing the sustainability agenda.

While companies can and do achieve some meaningful sustainability goals by acting alone, more deep-rooted structural issues inevitably require partnerships and collective action involving a wide range of stakeholders. For food companies, this may mean engaging with the likes of government agencies, NGOs, researchers, healthcare professionals, farmers, suppliers, retailers and/or peer companies.

Companies should not, and typically do not, see competition law as an insurmountable barrier to entering into sustainability collaborations with non-competitors: for example, in order to tackle issues that are linked to more than one level of the supply chain,[24] or are common to different product markets and/or industry sectors.

However, companies are understandably more cautious when it comes to engaging with a competitor, given that the potential financial and reputational consequences

---

made/data.pdf>; and Italy's increased flexibility towards the agri-food sector, <www.agcm.it/dotcmsdoc/allegati-news/Testo%20Comunicazione%20cooperazione%20e%20COVID-19.pdf>.

23   Indeed, the EU Parliament has already declared a climate and environmental "emergency": see "The European Parliament declares climate emergency" (29 November 2019) <www.europarl.europa.eu/news/en/press-room/20191121IPR67110/the-european-parliament-declaresclimate-emergency>.

24   If suppliers or customers of the company are involved, standard precautions related to vertical restraints (e.g. resale price maintenance) should of course be followed.

of being sanctioned for a competition law violation could very well outweigh the expected benefits of the initiative itself, and even jeopardise the company's entire sustainability programme. This is where competition policymakers, enforcers and advisers need to help.

From a practical perspective, collaboration with competitors may be indispensable to identifying and implementing some of the more ambitious, game-changing ideas that would otherwise take longer to achieve or never even materialise.[25] In those scenarios, companies are unable individually to make the necessary or desired impact, regardless of their genuine interest in (and commitment to) reaching the goal in question. Collaboration could, for example, be required in order to:

- Pool technical research, knowhow and expertise;

- Share otherwise prohibitive upfront investment costs;

- Achieve the required level of scale or market-wide adoption;

- Overcome a potential "first mover disadvantage"; and/or

- Enable and empower a critical mass of consumers to make more informed and sustainable choices – e.g., through education and enhanced supply chain transparency.[26]

In many instances, the sustainability objectives pursued through competitor collaboration would not entail any restriction of competition at all, in which case competition law should have no say in the matter whatsoever, and companies should be made to feel comfortable about proceeding with the initiative.

There may also be situations where the collaboration brings about economies of scale or scope which ultimately lead to lower prices; or where it can readily be demonstrated that consumers are willing to pay for the more expensive sustainability feature(s) in question.[27] Again, competition law should allow such initiatives to pass as a matter of course.

---

25 When surveyed, 93% of company sustainability leaders said that collaboration with peers is key to achieve progress on sustainability goals: Linklaters, "Competition law needs to cooperate: companies want clarity to enable climate change initiatives to be pursued" (April 2020) <https://lpscdn.linklaters. com/-/media/files/document-store/pdf/uk/2020/april/linklaters_competition-law-needs-to-cooperate_april-2020.ashx?rev=2c2c8c7d-91a8-496f-99fb-92a799c55cb2&extension=pdf&hash=6641BEDB36EC877 CA43C7D995BD6EEDA>.

26 Illustrative examples of actual and potential areas of competitor collaboration in the food sector can be found at <www.fooddrinkeurope.eu/publication/green-deal-and-competition-policy/> and <https:// sustainability.freshfields.com/post/102gkqb/competition-policy-and-the-eu-green-deal-freshfields-responds-to-the-commission>.

27 In practice, attempts to quantify consumers' willingness to pay for a given product or feature can be challenging to carry out, and laden with uncertainty. Therefore, this option might be of limited practical benefit and application, especially for companies seeking to conduct an *ex ante* competition law self-assessment.

In all other cases, for the reasons described above, competition law should systematically allow for (even require) any potential adverse effects on consumers to be balanced against – and, in appropriate cases, overridden by – the expected sustainability benefits, without the need for a full-blown economic impact assessment.[28]

Unfortunately, though, the impression that the current law excludes such a balancing exercise is stifling such initiatives from the very outset, and presents a significant (and unnecessarily rigid) obstacle to the realisation of sustainable practices that can only be unlocked through competitor collaboration.[29] By lowering this obstacle, competition policy could help pave the way for a much larger number of businesses to join forces in more impactful ways, thereby triggering tipping points that will lead to decisive systemic changes.

For as long as food companies lack the necessary reassurance that *bona fide* sustainability benefits will be viewed positively, the spectre of competition law sanctions (plus the associated reputational risks) will continue to have a chilling effect on their appetite to pursue them, and impede the sector's much-needed progression towards those goals.

Accordingly, more guidelines from competition authorities are urgently required in this area. It is hoped that these will begin to emerge from the European Commission during 2021, and that they will be sufficiently detailed and concrete to enable companies to take practical decisions in respect of real-life solutions.[30]

Ultimately, similar clarifications will also be needed from authorities beyond Europe, given the ubiquity of competition laws today and the international footprint of the most far-reaching sustainability initiatives. The fact that so many competition regimes recognise and apply the notion of "consumer welfare" should help to facilitate the adoption of similar, if not fully harmonised, approaches around the world.[31]

Naturally, this call for a more holistic and nuanced approach to such forms of competitor collaboration presupposes that they pursue genuine sustainability objectives, and that their scope remains within those bounds. It is clear that

---

28 Dolmans (n 16) and Holmes (n 16) make persuasive cases that the existing EU legislation and jurisprudence relating to agreements between competitors are perfectly capable of being read and applied in a way that enables environmental and climate benefits to be factored in.

29 When surveyed, 57% of company sustainability leaders said there were concrete examples of sustainability projects that they have not pursued because the legal risk was too high (Linklaters, n 23). See also Sophie Long, "Competition Law and Sustainability: A Study of Industry Attitudes Towards Multi-Stakeholder Collaboration in the UK Grocery Sector" (Fair Trade Foundation 2019) <www.fairtrade.org.uk/wp-content/uploads/legacy/Competition-Law-and-Sustainability---Fairtrade-Report.pdf>.

30 The Commission is expected to issue such guidelines following its public consultation on Competition Policy and the Green Deal <https://ec.europa.eu/competition/information/green_deal/index_en.html>, and in the context of its revised EU competition rules on horizontal agreements between companies.

31 See ICN (n 15).

sustainability can never be used as a smokescreen or defence for what would otherwise qualify as hardcore cartel behaviour.

IV. The Role of In-House Counsel

As frontline advisers to the executive committee, sustainability officer and business teams, in-house counsel can influence how bold or cautious a company is when defining its overall sustainability strategy or deciding whether to proceed with a particular initiative.

Even in cases where external advice is sought, it is in-house counsel who must ultimately interpret the level of potential legal exposure by reference to the commercial context, and help calibrate it against the company's values and longer-term business priorities. This is where in-house counsel must overcome any tendency towards risk-aversion, and embrace the opportunity to act as an accelerator, rather than an inhibitor, of sustainability goals.

Moreover, even after competition authorities have provided the additional guidelines called for in this area, novel scenarios will continue to arise in practice. It is hoped that authorities will be open to providing companies with bespoke guidance in such circumstances – however, it will not be feasible to take up that option in every situation, so companies will still have to conduct their own self-assessments more often than not.

Accordingly, in-house counsel will almost certainly have to continue making finely balanced judgment calls on a case-by-case basis. But this is nothing new. Operating in legal "grey zones", and taking decisions based on incomplete information, are an integral part of every in-house counsel's daily skillset – and, when it comes to matters involving sustainability improvements, excessive conservatism should be resisted.

More generally, modern in-house legal functions are increasingly expected not only to provide technical legal expertise, but also to contribute to the development and fulfilment of a company's broader corporate social responsibilities, and ultimately its sustainable economic growth (while, of course, remaining objective and independent). This shift of emphasis further reinforces the need for in-house counsel to give due weight to the targeted environmental and social benefits of each initiative, and to facilitate their progress to the maximum extent possible.

To that end, it is worth keeping in mind that the outcome when assessing any individual sustainability proposal need not be a binary "yes" or "no". Rather, in-house counsel armed with a close understanding of the business and industry can, where necessary, help to identify creative and pragmatic solutions that allow an initiative to move forward in alternative ways that pursue the same underlying sustainability objectives.

Of course, none of this means that in-house counsel should throw caution entirely to the wind. In practical terms, certain minimum principles and safeguards should always be followed in order to secure an appropriate level of governance, including:

–   Ensure the legal team is involved as early as possible in the design phase of a new sustainability strategy or project.

–   Verify, document and (if possible) quantify the sustainability objectives and consumer benefits behind each initiative, and record why the proposed form of action is necessary to achieve them.

–   Ensure that all participants are trained on the relevant competition law boundaries and commit to respecting them.

–   Avoid any adverse spillover effects, by ensuring that all activities undertaken in connection with the initiative remain strictly limited (in scope and in time) to its legitimate sustainability purpose.

–   If potentially sensitive information needs to be exchanged with other companies, especially competitors, implement a robust "clean room" process under the control of an independent (and duly qualified) third party.

V. Conclusions and Call to Action

The future of our planet, health and collective wellbeing is intrinsically linked to the sustainability of the global food system.

Food companies can – and must – play a leading role in transitioning the sector to a sustainable operating model, but they cannot achieve this on their own. Rather, a coordinated, multilateral approach is required, involving private and public sector actors alike.

While competition law is not the only (or even the most powerful) mode of state intervention in the quest for sustainability, every contribution counts.[32] Accordingly, sustainability considerations must become fully integrated into the fabric of competition assessments, alongside the other recognised parameters of consumer welfare. This requires a deliberate change of mindset and a new approach.

More specifically, it is critical that competition authorities interpret and apply competition law in a way that facilitates, rather than impedes, sustainability-enhancing business initiatives whenever possible, while of course continuing to give due protection to other elements of consumer welfare. At the same time,

---

32 For a broader assessment of the governance and policy reforms required to build sustainable food systems in Europe, see Olivier De Schutter, "Towards a Common Food Policy for the European Union" (IPES-Food 2019) <www.ipes-food.org/_img/upload/files/CFP_FullReport.pdf>.

in-house counsel must become adept at evaluating competition law risks in a purposeful way that empowers companies to pursue high-impact sustainability goals.

These demands may be challenging and require difficult judgments to be made. But they also provide hope. If the right balance is struck, competition policy can enhance and accelerate the food sector's transformation, thereby enabling food to fulfil its potential as "the single strongest lever to optimize human health and environmental sustainability on Earth".[33]

While the path to a sustainable future is a testing one, it is essential that all stakeholders in the food sector and the competition community rise to this challenge. The stakes are high, and it is time to act.

---

33   EAT-Lancet Commission (n 1), p 5.

An Environmentally and Socially Broken Global Food System: What Role For Competition Law?

Claudio Lombardi and Tomaso Ferrando[*]

KIMEP University | University of Antwerp

The contemporary food system represents one of the biggest obstacles between countries and the achievement of the Sustainable Development Goals, the Paris Agreement and the content of international and regional human rights obligations.[1] In a nutshell, the conventional food system appears incapable of achieving the fundamental purpose of any food system: protecting, respecting and fulfilling everyone's right to food by guaranteeing access to healthy, culturally appropriate, adequate and affordable food, while regenerating the planet and preserving it for the future generations.[2] If the goal is socio-environmental sustainability, the European food system is not an exception in departing from it: multiple challenges must be quickly addressed.

All over the world, increasing numbers of people are facing hunger, food insecurity, undernutrition and malnourishment.[3] The European Union is not an exception when it comes to hunger and malnourishment. Even before the

* Claudio Lombardi is an assistant professor, School of Law, KIMEP University and director of the Eurasian Centre for Law, Innovation, and Development at KIMEP University. Tomaso Ferrando is a research professor, Faculty of Law (Law and Development Research Group) and Institute of Development Policy, University of Antwerp.
1 Commission, "A Farm to Fork Strategy for a fair, health and environmentally-friendly food system" (Communication) COM/2020/381 final. See also Michael A Clark and others, "Global food system emissions could preclude achieving the 1.5° and 2°C climate change targets" (2020) 370 (6517) Science 705.
2 Olivier De Schutter, "Final report: The transformative potential of the right to food" A/HRC/25/57 (UN Human Rights Council, 24 May 2014).
3 Food and Agriculture Organization, *The State of Food Security and Nutrition in the World* (FAO 2020).

COVID-19 pandemic, 33 million people in the EU could not afford a quality meal every second day and depended on state assistance and private charity to satisfy their basic human right to food.[4] Moreover, over 950,000 deaths in 2017 (one in five) were attributable to unhealthy diets, mainly cardiovascular diseases and cancers.

Concentration and uneven distribution of power along the food chains are also crucial to the social unsustainability of the EU food system.[5] To give an example, although there are around 11 million farms in the EU, there are only 300,000 enterprises in the food and drink industry, which sell their products through the 2.8 million enterprises within the food distribution and foodservice industry, delivering food to the EU's 500 million consumers.[6] Even more importantly, the C5 concentration ratio widely varies across these industries, with the trading and retail sectors being of particular concern.[7]

Social fragility is not all. The production, distribution and waste of food account for over a quarter (26%) of global greenhouse gas emissions, mostly due to deforestation, land-use changes, livestock breeding, and the intense use of oil-based products (fertilisers, pesticides, gasoline, diesel, etc.).[8] At EU level, the "manufacturing, processing, retailing, packaging and transportation of food make a major contribution to air, soil and water pollution and GHG emissions and profoundly impact biodiversity."[9] For the European Commission, "food systems remain one of the key drivers of climate change and environmental degradation".[10]

Competition law, as we discuss in this paper, is gaining ground as a possible tool to address some of the issues that we have just mentioned: however, the focus on improving and adapting existing tools must go hand-in-hand with a reconsideration of the role of market-based mechanisms and the principles of competitiveness when it comes to adequately feeding people and regenerating the planet. The Farm to Fork Strategy (F2F), a vision for the future of the EU food system, represents a clear example of this renewed interest in the construction of the food market and – to a certain extent – competition law. Besides, other

---

4   Commission, "Farm to Fork Strategy" (n 1).
5   DG Agriculture and Rural Development, "The Food Supply Chain" (2017) <https://ec.europa.eu/info/sites/info/files/food-farming-fisheries/farming/documents/food-supply-chain_en.pdf>.
6   ibid.
7   ibid, see also Jennifer Clapp, "Mega-Mergers on the Menu: Corporate Concentration and the Politics of Sustainability in the Global Food System" (2018) 18 Global Environmental Politics 12 and, with regard to farmer's income ratio, EU Agridata, CAP Context indicator C.26 on Agricultural entrepreneurial income (2017) <https://agridata.ec.europa.eu/Qlik_Downloads/Jobs-Growth-sources.htm> accessed 13 November 2020.
8   Hannah Ritchie, "Food production is responsible for one-quarter of the world's greenhouse gas emissions" (*Our World in Data*, Oxford Martin School 2019) <https://ourworldindata.org/food-ghg-emissions> accessed 19 November 2020.
9   Commission, "Farm to Fork Strategy" (n 1).
10   ibid.

debates are unfolding that try to adapt and use competition law to achieve higher levels of (mainly environmental) sustainability in the food system and that need to be assessed in their logic, implementation and consequences.

I. Main EU Debates on Competition, Food Chains and Socio-Environmental Sustainability

Any consideration of the link between competition law and the EU agricultural sector must be based on the recognition that special treatment reserved by the EU legislator through Articles 39 and 42 of the Treaty on the Functioning of the European Union (TFEU). Article 42 TFEU allows to introduce special competition rules for agricultural products to pursue the Common Agricultural Policy (CAP) objectives of Article 39 TFEU,[11] namely increasing agricultural productivity, ensuring a fair standard of living for agricultural communities, stabilising markets, assuring supplies and ensuring reasonable prices for the consumer. Regulations 1308/2013[12] and 2017/2393[13] on competition in the agricultural sector also give a central role to social and environmental concerns.

Along with the TFEU, a wide body of sectoral policies and regulations define the European attitude towards the food system. In the context of fragmented interventions that look at specific aspects of the food system, the recently approved F2F represents a first attempt by the European Commission to adopt a holistic approach to the relationship between public authorities, the private sector and the multi-faceted nature of the food system (health, sustainability, fairness, accessibility, etc.). Inspired by the EU Green Deal of December 2019,[14] the F2F is based on the recognition that the EU food system represents both a threat and an opportunity in the fight against climate change and in the creation of a society that is socially and environmentally sustainable.

The F2F contains few references to the use of regulation to improve the competitiveness of food markets, including through the use of geographical

---

11 A new CAP regulation was proposed by the Commission on 1 June 2018, but it still needs approval.

12 Regulation (EU) 1308/2013 establishing a common organisation of the markets in agricultural products and repealing Council Regulations (EEC) 922/72, (EEC) 234/79, (EC) 1037/2001 and (EC) 1234/2007 (CMO Regulation) [2013] OJ L347/671. Articles 206 and following include detailed competition law provisions applicable to the agri-food markets.

13 Regulation (EU) 2017/2393 amending Regulations (EU) 1305/2013 on support for rural development by the European Agricultural Fund for Rural Development (EAFRD), (EU) 1306/2013 on the financing, management and monitoring of the common agricultural policy, (EU) 1307/2013 establishing rules for direct payments to farmers under support schemes within the framework of the common agricultural policy, (EU) 1308/2013 establishing a common organisation of the markets in agricultural products and (EU) 652/2014 laying down provisions for the management of expenditure relating to the food chain, animal health and animal welfare, and relating to plant health and plant reproductive material [2017] OJ L350/15.

14 Commission, "The European Green Deal" (Communication) COM(2019) 640 final.

indications, the redress of unfair trading practices and the subordination of competition law to the purposes and objectives of the CAP. However, the F2F does not represent the entirety of the debate that is currently taking place in the European context with regard to the changes that competition law should go through in order to foster sustainability.[15] In this section, we consider the 2019 Directive on unfair trading practices in business-to-business relationships in the agricultural and food supply chain (UTP Directive)[16] as one of the main regulatory interventions discussed by the F2F, then continue with a reference to other ongoing debates at EU level concerning sustainability and food systems.

1. The 2019 UTP Directive

The UTP Directive originated from the recognition that power imbalances between the actors of the food system lead, in almost 90% of the cases where they take place, to forms of unfair commercial treatment that have both social and environmental implications.[17] Although the UTP Directive "is not meant as a competition law amendment and does not make reference to the Commission's practice or EU acquis in the area of vertical restraints",[18] it may still have a significant impact on the way in which food chains are organised and on issues of economic dependence, superior bargaining power and buyer power.

The UTP Directive is based on the assumption that a difference in annual turnover easily translates into uneven bargaining power "likely to lead to unfair trading practices when larger and more powerful trading partners seek to impose certain practices or contractual arrangements which are to their advantage in relation to a sales transaction."[19] It starts therefore from the recognition of the unequal structure of the EU food system (including in its international components) and the negative consequences that it generates in terms of distribution of value, and conceives as a solution some new legal tools and judicial spaces to be leveraged by parties on the receiving side of unfair practices and contractual clauses.

The UTP Directive crystallises the fact that imbalanced commercial relationships in the agri-food system – even in the absence of dominant position – unequally impact smaller players, creating financial insecurity, loss of livelihood and poverty among suppliers, and represent an incentive towards cutting the costs of production, which is then detrimental for labour rights, food safety and environmental protections. Therefore, special protection must be provided by

---

15 Kate Raworth, *Doughnut Economics* (Random House 2017).
16 Directive (EU) 2019/633 on unfair trading practices in business-to-business relationships in the agricultural and food supply chain (UTP Directive) [2019] OJ L111/59.
17 ibid.
18 Victoria Daskalova, "The New Directive on Unfair Trading Practices in Food and EU Competition Law: Complementary or Divergent Normative Frameworks?" (2019) 10(5) JECL & Pract 281, 281.
19 UTP Directive, preamble.

Member States to prevent and sanction unfair trading practices, including by establishing a system of "Complaint and Confidentiality"[20] that protects the identity and the information of the complainants effectively, so that they can access enforcement authorities without fearing retaliation.[21]

The transformative capacity of the UTP Directive will depend on the way in which Member States implement it (by 1 May 2021), especially given that the Directive recognises that Member States can go beyond the minimum threshold of the UTP Directive in defining the list of unfair practices and establishing enforcement bodies with the power to initiate investigations, take decisions finding an infringement of the prohibitions contained, and impose or initiate proceedings for the imposition of fines and other equally effective penalties.[22]

Decisions made at Member State level could thus lead to very different trajectories and this regulatory space will need to be closely studied in the coming months. A successful implementation of the UTP Directive in favour of the victims of power imbalances and the environment may also trigger consideration of expanding its scope beyond the food and agriculture market. For example, national legislators could decide to sanction larger economic entities that pay prices below those that guarantee living income/wages, or the practice of dumping on smaller producers the full cost of improving sustainability practice standards.

The risk is that national regulations do not provide the UTP Directive with adequate teeth and therefore prevent the Commission's attempt to rebalance the food and agricultural chains that are entangled with high levels of uneven bargaining power, economic dependence, monopsony and oligopoly. In this sense, the space that the UTP Directive received in the F2F shall act as a nudge for Member States to be on the front line of the enforcement machine but also implement mechanisms for grievance and redress that recognise the financial and personal risks that small players face when they denounce unfair conduct and stand up to European retailers and the multi-billion-euro food industry.

2. Unsustainable anticompetitive practices and abuses of power

The previous section has considered certain aspects of the UTP Directive dealing with abuses of situational or relational superior bargaining power that, on analysis of the market share, are independent. However, when a party has market-wide or structural dominance, similar actions (e.g. abuse of dominant position)

---

20 UTP Directve, Article 5.
21 For the impact of the "fear factor" in B2B relationships in the food sector see Aneta Wiewiórowska – Domagalska, "Unfair Trading Practices in the Business-to-Business Food Supply Chain" PE 563.430 3 (European Parliament briefing, July 2015).
22 UTP Directive, art 6.

may fall within the competition law sphere.[23] Articles 101 and 102 TFEU have generally been used to punish anticompetitive conduct leading to economic exploitation or exclusion of competitors. However, a number of potentially anticompetitive practices may cause harms that are not expressed in price terms. Both abuses of dominant position and self-regulation of industry groups were the structural reasons underlying the worsening of food quality or the deterioration of the environmental sustainability of the food chain in several documented cases,[24] often facilitated by high level of concentration at processing and retailing level of the value chain.[25]

Article 102 TFEU is of relevance here, as it may give a basis for enforcing competition law in a way that punishes, prevents and deters anticompetitive conduct on the basis of negative environmental or social impact. As discussed above, although the UTP Directive directly tackles issues of unfair use of power imbalance, it has a different premise from Article 102 TFEU. It is thus important to recognise the role that the latter has to play in the construction of a socially and environmentally sustainable food system beyond the narrow content of the UTP Directive and how Members States will implement it.

This is particularly the case with regard to exploitative abuse that takes the form of excessive pricing. Although accepted in principle as a potential competition law violation under EU law,[26] excessive pricing is not a competition law infringement in all jurisdictions of the world. EU law considers this and similar abusive conduct as a violation of Article 102(1)(a) TFEU, whereby it is forbidden for a dominant undertaking to impose unfair purchase or selling prices or other unfair trading conditions.

Unfair conditions that fall under the scope of Article 102 TFEU can also consider the exercise of buyer power vis-à-vis a supplier (e.g. farmers) that is pressured to accept excessively low prices or other unfair trading conditions. In this regard,

---

23   For the difference between situational and structural dominance and its critique in the EU, see Michael J Trebilcock, *The Limits of Freedom of Contract* (Harvard University Press 1993), 94; Michael J Trebilcock, "The Doctrine of Inequality of Bargaining Power: Post-Benthamite Economics in the House of Lords" (1976) 26 U Toronto LJ 359; Ioannis Lianos, Claudio Lombardi and Justin Lindeboom, "Superior Bargaining Power and the Boundaries of Competition Law" in Ioannis Lianos, *Global Food Value Chains and Competition Law* (BRICS Draft Report 2017) <https://ssrn.com/abstract=3076160>.

24   Matthew Warning and Nigel Key, "The Social Performance and Distributional Consequences of Contract Farming: An Equilibrium Analysis of the *Arachide de Bouche* Program in Senegal" (2002) 30(2) World Development 255; Catherine Dolan and John Humphrey, "Governance and Trade in Fresh Vegetables: The Impact of UK Supermarkets on the African Horticulture Industry" (2000) 37 J Dev Stud 147; Thomas Reardon and others, "The Rise of Supermarkets in Africa, Asia, and Latin America" (2003) 85(5) American Journal of Agricultural Economics 1140.

25   Olivier De Schutter, "Addressing Concentration in Food Supply Chains" (UN Briefing Note 3, December 2010).

26   See, for example, Case 26/75 *General Motors Continental NV v Commission* [1975] ECR 1367; Case 27/76 *United Brands v Commission* [1978] ECR 207; *Deutsche Post AG* (COMP/C-1/36.915) Commission decision C(2001) 1934 [2001] OJ L331/40; *BHB Enterprises plc v Victor Chandler (International) Ltd* [2005] EWHC 1074 (Ch).

Article 39 TFEU and the CAP state that the EU should ensure a fair standard of living for the agricultural community. Simon Holmes suggests that "a purchase price is potentially 'unfair', and therefore potentially an 'abuse' if: a. it does not cover the true costs of production; or b. does not enable the farmer to make some reasonable mark-up (to feed his/her family and produce food on a sustainable basis)."[27] In this vein, the imposition of unconscionable contract terms that lead to the further deterioration of farmers' living standards may be caught by competition laws.

Vertical agreements, such as those between buyers and suppliers, may be also subject to the application of Article 101 TFEU when they do not imply a clear abuse of dominance. Weaker parties may conclude unfavourable contracts or acquiesce to unilateral conducts detrimental to them or their interests. Here, Article 101 TFEU may still apply if the Commission proves that such acquiescence might be based on cooperation or coercion.[28] For the purposes of this prohibition, the degree of market power required is less than the degree of market power required for a finding of dominance under Article 102 TFEU,[29] thus offering an additional basis for cases where the relational abuse of power is clear but dominance is disputed.

The primary function of Article 101 TFEU is to punish and deter horizontal cartels. Consideration should be given to collusions preventing or limiting the adoption of sustainable industry models. While there has been enforcement in this sense,[30] more emphasis should be given to sustainability factors in prioritising and deciding antitrust cases under Articles 101 and 102 TFEU.[31] As we discuss in the next section, Article 101 is increasingly considered not as a sanctioning tool but rather as an opportunity to carve out justifications to horizontal cooperation.

3. Horizontal cooperation for sustainability

We have mentioned that Articles 39 and 42 TFEU provide a potential safe harbour for cooperation between small-scale producers. When a practice, although potentially anticompetitive, is necessary for farmers to achieve the objectives assigned to them under EU law, this may escape the prohibition in Article 101 TFEU.[32] Allowing coordination among farmers is usually aimed at

---

27 Simon Holmes, "Climate Change, Sustainability, and Competition Law" (2020) 8(2)JAE 384.
28 Commission, "Guidelines on Vertical Restraints" SEC(2010) 413 [2010] OJ C130/1, [25].
29 ibid., [97].
30 An example would be the car emissions scandal concerning the collusion between three car manufacturers, BMW, Daimler and VW, on the development and adoption of technology to clean the emissions of petrol and diesel passenger cars, *see Car Emissions* (AT.40178), Commission, "Antitrust: Commission sends Statement of Objections to BMW, Daimler and VW for restricting competition on emission cleaning technology" Press release (IP/19/2008, 5 April 2019) <https://ec.europa.eu/commission/presscorner/detail/en/IP_19_2008>.
31 We acknowledge that more should be said about this but this paper does not allow for a deeper analysis.
32 See also Case C–671/15 *President of the Autorité de la concurrence v Association des producteurs vendeurs d'endives (APVE) and others* EU:C:2017:860; Anne-Sophie Choné-Grimaldi, "Common

creating countervailing power in the chain. However, this has rarely achieved the desired effect, with farmers usually getting the short straw in negotiations.[33]

Other industry stakeholders, in particular processors and retailers, have recently lamented the fact that cooperation to achieve higher and more sustainable standards is prevented by the application of competition laws.[34] In their opinion, competition law deters virtuous collaboration aiming at improving the sustainability of the food value chain by not allowing them to overcome the "first-mover disadvantage" and the financial burden associated with it. The crux of the matter would be the interpretation of Article 101(3) TFEU in a way that accommodates cooperation among industry stakeholders.

However, as seen before, EU laws encourage sustainable cooperation, but mainly among small-scale agricultural producers.[35] Moreover, the current approach to Article 101(3) TFEU, which considers almost exclusively economic efficiencies created by an agreement, generates several shortcomings from the perspective of recognising and respecting the socio-environmental needs of a truly sustainable world. Firstly, everything must be "commodified" in order to be visible to competition authorities. Negative externalities on, for instance, food quality, the environment, human rights and labour conditions have to be measured economically and accounted for, a process that it is inherently limited and reductionist.[36]

Secondly, this interpretation of Article 101(3) TFEU falls in the trap of a consumer-based vision of socio-environmental considerations, and subordinates the achievement of public goals with the benefit that is experienced by those consumers that are directly or indirectly affected by the agreement or anticompetitive practice. According to the Commission guidelines on Article 101, "The concept of 'fair share' implies that the pass-on of benefits must at least compensate consumers for any actual or likely negative impact caused to them by the restriction of competition found under Article [101](1)."[37]

Another element to consider is that collaboration among dominant industry stakeholders may easily transform into a form of self-regulation applicable to

---

market organization: In a preliminary ruling requested by the French Cour de cassation, the Court of justice clarifies the interplay between the EU rules applying to the agriculture sector and the various derogations to Article 101, §1 TFEU (*Association des producteurs vendeurs d'endives*) (2017) Concurrences N° 1–2018 Art N° 85799, 71–74.

33 See Regulation 2019/633 (n 16), recital 1 and ff.

34 Tomaso Ferrando and Claudio Lombardi, *EU Competition Law and Sustainability in Food Systems: Addressing the Broken Links* (FTAO 2019).

35 See Commission, "Staff Working Document Impact Assessment accompanying the proposal for a CAP Regulation" SWD/2018/301 final – 2018/0216 (COD).

36 Even the most progressive works suffer from this shortcoming, such as the Dutch ACM, "Draft Guidelines: Sustainability Agreements" (9 July 2020) <www.acm.nl/en/publications/draft-guidelines-sustainability-agreements>. For a critique outside competition law, see Davide Cerrato and Tomaso Ferrando, "The Financialization of Civil Society Activism: Sustainable Finance, Non-Financial Disclosure and the Shrinking Space for Engagement" (2020) 10(2) Accounting, Economics, and Law: A Convivium.

37 Commission, "Guidelines on the application of Article 101(3) TFEU" [2004] OJ C101/97, [85].

the whole industry sector. Moreover, it would be essential for the legislator and the judiciary to avoid that industry's requests for more horizontal cooperation justified by the desire to internalise only those externalities that are significant and/or materially relevant to their businesses: what about all those social and environmental externalities whose internalisation is not needed in order to guarantee the long-term financial sustainability of the business?

Additionally, Article 101(3) TFEU refers only to efficiencies created within a specific market, in the EU, where the anticompetitive distortion takes place. Hence, improvements in connected markets, perhaps even outside the EU, would not count for Article 101(3) purposes. However, even this more limited interpretation of Article 101(3) would permit consideration of environmental damages, as they have direct welfare-reducing effects that would impact all consumers, present and future. On the other hand, social concerns generally apply to a smaller fraction of society (e.g. specific groups of farmers or workers), so are more difficult to fit within Article 101(3) TFEU.

Although more leeway for food industries would be possible in theory, an interpretation of competition law coherent with the rest of the regulatory environment should discourage the concession of an Article 101(3) justification to non-small-scale farmers, if not necessary and proportional to the actual or potential competitive harm.

In addition, it must be noticed that objectives similar to those that some want to achieve through an expanded interpretation of Article 101(3) could be better obtained by an ad hoc judicial application of public interest concerns.[38] In particular, judges and administrative authorities, depending on the type and extent of their jurisdiction, may have the power to balance between conflicting public policy concerns, particularly on constitutional grounds.[39]

Finally, if industry truly considers sustainability, climate change and the respect of human rights as the "right thing to do" and an inevitable step towards long-term sustainability of their businesses, should enterprises not take advantage of being the first to go in the right direction, rather than waiting and losing their competitive advantage?

II. Systemic and Broader Engagement

Food systems entail the direct interaction of human labour, the ecosystem and access to food as an essential human right. In this vein, an unsustainable business practice and an imbalance distribution of power along the food chain may not

---

38 Christopher Townley, *Article 81 EC and Public Policy* (Bloomsbury 2009); Julian Nowag, *Environmental Integration in Competition and Free-Movement Laws* (OUP 2016).
39 Giovanni Pitruzzella, "Diritto Costituzionale e Diritto Della Concorrenza: C'è Dell'altro Oltre l'efficienza Economica?" (2019) 3 Quaderni costituzionali 597.

only have a negative impact on agricultural communities (e.g. infringing labour and constitutional rights) and on the environment (e.g. by reducing the quality of environmental industry standards), but also on society at a large and satisfaction of its basic needs.

In the EU, food chains have historically benefited from a number of specific actions providing guidance on the level of compromise between competition and socio-environmental sustainability, especially when they have a distributive impact and reinforce the position of smaller players. At the same time, the F2F suggests the adoption of a mix of public and private interventions aimed at developing food chains that are competitive while guaranteeing sustainability, healthy products and fair conditions of work and access to food.

In this regard, competition authorities should apply competition law in accordance with the overall EU regulatory framework. A first step would be to interpret competition law in the broader context of human rights and environmental obligations contained in the European Treaties, the international obligations assumed by the EU, and EU industry-specific laws. This would not only allow judges and administrative authorities to go beyond the mere economisation of individual interests, but it would also ensure a more uniform and coherent application of EU law.

Given the limitations of the current competition toolkit, it would be useful to create wider and shared competencies between administrative authorities. For example, the new competition tool[40] proposed by the Commission could be extended to include food markets. Moreover, infringements having a negative impact on the environment may be subject to supervision by the environmental authority, which could be vested with limited competition law powers.[41] In addition, behavioural remedies and commitments might be based on an industry code of practice. With specific regard to the negotiation of prices with farmers, third-party mediation could facilitate the process, while an independent institution could monitor the effective implementation of the agreements.[42]

In the long-run, however, issues are deeper and wider than simply improving enforcement and subordinating competition law to public objectives. For example, the internalisation of sustainability into the competition law realm risks normalising the representation of people and planet as figures, numbers to be accounted for when cost – benefit analyses are conducted. Moreover, without a reconsideration

---

40 Commission, "Single Market – new complementary tool to strengthen competition enforcement" <https://ec.europa.eu/info/law/better-regulation/have-your-say/initiatives/12416-New-competition-tool> accessed 28 January 2020.

41 Constituting a shared-competency competition model.

42 Similarly to what the Australian Competition and Consumer Commission (ACCC) is doing in the media industry: ACCC, "Mandatory News Media Bargaining Code: Concepts Paper" (19 May 2020) <www.accc.gov.au/system/files/ACCC%20-%20Mandatory%20news%20media%20bargaining%20code%20-%20concepts%20paper%20-%2019%20May%202020.pdf>, 7.

of the welfare standard applied, a "sustainable competition law" would subordinate global issues to the purchasing habits of selected groups of individuals, missing out the broader picture of an economy that is not only composed of sellers and buyers (more or less rational). In addition, solutions like an expanded interpretation of Article 101(3) TFEU should not be detached from the need to address the high levels of concentration and the unequal distribution of power across the food chain.

More importantly, the adaptation and enforcement of competition law cannot be separated from the economic and social imbalances that lay beneath the EU food system. Here, competition law should not preserve the very structure of the market that is the cause of the social, environmental and economic unsustainability that the rest of the legal framework attempts to fight.

The Footprint of Competition: Power, Value Distribution and Exploitation in the Food Supply Chain

MICHELLE MEAGHER AND SIMON ROBERTS[*]

University College, London | University of Johannesburg

I. Introduction

Given the essentiality of food to human survival and its cultural, social and political significance, food supply chains are of special importance in relation to the climate change agenda, while food consumption, production and distribution account for a significant proportion of emissions.[1] In addition, the impact of global warming is already being felt by farmers around the world.

---

[*]	Michelle Meagher is a senior policy fellow at the Centre for Law, Economics and Society at UCL. She is an expert in competition law and corporate governance. She has worked as a lawyer in private practice for global law firms (Linklaters LLP, Allen & Overy LLP), national regulators (the Office of Fair Trading in the UK and the Federal Trade Commission in the US) and the International Finance Corporation (World Bank Group). Simon Roberts is a professor of economics at the University of Johannesburg, where he founded the Centre for Competition, Regulation and Economic Development (CCRED). He has been an economics director at the UK Competition and Markets Authority (2019 to 2020) and the Chief Economist and Manager of the Policy & Research Division at the Competition Commission of South Africa from 2006 to 2012. Simon has been closely involved in the development of competition law in South Africa from the establishment of the authorities and has testified as an expert witness in major cases. He has also advised competition authorities, regulators and governments across Southern and East Africa, as well as further afield.
1	The food supply chain is estimated to account for around a quarter of greenhouse gas emissions, see Joseph Poor and Thomas Nemecek, "Reducing food's environmental impacts through producers and consumers" (2018) 360(6392) Science 987.

Within competition law, the changes required have led to an examination of the need for coordinated action and the ways in which competition law is an obstacle to such initiatives, including in this book.[2] Proposals have been made to reinterpret competition rules and widen exemptions in ways that would enable key businesses such as supermarkets and multinational food processing companies to implement sustainability agreements amongst themselves, that might otherwise fall foul of the prohibition on anticompetitive agreements.[3] It is argued that merger review should similarly take into account environmental implications, potentially as a justification for approval of an otherwise anticompetitive merger.

While these are important aspects of the debate, we approach the issue from a somewhat different standpoint in two regards.

First, we take as a starting point the critical need for rapid and radical decarbonisation of the global economy and a systemic rethink of resource use across the planet. This requires an analysis of the resources that are used by and, critically, for consumption in the developed world, and an assessment of the investment needed to adapt production in developing countries. This involves consideration of the geographical footprint of the food supply chain, the challenges of industrialisation and inclusive growth in developing countries, and the role of competition policy in opening up markets to wider participation.

Second, the approaches taken need to be based on an assessment of concentration and market power in food markets. It is evident that concentration is high and has increased at many levels of food production and supply. It is also important to understand how value chains are governed by large and leading companies, and how market power is entrenched and exerted within those chains. The concerns over market power have important implications for the design of any regulatory interventions, including under competition law, which may otherwise have the effect of further entrenching the position of large incumbents.

Each of these premises implies that the sustainability agenda will not be met through the facilitation under competition law of coordination by multinational corporations and, indeed, such coordination may in some cases undermine the changes required. We need a much broader reset.

As part of proposing the basis for such a reset, this paper will explore the two interrelated "footprints" of competition and markets along food supply chains: first, the geographical footprint of the agrifood sector; and, second, the footprint

---

2 Simon Holmes, "Climate change, sustainability and competition law" (2020) 8(2) JAE 354; Autoriteit Consument and Markt, Draft Guidelines: Sustainability Agreements (9 July 2020).
3 Unilever, "Sustainability cooperations between competitors & Art. 101 TFEU" (Submission to DG Comp, 2020) <www.unilever.com/Images/unilever_submission_sustainability_competition_law_tcm244-551751_en.pdf> accessed 14 January 2020.

of relational power within the food supply chain. We then consider how competition law can be strengthened to promote sustainability in light of the current distribution of power and wealth associated with food production.

II. The Geographical Footprint of Consumption and Competition

While obvious, it is nonetheless important to observe that industrialised economies have been built on high levels of past emissions. Today, while many of the most polluting industries have moved to developing countries, the high levels of consumption of the "Global North" include imports from around the world and the high carbon footprint of developing country production is often embedded in the supply chains of multinational corporations.[4] The burning of the Amazon to plant soya beans destined for animal feed for meat production overwhelmingly consumed by relatively wealthy urban consumers is just one example of this dynamic.

The intensification of international competition in fragmented global value chains forces countries to compete to deliver lower-priced products, which promotes short-termism and downward pressure on environmental and labour standards.[5] This is evident within, as well as across, countries as – often immigrant – farm labour is employed under exploitative conditions in industrialised countries as well as in countries from which produce is imported.

The temptation is to now place the burden of decarbonisation (and other changes to resource use) on the current emitters – i.e. developing country producers – through agreements on standards enforced by the leading "socially responsible" producers in value chains. This reflects a number of fundamental failures.

First, it fails to recognise that developing countries are, in the model of the Global North, seeking industrialisation. It also ignores the role that consumption in industrialised countries continues to play in resource-use globally. It is simply not realistic for the Global North to dictate sustainability requirements to the Global South that would require the Global South to forgo economic development. It is imperative that the concerns of developing countries are adequately addressed.

Second, investment in upgraded production capabilities of producers in developing countries is essential for their cooperation. A Green New Deal must be a deal for participants right the way along global value chains, ensuring a fairer

---

4   We use the terms "Global North" and "Global South" as a shorthand for relative privilege, to reflect the fact that inequality within countries mean that there are wealthy elites in developing countries which share more in common in terms of consumption and lifestyle with populations in industralised nations, while there are low income communities in industrialised nations who are in precarious and vulnerable positions.

5   Michelle Meagher, *Competition Is Killing Us* (Penguin Business 2020).

share of returns and the realisation of dynamic improvements – in the form of new business models and technologies consistent with a green transformation of production systems. Many middle-income and developing countries are stuck in a "technology trap" – competing against each other on a price basis – while the value creation from R&D, design and brands is captured by the increasingly concentrated global multinationals.[6]

Third, these changes require pressure by smaller developing-country producers and civil society movements to countervail the power of dominant buyers and to mitigate against the risks of price volatility and oversupply. This underscores the need for cooperation within the supply chain, but at the producer and farmer level, not just at the processor and manufacturer level.

This means that greater participation by developing-country producers, including small farmers, in food value chains is essential, and not only at the concession of multinational corporations. As we have seen in countries such as Brazil, high levels of inequality mean populist agendas backed by big business are attractive to voters. Imposing requirements from above, including through supermarkets and through industrialised-country taxation on imports from developing countries to reflect emissions, will simply exacerbate the sense of unfairness and injustice felt in developing and emerging economies.

III. The Footprint of Power and Governance

To make sense of the geographic footprint of competition, we must understand the footprint of power along value chains and, in particular, the governance of value chains by large and leading companies. We can distinguish between horizontal market power at any given market level and power that coordinates production and establishes rules and norms along multiple levels of value-addition, through varying degrees of vertical integration and differing institutional arrangements.[7]

There are high levels of concentration along food value chains, from seed, fertiliser and other agrochemicals, to processing, trading and retail. In the last two decades, concentration levels have increased, including through mergers of major seed and agrochemicals producers, and of major food product manufacturers.[8] In most countries, a few very large supermarket chains account for the majority of grocery

---

6   Antonio Andreoni and Fiona Tregenna, "Escaping the middle-income technology trap: A comparative analysis of industrial policies in China, Brazil and South Africa" (2020) 54(C) Structural Change and Economic Dynamics 324.

7   Stefano Ponte, *Business Power and Sustainability in a World of Global Value Chains* (Zed Books 2019); Mark P Dallas, Stefano Ponte and Timothy J Sturgeon, "Power in global value chains" (2019) 26(4) Rev Int'l Political Econ 666.

8   IPES-Food "Too big to feed: Exploring the impacts of mega-mergers, concentration, concentration of power in the agri-food sector".(October 2017) <www.ipes-food.org>; Carl Folke and others, "Trans-national corporations and the challenge of biosphere stewardship" (2019) 3 Nature Ecology and Evolution 1396.

sales. This affects the distribution of value in the supply chain, the bargaining position of producers and workers, the nature of production along the chains, and the changing patterns of land use and biodiversity.

Just 100 companies account for over 70% of global emissions.[9] A nexus between market power and unsustainable practices has been observed in EU findings of abuse of dominance by Iacovides and Vrettos, which cuts across sectors, with dominance facilitating the pursuit of firms of unsustainable practices.[10] The issues of market power are core concerns for competition authorities and are central, not peripheral, to sustainability concerns in food supply chains.

Incumbents have a natural incentive to limit the threats to their position through raising rivals' costs and barriers to entry. This can be achieved through:

- Using their dominance (if they are dominant) in traditional ways, which competition law is designed to address;

- The exercise of buyer power, abuse of a superior bargaining power, and unfair competition;[11]

- Seeking to shape private standards and, through lobbying, to influence public regulations and policy in their favour.

The point is that, even while many large incumbents are moving to take sustainability concerns into account in their businesses and along their supply chain, their interest is naturally to do so in ways that bolster their own positions. And, while large incumbents are aggressively marketing themselves in terms of their commitments to environmental, social and governance standards, the expansion of private standards organised by leading firms risks raising obstacles for smaller rivals and imposing the majority of adjustment costs on smaller input suppliers.[12]

The extensive body of research on governance in global value chains emphasises the role that the large and leading international businesses play in appropriating and distributing the value along the chains.[13] Environmental standards set by

---

9 Marios Iacovides, and Chris Vrettos, "Falling Through the Cracks no More? Article 102 TFEU and Sustainability I – the Nexus Between Dominance, Environmental Degradation, and Social Injustice" (25 September 2020) Faculty of Law, Stockholm University Research Paper No 79 <https://ssrn.com/abstract=3699416>, citing Paul Griffin, "The Carbon Majors Database – CDP Carbon Majors Report 2017" (CDP Report, July 2017).
10 Iacovides and Vrettos (n 9).
11 See Ioannis Lianos and Claudio Lombardi, "Superior Bargaining Power and the Global Food Value Chain: the Wuthering Heights of Holistic Competition Law?" ? in Ioannis Lianos, and others, "Competition law and policy and the food value chain" (2016) Concurrences N° 1–2016 Art N° 78014, 22; Tomaso Ferrando and Claudio Lombardi, *EU Competition Law and Sustainability in Food Systems: Addressing the Broken Links* (Fair Trade Advocacy Office, Brussels 2019). However, we note that there are differences in the antitrust community (enforcers and academics) on these issues.
12 See Elizabeth A Bennett, "Who Governs Socially-Oriented Voluntary Sustainability Standards? Not the Producers of Certified Products" (2017) 91(C) World Development 53.
13 Ponte (n 7); Stefano Ponte, Gary Gereffi, Gale Raj-Reichert, "Introduction" in Ponte, Gereffi and Raj-Reichert (eds) *Handbook on Global Value Chains* (Edward Elgar 2019).

multinationals appear to be adding a "sustainability-driven supplier squeeze" on developing country producers.[14] It also reinforces the governance position of these firms over global value chains. Even within the consumer welfare paradigm, the extraction of value by particular firms in the supply chain has implications for productivity and innovation that do not serve consumers, let alone the sectors, producers and countries that are impoverished by the extraction.[15]

The agenda on which we need to engage must therefore start from an understanding of the power of governing companies over the supply chain itself, the economies in which their products are most valued, the politics of those economies, and the societies and people impacted by or embedded within the supply chain. More broadly, we can see this type of power (governance of the supply chains) as the power to skew market outcomes in the lead firm's favour[16] – including the power to control rents in the chain, to undermine actual and potential rivals and to ensure norms and regulations that will bolster its position.

This poses a challenge to competition authorities. On the one hand, they can prioritise exemptions from competition law for large companies that are coordinating activities for the good of the environment. This could be agreements between supermarkets to assist them in making changes to plastic packaging or setting standards relating to carbon emissions by suppliers.[17] On the other hand, as institutions with in-depth knowledge about how markets work in practice, competition authorities can play a crucial role in developing the market-shaping measures that governments must implement to create a sustainable economy. These measures need to ensure that market power is curtailed and dynamic rivalry works to open up markets with opportunities for disruption by innovative smaller rivals and businesses with different ownership models.

The hyper-internationalised organisation of activity, the international scope of the businesses involved, and the pace of change required to address the climate emergency pose a fundamental challenge to a patchwork of national regimes. The agenda for more sustainable market outcomes must therefore be an international one, focused on the positive competition policies required for wider participation and production, organised in more resilient value chains. The adjustments required by climate change cannot be identified as a shopping list of discrete changes. Instead we need to think of the changes in more systemic ways, as a set of rules to reshape markets.

---

14 Ponte (n 7).
15 Ioannis Lianos, "Global Food Value Chains and Competition Law: BRICS Draft Report" (2017) CLES Research Paper series 11/2017, 57.
16 Marshall Steinbaum, Eric Harris Bernstein and John Sturm, "Powerless: Powerless: How Lax Antitrust and Concentrated Market Power Rig the Economy Against American Workers, Consumers, and Communities" (*Roosevelt Institute*, 21 March 2018).
17 Holmes (n 2); Nicole Kar, "Competition rules stymie co-operation on climate goals" *Financial Times* (London, 30 January 2020).

IV. Effective Competition Policy and Law Within a Wider Agenda For Sustainability

Once we recognise the complete footprint of competition – both geographically and in terms of power relations – it is evident that we need to combine competition law and policy, regulation, and appropriate industrial policies in order to open up value chains to wider participation and effective rivalry, while ensuring rapid changes in production systems to reduce emissions. It is not just about enforcing rules but about changing the rules to shape markets such that effective rivalry works towards different (better) outcomes. The market rules should prevent firms from unfairly competing through imposing costs on other parties in supply chains, and by addressing market outcomes that have substantial negative externalities (which are not reflected in prices and the decisions of market participants). Market arrangements involving abuse of dominance, unfair competition and negative externalities can be assessed in static terms, that is, in terms of a given market outcome and set of production choices.

In dynamic terms, we know that we need rapid changes that transform the way production and distribution happen. Investment and innovation are essential, for example, in the adoption of precision farming techniques to reduce the resources used (including fertiliser and water) in production. We know that market prices do not necessarily reflect the societal benefits of the changes required and thus may not set the appropriate incentives. The production changes therefore require industrial and agricultural policies on the part of governments. Many of the changes are cross-border – to reduce the European consumption footprint, farmers in developing countries need to be able invest to change their production methods.

Beyond the internalisation of externalities, a dynamic recalibration of markets along dimensions of future sustainability and in accordance with principles for a just transition to ecosystem resilience must also account for historic harms inflicted by the Global North, both environmental and social, before enjoining all countries to begin to engage in sustainable and just competition going forward.

In this context, enabling cooperative agreements amongst multinational corporations may lead to marginal benefits but also risks perverse outcomes. Nor will it be transformative on the scale that reordering competition and redistributing power within global value chains can be.

The contours of the intersection of power and sustainability are well-understood within civil society that (i) globally powerful transnational firms are able to govern the sustainability of their supply chains and the sustainability of industry as a whole; (ii) sustainability is meaningless without fairness, equality and justice, which are each impacted by the existence of corporate power; and (iii) the distribution of value within and across markets and nations is paramount. The processes to address sustainability must be democratic, with a leadership played by states and multilateral bodies, consulting with stakeholders including leading firms, but not derogating decision-making to them.

It is now becoming better appreciated that competition law has a fundamental role in challenging the power of such firms on the market and within the global value chains that they govern.[18] A failure to do so in the past can be attributed primarily to a historic lack of willingness on the part of the competition community to apply its expertise on these broader issues of corporate power. Work to align competition law with these concepts has just begun.[19]

There are several ways in which competition law enforcement and competition policy can be strengthened as part of a comprehensive sustainability agenda.

i. *Holistic market regulation and sustainability* – sustainability is not a separate agenda from the agenda of competition law, rather both concepts are subsumed within broader notions of making markets work well within planetary boundaries and the ideas of fairness, equality and justice embodied by the UN Sustainable Development Goals and the EU treaties. In short, we must solve for sustainability first and embrace whichever forms of economic organisation and regulation are compatible with a sustainable economy.

ii. *Foregrounding power* – concepts of power have been relatively absent from competition law as there has been an overwhelming focus on power only over price and output. In light of the complex power of multinational firms governing food supply chains, richer concepts of power must be explored within competition, particularly vertical power within integrated or coordinated supply chains[20] and how power is both exercised and entrenched.

iii. *Distribution and exploitation* – the global value chain literature makes clear that within value chains companies compete to extract value from the chain itself, as well as competing with other value chains. Dominant companies within the value chain have (a) the power to inflict costs on other parties within the value chain, on host countries and communities, and on the environmental ecosystem (externalised costs); (b) superior bargaining power, including buyer power to impose low input prices; (c) the power to seek and protect rents through lobbying; and (d) the market power to draw more value into the value chain from consumers

---

18 IPES (n 8); Lianos (n 15); Sophia Murphy, "Concentrated Market Power and Agricultural Trade" (2006) Ecofair Trade Dialogue Discussion Papers 1; Meagher (n 5).

19 See e.g. Ioannis Lianos and Amber Darr, "Hunger Games: Connecting the Right to Food and Competition Law" (2019) CLES Research Paper series 2/2019.

20 Lianos (n 15), 46 *et seq.*; Dallas, Ponte and Sturgeon (n 7); Pamela Mondliwa, Stefano Ponte and Simon Roberts, "Competition and Power in Global Value Chains" (2020) Competition and Change doi:10.1177/1024529420975154.

through raising prices. All these mechanisms for the extraction of value should be relevant to a competition analysis.

Distribution of value throughout the value chain has profound implications for the quality and standard of life of people living and working within those value chains. Exploitative conduct should be taken more seriously by competition authorities, as it has been in the COVID-19 pandemic (such as in tackling price gouging against vulnerable consumers).

In conclusion, we return to the over-arching risk that interventions can entrench incumbents and existing power structures under a "greening" banner. Support for sustainability cooperation between multinationals risks doing just that. Relatedly, there is a myth that dominant companies are better able to pursue sustainability objectives because they have more resources at their disposal and their consumers may be less sensitive to price (as they are able to charge a monopolistic price). The broader concept of power as "power to skew market outcomes in a firm's own favour" needs to be deployed in analysing alternative paths to more sustainable production. If this is not done then the measures taken risk continuing to allow powerful firms to inflict unsustainable outcomes on other economic actors. It is a fundamental contradiction to argue that a dominant firm may achieve higher sustainability outcomes when it is sometimes the existence of the dominant, market-governing firm itself that generates the unsustainable outcomes with which this paper is concerned.

Chapter 6
Industrial Products

How EU Antitrust Law Elevates Sustainability – And How Not: An In-House Practitioner Perspective on the Relationship Between Antitrust Law and Sustainability Objectives

BORIS KASTEN AND HENDRIK REFFKEN[*]

Schindler Management Ltd

I. Introduction

In 2015, the United Nations General Assembly committed on 17 interlinked goals aiming to achieve a better and more sustainable future – the so-called 2030 Sustainable Development Goals (SDG).[1] In the same year, the landmark Paris Agreement was concluded at the 21st Conference of the UNFCCC aiming to decrease global warming, in particular by reducing carbon dioxide (CO_2) emissions.[2] Unsurprisingly, as antitrust policy is not the prima ballerina when

---

[*] Dr Boris Kasten, LLM (Univ Chicago) is Deputy Group General Counsel and General Counsel Europe/ Competition Law at Schindler Management Ltd. He is a member of the bar in New York State and in Germany. Dr Hendrik Reffken is General Counsel Germany at Schindler Deutschland AG & Co KG and a member of the bar in Germany.

The views expressed in this article reflect our personal opinion. The authors would like to thank Adrian Raass, Senior Regulatory Manager, Swisscom (Schweiz) AG, and Simon Bishop, Partner, RBB Economics, for their extremely valuable thoughts on economic aspects raised by the sustainability/competition law debate, and Andre Podleisek, Head Sustainability Office, Schindler Management Ltd, for sharing his deep knowledge about sustainability policies. Any errors remain our own.

1 UN General Assembly Resolution on 25 September 2015, "Transforming our world: the 2030 agenda for sustainable development" UN document A/RES/70/1 (21 October 2015).

2 *Paris Climate Agreement* Treaty Series 2016 no 162 (12 December 2015).

it comes to sustainability and (particularly) protection of our environment, these events did not receive much attention in the global antitrust law community at the time. In fact, private enforcement has been the hot topic for antitrust lawyers in the last decade. This changed at the beginning of the 2020s – at least in Europe. The relationship between sustainability and antitrust law has become the "(wo)man of the match topic" at many conferences and webinars. This new, more political, and certainly less technical "green" topic seems to have been warmly welcomed by many antitrust lawyers. After years of dealing with the nitty-gritty of civil procedure and economic regression analysis, in a year which many would like to delete from their calendars, sustainability is a *Wohlfühlthema* (feel-good topic) which antitrust experts seem glad to embrace. It is not about the past but about the future, the Green Deal and, simply, about a better world. At the same time, it is certainly not a trivial topic. Global warming, on which much of the antitrust/sustainability debate is focused, is a concerning development. Experts claim that we must massively reduce CO_2 emissions within a short time frame.

Consequently, as Commissioner Vestager pointed out in her speech on the Green Deal and competition policy on 22 September 2020,[3] antitrust enforcers have to play their part in supporting the European Commission's ambitious Green Deal objective that Europe becomes the first climate-neutral continent by 2050. This raises the crucial question of how antitrust law can support sustainability. Numerous legal experts, organisations and antitrust enforcers have already contributed to this discussion in various interesting formats. Remarkably, two of the smaller agencies in Europe sped up the discussion with innovative contributions. First in line – and definitely without any first-mover disadvantage – was the Netherlands Authority for Consumers and Markets (ACM) with its Draft Guidelines on sustainability agreements of July 2020.[4] The Greek Competition Authority (HCC) followed with a draft staff discussion paper on sustainability issues and competition law in September 2020.[5] In October 2020, the German Bundeskartellamt published a comprehensive and sophisticated "background paper" on the relationship of sustainability initiatives and competition law.[6] In December 2020, the OECD held a virtual meeting with competition authorities to address sustainability-related questions and it

---

3   Margrethe Vestager, "The Green Deal and competition policy" (Renew webinar, 22 September 2020) <https://ec.europa.eu/commission/commissioners/2019-2024/vestager/announcements/green-deal-and-competition-policy_en>.
4   ACM, "Draft Guidelines: Sustainability agreements, Opportunities within competition law" (9 July 2020) <www.acm.nl/en/publications/draft-guidelines-sustainability-agreements>.
5   HCC, "Draft Staff Discussion Paper on 'Sustainability Issues and Competition Law'" (September 2020) <www.epant.gr/en/enimerosi/competition-law-sustainability.html>.
6   Bundeskartellamt, "Offene Märkte und nachhaltiges Wirtschaften – Gemeinwohlziele als Herausforderung für die Kartellrechtspraxis" (Virtual meeting of the Working Group on Competition Law, 5 October 2020) <www.bundeskartellamt.de/SharedDocs/Meldung/EN/Pressemitteilungen/2020/05_10_2020_AKK_2020.html>.

is planning to revisit the topic during its February 2021 OECD Competition Open Day.

The vibrant discussion dives deep to the bottom of the antitrust law ocean. It deals with fundamental questions of antitrust law such as how to define consumer welfare, how to quantify efficiencies and even how to interpret the objectives of EU competition policy.

II. Competition Law Objective in the Treaties and Economic Foundation of EU Competition Law

Where policy conflicts exist, they are traditionally solved either by regulatory law setting binding minimum standards or by incentive-based regulation such as tax subsidies or procurement law. For instance, EU procurement law allows public sector customers to consider sustainability aspects in the context of specifications, suitability or award criteria of the tendering documents.[7] Regulation (EU) 2019/631 sets binding legal CO_2 emission performance standards for new passenger cars and for new light commercial vehicles.[8]

Having said that, it is argued that the ambitious objectives of SDG and the Paris Agreement cannot be reached by traditional state regulation only. They may require additional initiatives by society, particularly by business, going beyond the requirements and incentives of regulatory law. Regulation is often slow and limited in scope. While the scope of global warming is literally global, the scope of EU regulation is limited to Europe. Businesses that are active worldwide, on the other hand, are in a position to roll out sustainability initiatives globally. Furthermore, regulation is always the result of a political compromise, taking care of the interests of many members of society. This need not be seen as a political failure. However, such compromise always leaves room for market players to go beyond the politically agreed standard. Indeed, compromises often include the expectation that certain parts of society are going beyond the set minimum. Finally, though regulatory law is a strong policy tool for achieving certain sustainability objectives, it is not the only tool. The governmental toolkit has been complemented by more modern and less authoritarian tools. For instance, government can moderate a process at the end of which major market players can agree on sustainability standards above the standard set by law. Government and undertakings might also conclude a voluntary or binding public – private agreement to act in a certain more sustainable way. For instance, in 2016, as a substitute for legislative actions,

---

7   See Directive 2014/24/EU on public procurement and repealing Directive 2004/18/EC [2014] OJ L94/65, art 76.
8   Regulation (EU) 2019/631 setting CO_2 emission performance standards for new passenger cars and for new light commercial vehicles, and repealing Regulations (EC) No 443/2009 and (EU) No 510/2011 [2019] OJ L111/13.

the German minister for environmental affairs reached a voluntary agreement with retailers according to which they would significantly reduce the use of plastic bags.[9]

In the debate about such measures, there are good reasons to separate arguments about sustainability from arguments about economic efficiency. The two can be (and in our view often are) aligned but need not be. If policy goals conflict, there is a benefit to understanding the cost at which one objective is pursued at the expense of another. It therefore seems useful to distinguish between conduct that is both economically efficient and improves sustainability (which we call "Type A" cases) and conduct that improves sustainability but cannot be justified on grounds of economic efficiency alone (which we refer to as "Type B" cases). A practical example of a Type B case is where a territorial delineation agreement between competitors across EU Member States leads to lower road traffic and therefore reduces carbon emissions. In many cases, however, it also decreases consumer welfare (customers are left with only one supplier, which is likely to negatively affect allocative and productive efficiency) and would be incompatible with the internal market objective.

Elevating sustainability can be understood as an increase in quality of products or services. The best quality assurance mechanism is, generally, competition. It has been stressed in the sustainability/antitrust debate, however, that several Treaty provisions require the promotion of sustainable development and environmental protection to be integrated into the definition of EU policies and activities (Article 11 TFEU). This has led to demands that the current economic interpretation of the competition provisions, the existence of which are itself a fundamental requirement under European economic constitutional law,[10] should be revised.[11]

We are not convinced that this is needed. It is a fair observation[12] that fear of antitrust law can prevent efficient and at the same time sustainability-enhancing collaborative market conduct.[13] In our view, however, the deterrent effect is not

---

9   See German Federal Government, "Plastiktüten ab Juli kostenpflichtig" (Press release, 26 April 2016) <www.bundesregierung.de/breg-de/aktuelles/plastiktueten-ab-juli-kostenpflichtig-474674>.

10 The Treaty rules ensuring a system of undistorted competition (Protocol (No 27) TEU on the internal market and competition [2008] OJ C115/309) are of a "vital nature"; Case C–496/09 *Commission v Italian Republic* [2011] ECR I-11483, [60]; Jean-Yves Chérot, "**Obligation de récupération**: La Cour de Justice prononce une astreinte dont le montant évolue dans le temps en proportion de l'avancement de l'exécution de la décision de la Commission *(Italie)*" (2012) Concurrences N° 1–2012 Art N° 42217, 161–162.

11 Simon Holmes, "Climate change, sustainability, and competition law" (2020) 8(2) JAE 354, 363 *et seq.*, 400; Simon Holmes, "Consumer welfare, sustainability and competition law goals" (2020) Concurrences N° 2–2020 Art N° 93496; Simon Holmes, preface to Part I of this book.

12 See Simon Holmes, "Climate Change and Competition Law – Note for the OECD" DAF/COMP/ WD(2020)94 (OECD 1 December 2020), [8] – [9], [30], [39], [42]; Holmes, "Climate change, sustainability, and competition law" (n 11), 357, 389.

13 This also applies to other efficient behaviour, e.g. unilateral conduct or mergers. In this paper we focus on collaborations between competitors.

so much driven by the industrial economics – focused consumer welfare standard, but by flawed legal enforcement concepts. The emphasis on economic principles has generally served EU competition law well. It helped give greater rationality to many of its policies and continues to be preferable to competing – and partly populist – notions about expanding the objectives of competition law. "Public interest" standards risk producing arbitrary outcomes. We recognise that, in the context of the sustainability debate, specific – emotionally appealing – "environmental" arguments are raised to justify abolition of the consumer welfare standard.[14] In substance, however, the call to look at "sustainability" to distinguish good from bad arrangements is, we fear, yet another example of the surge of new concepts that value desirability of specific market outcomes higher than an intellectually convincing analytical framework.[15] On that basis, any kind of sustainability arrangement could be justified, whatever it takes and regardless of cost, including Type B cooperation such as the road traffic – reducing geographic delineation agreement in our example. Instead of insubstantial assessments based on broad "public interest" tests ("sustainability", "fairness" or other standards), it should remain clear what the specific objectives of competition policy are. The economic efficiency (or consumer welfare) standard provides such clarity.

III. Flawed Legal Doctrines, Not Flawed Economics

The table summarises our interpretation of the interplay between antitrust law and sustainability in Type A and Type B cases:

	Economic efficiency analysis	Sustainability analysis	Legal analysis
Type A sustainability cases (e.g. quality-enhancing standards)	Increase of economic efficiency (or neutral)	Increase of sustainability (or neutral)	**Enforcement status quo:** Generally allowed *within* antitrust framework, but current enforcement practice may still deter conduct due to legal uncertainty regarding all competitor contacts (toxic cocktail).[16]

---

14 For example, Simon Holmes, "Climate change, sustainability and competition law, Lesson from COVID 19" (2020) University of Oxford working paper – CCLP(L)50, 4: "Against this background, is it really too much to ask the competition authorities for a little breathing space for business to cooperate to rid us of this dirty air?"; Holmes, "Climate change, sustainability, and competition law" (n 11), 380: "What weight should we attach to reducing carbon emissions and giving our children and grandchildren clean air to breathe?"

15 For a description of this phenomenon see Pablo Ibáñez Colomo, "Whatever Happened to the 'More Economics-Based Approach'?" (2020) 11(9) JECL & Pract 473. See also Alfonso Lamadrid de Pablo, "Competition Law as Fairness" (2017) 8(3) JECL & Pract 147.

16 See section III(1).

	Economic efficiency analysis	Sustainability analysis	Legal analysis
Type A sustainability cases (e.g. quality-enhancing standards)	Increase of economic efficiency (or neutral)	Increase of sustainability (or neutral)	**Potential for reforms:** Clarifications and changes of legal doctrines needed to overcome toxic cocktail creating legal uncertainty: – Clarifications for permissible information-sharing (particularly technical information). – Narrower restraint "by object" category (restricted to naked price-fixing). – Broader use of sanction toolbox, including agency non-fining commitments[17] and negotiated commitment decisions. – Reintroduce formal and informal procedures for agency guidance. – Allow margin of discretion for self-assessments, recognise legal and economic opinions.
Type B sustainability cases (e.g. geographic delineation)	Decrease of economic efficiency	Increase of sustainability (e.g. reduction of carbon emissions)	**Enforcement status quo:** Not allowed under traditional antitrust analysis. **Potential for reforms:** – *Political* decision whether to add sustainability justification *outside* of traditional antitrust (despite decrease in economic efficiency). – Foreseeable test, legal certainty and judicial review needed.

1. Type A cases

The vast majority of over-deterrence scenarios discussed in the sustainability/ antitrust debate seem to be Type A cases. They can be thought of as scenarios that promote both sustainability and economic efficiency through higher quality standards (e.g. product safety, environmental protection).[18] In our view, if the desired cooperation does still not occur, the main culprit of the "fear of competition law" is the rise in *legal* uncertainty about the boundaries of enforcement, rather than flawed economics. If in certain cases an overly narrow interpretation of economic efficiency contributes to over-deterrence, this can be easily overcome.

---

17 See ACM (n 4), at para. 62.
18 This applies to many "first-mover disadvantage" scenarios, with or without quantitative analysis, e.g. examples 4 and 5 discussed in ACM (n 4).

A. *Legal flaws*

We agree there is a real problem that fear of antitrust law can prevent beneficial market conduct. At least five EU law enforcement developments have gravely affected legal certainty as well as creating a chilling effect for benign, innovative conduct.

(1) The category of illegal arrangements or sharing of information has been considerably widened over the years. For example, it is exceedingly difficult in practice to predict with any satisfactory degree of certainty whether an exchange of technical information is permissible, particularly in light of the Commission's emission-cleaning technology case.[19]

(2) The category of "by object" restraints has grown considerably over the years. This has freed authorities from demonstrating anticompetitive effects. For corporate practitioners, however, this massively increases risk exposure, as nearly all contacts with competitors, regardless of content, are considered with a high degree of suspicion. As a practical result, the compliance burden is often too onerous to even begin considering a collaboration.

(3) The reliance of authorities on fines (and mega-fines) as the sanction of choice is unprecedented. Alternative sanctions (e.g. commitment decisions) are only considered in very rare circumstances. Cautious practitioners can hardly take these exceptions as a foundation for gauging risk levels.

(4) There are insufficient countervailing procedural safeguards at EU level to compensate for the elevated risk exposure in light of the previous three factors for nearly any competitor collaboration. Since the introduction of Regulation 1/2003, there is a near-exclusive reliance on corporate self-assessments and – with the exception of the COVID-19 – induced limited return to comfort letters[20] – insufficient formal or informal agency guidance.

(5) There are insufficient foundations on which self-assessments can be reliably built. Due to the absence of agency procedures for checking the legality of market conduct, business is left to itself. While agencies in light of factors (1) – (3) above enjoy a broad margin of discretion in determining the legality of conduct, there is no corresponding mechanism for market participants. Self-assessments, even if based on robust legal (or economic) advice, do not preclude agencies from imposing fines, according to the CJEU's judgment in *Schenker*.[21]

---

19 Commission, "Antitrust: Commission sends Statement of Objections to BMW, Daimler and VW for restricting competition on emission cleaning technology" Press release (5 April 2019, IP/19/2008).

20 Commission, "Guidelines on the optimal and rational supply of medicines to avoid shortages during the COVID-19 outbreak" (Communication) [2020] OJ C116I/1, 7–10.

21 Case C–681/11 *Bundeswettbewerbsbehörde v Schenker* EU:C:2013:404, , [43]; Alexandre Lacresse, "Liability exemption: The Court of Justice considers that an undertaking can be punished for having participated to an antitrust practice even if that is the consequence of its error resulting from a legal advice given by a lawyer and gives the right to national competition authorities to grant immunity from

In practice, these factors combined create a "toxic cocktail". They deter also sustainability-enhancing Type A competitor contacts. If we are serious about improving sustainability through competitor collaboration, it is important to revisit the expansive enforcement as outlined in the table at the beginning of this section.

B. *Economic analysis sufficiently flexible to account for Type A sustainability arrangements*

The economic efficiency standard seems generally well-equipped to analyse Type A cases. For example, the ACM[22] and the Bundeskartellamt[23] point out that competition and sustainability often go hand in hand. By stimulating innovation in the form of new or improved products and processes, antitrust law also stimulates sustainability. In general, the objectives of competition and public welfare are complementary. Moreover, older agency practice demonstrates that arrangements between competitors, including through industry associations, to enhance quality or sustainability (broadly defined), are often compatible with competition law. For example, the Bundeskartellamt determined, in the early stages of German antitrust law, that the cartel prohibition does not seek to prohibit agreements between competitors that solely serve technical safety and protection of people or goods against hazards.[24]

Concerns that the consumer welfare standard may be inadequate to account for sustainability therefore seem at least exaggerated. They could be attributable to (at least) three factors:

(1) Some observers may focus too much on price effects which leads to concerns that the mere finding of a price increase is always viewed negatively. "Chicago-style" antitrust analysis need not, however, be a

---

a fine when applying UE law on an exceptional basis *(Schenker & Co)*" (2013) Concurrences N° 3–2013 Art N° 53840, 142.

22 ACM (n 4), [2].

23 Bundeskartellamt n 6), 6, 8.

24 See Bundeskartellamt, "Activity Report 1959" (BT-Drucks 1795), 18: "... § 1 will nicht Abreden verbieten, die nur der technischen Sicherheit und dem Schutz von Menschen oder Gütern vor Gefahren dienen." Specifically, the Bundeskartellamt had to decide about intervening against an agreement between car manufacturers to abstain from using car hood ornaments. It held the arrangement compatible with GWB, s 1, as its intention was to minimise risk for other road users. In addition, at the level of industry association arrangements, the Bundeskartellamt had to deal with a provision which declared the use of certain "outdated" power plugs no longer permissible. The industry association's rules, while legally non-binding, were generally widely followed and therefore, effectively, amounted to a "ban" of the plugs. Several complaints were filed. The Bundeskartellamt, however, refused to intervene. It considered the association a not-for-profit organisation that supported electrical engineering. Its statutory tasks included drafting, publishing and interpreting industry standards as well as compliance testing and auditing. Its standards, which were developed based on set guidelines, aimed to prevent hazards for persons and livestock as well as fire, damage to property and disruption of operations. They were deemed as state-of-the-art under a specific ordinance to the German Energy Industry Act, and a certificate of conformity was considered a legitimate safety sign. For this reason, the Bundeskartellamt declined to consider the association's recommendation to manufacture, distribute and install only products carrying this certificate as a circumvention of GWB, s 1.

foe of sustainability arrangements. It will simply analyse them through the lens of whether they result in allocative inefficiencies (i.e. output restrictions leading to a deadweight loss) or productive inefficiencies.[25] Agreements with the object of increasing sustainability can be perfectly legitimate, regardless of whether or not they lead to higher prices, if they are ultimately efficient and in line with consumer (or "social") welfare. Thus, "efficiency" should not be misunderstood as impossible to exist in situations where prices may remain constant or increase as a result of an agreement on qualitative features of a product or service, for instance to overcome first-mover disadvantages.[26]

(2) There may also be concerns that the economic efficiency standard accounts only for the interests of direct customers or "consumers", that it lacks clarity about what are competitive benefits (particularly outside of the "price effect" category), and which time horizon applies. There is, however, a broad argument that the term "consumer" should comprise consumers in general.[27] This is relevant for the application of the consumer welfare standard in Article 101(1) TFEU and for the question as to whether consumers are allowed a fair share of the benefit resulting from an agreement under Article 101(3) TFEU. In measuring whether sustainability agreements increase efficiency (i.e. their benefits exceed the costs), economics also seems well-equipped to take into account broader groups of third parties than direct customers, against which to measure externalities. It seems also possible to give greater weight to quality and innovation aspects (in addition to price and quantity), to broaden the forecast horizon or otherwise expand the analytical tools to obtain a more comprehensive picture of consumer welfare.[28] This flexibility is exemplified by the ACM's Draft Guidelines.[29] We also do not believe that

---

25 For example (to cite two Chicago school classics), see Robert H Bork, *The Antitrust Paradox* (Free Press 1993), 107 *et seq.*; Richard A Posner, *Antitrust Law* (University of Chicago Press 2d ed. 2001), 12 *et seq.*

26 See various examples in ACM (n 4), which also take this view. See also this exchange between Justice Scalia and counsel to petitioner in *Leegin*: "JUSTICE SCALIA: Is it the object of the – is the sole object of the Sherman Act to produce low prices? MR OLSON: No. JUSTICE SCALIA: I thought it was consumer welfare. MR OLSON: Yes, yes, it is. JUSTICE SCALIA: And I thought some consumers would prefer more service at a higher price. MR OLSON: Precisely. JUSTICE SCALIA: So the mere fact that it would increase prices doesn't prove anything." *Leegin Creative Leather Products, Inc v PSKS, Inc* 551 US 877 (2007), transcript of oral argument (26 March 2007), 15 *et seq.*

27 See Holmes, "Note for the OECD" (n 12); Kevin Coates and Dirk Middelschulte, "Getting Consumer Welfare Right: the competition law implications of market-driven sustainability initiatives" (2019) 15 (2–3) ECJ 318; Luc Peeperkorn, "Competition and Sustainability: What can competition policy do?" in Guy Canivet and others, "Sustainability and competition law" (2020) Concurrences N° 4–2020 Art N° 97390, 26–65, [30] *et seq.*; ACM (n 4), [38] *et seq.*

28 For an expansion of the consumer welfare paradigm into the dimension of time (accounting both for existing and future generation consumers) see Roman Inderst and Stefan Thomas, "Prospective Welfare Analysis, Extending Willingness-to-Pay Assessment to Embrace Sustainability" (Version 06/10/2020). For considerations about an expansion of consumer welfare analysis beyond revealed preferences through actual purchases see Roman Inderst and Stefan Thomas, "Reflective Willingness to Pay, Preferences for Sustainable Consumption in a Consumer Welfare Analysis" (Version 27/12/2020). Both articles available at www.ssrn.com.

29 n 4.

EU case law suggests a very narrow interpretation of the term "consumer". The CJEU ruled that not only customers in the affected markets can claim cartel damages, but that the scope of potential claimants is much broader.[30] Why then should Article 101 TFEU necessarily be restricted to effects on customers in the affected market only?

(3) A third reason may lie in the fact that Type B cases cannot be validated by the economic efficiency standard. If that is the concern, it would be intellectually honest to concede that there are conflicting policy objectives that cannot be reached through the same instrument. Rather than using a "mixed" standard to provide Type B arrangements with a (false) "procompetitive" label, it seems preferable for reasons of transparency and predictability to analyse such scenarios through a separate "sustainability test" outside of the economic efficiency toolbox.[31]

In sum, abandoning economics-based antitrust analysis to allow Type A sustainability arrangements to pass competition law scrutiny seems unnecessary. It seems possible to use several economic techniques to integrate sustainability aspects into a consumer welfare assessment. Retaining the consumer welfare paradigm, and possibly broadening its conception, has the benefit of maintaining commensurability for the purposes of counterfactual analysis.[32] For Type B conduct, a separate sustainability test might be considered as part of a political decision about policy priorities.

2. Some initial thoughts on Type B cases

Type B cases are characterised by diverging assessments on the economic efficiency side and the sustainability side. The Bundeskartellamt recognises that there can be conflicts between competition and public welfare due to allocation deficits or market failure.[33]

Economic efficiency is not the only objective of society or the treaties, and sustainability is an important policy goal. The economic Tinbergen rule suggests that using the same instrument to achieve two policy objectives should be avoided. For the obvious policy conflict in Type B cases, it thus seems preferable to consider adding a separate sustainability justification. Any reforms should inter alia consider the following three aspects:

(1) Structural integration: The Ministerial Authorisation for Mergers under German Antitrust Law (*Ministererlaubnis*, GWB, s 42) is one example

---

30 Case C–435/18 *Otis v Land Oberösterreich* EU:C:2019:1069, [32]; Pascal Cardonnel, "**Private enforcement:** The Court of Justice of the European Union rules that a public body which granted promotional loans to purchasers of products covered by a cartel may request compensation for loss caused by the cartel (*Otis/Land Oberösterreich*)" (2019) Concurrences N° 2–2020 Art N° 94919, 157–158.
31 See section III(2).
32 Inderst and Thomas, "Reflective Willingness to Pay" (n 28), 20–21.
33 Bundeskartellamt (n 6), 9.

of how such an instrument for Type B cases could be integrated structurally into EU antitrust law. To be sure, a potential amendment of the EU Treaties, particularly of Articles 101 and 102 TFEU, which as primary law can only be amended by EU Member States, would be a challenging task. But wouldn't it be a worthwhile investment?

(2) Legal certainty: If the possibility of government or self-assessment permissions for Type B cases were introduced, it would be important to provide business with a clear procedural framework to assure legal certainty and thus avoid perverse incentives. Hence, it would seem good policy to require some sort of a quantitative assessment of purported sustainability benefits. These could be compared with the negative effects on economic efficiency. Such a comparison will only work if identical or similar measurement units are used. It would therefore be helpful if sustainability benefits could be expressed in monetary terms. This means that some sort of "price" or "cost" needs to be put on the benefit, and some sort of "exchange rate" identified and applied. At first glance, such an exercise looks very complex. However, economists have also attached "prices" on sustainability in other policy areas. Numerous examples can be found in the context of "CO_2-neutral" travel offers by airlines and railways for which extra fees are charged. A more sophisticated example is the trading of CO_2 emission permits. Similarly, in the field of EU public procurement law – which from a policy objective standpoint is closely linked to EU antitrust law – contracting authorities have been required for many years now to put a price on sustainability aspects. This is always the case if sustainability aspects are part of the award criteria for the tender. Hence, for antitrust lawyers who also advise on procurement law it is not entirely novel that sustainability aspects could be quantified and weighed against other costs. One option to increase legal certainty would be to integrate precise legally binding quantification criteria for sustainability aspects in EU law. This could be done by means of a block exemption regulation[34] which could also bind antitrust agencies of Member States (or other government bodies, should the competence for "sustainability permission" deviate). Business could apply these rules in a self-assessment (but with clearer criteria than under current antitrust rules for competitor collaborations).[35] This may, however, not be a short- or mid-term solution. Today, there is little case law or other practical experience regarding the quantification of sustainability aspects that can easily be developed into legislation. Hence, we assume that initial legislation to allow justifications for Type B cases has to be rather generic. However, this is also true for procurement law, which is a few years ahead in accounting for sustainability, and where

---

34 See Bundeskartellamt (n 6), 14.
35 See section III(1)(A).

this has turned out to be manageable in practice. It should therefore
not be a problem taking sustainability into account for other market
conduct.

(3) Judicial review: Finally, a separate sustainability justification tool would
need to be subject to adequate procedural safeguards, including judicial
review.

IV. Summary

The debate about the relation between EU antitrust law and sustainability objectives has led to calls to reconsider established antitrust concepts. We agree that
fear of competition law can have the practical effect to deter also benign, and
in particular innovative, market practices. At the same time, we are sceptical that
the standard of economic efficiency is responsible and should be overhauled.
Instead, we hold several legal developments accountable for the chilling effect
of current EU antitrust enforcement. Several interpretations of the law have led
to a situation in which conduct that satisfies both the principle of economic
efficiency and sustainability objectives (what we call "Type A" cases) may still
occur less frequently than would be desirable. Business would make broader use
of such conduct if these flaws were remedied. However, it must remain clear
what the objectives of competition policy are. If the economic efficiency (or
consumer welfare) standard was abolished or radically reinterpreted in the sense
of a broad "public interest" test (be it "sustainability", "fairness" or any other
standard), this would lead to wobbly substantive assessments. Many factors
could be relevant, but it would be unclear which are of higher priority and
ultimately determinative. Business would arguably have more, not less, difficulties
to predict what is allowed and what not. To be sure, economic efficiency need
not be the only objective of society. For arrangements which benefit sustainability
but are economically inefficient (what we call "Type B" cases), it should, however,
be avoided to inject a vague "sustainability" (or other "public policy") objective
into the substantive antitrust standard. It seems preferable to administer such
tests outside of – and in addition to – the substantive economic antitrust
assessment. This would assure analytical transparency and increase predictability
of outcomes. It would also be in line with the economic Tinbergen rule: using
one instrument to achieve several – incongruent – policy objectives should be
avoided.

We have focused on beneficial collaborations and practical suggestions to improve
legal certainty. Our analysis assumed a broad understanding of sustainability
which covers not only climate change or environmental protection but also other
product lifecycle aspects relevant for responsible corporate citizenship along the
value chain, such as anti-discrimination and harassment and, importantly,
product safety.

We conclude that competition law as such elevates sustainability through promoting higher quality. In practice, however, legal uncertainty deters desirable collaborations. Revisiting several expansive legal enforcement doctrines would help overcome the practical deficiencies of the self-assessment framework. Additional sustainability considerations can be considered "outside" economic antitrust assessments based on public interest objectives. This latter category raises specific difficulties and it may warrant legislative activity.

A Grey Area in Green Cooperation Between Competitors: Exchanging Non-Price Information Within a Trade Association

Gianni De Stefano*

AkzoNobel

Sustainability has become part of most companies' action and strategy. Competition law authorities and literature have made clear that firms can legitimately cooperate when it is necessary and proportionate to meet certain sustainability objectives. There remains a grey area, however, where companies do not know whether antitrust authorities will investigate them and possibly fine their sustainability-driven initiatives: one example is that of non-price exchanges between competitors within a trade association. There is therefore a need for general yet practical guidance from competition authorities as to what information firms can exchange.

* Gianni De Stefano is the Global Director Competition Law, Anti-Bribery and Trade Compliance at AkzoNobel. He previously spent over 10 years in private practice as an antitrust lawyer at international leading law firms. He is currently a non-governmental adviser to the International Competition Network, a convenor of the European Roundtable of Industrialists' competition policy working group, and a general editor of the Journal of European Competition Law & Practice. This paper contains the author's personal views and does not necessarily represent the views of AkzoNobel or any other bodies with which he has an affiliation. Thanks to Pablo Ibáñez Colomo and Teresa Vecchi for their comments and Jéssica A. Nemeth Garcia for the support; any errors are the author's.

I. Sustainability Is Part of the Ordinary Course of Business for Most Firms

Today, it is customary for firms to adapt their business model to address climate change and other sustainability objectives.[1] This is not only because of international and national regulations or pressure from customers and shareholders, but also because most companies genuinely believe that it is their corporate responsibility to promote sustainable development.

The United Nations 2030 agenda highlights the need for companies to adopt more sustainable business practices.[2] In the European Union, the EU Green Deal is not only an action plan to make the Union's economy sustainable,[3] but it also includes regulations addressed to the Member States that indirectly affect the course of action of companies, for example, firms investing in environmentally sustainable activities and which can benefit from EU or national support.[4]

Most corporations have dedicated personnel or departments to sustainability issues and regularly issue ESG (environment, social and governance) reports, showing the topicality of the matter and the dedication of resources. EU rules require large companies to publish regular reports on the environmental and social impacts of their activities.[5]

This also applies at industry level. For example, the supply of chemical products is regulated through EU and national regulations and codes aimed at improving

---

1   We do not address here the issue of whether "sustainability" should cover only environment-related sustainability or also "social" sustainability. While the EU Green Deal and most national frameworks refer to climate change, there is a lively debate on whether considering benefits to society should also be relevant in assessing cooperation in complementary areas, such as improved living and working standards, eliminating child labour, increasing the health benefits of products, and increasing educational and training opportunities. Interestingly, the Dutch Competition Authority (ACM) draws a distinction between environmental-damage agreements and other sustainability agreements, see ACM, "Draft Guidelines: Sustainability agreements" (9 July 2020) <www.acm.nl/en/publications/draft-guidelines-sustainability-agreements>, [6], [39], [42].
2   Julian Nowag, "Sustainability & Competition Law and Policy – Background Note" DAF/COMP(2020)3 (OECD, 1 December 2020), [24].
3   The EU has stepped up its 2030 climate ambition: reduction of greenhouse gas emissions of at least 55% compared with 1990, see Commission, "Stepping up Europe's 2030 climate ambition" (Communication) COM(2020) 562 final. See also Commission, "Proposal for a Regulation establishing the framework for achieving climate neutrality and amending Regulation (EU) 2018/1999 (European Climate Law)" COM(2020) 80 final. By June 2021, the Commission will present legislative proposals to implement the new target, including revising and possibly expanding the EU Emissions Trading System.
4   Regulation (EU) 2020/852 on the establishment of a framework to facilitate sustainable investment and amending Regulation (EU) 2019/2088 [2020] OJ L198/13, setting out an EU-wide classification system, or "taxonomy", which will provide businesses and investors with a common language to identify those economic activities that are considered environmentally sustainable.
5   Directive 2014/95/EU amending Directive 2013/34/EU as regards disclosure of non-financial and diversity information by certain large undertakings and groups [2014] OJ L330/1, lays down the rules on disclosure of non-financial and diversity information – including environmental protection – by large public-interest companies with more than 500 employees.

the environment, such as the EU REACH Regulation[6] or the EU Regulation on classification, labelling and packaging of substances and mixtures.[7]

Sustainability has also become part of industry technical discussions within trade associations and other industry forums. We will not deal here with the issue of whether firms should be allowed to collaborate to advance sustainability.[8] However, one can safely assume that the agendas of trade association meetings do include non-price-related topics on sustainability.

The fact that firms discuss about sustainability initiatives within trade associations does not mean that they collude to restrict competition on parameters such as price, quality or innovation. In fact, most businesses rely on their sustainability efforts to highlight how much they depart from their peers.[9] These efforts include the use of "performance indexes" tracing their improvement, over the years, relative to their competitors.[10]

Companies are keen to adhere to competition law. For example, most companies find helpful to state, for the avoidance of doubt, that their sustainability-related cooperation occur in a "pre-competitive" phase.[11] If anything, firms are fearful of discussing sustainability because they are mindful of remaining within the boundaries of what is allowed from an antitrust perspective (or what they understand such boundaries to be).[12]

---

6   Regulation (EC) 1907/2006 concerning the Registration, Evaluation, Authorisation and Restriction of Chemicals (REACH) [2006] OJ L396/1.

7   Regulation (EC) 1272/2008 on classification, labelling and packaging of substances and mixtures [2008] OJ L353/1.

8   The European Commission has recognised that "the approach of industrial alliances could be the appropriate tool. This has already shown its benefit in the area of batteries, plastics and microelectronics": see Commission, "A New Industrial Strategy for Europe" (Communication) COM(2020) 102 final.

9   Many companies refer to their "leadership" on sustainability, and certainly refer to how they are better than competitors. For example, a textile company states "we've differentiated ourselves from competitors in our original raw materials business"; for a telecommunications company "the pressure to prioritize sustainability comes from many sources... competition"; for a food company "staying ahead of competitors means... sustainability and fair trade certification"; for a telecommunications company "to compete effectively in today's dynamic marketplace... we are creating business value by... limiting our environmental impact".

10 Of the 35 highest ranked firms in each industry sector in the Fortune Global 500 2019, at least 25 (71%) companies publicly expressed the understanding that sustainability is parameter of competition: we considered statements from the most recent annual reports and websites in which the company recognised its leadership position in sustainability, competitive pressure created by environmental issues or sustainability as differentiator from other competitors.

11 For example, a food company outlines that "where collaboration is needed to move the needle on an industry-wide issue, we engage with relevant partners... to identify pre-competitive solutions". It is unclear what "pre-competitive" means: it could refer to exchanges of non-commercially-sensitive information.

12 Gianni De Stefano, "EU Competition Law & the Green Deal: The Consistency Road" (*Competition Policy International*, 28 July 2020), on a survey of a pool of the largest multinational firms within the Fortune 500 list. See also International Chamber of Commerce, "Competition Policy and Environmental Sustainability" (*ICC*, 26 November 2020) <https://iccwbo.org/content/uploads/sites/3/2020/12/2020-comppolicyandenvironmsustainnability.pdf>.

II. Straightforward Scenarios: Cartel Greenwashing Is Illegal While Non-Binding Recommendations Are Allowed

The way competition law applies to sustainability initiatives is straightforward in certain cases at the extremes of the spectrum. On the one hand, sustainability does not provide a cover for any anticompetitive practices or cartels; on the other, competitors adopting non-binding recommendations on sustainability are generally allowed.

First, sustainability should not be an excuse for businesses to cartelise or otherwise engage in conduct that goes beyond a specific and measurable initiative addressing climate change.[13] That is referred to as "cartel greenwashing", where competitors attempt to use sustainability as a "free pass" to collude.[14] Cartel greenwashing is different from the unilateral practice of deceitfully marketing a product as environmentally friendly when in fact basic environmental standards have not been met (which is often referred to as greenwashing, too).[15]

In 2011 the European Commission fined three suppliers of laundry detergent powder which, during the implementation of an environmental initiative, agreed to keep the price of the laundry products unchanged.[16] The initiative targeted the weight reduction of the products and their packaging, was adopted within a trade association representing the suppliers and was even endorsed by a European Commission's recommendation.

From the Commission's 25-page decision,[17] it is clear that the problem lay in the price discussions: "although the... environmental initiative neither foresaw nor necessitated price discussions, the industry agreements and the discussions on the occasion of that initiative led to anticompetitive conduct... the ultimate aim of which was to achieve market stabilisation as well as to coordinate prices at European level."[18] In practice, the parties exchanged information on pricing and

---

13   See ACM, "The assessment of anticompetitive practices as a result of sustainability initiatives in practice" (memorandum, 2013), which offers an overview of anticompetitive practices that could arise because of arrangements made as part of sustainability initiatives.

14   Maarten Pieter Schinkel discusses why horizontal agreements between competitors do not assist firms in internalising environmental negative externalities and do not have a positive impact on investments in green initiatives: see, for example, his recent paper with Lukáš Tóth, "Compensatory Public Good Provision by a Private Cartel" (2020) Tinbergen Institute Discussion Paper 2019-086/VII.

15   See e.g. Regulation 2020/852 (n 4), recital 11. This unilateral greenwashing is dealt with by the consumer protection powers of certain national competition authorities, see e.g. ACM, "Draft Guidelines: Sustainability claims" (22 September 2020) <www.acm.nl/sites/default/files/documents/2020-09/acm-publishes-for-consultation-its-draft-guidelines-regarding-sustainability-claims.pdf>; or the announcement of the UK Competition and Markets Authority (CMA), "CMA to examine if 'eco-friendly' claims are misleading" Press release (2 November 2020) <www.gov.uk/government/news/cma-to-examine-if-eco-friendly-claims-are-misleading>.

16   *Consumer Detergents* (Case COMP/39.579) Commission decision C(2011) 2528 final [2011] OJ C193/14.

17   The *Consumer Detergents* cartel was settled through the EU cartel settlement procedure and therefore the final decision is streamlined and offers limited insight into the detail of the investigated conduct.

18   *Consumer Detergents* (n 16), [22].

agreed to keep the price unchanged during the implementation of the different phases of the environmental initiative, including by not passing the benefit of cost savings (reduced raw materials, packaging and transport costs) on to consumers.[19] There was no justification for that behaviour: "since restriction of competition is the sole object of the practices aimed at market stabilisation and price coordination... there is no indication that those restrictive practices... entailed any efficiency benefits or otherwise promoted technical or economic progress."[20]

Another clearly illegal behaviour would be for companies to agree to avoid or delay the adoption of sustainability. The European Commission is currently investigating the behaviour of car makers that would have avoided or delayed the introduction of less polluting cars.[21] The European Commissioner for Competition, Margrethe Vestager, said: "companies can cooperate in many ways to improve the quality of their products. However, EU competition rules do not allow them to collude on exactly the opposite: not to improve their products, not to compete on quality". It will be interesting the see how this investigation unfolds and whether the published decision (if any) offers insight on the contours of the problematic behaviour.

Second, and on the other side of the spectrum, non-binding recommendations on sustainability are allowed. For example, the European Commission cleared a commitment on reducing car emissions by two associations of car makers because the companies remained "free to develop and introduce new CO_2-efficient technologies independently and in competition with each other".[22] The non-binding nature of the recommendation has also been a factor in other cases.[23]

By the same token, non-binding environmental standards are allowed. Commissioner Vestager stated that "businesses can... get together to agree standards for

---

19   ibid, [25].
20   ibid, [53].
21   Commission, "Antitrust: Commission sends Statement of Objections to BMW, Daimler and VW for restricting competition on emission cleaning technology" Press release (IP/19/2008). The Commission's preliminary view is that certain car makers would have colluded to restrict competition on the development of technology to clean the emissions of cars by "den[ying] consumers the opportunity to buy less polluting cars, despite the technology being available to the manufacturers".
22   Commission, "Commitments by Japanese and Korean Car Manufacturers to reduce CO2 emissions" Press release (1 December 1999); *Association of Japanese Automobile Manufacturers (JAMA)* (Case IV/F-2/37/634) and *Association of Korean Automobile Manufacturers (KAMA)* (Case IV/F-2/37.611).
23   European Commission's comfort letters of 21 April 1998 in *EACEM* (Case IV/C-36.494) (commitment by a large part of the members of the European Association of Consumer Electronics Manufacturers to reduce energy consumption by televisions and video recorders); and of 13 October 1998 in *ACEA* (Case COMP/37.231) (commitment by the Association of European Automobile Manufacturers to reduce CO₂ emissions in the automotive industry). See by analogy also the agreements about the creation of firms operating for the collection and recycling of used packaging at national level, where the adhesion to the systems is voluntary: see *DSD and others* (Case COMP/34493 and others) Commission decision C(2001) 2672 [2001] OJ L319/1; and *ARA and another* (Case D3/35470) Commission decision C(2003) 3703 [2003] OJ L75/69. Since 2004 we no longer have a notification system in the EU, which explains the lack of more recent examples.

sustainable products... without breaking the competition rules".[24] The current Horizontal Cooperation Guidelines recognise that "standards on... environmental aspects of a product may also facilitate consumer choice and can lead to increased product quality [or] innovation" and offer examples: washing machine makers agreeing to no longer manufacture energy-inefficient products, or standardised packaging.[25] At the same time, the Guidelines indicate that these standards are not concerning when they are non-binding: "restrictions in a standardisation agreement making a standard binding and obligatory for the industry are in principle not indispensable".[26]

Is it always straightforward the way that competition rules apply to sustainability initiatives? We will see below how certain aspects are not fully addressed.

III. Case Study: the *Trucks* Cartel in Europe

Let us assess an actual European antitrust case which will uncover a grey area: in 2016 and 2017 the European Commission hit with a record fine truck makers that coordinated – among other things – pricing and timing of the introduction of emission technologies for trucks to be compliant with newly introduced environmental standards.[27] While this case is clear in labelling pricing discussions as illegal, it also uses language referring to other exchanges, which is not as straightforward.

Two features of the *Trucks* cartel are relevant: sector regulation and discussions happening within a trade association. The decision explains that "the trucks have been subject to various European environmental standards, such as the EURO-emission standards... [which] were defined by various Commission directives setting obligatory deadlines".[28] It also refers to a European trade association where "major international automobile companies work... together to ensure effective communication and negotiation with... environmental... interests".[29]

---

24 Margrethe Vestager, "Sustainability and Competition Policy" (Conference, 24 October 2019) (phrase added at delivery, see <www.youtube.com/watch?v=7mpWAOhkQbY>).
25 Commission, "Guidelines on the applicability of Article 101 of the Treaty on the Functioning of the European Union to horizontal co-operation agreements" [2011] OJ C11/1, [329] and [331].
26 ibid, [318]. See also paras 306: "if the use of standard terms is binding, there is a need to assess their impact on product quality, product variety and innovation" and 320: "The possibility cannot, however, be ruled out that making standard terms binding may, in a specific case, be indispensable to the attainment of the efficiency gains generated by them".
27 *Trucks* (Case AT.39824) Commission decision C(2016) 4673 [2016] OJ C108/6 and Commission decision C(2017) 6467 [2017] OJ C216/9. The first decision (19 July 2016) is a cartel settlement decision that involves four truck markers, while the second decision (27 September 2017) is an infringement decision against one truck maker. The publicly available decision for the second decision is "provisional" and has many redactions.
28 *Trucks* (Case AT.39824) C(2017) 6467 [2017] OJ C216/9, [6].
29 ibid, [16].

Any restriction of competition on environmentally friendly technologies may constitute an infringement of competition rules: "it is... very important that the truck producers compete on new environmentally friendly technologies and try to bring these to market as early as possible. This is not only necessary to give customers a choice to adopt these technologies but it is also of great value to our environment".[30] In the case at hand, the companies "discussed and occasionally agreed on the timing and the passing on of costs for the introduction of emission technologies",[31] i.e. "the date and the additional costs of the market introduction of news trucks complying with emission standards".[32]

Exchanges about the pricing decisions of companies were defined as illegal: "by discussing... the additional costs triggered by the new technology... the [companies] obtained knowledge of the intended level of gross prices",[33] "they also colluded on the... increases to their EEA-wide gross price lists in connection with the launch of those new models",[34] "with respect to the collusion on... additional costs to the new environmental standard... [the companies] discussed... the additional costs triggered by the new standards during the same meetings or respectively in the same e-mails... Consequently the nature of the discussions [redacted] was related and complementary to the parties' collusion concerning prices and gross price increases".[35] That was part of a "a common plan with the single anti-competitive aim of restricting competition on the market for medium and heavy trucks in the EEA".[36]

By the same token, the exchanges about the timing of the introduction of the clean technology were also considered illegal: "another important factor for competition was the uncertainty about competitors' introduction of new models... in particular in the context of the introduction of new models complying with new EURO emission standards. In a competitive environment competitors strive to get ahead of the competitors in presenting more advanced technology".[37]

What about other (non-price) exchanges between competitors? The *Trucks* decision refers to a single discussion regarding "environmental issues and related political initiatives and that a key topic was the transition from Euro 3 to Euro 4 [and] the consequences of those environmental standards for trucks engines",[38] but it does not offer further detail on non-price exchanges.

---

30 "Statement by Commissioner Vestager on fining Scania for participating in trucks cartel" (STATEMENT/17/3509, 27 September 2017).
31 *Trucks* (2017) (n 28), [79], see also [207] and [212(b)], [237] and [238(b)].
32 ibid, [237].
33 ibid, [243].
34 ibid, [266].
35 ibid, [321]. One piece of evidence cited is a handwritten note for a single meeting where the exchange involved "sensitive market information... concerning the timing, prices and additional costs of Euro 4 and 5 emission standards" ([135]).
36 ibid, [317], see also [320] – [322], [326] and [330].
37 ibid, [286], see also [243], [266], [321] and [394].
38 ibid, [115].

Could non-price exchanges be justified by the need to better understand the environmental requirements? The *Trucks* decision recognises that a justification is possible, though it does not offer indication of what that justification could be in practical terms: "the collusion related to delaying the introduction of new emissions standards technologies and the passing on of costs related to the introduction of such technology does not present any discernible advantages for customers and cannot qualify as legitimate benchmarking within the meaning of the Horizontal Guidelines".[39]

The existence of an environmental requirement certainly cannot be a blanket excuse for discussions.[40] Should not firms be allowed to discuss sustainability standards or environmental rules, to make sure they interpret them correctly? Could firms adopt industry best practices to the benefit of the markets, the customers, and the environment?

IV. A Grey Area: Non-Price Exchanges Within a Trade Association

The questions emerging from *Trucks* are very pertinent, as it is often unclear if/how competing firms can exchange non-price information to best address climate change and/or meet newly introduced environmental requirements.

Sustainability exchanges within trade associations are unavoidable nowadays, due to the deep involvement of most companies in sustainability initiatives in a way that affects the entire relevant industry. Yet this is a grey area where it is difficult for firms to understand where exactly the legality threshold is and for lawyers to advise the best course of action.

In the European Commission's pending investigation in *Car Emissions*, the press release clarifies that the investigated behaviour of delay of introduction of less polluting technology "is to be distinguished from forms of cooperation between companies aimed at improving product quality and innovation which do not raise concerns under EU competition law".[41] The question is, what are the precise contours of this allowed cooperation?

Businesses need to discuss sustainability because often there is a lack of transparency or standards in the relevant industry, or even the presence of "bad" business models that increase costs without bringing any added value. It rarely happens that every player follows the applicable environmental rule and realise a good outcome for the environment and consumers. For example, other

---

39 ibid, [264], see also [225].
40 ibid, [304]: "the fact that the parties were under a legal obligation to introduce new emission technology by a specific date did not prevent the parties from offering such new technology to customers prior to the regulatory deadline for introduction, or choosing not to increase prices for trucks equipped with the new technology".
41 See *Car Emissions* (n 21).

stakeholders within the industry may complicate things; customers may require different (and sometimes more stringent) requirements in their tender procedures.

Let us consider a hypothetical case study of competing suppliers of widgets: competitors Alpha, Beta and Gamma. First, Alpha, Beta and Gamma are subject to EU and national environmental rules applicable to the supply of widgets. Second, their customers require in their tender documentations that a widget supplier has a green certification to be qualified to bid its widgets in response to a tender; customer X requires a self-certification by the widget supplier of adherence to the applicable environmental rules; customer Y requires a certification from a third-party vendor; and customer Z specifies certain green factors that, however, are not fully consistent with the applicable environmental rules.

Because of this complex industry scenario, it has become customary for widget suppliers Alpha, Beta and Gamma to obtain green certifications from third-party vendors Tom, Dick and Harry. These vendors use different methodologies and/or factors to offer their green certification: Tom relies on self-certification from the widget supplier based on a range of factors; Dick uses the same factors as Tom, but conducts actual controls rather than relying on self-certification; and Harry conducts controls but based on different factors from Tom or Dick. Since Alpha, Beta and Gamma want to make sure that they can participate in all possible tenders from all their customers X, Y, Z, they obtain all green certifications from all third-party vendors Tom, Dick and Harry.

This business situation increases costs and complexity for widget suppliers Alpha, Beta and Gamma without bringing any benefit to the customers X, Y and Z or, indeed, the environment: it is a complex or "bad" business model. To address this bad business model, competitors Alpha, Beta and Gamma would like to discuss between them how they can best adhere to the applicable environmental rules and their customers' requirements. For example, they would like to determine whether there are best practices to meet the objective of complying with the rules and the customers' requirements but in a more efficient manner: for example uniform criteria and/or methodologies to obtain a green certification.

Alpha, Beta and Gamma are members of an industry association, Widget Association, which has been meeting for years to discuss technical matters in compliance with competition rules. They wonder whether and how they could now address these sustainability issues within the Widget Association. Any exchanges between Alpha, Beta and Gamma within the Widget Association would not be price-related (or relate to any other parameter of competition) and would benefit the customers, the industry, and ultimately the environment and all consumers.

Can competitors Alpha, Beta and Gamma exchange information within the Widget Association to address a bad business model (provided they do not discuss price or other parameters affecting competition)?

V. Practical Guidance on this Grey Area
Would Be Welcome

Businesses would certainly welcome guidance from competition authorities on which sustainability exchanges they can entertain in trade associations or other industry contexts. It is true that the European Commission,[42] as well as other competition authorities,[43] has already sent a clear message that competition policy is keen to contribute to the effectiveness of green policies.[44]

However, more practical and example-based (and ideally industry-based) guidance would be warranted. For example, it would be helpful to have an express statement that exchanges between competitors about environmental requirements or standards are presumed not to infringe competition rules when they do not relate to price or other competition parameters.

The European Commission has declared its willingness to offer guidance in the future: "if companies come to us and they say 'this we want to do', we'd be happy to look at it, and... tell you about the results".[45] The Commission has now several tools in its toolbox: inapplicability decisions,[46] guidance letters[47] or comfort letters.[48] COVID-19 – dedicated mailboxes of competition authorities could be maintained in future months also for sustainability initiatives.[49]

However, businesses cannot seek guidance from the competition authorities each time they have query on a specific sustainability initiative, as that would have a cost, such as the delay in the implementation of the proposed arrangement.

---

42 Commission, "Competition Policy supporting the Green Deal: Call for contributions" (13 October 2020). The Commission is also dedicating its 2020 Management Plan to the "General Objective 1: A European Green Deal", holding a conference with interested parties on 4 February 2021.

43 See ACM, "Draft Guidelines: Sustainability agreements" (n 1), and the Hellenic Competition Commission, "Draft Staff Discussion paper on 'Sustainability Issues and Competition Law'" (September 2020) <www.epant.gr/en/enimerosi/competition-law-sustainability.html>.

44 The European Parliament has asked to "reconcile the EU competition rules, industrial policy and international trade, which must go hand in hand with sustainability and respect for the environment", see its resolution of 18 June 2020 on competition policy: European Parliament, "Competition Policy – annual report 2019" (2019/2131(INI)) <https://oeil.secure.europarl.europa.eu/oeil/popups/fichepro-cedure.do?lang=en&reference=2019/2131(INI)>, and indeed the draft European Climate Law (n 3), reads: "all EU actions and policies should pull together to help the EU to achieve a successful and just transition towards climate neutrality and a sustainable future" and that "by 2023, and every 5 years thereafter, the Commission shall review... the consistency of Union measures with the climate-neutrality objective".

45 See Vestager (n 24).

46 Regulation (EC) 1/2003 on the implementation of the rules on competition laid down in Articles 101 and 102 of the Treaty [2003] OJ L1/1, art 10.

47 Commission, "Notice on informal guidance relating to novel questions concerning Articles 101 and 102 of the EC Treaty that arise in individual cases (guidance letters)" [2014] OJ C101/78.

48 Commission, "Temporary Framework for assessing antitrust issues related to business cooperation in response to situations of urgency stemming from the current COVID-19 outbreak" [2020] OJ C116I/7.

49 Gianni De Stefano, "Covid-19 and EU Competition Law: Bring the Informal Guidance On" (2020) 11(3–4) JECL & Pract 121.

Certain grey areas, such as the exchanges between competitors of non-price sustainability information, would best be addressed with general guidance from the authorities.

Such guidance could come in the form of soft law, such as a notice or communication or even an enforcement priorities guidance (like the European Commission's 2009 guidance for exclusionary abuses of dominant position). In any case, the authorities should consider their audiences: businesses (which already use the authorities' guidance notes when they offer a practical format and actual examples)[50] as well as competition practitioners (who already advise on exchanges between competitors or are even involved in the works of trade associations).

VI. Conclusion

While it is straightforward that a cartel in disguise would hardly be justified by a sustainability objective, or that certain forms of cooperation (such as non-mandatory recommendations by a trade association) are allowed, grey areas remain regarding how competition and green policies can interact. Businesses would welcome guidance on whether (and, if so, how) competitors can exchange non-price information regarding sustainability requirements (or initiatives they are involved in).

The European Commission would be best placed to draft and issue such guidance in the EU, to avoid divergent approaches between not only the Commission and national authorities, but between national authorities themselves.[51]

Such guidance would not only clarify for practitioners how to interpret competition rules in the sustainability context, but it would also offer a practical tool for businesses to discuss how best to address climate change and/or environmental requirements or standards. The outcome would be win-win-win: for companies that could avoid ineffective business models, for customers and the industry overall, and for the environment.

---

50 See, for example, the format of the guidance notes of the UK CMA, e.g. "Competition law: information for trade associations" <www.gov.uk/government/publications/competition-law-dos-and-donts-for-trade-associations>.

51 While the Greek and the Dutch competition authorities seem to be more forthcoming (for example, the former welcomes "necessary investments in redefining their role and objective function in a broader context that takes into account various sorts of externalities" and the latter observes that "with regard to environmental-damage agreements, it should be possible to take into account benefits for others than merely the users"), the German Competition Authority is more cautious in its paper "Offene Märkte und nachhaltiges Wirtschaften" (Virtual Conference of the antitrust law working group, 1 October 2020), <www.bundeskartellamt.de/SharedDocs/Publikation/DE/Diskussions_Hintergrundpapier/AK_Kartell-recht_2020_Hintergrundpapier.pdf?__blob=publicationFile&v=2>, noting how environmental protection should probably not be used to justify forms of cooperation based on private self-regulation. See also Charley Connor, "Warming to sustainability" (*Global Competition Review*, 17 December 2020).

PART III
Agency Outlook

Preface:
Can Competition Authorities Consider Sustainability in their Decision-Making?

Martijn Snoep[*]

Netherlands Authority for Consumers and Markets

Like everyone else, competition lawyers and economists around the world – regardless of whether they are working in the private or public sector – are considering what they can do to help to prevent a global climate crisis. Our children and our children's children will look back at us, many years from now, and ask themselves what we did to create their living conditions. That is no different for competition authorities. Even small contributions, such as removing obstacles for other government agencies or businesses to do their part, will help do what's right for future generations.

In most jurisdictions, competition is not a constitutional right like freedom of speech or privacy. It is a means to achieve one or more public goals such as maximising consumer welfare, innovation, market integration, fairness or redistribution of economic power. If competition law stands in the way of reaching certain other public goals, someone must balance the weight of the different objectives. Ultimately the law prescribes whether that balancing may or must be done by an independent competition authority, by the executive branch of government or by the legislature. So the first question a competition authority must ask itself is whether the law *requires* that it takes into account

* Martijn Snoep has been the chair of the Netherlands Authority for Consumers and Markets (ACM) since September 2018.

the effects on sustainability of any agreement, unilateral behaviour or merger it is about to assess. This is a matter of law. The second question a competition authority must ask when the law does not *require* the effects on sustainability to be taken into account, is whether the law *allows* the authority to do this. Then this becomes a matter of policy. And finally, the third question a competition authority must ask when it intends to take these effects into account, is *how* this must be done. In essence, this is a matter of practical application. The formidable authors of this Part III tend to focus on the policy matter, but sometimes also venture out into the practical aspects of incorporating sustainability in the authority's practice. More importantly they show us that if there is a legal basis, it is really possible to do this.

The legal and policy questions have also been extensively assessed in other chapters of this book, but mostly from the perspective of private practitioners, academics or industry. The authors of this Part take the perspective of the competition authorities. One of the points that has not been raised explicitly by them, however, is the legitimacy of competition law and the authorities entrusted with its enforcement. In many jurisdictions, competition law and enforcement, particularly the prevailing short-term consumer welfare – oriented interpretation of it, is closely connected with the dominant neo-liberal ideology of the late 1990s and early 2000s. But the world has moved on since then. First, a devastating financial crisis showed shocking market failures. This was followed by significant social unrest, that can be attributed to increased income equality and the removal of government safety nets, leading to the rise of populist political parties. And, finally, the world is facing a unprecedented health and economic crisis as a result of the COVID-19 virus that is leading to a worldwide revaluation of the role of government in the economy. As a result of these developments, in many countries the idea of maximising short-term consumer welfare and the connected concept of the "trickle-down economy" has been traded in for a genuine desire for a fairer economy and a not-yet-fully-developed view on "citizen welfare" for present and future generations. Competition authorities and competition law can bring many good things to this new view, such as analytical rigour, independence from politics, fact-based intervention and transparent procedures. But this can only be done if authorities are willing to fundamentally adjust their old views to new realities, which often does not even require a change in the law. If, on the other hand, authorities decide to stick to the orthodox neo-liberal interpretation of the law, they should fear their extinction as they are likely to be replaced by new laws and new institutions. Or, in the words of Prince Tancredi to his uncle Don Fabrizio, in Giuseppe Tomasi di Lampedusa's novel *The Leopard*, set in a revolutionary 19th-century Sicily: "If we want everything to stay as it is, everything has to change."

As chair of the Netherlands Authority for Consumers and Markets (ACM), this was exactly the dilemma I faced when I took office in September 2018. With my fellow board members, we set in motion a programme of granular change. The first step the ACM took was to change its mission to: making markets work well for people and businesses, now and in the future. This was to show that competition is not a goal but a means to get good results for people (not only consumers!) and businesses. There is more to tell about this mission change, but that falls outside the scope of this book. After that, the ACM set new guidelines for regional horizontal cooperation among healthcare providers, who claimed that competition laws stood in the way of providing good healthcare, particularly in less-populated areas. These guidelines were welcomed by all sides of the table: healthcare providers, health insurers, patients (to whom we gave a bigger role) and the Ministry of Health. The ACM also set new guidelines for collective bargaining by the self-employed, allowing them to jointly negotiate fees up to a level of a reasonable minimum income. Again, labour unions (who were not the ACM's natural ally), the Ministry of Labour and Social Security and even business interest groups were happy with the balanced result after the consultation process. Finally, the ACM prepared new sustainability guidelines with the aim to: (1) remove the myth that competition law stands in the way of cooperation among competitors to achieve sustainability goals; (2) communicate our belief that in case of environmental damage agreements, i.e. agreements that reduce negative environmental externalities, benefits for the society at large should be included in the Article 101(3) TFEU assessment; and (3) propel a European, if not global, debate on the need to issue guidance to companies along the lines of our draft guidelines. This initiative was also near-unanimously supported by private practitioners, business interest groups, non-governmental organisations and the Ministry of Economic Affairs, at least in the Netherlands..

In parallel with these policy changes, the ACM continues to enforce competition laws strictly. Significant fines were imposed for illegal horizontal information exchanges and bid-rigging. New investigations with strict deadlines were launched into, among others, purchasing cartels, retail price-fixing, excessive pricing and conditional discounts in pharma, and the terms and conditions of app stores. Merger scrutiny also intensified with a record number of phase 2 investigations. So it is possible to combine strict competition law enforcement with an open mind towards the call for fairness, sustainability and other public interests. The ACM is not alone in finding a new balance. As some of this Part's authors show, there are already authorities with a long history in this area and there are others who are at the beginning of finding new ways to protect or even increase the legitimacy of competition law and competition authorities.

In the very interesting Australian outlook (especially interesting for non-Australian audiences), the authors, all lawyers in private practice, describe the authorisation framework by which the Australian Competition and Consumer Commission (ACCC) may grant immunity (authorisation) for anticompetitive conduct that would otherwise be prohibited. The basis for the authorisation is a public interest test that without any doubt includes environmental benefits for the society at large. A number of authorisation cases show how the ACCC is able to strike a careful balance between looking at short-run price effects for consumers and longer-term benefits to society as a whole, not only relying on quantitative evidence but also through qualitative submissions. The authorisation process is based on a pragmatic and measured statutory framework to help ensure that the right decision is reached. Authorisations are only granted after a thorough and public multi-stakeholder consultation. The authors clearly show how the Australian experience may provide a possible blueprint for other authorities.

The author of the European Union outlook, Luc Peeperkorn, is a former European Commission official, here giving his personal views. His central theme is that the discussion on the role that competition policy should play in helping to solve the climate crisis can be summed up in one question: should we assess the effects of possibly anticompetitive agreements only within their relevant market or should we assess their effects for society at large? He answers this question negatively, not from a legal but from a policy point of view. Peeperkorn believes that if so-called "out-of-market efficiencies" were included in the competition authorities' assessment it would be bad for the rigour, effectiveness and uniformity of EU competition policy and bad at tackling the climate crisis. This is not the appropriate place to debate the author's point of view, because ultimately it is up to the European Court of Justice to answer the so-far-unanswered legal question if, and under what circumstances, benefits for society at large should be included in the assessment. The ACM explained in its draft guidelines that societal benefits that are the result of reduced negative environmental externalities must be accepted under European competition law as a defence against an allegation of infringement of Article 101(1) TFEU. It will be interesting to see how the Court of Justice is going to deal with this question, either on appeal or after a preliminary reference from national courts.

It is not that Peeperkorn proposes administrative inaction, as he confirms, there are many other things that competition authorities can and should do. He advocates for the Commission and the European Competition Network to provide more specific guidance for sustainability agreements. Such guidance should make clear that genuine sustainability agreements will not be considered "by object" restrictions and that fines will only be imposed where sustainability agreements are used as a disguise for a horizontal cartel. In addition, the Commission and national competition authorities could use their discretion to set priorities and adopt a more hands-off approach to agreements and conduct that are expected to produce significant environmental benefits. On that basis, firms would have more freedom to experiment with new types of sustainability initiatives and agreements, without undue fear that EU competition policy will create obstacles.

In France, there is ample experience of taking on board sustainability aspects, as Isabelle de Silva, president of the French competition authority, demonstrates in her chapter. She emphasises that the connection between sustainability and competition policy is not without ambivalence and that authorities should find the right balance between over- and under-enforcement. President De Silva describes the organisational changes her authority made, including cooperation with sector regulators, to strengthen its experience in this area and coordinate the fight against climate change. The French authority has been particularly active in fighting anticompetitive practices that harm sustainability, for example in the floor-coverings trade, where market players with their trade organisation had entered into a non-competition agreement relating to environmental marketing practices. Few practices came to the authority's attention that actually benefit sustainability, with a notable exception in the candy-manufacturing market. According to President De Silva, an "attitude of openness yet of strong resolve" is what we need to address the challenges of sustainability in the framework of competition law.

Ioannis Lianos, president of the Hellenic Competition Commission, takes a policy perspective in his contribution, emphasising that competition authorities should facilitate the transition to a green economy. They should adapt their enforcement strategies to avoid jeopardising genuine public and private sustainability initiatives. They should also reflect on their role, taking into account unwanted externalities and intergenerational effects. This could lead to cooperation with other authorities and regulators, domestically and abroad. Finally, President Lianos further promotes his idea of creating "competition law sustainability sandboxes" to allow businesses to experiment with new business models and to stimulate innovation.

A fresh perspective to the debate is provided by Commissioner Tembinkosi Bonakele. He elaborates on the well-developed practice in South Africa of including social objectives, in particular the support for small and medium-sized businesses, in the application of competition law in merger and cooperation cases. He also shines a light on a few sustainability cases in the areas of waste management and seeds. Commissioner Bonakele emphasises that competition law exists in a social context and that competition policy can address social objectives, but warns that a successful policy also depends on the resolve of the authorities to be "courageous, consistent and transparent". South Africa's experience demonstrates that it is possible to balance robust competition assessment with social objectives.

Sandrine Delarue and Mike Walker from the UK's Competition and Markets Authority also focus on the policy question of whether authorities should take into account the effects on sustainability of any agreement, unilateral behaviour or merger it is about to assess. However, they take a more cautious approach than some other authors. They argue that the existence of precedents of competition authorities looking into sustainability initiatives demonstrates that competition law is capable of taking sustainability considerations into account. The authors submit that it is for competition authorities to alter their approach in order to take greater account of sustainability issues, by considering the welfare of all consumers, rather than just those in the market where competition is harmed, and by explicitly including long-term environmental degradation as part of the consumer harm analysis. They warn, however, that this approach raises concerns around the optimal use of policy instruments and around judgments as to what to include in the consumer welfare function. Therefore, they believe that there is much merit in competition authorities pushing the boundaries of what the law currently allows (the legal question), while encouraging the democratic legitimacy, and clarity, that should come from a policy debate leading to clear guidance.

Clearly, all the authors of this Part III provide inspiration to competition authorities around the world by showing a way to incorporate sustainability in their day-to-day practices. So, in light of the urgency of the climate crisis, *now* is the time to act.

Australia

GEORGINA FOSTER, GRANT MURRAY AND WENDY THIAN[*]

Baker McKenzie

Under pressure from consumers, employees and investors, and witnessing a shift from voluntary sustainability reporting to mandatory reporting and growing corporate accountability, it is hardly surprising that many organisations now treat sustainability as a board-level issue.

The COVID-19 pandemic has also played its part here, accentuating the importance of the climate crisis, the fragility of the planet and underlined the human element in the supply chain. As a result, many companies are looking to exit the pandemic with renewed or accelerated sustainability efforts.

Of course, the sheer scale of an environmental challenge will often mean that individual action by a company – no matter how laudable – is unlikely to bring about meaningful change, or to achieve it within an acceptable timeframe.

At the same time, competition compliance concerns have emerged as a significant hurdle to industry collaboration.[1]

It is laudable that many competition authorities are now considering the relationship between competition policy and sustainability and how they can be part of the solution without distorting the established objectives of their competition laws.

---

[*] Georgina Foster is a partner in Baker McKenzie's Sydney office and leads the firm's Australian competition practice. Grant Murray and Wendy Thian are knowledge lawyers in Baker McKenzie's Global Antitrust & Competition Group.

[1] FoodDrinkEurope, "FoodDrinkEurope's contribution on 'Competition Policy supporting the Green Deal'" (20 November 2020) <www.fooddrinkeurope.eu/uploads/publications_documents/FoodDrinkEurope_contribution_Green_deal_and_competition_policy.pdf>.

A number of these authorities are making efforts to develop guidance and offer greater legal certainty to companies, including through potential safe harbours. In some parts of the world, there are hints of scepticism towards the benefits of sustainability arrangements. In the flurry of consultations, conferences and discussions in 2020, Australia stands out as a potential framework for others to consider.

I. The International Stage

On 1 December 2020, the OECD's Competition Committee held a hearing with experts and antitrust agencies on sustainability and competition. This was an opportunity to broaden the conversation and engagement, as the antitrust policy debate so far seems to be driven primarily from Europe (despite the fact that many sustainability agreements are likely to be focused on supply chains etc. with their origins outside Europe).

The OECD Competition Committee's background note is a useful road map of the primary issues encountered when applying competition law in a sustainability context.[2] Attempts to reconcile competition policy and sustainability within established economic frameworks seem to be an area of contention.

Some authorities have responded to the global momentum by trying to develop policy and guidance that will be crucial to unlocking more ambitious forms of cooperation. Draft guidelines produced by the Netherlands' Authority for Consumers and Markets are bold and progressive – at least conceptually. The Hellenic Competition Commission's recent paper is a thoughtful contribution with pragmatic suggestions such as the use of a regulatory sandbox, where companies can experiment under the supervision of the competition authority and would not be punished for things that might otherwise be violations of the law.

The European Commission also seems alive to change. Comparing a 2019 speech[3] with the recent much more upbeat call for contributions relating to its Green Deal,[4] that change appears to already be underway.

But the joint written contribution from Australia and New Zealand for the OECD hearing makes a compelling case for a possible blueprint for others to follow.[5] Both have provided examples showing the advantages of having an exemption framework that enables enforcers to give the green light to

---

2   OECD, *Sustainability and Competition, OECD Competition Committee Discussion Paper* (OECD 2020) <www.oecd.org/daf/competition/sustainability-and-competition-2020.pdf>.
3   European Committee of the Regions, "Sustainability and Competition Policy: Bridging two worlds to enable a fairer economy" (Conference, 24 October 2019) <https://europa.eu/newsroom/events/sustainability-and-competition-policy-bridging-two-worlds-enable-fairer-economy_en>.
4   Commission (DG COMP), "Competition Policy supporting the Green Deal: Call for contributions" (13 October 2020) <https://ec.europa.eu/competition/information/green_deal/call_for_contributions_en.pdf>.
5   OECD, "Sustainability and Competition – Note by Australia and New Zealand" DAF/COMP/WD(2020)6 (6 November 2020) <https://one.oecd.org/document/DAF/COMP/WD(2020)62/en/pdf>.

sustainability-focused initiatives in the public interest in certain circumstances, while still keeping the focus of competition law on protecting competition by applying a consumer welfare standard.

The Australian examples, in particular, are worthy of closer examination. Although the Australian regime features a flexible public interest approach, the principles and analysis adopted by the ACCC and the courts will seem familiar to a competition authority conducting an "effects" or "rule of reason" analysis, and may well serve as a new framework for others.

II. The Australian Authorisation Framework

Australia has a long-established process by which the ACCC may grant immunity (known as "authorisation") for conduct that would or might otherwise contravene the substantive competition prohibitions, even for cartels. The ACCC typically makes a determination within a six-month statutory time frame.

The ACCC will grant the authorisation if it is satisfied that the proposed conduct would not lead to a significant lessening of competition or if the public benefits outweigh the public detriments (i.e. there is a net public benefit). Parties seeking authorisation bear the onus of satisfying the ACCC that the test is met. There must be a real chance, and not a mere possibility, that the benefit or detriment will eventuate.[6] In applying the test, the ACCC compares the likely future *with* the proposed conduct to the likely future in which the proposed conduct *does not* occur.

"Public benefit" is not defined by law, though authorisation decisions have confirmed that the term should be given its widest possible meaning. Public benefit refers to "anything of value to the community generally, any contribution to the aims pursued by society including as one of its principal elements… the achievement of the economic goals of efficiency and progress".[7]

There is well-established precedent for applying a modified total welfare standard.[8] The focus of public benefits is often on efficiencies, with environmental benefits fully recognised as being of relevance. And yet this does not lead to a "black box" approach since often the benefit will come from addressing an identified environmental externality.

The ACCC follows a rigorous process when assessing public benefits. Applicants must provide evidence in support of the claimed benefits that flow from the proposed conduct, and the conduct must be likely to bring about the public

---

6   *Re Qantas Airways Ltd* [2004] ACompT 9.
7   *Re 7-Eleven Stores* (1994) ATPR 41-357, 42,677. See also *Queensland Co-operative Milling Association Ltd* (1976) ATPR 40-012, 17,242.
8   *Australian Competition and Consumer Commission v Australian Competition Tribunal* [2017] FCAFC 150; *Re Qantas Airways Ltd* [2004] ACompT 9, [185].

benefit claimed. While the benefits must not be speculative, they do not have to be explicitly quantifiable in all instances. Any estimates should be "robust and commercially realistic, in the sense of being both significant and tangible".[9]

1. Parties protected by authorisation

While an authorisation is in force, parties under statutory protection from legal action include the applicant as well as any others referenced in the application as a person who it is proposed will be engaged in the conduct. This includes those who subsequently become parties to the proposed conduct, where that is its expressed effect and the other parties are identifiable with sufficient certainty.

2. Time limits and revocation of authorisations

An authorisation will usually be granted for a specific time period, although in some cases that time period can be 10 years or longer. For proposed ongoing conduct beyond the period of a granted authorisation, parties can seek to revoke an existing authorisation before it expires and substitute a new one in its place.

Immunity can also be reviewed and potentially revoked/replaced at any time in certain circumstances, including where there has been a material change in circumstances. Interim authorisation may also be granted, usually within 28 days (in the early stages of the pandemic, the ACCC granted interim authorisation for an urgent application within one business day). Such interim authorisations may be revoked at any time if the arrangement does not demonstrate the expected benefits, or if no longer necessary. These mechanisms ensure there is limited risk of negative longer-term impacts arising from ACCC authorisations.

III. Authorisations for Conduct

The Australian authorisation process has facilitated various sustainability initiatives. Industry action to address ozone depleting chemicals was authorised by the ACCC as far back in the 1990s.

A number of authorisation cases show how the ACCC is able to strike a balance between looking at short-run price effects and take into account broader, longer-term benefits. The ACCC's "stewardship cases" – which have related to batteries, chemical containers and tyres – are among the most notable. In these cases, the ACCC authorised schemes that fixed levies on consumers in order to fund programmes for the collection and disposal of waste or end-of-life products.

One example discussed in Australia's OECD submission related to a voluntary industry-led scheme aimed at improving the recycling rate of tyres. It proposed

---

9   *Re Qantas Airways Ltd* (2005) ATPR 42-065, [206].

a levy per tyre on importers and obligations on participants to commit to certain environmentally friendly practices and to deal only with accredited businesses along the supply chain. In its 2018 decision to grant a six-year authorisation to the Tyre Stewardship Scheme, the ACCC acknowledged that there was room to improve the arrangement for better outcomes and that it would closely review the result of a revised scheme, should the applicant seek re-authorisation.[10]

A more recent example is the conditional authorisation granted by the ACCC in September 2020 to the Battery Stewardship Council.[11] The ACCC granted a five-year authorisation for its proposed industry-led voluntary scheme designed to enable responsible disposal of used batteries.

1. Battery Stewardship Scheme

Under this national scheme, competitors agreed to a fixed surcharge on batteries imported by members of the programme, which would be passed through the supply chain to the consumer as a visible fee. Rebates would then be paid to recyclers to help offset the cost of collecting, sorting and processing expired batteries. To prevent free riding, members of the scheme would deal only with other members along the supply chain. Each member was required to make a number of other commitments (e.g. relating to branding and auditing) according to its role in the supply chain, such as government agency, supplier, retailer, collector or processor.

In accordance with the prescribed practice for authorisations, the ACCC conducted a thorough public consultation process, inviting submissions from a range of potentially interested parties including major industry associations, manufacturers, retailers, recyclers, consumer groups, and state and federal government representatives. It received submissions both for and against the scheme.

Despite the "public interest" test under the Australian statutory framework, the analysis involves elements and a process that will be familiar to a competition authority conducting an "effects" or "rule of reason" assessment:

–   Affected markets: the ACCC looked at the impact on competition in all relevant areas, which involved consideration of the wholesale, retail, collection, sorting and processing of batteries.

–   Impact on prices: the ACCC acknowledged that the uniform fee passed on to consumers would be less competitive than independent pricing. While the ACCC calculated that the scheme could result in an increase

10   ACCC authorisations register, *Tyre Stewardship Australia Limited* (granted 24 May 2018) <www.accc. gov.au/public-registers/authorisations-and-notifications-registers/authorisations-register/tyre-stewardship-australia-limited>.
11   ACCC authorisations register, *Battery Stewardship Council* (granted with conditions 4 September 2020) <www.accc.gov.au/public-registers/authorisations-and-notifications-registers/authorisations-register/battery-stewardship-council>.

of up to 6% in the price of certain batteries, it also considered that, if consumers paid closer to the full cost of the use and disposal of batteries, the price increase that might occur due to the levy was likely to signal a more (rather than less) efficient allocation of resources in the economy.

– Environmental benefits: the ACCC accepted that the scheme sought to avoid significant environmental harm to land and water resources and the need for costly remediation, which was not reflected in the current price of batteries. The levy and rebate system was therefore likely to better align pricing with the cost of responsible disposal and increase the incentive for businesses to facilitate their recycling.

– Qualitative benefits: there was a concern that the scheme might put participating businesses at a disadvantage when selling goods that consumers could purchase directly from overseas suppliers. But, on balance, the ACCC considered that any loss of sales faced by partici-pating businesses due to higher prices incorporating the levy was likely to be offset by the ability for businesses to signal their environmental credentials by participating in the scheme.

– R&D and innovation: the ACCC also accepted that the scheme was likely to support increased levels of innovation and research and devel-opment activities concerning end-of-life batteries.

– Indispensability and residual competition: the ACCC acknowledged first-mover disadvantage. Battery importers would not have an incentive to act unilaterally to impose a levy to fund the collection of end-of-life batteries. Therefore, to achieve the public benefits identified, the ACCC saw the need for importers to agree on a levy, to be clearly signalled to consumers. At the same time, the ACCC did not believe that the scheme would increase the likelihood of coordination among importers, wholesalers and retailers on price and in other areas in which they currently compete.

– No requirement for arithmetic or mathematical balancing: while the assessment of benefits and detriments must be complete and they must be weighed, this is not necessarily an arithmetical or accounting process.[12] As the Australian Competition Tribunal has previously noted, it may involve "an instinctive synthesis of otherwise incommensurable factors".

IV. A Possible Blueprint?

The flexibility of the Australian authorisation model allows competition regulators to account for sustainability impacts. At a time when some competition authorities are grappling with this balancing exercise, the ACCC's public benefit

---

12 *Australian Competition and Consumer Commission v Australian Competition Tribunal* [2017] FCAFC 150 (20 September 2017), [68].

approach could be a useful way to enable and encourage sustainability-focused cooperation that seeks to address market failures or a lack of government action.

The ACCC considers factors and evidence that competition authorities of all stripes are accustomed to assessing, and is able to do so in a sustainability context without opening a potential Pandora's box of issues regarding the consumer welfare standard. This includes likely impact on price; qualitative benefits (such as environmental credentials that may form part of a product's value proposition); improvements to R&D and innovation; and indispensability and proportionality.

Although the ACCC carefully assesses claimed benefits, they do not have to be explicitly quantifiable and mathematically calibrated in all cases. That is not radical. Even the exemption criteria under Article 101(3) of the Treaty on the Functioning of the European Union look beyond the exclusively "economic" to include three other elements: improving production, improving distribution and promoting technical progress. Most questions in competition law will require the decision-maker to weigh up quantitative and qualitative evidence and reach a judgment based upon that evidence.

The authorisation process is based on a pragmatic and measured statutory framework to help ensure that the right decision is reached. Authorisations are only granted after a thorough and public multi-stakeholder consultation and, like the useful interventions of authorities in the COVID-19 pandemic, are limited in time. If the parties seek longer-term protection, then they can apply for a re-authorisation, at which point the ACCC can actually verify whether the claimed benefits materialised, as it did in relation to CFC refrigerant authorisations, where the parties were able to show how much emissions had been reduced.[13]

Equally, the ACCC retains the power to claw back authorisations in certain circumstances, including where there has been a material change in circumstances. That it rarely uses these powers is perhaps testament to its robust processes and legitimacy. It may also indicate its appropriateness to serve as a guide for other competition authorities.

Taken as a whole, the ACCC's approach certainly offers a practicable framework within which competitors can work and obtain some certainty when they seek to achieve sustainability goals together. While public interest considerations are expressly mandated by Australian law – something that European and other enforcers might say they are lacking – the EU treaties do contain a number of sustainability-related provisions. In any event, an examination of the ACCC's principles and methodology suggests it is not the outlier that it first appears.

---

13 *Determination: Application for revocation and substitution of authorisation A91008 lodged by Refrigerant Reclaim Australia Limited* (ACCC, 14 May 2008) <www.accc.gov.au/system/files/public-registers/documents/D08%2B42141.pdf>.

These are all important issues that merit a robust conversation at an international forum. Climate change and sustainability are global concerns, and the solutions will need to be appreciably broader. Price effects of sustainability projects may be felt not just by consumers but also by those in places where products are sourced. Environmental benefits may be enjoyed by an even wider group. Legal certainty is critical, and a patchwork of approaches and unknowns will only continue to hamper companies from collaborating to achieve sustainability goals.

Attention now turns to the OECD and other international bodies like the International Competition Network, and their role to play in advancing the debate and helping different national governments and authorities find common ground.

European Union

Luc Peeperkorn[*]

Brussels School of Competition / College of Europe

I. Introduction

The discussion about the role that competition policy should play in helping to solve the climate crisis and supporting the European Green Deal can be summed up in one question: should we assess the effects of possibly anticompetitive agreements (only) within their relevant market(s) or should we assess their effects for society at large?[1] In other words, the key question is whether the current focus of competition law on the harm and benefits caused by an agreement in a particular market should be changed to a focus on the harm and benefits caused across markets, and effectively for society at large. A consumer welfare test versus a total/societal welfare test.[2] In the jargon of competition specialists: whether

---

[*]   Luc Peeperkorn is professor at the Brussels School of Competition and at the College of Europe, Natolin. He was previously Principal Expert Antitrust Policy, DG Competition of the European Commission, Brussels. luc.peeperkorn@gmail.com.
    I would like to thank Paul Bridgeland for his valuable comments. The opinions expressed in this chapter are strictly personal. While I previously worked for the European Commission, nothing in this chapter represents the views of the European Commission, DG COMP or any other institution, entity, person, etc. All errors and omissions are mine. This chapter is based in good part on Luc Peeperkorn, "Competition and sustainability: What can competition policy do?" in Guy Canivet and others, *Sustainability and competition law* (2020) Concurrences N° 4–2020 Art N° 97257, 26–65.

1   This paper only deals with what is also called antitrust policy: the application of Articles 101 and 102 TFEU. It does not deal with the control of state aid under Articles 107–108 TFEU, where there is a more direct link with the climate crisis, among others through the vetting of environmental aid schemes.

2   Some proponents of a wider balancing exercise propose a total welfare test on condition that consumers in the relevant market receive at least some, unspecified, benefit, even if on balance they are worse off as a result of the agreement. This is still a total welfare test, but with an (undefined) minimum consumer welfare constraint. In "Competition and sustainability: What can competition policy do?" in Guy Canivet and others, *Sustainability and competition law* (2020) Concurrences N° 4–2020, Art N° 97257, 26–65, in particular section V, I explain why such a test, even though it (unsuccessfully) tries to respect the wording of Article 101, is patently illogical and unworkable.

the assessment should be limited to "in-market" negative effects and efficiencies or whether it should also include "out-of-market" effects.

The discussion is not about whether the climate crisis is the biggest problem of our time. Some may still argue with this, but science overwhelmingly indicates that, unless we take drastic action, our world will be hit hard. For all those involved in the discussion, it is clear that sustainability must be a top priority for governments, policymakers and society at large.

Nor is there much debate that, for most climate-related problems, regulation is the best policy solution. In economic terms, that it is best to internalise the external effects that cause the climate crisis, either by prohibiting certain conduct, by taxing that conduct or by subsidising preferred alternatives.[3] By internalising the external effects, regulation induces firms and consumers to make climate-friendly choices when they decide on what and how to produce, distribute and consume.

There is also a consensus that there is no need for firms to agree on actions to address climate concerns if regulation is already properly internalising external effects. In that case, each firm is already incentivised to produce and sell its products in a climate-friendly way. This means that firms will also reduce their environmental impact to optimal levels without an agreement.

Nonetheless, based on a desire to help tackle global warming and to be "part of the solution and not part of the problem", a number of competition practitioners have proposed to change the test applied in (EU) competition policy. While the details of their proposals may differ, the essence is always to take a broader look at the effects of agreements and conduct by firms and to assess the effects for society at large.[4] In this paper, I will argue why that would be a bad approach.[5] Bad for the rigour, effectiveness and uniformity of EU competition policy and also bad for tackling the climate crisis.

---

3 Taxes and subsidies are seen by economists as the classic instruments to internalise an external effect. Taxes and subsidies work directly through the price system, by increasing (taxes) or reducing (subsidies) the prices of the products involved. However, prohibitions, including caps – if properly monitored and enforced – will also incentivise firms to take climate-friendly decisions, adapt their production and distribution, and internalise the external effects.

4 See, for instance, Maurits Dolmans, "Sustainable Competition Policy" (2020) 5(4) and 6(1) Competition Law & Policy Debate; Simon Holmes, "Climate change, sustainability, and competition law" (2020) 8(2) J Antitrust Enforcement 354; Jordan Ellison, "A Fair Share: Time for the Carbon Defence?" (21 February 2020) <https://ssrn.com/abstract=3542186> accessed 17 January 2021; Fair Trade Advocacy Office, "EU Competition Law and Sustainability in Food Systems: Addressing the Broken Links" (February 2019). See also ACM, "Draft Guidelines: Sustainability Agreements" (9 July 2020) <www. acm.nl/en/publications/acm-opens-more-opportunities-businesses-collaborate-achieve-climate-goals>.

5 See also Maarten Pieter Schinkel and Lukas Tóth, "Compensatory Public Good Provision by a Private Cartel" Tinbergen Institute Discussion Papers 19-086/VII (March 2020).

II. Effectiveness Requires Focus

Where public authorities have to take occasional major investment decisions, for example to choose between spending €10 billion on rail infrastructure or on road infrastructure, it may be possible and appropriate to undertake an extensive cost – benefit analysis in order to try to weigh up the effects of the investment in relation to various societal goals. However, the same is not true of a policy like EU competition policy, where the Commission, the national competition authorities and national courts are continually taking multiple decisions concerning differing markets and where, in addition, private firms are required to self-assess thousands, if not millions, of agreements and forms of conduct. For this type of public policy, it would not be possible, let alone appropriate, to require a balancing of a range of goals. A requirement, as proposed by some, to weigh up different policy goals in every competition case would destroy the effectiveness of EU competition law enforcement.

This is not a novel insight. Jan Tinbergen, the first Nobel Prize winner in Economics, already demonstrated that it is optimal to have (at least) as many policy instruments as goals, and to allocate one goal to each instrument.[6] The various goals can then be achieved by applying the appropriate mix of policy instruments, complemented where necessary by a hierarchy of instruments and goals. Although it was developed some decades ago, this insight has not been superseded or lost any of its relevance, as shown by Jean Tirole, also a winner of the Nobel Prize in Economics, in a recent speech in which he warned against trying to achieve industrial policy goals with competition law instruments.[7]

An examination of how environmental external effects might be taken into account provides a good example of some of these practical difficulties. Proponents of a wider societal balancing, like Dolmans, often refer to environmental prices, calculated by research institutes, as a practical tool that could be used to assess environmental efficiencies under Article 101(3) TFEU. Environmental prices are indices that measure the social marginal value of interventions such as reducing emissions or noise. They try to indicate the loss of welfare caused by the emission of one additional kilogram of pollutant or one extra decibel of noise. In that sense, environmental prices are often the same as external costs.[8]

---

6   On the virtues of having one goal per policy and having as many policies as goals: Jan Tinbergen, *On the Theory of Economic Policy* (North Holland Publishing Company 1952). For an application to competition policy, see Alexander Italianer and Luc Peeperkorn, "Schoenmaker blijf bij je leest" ESB Dossier 2014, no 4683S, 71–74.

7   Jean Tirole, "Competition Policy at a Crossroad" (keynote address, OECD Global Forum on Competition, 5 December 2019).

8   This definition is taken from two reports: Sander de Bruyn and others, *Environmental Prices Handbook 2017* (CE Delft 2018) and CE Delft, *Shadow Prices Handbook* (March 2010), both available at: <www.cedelft.eu>.

Because a market for environmental quality is lacking, environmental prices cannot be observed directly via market prices, but must be calculated using the results of studies on human preferences for avoiding the impacts of pollution. These prices are therefore usually based on a combination of different studies about the estimated impacts of pollutants on a number of themes or so-called midpoints – such as ozone depletion, climate change, eutrophication and human toxicity – and the resulting effects on certain endpoints – such as human health, ecosystem services including agriculture, buildings and materials, and resource availability. The effects on these endpoints are then monetised through a mix of willingness to pay studies and translated back to damage per intervention (kilo of substance, etc.).[9]

This monetisation and the resulting environmental price are necessarily not very precise. Not only are the estimates complex, but they also show large variations, both in the estimated physical impacts and the price effects, often varying by a factor 10 or more. In addition, not all impacts can be estimated and monetised, and there is also debate about which midpoints and endpoints to use, which further complicates the calculation. Moreover, environmental prices are usually average prices for a particular year, from an average source, at an average location (with average population density and average income, for example). Environmental prices are thus rough-and-ready estimates, which can be useful for general policy discussions and the formulation of general policy measures such as eco-taxes. However, they are not necessarily valid or useful for assessing specific situations, as required in competition cases. For example, it is highly questionable whether, for the assessment of an individual agreement or conduct under competition law, it would be appropriate to apply existing studies on average effects. Firms would be likely to claim that in their particular case the effects, given the specific circumstances, are (much) higher/ lower than what the averages indicate.[10]

In other words, if EU competition policy were to be used to try to achieve different EU goals, this would only lead to slow, costly and unpredictable case outcomes. The consequences would be even more dramatic for the continuous self-assessment that the competition rules require of firms for their commercial agreements and, once they hold a dominant position, for their unilateral conduct.[11] It would also put a very heavy strain on national courts, where many competition cases are brought. In view of the high number of actors (the

---

9   The description of the estimation of environmental prices in this and the next paragraph is based on the reports of CE Delft, ibid.
10 While this may not be an issue for a few substances, such as CO_2, where the effects are never local, it would be relevant for all other forms of pollution, such as emissions of NO_x, small particles, soil and water pollution, where the effects are to a certain degree local, and will therefore also depend on local land use, population density, etc.
11 The analysis in this paper focuses mainly on the assessment of agreements under Article 101 TFEU, but it applies equally to the assessment of unilateral conduct under Article 102 TFEU and the assessment of mergers.

Commission, national competition authorities, national courts, firms required to self-assess) and the very high number of agreements/mergers/conducts concerned, it would be impossible, and excessively costly, to carry out such wide-ranging cost – benefit analyses. Such a requirement would undermine, if not destroy, effective enforcement.[12]

III. A Total Welfare Test Will Undermine the Rigour and Uniform Application of the EU Competition Rules

The rationale underlying the current approach of EU competition policy is that, for an anticompetitive agreement to be allowed, the consumers that are harmed by the negative effects of the agreement must at least be compensated by sufficient pass-on of the efficiencies created by the agreement. In other words, the negative and positive effects are weighed up for the consumers per relevant market and not across different groups of consumers in different markets or across citizens in society at large.

Even leaving aside the issue whether or not to take possible external effects into account, EU competition policy has always considered that there are good practical reasons for limiting the assessment to each relevant market, and to the customers in that market. For instance, a merger in the pharmaceuticals sector may involve hundreds of products; weighing up the possible negative effects and efficiencies across markets would be excessively difficult and costly. These practical objections would be even stronger if it were necessary to extend the weighing-up exercise beyond markets, for instance to also take into account the interests of citizens who do not use the product(s) in question, or the interests of society at large.

Extending the assessment of effects beyond markets in this way would necessarily politicise EU competition policy. The resulting loss of rigour and certainty might not harm the very large firms, with their armies of lawyers, economists and lobbyists, but it would harm the many smaller firms and, behind them, their customers and European consumers, all of whom depend on a rigorous and predictable competition policy for their protection.

---

12 It is sometimes argued, for instance by Holmes (see n 4), that competition law is based on weighing-up positive and negative effects, and that balancing different goals should thus not create an (insurmountable) problem for firms and enforcers. This argument misses the fundamental difference between, on the one hand, trying to assess whether the positive effects of an agreement or conduct outweigh its negative effects for a particular group of customers and, on the other, trying to weigh up the effects of an agreement or conduct on different goals and therewith, by necessity, also across different groups. Asking one group of consumers that are equally affected whether they feel on balance that they are better or worse off as a result of the agreement does not necessarily require any quantification, and in practice often surveys, etc. suffice. By contrast, the second kind of balancing exercise, involving multiple markets and groups, necessarily requires quantification to avoid arbitrariness and is rare in competition cases.

Uniformity of application, predictability and rigour would be undermined not just because it is extremely difficult for competition authorities and national courts to weigh different interests and goals. It would also be undermined because (environmental) regulations differ between Member States, and so do opinions about the extent to which current regulations are optimal from an environmental point of view.

As indicated in the introduction, there is (or should be) agreement that there is no need for firms to agree on actions to address climate concerns if regulation properly internalises external effects. In that case, each firm is already incentivised to produce and sell its products in a climate-friendly way and to reduce its environment impact to optimal levels without any agreement.

It should also be clear that if regulation is already internalising external effects, there is no need to change the test currently applied by EU competition policy. In that case, firms will at most be able to claim an efficiency under Article 101 TFEU if they can show that collective action is a more efficient way of reducing their environmental impact than doing so individually, for instance because of economies of scale. The efficiency they can claim is not the reduction in the environmental impact itself, but only the reduction in the costs incurred to achieve that reduction. For this type of cost reduction, there is no need to take out-of-market efficiencies into account, because the cost reductions do not concern the reduction in environmental impact itself and will all be in-market. These cost efficiencies will benefit the consumers of the product in question and therefore do not require a change in the test applied under competition law.[13]

However, if a total welfare test were to be introduced, this would affect the consistency and rigour of enforcement. To the extent that regulations differ between Member States and to the extent that the opinions of competition law enforcers will differ about the degree to which such regulation is properly internalising all external effects – and such differences cannot be avoided – the cases in which and the degree to which effects for society at large will have to be taken into account will differ. This would undermine a uniform application of the EU competition rules and undermine legal certainty.

For instance, in the presence of a cap-and-trade system, the parties to an agreement can only claim a reduction of pollution as a possible efficiency if they agree to go beyond what the cap-and-trade system already requires of them.[14] In practice, this would mean that they would not only have to agree to reduce their own pollution, but also to destroy, or at least not sell, the allowances freed up by their own reduction in pollution. In other words, the parties to the agreement would agree to apply the cap-and-trade system more strictly than was decided by the democratic policy process.

---

13   For a more detailed argumentation, see in particular section VIII of Peeperkorn (n 2).
14   The same applies to cases where firms want to go beyond what is already incentivised under current tax and subsidy schemes or beyond what is required under current regulation in general.

While firms are at liberty to do so, it is not evident why it would be for a competition authority or indeed for the competition department of the Commission to substitute their views on what is the optimal level of pollution or the optimal societal balancing of effects for the views embodied in the democratically decided cap-and-trade system. If there is a regulation in place, there has arguably already been a political decision about what should be the optimal level of pollution for society.[15] If a competition authority were to decide that the cap-and-trade system does not sufficiently internalise the external effects and that a further reduction in pollution should be assessed as a benefit for society in general, this would raise questions about the democratic legitimacy of the competition authority's assessment. It can also be expected that competition authorities will differ in their assessment of the sufficiency of current regulations, if only because they are not well equipped to carry out the necessary assessment of the pros and cons for society at large.

Even where there is clear political demand for increased regulation and a consensus that current regulations are not doing enough, the fact that the appropriate policy instruments have not yet been adopted indicates that it is no simple matter to determine, from a societal point of view, what the optimal level of pollution for a particular substance should be. In that case also, it cannot be expected that competition agencies, national courts or private firms will be well placed to make that assessment.

For all these problems, the recent proposal of draft guidelines by the Dutch competition authority (ACM) provides an instructive example.[16] In the Netherlands, parliament has adopted a binding climate goal, giving Dutch citizens the right to demand that their government delivers on the goal, as confirmed by the Dutch Supreme Court in *Urgenda*.[17] However, the Dutch government and parliament have not adopted the necessary legislation or other measures to achieve the goal. It is in that context that the ACM made its proposal to widen the test of Article 101(3) TFEU to include "out-of-market" effects, but only for agreements that contribute to the achievement of an adopted societal goal that binds the state.

Not only is the Dutch situation rare – states are generally unlikely to adopt goals that legally bind them without also adopting the necessary measures to achieve those goals – but it can also be better addressed by adopting the missing legislation and other implementing measures. It is certainly not good for the uniform application and predictability of EU competition policy if the test to be applied depends on the areas in which different states have adopted binding obligations. Not only because of the fragmentation this would create, but also because the chosen goals will reflect differing national concerns and priorities. If, on the other

---

15 For the concept of the optimal level of pollution, see the CE Delft reports (n 8).
16 See the ACM guidelines (n 4).
17 Dutch Supreme Court Case 19/00135 *Netherlands v Urgenda* NL:HR:2019:2007: the Dutch government was held liable on the basis of its obligations under the European Convention on Human Rights to reduce greenhouse gas emissions at a higher minimum rate than that planned by the Dutch government.

hand, the state adopts the necessary implementing measures, its goal becomes binding also for the industry (the external effects are internalised) and, as explained earlier in this section, there is no need to change the test currently applied by EU competition policy.

The societal welfare test proposed by the ACM, if adopted, would require the ACM to assess possible gains and losses in societal welfare resulting from the environmental impact of agreements.[18] This will bring with it the complexities of estimating environmental prices in the specific circumstances of individual cases (see the previous section). Estimating the (avoided) damage to society is difficult, costly and uncertain. In its proposal, the ACM suggests that it can bypass these difficulties by using the so-called abatement cost approach: the positive contribution of the agreement to societal welfare is calculated as the costs that other firms/the rest of society no longer have to bear in order to achieve the environmental goal set by the state.[19] However, not only is estimating abatement costs not without its own difficulties, but this approach is not consistent with the way benefits are assessed and quantified under Article 101(3) TFEU. The abatement costs will generally be (much) lower than the damage costs.[20] Article 101(3) TFEU entitles the parties to an agreement to claim as efficiencies the total benefits that their agreement creates, which in this case would be the value to society of the reduced damage to the environment, and not just the costs that other firms/the rest of society would incur if they decided to help the state to achieve the goal that currently only binds the state.

IV. An Effective and Predictable Competition Policy Will Help to Tackle the Climate Crisis

Protecting competition will also protect sustainability. As sufficiently demonstrated elsewhere, competition spurs innovation, and it is widely recognised that innovation is key to addressing the climate crisis.[21] Competition also forces firms to use scarce resources efficiently and to listen to consumers when the latter demand more sustainable products. In other words, by protecting competition, competition law will indirectly support climate policy (as well as other sustainability goals).

---

18 While the ACM proposal only addresses how to take possible positive environmental impacts resulting from an agreement into account under Article 101(3) TFEU, it seems obvious that if positive impacts are to be taken into account, then also any negative impacts of the agreement on societal welfare should be taken into account, under Article 101(1) TFEU.
19 For more details on the ACM's proposal, see the contribution in this book from Theon van Dijk.
20 This is because, in many cases, actual environmental quality will be "sub-optimal", as a result of insufficiently effective environmental policy. In those cases, it "pays" to further reduce pollution. See the CE Delft reports (n 8).
21 For some references to the literature on the positive role played by competition as a driver of innovation, see section II of Peeperkorn (n 2).

In situations where external effects are not sufficiently internalised through adequate regulation, competition may not deliver the desired sustainable outcomes. In that case, (additional) regulation will be necessary, and will in most cases be the most effective means of achieving the policy goal. Once markets are adequately regulated, competition can then again play its positive role, as set out above. Recognising that, to internalise negative effects, it is advisable to make the polluter pay does not mean that it should be the role of competition law to make the polluter (or its customers) pay.

Some authors point to an unwarranted fear "in the market" that genuine and well-intentioned agreements to reduce pollution or contribute to other laudable sustainability goals may be prohibited, even where they do not lead to appreciable anticompetitive effects, and – even more frighteningly – may expose their participants to fines.[22] Addressing such fears is important, but doing so does not require any change to the substantive tests applied by EU competition law.

Current enforcement practice and Commission guidelines already make clear that all types of possible benefits for consumers in the relevant market can be taken into account.[23] From clearly quantifiable technical improvements in the production or distribution of goods or other forms of technical or economic progress – such as lower costs, wider choice, improved or new products etc. – to less tangible benefits that consumers (may) value – such as the luxury image and aura of products. Appreciation by consumers of products which pollute less, are made by workers that are paid a living wage, involve higher standards of animal welfare etc. can be and is sometimes already integrated in the assessment of positive and negative effects for the consumers in the relevant market.

It would be sufficient for the Commission and the European Competition Network to provide more specific guidance for sustainability agreements.[24] Such guidance should make clear that genuine sustainability agreements, which will often be a form of standardisation agreement, will not be considered "by object" restrictions. It would also be helpful for such guidance to make clear that fines will not normally be imposed in cases involving genuine sustainability agreements, i.e., that fines will only be imposed where sustainability agreements are used as a disguise for a horizontal cartel. This would do no more than confirm explicitly what is already good current practice – namely, that fines are generally not imposed for agreements that restrict competition "by effect" and which are only prohibited after a full assessment of their effects. In addition, the Commission and national competition authorities could use their discretion to set priorities

---

22 See Holmes and the report of the Fair Trade Advocacy Office (n 4).
23 Commission Guidelines on the application of Article 81(3) of the Treaty [2004] OJ C101/97; Commission Guidelines on the applicability of Article 101 TFEU to horizontal co-operation agreements [2011] OJ C11/01. See also Cristina Volpin, "Sustainability as a Quality Dimension of Competition: Protecting Our Future (Selves)" *CPI Antitrust Chronicle* (28 July 2020).
24 For some guidance on the application of Article 101 TFEU to sustainability agreements, see section IX of Peeperkorn (n 2).

and adopt a more hands-off approach to agreements or conduct that are expected to produce significant environmental benefits, while exercising extra vigilance in respect of agreements or conduct where the consumer harm is wholly or partly the result of environmental damage caused by the agreement or conduct, or where the consumer harm is accompanied by such environmental damage.

On that basis, firms would have more freedom to experiment with new types of sustainability initiatives and agreements, without undue fear that EU competition policy will create obstacles.

France

ISABELLE DE SILVA*

French Competition Authority (Autorité de la concurrence)

Sustainability has become a major concern for both consumers and undertakings. Awareness of the consequences of climate change, in particular, has much increased, and a lively public debate on how to tackle the considerable challenges it raises is now ongoing in our communities, in Europe and elsewhere. When every public institution has a duty to consider how to contribute to the global goal of achieving sustainable development, it is only natural for competition enforcers to engage in this discussion, and to seek to identify what input competition policy may have.

Clearly, while acknowledging the magnitude of environmental issues, competition authorities do not see themselves as being on the front line of this fight. It is primarily the role of policymakers to devise and implement appropriate regulation, for the safeguarding of the environment.

This said, while staying within their remit, which is solely about enforcing and promoting competition rules, competition authorities have a part to play in this debate.

The connection between sustainability and competition policy has a certain ambivalence.

---

* Isabelle de Silva has been the president of the French Competition Authority (*Autorité de la concurrence*) since her appointment by the President of the French Republic in October 2016. She is a member of the French Council of State (*Conseil d'Etat*), of which she chaired the Sixth Chamber. She held various Government positions, as an adviser to the Minister of Culture and Communications, in charge of the press and the radio, director of legal affairs of the Ministry of Ecology, Sustainable Development, Transport and Housing, and a member of the sector regulator for press distribution. She has, in addition, been a member of the board of the *Autorité de la concurrence* since 2014.

Competition law can sometimes be presented as a hindrance to achieving sustainability, because of the prohibition of anticompetitive agreements, which may come in the way of joint initiatives by market players to upgrade the sustainability of their products or processes. Furthermore, state aid rules may constitute a constraint on the support needed by an industry to advance sustainability goals. While they are keen not to obstruct efforts toward greater sustainability, it is the mission of competition agencies to uncover, investigate and punish harmful antitrust practices, whether collusive or unilateral, despite claims that such conducts serve high-level objectives. We also realise that we need to be alert to those anticompetitive behaviours that may be detrimental to the environment.

Against this background, it is imperative to strike the right balance and avoid being caught between two evils, namely: maintaining principles that may seem too rigid or short-sighted, and granting a "green" excuse to would-be competition infringers.

We are not alone trying to delineate the right path to follow. Various initiatives have been launched and are beginning to thrive. In October 2020, the European Commission launched a call for contributions on the topic "Competition policy supporting the Green Deal", in order to gather ideas from all stakeholders, within and beyond the competition community.

Internationally, the topic is on the agenda of the International Competition Network, as a project led by the host agency of its 2021 annual conference, and it was discussed at length in the course of the 2020 December meetings of the OECD competition committee.

At national level, some competition authorities have also shared their thoughts. The Dutch ACM, which has been very proactive in this debate, published draft guidelines (July 2020) to offer guidance to companies on market initiatives they might want to implement to improve sustainability,[1] while the Greek HCC released a "staff discussion paper" (September 2020), to kick-start its public consultation on how competition law rules might be adapted to promote more sustainable business practices.[2]

In France, the *Autorité* has taken also an active stance toward the challenges posed by sustainability objectives in the course of antitrust enforcement. Our first move was to strengthen our expertise. To that effect, we have put together a dedicated working group of volunteer case-handlers who are willing to devote a portion of their time to this topic, with a view to levelling up our understanding of these issues, collecting possible leads, and eventually looking for anticompetitive practices.

---

1   ACM, "Draft Guidelines: Sustainability agreements, Opportunities within competition law" (9 July 2020) <www.acm.nl/en/publications/draft-guidelines-sustainability-agreements>.
2   HCC, "Draft Staff Discussion Paper on 'Sustainability Issues and Competition Law'" (September 2020) <www.epant.gr/en/enimerosi/competition-law-sustainability.html>.

Ultimately, what we seek to achieve by pulling together our resources is to be able to develop cases. We believe there is merit in exploring the many aspects of the interrelation between competition policy and sustainable development only insofar as it eventually makes our institution better at performing its core mission, that is: to fight anticompetitive practices, to assess proposed mergers, and to advise public and private stakeholders through robust, reasoned and fair decisions and opinions.

Because sustainability has become a prominent concern for consumers over the years, it is growing into a parameter for product differentiation. Companies are also faced with demanding regulations that lead them to adapt their product range or production processes. For these reasons, sustainability is now a key part of their global strategy, and therefore anticompetitive practices may occur in connection with this new feature of competition. One clear illustration of this can be found in a case adjudicated by the *Autorité* in 2017.[3]

In that case, the main market players in the floor coverings sector, together with their trade association, had entered into a non-compete agreement relating to environmental communication. This charter barred each company involved from advertising the individual environmental performance of its products. Manufacturers were permitted only to communicate on this performance through joint data sheets produced by the trade association, based on an average of the results from the different companies.

According to the terms of the charter, it aimed to eliminate "competitive marketing practices based on environmental characteristics" and to "avoid unnecessary controversy relating to particular products and adopt a consistent marketing approach" in order to prevent "reckless green marketing". A request from one large distributor of the products in France, who wanted to know about the volatile organic compound emissions of each product in order to pass on the information to its customers, was met with a blunt refusal.

Neither retailers nor consumers, increasingly sensitive to how air quality impacts human health, especially at home or in the workplace, could receive the standard of information that they would have obtained without this agreement, and that would have assisted with their purchasing decisions. Furthermore, this agreement was clearly a disincentive for manufacturers to innovate in order to offer products with better environmental performances. These practices persisted for no less than nine years, from 2002 to 2011.

I believe this is an exemplary case regarding the interrelation of competition law and sustainable development. While sustainability is not in and of itself an objective that competition enforcers are bound to pursue, the very implementation of competition rules can help achieve it.

---

3   Autorité de la concurrence, Decision n° 17-D-20 of 18 October 2017 regarding practices implemented in the floor coverings sector

While it may be somehow less obvious, this is true also of antitrust enforcement against abuses of dominance.

Unilateral behaviour can harm sustainability all the same, as dominant firms can place barriers to entry against innovative market players. In a decision of 2014,[4] the *Autorité* ruled on a complaint filed against alleged exclusionary practices by Nespresso, whereby this firm would tie the purchase of its coffee pods to that of its coffee machines. The *Autorité* found that these practices were liable to constitute an abuse of dominance by preventing the development of competing coffee pods, including innovative products such as those incorporating recycling features. In response to these competition concerns, Nespresso offered a series of commitments that the *Autorité* accepted and made mandatory, resulting in a more diverse range of products. This substantiates the notion that sound competition enforcement can, albeit to an extent limited to its own purview, support sustainability.

This approach is in line with the overarching principles set by European law.

These principles have established sustainability as an objective to be integrated in the European Union's policies, among which is competition policy. The EU Charter of Fundamental rights, article 37, provides that "a high level of environmental protection and the improvement of the quality of the environment must be integrated into the policies of the Union and ensured in accordance with the principle of sustainable development". Article 11 TFEU states quite similarly that "environmental protection requirements must be integrated into the definition and implementation of the Union's policies and activities, in particular with a view to promoting sustainable development".

This makes for a strong legal basis for competition enforcers to place sustainability on top of their agenda, as the *Autorité* has done for 2020 and again for 2021 – all the more so now that the transposition of the ECN+ Directive makes it the prerogative of all national competition authorities in Europe to decide on their priorities.

With this in mind, the message to be sent to the business community is twofold.

Anticompetitive behaviour that adversely affects the environment is bound to be severely punished. At the same time, special attention should be given to sustainability-enhancing conduct. While there is obviously no blanket exception to the application of competition law when sustainability issues are at stake, the *Autorité* is willing to assist companies that would, in good faith, seek to cooperate toward a genuine green initiative. Companies should know we are open and ready to hear from them. However, it is worth noting that, thus far, no undertaking has reached out to us with a request that we offer clarity on what may lawfully be agreed upon.

---

4   Autorité de la concurrence, Decision 14-D-09 of 4 September 2014 regarding practices implemented by Nestlé, Nestec, Nestlé Nespresso, Nespresso France and Nestlé Entreprises in the sector of single-portion espresso coffee machines

The *Autorité* looks forward to having more opportunities to proceed with an actual case-by-case assessment.

Among very few examples, one may cite the candy manufacturing market, where French producers publicly agreed to no longer use titanium dioxide as an ingredient in their products, following a 2017 study that pointed to this food additive being associated with early stages of carcinogenesis. This agreement, reached under the aegis of the candy manufacturing trade organisation, came a year before E171 was banned. The *Autorité* decided not to formally investigate the case. Yet this type of agreement may be a candidate for competition analysis, to be conducted against an assessment of the possible efficiencies deriving from it.

In any case, it would not be unprecedented for the *Autorité* to take account of other public interests in the framework of its analysis, with a view to encouraging an environmentally-friendly or sustainability-enhancing initiative to proceed.

In 2005, the then *Conseil de la concurrence* accepted the objective justification by a dominant company – a religious community – regarding the restrictions it imposed on passenger transport to the small island of which it was the sole owner and resident.[5] It was found that its monopoly on ferry service was warranted by the geography of the place, and the need to preserve this listed natural site.

Beside this rather atypical decision, the *Autorité* has demonstrated on several occasions that it takes a broad view of the interests that may be part of its assessment.

Despite enduring criticism to the contrary, it is a fact that competition enforcers do not limit their assessment of the impact of a merger to the issue of prices. In the course of merger control, the *Autorité*, like many of its counterparts, has shown time and again that it will consider the impact of the transaction on a range of parameters that are relevant for consumers, not just on prices.

In several decisions in the broadcasting[6] and printed press[7] sectors, the *Autorité* took account of the impact of the proposed takeover on pluralism and diversity, and imposed commitments accordingly. Likewise, on an occasion when the *Autorité* had to assess a major merger in the retail sector, it examined how the transaction would affect inter alia the quality of service for the distribution of

5   Conseil de la concurrence, Decision n° 05-D-60 of 8 November 2005 regarding practices implemented by the Immaculate Conception Cistercian Order, the Planaria company and the municipality of Cannes
6   Autorité de la concurrence, Decision n° 12-DCC-100 of 23 July 2012 regarding the acquisition of TPS and CanalSatellite by Vivendi Universal and Canal Plus; Autorité de la concurrence, Decision n° 17-DCC-92 of 22 June 2017 reviewing the injunctions of Decision n° 12-DCC-100 of 23 July 2012.
7   Autorité de la concurrence, Decision n° 11-DCC-114 of 12 July 2011 regarding the acquisition of sole control of the Est Républicain Group by the Crédit Mutuel; Autorité de la concurrence, Decision n° 13-DCC-46 of 16 April 2013 regarding the acquisition, by the Rossel group, of the Champagne-Ardenne-Picardie Hub of the Hersant Média group; Autorité de la concurrence, Decision n° 15-DCC-63 of 4 June 2015 regarding the acquisition of Les Journaux du Midi by La Dépêche du Midi.

electronics (so-called "brown" and "grey" goods).[8] An online survey commissioned from a polling organisation identified a risk that the quality of the parties' products and services could be negatively impacted by the merger under review. It showed that, with service quality being a key factor in competition for consumers on that market, a reduction in quality would cause a shift in demand, thus providing a measure of the non-price effects of the transaction. This type of analysis could provide a benchmark for an assessment of the effect of a merger on other qualitative parameters.

Our consultation function also offers an illustration of how a variety of interests can be factored into our analysis.

In agriculture, a sector that is of prime importance to the French economy, the *Autorité* has been keen to explore all aspects of the combination of competition rules with the particular constraints of producers that are often of small size and caught up in a tense relation with powerful buyers. In the opinion we issued in 2018 on "agriculture and competition", we sought to clarify the conditions of applying competition law in this sector and to explain to stakeholders how these rules, together with sector regulations and the latest case law, make room for them to structure their activities and better balance supply and demand.[9] Exchange of information, collective setting of minimum sales prices, agreements on volumes … The *Autorité* stated in detailed and practical terms what is and what is not permissible, and under which conditions, with special reference to the types of formal horizontal and vertical agreements that agriculture producers can enter into. This type of approach, offering guidance to market players, while acknowledging the specific interest attached to their sector, could serve as an inspiration for advocacy-supporting sustainability initiatives that are compliant with competition law.

Taking better account of environmental challenges in the course of our mission is a duty not only for competition policy.

In France, the *Autorité* has teamed up in an informal group with sector regulators in order to share good practices and to coordinate the fight against climate change. Eight of them (the *Autorité* and the authorities overseeing respectively financial markets, telecoms, transport, data privacy, energy, broadcasting and the protection of literary and artistic property rights on the Internet) issued a working paper in May 2020, on their roles and tools to include pressing environmental issues into the definition and implementation of their policies.[10]

---

8   Autorité de la concurrence, Decision n° 16-DCC-111 of 18 July 2016 regarding the acquisition of the Darty company by the Fnac group.
9   Autorité de la concurrence, Opinion n° 18-A-05 of 3 May 2018 regarding the agricultural sector.
10 Autorité de la concurrence, "Eight French regulators publish a working paper on their role and tools in the face of climate change" Press release (5 May 2020) <www.autoritedelaconcurrence.fr/en/press-release/eight-french-regulators-publish-working-paper-their-role-and-tools-face-climate>.

Against the background of the objectives set by the Paris Agreement of December 2015, these regulators have exposed how they may help and monitor businesses in this respect, level-up consumer awareness and fight greenwashing, and strengthen their own expertise. All authorities in this group have integrated climate and environmental concerns into their priorities, and agreed to further advance their discussions on possible avenues for collaboration.

This attitude of openness yet strong resolve is likely the one we need to maintain in our attempt to address the challenges of sustainability in the framework of competition law and policy. It is by incorporating sustainability and climate change in the agenda of the different public agencies that, jointly with the actions of the private sector, we will be able to achieve lasting results.

Greece

IOANNIS LIANOS[*]

Hellenic Competition Commission

Environmental degradation and "climate emergency" pose important economic and social challenges for public authorities, including competition authorities, which are confronted with the transition to an economy that is environmentally (and socially) sustainable. Systemic resilience becomes a goal for all dimensions of public action, including competition law and policy.[1]

Sustainability-oriented policies will benefit the wellbeing of citizens and consumers but may also be a means of acquiring a competitive advantage for undertakings in Europe, thus serving a broader European industrial policy agenda, as has been put forward by the EU[2] and some Member States.[3]

The front-end costs of efficiency improvement and renewable energy use, if we take this aspect of the sustainable development goals, are indeed high, and financing of investment remains key in order to realise potential benefits. However, with benefits subject to greater uncertainty (in terms of the systemic effects) than is faced on the costs side (e.g. considerable investment costs for

---

[*] President, Hellenic Competition Commission (HCC); professor of global competition law and policy, UCL Faculty of Laws (on leave).
1   Ioannis Lianos, "Competition Law as a Form of Social Regulation" (2020) 65(1) Antitrust Bull 3.
2   European Commission, "Reflection Paper Towards a Sustainable Europe by 2030" (March 2019), 14; Commission, "The European Green Deal sets out how to make Europe the first climate-neutral continent by 2050, boosting the economy, improving people's health and quality of life, caring for nature, and leaving no one behind" (IP/19/6691, 11 December 2019); Commission, "The European Green Deal" (Communication) COM(2019) 640 final; Commssion, "Recovery Plan for Europe" <https://ec.europa.eu/info/live-work-travel-eu/health/coronavirus-response/recovery-plan-europe_en> accessed 26 January 2021.
3   See, for instance, in Greece, Christopher Pissarides Committee, "Plan for Growth" (14 November 2020) <https://government.gov.gr/wp-content/uploads/2020/11/growth_plan_2020-11-23_1021.pdf> (in Greek)
.

renewable energy projects), the prospects of corporate financing of the transition to green economy may not be optimal. Public funding, which is a necessary for this "green transition" to work, may not fill the funding gap, particularly as most EU countries are struggling to regain economic strength during the COVID-19 pandemic. Furthermore, with regard to public funding, an assessment of net benefits between climate investment and non-climate investment should be made in order to decide the allocation of scarce public funds among competing sustainable goals. There are important choices to be made and opportunity costs to be assessed. In view of the funds required, this transition to a sustainable economy will be successful if it is supported by both private and public actors and indeed some net-saving sectors should become net-investing sectors in the next few years.

This may not be easy, as it is difficult to assess climate disruption risks and the incentives of some business actors may be affected by legacy investments in non-environmentally friendly production processes, with the result that their assets may depreciate if stricter environmental regulation is passed or CO_2 emission pricing increases.

A regulatory public intervention approach for the green transition at EU level may not be possible for political reasons, and the policy space available to each national government depends on a number of factors, including institutional capabilities and a relatively tight budgetary constraints.

In Greece, the financial uncertainty inherent to such long-term investments is reinforced by two additional difficulties:

- First, most Greek businesses are small in size and would need to scale up in order to achieve the efficiencies needed to be competitive on a global scale and thus produce high returns on the green investment made. This can be done either with various processes of M&A or through the constitution of business and public – private ecosystems.

- Second, differences in financing capacity are enormous among EU Member States, despite the significant efforts for public EU funding in support of the green growth agenda. In Greece, in particular, considering the significant economic and financial crisis during the last decade, the funding gap may be severe. Hence, an important effort needs to be made in order to limit uncertainty, in particular regulatory uncertainty, and provide incentives for banks and institutional investors to make the necessary investments for green growth.

Business requires some legal certainty, as well as a complex system of nudges and incentives, in order to integrate sustainability objectives in its strategies. Of course, governments need to develop overall strategies for the green transition and use a mix of policies, such as innovation support for green energy, fiscal policies (tax and subsidies), carbon pricing and issue of green bonds.

Competition authorities should also aid this transition to a green economy, although the impact of their intervention may vary according to the severity of the problem and the need for a global response. For instance, their capacity to significantly contribute to climate change policies may be minimal, unless there is an intense effort of international cooperation in this area, such as competition authorities in jurisdictions that make a significant contribution to climate change in their economic activities and the structure of their economic production. But there are different ways in which competition authorities may play a role in promoting (environmental) sustainable development goals.

First, they should make efforts to enforce competition law in a way that does not only not jeopardise private and public sustainability strategies, but may also actively and directly contribute to the attainment of sustainability aims. This is not about authorising what some have called "green cartels", but rather to adopt an approach similar to that followed for R&D horizontal cooperation agreements and agreements promoting innovation. Hence, we should be careful not to "greenwash" cartels, although it is important to note that those consumers affected by higher prices, in regard to restriction of competition, are those that also have the lowest appreciation for the specific public good linked to environmental sustainability, and are therefore the hardest to compensate. This is acceptable in the context of a transformational effort to shift consumer preferences towards more sustainable products under the guidance of the "polluter pays" principle. Of course, one needs to also take into account the broader distributional implications of such policies, as these consumers may also be among the poorest in society. For this reason environmental and social sustainability are closely interlinked.

Second, competition authorities should make the necessary investments to redefine their role and objective function in a broader context, taking into account various sorts of externalities and their intergenerational effects, rather than focusing on the simple price effects of market power. This may also require the reliance on other tools than "willingness to pay" approaches in understanding consumer behaviour. Discounted values of profits over time should also be weighted with discounted values of costs for environmental and other sustainability goals. However, discounting should be done with caution: first, even an apparently low discount rate can reduce sustainability benefits to virtually nothing when looking long-term (as we do for many sustainability concerns – especially climate change), and second, we still grossly underestimate the future costs of climate change. The assumptions on which theories of harm to competition are based must also encompass some notion of long-term sustainability effects and eventually intergenerational equality.[4] Competition law should break its insularity and, in accordance with the principle of consistency and that of policy coherence,

---

4   Consider competition law and policy that integrates sustainability goals by design: John R Ehrenfeld, *Sustainability by Design* (Yale University Press 2008).

become more synchronised with the broader constitutional values and program-matic aims regarding sustainability, at international, EU and national levels. In the next few months, the HCC plans to explore new methodological approaches and metrics in order to integrate sustainability concerns in competition law, with the drafting and publication of a technical note in collaboration with the Dutch Competition and Markets Authority (ACM) and a group of experts.

In a recently published discussion paper,[5] HCC staff suggested that, in view of the legal uncertainty and the recognised need for a rapid transition to the green economy, more efforts should be made in order to provide undertakings with the legal certainty they need in order to make the necessary investments. This requires more targeted competition law interventions that provide a clear set of rules to follow. Collecting information on the various business strategies and the issues they face in proceeding to this green economy transition is also crucial, so as to adapt competition law enforcement to the specific circumstances faced by each national economy in managing this major economic change.

This may also involve close collaboration with other regulatory authorities, in particular through discussions in the suggested national regulatory network for competition and regulatory policy, in light of the collaboration between the competition authority and sector-specific regulators in other jurisdictions.

Eventually, a common "advice unit", made up of personnel from a variety of regulatory authorities, may be formed in order to provide informal steers on proposed sustainability-related innovations, across all fields of regulatory activity, to enable more direct communication between firms, the government and other stakeholders. This may help establish, if necessary, bespoke regulatory frame-works that would promote investments for green growth, following a process of public engagement with all stakeholders, including representative citizens' groups (civil society, NGOs).

This process may be facilitated by the development of a competition law sustain-ability "sandbox" in order for the industry to experiment with new business formats that aim to realise sustainability goals more quickly and efficiently, and which require cooperation between competing undertakings or even more permanent changes in market structure in order to be accomplished.[6] This could be done under some form of time-constrained authorisation, a periodical targeted supervision of the HCC, after balancing possible anticompetitive effects with the need to provide incentives for sustainability investment, and following a process of public consultation, as is best practice for environmental infrastructure

---

5   HCC, "Draft Staff Discussion Paper on 'Sustainability Issues and Competition Law'" (September 2020) <www.epant.gr/en/enimerosi/competition-law-sustainability.html>.
6   A sandbox is "a safe space where both regulated and unregulated firms can experiment with innovative products, services, business models and delivery mechanisms without immediately incurring all the normal regulatory consequences of engaging in such activity": Financial Conduct Authority, "Regulatory Sandbox" (November 2015).

projects. In addition, even if such arrangements produce anticompetitive effects, as long as they are part of the sandbox the HCC will not impose any fines and sanctions, although it will proceed with other remedies.

Systematic post-implementation reviews that integrate both competition and sustainability assessments of past mergers and/or antitrust infringement cases would also be helpful.

Another avenue could be for national competition authorities to issue general guidelines to clarify under which conditions the private sector may take cooperative action to promote the attainment of sustainability objectives, and what form of public accountability mechanisms should be put in place, including the enforcement of competition law, such as the recent draft guidelines from the Dutch ACM.[7] These initiatives at national level may provide interesting spaces for experimentation in EU competition law and policy. To the extent that cases involve an effect on EU trade, ultimately, they could be moved from the national level to the Court of Justice of the EU in order to set useful legal precedents for the future that could also influence the private enforcement of competition law.

The process of green transition provides an opportunity for citizens, workers and ultimately consumers to benefit from the dividends of innovation, creativity, green growth and, of course, a more sustainable environment and society, in accordance with the European preference for a social market economy. We need to embrace this democratic approach in competition law, which focuses on citizens' preferences for a sustainable and circular economy, and implement a high standard of environmental and social protection that could preserve adequate resources and quality of life for future generations.

---

7   See ACM, "Draft Guidelines: Sustainability agreements, Opportunities within competition law" (9 July 2020) <www.acm.nl/en/publications/draft-guidelines-sustainability-agreements>.

South Africa

TEMBINKOSI BONAKELE[*]

Competition Commission of South Africa

I. Can Competition Regulation Promote the Cause of Environmental Sustainability?

At first it may seem that environmental sustainability does not obviously intersect with competition policy. Some may even argue that competition policy is hardly a tool that can be used to achieve environmental sustainability, or indeed any other social goal. South Africa's first democratic government faced the same scepticism in the years it spent crafting South Africa's current competition law: the Competition Act 89 of 1998 (the Competition Act). The Competition Act sought to include development objectives in the law but several stakeholder groups, both within our borders and beyond, questioned the relevance of development objectives in competition legislation. They frequently cited the existence of other laws that were better suited to address the various social goals the Competition Act sought to include – such as labour laws to address unemployment – and reminded those charged with administering the Competition Act about the traditional aims of competition law: consumer welfare and the promotion of market efficiency.

---

[*]   Tembinkosi Bonakele is commissioner at the South African Competition Commission in Pretoria. He has occupied various positions in the Commission's core divisions: he was appointed deputy commissioner in 2008, and prior to that worked as head of mergers, head of compliance and senior legal counsel respectively. He established the Commission's cartels division and worked on all of the Commission's major cases over the past decade, including the bread & flour and construction bid-rigging cartel cases, Telkom and SAB abuse of dominance cases and a number of high-profile mergers. Mr Bonakele is an admitted attorney and previously practised with Cheadle Thompson and Haysom in Johannesburg primarily in the areas of labour law, regulation and health and safety. Mr Bonakele currently serves as the chair of the African Competition Forum and is a member of the International Competition Network Steering Group.

In this paper I suggest that competition law can indeed promote the cause of environmental sustainability, as well as any other social goals most relevant to the development of any jurisdiction. One way in which this can be done is to follow a framework similar to that adopted by the South African regime, which has delivered much success for South Africa's competition agencies in their 22 years of existence.

II. South Africa's Model for Including Social Goals in Competition Law

South Africa's historical reality of economic development skewed in favour of the white minority formed the backdrop against which the Competition Act was promulgated. The stated purposes of the Act demonstrate the desire of the legislature to pursue more than the traditional American or European aims of competition law.

When presenting the Competition Bill to lawmakers in the years leading up to its promulgation, the government department responsible for drafting it, the Department of Trade and Industry (DTI), said that it considered the Competition Bill as an important pillar in the overall economic policy framework. In addressing the need for competition policy in the South African economy, the DTI stated that:

> The Bill seeks to encourage competition, not because we wish to adhere to some textbook ideal, but rather because of what it can contribute to realising some of these important economic and social objectives… It is essential that we see the development of a vibrant small, medium and micro enterprise sector. There is necessity for a diversification of ownership in favour of historically disadvantaged communities. These are the potential outcomes of high levels of competition and these are the objectives enshrined in the Bill before this House.

The DTI thus made it clear that South Africa's competition legislation would go beyond textbook ideals and cover both economic and social objectives. Some of those objectives listed here, which would later find their way into the statute, were the development of small business and the spread of ownership in favour of the black majority.

Today the preamble to the Competition Act states clearly that it aims to achieve, among other things, fair participation in the economy and the "transfer of economic ownership in keeping with the public interest".

In the substantive provisions of the Act, social objectives are contained expressly in (1) public interest grounds that the competition agency must take into account when assessing mergers and acquisitions; and (2) provisions that allow firms to apply for an exemption from the application of the Competition Act.

1. Public interest grounds

Section 12A(1)(b) of the Competition Act states that:

> Whenever required to consider a merger, the Competition Commission or Competition Tribunal must initially determine whether or not the merger is likely to substantially prevent or lessen competition, by assessing the factors set out in subsection (2), and… otherwise, determine whether the merger can or cannot be justified on substantial public interest grounds by assessing the factors set out in subsection (3).

Section 12A(3) further provides that:

> (3) When determining whether a merger can or cannot be justified on public interest grounds, the Competition Commission or the Competition Tribunal must consider the effect that the merger will have on:
>
> a) a particular industrial sector or region;
>
> b) employment;
>
> c) the ability of small businesses, or firms controlled or owned by historically disadvantaged persons, to become competitive; and
>
> d) the ability of national industries to compete in international markets.

Amendments to the Act introduced in February 2019 further enhance the public interest factors to be taken into account in merger assessments. The competition agencies' mandate now includes an additional public interest factor, namely the "promotion of a greater spread of ownership, in particular to increase the levels of ownership by historically disadvantaged persons and workers in firms in the market".

In addition, section 12A(3)(c) was amended slightly to enable the agencies to take into account the "ability of small and medium businesses or firms controlled by historically disadvantaged persons to effectively enter into, participate in or expand" within a market.

Separately, when determining whether a proposed transaction is to be approved or prohibited, the competition agencies must also consider the following three additional factors:

- The extent of ownership by a party to a merger of other firms in a related market;

- The extent to which a party to the merger is related to other firms in related markets, including through common members or directors; and

- Any other mergers engaged in by a party to a merger for a period to be stipulated by the Commission.

When the public interest criteria were included in the Competition Act during the policy and legislative process, entrenched business interests became concerned about the possible arbitrary use of public interest criteria. However, the argument that triumphed contended that competition policy could not ignore the social needs of the people and that competition was not a value in its own right but only insofar as it met socially desirable objectives. Therefore, in addition to the key competition objectives of efficiency and consumer welfare, the Competition Act includes objectives such as protection of small and medium sized enterprises, the promotion of employment and the growth of black-owned enterprises.

Public interest criteria, as a standalone factor in competition assessment, was an uncommon phenomenon amongst competition agencies at the time. Recognising this, while describing the Competition Tribunal's approach to public interest grounds when assessing mergers, David Lewis, who was the first chairperson of the Competition Tribunal said:

> I've come to treat our task in dealing with public interest in much the same way that I treat my mad uncle, in much the same way that every family treats its mad uncle – with wary respect. We may try and ignore him; we may even deny his existence. But he somehow manages to turn up, invited or not, at every major family event. For the most part he turns out be quite an amiable, agreeable old chap, but he does have the potential to behave in a very unpredictable manner, one that causes severe embarrassment to a smug, complacent family, often threatening to tear it apart and reduce its reputation and standing in the society at large. He is nevertheless often respected by the younger members of the family, who feel that he has insights about the real world lacking in the more staid leaders of the family.[1]

Lewis went on to acknowledge that few, if any, regimes specified – let alone employed – a pure public interest test to evaluate mergers. Even those competition statutes that explicitly required a consideration of public interest generally also specified that the competition impact be determined by reference to one or other of the dominant paradigms, these being the substantial lessening of competition test or the dominance test. However, Lewis stated, South Africa's unique circumstances had necessitated the consideration of development criteria in the implementation of the Competition Act.

While the suggestion to include public interest objectives threatened to derail the consensus-seeking policy process in its earlier phase, its detractors were appeased once the technical mechanics of the law were worked on. Soon they realised that despite the public interest objectives, the substantive technical content of the law did not stray from a primary focus on efficiency within a

---

1   David Lewis, "The Role of Public Interest in Merger Evaluation" (Paper presented at the Merger Working Group, ICN, Naples, 28–29 September 2002), 1–4.

market paradigm. The Competition Act set out clear criteria for assessment but assumed that economic efficiency and the public interest were not inconsistent. In the same vein, Lewis concluded that:

> … we should take a pragmatic view of the introduction of public interest factors into a competition analysis. It is not evidence of a fatally compromised competition regime. In one way or another it is a feature of most regimes and, in those regimes where it is a particularly strong feature, serious consideration of the public interest by the competition authorities is likely to underpin the credibility of fledgling authorities. Moreover, it is possible to structure the evaluation in such a way that competition considerations occupy pride of place in the ultimate decision, indeed, in such a way that the competition authorities are able to use the public interest investigation to educate key public stakeholders about competition, rather than have them massively constrain the application of competition law.[2]

To date the competition agencies have not decided the outcome of a merger solely on public interest grounds, though the Competition Act enables the agencies to. Instead, in the first 20 years of its existence the Competition Commission approved 369 mergers (out of 6,490 notified) with conditions aimed at addressing public interest concerns such as unemployment or the development of small business.

2. Exemption provisions

A further provision which clearly reflects the development objectives of the Competition Act is section 10, which provides that firms wishing to engage in anticompetitive conduct may apply to the Competition Commission for an exemption from the provisions of the Competition Act for the firms' practices or agreements. The Competition Commission may grant the exemption under section 10(3) if:

a) Any restriction imposed on the firms concerned by the agreement or practice concerned, or category of either agreements or practices concerned, is required to attain an objective mentioned in paragraph (b); and

b) The agreement or practice concerned, or category of agreements or practices concerned, contributes to any of the following objectives:

   i. maintenance or promotion of exports;

   ii. promotion of the ability of small businesses, or firms controlled or owned by historically disadvantaged persons, to become competitive;

---

2   ibid.

iii.change in productive capacity necessary to stop decline in an industry; or

iv.the economic stability of any industry designated by the Minister, after consulting the Minister responsible for that industry.

In the recent amendments to the Competition Act, section 10(3)(b)(ii) has been amended to promote the effective entry into, participation in and expansion within a market by small and medium businesses, or firms controlled or owned by historically disadvantaged persons. Section 10(3)(b)(iv) is now extended to the development, growth and transformation of a designated industry, not only its stability. Finally, a new ground for exemption was added, namely competitiveness and efficiency gains that promote employment or industrial expansion.

In enacting the above provision, the legislature intended that firms controlled by historically disadvantaged persons would be permitted to engage in anticompetitive conduct for a limited period, if its restriction on competition was necessary for such a firm to become competitive. This provision furthered the legislature's intention to enact legislation that would correct the imbalances of the past.

Using the exemption provisions, over the last 22 years the Commission has been able to contribute to South Africa's development goals by improving market conditions for small and medium-sized businesses.

III. Competition Cases Covering Environmental Sustainability

1. Environmental sustainability as a factor in defining the market

In an August 2020 merger filed with the Competition Commission, the market definition hinged partly on whether customers of the merging parties considered the environmental sustainability of waste management processes as a significant factor when choosing a healthcare waste management supplier. A key question in defining the market here was whether incineration technology and thermal desorption – a form of burn technology that treats waste via pyrolysis technology, not combustion – were interchangeable processes in the treatment of pharmaceutical waste.

According to the customers the Commission contacted in its assessment, the extent to which either process was environmentally sustainable featured in their choice of supplier. For example, customer 1 and customer 2 submitted that thermal desorption was the preferred technology because the process was more environ-mentally friendly than incineration. However customer 3, who was one of the target firm's main customers, submitted that thermal desorption was not neces-sarily their preferred technology in the treatment of pharmaceutical waste. Customer views thus varied regarding the extent to which these two technologies were considered substitutable. In addition, customer preferences between the technologies were not only based on price differentials. For instance, customer 1 highlighted that if the price of treating pharmaceutical waste using thermal desorption were to increase significantly, they would consider a number of factors but were more inclined to consider environmental sustainability, while customer 2 submitted that they would switch to incineration but that price was not the only factor. Customer 2 highlighted that the treatment facility that it would use for incineration needed to comply with certain requirements, for example the presence of a pharmacist at the incineration plant, as well as their licensing status.

In the final analysis, the Commission found that although customers considered environmental sustainability as a factor, they ultimately had to weigh up several factors – such as licensing, the presence of adequate on-site expertise at an incineration, regulatory requirements and price – in choosing a process and supplier. Given this, the Commission concluded that incineration technology and thermal desorption were sufficiently interchangeable to consider them part of the same market.

In October 2020 the Commission prohibited the merger as it believed it would remove an effective competitor from the market and it would hamper the ability of small businesses to become competitive in the identified markets. Box 1 contains the media statement the Commission issued after prohibiting the merger.

Box 1: Competition Commission prohibits waste management merger
29 October 2020 (weekly media statement)

The Commission has prohibited the proposed merger whereby Averda SA intends to acquire the Target Firms.

Averda is an end to end provider of waste management services globally and in South Africa. Averda's activities in South Africa include the collection, transportation, treat-ment and disposal of general waste (domestic and industrial) and hazardous waste (which includes general hazardous and hazardous healthcare risk waste (HCRW)). HCRW includes anatomical waste, pharmaceutical waste, sharps waste and infectious waste. Of relevance to this merger assessment are Averda's HCRW treatment activi-ties using burn technology (i.e. incineration) and non-burn technology (e.g. electro thermal deactivation and autoclaves) to treat/neutralise waste. Averda's waste treat-ment facilities are located in Gauteng, North West and Western Cape.

Through A-Thermal, the Target Firms operate an incinerator which can treat all forms of healthcare risk waste. A-Thermal also operates a thermal desorption facility which is a form of burn technology that treats waste via pyrolysis technology. Unlike an incinerator, the waste is not combusted. The thermal desorption plant is licensed by DEFF to treat hazardous pharmaceutical and chemical waste. Through Cecor, the Target Firms oper-ate an autoclave which is a technology that treats healthcare risk waste such as medical sharps waste via disinfection. The Target Firms' waste treatment facilities are in Gauteng.

The merging parties both treat general hazardous waste and HCRW. The more signifi-cant overlap between the merging parties is regarding the treatment of HCRW. The Commission thus assessed the impact of the merger on the treatment of HCRW both nationally and regionally as follows:
– The market for the treatment of HCRW using burn technologies.
– The market for the treatment of HCRW using non-burn technologies.
– The market for the treatment of pharmaceutical waste using burn technologies.
– The market for the treatment of anatomical/pathological waste using burn incinera-tion technologies.
– The market for the treatment of infectious and sharps waste using non-burn and burn incineration technologies.

The Commission found that the merger will result in the merged entity having high market shares in most of the relevant markets assessed. The investigation showed that the Acquiring Firm has a history of expanding through acquisitions and has engaged in several acquisitions over the past 5 years, several of which were small mergers. The Commission found that Averda's acquisition of the Target Firms' additional burn technology capacity enables the merged entity to withhold supply of capacity to com-petitors, or price it at a level that makes rivals less competitive. The merged entity's acquisition of a portfolio of technologies used in HCRW treatment places it in a unique position to contest contracts/tenders. This may hinder the effective operations of the competitors, particularly SMMEs and HDI-controlled competitors, that traditionally rely on outsourced capacity to effectively compete in HCRW treatment markets. In addition, barriers to entry are high and there is currently insufficient burn capacity available due to various reasons. Thus, the Commission found that the merger is likely to substantially prevent or lessen competition in the relevant markets post-merger.

The Commission found that the merger has a negative effect on the ability of SMME and/or HDI competitors to effectively enter into, participate in or expand within the waste management (and treatment) sector. Waste management in particular has more scope for the entry and expansion of SMMEs and HDI competitors, but this requires that they are able to access treatment capacity on competitive terms. The Commission is therefore of the view that the merger raises significant public interest concerns.

The Commission and the merging parties were not able to agree on remedies to address the competition and public interest concerns identified. Accordingly, the Commission prohibited the merger.

2. Fighting for the sustainability of South Africa's food resources

According to Tejvan Pettinger, environmental sustainability is concerned with several issues, including the long-term health of ecosystems, that is, protecting the long-term productivity and health of resources to meet future economic and social needs, e.g. protecting food supplies, farmland and fishing stocks.[3]

---

3   Tejvan Pettinger, "Environmental Sustainability, definition and issues" (2018) accessible from <https://economicshelp.org>.

The protection of South Africa's food supplies is precisely what two environmental non-governmental organisations – Biowatch and The African Centre for Biodiversity (ACB) – were concerned with in 2011 when they applied to intervene in legal proceedings on the merger between Pannar Seeds and Pioneer Hi-Bred International. Pannar Seeds was a South African family-owned business founded in 1958 and South Africa's largest independent seed company. Pannar had an extensive maize germplasm inventory which, according to environmental groups, presented great opportunities for development. Pioneer Hi-Bred International, on the other hand, was a major US-based subsidiary of the global chemical giant DuPont, looking to assume control of Pannar. Box 2 perhaps illustrates more succinctly the motivation behind the ACB's application to intervene in the merger.

Box 2: Mariam Mayet, executive director and founder, ACB, "The roots of hunger and inequity in South Africa's corporate seed system" (*inf'OGM*, 15 March 2017)

Seed diversity: its importance for the environment, food systems and small-holder farmers

Seeds are the very basis of human society and have been for all of human history. They are at the heart of a healthy food system and form the basis of the food we consume. The harvesting of seed from preferred plants is the basis of crop domestication over the 10,000 years of agriculture. Farmers have nurtured thousands of varieties; adapting these to changing conditions with each growing season. Some varieties are resistant to diseases or pests. Others are tolerant of weather extremes like drought or floods or early frosts. Some have better yields or better nutrition as well as other desirable qualities such as taste and aroma, ease of cooking and processing or long storage capacity. Some varieties may also be prized for specific cultural or ceremonial purposes. This nurturing and maintenance of diversity has been made possible through intricate connections between families, communities and generations, where sharing and exchange of seed was seen as an obligation. For example, in West Africa the kola nut has cultural and medicinal uses as well as a deep ritual and spiritual significance (Hosken, L (ed) Undated). In Nigeria it is presented to elders at first meetings, and often forms part of a dowry; among the Igbo a kola nut is broken open and prayed over; while among the Tikari in Cameroon, kola trees are sacred and, as such, collectively protected by the whole community. (Hosken, L (ed) Undated).

The transaction was prohibited by the Competition Commission in December 2010 on the grounds that it would substantially lessen competition in the maize seed market. The merging parties appealed this decision to the Competition Tribunal. The two environmental groups were granted the right to intervene in the Tribunal's proceedings on limited grounds. These related to the effect of the proposed merger on pricing and the availability of alternative products if the merger were to be approved; the effect on smallholder farmers, small-scale commercial black farmers and consumer choice; the resultant barriers to entry; and the public interest effect of the proposed merger, particularly in light of Pannar's extensive maize germplasm inventory and the opportunities that it presented for development.

The environmental groups saw the merger as part of the commercialisation and consolidation process that had characterised the global seed market during the preceding two decades. This had resulted in the sale of seeds across the globe being dominated by three powerful companies – DuPont, Monsanto and Syngenta.

At the time, Glenn Ashton of Biowatch said that the loss of an "independent" Pannar "would remove our last remaining major seed company from the market, which would mean that our food supply would effectively be controlled by two US corporations, Pioneer and Monsanto".[4]

The ACB raised a number of concerns with the transaction, such as the likely genetic modification of maize seed that would likely follow the transaction; the suitability of a foreign-controlled maize seed for local farming conditions and the broader impact the merger would have on maize seed prices and quality into the future.

The Competition Tribunal, after hearing the Commission, the merging parties and the ACB, prohibited the deal in 2011. The matter would later be approved with conditions by a higher court, but ACB issued the statement in Box 3 when the Tribunal's decision was announced. ACB's statement highlights the concerns that both ACB and Biowatch had with the merger, although Biowatch withdrew its intervention before the hearing, stating that it no longer believed it had more to add than what the Commission's case already covered.

**Box 3: ACB Applauds Tribunal decision to prohibit Pioneer
Hi Bred and Pannar seed merger**
Press Release, 14 October 2011

The African Centre for Biosafety (ACB) applauds today's decision of the Competition Tribunal (Tribunal) to prohibit the seed merger between multinational seed company Pioneer Hi Bred, and South Africa's largest seed company, Pannar Seed. During December 2010, the Competition Commission prohibited the merger and the merging parties referred the Commission's decision to the Tribunal for reconsideration. After a three-week-long hearing, the Tribunal has decided to similarly prohibit the merger. Reasons for the decision are still forthcoming and no further information is at this stage available. The ACB was granted leave by the Tribunal on the 19th August 2011, to intervene in the merger proceedings on public interest grounds, particularly with regard to the effect the merger would have on small scale farmers. This was itself precedent setting in that it was the first time the Tribunal had allowed NGOs to intervene in merger proceedings. The ACB has in fact been involved in the merger proceedings since October 2010. The ACB participated in the proceedings and led the expert evidence of an agricultural economist working directly with smallholder farmers, who outlined the devastating impacts the merger would have on smallholder farmers and food security. According

---

4   Ann Crotty, "Tribunal allows two NGOs to intervene" (*IOL*, 23 August 2011) <www.iol.co.za/business-report/economy>.

to Mariam Mayet, director of the ACB, "The prohibition is a victory for smallholder farmers in South Africa and all those who advocate for a more equitable food system. The Tribunal's decision will create much needed breathing space for the development of an appropriate seed system for South Africa that responds to the needs of smallholder and resource-poor farmers rather than those of profit-seeking multinational corporations." The ACB notes that the South African government has prioritised the development of black smallholder farmers. Government must now do the right thing by building on the Tribunal's decision and work in partnerships with farmers to develop smallholder capacity to produce and distribute seeds that are appropriate to farmer conditions and needs.

"Government must stop pushing for the further propagation of the industrial agricultural model, including for smallholder emerging and resource poor farmers. Far too little resources have been devoted to utilizing local knowledge and local varieties as genuine solutions to food insecurity," said Mayet.

As mentioned above, the merger was ultimately approved with conditions by a higher court. The ACB, however, has continued its fight for the long-term sustainability of South Africa's food resources as its concerns with the 2011 merger came to pass. In February 2019 it was reported that the ACB had lodged an objection against Pioneer Hi-Bred's application for field trials of a gene-silencing genetically modified maize. ACB said it refused to allow South African citizens and the environment to be used as "guinea pigs" for the untested and unproven technology.

Pioneer's regional media liaison in Africa, Barbara Muzata, said that South Africa was chosen for the trial for three reasons: it had a high-level presence of expertise in the public and private sector; it was a conducive environment for science and technological investment; and it needed high-yielding agricultural technologies. Muzata said the end vision of the trial was to gain approval for use of the technology in South Africa and thereby contribute to increased maize yields and food production.

The ACB argued that the risks of the trial were untested, therefore it was premature to allow the seeds to be approved for environmental release as they could contaminate farmers' varieties and hence South Africa's food supply.

IV. Conclusion

Competition law exists in a social context, which often requires a policy mix with complementarities and potential contradictions. This often imposes the need for trade-offs. Where one lands on these is a matter of one's own objectives. For developing countries, especially South Africa, which has a history of racial exclusion, the pursuit of fairness, equality and equity is a necessary trade-off. The time may have also come to complement competition law with environmental sustainability and allow for coordination of these. South Africa, in its own way, shows that there is a workable framework for doing this, namely (1) public interest factors in merger assessments and (2) grounds for exemption that are rooted in the country's social objectives.

I hope I have demonstrated the ability of competition policy and legislation to directly address ancillary social objectives. Although South Africa's Competition Act does not mention environmental sustainability as a desired outcome of implementing competition law, it covers the social objectives that were a priority to lawmakers at the time of drafting. Those objectives – mainly employment, black economic empowerment and the development of small and medium-sized businesses – remain a priority in South Africa today, which is why the competition agencies were granted additional powers in 2019 to pursue these objectives in the Competition Act.

That being said, it is also clear to me that the successful pursuit of ancillary social objectives – such as environmental sustainability – through competition law does not depend solely on lawmakers. It also depends on the resolve of administrators tasked with implementing the law to be courageous, consistent and transparent in their quest to achieve the social objectives set out in the law. In the policy formulation process there is bound to be disagreement and opposition from competition purists and traditionalists who fear the dilution of competition policy with evolving social objectives and national priorities. But I believe that South Africa's experience over the last 21 years, as outlined above, demonstrates that it is possible to balance robust competition assessment with the prevailing social priorities of any jurisdiction, and thus have competition law contribute to the overall development objectives of society at large.

United Kingdom

SANDRINE DELARUE AND MIKE WALKER[*]

I. Introduction

The issue of the relationship between competition law and environmental sustainability concerns has become very topical in recent months. There have been a number of important agency contributions to advancing the debate, such as the Dutch ACM's Draft Guidelines on Sustainability Agreements and the Greek competition authority's Staff Discussion Paper on sustainability issues and competition law.[1] Recent publications have also made some excellent contributions to the debate and consider a wide range of solutions.[2]

This short paper discusses some of the arguments around incorporating environmental sustainability concerns into competition law from the perspective of a lawyer and an economist working within an agency. The views expressed in this paper are personal views, not necessarily those of the agency.

---

[*] Sandrine Delarue is an assistant director in the Policy and International team at the UK Competition & Markets Authority. Mike Walker is the chief economic adviser at the UK Competition & Markets Authority. He is also a professor at the College of Europe in Bruges and a visiting fellow at King's College London.

1 ACM, "Draft Guidelines: Sustainability Agreements" (9 July 2020) <www.acm.nl/en/publications/draft-guidelines-sustainability-agreements>; Hellenic Competition Authority, "Staff Discussion paper on sustainability issues and competition law" (September 2020), <www.epant.gr/en/enimerosi/competition-law-sustainability.html> accessed 17 January 2021.

2 OECD, "Sustainability and competition" (virtual meeting, December 2020) <www.oecd.org/daf/competition/sustainability-and-competition.htm> accessed 17 January 2020. See in particular Julian Norwag, "Sustainability & Competition Law and Policy – Background Note" DAF/COMP(2020)3 (OECD 1 December 2020); Luc Peeperkorn, "Competition and sustainability: What can competition policy do"; Julian Nowag and Alexandra Teorell, "Beyond Balancing: Sustainability and Competition Law"; Michael Ristaniemi and Maria Wasastjerna, "Sustainability and competition: Unlocking the potential" in Guy Canivet and others, *Sustainability and competition law* (2020) Concurrences N° 4–2020 Art N° 97257, 26–65.

II. Setting the Scene, the Practical Realities

In the OECD background note, the normative question considered by the author is whether competition law and policy should at all "be influenced by sustainability". From a practical perspective, it seems to us that the answer to the question will inevitably be "yes". Competition law applies to markets and considers issues arising on those markets at a particular point in time. So, if the main challenge for businesses at a certain point in time is to adapt to a low carbon economy, then their conduct will be influenced by, if not driven by, such considerations. The result is that competition authorities will have to grapple with issues related to sustainability concerns. These issues will arise in merger analysis and in allegations around anticompetitive agreements, cartels and abuses of dominant positions. Competition authorities will need to develop their understanding of what businesses are trying to achieve and whether, in doing so, they are complying with competition law.

Competition law already allows for efficiencies to be taken into account and it is right that competition authorities carefully consider these arguments.[3] Precedents where competition authorities have looked into sustainability initiatives demonstrate that authorities consider that competition law is capable of taking account of sustainability considerations (see below for two well-known examples).

It can therefore be argued that competition law is already capable of dealing with environmental sustainability concerns. However, it seems to us that while this is true, it is true only to a limited extent.

III. Setting the Scene, the Legal Perspective

This section of the paper attempts to highlight some of the problematic areas of the interplay between competition law and environmental sustainability concerns within the context of Article 101 TFEU. The first part briefly reminds us that currently competition law will not interfere with many sustainability agreements.[4] The second part focuses on where some tensions have been identified.

First, competition law is currently unlikely to interfere with a sustainability initiative in the form of an agreement (formal or informal) between businesses[5] when it is imposed by state regulation or it does not appreciably restrict competition. Relevant considerations in the latter case will be parties' market shares and the extent to which the agreement affects one or more of the key parameters of competition.[6] Competition

---

3   Article 101(3) TFEU, Article 102 TFEU objective justification, merger control.
4   In this part of the paper, interfere means to prevent (a process of activity) from continuing or being carried out properly.
5   Or a decision by a trade association.
6   See more details in Richard Whish and David Bailey, *Competition Law* (9th edn, OUP 2018) , 147–150.

law is currently unlikely to prevent standard-setting sustainability agreements, as long as the parties follow the guidance on standards as set out in the horizontal guidelines.[7] Lastly, if a sustainability agreement restricts competition but meets the conditions of a block exemption, for example on research and development or specialisation, competition law will not prevent such agreements.[8]

Outside those situations, when a sustainability initiative restricts competition, it would have to meet the four cumulative conditions of Article 101(3) TFEU and this is where the interplay between competition law and sustainability concerns is most problematic. Under Article 101(3), the agreement will not be prohibited if it generates efficiencies, the efficiencies cannot be achieved by a less restrictive means, consumers receive a fair share of these efficiencies and the agreement does not lead to the elimination of competition in that market. One of the conditions that can be difficult to satisfy in the context of sustainability agreements is the "fair share" requirement, more specifically the current requirement that the category of consumers harmed by the agreement should also be the ones who receive the benefits generated by the agreement that restricts competition. This approach does not support taking into account the positive externalities created by the product or service covered by the agreement that restricts competition.[9] As explained later further down in this paper, this current approach does not seem economically rational, and a better approach, at least from an economic perspective, would seem to be to take into account the total costs and total benefits for society. However, this raises significant concerns over whether competition policy would be seeking to achieve goals that are beyond its current remit and which might be better pursued through other means. As Luc Peeperkorn argues, using one policy instrument to pursue a variety of goals may "lead to slow, costly and unpredictable outcomes for every policy instrument" and may "undermine, if not destroy, effective enforcement".[10]

1. Two examples of the interplay between competition law and sustainability

Two well-known cases which are often referred to are those of the Dutch *Chicken of Tomorrow*[11] and the European Commission's *CECED* decision.[12] Without wanting to get into a detailed legal discussion, neither of these cases seem to be very compelling support for the proposition that competition law can handle environmental sustainability concerns separately from consumer welfare.

---

7   Which include market share thresholds.
8   Which also include market share thresholds.
9   Peeperkorn (n 2), [31] – [32].
10   ibid [39] – [42].
11   ACM, "Industry-wide arrangements for the so-called Chicken of Tomorrow restrict competition" (ACM news, 26 January 2015) <www.acm.nl/en/publications/publication/13761/Industry-wide-arrangements-for-the-so-called-Chicken-of-Tomorrow-restrict-competition>.
12   *CECED* (Case IV.F.1/36.718) Commission Decision C(1999) 5064 [2000] OJ L187/47.

The Dutch case seemed to focus only on the willingness of current consumers of chicken to pay for higher chicken welfare standards. *CECED* seems more on point, as the Commission did note in that case that the agreement would lead to lower carbon emissions. In that case, producers of washing machines agreed to produce machines that used less electricity and water, and to stop producing and selling older types of washing machines that were less environmentally friendly. When assessing the agreement under Article 101(3), the Commission considered that the direct benefits for buyers of washing machines outweighed the negative effects for the buyers resulting from the agreement to limit the variety of washing machines available by eliminating less efficient but cheaper washing machines from the market.[13]

2. Additional considerations

Another argument in favour of competition law already being able to deal with environmental concerns is that it is able to do so where firms compete on the basis of sustainability concerns. This is of course true, but it is a limited claim in two senses. First, this form of competition is relatively infrequent (but this may change) and where it does occur there are often concerns over "greenwashing". Second, it still only focuses on the specific consumers of the product in question. The decisions that these consumers make about whether or not to buy environmentally sustainable products may not coincide with the optimal outcome for society as a whole.

Some also argue that competition law promotes economic efficiency and thus the efficient use of scarce resources, which is good for environmental sustainability. Again, to a limited extent, this is a reasonable observation. But it should also be noted (as argued below), that competition does not always promote efficient outcomes when positive or negative externalities are involved. It is also worth noting that another effective way to reduce the use of scarce resources would be to raise the prices of products to reduce demand. Raising prices is usually considered anathema to competition law.

IV. An Economist's Perspective

This section of the paper focuses on how an economist thinks about the issue of whether environmental sustainability concerns should be integrated into competition law. The discussion is in two parts. The first deals with conceptual issues; the second with practical issues.

---

13 Peeperkorn (n 2). It is also worth noting that when this case was used as an example in the Horizontal Cooperation Agreements Guidelines (para 329), there was no mention of wider environmental benefits but only of the benefits to the consumers buying the washing machines in terms of reduced consumption of energy, water and soap. Not exactly a ringing endorsement of taking environmental sustainability concerns into account.

1. Conceptual issues

To an economist, competition law is about protecting consumer welfare.[14] There is a tendency for people to interpret this as meaning that economists think that competition law is only about prices. This is the interpretation that is often suggested by the neo-Brandeisians, but there is no basis for the claim. Economics is clear that the consumer welfare standard should include more than just price effects. For instance, it is standard that quality, product range and innovation are relevant to consumer welfare. Many jurisdictions include national security concerns within merger control and this could be justified on consumer welfare grounds. The South African competition authority has been at the vanguard of including wider factors in its welfare standard, such as protecting SMEs and increasing the ownership of firms by historically disadvantaged groups. So there is nothing conceptually difficult about also believing that things such as sustainable production, decarbonisation, reducing environmental degradation and so on should also be included in a consumer welfare standard.[15]

The interesting question here is not whether the consumer welfare standard should include more than just price, quality, innovation and so on. The interesting question is what is the limiting principle that determines what aspects of consumer welfare are taken into account in competition law and what aspects are not? A consumer welfare standard without a limiting principle has the potential to become both all-encompassing and arbitrary.

This question should not be left up to competition authorities to decide. It seems to be a much wider societal question, which means in practice that it probably becomes a political question.[16] What does society want competition authorities to be concerned with, in addition to the standard concerns? Clean air? Distributional fairness? Ensuring that firms do not have political power in addition to market power? All of these can be tied back to the welfare of consumers, so there does not seem to be an easy principled way to make this decision. Thus, it becomes a decision for society, and hence for government.

Once society has made its decision, the technocrats inside competition authorities can then apply the relevant criteria to specific cases. Economists would generally view this as uncontroversial: once we know what is in the "objective function", then we can happily maximise that objective function (i.e. find the best outcome for consumers based on the criteria that society has decided that the competition authority should care about).

---

14 The debate about total welfare or consumer welfare is moot in this discussion. This is because the discussion is about consumer welfare in the long run. In the long run, consumer welfare and total welfare are effectively the same.
15 The CMA already has decarbonisation as one of its priorities in its latest Annual Plan.
16 The argument here is similar to that from Paul Tucker in *Unelected Power* (Princeton University Press 2018). He focuses on central banking, but the basic argument applies more widely to regulatory bodies.

It is important to note that this society question is not just about what society thinks matters. It is crucially also about where it thinks what matters is best dealt with. The key point here is that competition law will not always be the best solution to consumer welfare concerns around sustainability.[17] For instance, there has been discussion around allowing horizontal cooperation between firms in order to achieve sustainability objectives. The concern is that if it is costly for firms to operate in an environmentally sustainable manner, then they will not do this unilaterally. If just one firm took on the higher costs of being environmentally sustainable but its competitors did not, then it would lose demand and potentially go out of business. However, if all firms act in an environmentally sustainable manner, and accept the associated higher costs, then each firm is still able to compete. So without horizontal cooperation it seems that there is a danger of bad competitive equilibria whereby each firm individually has an incentive to underprovide environmental goodness. For instance, competition between firms could lead to the adoption of low-cost, but polluting, technologies. Is there a role for competition law to solve this sort of problem?

Consider an agreement between firms in an industry to agree collectively to use a less polluting, but more expensive, production process. No firm would individually make this choice, as it would lead to their costs being too high for them to be competitive. The agreement might well have good environmental outcomes, but it also involves cooperation between horizontal competitors, which often leads to bad outcomes for consumers. Is this a worthwhile trade-off: reduced pollution compared with potentially reduced competitive intensity? Maybe, but it is not clear that we need to make this trade-off. In this case, a better approach is likely to be that government subsidises the less polluting technology. This would lower the cost to firms to use it and so they would make it a *unilaterally* rational decision to adopt it. This approach could lead to the widespread adoption of the technology without creating an environment of horizontal cooperation. The basic logic here is the same as that underpinning the practice of carbon pricing: by putting a price on the act of polluting, carbon pricing changes the unilateral incentives of firms. Another alternative approach would be for the government just to impose a regulation that forces all firms to follow the higher environmental standards, but without funding the additional costs through a government subsidy.

A final conceptual issue arises around the competition law requirement that the benefits to consumers from a reduction in competition must be felt by consumers within that market. This does not seem very economically rational. Consider the example above of the technology that raises production costs but lowers pollution. It is quite possible that the harm to consumers of the product from higher prices is greater than the benefit to them from reduced pollution, but smaller than the

---

17   See Maarten Pieter Schinkel and Abel d'Ailly, "Corona Crisis Cartels: Sense and Sensibility" Amsterdam Law School Research Paper No. 2020-31 (9 June 2020) <https://papers.ssrn.com/sol3/papers.cfm?abstract_id=3623154>.

benefit to all consumers from reduced pollution. It is not clear from an economic perspective why competition law would not want to facilitate the use of this technology. Good public policy decision-making should focus on the total benefits compared with the total costs for society, not just the costs for a narrow section of it.[18,19] In this regard, the Dutch ACM's recent Draft Guidelines on Sustainability Agreements are a welcome step in the right direction: benefits to wider society, and not just consumers in a relevant market, can be taken into account under an Article 101(3) assessment. The Greek Staff Discussion paper also has an interesting discussion of this issue.

2. Practical issues

The basic message of this section is: it is not as hard as it looks. Many of the practical difficulties that people raise in the context of competition law and sustainability issues are issues that are common in other areas of policy and where there are already well-established solutions.

Many of the issues that sustainability concerns raise in competition law involve trading off the positive externalities of improved sustainability against reduced competition within some markets. This leads to the claim that competition authorities should not seek to make this trade-off because it is too hard to estimate the value of the uncertain positive externalities. It is certainly true that it is difficult to estimate the long-term benefits of things like reduced environmental degradation. However, this is not a new problem and has been a significant focus of welfare economics for decades.[20] So there are well-established analytical tools already available that are routinely used within policymaking.[21] This is also true of concerns around "Black Swan" events (i.e. low probability, very high damage events).[22]

Another concern that has been raised is that the quantification of long-term sustainability benefits is very uncertain and that therefore such potential benefits should not be taken into account as compared with clearer near-term competition harms. Again, this does not strike me as a strong argument. To the extent that future benefits are uncertain, they should be discounted to some extent, as is standard in welfare economics. But they should not be discounted to zero. It can however be observed that the legal community does tend to discount uncertainty to zero, but this is very rarely the correct response.

---

18 The situation is actually worse than I suggest in the main text. Competition law would allow horizontal cooperation if the benefits to consumers in the relevant market outweigh the costs to those consumers, even if the cost to all other consumers is vastly greater than the benefit to all other consumers.
19 As noted above, the Dutch *Chicken of Tomorrow* case and *CECED* both fail this criterion.
20 See, for instance, A Pigou, *The Economics of Welfare* (Macmillan and Co 1920).
21 A heavy focus on consumers' willingness to pay is not, however, one of them. This approach will fail to capture externalities, fail to capture intergenerational concerns and will be hampered by consumers not being fully informed.
22 See, for instance, Nassim Nicholas Taleb, *The Black Swan: The Impact of the Improbable* (Penguin 2008).

V. Conclusion

While competition law may currently be able to include some sustainability concerns, it seems likely that, with some suitable adjustments, it could capture many more. There seems to us to be two ways forward.

One approach would be for competition authorities to alter their approach in order to take greater account of sustainability issues. A competition authority could choose to broaden its mandate by taking account of the welfare of all consumers rather than just those in the market where competition is harmed and by explicitly including long-term environmental degradation as part of the consumer harm analysis. It could justify this by reference to the urgency of climate change concerns, the lack of legal limits to the concept of consumer welfare and the growing set of laws adopted by individual countries to move urgently towards net zero.

However, as discussed above, this approach raises concerns around the optimal use of policy instruments and around judgments as to what to include in the consumer welfare function. The correct answers to these concerns depend on society-wide views on the relative importance of environment sustainability and on whether there are better tools to promote it than competition policy. This is a question for a wider (but urgent) policy debate, rather than unilateral action by competition authorities. So the second way forward would be for policymakers urgently to engage in this debate.

These are not mutually exclusive approaches. We believe that there is much merit in competition authorities pushing the boundaries of what the law currently allows them to do, while encouraging the democratic legitimacy and clarity that should come from a policy debate leading to clear guidance.

PART IV
Alternative Perspectives

A Sustainable Competition Policy is a Shared Responsibility

MARTIJN HAN[*]

True Price Foundation

One of my favourite words is the word *responsibility*.

It is composed of *response-ability*, or put differently: *the ability to respond*. The capacity to look into the world, and into ourselves, with wide-open eyes, observing all the beautiful and messy things that are happening around and within us, and realising we actually have the *ability to respond* to those happenings. Isn't that a great human gift?

We live in such intricate human bodies with all kinds of amazing sense perceptions and possibilities of action. Our hands can bring food to our mouths and build the most amazing instruments. And our minds! Let's take a moment to be in wonder of the great capacities of our minds. By the power of thought we are able to create, sustain and (creatively) destruct a whole bunch of stuff in the physical world. You think of cooking a meal and, the next thing you know, you're eating a self-cooked meal. You think of creating a competition policy and the next thing you know is that the entire economy is largely obeying a competitive system created by human hands and minds. All by the power of thought and action. All by the power of the *ability to respond* to what is presented to us in life. This is truly amazing.

We use our *abilities to respond* continuously throughout the day, from the most mundane to the most complex matters. From building houses (our ability to

---

[*] Martijn Han is chief economist at the True Price Foundation and previously served as senior enforcement official at the Netherlands Authority for Consumers & Markets (ACM). This article reflects Martijn's personal views and opinions.

respond to the desire to live comfortably) to listening to music (our ability to respond to the desire for beauty). From choosing which foods to eat (our ability to respond to the desire to sustain and take care of our bodies) to making phone calls (our ability to respond to the desire for communication).

When you think of it, *everything* we do is rooted in our human *ability to respond*.

From this perspective, let's look at the current state of our competition policies in relation to probably the single most important outward challenge of our times: climate change.

We live in market economies that are rooted in competitive processes. While a fair amount of competition is good for everyone, fierce competitive market processes have led to economic activities that destroy and continue to destroy our planet and climate.

Looking at these facts, the simple question arises: what is our *ability to respond?*

The answer is pretty simple. We need to fix our economic system so that we live, create and produce in accordance with planetary boundaries. We need to act on climate change.

We need to act on climate change with the instruments that are given to each of us.

Law-makers are given the instrument of law-making: they can create greener competition laws. Politicians are given the instrument of policymaking: they are in the position to create truly green (inter)national policies. Bankers are given, among other instruments, the instrument of investing: they can choose to invest in green initiatives. And so on.

Likewise, competition professionals are given a whole lot of instruments that can help steer markets in a direction that prevents climate change from reaching a tipping point.

In the remainder of this paper, I will outline a few of those instruments that are on the top of my mind, as an inspiration for competition professionals to further explore and put them into action. Some of them may be obvious to you, others may be new lines of thought.

I. First Things First: Recognition of a Shared Ability to Respond

Any meaningful change starts with the recognition that we have agency over the challenge before us, and that we actually are willing to tackle the challenge. Our decisions and actions have a direct impact, and not-taking-a-decision is also a decision with a resulting impact.

Since the market economy is essentially driven by the underlying principles of competition law, the first thing is to recognise that the entire competition community is fundamentally responsible for moving towards greener economies.

Competition authorities have the response-ability to redesign the application of competition policies in a greener way. Judges have the response-ability to interpret competition laws in a holistic way in resonance with emerging climate laws. Academics have the response-ability to figure out how competition laws can be made greener in a smart way. And, very importantly: corporations, as well as competition lawyers and economists, have the response-ability to not misuse greener competition policies for greenwashing.

II. Statement of Integrity for Competition Lawyers and Economists

An essential step in the recognition of a shared response-ability of the entire competition community for creating and sustaining a greener competition policy, is to adopt a common statement of integrity for commercial competition lawyers and economists. When competition lawyers and economists declare that they will not misuse the possible openings of greener competition policies, then competition authorities have much more possibilities to work on the sustainability of competition policies. This may take the simple form of law firms and economic consultants publishing statements of integrity, such as:

> I, as a commercial competition lawyer/economist, take up the responsibility to move towards a greener competition community. I will not misuse the openings that a greener competition policy offers to design and defend anticompetitive greenwashing practices.

III. Aggravating Circumstances in Case of Misuse

Competition authorities may consider misuse by parties – for example: smartly misusing Article 101(3) TFEU exceptions to design a greenwashing deal – as aggravating circumstances in their competition analyses, resulting in higher fines and public naming of those companies and law offices that misused greener competition policies. This very simple instrument can keep the whole community in line, moving towards a more sustainable competition practice.

IV. Human Wellbeing Standard

Almost needless to say because it's so obvious: we need to move from a consumer welfare standard to a human wellbeing standard, which incorporates climate effects (CO_2 emissions, pollution, biodiversity degradation, etc.) for the simple reason that they impact the wellbeing of us, our children, their children, etc. While the consumer welfare standard has served us quite well in setting up a coherent set of competition policies, this standard is no longer good enough to ensure that competition policies steer the economy in a greener direction. We need to implement a practical human wellbeing standard that brings competition analyses in line with what matters most to us.

V. Assess Concentrations Against Human Wellbeing Standard and Climate Effects

In addition to guidelines on sustainability cooperation between undertakings from an Article 101(3) TFEU perspective,[1] competition authorities need to assess mergers and acquisitions from the point of view of a human wellbeing and climate perspective. Concentrations that reduce negative climate effects significantly, even when they somewhat increase the price in relevant markets, should be cleared. Likewise, concentrations that substantially increase dirty climate effects, even when they somewhat reduce prices in relevant markets, should be blocked. The underlying principle can be straight and simple: allow green concentrations that do not unnecessarily restrict competition, and block not-green concentrations even when they lead to lower prices. In that way, we take up the responsibility to not pass on the "true price" of not-green concentrations to future generations.

VI. Avoiding Green Measures is an Abuse of a Dominant Position

Undertakings that enjoy a dominant position in their market(s), have the moral obligation to implement green technologies and move towards a greener mode of operation on all levels of their business processes. Competition authorities should adopt the view that dominant undertakings that avoid implementing obvious green measures are actually abusing their dominant position. After all, such a dominant company essentially charges a price to their consumers that is unfairly high: in addition to the monetary price that consumers pay for the product, consumers and their children also pay the price of negative climate effects.

VII. True Pricing in Competitive Assessments

Is the price we pay for a product confined to the monetary price of that product? By now, we know that we may pay on other dimensions as well, such as our

---

1   Such as the draft Guideline of the Netherlands Competition Authority (ACM) (9 July 2020) <www.acm. nl/en/publications/draft-guidelines-sustainability-agreements>.

health, degradation of biodiversity, increased CO_2 emissions, etc. Competitive analyses based on an integrated concept of what the "true price" is of products may be an elegant way to internalise climate effects into competitive analyses. When adopting a more holistic concept of what a price truly is, no major changes in our competition policies are necessary. The same competitive analyses could be applied as usual, but now on the basis of a true price that adds the relevant externalities to the monetary price. Principles for such a true price methodology are published by the True Price Foundation;[2] the underlying monetisation factors of climate effects are available on an open-source basis to be used by anyone looking to calculate true prices.[3]

VIII. Final Words: Let's Just Do It

Competition professionals have great tools in their toolbox to steer the economy in a greener direction. Let's use those tools, and refine our competition policies into a robust and sustainable set of measures that guarantee the wellbeing of future generations.

---

2   True Price, "Principles for true pricing": <https://trueprice.org/principles-for-true-pricing/>.
3   True Price, "Monetisation factors for true pricing" (2020): <https://trueprice.org/monetisation-factors-for-true-pricing/>.

"It Ain't Necessarily So..."

WILLEM VRIESENDORP[*]
#SustainablePublicAffairs

"It Ain't Necessarily So"… is one of my favourite songs, but this song of Gershwin's opera *Porgy and Bess* also holds a life lesson to never take things for granted and to always remain curious, inquisitive and creative.

One of the highlights of the song is when Sportin' Life sings:

> It ain't necessarily so
> The things that you're liable
> To read in the Bible
> It ain't necessarily so

Like the Bible, any rule book is a mere codification of the societal conventions of its time. Its text always needs to be interpreted in the context of the here and now. That also goes for competition law.

Simon Holmes, one of the leading thinkers on this topic, argues in the article "Climate Change, Sustainability, and Competition Law" that "it's not the law that needs to change but our approach to it".[1] Inge Bernaerts, director of policy and strategy at the European Commission's Directorate General for Competition, calls this the "in-built flexibility" of competition rules.[2]

---

[*]   Willem Vriesendorp is the founder of #SustainablePublicAffairs, the first public affairs consultancy that only takes on cases that have a positive impact on the environment. He works exclusively for sustainable frontrunners and helps them to improve regulatory conditions – so their leadership on sustainability becomes a competitive advantage. Willem studied law and started his career with Allen & Overy in Amsterdam, where he qualified as a competition lawyer. He would like to thank Andrew Boyce for the many lively discussions about this topic!
1   Simon Holmes, "Climate change, sustainability, and competition law" (2020) 8(2) JAE 354.
2   Inge Bernaerts, speech ("Sustainable development and competition law, Towards a Green Growth regulatory osmosis" conference, organised by the Greek competition authority, 28 September 2020).

That is why "practising" the law is an active, creative profession of great responsibility, in which legal knowledge is as important as the understanding of its political and societal context.

This symbiosis of text and context is typically the domain of public affairs professionals who could, therefore, become more serious contributors to the interpretation of competition law, and with that, play a role in its evolution. In essence, are competition policies anything other than public affairs?

With my contribution, the hope is to provoke a rethink of some interpretations of competition law that we have come to take for granted – and that ain't necessarily so.

I. Why Do We Have Competition Law?

In any piece of legal text, I find that the preamble, the "whereas" clauses or considerations almost always contain the most interesting and essential context for interpretation.

That is why any discussion about EU competition law should start with the preamble of the Treaty on the Functioning of the European Union (TFEU),[3] which provides helpful guidance on the field's *raison d'être*.

It says that the signing Member States are, among others (emphasis added):

> AFFIRMING as the essential objective of their efforts the constant improvements of the living and working conditions of their peoples,

> RECOGNISING that the removal of existing obstacles calls for concerted action in order to guarantee steady expansion, balanced trade and *fair competition*.

This is the reason why the European Union has "competition rules necessary for the functioning of the internal market", as stated in Article 3 TFEU, and this principle is further operationalised in Article 101 TFEU and so on.

In that light, competition law has a very broad, societally relevant function.

And society is changing fast.

While the Juncker Commission (2014–2019) was very much focused on "jobs and growth", President von der Leyen is attempting to address the changes in society with her ambitious Green Deal,[4] touted as Europe's new growth strategy.

---

3   Consolidated version of the Treaty on the Functioning of the European Union [2012] OJ C326/47.
4   Commission, "The European Green Deal" (Communication) COM (2019) 640.

The economic and employment policy strategy to deliver on this Green Deal, as set out in the Annual Sustainable Growth Strategy,[5] marks a paradigm shift in economic policy, where it says: "Economic growth is not an end in itself. An economy must work for the people and the planet."

And the Commission is not alone in this. The Council[6] and the European Social and Economic Committee[7] have also called for measuring economic performance and societal progress "beyond GDP" and shift towards using "wellbeing" as a compass for policy, a move also supported by the Organisation for Economic Co-operation and Development.[8]

Such a change in the notion of what economy and growth actually mean should have a bearing on all public affairs, including competition policy. Once called "hipster antitrust", this is rapidly becoming "the new normal".

II. Impact of the New Normal On Competition Law

What then, is the concrete impact of this "new normal" on the application of competition rules that exist for the "constant improvements of the living and working conditions of the peoples"?

It all starts with a changed interpretation of the term "cost". That is because cost plus margin makes for a price, and price is (next to choice) one of the most important yardsticks in competition policy. But what exactly should we consider a cost in a society that has developed such a different understanding of growth and strives for an economy that should "work for the people and the planet"?

The answer is clear: in the new normal, the notion of cost should contain an integral valuation of the cost to our common good that is necessary for the production of a product or a service. Briefly, any cost should internalise environmental externalities and therefore lead to a different price.

This is not a novel concept and the European Commission itself was an early adopter – for example, in the pricing of carbon emissions under the emissions trading scheme (EU – ETS).

This logic is now mainstream thought and is even supported by free market – economy champions like Henry Paulson, who argues in the report "Financing

Nature: Closing the Global Biodiversity Financing Gap",[9] that the "only way to slow and stop global biodiversity loss is to ensure that nature is appropriately valued in all economies".

Similarly, McKinsey & Company describes a methodology for quantifying the benefits of protecting the planet's natural capital in their report "Valuing nature conservation".[10]

Others, like True Price, have written much more eloquently on this topic, so I will not dwell on it. But I do want to explore what this emerging notion of cost – this new paradigm – means for the interpretation of some of competition policy's core principles.

1. Fair prices

The first change that a new notion of cost would bring about would, of course, pertain to the topic of fair prices as set out in Article 102 TFEU.

Imagine that a dominant company that makes, for example, chocolate spread starts to effectively internalise environmental externalities in its prices from tomorrow. From one day to the next, it would have to account for, say, the cost of deforestation in Indonesia, caused by its use of palm oil. This would then have to be accounted for in the cost of a pot of chocolate spread.

If this would be passed on to the consumer, does that actually result in a price increase or even the possibility of (the illegal use of) *excess prices*? Or could one argue that such a price hike is more of a price normalisation, and that the prices offered by competitors are actually too low – i.e. below production costs because they do not account for the loss of biodiversity and the pollution or air, which are our common goods.

Conversely, could this mean that a company that does internalise environmental externalities in its prices – for example, a producer of chocolate spread that has developed a sustainable substitute for palm oil – may claim *predatory pricing* by its (dominant) competitor who does not include the use of externalities related to the use of palm oil in its prices?

Furthermore, could the non-palm-oil chocolate spread producer argue then that the market power of its discounting competitor constitutes a *barrier to entry* to the market for chocolate spread, resulting in unfair competition?

---

9   Paulson Institute in cooperation with the Nature Conservancy and Cornell Atkinson Centre for Sustainability, "Financing Nature: Closing the Global Biodiversity Financing Gap" (2020) [6].
10 McKinsey & Company, "Valuing nature conservation: a methodology for quantifying the benefits of protecting the planet's natural capital" (2020) <www.mckinsey.com/business-functions/sustainability/our-insights/valuing-nature-conservation>.

2. Market definitions

Of course, this has everything to do with the powerful practice of product market definitions. Are the two actors from the chocolate spread example operating on the same product market? If not, they are out of scope of competition policy, altogether.

This backward-looking process of defining markets – the focus on detail, precedents and legal certainty – has often led us to interpret product markets more narrowly than, for example, anyone involved in research and development for the same product would do.

These kinds of static, narrow market definitions can create competitive disadvantages for companies who are aiming to go further for the environment, and they also stifle innovation in the field of sustainability.

Let me give a real example of a company that has developed iron-ore pellets in order to make hot steel in a 15% more carbon efficient way than by using traditional sintered ore. Instead of looking at the product itself (hot steel), the Commission defines the relevant market by looking at the two different inputs for it and defines one market for pellets and one for sinter – the court gives it "broad discretion" to do so.[11]

As a result, the sustainable innovator is found to operate in a different product market from its more traditional competitors. This has a number of unintended consequences for competition.

First, a potential acquisition of a sustainable innovator by a more traditional company could be completely out of the scope of competition law. And this could turn out to be detrimental for society and the climate, as the acquirer could do whatever it wants with its acquisition's innovations – without any "innovation theory of harm"[12] to police this.

But, also, such restricted definitions of product markets have negative ripple effects on other environmental policies that are supposed to enhance competition. One example is the EU – ETS, whereby the difference in product market definitions between pellets and sinter results in unfair competition because the more polluting sinter gets more free allowances than its sustainable substitute. This incentivises the status quo, rather than facilitating the sustainable innovation that is needed to achieve the European Commission's own climate ambitions.

In order to develop more innovation-enhancing product market definitions, should we not be looking more closely at what societal needs are served by

---

11 Case C–80/16, Request for a preliminary ruling under Article 267 TFEU from the tribunal administratif de Montreuil (Administrative Court, Montreuil, France) (2016/C 136/24).

12 Case M.7932 *Dow/DuPont* [2017] OJ C353/9; Jean-François Bellis, Valérie Lefever, "Commitments: The European Commission, following an in-depth review, clears a merger between two American groups active in crop protection and seeds, subject to structural commitments aiming at maintaining price competition and innovation for pesticides (*Dow/DuPont*)" (2017) Concurrences N° 1–2018 Art N° 86220, 121–123.

different market operators, to determine whether they actually compete or not? In other words, should we not just look at the market for (hot) steel, instead of distinguishing markets for pellets and sinter?

Questions like these will only become more relevant with novel economic concepts that are essential for sustainability, like servitisation,[13] the shared economy, and so on.

They would all require more dynamic, future-proof product markets based on technologically neutral approaches to help the most innovative performers in a market set the norm for others. This is key if we want to make sustainability a competitive advantage and raise the bar environmentally.

This, again, is not novel.

Introduced in 1999, the Japanese Top Runner Programme is a set of energy efficiency standards for energy-intensive products, such as home appliances and motor vehicles.[14] Under that scheme, energy efficiency targets are set to be achieved within a given number of years, *based on the most efficient model on the market* (the "Top Runner"). The same applies to the "bell curve" concept in universities, where the best performers set the benchmark for the rest.

In that respect, it is encouraging to see that the new Circular Economy Action Plan (CEAP) has now effectively introduced this concept, when it proposed that "the performance of front-runners in sustainability progressively becomes the norm".[15] For more detail, may I draw your attention to my firm's (#Sustainable-PublicAffairs) plea for this in the consultation on the CEAP.[16]

Hopefully this is the start of an evolution towards more innovation-enhancing product markets that create a race to the top – not the bottom.

3. Merger control

Determining product market definitions is akin to predicting the future and that is very difficult. But we can simply start by correcting the discount rate that we as a society have traditionally applied to our future.

The "discount rate" is the rate at which society is willing to trade off present benefits for future ones. High discount rates tend to discourage projects that

---

13 A good example of servitisation is Philips Circular Lighting, which has gone from only selling light bulbs to selling "lighting", more broadly. This aims to unite the different product markets for light bulbs and for LED lights under a new outcomes-based definition: "light".

14 FuturePolicy.org, "Japan's Top Runner Programme" <www.futurepolicy.org/ecologically-intelligent-design/japans-top-runner-programme/>.

15 Commission, "A new Circular Economy Action Plan For a cleaner and more competitive Europe" (Communication) COM (2020) 98.

16 Feedback from #SustainablePublicAffairs (20 January 2020), <https://ec.europa.eu/info/law/better-regulation/have-your-say/initiatives/12095-A-new-Circular-Economy-Action-Plan/F503052>.

generate long-term benefits and favour those that create short-term benefits and significant long-term costs.

This *present bias* has been one of the defining undercurrents of our current economic thinking – and it is therefore the basis for typically future-orientated market-ordering tools, like merger control policy.

The problem with the current approach is that it is far too one-dimensional, as it is solely based on GDP growth and does not take environmental considerations and resource exhaustion into account (which explains why a tree or a whale is "worth" more dead than alive).

If we were better at valuing these factors, and if we were indeed to measure economic performance and societal progress "beyond GDP" and shift towards using "wellbeing", would we still discount the future based solely on GDP growth?

And if not, would this influence, for example, merger control?

How would we predict *market shares* in markets that do not grow in monetary value? Or what about the ones that might even get smaller, but grow in terms of environmental benefit? Should we not urgently improve our ability to demonstrate and recognise *qualitive efficiencies* as environmental efficiencies?

An interesting case on this topic is that of *Aurubis/Metallo*,[17] where parties had been arguing throughout the merger review that their deal would boost sustainability by bringing about environmental efficiencies – for example, by lowering emissions and reducing their need to mine new materials. Officials ultimately conceded their concerns about buyer power and concluded that the deal could result in savings in refining copper scrap, considering Aurubis and Metallo's complementary technological focuses.

It is certainly encouraging to hear that DG COMP's chief competition economist, Pierre Régibeau, wants to recognise "out-of-market efficiencies". For instance, he noted that "it's not just the people who use the better washing machines and use fewer chemicals – they're not the only ones who benefit from cleaner water".[18]

But more guidance is already in development. The Dutch and Greek competition authorities and their trailblazing chiefs, Martijn Snoep and Ioannis Lianos, have also suggested ways authorities could look at sustainability in merger reviews, in line with this article. The Greeks argued:

> Under the current EU merger control regime, there are various options to address wider in scope sustainability issues: a) to delve into the substantive assessment of mergers under Article 2 of the EU Merger

---

17   *Aurubis/Metallo Group Holding* (Case M.9409) Commission Decision C(2020) 2752 final.
18   Pierre Régibeau, speech ("Sustainable development and competition law, Towards a Green Growth regulatory osmosis" conference, organised by the Greek competition authority, 28 September 2020).

Regulation ("EUMR") in particular by considering sustainability concerns in defining relevant markets or, b) by integrating these concerns in the "efficiencies" examined under the EUMR.[19]

4. Consumer

Taking the future into consideration when applying competition law also introduces a new actor or benchmark: the future generation.

Again, this is (or should not be) new. As early as 1987, the Brundtland Commission famously defined sustainable development as development that meets the needs of the present without compromising the ability of future generations to meet their own needs.[20]

Still, younger or future generations have been largely neglected so far in (competition) policymaking. This has led to young people taking to the streets in massive protests. They feel the generational contract is broken[21] and they have less standing.

So how do we give these stakeholders and even future generations their rightful place, and what does the introduction of such a new actor mean for competition law more broadly?

If we, for instance, look at the notion of "consumer" in Article 101(3) TFEU, or in the widely debated notion of consumer welfare as a yardstick for competition law, then who is that consumer?

Is it the one holding the wallet? It ain't necessarily so…

The concept of consumer also refers to the "wider group" (society at large), which the draft Dutch sustainability guidelines introduce as the beneficiary of, in this case, a sustainability agreement. This could well mean that the "consumer concept" could take us even beyond human beings – and would be able to also take into account animals and rivers, forests, etc.[22] We can call that the *horizontal* enlargement of the notion of consumer.

But is there also room for a *vertical* enlargement of the notion of consumer, i.e. the consumers' children, or even a future generation?

I believe this is undeniably the intention of the TFEU, as its preamble states that the main reason to have fair competition (policy) is the constant "improvements

19 Hellenic Competition Commission, Staff Discussion Paper <www.epant.gr/en/enimerosi/competition-law-sustainability.html>, 39.
20 Wikipedia, "Brundtland Commission" <https://en.wikipedia.org/wiki/Brundtland_Commission> accessed 29 December 2020.
21 Bernhard Hammer, Tanja Istenič and Lili Vargha, "The Broken Generational Contract in Europe: Generous Transfers to the Elderly Population, Low Investments in Children" (Agenta Working Paper 1/2017) <www.agentaproject.eu/Jacomo/upload/publications/generational_contract_paper.pdf>
22 Kennedy Warne, "A Voice for Nature" *National Geographic* (24 April 2019).

of the living and working conditions of their peoples". The term "peoples" has, almost by definition, a transgenerational scope.

So, if you combine the horizontal perspective of the word consumer with the vertical one, you must conclude that a future generation could well be unborn people in any region of the world: or simply humanity as a whole. This is certainly true for any benefit stemming from sustainability, as the effects of climate change and environmental pollution are inherently cross-border.

More concretely, it means that the benefits for the generations to come – from Siberia to the Philippines – could be the appropriate benchmark for determining whether a sustainability agreement between supermarkets in Europe is a violation of Article 101 or can pass the test of Article 101(3).

This is still the passive manifestation of future generations in competition law, but simply imagine if it is brought into action.

What would prevent the future generations of the Democratic Republic of Congo from launching a case based on Article 102 TFEU against an electronic equipment – maker in Europe for predatory pricing, as the cobalt used in such devices is not priced in a way that internalises environmental externalities.

This might be an interesting topic for academic debate, but we might not even need these exotic concepts, as the Intergovernmental Panel on Climate Change (IPCC) predictions[23] help us understand that we do not have to look very far into the future (2030) to see the impact of rising temperatures, extreme weather and plastic waste in the ocean.

Yes, climate change will affect future generations, but it also entails costs for consumers here and now. This reinforces the need to act, now.

III. Conclusion and Call to Action

The place of non-economic objectives in EU competition law – particularly in relation to Article 101 TFEU and the others – has been a topic of debate for many decades. I hope that this article helps to put an end to that debate.

In the context of today, where the economy should work for people and planet, what used to be seen as non-economic benefits are actually just economic benefits like any others.

This is not as revolutionary as it might seem, as the term "economy" comes from the Greek word *oíκoς* which means "household" and *νέμομαι*, which means

---

23 IPCC, "Summary for Policymakers of IPCC Special Report on Global Warming of 1.5°C approved by governments" (2018) <www.ipcc.ch/2018/10/08/summary-for-policymakers-of-ipcc-special-report-on-global-warming-of-1-5c-approved-by-governments>.

"manage". It is defined as an area of production, distribution and trade, as well as the consumption of goods and services by different agents. Understood in its broadest sense, the economy is defined as a *social* domain that emphasises the practices, discourses and material expressions associated with the production, use and management of resources.

So, could such broader definition give us the (legal) certainty we need to be proactive and play our part? Or are we waiting around for more guidelines and comfort letters?

Climate change gives us the answer. There is no time to waste.

And, even if there were time, there will never be real upfront certainty about what we do or advise, so we cannot wait around if we want to see real progress happening.

Professor Richard Feynman, who won the Nobel Prize in Physics in 1965, once famously said: "We absolutely must leave room for doubt or there is no progress and there is no learning. There is no learning without having to pose a question. And a question requires doubt. People search for certainty. But there is no certainty." So, as competition law practitioners, we have to continuously remind ourselves of that and tell ourselves: it ain't necessarily so.

And if we do that, I would argue that there is now a great potential to make a difference.

We are living through plastic hours, what philosopher Gershom Scholem called the "unique moments in time when ossified social order suddenly turns pliable, prolonged stasis gives way to motion, and people dare to hope. Plastic hours are rare. They require the right alignment of public opinion, political power, and events – usually a crisis. They depend on social mobilisation and leadership. They can come and go unnoticed or wasted. Nothing happens unless you move."[24]

I am hopeful that competition law and its practitioners take that leadership and do move, and I see it happening with things like the Inclusive Competition Forum or the initiative "JURIST DOET WAT" of the Netherlands Association of Company Lawyers (NGB) that wants to make an active contribution to the sustainability of the economy and society, across the entire legal sector in the Netherlands.

The foundation of #SustainablePublicAffairs, and its decision to only take on cases that have a positive impact on the environment, has been my contribution to that leadership from a public affairs perspective, and I am confident that others will follow. That is because, in light of tomorrow's challenges, the best comfort or legal certainty we can get is advising our clients not in the safest direction – but in the right direction.

---

24   George Packer, "America's Plastic Hour is Upon Us" *The Atlantic* (Washington DC, October 2020) <www.theatlantic.com/magazine/archive/2020/10/make-america-again/615478/>.

Concurrences
Competition Laws Review

Concurrences Review

Concurrences is a print and online quarterly peer reviewed journal dedicated to EU and national competitions laws. It has been launched in 2004 as the flagship of the Institute of Competition Law in order to provide a forum for academics, practitioners and enforcers. Concurrences'influence and expertise has garnered interviews with such figures as Christine Lagarde, Bill Kovacic, Emmanuel Macron and Margarethe Vestager.

CONTENTS

More than 12,000 articles, print and/or online. Quarterly issues provide current coverage with contributions from the EU or national or foreign countries thanks to more than 1,500 authors in Europe and abroad. Approximately 35 % of the contributions are published in English, 65 % in French, as the official language of the General Court of justice of the EU; all contributions have English abstracts.

FORMAT

In order to balance academic contributions with opinions or legal practice notes, Concurrences provides its insight and analysis in a number of formats:

- Forewords: Opinions by leading academics or enforcers
- Interviews: Interviews of antitrust experts
- On-Topics: 4 to 6 short papers on hot issues
- Law & Economics: Short papers written by economists for a legal audience
- Articles: Long academic papers
- Case Summaries: Case commentary on EU and French case law
- Legal Practice: Short papers for in-house counsels
- International: Medium size papers on international policies
- Books Review: Summaries of recent antitrust books
- Articles Review: Summaries of leading articles published in 45 antitrust journals

BOARDS

The Scientific Committee is headed by Laurence Idot, Professor at Panthéon Assas University. The International Committee is headed by Frederic Jenny, OECD Competition Comitteee Chairman. Boards members include Bruno Lasserre, Mario Monti, Howard Shelanski, Richard Whish, Wouter Wils, etc.

ONLINE VERSION

Concurrences website provides all articles published since its inception, in addition to selected articles published online only in the electronic supplement.

WRITE FOR CONCURRENCES

Concurrences welcome spontaneous contributions. Except in rare circumstances, the journal accepts only unpublished articles, whatever the form and nature of the contribution. The Editorial Board checks the form of the proposals, and then submits these to the Scientific Committee. Selection of the papers is conditional to a peer review by at least two members of the Committee. Within a month, the Committee assesses whether the draft article can be published and notifies the author.

e-Competitions Bulletin

Case law database

e-Competitions is the only online resource that provides consistent coverage of antitrust cases from 55 jurisdictions, organized into a searchable database structure. e-Competitions concentrates on cases summaries taking into account that in the context of a continuing growing number of sources there is a need for factual information, i.e., case law.

- 18,000 case summaries
- 3,000 authors
- 85 countries covered
- 30,000 subscribers

Sophisticated editorial and IT enrichment

e-Competitions is structured as a database. The editors make a sophisticated technical and legal work on all articles by tagging these with key words, drafting abstracts and writing html code to increase Google ranking. There is a team of antitrust lawyers – PhD and judges clerks - and a team of IT experts. e-Competitions makes comparative law possible. Thanks to this expert editorial work, it is possible to search and compare cases by jurisdiction, legal topics or business sectors.

Prestigious Boards

e-Competitions draws upon highly distinguished editors, all leading experts in national or international antitrust. Advisory Board Members include: Sir Christopher Bellamy, Ioanis Lianos (UCL), Eleanor Fox (NYU), Frédéric Jenny (OECD), Jacqueline Riffault-Silk (Cour de cassation), Wouter Wils (King's College London), etc.

Leading Partners

- Association of European Competition Law Judges: The AECLJ is a forum for judges of national Courts specializing in antitrust case law. Members timely feed e-Competitions with just released cases.

- Academics partners: Antitrust research centres from leading universities write regularly in e-Competitions: University College London, King's College London, Queen Mary University, etc.

- Law firms: Global law firms and antitrust niche firms write detailed cases summaries specifically for e-Competitions: Allen & Overy, Baker McKenzie, Cleary Gottlieb Steen & Hamilton, Jones Day, Norton Rose Fulbright, Skadden, White & Case, etc.

The Institute of Competition Law

The Institute of Competition Law is a publishing company, founded in 2004 by Dr. Nicolas Charbit, based in Paris, London and NewYork. The Institute cultivates scholarship and discussion about antitrust issues though publications and conferences. Each publication and event is supervised by editorial boards and scientific or steering committees to ensure independence, objectivity, and academic rigor. Thanks to this management, the Institute has become one of the few think tanks in Europe to have significant influence on antitrust policies.

AIM

The Institute focuses government, business and academic attention on a broad range of subjects which concern competition laws, regulations and related economics.

BOARDS

To maintain its unique focus, the Institute relies upon highly distinguished editors, all leading experts in national or international antitrust: Bill Kovacic, Mario Monti, Eleanor Fox, Laurence Idot, Frédéric Jenny, Ioannis Lianos, Richard Whish, etc.

AUTHORS

3,800 authors, from 55 jurisdictions.

PARTNERS

- Universities: University College London, King's College London, Queen Mary University, Paris Sorbonne Panthéon-Assas, etc.

- Law firms: Allen & Overy, Cleary Gottlieb Steen & Hamilton, Baker McKenzie, Hogan Lovells, Jones Day, Norton Rose Fulbright, Skadden Arps, White & Case, etc.

EVENTS

Brussels, Hong Kong, London, New York, Paris, Singapore and Washington, DC.

ONLINE VERSION

Concurrences website provides all articles published since its inception.

PUBLICATIONS

The Institute publishes Concurrences Review, a print and online quarterly peer-reviewed journal dedicated to EU and national competitions laws. e-Competitions is a bi-monthly antitrust news bulletin covering 85 countries. The e-Competitions database contains over 18,000 case summaries from 4,000 authors.

Concurrences+
ANTITRUST LAW PORTAL

17 years of archives
30,000 articles

4 DATABASES

Concurrences Review
Access to latest issue and archives

- 12,000 articles from 2004 to the present

- European and national doctrine and case law

e-Competitions Bulletin
Access to latest issue and archives

- 18,000 case summaries from 1911 to the present

- Case law of 85 jurisdictions

Conferences
**Access to the documentation
of all Concurrences events**

- 450 conferences (Brussels, Hong Kong, London, New York, Paris, Singapore and Washington, DC)

- 250 PowerPoint presentations, proceedings and syntheses

- 300 videos

- Verbatim reports

e-Books
Access to all Concurrences books

- 42 e-Books available

- PDF version

NEW

New search engine
Optimized results to save time

- Search results sorted by date, jurisdiction, keyword, economic sector, author, etc.

New modes of access
IP address recognition

- No need to enter codes: immediate access

- No need to change codes when your team changes: offers increased security and saves time

Mobility

- Responsive design: site optimized for tablets and smartphones

Lightning Source UK Ltd.
Milton Keynes UK
UKHW020352160421
382065UK00003B/42